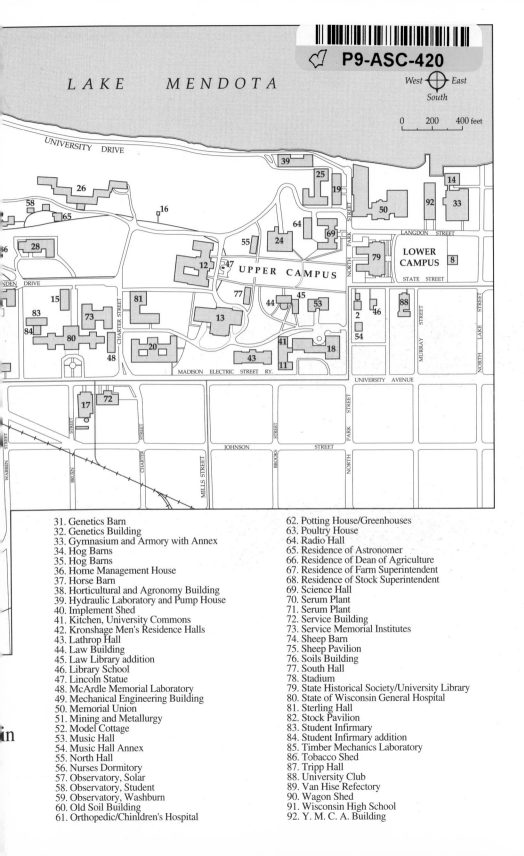

LAKE MENDOTA

P9-ASC-420

West — East
South

0   200   400 feet

UNIVERSITY DRIVE

26

58
65

16

39
25
19

14

92   33

50

64
69

LANGDON   STREET

55
24

79

LOWER
CAMPUS

8

28

12   47   UPPER CAMPUS

STATE   STREET

INDEN DRIVE

15

81

77   45
44   53
88

2   46

54

79

13

83
84
73
80

20

41   18

43   11

48

MADISON   ELECTRIC   STREET   RY.

UNIVERSITY   AVENUE

17   72

STREET

STREET

STREET

PARK

STREET

JOHNSON   STREET   STREET

MILLS STREET

BROOKS

NORTH

WARREN

BRUEN

CHARTER

31. Genetics Barn
32. Genetics Building
33. Gymnasium and Armory with Annex
34. Hog Barns
35. Hog Barns
36. Home Management House
37. Horse Barn
38. Horticultural and Agronomy Building
39. Hydraulic Laboratory and Pump House
40. Implement Shed
41. Kitchen, University Commons
42. Kronshage Men's Residence Halls
43. Lathrop Hall
44. Law Building
45. Law Library addition
46. Library School
47. Lincoln Statue
48. McArdle Memorial Laboratory
49. Mechanical Engineering Building
50. Memorial Union
51. Mining and Metallurgy
52. Model Cottage
53. Music Hall
54. Music Hall Annex
55. North Hall
56. Nurses Dormitory
57. Observatory, Solar
58. Observatory, Student
59. Observatory, Washburn
60. Old Soil Building
61. Orthopedic/Children's Hospital

62. Potting House/Greenhouses
63. Poultry House
64. Radio Hall
65. Residence of Astronomer
66. Residence of Dean of Agriculture
67. Residence of Farm Superintendent
68. Residence of Stock Superintendent
69. Science Hall
70. Serum Plant
71. Serum Plant
72. Service Building
73. Service Memorial Institutes
74. Sheep Barn
75. Sheep Pavilion
76. Soils Building
77. South Hall
78. Stadium
79. State Historical Society/University Library
80. State of Wisconsin General Hospital
81. Sterling Hall
82. Stock Pavilion
83. Student Infirmary
84. Student Infirmary addition
85. Timber Mechanics Laboratory
86. Tobacco Shed
87. Tripp Hall
88. University Club
89. Van Hise Refectory
90. Wagon Shed
91. Wisconsin High School
92. Y. M. C. A. Building

THE UNIVERSITY OF WISCONSIN

A History, 1945-1971

Volume IV

The University of Wisconsin

1945   *A History*   1971

Renewal to Revolution

E. David Cronon
&
John W. Jenkins

Volume IV

THE UNIVERSITY OF WISCONSIN PRESS

The University of Wisconsin Press
2537 Daniels Street
Madison, Wisconsin 53718

3 Henrietta Street
London WC2E 8LU, England

1 3 5 4 2

Printed in the United States of America

Library of Congress Catalog Card Number 48-47638

·ISBN 299-16290-7

For Merle Curti and Edith Frances Eells

Contents

Illustrations   ix
Preface   xi
Acknowledgments   xiii
Abbreviations   xv

Introduction   1
1. Handling the GI Invasion   7
2. The Insider President   55
3. A Caretaker President   109
4. The Imperial President   163
5. The Academic Enterprise   225
6. Reshaping the Wisconsin Idea   295
7. The Rise of Student Power   383
8. From Rights to Revolution   447
9. The UW System Merger   521
10. End of an Era   597

Appendix   611
Bibliographical Note   614
Index   615

Illustrations

Political science class at Congregational Church; Memorial Union food line	22
"Sow and Six piglets; "Sow" interior	23
Veterans applying for housing; Camp Randall trailer parks	29
Camp Randall trailer kitchen; Co-op Grocery	30
Truax Field veterans housing; single men's quarters	36
Badger Village veterans housing; row house interior	42
University Houses; Fred, Rennebohm, and Eisenhower	81
Gov. Kohler's budget cut message; Memorial Library ground-breaking	87
Fred and janitors' crew; Freds at student banquet	104
Wisconsin Center cornerstone laying; Wisconsin Center	105
Bohrod collage of President Elvehjem	116
Elvehjem at lab bench; Sperry 1604 computer	125
Social Science Building under construction; Sellery Hall under construction	126
President Harrington in Van Hise Hall office	167
Harrington inaugural at Field House; Harrington, Iacocca, and Clodius	173
UW chancellors of 1960s; Humanities construction site	212
Van Hise Hall excavation; Van Hise looms over Bascom	213
Peterson Building sit-in; Bascom Hill rally	220
Bascom Hill "Cemetery"; Harringtons' final exit	221
Historical Society library stacks; first book into Memorial Library	235
Atom smasher; Social Science Building	262
Prof. Harlow at Primate Lab; McArdle Labs model	263

ix

Illustrations

Profs. Bryson and Suomi; Meteorology and Space Science Center	276
Ag Extension in the field; University Extension leaders	302
Speech class using WHA-TV equipment; Prof. Durand's WHA radio lecture	309
Presidents Harrington and Johnson; exchange program	324
Chancellors McNeil and Adolfson; Extension Building	351
"Freshman Forum"; dignitaries at Eagle Heights map	373
Panty raider; registration line	374
Coeds sweep off Lincoln Statue; broom hockey	375
Alan "the Horse" Ameche; Gov. Kohler leads "Varsity"	376
Installing Tartan Turf at Stadium; Rose Bowl	377
Union Terrace; Part St. bridge	378
Historical Society reading room; White Hall library	379
Modern west campus; new lower campus	380
Southeast Dormitories; between classes on Bascom Hill	381
UW Presidents Harrington, Weaver, and Fred; Edwin Young and Donald Percy	382
Officers Hammersley and Dohse; ROTC protest	420
"Wild Bill" Kiekhofer's class; Rathskeller	421
Professor Hartshorne; panty raid	428
Daily Cardinal front page; State Street at night	429
UW freedom marchers; civil rights bus	434
Before Dow II; end of Dow II	464
Chancellor Young during black strike; National Guard on Bascom Hill	480
Anti-war demonstration; Kent State-Cambodia protest	513
Tear gas on Bascom Hill; Sterling Hall bombing	514
Regent DeBardeleben; Van Hise Hall	548
President Weaver news conference; UW System merger bill signing	594

Preface

This is the fourth volume in *The University of Wisconsin: A History* series. The first two volumes were written by Merle Curti and Vernon Carstensen and published by the University of Wisconsin Press in 1949 as a part of the institution's centennial celebration that year. Our two volumes, the first published in 1994, pick up the Curti and Carstensen story in 1925 and take it into 1971, the year the Wisconsin Legislature merged the University of Wisconsin with the nine Wisconsin State Universities to form a new University of Wisconsin System.

Volume 3 recounted the University's recurrent travails with Wisconsin politicians in the 1920s and 1930s and the often traumatic experiences during the Great Depression and the Second World War. The present volume, which is being published in conjunction with UW-Madison's sesquicentennial celebration, deals with the return of the veterans after the war, the great institutional expansion and reorganization of the 1950s and 1960s, the student protests and campus violence associated with the Vietnam War, and culminates with the legal end of the original University of Wisconsin in the 1971 merger. As in Volume 3, we have viewed the University from both a top-down and a grassroots perspective. Several chapters view developments through the eyes and experience of the Board of Regents, the UW presidents, and other top administrators of the period. Other chapters give related student and faculty perspectives of the same years, showing how their concerns were sometimes different, both from each other and from the University leadership.

Although we did not know each other then, both of us were on campus during parts of the period covered in Volume 4. While there are aspects of that experience we are happy to have behind us, we wouldn't want to have missed the excitement and challenges of those years. Reliving them for this volume, we have come away with renewed respect for the resiliency of the University and the commitment and dedication of the many thousands of UW students and staff members over the past 150 years who have helped make it one of the great institutions of higher learning in the world. We hope our readers will feel we have succeeded in conveying this respect in these pages.

E. D. C.
J. W. J.

Acknowledgments

The University History Project began in 1981 as a reunion initiative of the Class of 1925, two of whose members, the late Dorothy King Knaplund and John L. Bergstresser, were particularly interested and helpful. Over the years UW-Madison Chancellors Irving Shain, Donna E. Shalala, and David Ward provided generous financial support and encouragement that made possible this and the preceding volume in the *University of Wisconsin: A History* series.

A number of student researchers were employed to work on this volume by the University History Project. Karen H. Cotlar gathered and made computer notes on the basic official institutional records; Mark R. Goodale and John M. Murphy, conducted archival work during the early part of this effort; and Joseph F. Cullon, Susan O. Haswell, Flannery Haug, John Murphy, Eric D. Olmanson, and Greg Summers were instrumental in bringing the volume to fruition, providing not only high quality research but also valuable insights and an enthusiastic willingness to get the job done correctly and on time. John P. Kaminski, director of the UW-Madison Center for the Study of the American Constitution, prepared the index, as he did for the third volume.

The University History Project also received substantial assistance from a number of other individuals: Jean Cronon, the wife of one of the authors and working as an unpaid volunteer, produced invaluable computer notes on the *Daily Cardinal* throughout our period; Director J. Frank Cook, Cathy Jacob, Bernard Schermetzler, and Barry J. Teicher, all of University Archives and Records Management, helped track down and make available the great bulk of data upon which this volume is based. The History Project further benefitted from the timely and generous administrative support provided by the UW-Madison

Acknowledgments

College of Letters and Science. Particularly interested and helpful was Dean Phillip R. Certain and some of his staff: Jim Duff, Anne C. Gunther, Sharon L. McCarthy, Michelle R. Massen, Diane Pladziewicz, and Margaret M. Sullivan.

While any errors of fact or interpretation are entirely ours alone, we have benefitted greatly from the knowledge and insights of a sizeable number of people who read portions of the manuscript: Henry L. Ahlgren, Marvin T. Beatty, Albert J. Beaver, Patrick G. Boyle, Robert L. Clodius, Joe Corry, Robert H. DeZonia, James W. Gooch, Arthur O. Hove, Harland Klagos, Luke F. Lamb, Ann Litchfield, Harold Montross, Donald E. Percy, Glenn S. Pound, Charles J. Stathas, Theodore J. Shannon, Rosemary Stare, Barry Teicher, Gale VandeBerg, Wilson B. Thiede, Leo M. Walsh, and Grace W. White.

Abbreviations

The following abbreviations and short titles are used throughout:

CCHE	Coordinating Committee [Commission after 1968] for Higher Education
UW BOR	University of Wisconsin Board of Regents
SHSW	State Historical Society of Wisconsin
UA	University Archives, University of Wisconsin-Madison
UHP	University History Project, a special project of the University of Wisconsin-Madison
WAM	*Wisconsin Alumni Magazine* or *Wisconsin Alumnus*
WSC/WSU BOR	Wisconsin State College/Wisconsin State University Board of Regents

THE UNIVERSITY OF WISCONSIN

A History, 1945-1971

Volume IV

Introduction

On February 5, 1849, Chancellor John H. Lathrop welcomed the University of Wisconsin's initial seventeen students to their first classroom exercises. All were inadequately schooled young men enrolled in the Preparatory Department, a remedial unit of the Department of Science, Literature, and the Arts, which had no other students. Nor did the University in 1849 offer any college-level programs or have any buildings of its own. As yet it possessed only part of what was known as University Hill (eventually renamed Bascom Hill). Lathrop constituted the institution's entire salaried administration and faculty and taught his new charges in a borrowed classroom of the Madison Female Academy downtown. The newly appointed Board of Regents had plans for obtaining a sizable lakeside campus, constructing impressive academic and residential buildings, shaping a substantial collegiate curriculum, gathering a solid nucleus of faculty-scholars, and arranging for adequate financial support. None of this had yet come about, however. The University's history was all in its future.

Women would not be admitted for more than a decade, after the shortage of male students during the Civil War led University authorities to open its back door a bit by creating a Normal Department to train teachers for the common schools of the state. President Paul A. Chadbourne (1867-70), an opponent of coeducation, decided this program was not sufficiently demanding for the University. He therefore converted the Normal Department into a Female College in 1868. The college was located initially in South Hall with a separate curriculum and instruction, though its women students were permitted to attend other classes as well. Following Chadbourne's departure, the regents abolished the Female College in 1874 and established the policy, never seriously challenged thereafter, that women were eligible for admission to any course of study at the University.

1

Over the next century the University of Wisconsin developed into one of the premier institutions of higher learning in the world. The transformation from preparatory school to college to university was already apparent by the time of the appointment of Charles R. Van Hise as UW president. His inaugural in 1904 celebrated the jubilee anniversary of the University's first graduation ceremony fifty years earlier. The first Wisconsin native and UW graduate to serve as president, Van Hise was well-prepared to move the institution ahead. A member of the Class of 1879, he had been strongly influenced by President John Bascom (1874-87), who was in the process of recruiting a stronger faculty and developing a solid undergraduate liberal arts instructional program. Van Hise subsequently earned the University's first Ph.D. degree in 1892 for graduate work with Bascom's successor, the prominent geologist Thomas C. Chamberlin (1887-92). For the next several years, Van Hise taught at both UW and the new University of Chicago, where Chamberlin served as chairman of the geology department after leaving Wisconsin. Chamberlin was succeeded as president by historian Charles Kendall Adams (1892-1901), who advanced graduate education, academic freedom, and intercollegiate athletics and school spirit. During the 1890s a rigorously science-based College of Agriculture emerged on the western edge of the campus; it was to be instrumental in developing Wisconsin's dairy industry. The University of Wisconsin was becoming a true university of recognized stature.

Van Hise became president during the tenure of Wisconsin's famous progressive governor Robert M. La Follette, a UW classmate who had helped to arrange his friend's appointment to head the University. As undergraduates, both men had been inspired by the moral philosophy and social activism taught and exemplified by President Bascom. They shared his view that the University had a responsibility to devote its intellectual resources to improve the quality of life in the state and nation. In his inaugural address Van Hise proclaimed his vision of a "combination university," involving a tripartite academic structure combining high quality instruction, ground-breaking scholarship and research, and effective social service, all tied together in a mutually reinforcing academic community of faculty and student scholars. The goal was unprecedented among American institutions of public higher education.

Van Hise and his colleagues achieved mixed results during his presidency until his unexpected death in 1918. Especially during his first decade in office when La Follette's influence and backing were strong, the UW president succeeded in persuading the largely progressive legislature to provide a number of new classroom and laboratory facilities for the growing institution. Yet he consistently failed to obtain state funding for his extra-curricular, community-related initiatives, such as men's dormitories, commons, and a men's union comparable to the state-funded Lathrop Hall for women, opened in 1910. He also encountered legislative reluctance to recognize and adequately fund research as a basic function of his state-supported enterprise.

The president had more success in promoting a campus community spirit among the faculty by orchestrating the organization of a University Club and helping it acquire and develop a club house on the lower campus. Van Hise was the first UW president to encourage significant and broad faculty participation in University governance by setting up numerous faculty committees through which much of the University's academic business was transacted. Similarly, his administration institutionalized public service with the founding of separate agricultural and general extension services, both of which quickly became national leaders in their respective fields. As one of its first actions, prior to World War I general extension began offering adult education courses in Milwaukee; in the early 1920s the Milwaukee program expanded to include freshman-sophomore credit offerings in a downtown University Extension Center. This helped to counter the efforts of Milwaukee boosters seeking a second full-fledged UW campus for the city. Van Hise and the regents feared such a development would threaten the primacy of the Madison campus.

Although Van Hise died in 1918, the inter-war period witnessed the flowering of his combination university. During the 1920s, for example, committed alumni and University authorities found imaginative ways–in the form of the Wisconsin Alumni Research Foundation and the Wisconsin University Building Corporation–to fund research and develop facilities the state refused to provide. By 1940, the lakeside Tripp-Adams-Kronshage men's dormitory complexes, Van Hise Commons, Elizabeth Waters women's residence hall, and the Memorial Union, along with the faculty's University Club, supported a vital campus community of scholars. During the darkest days of the Great Depression, WARF emergency aid protected and nurtured the scholarly nucleus of the University, making possible the recruitment and retention of some of the nation's brightest graduate students and new Ph.Ds. All of this grew directly out of the inspiration of the great Van Hise.

Several additional developments helped to shape the combination university, although they were less directly associated with Van Hise. During the first half of the twentieth century the University developed an elaborate array of *in loco parentis* policies governing student life and extra-curricular activities. These evolved under the aegis of the faculty Committee on Student Life and Interests after 1914 and were enforced through the deans of men and of women. Mostly designed to protect the individual and collective interests of the undergraduates, by mid-century students began to view these constraints as increasingly outmoded and irksome. On the other hand, academic freedom, for both faculty and students, enjoyed continuous and solid support from UW leaders. In 1922 the regents reaffirmed and broadened their commitment to the "sifting and winnowing" principle first promulgated by the board in 1894. Later President Glenn Frank (1925-37) spoke out eloquently in its defense. Wisconsin's well-publicized commitment to free speech and association, as well as its non-discriminatory open admissions policy, began attracting sizable numbers of Jewish students from the eastern seaboard in the 1920s, who often experienced quotas and other barriers at colleges and universities in their own region. The resulting UW campus environment supported a diverse and frequently noisy culture of student political and social activism, some of it well-publicized and far left of center. While the diverse student body enriched the intellectual life of the University, these latter aspects sometimes raised eyebrows and worse at the capitol and across the state.

Faculty participation in University governance progressed markedly during and after the Frank administration. An urbane New York magazine editor and masterful orator of moderately progressive views, Frank had appealed to the Board of Regents in 1925 as the perfect candidate to refurbish the University's tarnished post-war image throughout the state. He thus tended to focus his presidential attention on public relations while allowing his deans and other subordinates and the faculty unprecedented leeway in their work. Unfortunately for Frank, who was a well-read generalist possessing no advanced degrees, most of the deans and the faculty never appreciated the advantages of the president's laissez faire administrative style. Instead they largely snubbed him as an academic pretender. Frank's appointment also lacked the La Follette family imprimatur. In 1937 Governor Philip La Follette engineered Frank's firing while the faculty stood quietly by, offering little support for their ousted leader. In return for this prearranged acquiescence, College of Letters and Science Dean George C. Sellery obtained assurances from the regents that the faculty would be consulted about Frank's successor. After a search influenced by the La Follette family, the regents settled on Cincinnati City Manager Clarence A. Dykstra (1937-45), an applied political scientist of limited academic experience. Sellery took every opportunity to impress on the new leader the crucial importance of extending the faculty's role in shared governance at Wisconsin.

Ironically, as these developments and others brought Van Hise's combination university to fruition, events overshadowed recognition of this accomplishment. Almost immediately President Dykstra and the regents had to confront a series of drastic budget cuts directed by Governor Julius Heil, a conservative Milwaukee industrialist who had been stung by the unexpected attacks of student radicals. Simultaneously, as the United States moved closer to involvement in the European war, Dykstra accepted the call of President Franklin Roosevelt to serve as civilian head of the Selective Service program. His frequent absences from Madison in this role and subsequently as a leading wartime manpower expert led the regents to establish an administrative support committee to act in his behalf. The members of this group included three long-time campus stalwarts: L&S Dean George C. Sellery, Graduate School Dean E.B. Fred, and Comptroller A.W. Peterson. Thus even before the Japanese attack on Pearl Harbor, the University was effectively on an emergency wartime footing that would endure throughout the war and in some respects well beyond.

President Dykstra left Madison in early 1945 to head the emerging University of California at Los Angeles. His departure led to a series of three "insider" UW presidents drawn from the Madison faculty: Edwin B. Fred (1945-58), Conrad A. Elvehjem (1958-62), and Fred Harvey Harrington (1962-70). Their administrations, viewed from above and below, span this volume, which traces the stunning evolution of the University from its unitary "combination" structure in 1945 to a centrally managed and considerably more bureaucratic multi-campus, multi-function, megaversity a quarter century later. Along the way the volume reviews the rise of a broad student power movement, whose increasingly violent response to the Vietnam War culminated in the tragic Sterling Hall bombing in August, 1970. This, and other forces set in motion during the 1960s, especially the development of a number of new two- and four-year UW campuses, helped prepare the way for the merger of Wisconsin's two systems of higher education the following year. With it came the legal end of the original University of Wisconsin after 122 years.

1.

Handling the GI Invasion

Following hard on the trauma of the Great Depression, the Second World War brought unprecedented upheaval to the University of Wisconsin. Its dislocation was more profound and far-reaching even than that of the Civil War eighty years earlier, when women were first admitted to help offset the decline in male enrollment. This time, too, Wisconsin men departed the campus in ever-mounting numbers. Overall University enrollment declined by more than half during the two years following the Japanese attack on Pearl Harbor on December 7, 1941. The number of male students plunged more than threefold, from about 7,700 in 1940 to fewer than 2,300 in 1944, and many of those remaining were eighteen-year-olds awaiting draft calls. For the first time women outnumbered men in the regular student body and held most of the leadership positions in student organizations. During the conflict more than 12,500 UW students and alumni, some of them women, served in the armed forces in all parts of the globe; 485 of them gave their lives.[1] A number of UW faculty members went to war as well, some in uniform and some working for various war agencies on campus and elsewhere. The University's two nuclear accelerators and a number of UW scientists, for example, spent most of the war at Los Alamos, New Mexico, assigned to the top-secret Manhattan Project to develop the atomic bombs that ended the war with Japan.

---

[1] A list of the University's gold star honor roll was published in advance of an all-University memorial convocation service held in the Field House on May 8, 1946. *Wisconsin State Journal*, May 5, 1946. For a discussion of the University during the war, see E. David Cronon and John W. Jenkins, *The University of Wisconsin: A History*, vol. 3, *Politics, Depression, and War, 1925-1945* (Madison: University of Wisconsin Press, 1994), pp. 407-63.

Graduate School Dean Edwin B. Fred, before his appointment as UW president in January, 1945, spent considerable time in Washington advising the federal government on science issues. Fred was primarily responsible for the selection of UW bacteriology Chairman Ira L. Baldwin to direct the nation's biological warfare research program at Camp Detrick, Maryland.[2] Law School Dean Lloyd K. Garrison also served in Washington as general counsel and then executive director of the War Labor Board. Medical School Dean William S. Middleton spent many months in Europe as a colonel with the Army Medical Corps helping to develop a sophisticated network of army field and base hospitals. On the other side of the world a substantial number of Middleton's clinical colleagues in the UW Medical School had departed the campus en masse to serve in the South Pacific as the U.S. Army's 44th General Hospital.

Those University staff members who remained in Madison mobilized the campus for the war emergency under the skillful leadership of UW President Clarence A. Dykstra, himself a frequent Washington consultant on manpower issues. Early in the conflict the University adopted a modified trimester calendar with a fifteen-week summer session, which enabled diligent students to complete a full undergraduate program in two years and nine months. The faculty added a number of new war-related courses to the curriculum, and many campus-based researchers turned their attention to war needs. At the request of the War Production Board, for example, biochemist William H. Peterson and botanist Myron P. Backus led a UW team of more than fifty scientists that developed techniques for the production of the recently discovered antibiotic penicillin in vastly greater quantities, and in less time and at lower cost, than previously possible.[3]

To bolster declining enrollment and make full use of University resources for the war effort, Dykstra energetically sought to attract various army and navy training programs to the campus. Some, like the Navy V-12 Program and the Army Specialized Training Program, involved regular college-level academic work. Others, especially the large Navy Radio School and the Army Cooks and Bakers School, involved short-term, purely vocational instruction that made little use of the University's intellectual resources. In time

---

[2]*Daily Cardinal*, January 4, 1947; Ira L. Baldwin, *My Half Century at the University of Wisconsin*, (Madison: Ira L. Baldwin, 1995), pp. 121-31.

[3]"UW's Role in Penicillin Research Is Disclosed," *WAM*, 46 (June 15, 1945), 7; Baldwin, *My Half Century*, pp. 118-20.

President Dykstra came to doubt the wisdom of using the campus primarily as a hotel to house such programs. The number of war programs and servicemen and women assigned to them fluctuated with bewildering rapidity, with the military occupation of the campus reaching its peak in 1943. For a time this expanding military use more than offset the decline in regular male enrollment, so much so that Badger coeds of the war years experienced little sense of male deprivation. Altogether, more than 18,000 servicemen and women spent part of their World War II training at the University of Wisconsin.[4] In addition, many thousands more received communications training at the Army Air Corp's Truax air base outside of Madison, which during its peak use housed 35,000 airmen. Many of these spent some of their off-duty recreational time on campus. Few if any aspects of the University's operation were untouched by the war. The institution was mobilized for national service as never before.

Planning for the Post-War Era

Even before the tide turned definitely toward an allied victory, UW authorities were giving thought to the eventual reconversion of the University to regular peacetime activities. As early as the spring of 1943 President Dykstra asked the faculty through its University Committee to begin to identify likely post-war problems. Basing its judgment on the experience after World War I, the committee early concluded that the campus might anticipate an enrollment of as many as 17,000 students after the war, in contrast to the previous peak of fewer than 12,000 in 1940.[5] The following October, in his annual address to the faculty, Dykstra called for the creation of a special commission for post-war planning:

> If the experience of the years following the last war has any significance, we must look forward to student numbers which will tax our facilities to the breaking point. . . . We were crowded in 1940 with eleven thousand. What can we

---

[4]Walter J. Hodgkins, "Is Our University Slipping," *WAM*, 46(March 15, 1945), 4. During three years of operation from 1942 to 1945, the UW navy programs alone trained over 15,000 sailors and WAVES, more than 9,000 of them in the 20-week radio course. "Navy Radio Schools Close," ibid. (May 15, 1945), 6.

[5]UW Faculty Document 672, University Committee, "Statement on Post-War Problems," April 5, 1943, UA; *Press Bulletin*, April 21, 1943; *Daily Cardinal*, April 23, 1943.

do for fifteen thousand or more? What classrooms and laboratories shall we use and what library facilities can we offer? Certainly there will have to be increases in the teaching staff and, in the second place, room in which to teach. Staff and space; space and staff![6]

More specifically, the key issue was how to handle the expected influx of student veterans when the conflict ended. Already by the fall of 1943 nine discharged servicemen enrolled under the provisions of Public Law 16, which Congress had enacted earlier that year to provide medical care and educational and other services for disabled veterans. The University promptly arranged a series of contracts with the U.S. Veterans Administration to provide correspondence and campus-based instruction for disabled veterans.[7] Much more significant in terms of the numbers covered was Public Law 346, enacted the following year as the allied invasion of Europe was getting under way, essentially as an amendment to Public Law 16. Entitled the Servicemen's Readjustment Act of 1944, this landmark legislation was quickly dubbed the GI Bill of Rights because of its unprecedentedly generous and sweeping benefits for all World War II veterans. Based partly on the Wisconsin Educational Bonus Act of 1919, among other assistance the law provided up to $500 a semester for tuition, books, and a living allowance while any veteran was enrolled in an accredited training program or educational institution after the war. The duration of these educational benefits depended upon the length of the individual's military service, with every veteran receiving twelve months of eligibility plus one month for each month of service up to a maximum of forty-eight months.[8]

The GI Bill quickly proved to be even more important than the Morrill Land Grant Act of 1862 in opening up higher education to

---

[6]UW Faculty Minutes, October 4, 1943, UA; *Daily Cardinal*, October 5, 1943; *Press Bulletin*, October 20, 1943; Clarence A. Dykstra, "A Look Ahead," *WAM*, 45 (November and December, 1943), 33-34, 65-66. The quotation is from Dykstra's adaptation of his faculty address for the alumni in ibid., 65.

[7]See UW BOR Minutes, September 18, 1943, April 26, June 15, August 28, and September 30, 1944, January 25, and March 21, 1945, UA; "War Veterans," *WAM*, 45 (October, 1943), 35.

[8]Title II, Chapter IV, "Education of Veterans," Public Law 346, 78th Congress (1944), *The Serviceman's Readjustment Act*. As early as the summer of 1942 the Veterans Administration had studied the 1919 Wisconsin legislation as an example of the sort of educational benefits that might be provided to veterans by the federal government after the war. Keith W. Olson, *The G.I. Bill, the Veterans, and the Colleges* (Lexington: University Press of Kentucky, 1974), p. 7.

millions of American young people, many of whom had not previously aspired to or could not afford post-secondary schooling.[9] As a result, ex-GIs dominated American campuses for half a decade after the war. Altogether more than a third of all World War II veterans made use of their education benefits. Of these, over 2.2 million enrolled in college-level undergraduate, graduate, and professional programs at a cost to the taxpayers of $5.5 billion.[10] The GI Bill sparked a boom in higher education far surpassing anything the United States had previously experienced.

At first few educators in Madison or elsewhere foresaw the full dimensions of the problems the post-war enrollment deluge would bring to their institutions. Instead, the thinking behind the GI Bill reflected very much the country's recent experience with the Great Depression of the 1930s. Congress and the Roosevelt administration assumed that peace would very likely bring a resumption of the Depression, and with it the problem of dealing with millions of unemployed workers. The immediate adjustments confronting the returned veterans thus seemed likely to be economic. The unpublicized report of the first government task force to study demobilization issues predicted flatly in June, 1943, that within a year after the end of the war there would "exist the likelihood, if not the certainty, of a large volume of unemployed, involving as many as 8 or 9 million."[11]

Mindful of the ill-fated bonus march on Washington by desperate unemployed veterans in 1932, a number of commentators shuddered at the likelihood of "chaotic and revolutionary conditions" if the nation did not provide adequate economic opportunities for the

---

[9]Comparing these two landmark education acts involves, of course, mixing apples and oranges. The GI Bill's educational benefits were provided to individual veterans without regard to the nature of their studies; the duration of the support was finite and only indirectly benefitted the institutions in which the veterans enrolled. The Morrill Act, on the other hand, provided a large grant of federal land to each state to help subsidize its public university, in return for which the institution was required to offer certain applied educational programs deemed of national importance. If the state and its university treated the land grant as a quasi-endowment (few did), this federal support was on-going, as was Congress' subsequent interest in funding agricultural research and education through the network of public land-grant universities.

[10]Keith W. Olson, "The G.I. Bill and Higher Education: Success and Surprise," *American Quarterly*, 25 (December, 1973), 596-610. The total cost for all parts of the GI Bill was far higher, about $14.5 billion. LeRoy E. Luberg, *Characteristics of Recent Federal Support at the University of Wisconsin* (Madison: School of Education, 1964), p. 13.

[11]Olson, *G.I. Bill, Veterans, and Colleges*, p. 1.

GIs after the war. As early as April, 1942, Eleanor Roosevelt had warned against creating "a dangerous pressure group in our midst" if there were no jobs for the returning veterans, or else "we may reap the whirlwind."[12] Not surprisingly, the GI Bill's main provisions dealt not with education but with unemployment payments of $20 a month for up to a year, subsidized home mortgages, and various types of job-related education, especially on-the-job training. Government studies and surveys of servicemen during the war estimated that between 7 and 12 percent of the veterans would probably return to school, and most of these would enroll in technical and vocational institutions. This led the War Department and the Veterans Administration to reach the conclusion that fewer than 700,000 of the more than 15 million World War II veterans were likely to attend school or college on a full-time basis, and this enrollment would be distributed over several years.[13]

Academic opinions varied decidedly about the potential effect of the GI Bill's educational provisions. A few spokesmen, most of them representing elite private colleges and universities, objected to the sweeping nature of the educational benefits. In a widely circulated *Collier's* article entitled "The Threat to American Education," President Robert M. Hutchins of the University of Chicago dismissed what he termed the "absurd" educational provisions as simply "a method of keeping the veterans off the bread line." He predicted that many schools would prostitute themselves through lowered academic standards in order to attract more of these easy federal dollars. "Education is not a device for coping with mass unemployment," he admonished. "Colleges and universities will find themselves converted into educational hobo jungles." Harvard President James B. Conant likewise thought the educational provisions should be limited to a carefully selected group of academically well-prepared veterans; otherwise, he said, "we may find the least capable among the war generation . . . flooding the facilities for advanced education."[14]

Less elitist educators worried that because the ex-GIs were older than typical undergraduates and many were married with

---

[12]Quoted in ibid., p. 21.

[13]UW Personnel Council, "Student Veterans at the University of Wisconsin," March 20, 1945, Series 1/1/3, Box 62, UA; Olson, "G.I. Bill and Higher Education," 601-2; *Wisconsin State Journal*, September 15, 1945.

[14]Robert M. Hutchins, "The Threat to American Education," *Collier's*, 114 (December 30, 1944), pp. 20-21, quoted in Olson, *G.I. Bill, Veterans, and Colleges*, pp. 25, 34. Conant is quoted in ibid., p. 33.

children, they would constitute a new and decidedly anomalous student group disruptive of the traditional campus atmosphere and routines. While some believed the veterans would have no problem readjusting to student life, others feared the ex-GIs would resent civilian authority or were likely to have been so traumatized or brutalized by their combat experience as to make their campus assimilation difficult if not impossible. UW Assistant Dean of Men W.W. Blaesser predicted in July, 1944, that most of the veterans would have trouble adapting because they "are used to being told what to do and find it difficult adjusting to a situation where they have to go out on their own."[15] To prepare for such problems a number of colleges and universities added special trauma counselors to their student health services.

In Madison, newly appointed President Fred rejected this course and decided to rely on the University's regular student services personnel for any counseling the veterans might need. Working with the U.S. Veterans Administration, the University early created a general veterans center to provide testing and advice to ex-GIs living in and around Madison on how to obtain their federal and state benefits and meet the educational requirements of the GI Bill. In the fall of 1945 the University added two more administrative units for its own growing number of student veterans: an Office of Veteran Affairs to advise veterans of their rights under state and federal law and assist them in developing their educational programs, and a Veterans Business Office to handle the financial aspects of veteran enrollment under the GI Bill. Additional staff was added as the number of ex-GIs increased, but the focus remained on administering the educational benefits of student veterans efficiently rather than providing special academic or personal counseling. Veterans received preference in admission, but once enrolled they were regarded as regular UW students. The student services staff described it as a "policy of *assimilation*, with provision for specialized assistance when necessary." This, they expected, would mostly involve helping the veterans "to curb restlessness and to develop proper study habits," since some were probably "not prepared physically or mentally, for rigorous study."[16]

---

[15]*Daily Cardinal*, July 7, 1944.

[16]Personnel Council, "Student-Veterans at the University of Wisconsin," March 20, 1945; Olson, "G.I. Bill and Higher Education," 603-4; UW BOR Minutes, April 26 and June 15, 1944; *Badger Quarterly*, September, 1944; "Veterans Center," *WAM*, 46 (November, 1944), 5; UW Faculty Document 698, "Report of the Steering

One innovative feature of the University of Wisconsin's post-war planning dated back to early 1942, when the general faculty agreed to permit the University's various schools and colleges to award a modest amount of academic credit for wartime military service. Proponents argued that the physical education and military science (ROTC) requirements should be waived for veterans and in addition that some military training was of a sufficiently intellectual character to deserve academic credit. The faculty charged a committee of academic deans with developing reasonably uniform policies for implementing this decision, a process that was eased when the American Council on Education eventually sponsored a data base to assist colleges and universities in evaluating the academic content of the various military training programs. The initial UW policy granted up to ten elective credits for service as an enlisted man and as many as fifteen for service as a commissioned officer. Whatever the merit of this distinction between the two levels of service, it was unlikely to stand in a state with Wisconsin's democratic traditions. When the veterans began flooding onto the campus after the war, the policy was quietly modified to provide a blanket grant of fifteen elective credits to all who had been honorably discharged after service of three months or longer. Although UW administrators did not emphasize it, they were well aware that the fifteen war service credits reduced the time a veteran needed to be in school by as much as a semester, no small consideration as enrollment pressures mounted.[17]

By early 1944, months before the allied invasion of Europe and with the end of the war more than a year away, University planning for handling the return of the war veterans to the campus got seriously under way. In response to a faculty recommendation, on

Committee on Post-War University Problems," February 7, 1944; E.B. Fred to Malcolm Willey, June 26, 1945, Series 4/16/1, Box 21, UA; UW Faculty Document, 735p, Fred, "President's Report to the Faculty," October 1, 1945; *Wisconsin State Journal*, September 16, 1945.

[17]UW Faculty Document 640, Administrative Committee, "Recommendations on War Credits and Credits for Civil Pilot Training Courses," February 9, 1942; UW Faculty Document 672, University Committee, "Statement on Post-War Problems," April 5, 1943; UW Faculty Documents 701, 701a, and 701b, Recommendations on War Credits from the Faculties of the Colleges of Letters and Science, Agriculture, and Engineering, March 6, 1944; UW BOR Minutes, March 11, April 15, 1944, and January 19, 1946; "UW Credit for War," *WAM*, 47 (October, 1945), 7; "Student Veterans Get the Breaks When They Come to Wisconsin," ibid. (February, 1946), 4; *Daily Cardinal*, February 1, 1947. The war service credits essentially applied to undergraduate degree work, since graduate study was based less on credits than on mastery of a subject area.

February 18 President Dykstra appointed a Special Committee on Educational Problems for War Veterans chaired by English Professor Henry A. Pochmann.[18] One of the first actions of the Pochmann Committee was to secure more flexibility in applying admissions requirements to veterans lacking some preparatory work, a change the committee noted was urgent because already a few discharged service-men were seeking to enroll. The committee also declared that ex-GIs should be welcomed as regular students, not some exotic species: "The general policy of the University should be to absorb the war veterans into the general student body as far as possible and to organize separate courses and provide special services only as the desirability for these is clearly evident."[19]

In May, 1944, a month before the allied invasion of Europe, the Pochmann Committee hosted a conference for midwestern colleges and universities to consider likely post-war educational problems. For two days nearly two hundred educators representing more than sixty institutions gathered at the Memorial Union. The most obvious issue was how to deal with the returning GIs, especially what sort of counseling they might need and whether and to what extent to give academic credit for their training while in service. Some of those present believed an equally important educational challenge facing the country was how to persuade high school and college dropouts now working in war plants to resume their abandoned studies.[20] If the Madison conferees underestimated the difficulties their institutions would eventually confront in absorbing the war veterans, their opti-mism was understandable. Although the academic community was generally aware that Congress was considering additional veterans legislation (and indeed the national educational associations helped to shape the measure's educational provisions), the landmark GI Bill of

---

[18]Other members of the committee were Professors Phillip G. Fox (commerce), Vincent E. Kivlin (agricultural education), J. Kenneth Little (education), Villiers W. Meloche (chemistry), Albert G. Ramsberger (philosophy), and Leslie F. Van Hagen (civil engineering). Dykstra to members of the Special Committee on Educational Problems for War Veterans, February 18, 1944, Series 5/102, Box 1, UA.

[19]*Press Bulletin*, February 23, 1944; UW Faculty Documents 702 and 702a, Reports of Special Committee on Educational Problems for War Veterans, March 6 and April 3, 1944.

[20]See Henry A. Pochmann to E.F. Lindquist, April 1, 1944; Agenda for Regional Conference on Post-War Education, May 8, 1944, Series 5/102, Box 1, UA; *Daily Cardinal*, April 9, 1944.

Rights would not be passed and signed into law until more than a month after the Madison conference adjourned.[21]

Whatever the estimates of the size of the post-war UW student body, there was recognition at both ends of State Street that the University would need expanded facilities in order to handle any substantial increase in its enrollment. Federal Depression-era Public Works Administration funds had supported the construction of the Kronshage men's and Elizabeth Waters women's dormitories, the Memorial Union Theater, and the Law School library wing during the 1930s. Apart from some remodeling, however, there had been no construction of classroom and laboratory space or other academic facilities since the completion of the Mechanical Engineering Building in 1931. Some high-priority projects, such as a badly needed new library building, had languished for more than two decades for lack of state funding. In October, 1943, the Board of Regents approved a seven-point post-war construction request totaling more than $7 million.[22] Apart from the perennial call for a new campus library and another engineering building, most of the projects identified–for example, a new dairy building and expansion of the Home Economics Building–reflected earlier priorities rather than a realistic appraisal of what would be most needed after the war: more classrooms, instructional laboratories, and student housing. Following a review of University physical plant needs by a friendly legislative committee in the fall of 1944, the regents approved an expanded construction request totaling $12.3 million.[23] A new library remained a high priority, but much of the list was not immediately relevant to what would emerge as the University's most pressing building needs after the war.

Like their counterparts across the country, UW administrators from the first tended to underestimate the magnitude of the pent-up demand for the University's services. Shortly after the enactment of the GI Bill in the summer of 1944, Registrar Curtis Merriman predicted that between 125 and 150 ex-GIs would enroll under the new

[21]American Council on Education announcement, June 29, 1944, Series 5/102, Box 1, UA. The council informed its member institutions that Public Law 346 was effective immediately.

[22]"Post-War Building," *WAM*, 45 (November 15, 1943), 35-36.

[23]See UW BOR Minutes, October 28,1944; "The Real Need of the University," *WAM*, 46 (December 15, 1944), 2-3; *Capital Times*, December 31, 1944.

federal program that fall. Nearly 200 showed up.[24] A year later, with the war just over but demobilization not yet in full swing, enrollment jumped by a third to 9,000 students, of whom a third of the men were veterans.[25] Predicting enrollment, never easy, was particularly difficult during the early months of demobilization. As the number of discharged servicemen seeking admission steadily increased, University authorities arranged for their immediate enrollment during the semester in special refresher courses without regard to regular entrance requirements. A number of promising veterans were admitted even though they had not graduated from high school.[26]

Mounting Enrollments

Apart from the increasing number of veterans, easily identifiable in their used GI clothing, the return of peacetime conditions in September, 1945, brought some other changes to the campus. The Memorial Union, for example, reopened Tripp Commons to general use after three years as an army mess hall. It also began serving a full pat of butter with every meal. The end of the Navy Radio School released Tripp and Adams halls initially to women residents and three of the Kronshage dormitories reverted to use by regular men students. Only ten of the more than fifty fraternities operating before the war were able to reopen their houses initially, however. A number had to wait until wartime leases expired before they could reclaim their houses; two were obliged to operate as men's rooming houses until they could rebuild their membership. Thirteen fraternities had lost their houses during the war and were forced to seek new space.[27] The number of students on campus grew substantially throughout 1945-46, from 7,779 in September, 1945, to 12,429 the following May. Summer session enrollments, which averaged about 1,100 in 1944 and 1945, jumped to 4,300 in 1946, with most of the increase made up of veterans.[28]

---

[24]Ibid., September 24, 1944; *Daily Cardinal*, October 18, 1944.

[25]L. Joseph Lins, "Fact Book for History of Madison Campus," notebook, 1983, UHP.

[26]"Highlight Facts about Enrollment, Housing, and War Veterans," November 9, 1945, Series 4/16/1, Box 32, UA.

[27]*Daily Cardinal*, September 21, 1945, March 21, 1959.

[28]"The University of Wisconsin's Program for Veterans," June 26, 1946, Series 1/1/3, Box 64, UA.

Reluctantly, University authorities began taking steps to restrict admission of non-resident, non-veteran applicants to keep the campus from being swamped. Such controls, President Fred told the regents in November, 1945, were necessary in order "to protect the interests of new students from Wisconsin and veterans."[29] For the fall semester of 1945, non-resident women students were required to be in the upper 30 percent of their high school graduating class or to have a 1.4 grade point average (on a 3 point scale) if they were transferring from another institution. This excluded about 450 non-resident women, an action that led to rumors–vigorously denied–that its real purpose was to reduce the number of Jewish students at the University.[30] Before the next semester rising enrollment pressures led UW authorities to suspend the admission of all new non-resident applicants except for veterans, who were treated as if they were Wisconsin residents. Applications from non-residents, unless from former students or veterans, were held up pending availability of housing. During 1946 the University stopped accepting transfers from Wisconsin colleges, even of state residents, if the student was able to continue where enrolled.[31] "We deplore the situation which requires that students must be turned away," President Fred told the regents. "We are exploring every possibility for housing which will enable us to accommodate the maximum number."[32]

Not only were veterans seeking admission in unexpected numbers, but the end of draft calls increased the number of high school graduates wanting to move directly on to college. By the summer of 1946 the flood of Wisconsin applicants–veterans and non-veterans alike–led the University to reject all new non-resident undergraduate students, including non-resident veterans. Even so, UW housing officials predicted that as many as 2,750 students were unlikely to find housing in Madison.[33] Assessing enrollment pressures across the state,

[29]Fred to Board of Regents, November 26, 1945, Series 1/1/3, Box 63, UA.

[30]"It Can't Be Helped," *Wisconsin State Journal*, September 7, 1945; Kenneth Little to Dear Faculty Member, December 10, 1945, Series 4/16/1, Box 36, UA. There is no evidence for the suspicion that the enrollment restrictions reflected any underlying anti-Semitic policy.

[31]*Daily Cardinal*, October 15, 1946.

[32]Fred to Board of Regents, November 26, 1945; Little, "Some Interesting Facts about Current University Enrollment and Guesses for Next Year" [May 4, 1946], Series 1/1/3, Box 63, UA.

[33]"Enrollment in the University of Wisconsin and Provisions for Veterans" [August, 1946], Series 4/16/1, Box 32, UA.

President Fred soberly told the regents that a large number of qualified Wisconsin residents–he thought as many as 4,000–"will not find it possible to gain admission to any college."[34] That fall the University was forced to turn away more than 10,000 non-resident applicants, three-fourths of them veterans.[35]

Yank *Magazine's Sad Sack Confronts UW Registration Lines*

With the opening of the fall term in 1946, enrollment in Madison had doubled to a record 18,598 students, 40 percent above the pre-war peak and triple the number enrolled only two years earlier. Of these nearly 12,000 were veterans, or 62 percent of the total student body. "How did it happen," a University fact sheet attempted somewhat lamely to explain, "that over 3,000 students in excess of the estimated 15,500 were permitted to come?" The simple answer was that more than 6,000 additional veterans, double the number of the previous semester, had been admitted. Moreover, the University had enrolled its largest freshman class in history: 3,800 in all, including about 2,000 veterans.[36] "The University has not sought the increases in responsibilities that have come," President Fred told the Board of Regents in October:

[34]Fred, "A Look at the Future" [September 14, 1946], Series 1/1/3, Box 64, UA.

[35]Keith W. Olson, "World War II Veterans at the University of Wisconsin," *Wisconsin Magazine of History*, 53 (Winter, 1969-70), 85.

[36]"Some Questions and Answers about the University's Record Enrollment," September 27, 1946, Series 4/16/1, Box 57, UA.

> All colleges and universities in the nation are faced with a
> great increase in the number of students and in the number
> of problems to be studied. This is a challenge that the
> University of Wisconsin faces gladly albeit with consider-
> able apprehension. The faculty and staff are doing their best
> under very difficult circumstances.[37]

University authorities reduced some of the pressure on the Madison
campus by reestablishing the network of freshman-sophomore extension centers around the state that had been created during the Depression. By the fall of 1946 these centers had enrolled nearly 5,400
freshmen and sophomores in 34 Wisconsin communities.[38] Even so,
the doubling of enrollment in Madison brought unprecedented,
massive, and sleep-robbing administrative problems on a scale never
before experienced.

   To provide more classroom space the University expanded its
normal class timetable, continuing the wartime trimester summer
session and scheduling classes from 7:45 a.m. to 9:30 p.m. on week-
days and from 7:45 a.m. to noon on Saturdays. Classes doubled and
tripled in size, with a few large classes even moving to the Memorial
Union Theater and nearby church auditoriums.[39] For the first time
public address systems came into regular use in large lecture halls. The
traditionally popular History 3a, the introductory survey of European
civilization between 800-1660, had regularly drawn enrollments of
350-500 before the war. In the fall of 1945 the history department
offered two sections, each taught by a full professor and enrolling 450
and 525 students. By the second semester, with only one professor
available to teach the course, the department stopped enrollment at
1,030 students and broke the course into three sections, two of them
taught by graduate acting instructors lecturing to 400 students each.[40]
Other departments made similar adjustments and improvisations, often

---

[37][Fred,] "Statement Concerning the University Budget for 1947-49" [October
20, 1946], Series 1/1/3, Box 64, UA.
   [38]Ibid.; "The UW Campus Means 40 Places," *WAM*, 48 (November, 1946), 7.
   [39]In September, 1946, the University began using the main auditorium of the
First Congregational Church to teach large political science and sociology classes. The
arrangements were oral until set down in writing several months later with the University
paying no rent, only for utilities and maintenance. Peterson and First Congregational
Church, Memorandum of Agreement, December 26, 1947, and January 8, 1947, Series
1/1/3, Box 65, UA. The accelerated trimester plan ended in 1948 as the pressure of
veteran enrollments declined. *Daily Cardinal*, January 22, 1947.
   [40]Robert L. Reynolds to Fred, February 27, 1946, Series 1/1/3, Box 63, UA.

limited by the shortage of large classrooms and qualified teaching staff.

The existing physical plant could be stretched only so far, however, so the Board of Regents delegated broad authority to President Fred and the UW business and finance director, A.W. Peterson, to move quickly in obtaining wartime temporary buildings being declared surplus by the federal government at military bases and war plants around the country.[41] Peterson was remarkably agile and imaginative in carrying out this directive. During 1946-47, construction crews disassembled, moved to the campus, and re-erected thirty-nine Quonset huts and other assorted prefabricated buildings. To augment the tight Madison labor market University authorities appealed to student veterans with wartime army or navy construction experience to help with these emergency building projects.[42] Typical were the seven Quonset huts installed on the lower campus playing field in front of the State Historical Society. The six smaller huts were each divided into two classrooms, while the seventh large unit became the library's reserve book reading room, enabling its smaller predecessor in Bascom Hall to be reconverted back into classrooms. Irreverent students quickly dubbed these new campus additions "the Sow and Six Piglets." The balance of the field was turned into a temporary parking lot for the increased number of commuting staff and students. When the fabled Kiekhofer Wall on Langdon Street was demolished in 1946, students quickly substituted the exterior of the lower campus Quonset huts for painting announcements and slogans.

Particularly useful were former War Department prefabricated barracks that could quickly be converted into classroom and office space with minimal alteration. Three of these were relocated onto the Hill behind Bascom Hall, two of them sited in the former outdoor theater immediately west of the building and assigned to the recently autonomous School of Commerce. Another three of the barracks were installed on the lawn in front of Barnard Hall; others were scattered across the campus. University crews moved the newest section of the school building at the Badger Ordnance Works near Baraboo to the campus for temporary classroom space. One of the most ambitious projects involved relocating two large buildings from the former army air base at Truax Field to serve as a 400-seat cafeteria at the corner of

---

[41]UW BOR Minutes, September 14, 1946.

[42]*Daily Cardinal*, October 2, 3, 1946, April 1, 1947; Luberg, *Characteristics of Recent Federal Support*, p. 14.

Political science class at First Congregational Church, 1947. UA, 631-M.

Memorial Union food line, 1946. UA, X25-3382.

"Sow and Six Piglets" Quonset huts with parking lot, on site of future Memorial Library and Library Mall, photo by Phil Harrington. UA, X25-3404.

"Sow" Quonset hut on lower campus as reserve reading room. UA, X25-1485.

University Avenue and Breese Terrace. Opened in late October, 1947, the new food service brought immediate relief to the hard-pressed Memorial Union, where serving lines of hungry students had some- times snaked for a hundred yards or more outside the building.[43]

The growth of enrollment and the resulting need for these temporary buildings to meet the emergency led the Board of Regents to decide in the fall of 1946 that the University's physical plant "should be so expanded that it can adequately accommodate 22,500 students," including "a fair proportion of freshmen and sophomores on the campus." The latter observation made clear the administration and regents did not agree with suggestions that the Madison campus should be primarily an upper division and graduate institution.[44]

More students required more staff, of course. Not all of the faculty members who had left for various forms of service returned to Madison after the war, requiring departments to move aggressively in recruiting replacements and additions to their teaching staff. Because competition for experienced faculty was keen nationally, much of the expansion had to be at the junior level. Fortunately, the GI Bill stimulated a great increase in the number of students seeking advanced degrees and supported a ready pool of instructors and graduate teaching assistants eager to acquire some instructional experience. By 1947-48 the University employed 1,402 graduate assistants, compared with 665 in 1939-40. The increase in the number of instructors–the lowest, non-tenured faculty rank and an appointment usually held briefly by an advanced graduate student–was nearly as great, from 418 to 870. The faculty as a whole more than doubled in size over the decade, with even the two tenured ranks (professors and associate professors) growing by 40 percent. The lopsided nature of the expan-

---

[43]See UW BOR Minutes, May 4, June 28, July 25, October 12 and 30, and December 14, 1946, June 25, 1947, and June 16, 1949; Olson, "World War II Veterans," 89; Mueller, *Badger Village and Bluffview Courts (The Town That Would Not Die),* (Badger: Bluffview Acres, Inc., 1982), pp. 86-87.

[44]UW BOR Minutes, October 30, 1946. UW faculty and administrators consistently stressed that enrollment pressures should not be permitted to change the balanced nature of the University. The faculty Committee on Enrollment Policy emphasized in March, 1946, that any enrollment restrictions should not apply to graduate students because "they are necessary for the continuance of the instructional program of the University." The University increased its use of graduate teaching assistants and instructors substantially during the postwar boom and very likely could not have handled the burgeoning undergraduate enrollment in Madison and at the two-year centers otherwise. "Report of the Committee on Enrollment Policy," undated but approved by the Board of Regents on March 9, 1946.

sion was evident, however, in comparing the role held by the junior teaching staff in the two periods. Before the war tenured faculty constituted 24 percent of the total instructional staff; by 1947-48 their percentage had declined to 18 percent.[45] The increase in class sizes and in the number of inexperienced teachers may well have eroded academic quality in these years, but it was a way of assuring maximum student access at a time of severe institutional stress.

Hustling for Housing

The thousands of students clamoring for admission presented the University with a number of daunting challenges, of which probably the most immediate and severe was the critical shortage of housing in Madison. Wartime needs had converted to other uses much of the city's stock of privately owned student rooming houses, including a number of former fraternity houses. By war's end, moreover, most of the increased number of women students (1,400 more than before the war) were living in space previously earmarked for men. "We know that housing will present a serious problem at the close of the War," Donald L. Halverson, the director of the Division of Residence Halls, had written President Dykstra in the summer of 1944, "so I shall hope that work may start as soon as materials are available."[46] Halverson had in mind the construction of additional regular dormitories, the first of which–Slichter Hall–turned out not to be ready for its initial 200 male residents until the fall of 1947. Clearly the construction of regular dormitories offered no quick solution. Such projects required uncertain and lengthy state approval and funding and were subject to unpredictable construction delays because of the shortage of building materials in the immediate post-war period.

More aggressive steps were required to deal with the housing emergency. One approach was to restrict enrollment, especially of non-resident and even non-veteran Wisconsin applicants. As early as May, 1945, the Board of Regents warned that new Wisconsin high school graduates contemplating admission to the University for the fall semester should apply by June 20 and obtain their housing immediately. The regents decided to hold up registration permits for most non-resident women applicants until enrollment totals were known and to

---

[45]Olson, "World War II Veterans," 88-90.
[46]Halverson to Dykstra, July 18, 1944, Series 24/1/1, Box 188, UA.

develop comparable standards for transfer students.[47] The enrollment controls were steadily tightened over the next several years in large part because of the housing shortage.

As the University developed its admission priorities, there was clear agreement that top priority must go to qualified veterans, especially those from Wisconsin. Because of the tight housing situation in Madison, the regents directed Registrar Kenneth Little to tie the issuance of registration permits to the projected availability of student housing, a rather uncertain science. Little felt obliged to caution high school principals and graduating seniors that even though Wisconsin residents would receive priority for admission, the University could not guarantee rooming accommodations. The issuance of a permit to register does not insure a room," he warned. "Each student must arrange for his living quarters."[48]

Restricting enrollment did nothing, of course, to expand the supply of student housing needed for the rapidly growing number of qualified students–veterans and non-veterans alike–seeking admission. The only hope of meeting this urgent need was through a variety of temporary expedients, some of them remarkably creative. One approach was to appeal to faculty members and other Dane County residents to open their homes, citing the "desperate need" for more student accommodations.[49] Though it hardly solved the problem, this brought significant results. By the fall of 1946 more than 2,500 UW students, including 860 married students, were living in private homes not previously open to student roomers. By converting the larger single rooms into doubles, the residence halls staff expanded the capacity of campus dormitories by about a third. University officials also surveyed every inch of the campus for possible additional living quarters. They even sought federal approval to use the former Civilian Conservation Corps barracks at the University Arboretum, although this idea was dropped when it turned out the structures were too "ancient and dilapidated."[50] Assistant Dean Vincent I. Kivlin of the College of

---

[47]UW BOR Minutes, May 25, 1945.

[48]Kenneth Little to Dear Principal, March 7, 1946, Series 1/1/3, Box 63, UA. Little asked that a notice about UW admissions procedures and the shortage of housing be posted prominently for students to read. "It is urgent," the notice advised, "that, in view of the total situation, students of doubtful college aptitude do not use college facilities greatly needed by war veterans."

[49]*Wisconsin State Journal*, October 9, 1945.

[50] E.B. Fred, "The University and the G.I.," *WAM*, 48 (September-October, 1946), 3-4; "Life on the Wisconsin Campuses," ibid., 5; *Capital Times*, July 27, 1945,

Agriculture reported his unit could provide living space in several of its buildings: 6 places in the dairy barn, 1 in the poultry building, 1 in the swine barn, and 6 in the Stock Pavilion.[51] Athletic director Harry Stuhldreher relinquished space in the enclosed east side of the football stadium for barracks-type housing for 160 single men. This made possible two large dorms, appropriately named after two prominent Wisconsin athletes killed during the war: David N. Schreiner and Robert F. Baumann.[52] Most of the ground floor of the Women's Field House was turned into a temporary men's cooperative house.[53]

"And to think we've been waiting since we were freshmen for men to come back!"

The most difficult housing problem was the shortage of campus-area apartments and housekeeping rooms, because it turned out that about a third of the veterans seeking admission were married, many of them with children, present and prospective. Before the war very few undergraduates were married and the University made no provision for their housing. Now, however, it was clear that aggressive steps were needed to provide appropriate accommodations if these ex-

---

and January 23, 1946.
    [51]Vincent E. Kivlin to E.B. Fred, July 30, 1945, Series 4/16/1, UA.
    [52]UW BOR Minutes, November 23, 1946.
    [53]Division of Residence Halls lease agreement, October 11, 1946, Series 24/1/1, Box 214, UA.

GIs were to take advantage of their educational benefits. Accordingly, even before the end of the war the Fred administration was working to secure surplus government trailers for a University-operated trailer park for married veterans. He was assisted in this effort by Joseph W. Jackson of the Madison and Wisconsin Foundation, whose efforts had earlier been so critical in creating the University Arboretum. Fred also enlisted the political assistance of Robert M. La Follette, Jr., the state's senior U.S. senator in Washington.[54] By early August, 1945, plans were set for what came to be known as the Randall Trailer Park, perhaps the first such student veteran housing project in the country. Cutting through normal federal and state bureaucratic red tape with surprising speed, UW officials persuaded the Federal Public Housing Authority to release up to 100 surplus trailers at Prairie du Sac that had formerly housed war workers at the Badger Ordnance Works at nearby Baraboo. The State Emergency Board provided $40,000 to move and install the trailers in the Camp Randall Memorial Park east of the football stadium, though because of the need to move quickly the facilities and funds of the Wisconsin University Building Corporation were used initially.[55]

By the start of the fall semester 64 "standard" and 27 "expansive" trailers were ready for occupancy, along with 4 toilet/shower units and 2 laundry units, all connected by a series of wooden sidewalks. The Board of Regents set the rental at $25 per month for the standard and $32.50 for the larger expansive units, rates considerably

---

[54]J.W. Jackson to Fred, June 29, 1945; Fred to Robert M. La Follette, July 12, 1945, Series 4/16/1, box 36, UA; Barry Teicher and John W. Jenkins, *A History of Housing at the University of Wisconsin* (Madison: UW History Project, 1987), p. 48.

[55]"Trailer Housing for Married Veterans," report to the regents, August 11, 1945, Series 1/1/3, Box 62; UW BOR Minutes, August 11, 1945. The location of this first trailer park was a matter of some delicacy, because when the University acquired the Camp Randall site in 1893 the regents had pledged to maintain in perpetuity the 3-acre Camp Randall Memorial Park honoring Wisconsin's Civil War veterans. A Virginian by birth, whose relatives had fought for the Confederacy and who still displayed traces of his soft southern accent, President Fred was concerned that his background might stir up opposition to the trailer project from Wisconsin veterans organizations. He was more than a little upset, therefore, when the University news service released a story early in his presidency noting that he had a Confederate flag hanging in his house. Fred instructed the news service never to mention this again, explaining that he was merely honoring a promise made long ago to his late mother. Fortunately, the veterans groups accepted without question the University explanation that the trailer park was merely temporary housing designed to benefit and honor the latest group of Wisconsin veterans. See, for example, Fred to J. Stanley Dietz (draft), November 19, 1945, Series 24/1/3, Box 4, UA.

Veterans applying for housing, January 18, 1946. UA, X25-3403.

Camp Randall trailer parks, 1947. UA, 22/4-22/7/2, 257.

29

Camp Randall tiny trailer kitchen. UA, X25-2823.

Camp Randall Co-op Grocery. UA, 22/6/7/2, 557.

30

lower than the market price for similar space in Madison. The University incurred costs of $26,167 in moving, installing, and equipping the initial 91 units, or about $300 per unit, well below the $40,000 originally budgeted.[56] The accommodations were cramped; the small trailers measured only 7 feet wide by 21 feet long and provided about 600 cubic feet of space, compared with about 1,500 cubic feet in the larger units. The comforts were equally Spartan—no running water or drains, a small ice box, a two-burner electric hot plate for cooking, and, not least, a University-issued chamber pot for night use. Oil for the small heating stoves had to be carried from a central supply tank. Still, as the wife of one of the ex-GIs commented: "It's better than a fox hole—so why shouldn't we be content." The residents rejected the first names suggested for their community, Vetsville or Vetsburg, in favor of the more elegant Randall Park. [57]

As the need for married student housing continued to increase during 1945-46, the University moved quickly to develop a second trailer park nearby along Monroe Street, with government surplus units brought from as far away as Illinois and Indiana. By the start of the spring semester there were 190 student families including some 50 children living in the Randall and Monroe parks. In time some of the expansive trailers housed families with as many as three children; one had four. The residents quickly organized the two parks along the lines of small American villages, each with an elected mayor, a council of five aldermen, a secretary-treasurer, and several committees. Of the latter, the sanitary committee was considered the most important because of the problems inherent in cramped facilities and shared space.[58] With advice from economics Professor Harold M. Groves, the

---

[56]Lee Burns to A.W. Peterson, October 22, 1945, Series 24/1/3, Box 4, UA; Burns, "Report on Emergency Housing Projects at Wisconsin and Operating Estimates for 1946-47," March 8, 1947, UHP.

[57]Peterson, "Report on Veterans' Housing," October 27, 1945, Series 1/1/3, Box 63, UA; Svend Riemer and Marvin Riley, "Trailer Communities on a University Campus," *Journal of Land and Public Utility Economics*, 23 (February, 1947), 83; "Veterans and Wives Happy in U.W. Trailer Colony," *Milwaukee Journal*, October 21, 1945; *Daily Cardinal*, September 25, 1945.

[58]*Wisconsin State Journal*, November 2, 1945; *Milwaukee Sentinel*, November 3, 1945; Campus Planning Commission Minutes, November 9, 1945; Series 24/1/3, Box 4; William K. Divers to A.W. Peterson, November 14, 1945, telegram, ibid.; E.P. Grzybowski to D.L. Halverson, November 26, 1945, telegram, ibid; UW BOR Minutes, October 27, 1945. The overall cost of establishing the two trailer camps was $66,877, or about $350 per unit, for which the State Emergency Board advanced $65,000. The rent paid by residents was intended to operate the two parks on a break-even basis,

residents pooled their resources to create a cooperative grocery store. As the number of children in the camp increased, they persuaded President Fred to help them get the equipment and staff to start a nursery school, operated by the UW School of Education.[59]

"Hey, you've forgotten your change!"

Despite occasional complaints,[60] most of the residents were appreciative of their life at Camp Randall; turnover was low. Declared the wife of one veteran:

> Trailer life is certainly an 'adventure in living' which I wouldn't have wanted to miss. Our neighbors are congenial. My son has plenty of playmates. My husband enjoys the "sessions" with other fellows. We have air and sunlight, and best of all we have our own family unit together.

covering operating costs including the $1 nominal rent per unit charged by the Federal Public Housing Authority and repayment of the $65,000 advance from the state. The University did not charge residents for the costs of the Randall-Monroe nursery school. See also Constitution and By-Laws of Randall Park Village, January 24, 1946, and Monroe Park Village, March 22, 1946, Series 25/7/2, Box 13, UA.

[59]*Wisconsin State Journal*, September 22, 1946, and November 2, 1947; *Milwaukee Journal*, February 23, 1947.

[60]See, for example, Mrs. Chester A. Harlow to Fred, April 5, 1947; J.R. Hammersley to LeRoy Luberg, April 8, 1947; Arnold H. Dammen to Fred, April 15, 1947; A.W. Peterson to Glen R. Wilson, April 21, 1947, Series 4/16/1, Box 53, UA.

Another wife praised convenient location and the "friendly, helpful, cooperative management" of the parks and saw a virtue in the cramped nature of trailer life. "The small amount of work involved in house-work," she explained, "gives much time for leisure and special activi-ties–sewing, gardening, recreation."[61] Indeed, so popular were the Randall-Monroe parks among married veterans that for the fall of 1947 University authorities opened a third trailer park–East Hill–located on the eastern edge of the College of Agriculture's Hill Farms complex, along the gravel road that later became Midvale Boulevard. This park was just that; it merely provided 300 sites with access to water, electricity, and waste disposal for the considerable number of students and staff who needed space to park their own trailers.[62]

Recognizing that the trailer parks could accommodate only a small part of the growing student veteran population, President Fred and other UW officials also explored other housing possibilities. Quickly acting on a tip from a student, in September, 1946, the University paid $35,000 for the 16-unit Sullivan cabin court on University Avenue and promptly added 4 Quonset huts and 24 trailer sites.[63] Another option offering considerable space was the Army Air Corps training base at Truax Field northeast of the city. The site had formerly been the Madison airport, which was taken over by the army in the spring of 1942 to serve as a radio and radio mechanics training base. During the war it had housed as many as 35,000 airmen in a sizable complex of barracks, kitchens and mess halls, school buildings, a hospital, chapel, gymnasium, and other recreation facilities. Presi-dent Fred once again sought the help of Wisconsin politicians, includ-ing Senators La Follette and Alexander Wiley, in persuading the War Department to release the Truax facilities to meet the needs of veterans

---

[61]Riemer and Riley, "Trailer Communities," 83.

[62]UW BOR Minutes, June 28, 1946. In September, 1945, the regents had agreed to give the city of Madison an easement along the proposed Midvale Boulevard passing through the east 20 acres of the Hill Farms complex between University Avenue and the extension of Regent Street so the city could extend sewers and water mains to service new homes being built south of the University's farms. The regents drove a hard bargain, stipulating that the University and its successor property holders "shall be held free from property assessments for installation of sewers or water mains in either of these streets [Midvale Boulevard or Meadow Lane], but shall be allowed to make connections with said sewers and water mains for any residences or establishments which may be erected on said land." "Report of the Constructional Development Committee," Series 1/1/3, Box 63, UA; UW BOR Minutes, September 29, 1945. This action prepared the way for the siting of the East Hill Trailer Park the following year.

[63]Olson, "World War II Veterans," 92.

attending the University. "The housing problem in Madison has become desperate and all available space is exhausted," he explained to La Follette. "We could also use some of the buildings at Truax for instructional purposes and for messing. The use of Truax Field buildings for veterans attending the University would provide material relief to the housing, instructional and messing requirements of veterans."[64] After some hurried negotiations with federal officials, on January 5, 1946, the War Department released a sizable part of the Truax military reservation ("revocable at will by the Secretary of War") to the Federal Public Housing Authority, which in turn transferred the property to the University three days later.[65]

Even before the formal transfer, a month earlier the UW Division of Residence Halls with the army's blessing had opened an office in the base hospital. Newell J. Smith, a former housing staff member himself recently released from military service, was assigned to Truax as the resident director of the project.[66] Smith and residence halls workers quickly began renovating and furnishing the hospital as a giant student dormitory fitted out to house 562 single men and 100 married couples, all in time for the second semester of 1945-46. The State Emergency Board advanced $15,000 to cover the University's initial costs in converting the base hospital to student housing. By January 19, only eleven days after the University took formal possession of the property and scarcely a month after Smith and his staff had begun their whirlwind conversion work, the hospital complex was ready for its first student residents. Within a few weeks 80 married couples and 300 single students were living at Truax.

---

[64]Fred to La Follette, November 16, 1945, Series 4/16/1, Box 46, UA.

[65]Fred, Memorandum of Conversation with Captain Kirby, November 19, 1945; Major Joe C. Robinson, Entry Permit for the Federal Public Housing Authority, January 5, 1946; William E. Bergeron, Permit for the Regents of the University of Wisconsin, January 8, 1946, Bergeron to A.W. Peterson, January 7, 1946, all in ibid.; Burns, "Report on Emergency Housing Projects"; "University Uses Truax Hospital," *WAM*, 47 (January, 1946), 4.

[66]Smith suspected that President Fred might have pulled strings to secure his early release from the army, since he had no other explanation of why his departure from Camp Hood, Texas, was mysteriously expedited well ahead of others in his unit and just in time to help with planning the Truax project. Smith recalls Fred's writing to him in the fall of 1945 asking if he would be interested in returning to Madison to help find housing for the increasing number of student veterans. Shortly after responding affirmatively he received orders for his release. Newell J. Smith, conversation with Barry Teicher, February 27, 1996, Oral History Project, UA.

The Truax accommodations were Spartan at best. As many as twenty-seven single men lived in what had formerly been open hospital wards, now sparsely furnished with cots, chairs, and study tables, and including shared toilet and shower facilities. For this the veterans were charged $13.00 a month or $19.50 for the few single rooms. "Suites" for married couples (no children or cooking) consisted of two small adjoining rooms at a cost of $27.50 a month or $30.00 if there was an attached private bathroom. For these quarters the University supplied double deck bunks, an easy chair, one or two other chairs, a dresser, a study table, lamps, and linen. Susan Burdick Davis, who was hired to serve as educational adviser and house mother at Truax, reported that many young couples expressed great disappointment when they first viewed their "suites." "Have I come from Georgia for this!" exclaimed one young wife in dismay:

> "We went right back to Chicago for three days," said a couple; "Just another fox hole," said a third, "but we were mighty thankful when the letter came saying we had been assigned to one." "We soon found, moreover," they went on, "that it was fun to go to work to dress it up for our first home." . . . Of course there have been tormenting inconveniences and many a gripe, but the veterans appreciate the fact that the University has made a sincere effort to make family living possible for them.[67]

The lack of cooking facilities for the Truax residents led residence halls to operate a cafeteria and snack bar open for all meals at prices comparable to the Memorial Union.

In May of 1946 the University took over a second section of the Truax base to provide accommodations for an additional 960 single veterans. It also worked with the city of Madison to convert part of the Truax military reservation into general veterans housing. The Federal Public Housing Authority agreed to remodel as UW dormitories three large buildings formerly used for radio instruction, and residence halls personnel undertook to turn several nearby auxiliary buildings into the kitchen, cafeteria, snack bar, library, gymnasium, and related support facilities needed for expanding this student housing complex. Remodeling of the three dormitory buildings continued for nearly a full year,

---

[67]Burns, "Report on Emergency Housing Projects"; Susan Burdick Davis, "The First Year at the University of Wisconsin Truax Project," n.d., Series 25/8/1, Box 1, UA.

Truax Field housing for UW veterans, left-center and center. UA, 2993-A.

Truax Field single men's living quarters, four men per room, rent $30 month.
UA, X25-3378.

although the first two units were partially ready for use by some residents at the beginning of the 1946-47 academic year. The Emergency Board once again came through with an advance of $62,500 for this second Truax project.[68] Subsequently the University appealed for the formal release by the FPHA of additional facilities already being used by the residence halls staff to service the growing Truax project, including a number of maintenance shops and storage sheds, a garage for servicing campus buses, and a trestle for unloading coal.[69] By November, 1947, the Truax project was essentially complete, a veritable small town able to house 1,522 single veterans and 104 married couples in 46 buildings or building wings, each named after a UW alumnus killed during the war.

Because of the distance from campus and the lack of nearby city bus service to the project, the University sought to acquire surplus army buses for its own Truax bus line. When these were not at first available, UW officials prevailed upon the Madison Transportation Company to offer occasional bus service to Truax. The company cut back this service in September, 1946, however, leading the University to operate several express bus runs to and from the campus and more frequent shuttle service to the nearest city bus line. One of the student drivers was Robert S. Korach, whose UW education had been interrupted by wartime service in the Army Transportation Corps. Korach quickly rose to be the manager of the growing UW Truax bus system, eventually supervising twenty student and full-time drivers and being responsible for the maintenance of the fleet of dilapidated school and army buses. His most vivid memory of his Truax bus experience was coping with the massive snow storm of February, 1947. After graduating in 1947 with a major in economics, Korach entered the field of public transportation, first in New Jersey and finally as operating manager of the sprawling Los Angeles bus and rail system. More than his course work, he credited his student training with the ramshackle Truax bus system as providing the basic preparation for his subsequent career.[70]

---

[68]Ibid.; "Report to Regents on the Truax Project," March 8, 1946, Series 4/16/1, Box 46; UW BOR Minutes, March 9, 1946; Federal Public Housing Authority, Contract with the Regents of the University of Wisconsin to Provide Temporary Housing, June 21, 1946, Series 25/8/1, Box 1; UW BOR Minutes, June 28, 1946.

[69]Burns to Olmsted, October 1, 1946, Series 25/8/1, Box 1, UA.

[70]Robert S. Korach, oral history interview, 1993, UA.

Largely because of the Truax project's inconvenient location and the lack of real housekeeping facilities for married students, turnover was high, with residents moving out on short notice as soon as they could locate more suitable housing. University authorities nevertheless viewed the project as an essential safety valve at the start of the academic years in 1946 and 1947 when Truax made it possible for many veterans to be in school until other Madison housing opened up.[71] In spite of the *Daily Cardinal*'s editorial hope as early as 1947 that the Truax project would soon be unnecessary, there were still about 500 students living at the former air base two years later when residence halls staff finally concluded they could safely close down the project at the end of the fall semester of 1949.[72]

Within the limitations imposed by the site, Newell Smith and his staff sought to make Truax as attractive as possible, using the well-established house fellow system in the single male dormitories. In her role as adviser and house mother, for example, Susan Burdick Davis helped the Truax wives organize a women's club that sponsored various educational and social activities such as craft groups, lectures, and faculty teas. Although a few of the veterans declared they had had enough of regimentation and group activities, most of the residents quickly developed a Truax Student Association that created radio and camera clubs, sponsored a forum program, developed the Truax library, and organized dances and other social activities. There was even a mimeographed newspaper, the *True Axe*, whose motto was "All the News That's Print to Fit." The Memorial Union recognized its obligation to these off-campus students by showing movies twice a week.[73]

Simultaneously with the development of the Truax project, President Fred and A.W. Peterson were also moving to secure use of the housing and other facilities at the Badger Ordnance Works near Baraboo. Located in Sauk County thirty-five miles northwest of Madison, the sprawling BOW plant had been hastily constructed early in the war for the manufacture of gunpowder at a cost of $120 million. It was spread over forty-nine square miles because of the dangers involved in its highly explosive manufacturing processes. With the end

---

[71]See *Daily Cardinal*, January 10, 1947.

[72]*Daily Cardinal*, March 13, 1947; Residence Halls Faculty Committee Minutes, October 13, 1949, Series 19/18, Box 1, UA.

[73]Ibid.; Davis, "Truax Project"; George W. Robinson, oral history interview, 1984, UA.

of the fighting the government contractor, the Hercules Powder Company, rapidly laid off most of the BOW workers and moth-balled the production lines.

The plant's isolated rural setting had led the Federal Public Housing Authority to construct a variety of housing and support buildings to accommodate the large wartime BOW work force both at the plant and in nearby communities. These included some single-family homes and a large number of row houses, barracks, and trailer parks. Located in an area adjacent to the plant known as North Badger, during the war each of the barracks had housed single workers in 60 single and double rooms facing a central hallway and sharing a common lounge and a large multi-stall shower and toilet room. South Badger Village consisted mostly of row houses–long one-story buildings divided into one- and two-bedroom and two-room efficiency apartments for married workers. The village also had a school building and various recreational and service facilities.[74] As the BOW workers began departing after the war, the FPHA offered to rent apartments to married veterans, but the lack of transportation for the remote site limited demand. The first allocation of FHPA trailers for the University's Randall Trailer Park came from the BOW trailer park in Prairie du Sac.

Even more than Truax, the remote Badger location required transportation for it to be useful to the University. Consequently, from the first UW officials emphasized the need to acquire not only housing but also some of the fleet of buses used by Hercules for transporting its workers during the war.[75] Peterson warned FPHA officials in Chicago that if the agency was unable to assign additional Baraboo dwelling units to the University "there is no alternative but to deny admission to veterans wishing to enroll at the University of Wisconsin." He also declared that without buses the Baraboo temporary housing would have to be dismantled and re-erected closer to the campus, an expensive option the FHPA staff declined to consider.[76] It may, in fact, have been Peterson who first suggested that the FHPA should press the War Department to transfer some of its surplus buses in order to make

---

[74]Mueller, *Badger Village,* pp. 1-3.

[75]Fred, Memorandum of telephone conversation with General Ralph Immell, November 23, 1945, Series, 4/16/1, Box 46, UA; A.W. Peterson to Fred, December 19, 1945, ibid., December 19, 1945, ibid., Box 36.

[76]Peterson to Clemons Roark, December 22, 1945, ibid.

remote housing sites like Badger usable for emergency student housing.[77]

By early January, 1946, federal officials had agreed to assign part of South Badger Village, the major housing complex at the gunpowder plant, to the University, but the critical issue of transportation at first remained unresolved because of the extreme national shortage of buses. In line with an early faculty recommendation, for a time UW officials considered using the Badger project as a satellite campus, with most of its faculty living on the site and offering freshman-level general education courses to the residents.[78] President Fred went so far as to recruit philosophy Professor Carl Bögholt to head the Badger campus and plan its curriculum, an appointment the Board of Regents approved in principle subject to authorization by federal authorities for non-veteran students and faculty members to live at Badger. Fred then forgot to inform Bögholt some weeks later when such permission was denied and the University was obliged to redeploy Badger Village as a purely residential site for married student veterans. Bögholt belatedly learned that his deanship had evaporated only after reading about the new plans in the press.[79] Meanwhile, some married student veterans, unable to find housing in Madison, had already begun renting Badger Village apartments from the Federal Public Housing Authority. By mid-February 1946, in fact, 75 married student veterans were living at Badger.[80]

Recruited as the University's resident manager of the Badger Village project was Lawrence E. Halle, who had been a house fellow and then for a year a residence halls staff member before he was drafted into the army in 1943. Following his discharge in March of

<hr/>

[77]Peterson to Fred, December 19, 1945, ibid.

[78]Recommendations of the Committee on the Educational Program at the Badger Ordnance Works, January 8, 1946, ibid., Box 27, and March 5, 1946, Series 19/2/6-10, Box 1, UA; Peterson to Orville R. Olmsted, January 5, 1946, Series 4/16/1, Box 27, UA; UW BOR Minutes, January 19, 1946; "Off-Campus School Will Be Set up At Badger Village 34 Miles from Madison," *WAM*, 47 (February, 1946), 5, and (April, 1946), 5; *Capital Times*, January 4, 5, 1946; *Milwaukee Journal*, January 4, 1946; *Milwaukee Sentinel*, January 5, 20, March 10, 1946. The faculty committee stressed that the satellite Badger campus should be residential and coeducational and open to veterans and non-veterans alike. Instruction was to be primarily at the freshman level. The students would be provided with two free trips to Madison weekly and should not live at Badger more than a year.

[79]Carl M. Bögholt, oral history interview, 1973, UA; UW BOR Minutes, March 9, 1946; *WAM*, 47 (April, 1946), 5, and (July-August, 1946), 5.

[80]Mueller, *Badger Village*, p. 9.

1946 he returned to Madison intending to resume his interrupted legal education. Fortuitously, he stopped in to chat with his old residence halls supervisors, Don Halverson and Lee Burns, just as they were planning the University's imminent takeover of Badger Village. In no time at all they persuaded Halle, who had been searching fruitlessly for an apartment for his wife and himself, to postpone law school and take over the day-to-day management of the Badger project, promising him free use of a two-bedroom house. Under the circumstances it was an irresistible offer. Halle stayed as the manager and de facto mayor of Badger Village until 1951, when the Korean War led the War Department to resume gunpowder production at the plant and cancel the University's housing lease. Federal authorities permitted the current student residents to stay until they completed their education, but the University closed down its bus service and ended its official connection with the project in June, 1952. Halle never went back to law school, working in a variety of positions in University housing before succeeding Newell Smith as Director of University Residence Halls in 1965.[81]

The University officially began operating married veterans housing at Badger Village on March 1, 1946, when it took over the BOW staff village consisting of 17 detached houses of varying sizes used during the war to house the plant's supervisory staff. The first 9 of these houses were assigned to UW staff members at monthly rentals ranging from $29.50 to $44.00 depending on size. The following December the FHPA and the War Department formally turned over management of the Badger Village row houses, consisting of 8 one-room efficiencies, 224 two-room units, 207 three-room units, and 12 four-room units, for a total of 451 apartments. Approximately 100 of these units were still occupied by former BOW war workers or non-student veterans, but as they moved out their apartments were assigned to married UW student veterans on a first-come, first-served basis. Meanwhile, Halle and his staff were busily remodeling 10 North Badger barracks that had formerly housed single war workers. These were transformed into two-room, shared-bath apartments, with the first units ready for occupancy at the time of the December transfer. By March 1, 1947, with the remodeling project half-completed, 103 families were living in these North Badger apartments. Monthly rentals in the project were based on apartment size and averaged $24.00 in the

---

[81]Lawrence Halle, oral history interviews, 1984 and 1989, UA.

Badger Village housing for UW veterans, front-center and extreme right-front, photo by Robert Yarnall Richie. UA, 26/10.

Badger Village row house interior. UA, X25-1908.

row houses and $26.50 in the barracks, but some were as little as $18. Eventually Badger Village was able to accommodate about700 student families in a variety of housing that for all its limitations was considerably better than the cramped Truax apartments.[82]

The Badger Village housing had been designed for temporary use and was hastily constructed and poorly maintained during the war. By 1946 it required considerable attention at a time when building materials were expensive and in short supply. Floors were sagging, water pipes broken. Exterior and interior walls alike consisted of uninsulated plaster board, which made the corner apartments especially difficult to heat in winter. Ellen Sawall, later the wife of U.S. Senator William Proxmire of Wisconsin but then married to a veteran living at Badger, recalled that the walls of their row house apartment were so ill-fitting that a match held near the corner would be blown out. "In the winter the wind whistled through the cracks," she remembered. "I used to dress my baby in outdoor clothes to keep her warm." The South Badger apartments were heated by so-called Warm Morning wood/coal cook stoves, through which water pipes ran to a water tank to provide the residents with hot water. This supply was uncertain in winter and unbearable on hot summer days, so residents increasingly cooked on one hot plate and strapped another onto the water tank for hot water. A top University priority understandably was to upgrade the wiring and add more transformers for the row houses, which were increasingly overloaded by the residents' electrical appliances. A serious electrical fire emphasized the urgency of this rewiring before it could be accomplished. Other repairs tended to follow crisis after crisis that sometimes kept Halle and his maintenance staff working around the clock. As with other UW temporary post-war housing projects, the State Emergency Board appropriated $50,000 to cover the initial remodeling and operating costs at Badger.[83]

Even before the student veterans–most without automobiles–began moving their families into Badger Village during the spring of 1946, the University concluded it would have to operate a transportation system for the residents. While the Greyhound Bus Company provided service six times daily into Baraboo and Madison, its schedule did not fit University class times, and the number of riders

[82]L.E. Halle, "The University of Wisconsin Badger Project," in Burns, "Report on Emergency Housing Projects"; Halle, oral history interview, 1989; *Life at Badger* (undated pamphlet for residents), pp. 2-4, Series 4/16/1, Box 75.

[83]Ibid.; Mueller, *Badger Village*, pp. 10-12, 15 (the Sawall quotation).

would soon have overwhelmed the service in any event. Residence halls accordingly purchased a used school bus for $2,200 early in 1946. On March 7 this bus, still with the slogan "Protect Our Children" painted on the rear, began operating between Badger and the campus at a fare of 25¢ each way, subsequently reduced to 10¢ for UW students and staff members. After the Federal Public Housing Authority gained the right to lease surplus government buses for use with federally sponsored emergency housing projects, the University moved aggressively to expand its bus system, not only for Badger but also for the Truax and East Hill projects. The staff sought out and reclaimed FPHA buses from as far away as Georgia, Virginia, Missouri, Ohio, Minnesota, and Illinois, as well as Wisconsin. Most were in poor condition and required considerable repair at the Truax motor pool before being put into service. In little more than a year the University's polyglot fleet included 35 buses of varied ages, makes, and condition. By 1950, when residence halls began to phase out its post-war transportation system, 80 percent of the fleet–then numbering 27–had run more than 100,000 miles and 6 of the buses had accumulated between 250,000 and 350,000 miles.[84]

Except for three full-time drivers who were used for shuttle service and mid-day trips when students were not available, the bus fleet was largely operated by student drivers living at Badger and Truax. The Badger service, managed by student resident Bruce L. Solie, a wartime navigator in the Army Air Transport Command, required the most organization on the part of the drivers and their passengers. One of the Badger buses had a padded bumper for use in pushing the other buses to get them started in cold weather. On especially frigid nights Solie or one of his drivers might start the buses twice during the night to keep them ready for morning use. There were four bus runs from Badger to the Memorial Union each morning Monday through Saturday, starting at 6:25 a.m. Returning, Badger residents had a choice of six departures on Monday through Friday and four on Saturday, with the earliest at 11:00 a.m. and the latest at 10:00 p.m. week days. Pickup points were at the Union and the University Avenue railroad tracks. In addition, the service operated one bus run

---

[84]Burns to Peterson, December 5, 1950, Series 24/1/1, Box 273, UA; Burns, "The University of Wisconsin Badger and Truax Bus System," in "Report on Emergency Housing Projects"; Mueller, *Badger Village*, pp. 48-50. For a photo of the first Badger-campus commuter bus, see *Capital Times*, March 10, 1946.

each way for shopping in downtown Baraboo on Wednesday after-noons and two on Saturdays. Those who missed a University bus had to hitchhike or hope to connect with one of the more expensive and less convenient Greyhound buses.[85]

The aging UW bus fleet provided bare-bones transportation and little else. In winter the buses were cold and drafty, heated mostly by body warmth that quickly fogged and iced-over the windows. Despite the cramped seating, riders quickly learned to bundle up as if they were outside. Those who sought to sit near the two small floor heaters found this presumed advantage offset by the rougher ride over the rear axle. The first two morning departures from Badger left in the dark during much of the year, as did the last four returns, so studying on the bus was difficult to impossible. Passengers usually talked, slept, or played cards–sometimes as many as three quick rubbers of bridge–during the hour-and-fifteen-minute ride. Occasionally in icy conditions the riders had to help push the bus up the steep Springfield Hill en route to Madison; more often in bad weather the driver would detour through Prairie du Sac, adding another fifteen minutes to the trip. Still, many of the veterans had experienced far worse privation during the war, and the regular commuting runs to and from campus brought a special camaraderie reminiscent of their wartime service.

Within a short time Badger Village was once again a self-contained small town of about 2,700 residents, complete with its own shopping center containing an A&P supermarket, drug store, post office, barber shop, and trading post. The University stationed one of its police officers at Badger and contracted with the BOW for fire protection. Located in the Badger School building was a health service staffed by two registered nurses and a physician for emergency medical treatment. By mid-1946 there were 167 pre-school children living in the village, resulting in a decision by residence halls to open a nursery school for the project with morning and afternoon sessions five days a week. Operated by the UW School of Education, the service was free for children of UW students and staff and open to others for $1 a week. The children were divided into five age groups and received a light snack and a daily health check by one of the project nurses. Older children from kindergarten through eighth grade attended the existing Badger School.[86]

---

[85]*Life at Badger*, pp. 16-17; Mueller, *Badger Village*, pp. 38, 49-50.

[86]John G. Fowlkes to L.E. Halle, June 5, 1946; C.J. Krumm to Kai Jensen, July 29, 1946; Halle to Fowlkes and Krumm, July 30, 1946; Peterson to Fred, August 31,

Badger Village offered much for its adult residents as well. The community building contained a large game room and snack bar, a sewing and craft room, two lounges with an adjacent kitchen, and an auditorium used variously as a gymnasium, movie theater, and concert and lecture hall. North Badger also had a sizable recreation room open for socializing during the day, as a study hall in the evening, and for parties on Saturday nights. Residents could check out books from the Badger School library and use it as a place to study in the evening. The Memorial Union provided a staff member for the village community building, equipment for the game room (billiards and pool, table tennis, and a juke box), and a $900 budget for entertainment. The latter included occasional dances to the music of Don Voegli and other popular campus bands as well as a regular schedule of movies on Fridays, an afternoon matinee for children (admission 12¢), and an adult evening show for 30¢. On Sundays Badger residents could choose from among five different denominational religious services in the school and community buildings. The Badger Wives' Club organized a variety of activities for the women during the day while their husbands were on campus and helped put out the weekly mimeo-graphed village newspaper, the *Badger Bulletin*. The club also sponsored a popular series of six lectures by UW faculty members each semester. Assisting "Mayor" Halle in governing Badger Village was a 29-member council elected from the various wards by the leaseholder residents, as well as a number of committees, including one to settle grievances and another to provide help with medical or financial emergencies. Law students living at Badger Village usually served as justice of the peace for the surrounding rural township. One of the most colorful of these was Kenneth Hurwitz, whose first exposure to the University was as a Truax airman during the war and who later became prominent as the flamboyant Madison attorney Ken Hur. Whenever Hurwitz was short of funds he would send his constable, Lee Dreyfus, out to patrol nearby highway 12 for speeders, since under state law a justice of the peace could keep the $2 court costs.[87]

Little wonder that despite the inconvenience of the location, turnover at Badger Village was low, and the residents generally left with happy memories of their stay there. Susan Dreyfus, who was born at Badger Village while her father, future Wisconsin Governor Lee Sherman Dreyfus was earning his three UW degrees, remembered that

---

1946, all in Series 25/7/2, Box 7, UA; *Life at Badger*, pp. 8-17.
    [87]Ibid., pp. 17-24; Mueller, *Badger Village*, pp. 10-24, 44, 47.

"getting along was necessary when you could smell someone else's popcorn through the walls." "It was a very difficult time, but a very positive time," her mother Joyce agreed. "Some of the dearest friends we have were made there."[88] More than four decades later when University radio station WHA put together a documentary radio program containing interviews with five former residents, each of them stressed the unusually strong sense of fellowship and community they had experienced at Badger, unique in their experience. One fondly recalled the communal Thanksgiving dinners the residents of his 24-apartment barracks building cooked and shared each year. Another remembered various neighbors insisting that he borrow shoes, suit, and topcoat so he would be appropriately dressed for a job interview in New York. Several commented on the regular visits of E.B. and Mrs. Fred to the village, the president once fixing a balky sewing machine. One woman summarized life at Badger Village as a challenge but not, she emphasized, a privation. "You knew everyone was going through the same thing," she explained, "there was an intensity of concern, a camaraderie." Indeed, she wished life "could be like that today."[89]

Finding creative ways to solve the Madison housing shortage and thereby accommodate the thousands of ex-GIs thronging to the University after the war was perhaps the Fred administration's finest achievement. Certainly General Omar Bradley, the post-war head of the Veterans Administration, thought so when he hailed the University's effort as the "most effective veterans housing program in the country."[90]

VA Largesse

Although the veterans' invasion of the campus after the war brought many difficult and unfamiliar problems, it also included a financial windfall of major proportions for the University and the State of Wisconsin. As enacted by Congress in 1944, the educational provisions of the GI Bill authorized the Veterans Administration to reimburse colleges and universities for veterans' tuition and other educational costs up to a maximum of $500 a semester. The Milwaukee VA office at first questioned whether the University was entitled

[88]Mueller, *Badger Village*, pp. 17, 26.
[89]Phyllis S. Young, William J. Schereck, Sr., Peggy Baime, August P. Lemberger, Marjorie K. Johnson, oral history interviews, 1990, UA.
[90]Luberg, *Characteristics of Recent Federal Support*, p. 14.

to tuition reimbursement for educating Wisconsin veterans because it did not charge state residents any tuition, only small fees (set at $48 per semester in 1945, $60 in 1947, and $75 in 1949). The regents protested that Congress clearly intended to help universities cover the costs they incurred in educating the veterans. A narrow interpretation of the law, they argued, would benefit primarily private colleges and universities that charged high tuition and would discriminate against public institutions with subsidized low or no tuition for their state residents. In June, 1945, the Veterans Administration in Washington accepted this logic and ruled that "institutions which have non-resident tuition may, if they so desire, charge for each veteran enrolled under part 8 such customary and incidental fees as are applicable to all non-resident students."[91]

Thus the first and succeeding VA contracts with the University provided for reimbursement of educational costs at the University's non-resident tuition rate–$100 in 1945, plus fees–regardless of whether or not a veteran was a Wisconsin resident. Ironically, the Wisconsin State Assembly promptly adopted a resolution objecting to this policy, on the ground that it would unfairly penalize Wisconsin veterans should Congress subsequently authorize a bonus for wartime military service, because their entitlements would be reduced by the cost of their educational benefits.[92]

The federal tuition reimbursement policy was an important source of revenue for Wisconsin and a number of other states during the immediate post-war years while the veterans were enrolled in large numbers. The additional UW revenue amounted to nearly a million dollars for the fall semester of 1946 alone, and totaled about $10 million for the veteran years.[93] President Fred reminded the regents in October, 1946, that Wisconsin taxpayers were receiving a significant windfall:

> The rate of increase in costs to the State has *been retarded for the time being by the payment by the federal govern-ment* of the equivalent of non-resident tuition and fees for all veterans regardless of their legal residence. Thus, the

---

[91]VA Instruction #6, Title II, Paragraph 2-A-2, quoted in letter from the presidents of the Association of Land-Grant Colleges and Universities and the National Association of State Universities to General Omar N. Bradley, December 17, 1946, Series 4/16/1, Box 70, UA.

[92]*Milwaukee Journal*, May 20, 1945.

[93]Olson, "World War II Veterans," 88.

federal government pays $200 more per school year for each Wisconsin veteran in the University than the student would pay individually if he were not enrolled as a veteran. Under present federal law this payment will not be deducted from any federal bonus. In the course of a few years when the veterans are replaced by non-veteran students, it will undoubtedly be necessary to accelerate the rate of financial support from the State for University operations.[94]

The burgeoning GI enrollment and tuition largesse enabled the legislature to reduce its contribution to the University budget by 7 percent in 1946.[95]

Not everyone agreed with this generous interpretation of the Servicemen's Readjustment Act of 1944, however. Some UW veterans, notably in the law and medical schools where book costs were high, argued that by charging non-resident tuition for them the University was unfairly eroding the $500 per semester maximum allowed by the law for their educational costs, thus preventing them from spending an additional $100 each semester on books and supplies. The protesters went so far as to enlist the assistance of Colonel Leo B. Levenick, the Wisconsin director of veterans affairs.[96] More serious was the continuing belief by some federal officials, especially as the educational costs of the GI Bill mounted far beyond initial estimates, that the VA's tuition reimbursement practice was neither authorized by the Servicemen's Readjustment Act nor fair to federal taxpayers. If states like Wisconsin chose to have a low or no tuition policy for residents attending their state university, the argument ran, why should they expect the federal government to reimburse them at a higher non-resident tuition rate for educating residents who also happened to be World War II veterans? From the federal perspective the practice smelled of pork on a gigantic scale.

[94]Fred, "Statement Concerning the University Budget for 1947-49," October 20, 1946, Series 1/1/3, Box 64, UA.

[95]Olson, "World War II Veterans," 88.

[96]Leo B. Levenick to Fred, February 16, 1946, Series 1/1/17, Box 45, UA. In response A.W. Peterson noted the basis for the policy–making sure that public institutions with low or no tuition for state residents received some federal reimbursement of their costs of educating the veterans. Peterson explained that VA policy prohibited reimbursement for any books and supplies not required of all students and said he doubted the tuition reimbursement policy worked any hardship on law students. He conceded there might be a problem for medical students and promised to discuss their situation with the regents. Peterson to Levenick, February 21, 1946, ibid.

As early as the spring of 1946 UW officials worried about a rumored change in the reimbursement policy, leading Peterson to wire the VA headquarters in Washington for clarification.[97] Although the response was reassuring, the issue continued to be confusing and controversial. Peterson felt obliged to issue a memo explaining the reasoning behind the tuition reimbursement policy. *"The University is not making a profit,"* he emphasized.[98] The following November the Veterans Administration shocked the academic world by notifying all institutions it was canceling the non-resident tuition basis for calculating veterans' educational costs. Instead, the reimbursement policy would be based on either "customary charges" or a determination of "the estimated cost of teaching personnel and supplies for instruction." The universities and their professional associations strenuously objected, noting that the new policy not only discriminated against public institutions whose states subsidized the education of their residents but that its implementation would create an accounting nightmare and budgetary chaos. Reimbursing universities only for the direct cost of instruction, moreover, would ignore the substantially increased operating, overhead, and administrative expenses resulting from the deluge of veterans. Congressional intent was clear, the higher education spokesmen argued, "that the federal government would bear the institutional cost of veterans education up to $500 per year."[99] The uproar led the VA to modify the new reimbursement policy, allowing either (1) the direct cost of instruction as calculated by a comprehensive VA-approved formula or (2) non-resident tuition if it did not exceed the formula cost. Since the UW non-resident tuition was approximately the same as the cost of instruction derived from the formula, with the VA's blessing the University continued to use its non-resident tuition as the basis for calculating the educational costs of the veterans.[100]

---

[97]Peterson to Nelson Hensen, March 3, 1946, telegram; Henson [*sic*] to Peterson, March 5, 1946, telegram, ibid. Hensen assured Peterson that "no changes contemplated with respect to payment of non resident tuition for Public 346 enrollees."

[98]Peterson, Veterans Fees at the University of Wisconsin, Series 4/16/1, Box 95, UA.

[99]Presidents of Association of Land-Grant Colleges and Universities and National Association of State Universities to Bradley, December 17, 1946. Actually, Congress had amended the law in December 1945 to clearly benefit the private colleges and universities. The change authorized the VA to reimburse tuition at a rate higher than $500 a year, with a proportionate reduction in the veteran's period of eligibility.

[100]Fred to Glenn R. Davis, February 24, 1948; Kenneth Little to Fred, February

The non-resident tuition reimbursement issue was still not dead, however. In 1949 U.S. Controller General Lindsay Warren, head of the congressional audit agency, singled out Wisconsin in challenging the right of the Veterans Administration to pay higher non-resident tuition rates for student veterans who were residents. In response Veterans Affairs Administrator Carl Gray settled the matter once and for all by promulgating as an official agency declaration the VA's right to use non-resident tuition as one of the "fair and reasonable" methods of calculating veterans' educational costs. Inasmuch as Gray was charged under the law with determining the "fair and reasonable" reimbursement rates, Warren backed off and directed his staff not to pursue the matter further.[101]

The GI Legacy

For a decade after World War II, the ex-GIs were a significant presence at Wisconsin, as well as on college and university campuses across the country. From 1946 through 1949 they comprised considerably more than half of the UW student body and dominated every part of the campus. Serious, mature, hard-working, wanting only to get on with their civilian lives as quickly as possible, most of the veterans showed little interest in a return to traditional student life, especially its juvenile pranks and expensive proms and balls. Casual dress–navy blue and army suntan or olive drab–replaced the more formal coat-and-tie garb UW men had worn to dinner and often to class before the war. Far from the GIs needing help to adjust to campus ways, their numbers were so overwhelming that most of the adjustment occurred among the faculty and the rest of the student body. For the University as a whole, absorbing the veterans provided some useful lessons for the next great enrollment surge, when their children–the baby boomers–began to reach college age in the 1960s.[102]

In the fall of 1944 the first group of veterans on campus organized the University of Wisconsin Veterans of World War II, whose lofty purpose was "to maintain good fellowship and understanding

---

17, 1948, Series 4/16/1, Box 95, UA. Beginning in 1949 the University switched over to the VA cost formula.

[101]Lindsay C. Warren to [Carl Gray,] Administrator of Veterans Affairs, March 29, 1950; Fred, press release, December 22, 1949, ibid., Box 138, UA.

[102]As will become apparent, however, the baby boomers were to prove less adaptable and more demanding than their parents.

among all mankind, and to foster those rights for which the people of our nation and of Allied countries are now engaged in preserving in this war."[103] Although the group was given use of a Quonset hut next to the Memorial Union, its idealism and sense of purpose faded, and by 1947 it had disappeared. Nor were student veterans much attracted to the David Schreiner Post of the American Legion after its organization on campus in the fall of 1946. The Legion's conservative politics and narrow veteran-centered program turned off most students. More UW veterans joined or identified with the American Veterans Committee (AVC) after its campus chapter organized in August, 1946. Like the national AVC, the campus group stressed that its members were citizens first and veterans second. Several of the chapter presidents–John A. Gronouski, Ivan Nestigen, and John Higham–went on to achieve considerable national prominence in their subsequent careers. The campus AVC was avowedly political, supporting an internationalist foreign policy and generally acting as the conscience of Wisconsin progressivism on domestic issues. It endorsed the Acheson-Lilienthal Plan for the international control of atomic energy, for example, and urged that the United Nations administer the Marshall Plan. AVC members opposed compulsory ROTC and backed price controls and government action to maintain full employment and provide low cost housing, along with higher faculty salaries and wages for student employees. When a local tavern refused to serve a Negro law student in the summer of 1947, the campus AVC organized a boycott and urged Madisonians to "practice a little real Americanism."[104]

Older than the typical undergraduate, more than a third of the veterans were married, many with children. Their presence obliged the University for the first time to take responsibility for providing married student housing and even nursery schools. If anything, marriage seemed to strengthen the purpose and discipline of student veterans. As a group, the veterans regularly outperformed their non-veteran classmates academically, with married veterans consistently heading the list. During the spring semester of 1946, for example–the first reporting period with substantial veteran enrollment–4,201 undergraduate veteran men earned a grade point average of 1.664 (on a 3 point scale), compared with the 1.569 gpa achieved by their 1,296 non-veteran male classmates. The gpa of 1,021 married veterans was

---

[103]*Daily Cardinal*, November 29, 1944.
[104]Olson, "World War II Veterans," p. 95.

even higher: 1.798.[105] One study of 114 UW veterans whose college education had been interrupted by military service found that 99 improved their academic performance after returning to school and only 9 registered a gpa decline, mostly minor.[106] The veterans' solid academic work, commented Paul L. Trump, the University's adviser of men, certainly refuted those who had predicted that American universities were "going to be filled with educational tramps who just wanted to take advantage of government allowances."[107] Indeed.

If most of the veterans were not interested in traditional high jinks or a frivolous social life, they quickly filled most student offices and dominated campus extracurricular activities for half-a-decade after the war. Some joined fraternities, often primarily to obtain housing close to the campus. Others sought the fellowship and organized recreational activities offered by the Greek houses. Whatever their motivation, the ex-GIs enabled some of the fraternities to expand their membership as much as four-fold after the war. The greater numbers and range of ages and interests, however, tended to undermine the close bond of fraternal brotherhood that had been the Greeks' traditional *raison d'être*. Thus, besides helping to reestablish many of the fraternities, the veterans may in fact have weakened them. For at a time when the closed Greek system was coming under increasing attack on campus and nationally, these new recruits lacked the strong loyalty and commitment felt by earlier generations of fraternity men.

Illustrative of the ex-GIs' active participation in student life was their domination of the *Daily Cardinal*, by far the most prestigious and influential student organization. Beginning with the editorship of John McNelly in 1945-46, veterans held the top leadership posts on the *Cardinal* until 1949.[108] Their broader interests and perspective gave the paper a strong focus on national and international affairs it had sometimes lacked in the past. As was the case with most other student organizations, the unintended downside of the veterans' control of the *Cardinal* in the early post-war years was their dislodging the women staffers whose first opportunity to run the paper had come only during the war. Karl E. Meyer, the first non-veteran editor of the *Cardinal* after the war, praised his predecessors for their "real concern for basic

---

[105]Paul L. Trump, Scholarship Averages - Veterans, Second Semester 1945-46, September 19, 1946, Series 4/16/1, Box 70, UA.

[106]Olson, "World War II Veterans," p. 87.

[107]*Wisconsin State Journal*, September 29, 1946.

[108]McNelly later became a professor in the UW School of Journalism.

problems of student and national welfare."[109] And as the GIs departed, Meyer lamented the passing of a unique era in University history. "Only three years ago the whole atmosphere of the campus was entirely different–and better," he declared in 1951 lamenting the departure of "the last of the hell-raising veterans who once made this University a stimulating and lively place for an all-too-brief post-war period."[110]

Meyer was not alone in his appreciation of the GI years. They constituted an extraordinary chapter in the history of the University.

---

[109]*Daily Cardinal*, September 21, 1949.
[110]Ibid., January 9, 1951.

2.

The Insider President

The resignation of UW President Clarence A. Dykstra in the fall of 1944 to head the University of California at Los Angeles left the University of Wisconsin leaderless just as the institution was beginning to plan for the conversion back to normal peacetime operations. Dykstra, like his predecessor Glenn Frank, was an "outsider" without previous ties to the state or strong academic or scholarly credentials. Both presidents had been recruited by the Board of Regents for their perceived talents in their previous positions: Frank for his superb oratorical and publicist skills as a prominent New York magazine editor, and Dykstra for his tested administrative experience as the city manager of Cincinnati during the terrible 1937 flood. Both men had also soon run afoul of Wisconsin politics–Frank because his appointment lacked the La Follette family's imprimatur though he was undeniably progressive in his political views, and Dykstra because he was appointed by a La Follette-dominated Board of Regents soon replaced by a suspicious and conservative anti-La Follette governor.[1]

Although following President Dykstra's resignation the regents gave consideration to conducting another wide-ranging presidential search, they were also more disposed than in the recent past to look inside the institution for leadership. One of those whose advice they sought about the needs of the University was the widely respected dean of the College of Agriculture, Edwin Broun Fred.[2] A bacteriologist,

---

[1]See E. David Cronon and John W. Jenkins, *The University of Wisconsin: A History*, vol. 3, *Politics, Depression, and War, 1925-1945* (Madison: University of Wisconsin Press, 1994), passim.

[2]Born in Middleburg, Virginia, in 1887, Fred earned a B.S. degree at Virginia Politechnic Institute in 1907 and a Ph.D. at the prestigious Göttingen University in

Fred had worked closely with the Frank and Dykstra administrations, serving as dean of the Graduate School from 1934 to 1943, when he shifted to the agriculture deanship. Both posts involved key units of the University with frequent contact with the Board of Regents, whose members came to appreciate Dean Fred's scientific acumen, national contacts, and self-effacing, low-key personal style. They also admired his dedication to and comprehension of the University as a powerful engine of intellectual, social, and economic development. It was hardly surprising, therefore, that as the regents consulted Fred informally about the qualities appropriate for a successor to President Dykstra and asked his opinion of individuals who might fill the bill, they soon raised the question of his own availability for the position.

There was widespread approval on and off campus when on January 25, 1945, the board announced the appointment of Dean Fred as the twelfth president of the University of Wisconsin. Characteristically shunning any formal inauguration ceremony, the new leader was quietly installed by the regents three weeks later on February 15.[3] The selection of Fred, the first "insider" to head the institution in twenty years, made eminently good sense. The University could ill-afford a lengthy and unpredictable national search under wartime constraints even as it was making plans for the coming post-war era. A UW faculty member since 1913, Fred offered both reassuring familiarity with the campus and the proven administrative experience needed to overcome future uncertainties. Indeed, probably only Letters and Science Dean Mark H. Ingraham commanded as much respect as a faculty leader, and Fred's experience in administration, research, and public service was far superior. Recognizing that post-war growth would bring new and severe

---

Germany in 1911. After teaching a year at VPI, he accepted a temporary position as assistant professor of bacteriology at the University of Wisconsin in 1912, winning a full professorship by 1918. Except for wartime service, Fred spent the remainder of his career at Wisconsin. See E.B. Fred, oral history interview, 1976, UA.

[3]UW BOR Minutes, January 15, February 15, 1945, UA. Fred disliked making speeches and avoided them whenever possible. He set the tone for his presidency at his installation. Observed board president Walter Hodgkins to Fred: "As you probably know by now, you have been elected president of the University of Wisconsin. The election came after the regents considered a great many names. We have thought of making a formal occasion out of this, but, knowing your repugnance to ostentation, the regents wish to induct you as simply as possible." Fred replied, "Mr. President and members of the Board of Regents, I will do the best I can to take care of the position to which you have elected me." This "inaugural address" surely set a record in the history of higher education, being exceeded in length by its introduction! Quoted in "President Fred Installed," *WAM*, 46 (March 15, 1945), 7.

challenges, Fred conditioned his acceptance on the board's agreement that he would be allowed to expand and reorganize the president's administrative and support structure. Almost certainly with Glenn Frank's messy 1937 firing in mind, Fred also promptly submitted his resignation so there could never be a conflict over his continuing in office at the pleasure of the regents.[4]

Shaping the Fred Administration

From the beginning, Fred tried to emulate the early twentieth-century presidency of the great Charles R. Van Hise, while at the same time retaining the University's most important contemporary strengths. Indeed, the bulk of Fred's brief statement issued on the day the regents named him president-elect described an important part of Van Hise's vision for the University: "President Van Hise conceived it as the University's duty to increase knowledge, and to make this knowledge live in the lives of the students and the people of the entire state. . . . His was a working concept of education and research."[5] The regents' Personnel Committee in "unanimously and enthusiastically" recommending Fred for the UW presidency reported glowingly on his qualifications:

> His interest in the University and its program was not limited to his particular field. His knowledge of the whole University, its personnel, its facilities and equipment as well as its obligations and objectives is as broad as, if not broader than, that of any living person. He has the knowledge and the interest required to think of the University as an entity and to correlate its units as a cooperative enterprise.[6]

Most UW faculty members agreed, welcoming the regents' decision to look within the institution for leadership to confront the inevitable post-war challenges.

---

[4]Fred, oral history interview.

[5]"Statement Made by President-elect Fred at the Meeting of the Board held on January 25, 1945," Series 1/1/3, Box 62, UA.

[6]UW BOR, "Personnel Committee Report," [January 25, 1945], ibid. A University press release issued about the appointment quoted liberally from Fred's statement and the Personnel Committee report. "Dr. Edwin B. Fred, Nationally Known Scientist and Educator, Becomes 12th President of U.W. Feb. 15," *University Press Bulletin*, February 7, 1945.

President Van Hise's fundamental task had been to complete UW's transition to a full-fledged comprehensive, democratically oriented, service institution, what he called in his inaugural a "combination university." President Fred's challenge was to preserve the quality of Van Hise's combination university in an environment of sweeping change. By early 1945 when Fred took office, normal University life had been suspended by several years of world war. While the military conflict was continuing, its end was definitely in view. During the next eighteen months, as the previous chapter of this volume has detailed, University enrollment more than doubled, due largely to the deluge of war veterans. Even after the great bulge of GI Bill students graduated, enrollments remained high relative to pre-war levels. Between 1948 and 1953 student numbers declined from 18,623 to what would turn out to be the post-war low of 13,346, which was still about 3,000 more than the pre-war peak. Thereafter gradual growth resumed, resulting in a student population of about 16,000 during 1957-58, the final year of the Fred administration. Faculty staffing, as might be expected, generally reflected enrollment, and rose from 809 in 1945-46 to 1,434 a decade later. Increased staffing did not occur automatically, however, and in fact was a major problem for an administration that sought to sustain high academic quality as well as appropriate numbers. Meanwhile, Fred oversaw a considerable expansion of the University's physical plant for the first time since the 1920s, providing much-needed new and renovated facilities for teaching, research, and residential living.[7]

Throughout his nearly thirteen-year tenure President Fred would both respond to and nurture a burgeoning University of Wisconsin, in the process expanding its administrative structure while retaining close presidential supervision. The new president moved quickly to hire a regent-authorized administrative assistant to whom he might delegate some of his work. His choice was Professor William B. Sarles, appointed in October, two months before he was released from wartime service in the navy.[8] New to high-level university administration, Sarles already had enjoyed a close twenty-year relationship with Fred, first as his student, later as a junior faculty colleague in the bacteriology department, and finally as a trusted wartime assistant in Washington and elsewhere. During the decade of the Depression, particularly after his promotion to associate professor in 1936, Sarles had regularly partici-

---

[7]L. Joseph Lins, "Fact Book for History of Madison Campus," notebook, 1983, UHP.

[8]UW BOR Minutes, February 15, October 21, 1945.

pated in University faculty meetings and committee deliberations, developed collegial relationships across the campus at the University Club, and established a close friendship with future L&S Dean Mark Ingraham as his frequent tennis partner.[9]

Sarles accepted Fred's summons to administrative duty with considerable reluctance, preferring to return to his department and full-time scholarship. He endured in the position only through mid-1946, when Fred replaced him with LeRoy Luberg, a highly personable war veteran who previously had been a part-time UW graduate student while employed as vice principal at Madison's West High School. Sarles could not escape Fred's reach for long, however, as the president soon thrust him into the difficult and time-consuming chairmanship of the UW Athletic Board the next year.[10] The Sarles appointment foreshadowed Fred's tendency to look to trusted colleagues from his department and elsewhere in the College of Agriculture for his close advisors and key administrative staff. By the end of his administration resentment was growing among other UW faculty members over the perceived disproportionate influence of the College of Agriculture and of scientists generally in shaping University policies and development.

Another important administrative change was the regents' creation of a permanent Campus Planning Commission to replace a succession of ad hoc bodies that had operated intermittently in response to occasional indications from the governor and legislature that funding for capital projects could be expected after the war. By early 1945 it had become apparent that the planning, funding, and construction of badly needed new facilities would soon become a major and continuing function at the University. For more than a decade E.B. Fred had been a close observer and quiet participant in such deliberations. Not only had he been involved in his capacity as graduate and then agriculture dean, he also for a time had served with L&S Dean George Sellery and Comptroller A.W. Peterson on a regent-appointed administrative committee early in the war to assist President Dykstra in his University duties while he split his time serving in Washington on selective service

---

[9]Ingraham succeeded George C. Sellery as dean of the College of Letters and Science on July 1, 1942, and served in that post as a widely respected faculty leader for the next nineteen years.

[10]William B. Sarles, oral history interview, 1982, UA. Sometime during 1946, while on a trip to Washington with the UW president, Sarles, wanting desperately to return to the academic life, accidentally encountered Luberg and introduced him to Fred. The two men chatted for nearly and hour, after which time Sarles strongly encouraged the new appointment.

and manpower issues. The formal appointment of the new Campus Planning Commission grew out of the work of a special Advisory Committee on Future Campus Development established by the regents in December, 1944, at the behest of the board's Constructional Development Committee. Fred was a member of this body and doubtless played an important behind-the-scenes role in its deliberations. The Advisory Committee reported twice in January, 1945, its main recommendation being that the regents establish a permanent planning commission, which the board did on February 15.[11]

Appreciating the CPC's intended central role in shaping the post-war University, President Fred was careful to assign his best institutional resources to it. At first this involved his own personal role mediating between the regents and more than two-dozen commission members representing a wide diversity of campus interests. Uncomfortable with an assignment that frequently required visible and aggressive leadership, Fred managed by August to maneuver the creation of a steering or executive committee for the commission, which he placed under the direction of his trusted long-time scientific and administrative protégé, Ira L. Baldwin.[12] Composed of a third of the full commission, the Steering Committee quickly began to perform most of the constructive work, which then was referred to the larger body for discussion and formal recommendations to the regents.[13] President Fred continued his oversight and mediating roles, only now more comfortably in the

---

[11]"Meeting of Advisory Committee on Future Campus Development," January 18, 1945, included with papers for January 25, 1945, UW BOR meeting, Series 1/1/3, Box 62, UA; "Report of the Constructional Development Committee to the Board of Regents," n.d., included with papers for February 15, 1945, UW BOR meeting, ibid.

[12]Baldwin joined Fred's agricultural bacteriology department in 1927 as a young assistant professor. By 1931 he had begun to move into administration as assistant dean of the College of Agriculture until he took over the chairmanship of the department a decade later. During World War II Fred, in his role as a federal science advisor, arranged for Baldwin to head up the government's chemical warfare research at Camp Detrick, Maryland. Even before he returned to the campus full-time, Baldwin was appointed dean of the Graduate School in the fall of 1944. A year later President Fred arranged his appointment as dean and director of the College of Agriculture.

[13]The original Steering Committee included Baldwin, Engineering Dean Withey, Business Manager Peterson, L&S Dean Ingraham, UW BOR Secretary Torkelson, Leon Smith (City of Madison), Superintendent of Buildings and Grounds Gallistel, and engineering Professor James G. Woodburn. UW BOR Minutes, August 11, 1945; Ira L. Baldwin, *My Half Century at the University of Wisconsin* (Madison: Ira L. Baldwin, 1995), p. 154.

background. Years later, Baldwin recalled the value of his work with the Steering Committee and full CPC:

> it . . . gave me another opportunity to look at the University very broadly, because the Campus Planning Commission was concerned with what the problems are today in terms of space, and how you use that space to the best advantage. It was also concerned with predictions for the future–as to what we might expect in the way of enrollments, in research, extension, and in public service, the staff you might have, which areas of the University could be expected to grow more rapidly–the total University planning activity.[14]

Between them Baldwin and Fred developed the CPC into an influential and effective agency for planning the post-war face of the campus, always under the close scrutiny of the president.

The Campus Planning Commission had a number of pressing issues to deal with in its first few years of existence. These included deciding where to put the numerous "temporary" Quonset huts, trailers, and other wartime buildings the University was acquiring during 1945-47 to handle the enrollment crisis, determining the sites for the proposed new University library building and other permanent construction, and, certainly not least, reaching the conclusion that the University was going to have to expand south of University Avenue in the future.

An important early task involved deciding what to do about the College of Agriculture's Hill Farms. A tract of more than 600 acres on Madison's west side located beyond Sunset Point between University Avenue and Mineral Point Road, the sprawling Hill Farms had been acquired over time since the 1890s for use as an experimental farm. After the war, housing developments were begun north and south of the Hill Farms and it was clear that the University land was blocking the westward expansion of the city. In 1945 the Board of Regents gave Madison an easement across the East Hill Farm along the proposed Midvale Boulevard to enable the city to improve the existing dirt farm road and provide sanitary sewers and water mains to new homes being built in the area. The following year the board allowed the city to annex twenty acres of the East Hill Farm.[15] As we have seen, at this time the University also established the temporary East Hill trailer park along what is now Midvale Boulevard to provide an emergency housing site

---

[14]Ibid., pp. 184-85.
[15]UW BOR Minutes, September 29, 1945, and June 28, 1946.

for UW married students and staff owning their own trailers.[16] It was increasingly evident that this longstanding UW experimental farm land would eventually have to give way to city housing needs.

In 1953 the legislature authorized the Board of Regents to dispose of all UW farm land between University Avenue and Mineral Point Road. The board established a committee headed by one of the newer regents, former Wisconsin governor and Madison businessman Oscar Rennebohm, to supervise the sale of the land. Although private developers offered as much as $1,000 an acre, far more than the price of comparable agricultural land, Rennebohm persuaded his colleagues the University could realize a larger return and exercise quality control by handling the residential development itself. He also insisted on reserving forty acres on the northeast corner of the tract for commercial use and a shopping center. With some of the proceeds from the sale of lots the College of Agriculture was able to acquire a much larger replacement experimental farm in the Arlington-Leeds area, about fifteen miles north of Madison. The Hill Farms development, a major University undertaking in these years, will be discussed later in this volume, but it is notable in the present context as an instance where the Board of Regents not only established a policy but also played an active role in implementing and administering it.[17]

Characteristically, President Fred moved slowly and carefully as he shaped his new administration. In the immediate post-war period much of his time was occupied in meeting the emergency challenge of educating and housing the veritable army of war veterans who sought to take advantage of the educational provisions of the GI Bill. At the same time the president had to address the longer-term institutional growth problems of a campus with two decades of deferred building and maintenance needs. During April of 1945 Fred and the regents worked out an arrangement whereby Business Manager A.W. Peterson was named to the new post of Director of Business and Finance with expanded responsibilities and assistants. This reorganization, which involved Peterson's reporting both to Fred and the regents, streamlined UW's business affairs considerably but also shifted more authority to

---

[16]See pp. 34, 45.

[17]See "Report on Relocation of University Farms," February, 1953, Series 4/16/1, Box 181, UA; UW BOR Minutes, June 17, 1954; Madison City Plan Division, "Report on Plan for Development of University Hill Farms," January, 1954, UHP; *Wisconsin State Journal*, March 3, 1955; "The Hill Farms Story," *WAM*, 62 (January 1961), 13-21; Baldwin, *My Half Century*, p. 475; see also pp. 135-37, 177, 254-55.

Peterson than Fred may eventually have desired.[18] At the urging of
President Fred and his Administrative Committee, the University faculty
directed its executive University Committee to evaluate and make
recommendations about the standing committee system, a key element
in the institution's shared academic governance structure. The result
was a strong reaffirmation of the value of faculty committee service and
several adjustments of the committee roster in the evolving post-war
environment.[19]

By 1948 President Fred had decided that more substantial
change was needed. On June 18 Regent Leonard J. Kleczka, chairman
of the board's Personnel Committee, reported to his colleagues:

> The size and complexity of the University have reached such
> proportions that it is no longer possible for one individual to
> handle the multitude of details associated with the Presi-
> dent's Office. As the chief executive officer of the institu-
> tion, the President must be the responsible head of all phases
> of University operations, but it is necessary that he be
> authorized to delegate some administrative duties to subordi-
> nate officers.

Kleczka then recommended and the full board concurred in the
appointment of Ira Baldwin as vice president of academic affairs, and
A.W. Peterson as vice president of business and finance. "The Vice
Presidents," concluded Kleczka, "shall be responsible to the President

[18]UW BOR Minutes, March 21, 1945; "Business and Finance," *WAM* , 46
(April 15, 1945), 4. The positions and personnel involved in the new arrangement were:
A.W. Peterson, director of business and finance; D.L. Halverson, associate director of
business and finance; M. E. McCaffrey, trust officer and director of investments; R.E.
Hammes, budget officer and chief auditor; A.F. Gallistel, superintendent of buildings
and grounds; C.W. Vaughn, personnel officer; N.G. Cafferty, chief accountant; C.B.
Horswill, bursar; and H.M. Schmelzer, purchasing agent.
[19]UW Faculty Minutes, December 3, 1945, November 4, 1946,UA; UW
Faculty Document 781, University Committee, "Annual Report for 1945-46 and
Recommendations," for faculty meeting of November 4, 1946, UA. In the section
entitled "Improved Functioning and Simplification of the Standing Committees of the
University," the University Committee observed: "Service on the committees of the
University, and of its Colleges, Schools, Divisions, and Departments, is the price
members of the Faculty must pay for democratic government. Such service often makes
heavy demands upon their time and energy, is sometimes wasteful and nearly barren of
results, but more commonly gets the necessary academic 'chores' done satisfactorily, and
frequently results in outstanding statements of educational policy." Of the forty-four
standing committees and five special committees of the faculty then in existence, the
University Committee recommended and the faculty affirmed that eight should be
dropped and important changes made in seven of the remainder.

of the University for their respective duties."[20] This action provided Fred with improved high-level administrative support, and it also created a structure of deputies with authority to act in the absence of the president. Peterson's promotion, to be sure, was largely symbolic, primarily maintaining symmetry within the administration's evolving bureaucratic structure.

The final piece of Fred's administrative reorganization fell into place during 1951. That September the regents approved a proposal by the president to change J. Kenneth Little's title from registrar and director of student personnel services to vice president of student affairs and that of LeRoy Luberg from assistant vice president of academic affairs to assistant to the president. The board also approved a series of "functional organization" charts defining the primary assignments of the institution's five top administrators. Vice President Baldwin's responsibilities encompassed several broad areas, including instructional programming, the hiring and promotion of faculty, relations with the State Teachers Colleges, and heading the Campus Planning Commission. Thirteen officials now reported to Vice President Peterson. In addition to the usual business and finance staff, these included directors of the residence halls, the housing bureau, and building and grounds. Vice President Little's responsibilities covered student records, student services, and student life. Reporting to him, for example, were the directors of admissions, registration and records, placement services, the Wisconsin Union, and the deans of men and women. LeRoy Luberg now handled liaison with educational, alumni, and civic organizations, supervised on- and off-campus speaking activity, kept track of the institution's Army, Navy, and Air Force ROTC programs as well as WHA radio operations. These four officers, of course, reported to President Fred, along with the school and college deans, the news service, intercollegiate athletics, the University Extension Division, and Summer Sessions. Compared with the relatively simple structure of a decade earlier, the campus administrative apparatus had certainly blossomed.[21]

Continuity and high quality characterized much of the University's academic administration throughout the Fred presidency. Letters and Science Dean Mark H. Ingraham, who had succeeded George

---

[20]UW BOR Minutes, June 18, 1948.

[21]Ibid., September 8, 1951; University of Wisconsin Functional Organization Charts, filed with Administrative Committee Minutes, September 7, 1951, Series 5/13, UA; "Little Gets Promotion to Vice President's Job," *WAM*, 53 (October, 1951), 13.

Sellery in 1942, not only administered UW's largest undergraduate college with wisdom and energy but also served as the institution's most articulate spokesman for faculty involvement in University governance. Ingraham continued to provide thoughtful academic leadership for his college and the University as a whole until his retirement in 1961. Conrad A. Elvehjem, a one-time Fred student and the chairman of the world-renowned biochemistry department, served as graduate dean from 1942 until 1958, when he succeeded Fred as president. Unlike Ingraham, whose interests were broad and eclectic, Elvehjem focused on developing the University's strong natural science base while continuing his departmental chairmanship and personal laboratory research. By the early 1950s faculty members in the social sciences and humanities were increasingly dissatisfied with the level of institutional support available for their work, as contrasted with the growing research funding provided to the natural sciences by the Wisconsin Alumni Research Foundation (WARF). Always sensitive to faculty criticism, President Fred brought history Professor Fred Harvey Harrington into his office in 1955-56 as a special assistant to seek research and program funds for the social sciences from such sources as the Ford, Rockefeller, and Carnegie foundations.[22] The College of Agriculture, which included much of the University's scholarly strength in the biological sciences, received rather passive leadership from Dean Rudolph K. Froker, who had succeeded Ira Baldwin in 1948. The college flourished, however, not only because its well-seasoned administrative support staff was fully competent to carry on without aggressive direction, but also because Fred and Baldwin kept a close watch over their home base.[23] Traditionally a laggard behind its sister colleges of Letters and Science and Agriculture, the College of Engineering in the post-war years began a long and steady ascent in quality under the leadership of Deans Morton O. Withey (1946-53) and Kurt F. Wendt (1953-71).

The Schools of Pharmacy, Nursing, Law, Commerce, Medicine, and Education hosted a variety of administrative mutations during the Fred era. Although largely unnoticed on campus, the major structural change occurred in Pharmacy, which transferred from departmental status within the College of Letters and Science to an independent school on July 1, 1950, thanks to strong legislative pressure the previous

---

[22]See below, pp. 119, 169, 243, 250, 310.
[23]See John W. Jenkins, *A Centennial History: A History of the College of Agricultural and Life Sciences at the University of Wisconsin-Madison* (Madison: College of Agricultural and Life Sciences, 1991), pp. 130-34.

year generated by the pharmacists of the state. President Fred, who had questioned the move as a potential threat to L&S, retained Director Arthur H. Uhl as dean, allowing this smallest of UW's college-level schools to carry on in its traditionally competent and quiet manner.[24] A similar move freed the School of Nursing from L&S oversight. Law Dean Lloyd K. Garrison, originally recruited by Glenn Frank, had spent most of World War II away from campus and by September, 1945, had finally decided not to return to Madison. The school had been headed by Acting Dean Oliver S. Rundell during the war, and Fred and the regents persuaded him to retain the deanship on a permanent basis until his retirement in 1953. He was succeeded by outsider John Ritchie, who barely got settled before leaving for Northwestern University. This time Fred and the regents turned to another long-time UW faculty member, George H. Young, in December of 1957.[25] The School of Commerce had been a rather isolated entity under its founding Dean Fayette H. Elwell, who resented its L&S parent and believed his school's primary constituencies lay outside the University. When the time came for his mandatory retirement, Elwell joined President Fred in recommending the promotion of Associate Dean Erwin A. Gaumnitz to the deanship on July 1, 1955.[26] When long-time Medical Dean William S. Middleton resigned in early 1955, President Fred played the major role in recruiting John Z. Bowers as dean, with a charge to strengthen all areas of the school. About the same time Lindley J. Stiles became the third dean of the School of Education, succeeding John Guy Fowlkes, who had served from mid-1947 through September, 1954, when he took a leave of absence for two years of study in India.[27] Of the deans mentioned in this paragraph, only Fowlkes played any meaningful role in campus-wide affairs during the Fred era, the others focusing instead largely on their more narrow areas of administrative responsibility.

President Fred's personal administrative style merits comment. In a word, he was cautious, sometimes to a fault. Nearly every recollection of the Fred administration includes prominent examples of the

---

[24]UW BOR Minutes, October 15, 1949, March 11, 1950, April 15, 1950; "The Voice of Pharmacy," *WAM*, 51 (November, 1949), 17;

[25]UW BOR Minutes, September 15, 27, 1945, December 14, 1957.

[26]Ibid., September 25, 1945.

[27]Ibid., September 27, 1947, September 25, 1954. In 1947 Fowlkes had succeeded C. J. Anderson, who had served as dean of the School of Education since it separated from the College of Letters and Science in 1930. Ibid., May 23, 1947. For an account of the founding of the School of Education, see Cronon and Jenkins, *University of Wisconsin*, vol. 3, pp. 94-107.

president's tendency to delay decisions while he sought advice from practically anyone on every subject of concern. He would even stop strangers walking on Bascom Hill to solicit their opinions, all the while keeping his own counsel. Sometimes he asked a faculty or staff member to draft a speech for him, not mentioning that he was making the same request of others. This no doubt angered and frustrated his associates, but it also directed their attention to the problem while leaving the president free to use whatever ideas and phrases best suited his needs.

President Fred nearly always moved indirectly rather than risk what might be an unpleasant confrontation. For example, students, faculty members, and state editors complained in 1947 that the School of Journalism was stagnating under the stodgy leadership of its long-time director, Grant M. Hyde, who had been on the J-School staff since 1910 and its director since 1935. The president's indirect handling of the problem was both characteristic and disarmingly simple. He created an academic department within the school, whose members were expected to follow the traditional University procedure of electing a faculty chairman annually. They promptly chose the younger and more vigorous Henry Ladd Smith as their leader. Hyde continued as the nominal director of the J-School, but Smith was now responsible for the journalism department's day-to-day operation. Hyde decided to resign the following year and the school then recruited a new director, Ralph O. Nafziger, a distinguished alumnus and former UW faculty member.[28]

Most people who got to know President Fred realized there was considerable shrewdness behind his folksy manner and soft Virginia accent. Scott Cutlip, who served as the president's public relations assistant for several years, recalled:

> President Fred always gave the untutored observer–and I was untutored until I got to know him–the impression of a man who was fumbling, who didn't know where he was going, didn't know what he wanted to accomplish. President Fred always knew what he wanted to do and how he wanted to do it, but he believed that you had to make haste slowly. One time he told me, he said, "You're just like Al Peterson. . . . You think that the shortest distance between two points is a straight line." And another time he told me, "You know,

---

[28]*Daily Cardinal*, October 16, 22, December 2, 3, 1947, August 18, 1948, February 12, 15, March 2, 17, June 3, 1949; "Jam in the 'J' School," *WAM*, 49 (January, 1948), 6; "Nafziger Comes Back," *WAM*, 50 (April, 1949), 12.

you've never learned enough to walk around a brush fire instead of plowing through it."[29]

Fred was particularly careful in making administrative appointments. Typically, as in the selection of his deans, he canvassed widely for candidates, both on and off campus, then prepared lists comparing candidates according to various criteria, and sought outside evaluations. Simultaneously, he appointed faculty advisory committees to make their own reviews and submit lists of acceptable individuals, usually containing between three and five names. With all these materials in hand, Fred and Vice President Baldwin would discuss the matter in depth until a consensus emerged. The final step was to seek the approval of the regents, some of whom might have been consulted informally along the way. Though time-consuming and cumbersome, on the whole this deliberate method worked well.

Occasionally, however, Fred's caution backfired. In deciding on Ira Baldwin's successor as agriculture dean in 1948, for example, the president's insistence on gaining general behind-the-scenes support for his hand-picked candidate–Floyd Andre, the associate director of the Agricultural Experiment Station--resulted in defeat.[30] While Fred delayed, two other self-declared candidates or their supporters–Vincent E. Kivlin and Henry Ahlgren–lobbied the regents and others so effectively that a deadlock occurred before the president felt prepared to announce his preference. The result was the compromise appointment of Rudolph Froker, a UW agricultural economist specializing in dairy pricing. Andre eventually left UW for a distinguished administrative career in Iowa. Ultimately, President Fred's failure to obtain his choice as dean may have meant that agricultural research at Wisconsin was not as well served during the 1950s as it might have been under Andre or a more imaginative and aggressive dean than Froker.

Perhaps learning from this experience, in 1955 Fred worked hard to hire a hard-driving, research-oriented dean for the Medical School, recruiting Dr. John Z. Bowers from the University of Utah. The

---

[29]Scott Cutlip, oral history interview, 1977, UA.

[30]In the College of Agriculture the chief administrative officer was called "dean and director," the former referring to matriculated instructional programming and the latter to district Experiment Station (research) and Cooperative Extension Service (extension) programs. Each of these three areas had evolved their own specialized administrations, instruction headed by an assistant dean and the other two headed by associate directors. Thus Andre, as associate director of the Experiment Station, was actually the lead administrator for the college's research function.

president's careful selection process seemed at first to have worked perfectly in this case, but as is revealed in the next chapter the Bowers administration eventually ended in disaster, at least partly because of a fundamental misfit between the dean and his faculty.[31] For the most part, however, E.B. Fred's careful search-and-screen methodology, which reflected the president's cautious personal style, served the institution well.

"Forming the Future"

During the latter 1940s the Fred administration orchestrated a number of initiatives designed to refurbish the University's image and position it to meet future challenges and opportunities. For the previous decade-and-a-half, the institution had been in more or less constant turmoil and its reputation as a great academic institution had correspondingly declined. The Depression of the 1930s had sorely challenged the University to maintain quality and access in the face of severely limited resources. Most of the faculty disdained the intellectual pretensions and reform ideas of the then UW president, Glenn Frank, and failed to provide support after he fell out of grace at the state capitol. After Frank's dismissal in 1937, following a highly publicized "trial," his successor, Cincinnati City Manager Clarence Dykstra, at first proved no match for the conservative and suspicious stalwart Republican Governor Julius P. Heil. Heil repeatedly slashed the University's budget on short notice, even after minimal state appropriations had been voted and approved. As the physical plant deteriorated, badly needed capital improvements on campus were next to impossible to obtain except through limited federal relief funding. Dykstra's forbearance led to improved relations with Heil and the legislature during 1940 and 1941, but Pearl Harbor transformed the University largely into a military training facility for the next four years.

It was in the context of all-out war that the regents directed board President Walter Hodgkins and UW President Dykstra in 1943 to confer about appropriate ways to celebrate the University's coming hundred-year anniversary in 1948-49.[32] The following month Dykstra proposed and the board agreed that he and Regent Hodgkins should appoint a Centennial Committee to make plans for the celebration. This

---

[31]See below, pp. 140-161.
[32]UW BOR Minutes, October 16, 1943.

"Working Committee" was charged with seven responsibilities: to organize the centennial celebration; suggest a budget; arrange for the writing of a University history; consider an alumni proposal to create a Centennial Gift Fund; appoint sub-committees for "specific tasks," such as arranging for symposia or publications; discuss the creation of an "honorary committee," which the Wisconsin governor might chair; and do any other "necessary things" for accomplishing the "undertaking."[33] The regents subsequently approved Dykstra's suggested committee roster. The membership was distinguished, including prominent faculty representatives from across the institution and was chaired by economics Professor and legendary classroom lecturer William H. "Wild Bill" Kiekhofer. Regent President Hodgkins was initially listed as honorary chairman, with ex officio members including Dykstra, State Historical Society Director Edward P. Alexander, and Alumni Association Secretary John Berge.[34]

The Centennial Committee met four times during 1944, including a formal dinner meeting hosted by the regents at the Madison Club on Friday evening, November 24. Committee members described their plans while individual regents expressed general approval and "deep interest." Before Dykstra departed for his new post at UCLA in early 1945, the committee had developed a budget for 1945-47, which the regents promptly approved. The most expensive item in the committee's request was $10,000 for work on a University history, eventually to be written by Merle Curti and Vernon Carstensen under the supervision of a Centennial History Subcommittee headed by history Professor Paul Knaplund, a member of the parent group. The Centennial Committee also considered an expected request from the Alumni Records Office for funds to support the preparation of a Centennial Directory of all UW alumni and former students.[35] Other committee suggestions were for a student exposition and a number of scholarly symposia.[36]

---

[33]Ibid., November 6, 1943.

[34]The faculty members were Paul Knaplund (history), R.A. Brink (genetics), Morton O. Withey (engineering), Harold C. Bradley (physiological chemistry), Andrew T. Weaver (speech), and John Guy Fowlkes (education). Also included was Frank O. Holt, dean of the University Extension Division. Ibid., December 4, 1943.

[35]This project was eventually dropped due to the great difficulty and expense involved.

[36]William H. Kiekhofer to C. A. Dykstra, January 4, 1944 [1945], with attachment, "Centennial Committee of the University," Series, 1/1/3, Box 61, UA; UW BOR Minutes, January 9, 1945. While regent enthusiasm and support remained constant, the budget did not. As would be expected, the planning process was fluid, and so too

Thus by the time E.B. Fred became University president in February, 1945, planning for the centennial celebration was well under way. Professor Kiekhofer was an excellent choice to head the organizing committee, and he conscientiously saw his assignment through to a successful conclusion in 1948-49. Meanwhile, President Fred took a more strategic view of the anniversary, emphasizing not so much the festivities as how they might be used to build public support for the University and position it to meet future challenges. He declared in 1948:

> We plan to celebrate our Centennial, not by glorification of the past, but rather by a relentless search for the ways we may best serve, in our second century, the people of Wisconsin, the nation, and the world. For us this Centennial marks, not the completion of one hundred years of such service, but rather the beginning of a second one hundred.[37]

Fred saw the coming celebration as an unrivaled public relations opportunity. Thus although the deluge of ex-GIs brought innumerable growing pains early in his administration, the president never lost sight of the importance of the centennial and acted decisively to make the most of it.

He began by recruiting Chester V. Clifton to prepare a "blueprint" for the centennial, a "brief study on publicity for the centennial observance of the founding of the University of Wisconsin." Ted Clifton submitted a 76-page report to Kiekhofer's Centennial Committee on September 10, 1947. He had come to President Fred's attention in 1946 after impressing agricultural journalism Professor Andrew Hopkins with his drive and creative ideas. Hopkins had earlier developed the College of Agriculture's highly effective news bureau and had recently been discussing the University's public relations problems with the president. Clifton, an army lieutenant colonel, arrived on campus in the summer of 1946 to participate in a special graduate program in

were the budget requirements. By the time the official University budget for 1945-46 was printed, for example, Centennial funding included nearly $5,000 for Vernon Carstensen, recruited to work on the general University history, and a similar amount to fund Wilbur H. Glover, who was writing a separate history of the College of Agriculture. Eventually the cost of research assistants and secretarial help for the Curti-Carstensen general University history amounted to considerably more than the $10,000 originally requested.

[37]E.B. Fred, introductory statement, *Centennial Announcement: An Outline of the Centennial Commemoration Program* (Madison: University of Wisconsin, n.d.), Centennial Subject File, UA.

the summer of 1946 to participate in a special graduate program in journalism and public relations for promising career military officers. He met Hopkins at a seminar run by Scott Cutlip, a young assistant professor who was heading the new program. Very soon thereafter President Fred arranged for Clifton to produce the centennial "blueprint."[38]

"Every element of the publicity," declared Clifton at the beginning of his report, "must contribute to the formation of a favorable public opinion about the University." Lest his readers misunderstand, he elaborated: "the purpose of the centennial publicity is to reach those people we desire to impress with the information we want them to have, at the time we want them to have it." He explained that his report gave careful consideration "to each suggestion and project [of the Centennial Committee] in light of its effect upon, and its relation to, the integrated over-all public relations program of the University." Clifton's report was a masterpiece—logical, clear, precise, and substantial in its orderly presentation. It addressed the challenges and resources at hand, general public relations techniques and opportunities, and promotional recommendations for the individual programs currently being planned. Clifton divided this latter category according to "academic projects," "fine arts projects," "selected demonstrations of the century-old University at work," "memorial projects," and "celebrations." Although plans for particular projects and events would continue to evolve as the centennial year approached, Clifton's "Blueprint" instantly established itself as the central organizing document of the entire celebration.

While Clifton worked on his report, President Fred was overhauling the University's public relations machinery. The key decision came in August, 1947, when Fred appointed Ted Clifton's journalism mentor, Scott Cutlip, to a new position as assistant to the president for public relations. Not wanting to abandon his academic work Cutlip was reluctant to take the assignment, but finally agreed if he could continue part-time teaching. Fred was willing, provided Cutlip could improve the University news bureau and assure a well-publicized centennial celebration. The resulting changes at the news bureau were particularly hard on Robert Foss, the incumbent UW news director. Foss

---

[38]C. V. Clifton, "Blueprint for Centennial: Commemorating A Century of Service," September 10, 1947, Series 0/5/7, Box 2, UA; Cutlip, oral history interview. Clifton eventually rose to the rank of major general, serving as the chief senior military aide and public relations adviser to President Kennedy and as a military aide to President Johnson.

had served the University for well over a decade in this and other capacities, and in 1938 had come up with the classic slogan defining University public service: "The boundaries of the campus are the boundaries of the state." By the mid-1940s, however, his physical strength was declining and he had lost control of a service that had spawned numerous and uncoordinated campus outlets. Cutlip considered the situation for a year and then moved decisively to reorganize and consolidate operations, in the process reassigning Foss and recruiting Robert Taylor as the news director.[39] Taylor, who had helped edit the *Daily Cardinal* as an undergraduate during the late 1930s, returned to the campus from a position as news director at WIBA radio in Madison. His distinguished service shaping UW public relations would continue throughout the period covered by this volume and well beyond.

To provide all-around staff support for the centennial preparations, Cutlip arranged for the hiring of another pre-war *Cardinal* editor, Clarence Schoenfeld. Following extensive World War II military service, Clay Schoenfeld had served as editor of the *Wisconsin Alumnus* magazine while working on a master's degree in journalism. When he enrolled in one of Cutlip's courses, the match was made. As executive secretary to the Centennial Committee, Schoenfeld had to serve several masters. He reported to Chairman Kiekhofer and his fellow committee members while at the same time receiving regular direction from Cutlip and President Fred. Before long, in fact, Schoenfeld's duties expanded to include speech writing and traveling around the state with the president. Encouraged by his close association with Fred as well as his own inclination, Schoenfeld's approach supported the UW administration's broader public relations objectives over the considerably more restrained and scholarly preferences of the Centennial Committee. Sometimes the committee's cautious approach prevailed. For example, Schoenfeld and Cutlip had to drop their plans for a centennial movie and radio series after Kiekhofer and his faculty colleagues insisted on closely reviewing the proposed scripts.[40] Still, Schoenfeld proved to be an excellent choice as executive secretary, and he was instrumental in putting together and orchestrating the University's most successful and extensive anniversary celebration ever.[41]

---

[39]The reorganization resulted in three publicity agencies: the overarching News Service, a separate news service for intercollegiate athletics, and another for agricultural journalism.

[40]Ibid.

[41]Some years later Schoenfeld commented: "Wisconsin PR people like to

The centennial celebration covered the entire 1948-49 academic year, with a few activities relating to the state's centennial occurring during the spring and summer of 1948. The University participated in the Statehood Day celebration of May 29, 1948, for example, and provided three display booths at the State Centennial Exposition in Milwaukee during the summer. But the major emphasis was naturally on the University's centennial. Special campus-based events throughout the year included Founder's Day on February 5, 1949, and a gala Commencement-Reunion Week, from June 12 to 19, 1949. Numerous forward-looking academic events crowded the calendar, beginning with a conference in October examining "Higher Education for American Society." Sixteen symposia, with topics ranging from "The Humanities in American Society" to "The Steroid Hormones," attracted scholars from across the academic world, and the University hosted the annual meetings of thirteen national learned societies. Fine arts activities also were plentiful, including performances by impressive local musical talent as well as by outstanding national attractions such as violinist Fritz Kreisler, pianist Vladimir Horowitz, and the New York Philharmonic Orchestra under conductor Leopold Stokowski. The Wisconsin Players dedicated their season to the works of Wisconsin playwrites, and Alfred Lunt and Lynn Fontanne staged the world debut of *Speak to Me of Love* in the Memorial Union Theater. A campus exhibition of old master paintings valued at $1 million borrowed from the New York Metropolitan Museum of Art reportedly drew 66,000 visitors.[42]

Throughout, the young publicists seized every opportunity to reach and impress the University's many publics. "Rooted in the past, serving the present, forming the future," became the centennial motto, proudly attributed to venerable University President Emeritus Edward A. Birge, who at 94 years of age was deemed "Mr. Centennial" for the duration. A centennial logo also appeared ubiquitously on University

---

think–with all its flaws–their Centennial was in a very real sense a distillation of all they had learned in 100 years about the role of a great university in the life of a state. It was concerned with teaching, with searching, with serving, and with building. It marked not only the completion of 100 years, but also the beginning of a second hundred. The Centennial like all good PR, in other words, was indigenous to the Wisconsin campus." Clay Schoenfeld, *The Outreach University: A Case History in the Public Relationships of Higher Education* (UW-Madison: Office of Inter-College Programs, 1977), p. 175.

[42]Clay Schoenfeld, "The University of Wisconsin Centennial: 1848-49–1948-49," *Wisconsin Journal of Education*, 81(January, 1949), pp. 3-7; "Calendar of University Centennial Events (As of September 1, 1948)," Series 0/5/7, Box 1, UA; Schoenfeld, *Outreach University*, pp. 170-73.

stationery and publications and across a sixteen-by-sixteen-foot backdrop adorning many events. Not only did Schoenfeld and his colleagues produce an amazing array of centennial brochures, invitations, calendars, and more, they also arranged for essentially constant press coverage in the *Wisconsin Alumnus* and state newspapers as well as positive comment in such national publications as *Look*, *Life*, *Newsweek*, *Holiday*, *Reader's Digest*, and the *Saturday Evening Post*. They even obtained an enthusiastic statement of congratulatory praise from President Harry Truman, who had campaigned at the Stock Pavilion in his recent come-from-behind election victory.[43]

Of course, more than well-publicized academic exercises and celebrations were necessary if the University were to take control of its future. Needed also were substantial new sources of funding–for instructional programming, scholarship, and facilities. An example of creative institutional bootstrapping was the Wisconsin Alumni Research Foundation (WARF), founded in 1925, which had proved of crucial value during the dark days of the Depression and since. Dedicated to the support of research at the University, WARF managed patentable discoveries by UW researchers, returning some of the proceeds to the campus while building an enviable endowment. The Board of Regents had also received and invested bequests and other gifts over the years, but to E.B. Fred and others it seemed clear that a better conduit for financial support from the University's friends was needed to supplement state appropriations. The University developed such a mechanism in early 1945 by creating a Gifts and Bequests Council. Its membership included Fred, Regent President Walter Hodgkins, A.W. Peterson, Regent Secretary M.E. McCaffrey, UW Public Service Director Frank O. Holt, Wisconsin Alumni Association (WAA) Executive Secretary John Berge, plus nine members of the Board of Regents and six WAA members. Two of the alumni members–George I. Haight of Chicago and William S. Kies of New York City–had been instrumental in the founding of WARF.[44] The following April the council transformed itself

[43]*Centennial Announcement: An Outline of the Centennial Commemoration Program*, n.d., Centennial Subject File, UA; Schoenfeld, *Outreach University*, pp. 174-75.
[44]Regent members were Herman Ekern, Clark Everest, A. J. Horlick, Glen V. Rourk, Ray Stroud, Reuben Trane, Robert Uihlein, Howard I. Potter, and F. J. Sensenbrenner. WAA members, in addition to Haight and Kies, were Harry Bullis, Howard Greene, George Luhman, and C. F. Van Pelt. *WAM*, 46 (February 15, 1945), 10. See also *WAM*, 47 (January 20, 1946), 6. The impetus for the Gifts and Bequests

and incorporated as the University of Wisconsin Foundation. With the ex officio members now limited to the University president and one regent, along with the WAA president and executive secretary, the foundation was at least formally a more independent agency than the old council. Yet among the eighteen elected directors, most of whom were alumni, were several regents. George Haight was elected to the Executive Committee and named chairman of the board.[45]

During the next few years, as the UW Foundation refined its organization and structure, it used the centennial celebration to focus its early fund-raising activities. In late 1945 the foundation created the post of executive director for William J. Hagenah.[46] Hagenah had earned a UW baccalaureate degree in 1903 and a UW law degree two years later. He had subsequently worked as a successful attorney, a public utilities expert, and most recently as chairman of the formerly German-owned Schering Corporation of New Jersey, seized by the American government during the war. In the past he had contributed generously to a Law School scholarship fund and lately had proposed the "Hagenah Plan" for developing and beautifying the lower campus. Now, in conjunction with the coming University centennial, Hagenah was charged with coordinating a $5 million UWF capital campaign. WAA Executive Secretary

Council was a resolution passed by the WAA in 1941, pledging the association "to the task of promoting specific gifts and bequests to the University." Quoted in "UW Foundation's Executive Director," *WAM*, 47 (December 20, 1945), 10.

[45]Named to the first board of directors as ex officio members were President Fred, Regent President Hodgkins, WAA President Philip H. Falk, and WAA Executive Secretary Berge; named to one-year terms were George Haight, Michael J. Cleary, and Howard I. Potter; named to two-year terms were Harry A. Bullis, Thomas E. Brittingham, Jr., and George B. Luhman; named to three-year terms were William S. Kies, William J. Hagenah, and Howard T. Greene; named to four-year terms were F.J. Sensenbrenner, Robert Uihlein, and Herman Ekern; named to five-year terms were C.F. Van Pelt, Oscar Rennebohm, and Ray M. Stroud; named to six-year terms were A.J. Horlick, Reuben N. Trane, and Glen Roark. Officers elected at the first meeting were Haight, chairman of the board; Potter, president; Luhman, vice president and treasurer; Frank O. Holt, secretary; Kies, vice president, and Bullis, vice president. The foundation Executive Committee included Haight, Potter, Luhman, Sensenbrenner, Greene, Van Pelt, and Ekern. The articles of incorporation provided for a maximum of one hundred directors of the foundation. *WAM*, 46 (April 15, 1945), 9.

[46]At about this time the UW Foundation absorbed the Wisconsin Educational Foundation, an agency established contemporaneously with UWF. While UWF encouraged gifts and bequests for buildings, scholarships, and other purposes, the educational foundation focused solely on raising scholarship support. The merger was designed to avert confusion among potential contributors as to which organization did what. "Foundations Merge," *WAM*, 47 (January 20, 1946), 6.

John Berge told his membership: "It's unquestionably one of the biggest jobs ever tackled by Wisconsin alumni, but it is also the most important."[47]

New and inexperienced, and dealing with an alumni base not accustomed to giving money to a state-supported institution, the UW Foundation managed to raise only $1.5 million by mid-1949; in fact, it took until 1960 to reach the full $5 million Centennial Fund goal. UWF support was valuable nevertheless. The foundation contributed directly to the centennial celebration by sponsoring several events and establishing important new scholarships and professorships. Early in 1948 UWF leaders announced plans to construct a long-needed campus conference center. Although for a variety of reasons the Wisconsin Center would not open for business until 1958, the foundation's commitment reaffirmed the University's longstanding support of public service outreach programming, which since early in the century had been popularized as the Wisconsin Idea.

Meanwhile, the Hagenah Plan came to partial fruition in 1953 with the opening of the new Memorial Library building.[48] By 1958 a well-developed mall linked the Memorial and State Historical Society libraries and featured the centerpiece Hagenah Fountain, providing for the first time an appropriate "front door" to the campus. Between 1946, when the new foundation paid out $9,437 to the University, and 1971, UWF contributed a total of more than $10.7 million. In the long run the creation of the University of Wisconsin Foundation as the institution's primary development mechanism was a major contribution of E.B. Fred's presidency. First under William Hagenah and beginning in 1955 under Robert B. Rennebohm for the next thirty-three years, the foundation functioned along with WARF to provide crucial supplemental funding for many of the University's most important needs.[49]

[47]"UW Foundation's Executive Director: William J. Hagenah Handles New Post," and John Berge, "Back the Foundation," both in *WAM*, 47 (December 20, 1945), 10, 11.

[48]See below, pp. 233-38.

[49]William H. Young, "The University's Supporting Resources, 1949-1974," in Allan G Bogue and Robert Taylor, *The University of Wisconsin: One Hundred and Twenty-Five Years* (Madison: University of Wisconsin Press, 1975), p. 83; "UW Foundation Celebrates 50 Years," *The Campaigner*, newsletter of the UW Foundation, Special Anniversary Issue (November, 1995), 1, UHP; William Hagenah, "Wanted: Front Door for the University," *WAM*, 47 (February, 1946), 10-14; "A Roof for the Wisconsin Idea," ibid., 49 (January, 1948), 18-19; "Campaign Report," ibid., 50 (June, 1949), 9; "Rennebohm Heads Foundation," ibid., 56 (October, 1954), 19; "Wisconsin Center for Adult Education," ibid., 59 (June, 1958), 14-24.

Because in its early years UWF lacked significant resources, during the planning for the centennial President Fred turned to the trustees of the Wisconsin Alumni Research Foundation for support of a key element of his centennial program–the strengthening of the faculty as scholars and University citizens. While serving as graduate dean, Fred had become interested in the problem of how to recruit and nurture outstanding young faculty members in an increasingly large and decentralized institution. He brought this concern to the presidency, enhanced now by a greater appreciation of the difficulties of recruitment and retention of faculty in the chaotic post-war environment. In Madison as throughout the nation, housing was in desperately short supply after the war, as the previous chapter has shown. Successful faculty recruitment often depended on availability of affordable housing, especially for junior appointees.

While the initial steps of the process were not documented, it is clear that sometime during the winter of 1946-47 the president brought the housing problem before the WARF trustees. Although the matter was outside of WARF's traditional purview, the trustees agreed to construct and operate a UW apartment complex for junior faculty members. Trustee William Kies took the lead for WARF in creating and presiding over University Houses, Inc., the corporation that constructed and formally owned the "150 urgently needed" family units on fifteen acres of the old Raymer Farm that belonged to the College of Agriculture. Located west of Picnic Point, the project was adjacent to the suburban Village of Shorewood Hills. In April of 1948 the first occupants moved into University Houses, trumpeted as "one of the first faculty housing projects in the Middlewest and the finest faculty housing project in the country."[50]

---

[50]The first quotation is from a BOR resolution, UW BOR Minutes, February 11, 1950; the second quote appears in "Houses for Homeless Profs," *WAM*, 49 (March, 1948), 20-5. See also Ira Baldwin, *My Half Century*, p. 189. Two decades later E.B. Fred observed: "We had people that would offer to come to Madison if we could give them a place to live, and we didn't know what we could do." E.B. Fred, oral history interview, 1967, UA. Perhaps only Fred could have persuaded the skeptical WARF trustees to break with tradition and invest $2.75 million in the University Houses project. Eventually, according to Mark Ingraham, WARF handed over ownership of the Houses to the University following a policy dispute over housing priorities after UW officials placed a black professor ahead of earlier applicants because of his presumed problems in finding suitable accommodations in town. Mark H. Ingraham, "The University of Wisconsin, 1925-1970," in Bogue and Taylor, *University of Wisconsin*, p. 74.

An oft-told anecdote about Fred and the University Houses project reveals much about the president's acumen and close-to-the-vest administrative style. When word of the project leaked out, a concerned group of Shorewood residents led by several prominent UW faculty members sought a meeting with the president to protest the building of an apartment project next door to their upscale village, worried that its residents, of uncertain background, might swamp their exclusive elementary school. President Fred exclaimed his happiness over the delegation's visit, as he needed its advice on a difficult administrative problem. He said he had been mulling over WARF's proposal to build an attractive faculty housing project near Picnic Point, but it seemed that the land in question was owned by the College of Agriculture, whose Department of Animal Husbandry wanted it for a badly needed pig farm! What should be done? Although the president was seemingly at a loss to decide between the two projects, the delegation instantly was not. Construction of University Houses was soon under way.[51]

The University Houses project and series of reports by a special faculty Committee on University Functions and Policies rounded out the centennial period of the Fred administration. On August 16, 1947, the regents approved a recommendation from President Fred's Administrative Committee to undertake the study. As recorded in the regent minutes, the president noted that "it would be most worthwhile for the State University to pause and take a searching inventory of itself as it completes one century of service, and contemplates a second century." In October, at the faculty's first meeting of the new academic year, the president explained:

> During the 1930's the state and the nation were facing the problems of depression and recovery. Since then our energies have been devoted to war and its aftermath. It is natural that now as the developing educational needs become clearer, and with the mushroom growth of our own institution, questions should be raised concerning the structure of higher education in the state. In particular we must assess our own role and decide not only how best to fulfill our traditional obligations but how to cooperate with the other institutions of the state to meet new needs. I welcomed the direction of the Regents that we make a careful study of the functions and policy of the University. This will call for the

---

[51]This anecdote has had many tellings, perhaps most authoritatively in Ira Baldwin's oral history interview with John W. Jenkins, July 6, 1988, UHP.

combined energy and wisdom of the entire faculty including
of course the administration.[52]

On the motion of L&S Dean Ingraham, the faculty authorized the
University Committee to consult with the president in naming the
members of a committee to carry out the assignment.

The University Committee and the president moved quickly to
appoint the functions and policies study committee, which held its first
meeting on October 22, 1947. The membership was impressive,
representing the best of UW's academic and administrative leadership.[53]
Heading the 23-member group was Mark Ingraham, perhaps the
University's most respected faculty leader. Twice elected to serve on
and chair the prestigious University Committee, Ingraham also had
chaired the Committee on the Quality of Instruction and Scholarship
during 1940-42. In recognition of the importance of the new committee's work, Dean Ingraham reduced his administrative assignment to
half-time while leading the study.

The Ingraham Committee issued its "First Report" in October,
1948, addressing the complex and controversial question of the
University's appropriate role in the structure of Wisconsin public higher
education. A brilliant piece of analysis and speculative educational
philosophy, the report laid out a controversial vision of a statewide
University of Wisconsin encompassing not only the Madison campus
and its many outreach activities and two-year centers, but also the
parallel State Teachers College system.[54] A year later, in November,
1949, the committee published a "Second Report: Internal Survey," a
detailed summary of the University's various programs and activities.
Based on the work of nine sub-committees and two University standing
committees, this second report paralleled the earlier work of the pre-war
Committee on Quality of Instruction and Scholarship. More than a

---

[52]Fred's statement is quoted in the forward of Committee on University
Functions and Policies, "First Report," October, 1948, UHP. The UW Faculty Minutes
for the October 6 meeting include only a cursory reference to Fred's comment.

[53]Initial membership included: Deans Mark H. Ingraham (chairman), I. L.
Baldwin, C. A. Elvehjem, and John Guy Fowlkes; Professors H. L. Ahlgren, R. A.
Brink, Charles Bunn, Anthony R. Curreri, Merle Curti, Helen Dawe, Glen G. Eye, E. A.
Gaumnitz, C. L. Huskins, J. L. McCamy, P. L. MacKendrick, V. W. Meloche, R. J.
Roark, George B. Rodman, Kurt Wendt, and Helen C. White; Directors Kenneth Little
and A. W. Peterson; and President Fred. By October, 1948, when the committee issued
its first report, Professor S. M. McElvain had also joined the group,

[54]The committee's far-sighted call for a merger of the two systems is dealt
with elsewhere in this volume. See below, pp. 523-24, 528, 575, 596.

University Houses under construction, January 6, 1948. UA, 26/11.

E.B. Fred, Gov. Oscar Rennebohm, Columbia University President Dwight Eisenhower
at Association of American Universities meeting in Madison
during the centennial year, October 28-29, 1949. UA, 7890-C-1.

hundred people participated in the work of the supporting committees, including a number of graduate and undergraduate students.[55] Throughout the spring semester of 1949-50, the University faculty formally considered and frequently amended each of the sub-committee studies. Faculty participation was broadly inclusive and the evaluation of the Ingraham Committee's report was thoughtful and comprehensive.[56] The entire exercise illustrated how seriously the UW faculty took its governance responsibilities after a century of University history. That the Board of Regents and state officials for a variety of reasons chose not to make much use of the massive study and its findings in planning for the University's next century should not detract from a later generation's appreciation of the care and insight with which Mark Ingraham and his colleagues on the Committee on University Functions and Policies approached their centennial assignment.

Battling for the Biennial Budget

Like their predecessors, President Fred and his administrative colleagues often must have felt the University was locked in a more or less constant struggle to obtain adequate financial support. Yet in spite of disappointing rebuffs, on the whole Fred was at least moderately successful in gaining state funding for the University. Even in 1953-55, when the governor and legislature slashed the UW appropriation below the previous biennium, the University arguably fared better than at any time during the Depression or World War II. The Fred era coincided with a state and national economy rebounding from fifteen years of hard times, when "make-do" and emergency measures defined the norm for

[55]The sub-committees included: Recruitment of Senior Staff, comprised of 8 staff members; Measurement of the Quality of Scholarship, 9 staff; Methods of Improving Instruction, 9 staff, 1 graduate student, 2 undergraduates; Recruitment and In-Service Training of Junior Staff, 9 staff, 1 graduate student; How Curricula Are Established and Changed, 10 staff, 1 graduate student; Student Dishonesty and Cheating, 3 staff, 5 undergraduates; Advising and Counseling Services, 11 staff, 1 graduate student, 3 undergraduates; Student Extra-Curricular Cultural Enterprise, 8 staff, 5 undergraduates; Internal Administrative Structure, 10 staff. The report of the Committee on Student Life and Interests considered student housing, student activities not associated with housing, and foreign students. The Research Committee reported on research facilities.

[56]The University faculty considered the sub-committee reports–formally identified as UW Faculty Documents 926, 926a, 926b, and 926c–at seven meetings. UW Faculty Minutes, December 12, 1949, and January 1, March 13, March 20, April 3, April 24, and May 1, 1950.

institutions and individuals alike. The occasional post-war economic recessions, moreover, surprised many by failing to bring a return of the depressed economy and massive unemployment of the 1930s. Although it was evident only in retrospect, the fundamental problem for state officials and University administrators had shifted from how to survive in adversity to how best to manage the growing prosperity.

For those charged with developing state budgets, the problems and prospects were immediate, however, and the longer-term benevolent economic trend was obscure. While state resources were growing from an expanding economy, so too was competition from various state agencies for tax support. This was especially evident at the state capitol, where a succession of governors and legislatures, mostly Republican in this period, grappled with the continuing challenge of meeting state needs. Wisconsin budgeting practice involved incredibly short lead-times for review of state agency requests by the governor and legislature. The governor was required to hold public hearings on agency requests only a few weeks after his election in November. Even for an incumbent governor this necessitated hasty decisions, often without adequate information or analysis. Any gubernatorial initiatives, moreover, inevitably involved fiscal commitments likely to disrupt the funding equilibrium established among the existing state agencies. This problem was especially evident during the three terms of Republican Governor Walter J. Kohler, Jr., from 1951 to 1957. Kohler sought to run a fiscally conservative administration while also trying to provide for major capital improvements, notably the construction of Wisconsin's part of the new interstate highway system.

Even under the most favorable circumstances, UW officials dreaded the uncertainty and intensive work of the biennial budget exercise. The process had several steps. First the University administration developed a proposed budget, sometimes in conjunction with a capital request for new construction or remodeling. The president then presented this budget to the Board of Regents, which officially adopted it (usually with only a few changes) and sent it to the governor. Along with the requests from other state agencies, the latter held public hearings and hastily compiled them into a recommended biennial budget for consideration by the new legislature during the winter and spring of each odd year. Over the next several months the legislature held further hearings (mostly conducted by its Joint Committee on Finance) and eventually approved a final biennial appropriation bill, which it transmitted to the governor for approval in late spring or early summer.

This was never the end of the process, however. Actual state spending over the biennium always turned out to be somewhat different than the original appropriation. Sometimes the legislature later approved "emergency" or "special" measures as needs arose; sometimes the State Emergency Board, composed of the governor and legislative leaders, released discretionary funds at its disposal; sometimes the governor withheld funds. Furthermore, it must be remembered that the University, more than other state agencies, enjoyed access to auxiliary sources of funding, such as income from student tuition and fees and grants from its Wisconsin Alumni Research Foundation and University of Wisconsin Foundation as well as increasingly from the federal government and national foundations. Thus, it would be a mistake to confuse the state appropriation of tax dollars in any given year with the University's total spending. Throughout the period of this volume, the *percentage* of support provided to the University by the state declined, while except in a single instance the *amount* of state funding increased. During the Fred era the state-funded share of the University budget hovered around the 50 percent mark.

The single budget reduction came in 1953-55 during a national recession, when the state appropriation for the University was cut by $2.4 million. Since the total state budget declined $6.18 million, other state agencies also did not escape unscathed. A notable exception was the rapidly growing Wisconsin State College system, UW's primary competition for public higher education dollars. The WSC budget received a modest increase of about $360,000.[57] That the University was in for difficult times should have been clear from the time Governor Kohler took office in early 1951. Kohler at first threatened to cut the University's budget,[58] but new to politics and office, he eventually recommended a nearly $6 million increase over the previous biennium. By late summer of 1952, the governor–now with plenty of time to plan and fully expecting to be re-elected in November–passed word to the University and other state agencies to expect severe cuts in 1953. President Fred's Administrative Committee discussed this troubling prospect in August. Fred speculated about how to manage the budget process, but the more decisive Graduate Dean Conrad Elvehjem

---

[57] *1953 Wisconsin State Budget* (Prepared for the use of the Governor and the Members of the 1953 Wisconsin Legislature by the Department of Budget and Accounts, January, 1953); *1955 Wisconsin State Budget* (ibid., 1955).
[58] "Opposition Looms for UW's $32,000,000 Operating Budget," *WAM*, 52 (January, 1951), 9-11, 30.

declared that the University Extension Division should be cut first in order to protect campus-based instruction and research.[59] In September, Governor Kohler assigned Claude Holloway of the state budget bureau to work with the University on its proposal, which the regents approved on October 25.[60]

, Although University leaders termed their $37.7 million proposal an "economy budget," it was immediately in trouble with the governor.[61] Instead of considering the requested increase of about $5.7 million, Kohler announced that he expected UW officials to appear at his budget hearing on December 16 prepared to describe how they would cut current support levels by 10 percent.[62] The skeptical governor, a Yale College graduate, came armed with a series of seventeen tough questions that cast doubt on all aspects of University operations, from the ordering of supplies and equipment to the decision to construct a new library within a hundred feet of the old one.[63] State Auditor J. Jay Keliher released a controversial analysis of the University's use of student fee revenues, characterizing UW reporting as "inaccurate, unfair and misleading."[64] Governor Kohler confirmed President Fred's worst fears in his budget message to the legislature on January 27. "I have concluded," he declared, "the people want less government, fewer regulations, smaller budgets and lower taxes." For the University he proposed a reduced appropriation of about $32.7 million, a sum, he asserted, that would allow UW to function at its 1951-52 level, with fewer state dollars offset by lower enrollment and curtailed activity at Badger Village. "It will probably not be easy for the University to adjust its operations to the recommended appropriation," Kohler conceded, but he was sure it could be done.[65]

Fighting back, President Fred orchestrated a broad UW defense of the original budget request, rallying the regents, addressing the faculty and appointing a special faculty advisory committee, and working energetically with his Administrative Committee on ideas and tactics to influence the legislature. The effort was probably doomed

---

[59]Administrative Committee Minutes, August 8, 1952.

[60]Ibid., September 16, 1952; UW BOR Minutes, October 25, 1952.

[61]"'Economy Budget' Sought by UW," *WAM*, 54 (December, 1952), 9.

[62]Administrative Committee Minutes, December 9, 1952.

[63]"Outline of Questions Asked by Governor Kohler at Budget Hearing, December 16, 1952," attached to ibid., December 18, 1952.

[64]"Regents Assail Auditor's Report," *WAM*, 54 (February, 1953), 13.

[65]Governor Walter J. Kohler, "Governor's Message," *Senate Journal*, 71st session, 1953, pp. 90, 98.

from the start, however, as the Republican-dominated Joint Finance Committee even removed another $2 million from the governor's recommendation for the University. Voting on party lines, the full legislature concurred–ironically on April Fools Day of 1953. This produced a final appropriation of just over $29.9 million, or about $2.4 million lower than the previous biennium. The governor had his leaner budget and the University had a major headache.

Perhaps the only positive aspect of the entire episode was the appointment of the faculty Budget Advisory Committee, reminiscent of the budget crisis of 1932-33 that had affirmed the faculty's role in helping resolve serious University policy questions in adverse circumstances.[66] Unfortunately, any sympathy the University might have earned among friendly legislators and the public was partly offset when the faculty voted during the legislative budget deliberations to reaffirm its longstanding opposition to Big Ten participation in the New Year's Day Rose Bowl football game. This action so displeased the legislature that it quickly passed a resolution condemning the faculty.[67]

The University was now faced with the problem of curtailing its operations to fit the reduced appropriation. President Fred wisely retained the Budget Advisory Committee, headed by a widely respected mathematician, Rudolph Langer. Fred also worked closely with the deans and other administrators and the regents on the problem.[68] By the fall of 1953, after many hours of study and analysis, the board approved a series of acceptable if not popular actions, including the elimination of 161 junior faculty and staff positions, dropping or rearranging of 60 courses, canceling or consolidating several research projects, cutting supplies, capital, and maintenance spending, and reducing a wide array of extension programming. A surprise decision allowed all eight of the two-year extension centers to remain open. At the same time, the University managed to provide $500,000 in faculty raises in an effort to keep salaries minimally competitive.[69] Overall, as the Langer Committee reported during the wrenching process, the University would probably

---

[66]See Cronon and Jenkins, *University of Wisconsin*, vol. 3, pp. 219-36.

[67]UW Faculty Minutes, March 2, 1953; "Faculty Criticized on Bowl Stand," *WAM*, 54 (March, 1953), 10.

[68]For an overview of austerity measures see "Budget Adjusting Is Under Way," ibid., (May, 1953), 13; Administrative Committee Minutes, March 24, April 1 and 14, and July 7, 1953; UW BOR Minutes, July 11, 1953.

[69]"Regents OK $34½ Million Budget," *WAM*, 55 (October, 1953), 10-11.

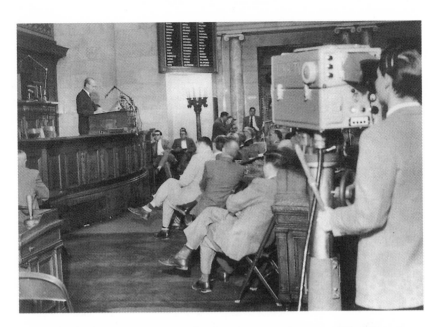

Gov. Kohler's budget cutting message to the legislature, January, 1953, *Milwaukee Sentinel* photo. UA, X25-3393.

Memorial Library ground-breaking ceremony, July 24, 1950; l-r: E.B. Fred, Regent Daniel H. Grady, Frederick V. Platz, Jr., Regent W.J. Campbell (foreground), O.T. Havey (electrical contractor, smiling in glasses). UA, 1824-M.

87

avoid any permanent harm from the budget cuts as long as they were not repeated in the next biennium.[70]

President Fred began to address this longer-term threat almost immediately by drawing on the experience and contacts of political science Associate Professor William H. Young as an informal budget officer. Former Wisconsin Governor Oscar Rennebohm, currently serving on the Board of Regents, probably brought Young to Fred's attention. During the late 1940s, Young had taken leave from his UW faculty duties to work for Governor Rennebohm as an executive assistant for budget and other matters. He had remained part-time to assist Governor Kohler at the beginning of his administration in 1951. In early 1953 the Keliher audit of state activities led Governor Kohler to subtract unspent tuition balances from the University's budget request, in effect resulting in a new state policy lapsing unspent student tuition and fee income back to the state treasury at the end of each year. This removed an important continuing source of budgetary flexibility the University had been using for emergency purposes. With this resource now apparently gone, it became Young's assignment to identify a replacement, which he partially found in the overhead income the University was receiving as part of its growing federal grant support. In December of 1953 President Fred assigned a faculty study committee to evaluate the idea, and the following April Professor Young sought and received permission from the State Emergency Board to spend some of the overhead proceeds on operations and remodeling. Thanks to this authorization, for example, in October of 1954 the regents were able to assign $40,000 in federal overhead funds for the landscaping of the lower campus library mall between the State Historical Society and the new Memorial Library.[71]

Fred gradually shifted responsibility for management of the University's overall budgeting to Regent Rennebohm's one-time assistant. A key need, Young believed, was to develop a more reliable and defensible method for setting student tuition rates. Young and UW Comptroller Neil G. Cafferty came up with a plan to establish undergraduate tuition for Wisconsin residents at 20 percent of instructional costs and for non-resident students at 100 percent of costs. This allowed tuition to be determined more or less mechanically after the legislature

---

[70]"Warning Sounded as UW Tightens Belt," ibid., (July, 1953), 21-22.

[71]William O. Young, oral history interview with E. David Cronon, September 12-13, 1995, UHP; Administrative Committee Minutes, December 23, 1953, and April 6, 1954; "Lower Campus Mall Gets Appropriation," *WAM,* 56 (October, 1954), 21.

had approved staff salary increases. Young worked quietly throughout the fall semester of 1953-54 to develop this fresh approach featuring a more intelligible and compelling case for meeting the University's funding needs. On at least two occasions he shared the evolving plan with Fred's Administrative Committee before presenting it in late October to the regents for their informal blessing.[72] In November, Young returned to the Administrative Committee for a discussion of "Principles Governing Preparation of the University Budget," which in December produced a decision for him to explain the new process to the several school and college faculties after President Fred announced its development at the University faculty meeting in January.[73] Meanwhile, Young put his state government contacts to good use as he and Cafferty met with Senator Arthur A. Lenroot, Jr., and Assemblyman Alfred R. Ludvigsen, the co-chairmen of the Joint Finance Committee, and obtained their approval of the new budgeting system.[74] President Fred characteristically sought academic involvement, appointing a faculty committee in January, 1954, to help develop the controversial new scholarly activities report forms that were at the heart of Young's system to calculate instructional costs. The president announced in April that he would convene the faculty as a committee of the whole for a comprehensive discussion of the entire budgeting process.[75] He explained: "We have attempted in the past to provide detailed and accurate statements of our expenditures and our needs. We are now redoubling our efforts to make future statements more meaningful, more understandable."[76]

The unusually well-documented 1955-57 University budget request was unveiled in the fall of 1954. Speaking before a gathering of UW alumni in Fond du Lac on November 5, President Fred observed, "In a very real sense, our [budget] statement is a financial interpretation of the University's hopes and plans for the future." The next day he presented the fruit of Young's labors to the regents, who approved the $35.8 million request for transmission to the governor. Not coincidentally, on December 1 the influential Wisconsin Legislative Council issued a highly supportive report on "University of Wisconsin Policies" to the governor and legislature outlining UW's functions, needs, and

[72]Administrative Committee Minutes, October 6, 21, and 27, 1953.
[73]Ibid., November 17, and December 1 and 23, 1953.
[74]Ibid., January 14, 1954.
[75]Ibid., January 26, and April 5, 1954.
[76]"UW Is Planning Budget Request," *WAM*, 55 (February, 1954), 15.

problems, and generally setting a positive tone for the budget debate soon to follow. Governor Kohler's recommended budget on February 1 cut only $600,000 from the UW request. Subsequent hearings before the Joint Finance Committee were cordial, producing no important challenges to the carefully crafted document. The process concluded successfully on May 5, 1955, with the approval of a $37 million appropriation, surpassing the 1953-55 figure by more than $7 million![77] Bill Young had proved his worth.

Concern over Communist Subversion

The report by the Wisconsin Legislative Council on "University of Wisconsin Policies" was influential in the 1955 budget-making process both for what it said and did not say. On the one hand, it portrayed the University so positively that the *Wisconsin Alumnus* published the full document as a special supplement to its January, 1955, issue, and provided a thousand copies to the council for its own use. The report offered eighteen recommendations covering five broad categories. The ensuing discussion of these subjects provided an affirmative and persuasive status report on the University. Emphasizing UW's "brilliant past," the report cautioned that the future almost certainly would bring both unprecedented enrollment growth and continued severe competition for state support. America had and would continue to flourish to the extent it cultivated its human resources, the council declared. "Continued adequate support of the University of Wisconsin and other institutions of higher learning is an investment which the state cannot afford to neglect."[78]

Each of the council's policy recommendations took the form of one or more short questions followed by a well-crafted discussion. The conclusions relied heavily on information and interpretations provided elsewhere in the report, most of which had been supplied by University personnel during several days of campus hearings. Under "Budgeting and Finance," for example, the report offered three recommendations

---

[77]Fred, "Untitled Address for Meeting with University Alumni of Fond du Lac," November 6, 1954, Series 4/16/5, Box 17, UA; UW BOR Minutes, November 6, 1954; "UW Budget Goes to Legislature," *WAM*, 56 (February 15, 1955), 11; *1955 Wisconsin State Budget*; *1957 Wisconsin State Budget*.

[78]Wisconsin Legislative Council, "University of Wisconsin Policies: Committee Report," submitted to the Governor and Legislature December 1, 1954, insert to *WAM*, 56 (January 15, 1955).

that combined to argue the legislature's obligation to appreciate UW's complicated funding needs, the University's solid accountability and integrity, the advisability of taking a flexible approach to controlling the outside income of faculty, and the fundamental value of maintaining a strong faculty of teachers and scholars. The other categories worked similarly. Six questions and answers, the most of any section, referred to "The Student and Instruction." The third asked, "Should the University . . . impose restrictions upon the student body in matters of freedom of press or assembly beyond those imposed by the laws of the state and nation?" The reply affirmed the "present policy" of no restrictions:

> We are trying to develop self-directing mature citizens capable of making their own evaluation of truth and false-hood. . . . We believe in freedom of discussion and that continued emphasis on the privileges and benefits of our government and our system of free enterprise will make the youth of Wisconsin better citizens.

Little would the uninformed observer realize that this seemingly innocuous entry–fully consistent with UW's classic "sifting and winnowing" tradition (shorthand for academic freedom in Wisconsin)–actually stood at the very heart of the report and the detailed investigation that informed it.

The genesis of this legislative review and report had come nearly two years earlier. On January 13, 1953, State Senator Gordon Bubolz, the conservative Republican chairman of the Wisconsin Legislative Council, had denounced the University for harboring dangerous radicals. Bubolz complained that a "subversive" student group, the Labor Youth League, was operating openly on campus, and he promised to investigate the matter. The occasion for his concern was an LYL-sponsored campus speech, scheduled for the following evening, by Abner Berry, the Negro affairs editor of the New York *Daily Worker*, the official newspaper of the U.S. Communist Party. The Labor Youth League, Bubolz pointed out, was on the official government list of subversive organizations and was currently under investigation by the House Committee on Un-American Activities.[79]

Bubolz's attack, coming as the governor's biennial budget recommendation was expected shortly, did not go unnoticed in Bascom Hall. The next morning President Fred responded with a formal

---

[79]*Daily Cardinal*, January 7, 8, 9, 14, 15, 16, 17, 1953.

statement. Acknowledging the communist "menace," Fred stated he would be "glad" to make available information about the Berry talk, as well as UW policy documents governing student groups. The LYL, he noted, was a "duly registered" student organization and was operating according to University rules. These were premised on "freedom of inquiry," the president pointed out, which at Wisconsin had "served to discredit Communism, not to strengthen its insidious influence." While UW did not allow convicted subversives or persons under indictment to speak, it would be "impractical" to try to censor lawful speakers and might even result unintentionally in "sponsoring" what the University, under current policy, "merely permits." "Speaking for myself personally," the president concluded, "I will not knowingly recommend the appointment of a member of the Communist Party to the staff of the University; and I shall recommend the termination of the services of any staff member whose activities are proved to be subversive of our government." Berry's speech took place as scheduled.[80]

The Bubolz attack was neither new nor unexpected, coming as it did during the height of the anti-communist crusade of the early 1950s. Wisconsin's junior U.S. Senator Joseph R. McCarthy had assumed a leading role in the campaign and indeed provided the name for the worst of the witch hunting excesses. By 1953 President Fred was well-practiced in responding to charges like those of Senator Bubolz, a McCarthy supporter who represented the senator's home town of Appleton in the legislature. As previous volumes of this history have recorded, the University had periodically been attacked for its alleged "radical" orientation, and E.B. Fred had witnessed a number of the previous uproars. Facing now perhaps the most threatening ideological environment in the institution's history, the president characteristically staked out a middle ground.

During 1948-49, for example, Fred fended off calls to censor a Marxist student discussion group and quietly defeated UW Regent William J. Campbell's efforts to impose a faculty loyalty oath similar to one adopted at the University of California. In a measured approach to the growing hysteria, Fred affirmed a UW policy of denying permission to speak on campus to those convicted of a serious crime, including communists Gerhard Eisler, under sentence for contempt of

---

[80]*Capital Times*, January 13, 1953; Michael J. O'Brien, "Senator Joseph McCarthy and Wisconsin, 1946-1957" (Ph.D. dissertation, University of Wisconsin-Madison, 1971) p. 337; "Statement by University of Wisconsin Pres. E.B. Fred," January 14, 1953, Series 4/0/3, Box 19, UA.

Congress, and Carl Marzani, convicted of concealing his Communist Party membership.[81] He also agreed to supply the House Committee on Un-American Activities with lists of texts and supplementary readings used in UW social studies courses while strongly asserting the inappropriateness, if not the illegality, of such a request.[82]

Between 1949 and 1953, the communist subversion/academic freedom themes played out in many contexts at the University. The Committee on Student Life and Interests (SLIC), the chief agency for faculty oversight of student activities, and the Board of Regents were called upon a number of times to reaffirm the University's traditionally generous policy on the right of student organizations to invite outside speakers.[83] President Fred spoke frequently and eloquently in defense of academic freedom at Wisconsin, usually in response to a particular controversy. During reunion weekend in June, 1950, the UW Class of 1910 added support by sponsoring a rededication of the "sifting and winnowing" plaque on Bascom Hall.[84]

The University made headlines on May 7, 1951, when Senator McCarthy–a graduate of Marquette University–made a speaking appearance on campus, presenting a patriotic address before several hundred students, faculty, and townspeople in the Union Theater. When McCarthy likened General Douglas MacArthur to Genghis Khan and referred to the liberal *Capital Times* as Madison's edition of the *Daily Worker*, boos erupted in the audience. McCarthy responded by calling his detractors "braying jackasses," producing a chorus of laughter and jeers that continued until the angry Senator departed.[85]

---

[81]"For UW, No Embarrassment," *WAM*, 49 (January, 1948), 3, 37; Cutlip, oral history interview.

[82]John S. Wood to Fred, June 21, 1949; Fred to Wood, June 30, 1949, both at Series 4/16/1, Box 116, UA; Administrative Committee Minutes, June 7, 1949; "Book Purge Halts," *WAM*, 51 (October, 1949), 14-15.

[83]On March 8, 1952, with regard to the Wisconsin Memorial Union Forum Committee, President Fred discussed in detail the issue "relating to off-campus speakers sponsored by student or faculty groups" at a meeting of the board. After full discussion, the regents voted unanimously "that this Board approves of the sentiments expressed in the statement presented by the President." UW BOR Minutes.

[84]"1910—Sifting, Winnowing," *WAM*, 51 (July, 1950), 10; E. B. Fred, "Re-Dedication of Bascom Hall Plaque," Series 4/16/5, Box 8, UA.

[85]O'Brien, "Senator Joseph McCarthy," pp. 119-20. The undergraduate assigned to host Senator McCarthy before his speech was Stephen Ambrose, a football player and Memorial Union leader who later became a prominent American historian. The senator expressed interest in touring the University library, during which he inspected the card catalog and professed outrage at the number of books dealing with

McCarthy's appearance may have resulted from an initiative adopted by the Board of Regents on October 15, 1949, when board President Frank J. Sensenbrenner, a friend and financial backer of the senator, proposed that the University sponsor a series of talks on "The American Way of Life." Sensenbrenner prefaced his suggestion by explaining: "An opportunity critically to study the proposals and claims of systems alien to our own is the intellectual right of every student. And freedom to explore and discuss the issues in the field of his special competence is the right of every teacher." Thus a well-chosen "series of distinguished speakers would give convincing evidence that the best defense of the 'American way of life' is an understanding of its meaning and an acceptance of its obligations."[86] Whether Sensenbrenner's friend, Joe McCarthy, agreed with this assertion seems unlikely, but President Fred could draw some comfort from the fact that even conservative regents like Sensenbrenner were committed to the University's academic freedom heritage.

Senator Bubolz's criticism in January, 1953, set in motion a number of responses. The University administration promptly initiated yet another review of campus policy on student organizations, this one lasting nearly a year. The result was both a reaffirmation of the University's traditional stand on academic freedom and a marvelously extended occasion for a campus-wide dialogue that defined and defended that cherished heritage. All elements of the UW community were involved, beginning with the elected Student Board, expanding to include SLIC and the institution's most eloquent academic spokesmen, and concluding with formal faculty debate and action. The dialogue was also leavened significantly by President Fred, who simultaneously was playing an influential role in the Association of American Universities and the National Association of Land-Grant Colleges and Universities as their member institutions struggled with similar problems. These larger issues included an attempt by the U.S. Department of Defense to control the employment of faculty members providing United States Armed Forces Institute correspondence courses and to require loyalty

---

Marxism, communism, and revolution. McCarthy demanded to see the library director, so Ambrose took him to see Louis Kaplan, the associate director. Both Ambrose and Kaplan recall that the latter listened patiently as the senator denounced the subversive materials in the library collection and demanded that Kaplan destroy them immediately. "Oh, I could never do that," Kaplan replied. "Why not?" sputtered McCarthy. "You see, those books are state property." The senator was so taken aback at this response that he left without another word. Ambrose and Kaplan conversations with E. David Cronon.

[86]"The American Way of Life," with UW BOR Minutes, October 15, 1949.

oaths of ROTC cadets. Throughout, the *Daily Cardinal* provided an excellent forum for news and the exchange of a wide spectrum of views.[87]

Senator Bubolz followed his attack with Joint Resolution 31S, which called for "a study of the fundamental and long-range policies of the state university and the subordinate agencies under its jurisdiction." Proposed in late March, and passed into law later in the 1953 session, the resolution seemed at first glance primarily concerned with the University's policy toward communist subversion, specifically the Labor Youth League and the radicals that organization invited to the campus. This was very likely Senator Bubolz's expectation. Friends of the University, however, viewed 31S more constructively. Vice President Baldwin recalls that after discussion with President Fred, a number of influential alumni and UW supporters in the legislature concluded that to quash Bubolz' call for an investigation would make it appear that communists might really be manipulating the institution. Rather, the proposed investigation should be embraced and broadened. The joint resolution called for the creation of a Joint Interim Committee, consisting of three senators, five assemblymen, and three citizen members appointed by the governor, to make the study and report its findings to the Legislative Council by November 1, 1954. The resolution mandated that "the committee have full authority to study and to make recommendations regarding any and all phases and functions of the university."[88]

[87]For President Fred's involvement with the national associations, see Fred to President Harold Dodds, Princeton University, March 24, 1953, Series 4/16/1, Box 182, UA; "Universities Protest New USAFI Contracts," *Higher Education and National Affairs,* 2, no. 13 (August 7, 1953), ibid., Box 201. For examples of problems with the military, see Fred to Dodds, April 8, 1953, Ibid., Box 182; Proposed Letter Re: Contract for Correction of Correspondence Study Courses, [June, 1953], ibid., Box 201; Harlan N. Hartness, Major General, Department of Defense, to Dr. Baldwin, June 15, 1953, ibid., Box 219; L.H. Adolfson, Memorandum: USAFI Lesson Service Contract for 1953-54, June 16, 1953, Series 5/1/2, Box 68, UA; Glenn L. McConagha, USAFI Director, to Fred, June 19, 1953, ibid.; Fred to John A. Hannah, July 17, 1953, Series 4/16/1, Box 219, UA; Fred to Hartness, July 27, 1953, Series 5/1/2, Box 68, UA; "U.W. Refuses 1 USAFI Contract," *Wisconsin State Journal,* August 21, 1953; *Daily Cardinal,* September 28, 1954.

[88]The only account of the discussions with Fred is found in Baldwin, *My Half Century,* p. 478. The Interim Committee, officially named the University of Wisconsin Policies Committee, included: Senator Warren P. Knowles, chairman, New Richmond; Mrs. Anita Webster, vice-chairman and public member, Milwaukee; Assemblyman Floyd Wheeler, secretary, Madison; Senators William W. Clark, Vesper, and Gaylord Nelson, Madison; Assemblymen William C. Giese, Racine, Milford C. Kintz, Richland

Here was a golden opportunity. LeRoy Luberg and Ira Baldwin promptly reported to President Fred that the legislative members appointed to the investigating committee were all men who would "approach their problem with an appreciation of the value of the University, and with sympathetic understanding." Furthermore, certain of the legislative members had suggested "that they would be happy to receive suggestions informally as to the subjects which should be considered." Luberg and Baldwin suggested four key topics, none involving communist subversion. First was "the role of the Extension Centers," the University's small freshman-sophomore programs around the state whose future seemed always in doubt. Second was the question of expanding UW instructional programs to include such professional areas as veterinary science, dentistry, forestry, and architecture. Third was expanding University research to put a stronger focus on "the economic future of Wisconsin." Finally, Luberg and Baldwin raised the issue of adult education and the functions and funding of the University's general and agricultural extension agencies. Knowing their president's tendency to mull over decisions at length, they urged him "to make up your mind" about what to suggest to the committee. "We believe that it would be advisable to move fairly rapidly in this matter," they emphasized, "before the committee meets to determine the course of its activities."[89]

In keeping with age-old bureaucratic practice, those who raise an issue often find themselves responsible for resolving it. Thus it was not surprising that President Fred assigned Baldwin the primary responsibility for developing the University's response to the legislative investigation. He reported to the Administrative Committee on March 2, 1954, that the Interim Committee had settled on the topical outline of its work: instruction and students, research, adult education and public service, capital needs, and budget. Five two-day meetings were envisioned "for which the University will be expected to furnish the agenda." Baldwin also proposed that a UW committee be appointed for each topic to prepare materials and present them to the Interim Committee.[90] A week later President Fred announced the five campus

---

Center, Ora R. Rice, Delevan, and J. Riley Stone, Reedsburg; and public members Norton E. Masterson, Stevens Point, and Peter Pappas, La Crosse. Knowles, Clark, Rice, and Stone were also members of the parent Wisconsin Legislative Council.

[89]Luberg and Baldwin to Fred, memorandum, December 31, 1953, Series 5/1/2, Box 79.

[90]Administrative Committee Minutes, March 2, 1954; J.H. and Charlotte Kolb

committee rosters, involving high administrators and prominent faculty members, and a "coordinating committee" of the UW committee chairmen, each also a member of the Administrative Committee, headed by Baldwin.[91] President Fred told the latter group, "I recognize that [the assignment] will require considerable work, but I feel it presents a very real opportunity for the University to present its story to an official legislative group."[92]

The Interim Committee functioned throughout most of 1954. Vice President Baldwin led off in April by presenting the University's case on instruction and students.[93] The committee apparently met four additional times through August, in the process covering most of the designated topics. The *Wisconsin Alumnus* reported in May that "the topic which seemed to provide impetus for the committee's formation was passed over with no comment from the legislators. . . . Evidently, this question had been decided to the satisfaction of the committee members, as a result of the strong statements by the University . . . and the rebuttals by students themselves to the speaker's arguments."[94] The Interim Committee even involved the University in the drafting of its report. While this made sense because of the mass of information involved and the well-documented and well-organized nature of the institutional response, it also showed the legislators' trust. The initiative came from the committee chairman, Senator Warren P. Knowles, a UW graduate who simultaneously was serving as president of the Wisconsin Alumni Association. In August he requested that Baldwin "draw

---

to Baldwin, March 4, 1954, Series 5/1/2, Box 79, UA. J.H. and Kolb were apparently staffers for the committee. They note in their letter that Baldwin's suggestion to invite the committee to meet on the University campus was a good one.

[91]Administrative Committee Minutes, March 9, 1954. The committees were: (1) Students and Instruction: Kenneth Little (chairman), I.L. Baldwin, C.A. Elvehjem, M.H. Ingraham, and K.F. Wendt; (2) Research: Elvehjem (chairman), D. Murray Angevine, F.H. Harrington, Virgil Herrick, W.D. Knight, William P. Marshall, Robert J. Muckenhirn, John Ritchie, and William H. Sewell; (3) Adult Education and Public Service: L.H. Adolfson and H.L. Ahlgren (co-chairmen), Paul J. Grogan, Harold B. McCarty, Robert C. Parkin, and Walter A. Rowlands; (4) Physical Plant: A.W. Peterson (chairman), A.F. Ahearn, A.F. Gallistel, C.A. Halbert, Robert E. Hammes, and Alden White; (5) Budget: William H. Young (chairman), R.A. Brink, Neil G. Cafferty, John Guy Fowlkes, Chester W. Harris, and Rudolph E. Langer.

[92]Fred to Little, Baldwin, Elvehjem, Ingraham, and Wendt, March 10, 1954, Series 5/1/2, Box 79, UA.

[93]"Summation of Remarks by I.L. Baldwin before the Legislative Committee on University Functions, Policies and Procedures," April 2, 1954, ibid.

[94]"Where Is the University Going?" *WAM*, 55 (May 15, 1954), 8.

together some of the public policy questions arising from the deliberations of the committee" for use either as a concluding chapter or "in
drawing up their conclusions and recommendations."[95] This Baldwin
did, assigning Clay Schoenfeld, who had worked so energetically on the
University centennial in 1948-49, to draft the bulk of the report. The
result, as Baldwin later recalled, was "one of the finest documents that
I have seen about the University over the period that I have been
associated with it."[96] More immediately, the Interim Committee's
findings undoubtedly helped to produce the generous UW appropriation
for 1955-57.

Creating UW-Milwaukee

The affirmative 1955 legislative session portended well for the
remaining three years of the E.B. Fred era at Wisconsin. The national
environment was turning positive as well. The Korean War had ended
with a stalemate and an armistice, and the red scare was on the wane
following the U.S. Senate's censure of Wisconsin's junior senator.
Americans were getting used to living with the Cold War, and somehow
the dangers now seemed not quite so immediate or grim as they had
appeared earlier. University authorities were able to focus their attention
and energies on educational matters more single mindedly than at any
time since the late 1920s. The organization of a new branch campus in
Milwaukee was one notable result, and the construction of the Wisconsin Center building in Madison provided a long-needed outreach
conference center while highlighting the growing success of the effort
to develop a base of private funding through the University of Wisconsin Foundation.

The creation of the University of Wisconsin-Milwaukee,
quickly known as UWM, was the culmination of a political debate in the
state dating sporadically back at least to the turn of the century. Local
Milwaukee boosters and interests had periodically called for a branch
of the University to be established in the state's largest city and
financial center. For their part, UW leaders and regents had over the
years steadfastly resisted such a development, considering it a likely

---

[95]Baldwin to Fred, A.W. Peterson, W.H. Young, and George Richards, August
31, 1954, Series 5/1/2, Box 79, UA.

[96]Baldwin added: "I wish that it could be compulsory reading for every new
governor, every new regent, every new legislator, every new University administrator.
I think it is an excellent report." Baldwin, *My Half Century*, p. 479.

long-term threat to the campus in Madison.[97] By 1955 there were several institutions of higher education in Milwaukee. One was Marquette University, a private Roman Catholic liberal arts institution offering some graduate and professional programs. Another was the Wisconsin State College-Milwaukee, the flagship unit of the system of normal schools launched in the nineteenth century to train teachers for the public schools of the state. A third was the UW Extension Center in downtown Milwaukee, which the University launched before World War I and expanded significantly during the 1920s. The center offered both credit and non-credit instruction and included a resident faculty teaching regular freshman-sophomore liberal arts classes. The Milwaukee Extension Center in fact became the model for the two-year centers developed by the University in communities around the state in the 1930s and after World War II.

As part of his effort to rein in state spending, in the early 1950s Governor Kohler proposed merging the University and the State Colleges under a single board of regents. The idea was resisted by the two boards of regents, and to head it off they collaborated on a proposal for greater cooperation between the two Wisconsin systems of public higher education. The eventual result was legislation establishing the Coordinating Committee for Higher Education (CCHE) in 1955.[98] A major part of the compromise legislation establishing CCHE also gave the new agency its first assignment: to superintend the merger of Milwaukee's two public collegiate institutions into the University of Wisconsin-Milwaukee by January 1, 1957. Not surprisingly in light of Vice President Baldwin's substantial involvement in the legislative drafting process, the statute prominently addressed the perennial concern in Madison to maintain the University's reputation and quality:

> Such merged institution shall be operated as an integral part of the university, and shall be under the government of its board of regents. . . . This unit of the university shall be under the supervision of a provost reporting directly to the president, with the same degree of self-government by its own faculty as is vested in other units of the university. All degrees granted upon the completion of prescribed courses

---

[97]The threat was perceived to be two-fold: first, they feared that state funding, already considered inadequate, would become even less effective when spread across two major institutions; second, in spite of the mandate of the state constitution, there was danger that the Madison campus might eventually be overshadowed by a Milwaukee branch located in an area of considerably greater population and political influence.

[98]See below, pp. 526-34.

shall be issued by the board of regents in the same manner and with the same status as degrees based upon work done in other units of the university.[99]

A daunting task lay ahead.

The initial planning for UWM was concluded by mid-January, 1956. President Fred took the lead in this effort, which had begun the previous November, when he had hosted a meeting with Baldwin, Milwaukee Extension Center Director George A. Parkinson, and Wisconsin State College at Milwaukee President J. Martin Klotsche to discuss the challenge before them. The conversation resulted in Fred's decision to set up an ad hoc planning committee of faculty members and administrators drawn equally from the two merging institutions and the Madison campus. The Committee of Thirty first met in Milwaukee on December 1, and two weeks later issued a report entitled "Suggestions on the Merger of Wisconsin State College, Milwaukee, and the University of Wisconsin." It offered advice on general principles and procedures, listed key decisions that had to be made and by whom, and suggested a timetable for concluding the merger by September 1, several months ahead of the legislative deadline. President Fred brought this report to the first meeting of the CCHE on January 5, 1956, which approved the suggested completion date and directed the two boards of regents to carry through with the merger. The UW regents, for their part, told President Fred to "take all necessary steps" to complete the assignment. Finally, on January 19, Fred met with the Committee of Thirty, outlined his plans, reconstituted the group as a policy review committee, and established a nine-member Executive Committee, with equal representation from each of the parent delegations.[100]

Fred named Ira Baldwin chairman of the Executive Committee, which met weekly throughout much of 1956 and presided over an extended frenzy of activity. Baldwin and his colleagues established, supervised, and received reports from twenty-five sub-committees

---

[99]Chapter 619, *Laws of Wisconsin*, 1955.

[100]Committee of Thirty members are listed according to institution and Executive Committee members are indicated by asterisks: *Madison*: Ira L. Baldwin*, Gladys Borchers, Conrad A. Elvehjem, Edwin B. Fred, Mark H. Ingraham*, J. Kenneth Little*, A.W. Peterson, R.U. Ratcliff, Lindley J. Stiles, and Kurt F. Wendt. *Wisconsin State College*: Ned Billings, Maxwell Freeman, Gordon Haferbecker*, Donald Hill, J. Martin Klotsche*, Charlotte Major, Lee Mathews, Robert Norris*, Adolph Suppan, and Charlotte Wollaeger. *Milwaukee Extension Center*: Joseph G. Baier*, Ross H. Bardell, Irene M. Bozak, Alfred F. Fiorita, Edwin R. Hodge, Edward D. Holst, George A. Parkinson*, Benjamin A. Sullivan, John W. Teter*, James G. Van Vleet.

dealing with various aspects of the merger. Their purview ran the entire gamut of institution-related subjects, large and small, ranging from faculty affairs and policies, calendar and catalogs, school colors, symbols and emblems, public relations, and space utilization.[101]

Three early substantive decisions set a constructive tone for the entire proceedings. First, the Executive Committee determined that the faculties of the two Milwaukee degree-sponsoring units–the Colleges of Letters and Science and of Education–would function parallel to their counterparts in Madison, while the remaining department-level programs–such as commerce and engineering–would be closely tied to the schools on the Madison campus offering degrees in those fields. Second, graduate programming at Milwaukee, as in Madison, would operate under centralized control to assure academic integrity, with an officer of the Madison Graduate School administering the work in Milwaukee. Finally, the appointment of faculty members in Milwaukee would be accomplished in a "completely parallel" manner to the procedures in Madison. The only difference would be that while the Madison deans reported directly to the UW president, in Milwaukee the deans would report to the UWM provost as the chief administrator of that campus. Once these important policy matters were settled, the Executive Committee easily came up with a statement of "Basic Principles and Policies" that guided the remainder of the effort. Only two or three times did the group find it necessary to consult formally with the full Committee of Thirty, the distinction between them at any rate becoming blurred after Baldwin took over the leadership of both following President Fred's unexpected hospitalization and recuperation from a severe case of bursitis.

The president was sufficiently recovered to address a convocation on October 15, 1956, marking the official opening of the University of Wisconsin-Milwaukee. In his remarks Fred stressed the cooperative spirit that had infused the merger exercise during the year following

---

[101]The full list of committees included: Admissions and Records; Art and Music (Education); Calendar; Catalogs; Colors, Symbols and Emblems; Credits for ROTC and Required Physical Education; Definition of Faculty of U.W.-M.; Enrollment Estimates; Faculty Welfare; Fee Structure; Fiscal Questions; Graduate Programs; Implementation of Policies; Intercollegiate Athletics; Long Range Building Program; Public Relations; Radio and Television; ROTC Programs; Space Utilization; Student Affairs; Student Financial Aids; Teacher Education Programs; Teaching Load; Advisory Committee on Provost. Exhibit H, "Summary Report of the Actions Leading to the Establishment of the University of Wisconsin-Milwaukee," September 25, 1956, Series 1/1/3, Box 80, UA.

Governor Kohler's approval of the legislation creating the new UW branch:

> It was anticipated that in the discussions of the problems of merger there might be a considerable amount of debate and diverse opinion. Actually, none developed. It was obvious that the ground each of the committee members held was the same ground–and that each of their goals was the same goal. They sought to create here a significant part of the University that would serve this area well and add to the resources of the entire University.[102]

Something truly impressive had been accomplished in Milwaukee over a remarkably brief period of time, he pointed out. While the organizers recognized that many of their arrangements were "temporary," the fact remained that the University of Wisconsin now had a notable presence in Wisconsin's major urban center and with it an enhanced opportunity to serve the state more effectively.[103]

A basic question remained: Just what was the relationship of the University of Wisconsin-Milwaukee to the parent University of Wisconsin? The 1949 report of the Committee on University Functions and Policies had hinted at the answer by arguing that the University, however it might grow or evolve in the future, must continue to have a single faculty, operate under a single administration and board of regents, and offer only one set of degrees. This is almost certainly what Ira Baldwin, who had served on the Functions and Policies Committee, meant as he drafted the 1955 legislation and used the term "integral" to state the fundamental relationship of UWM to UW. And it was no accident that Mark Ingraham, the main author of the functions and policies report, served with Baldwin on both the Committee of Thirty and its Executive Committee. Out of this unitary vision of the University the key merger policy decisions flowed. Thus, while the UWM schools, colleges, and departments would have their separate faculties, each UWM faculty member would also hold membership in the larger University faculty and would enjoy all of its benefits and obligations. UWM representatives soon joined essentially every Madison faculty

---

[102]E. B. Fred, untitled address, October 15, 1956, Series 4/16/5, Box 17, UA.

[103]In its "Summary Report of the Actions Leading to the Establishment of the University of Wisconsin-Milwaukee," September 25, 1956, the Executive Committee explained in the Forward "that many of the decisions reached in order to effect a merger were only tentative—subject to approval of University faculty and of the Regents, and that many, by their nature, even when approved, would be temporary."

committee, including the University Committee and the four Faculty Divisional Committees, which were consulted on new course proposals and faculty tenure decisions at Madison and Milwaukee. All UWM faculty members had the right to participate and vote in University faculty meetings. Provost Klotsche, previously the Milwaukee State College president and now the administrative head of UWM, represented it on President Fred's Administrative Committee essentially on the level of the Madison campus deans. UWM thus began as a sort of super-college of the University, with its degrees indistinguishable from those earned by students enrolled in Madison.

While this arrangement may have made sense from the Madison point of view, a divergent perspective soon began to develop in Milwaukee. UWM was, after all, an evolving institution in its own right, located nearly a hundred miles away from the president's office in Bascom Hall. Although UWM continued to serve students on both of its original campuses for several years, by the end of 1956-57 it already had completely merged its academic departments. This accomplishment encouraged a growing sense of unity among the UWM faculty and students that diminished whatever identity they might initially have felt with the Madison campus. Thus as time passed the tendency at UWM was to interpret initiatives and decisions made in Madison as unwarranted, intrusive, and inappropriate. For the time being, however, the smooth launching of the University's new branch in Milwaukee seemed one of the Fred administration's unqualified achievements.

End of the Fred Era

The opening of the new Wisconsin Center building in the spring of 1958 provided a fitting culmination of President Fred's thirteen eventful years at the helm of the University. Legislative appropriations were up, political and ideological unrest was down, and cordiality marked relations among the University administration, the Board of Regents, and the Wisconsin Legislature and governor. Long-sought improvements in the physical plant had been made or were in prospect. The new state coordinating body, the CCHE, was working quietly and apparently effectively, helping the University and the State Colleges to prepare themselves for the coming avalanche of baby boom generation students.

E.B. Fred with Bascom Hall janitors' crew for his birthday, March 20, 1957. UA, 3577-C-1.

The Freds at a student banquet, May 18, 1958. UA, 4320-M.

Cornerstone laying ceremony, Wisconsin Center, May 18, 1957; President Fred speaking; l-r, Father Kutchera, St Paul's Chapel; F.H. Elwell; K. Wendt; Oscar Rennebohm; W.J. Haganah; Rev. Morris Wee, Bethel Lutheran; Ellis Jensen, behind Wee; Howard Greene, UW Foundation. UA, 3929-C-1.

Wisconsin Center . UA, 961-H-1.

During the Fred years, the University had added more than two dozen new buildings. The most significant of these was the Memorial Library, opened in 1953 primarily to support the social science and humanities disciplines.[104] Yet in reality the Fred administration's construction program was unbalanced, favoring the biological and physical sciences, especially in agriculture and engineering. It had also provided a dedicated building for the School of Commerce, a limited amount of student housing, and an enhanced physical plant infrastructure. The Medical School had benefitted mostly from renovations and building additions. The longstanding objective of a general adult education and conference facility had long proved elusive to its strongest backers, President Fred and the UW Foundation, in spite of its key place in the foundation's Centennial Fund campaign in 1948.

The Wisconsin Center project had faced a number of obstacles. Funding was a major problem, of course. A legislative appropriation for this sort of facility seemed out of the question, and the foundation had greatly overestimated its timely ability to meet the $5 million Centennial Fund goal. Of the array of projects listed originally, the center was among the most expensive, with a price tag eventually reaching $2.4 million. The University was confronting the task of reshaping its campus beyond anything envisioned before the war, moreover, and the Campus Planning Commission had to balance a number of sometimes conflicting needs and visions. Several years of debate, in fact, centered on where the Wisconsin Center building should be located. The site originally proposed, the northwest corner of Lake and Langdon streets, turned out to be the final choice. In between, however, there was serious consideration given to Observatory Hill and other places. Once the site was decided, planning for the center building came into conflict with the projected Murray Street mall stretching from University Avenue to the shoreline of Lake Mendota, a goal yet to be realized. Questions regarding parking, overnight accommodations, and kitchen facilities, brought the Memorial Union and private hoteliers into the discussion. Only the most forceful importunities by such UW Foundation leaders as Oscar Rennebohm and Herbert V. Kohler were decisive enough to cut through the planning morass so that ground breaking for the facility could finally take place in 1956.[105]

---

[104]See below, pp. 233-38.

[105]See for example Campus Planning Commission Minutes, May 4, 1954, Series 5/24, Box 1, UA; "Ground Breaking For Adult Education Center," *Daily Cardinal*, September 28, 1956; "Wisconsin Center Hailed at Ground Breaking

Designed in a straight-line contemporary style, the Wisconsin Center was an impressive addition to the campus. It consisted of three floors and a finished basement, twenty-two rooms in all, outfitted for lectures, conferences, and large- and small-group meetings. Supporting equipment included the latest in motion picture, slide, and film strip projectors, as well as up-to-date audio and mimeographing machinery. The exterior combined brick, marble, metal, and glass to create, as a UW Foundation "Progress Report" put it, "an outstanding addition to America's most beautiful college campus."[106] The interior was equally opulent and substantial, featuring the best in materials and workmanship.

A full day and evening of festivities ushered the new facility into operation on Friday, April 11, 1958. UW Foundation President Frank V. Birch acted as master of ceremonies for the morning dedication ceremony. Foundation board Chairman Howard I. Potter officially presented the center to the University "to help it carry on the Wisconsin idea of service." UW Regent President Wilbur N. Renk accepted the new facility, observing "that a university cannot continue to be great with only state appropriations. . . . Gifts such as these are needed to maintain the University of Wisconsin's greatness." President Fred promised that the center would "enhance our program of conferences, short courses and institutes to an extent we can only dream about today."[107] Other speakers at the following luncheon and dinner festivities included Wisconsin Governor Vernon W. Thomson, Graduate Dean Conrad A. Elvehjem, and Herbert V. Kohler, the chairman of the UW Foundation Centennial Fund Campaign. All agreed the center was a fitting symbol of how far the University had come since the war.

There was, however, a small but prophetic dissent to the general congratulatory speeches. At an opening-day forum to inaugurate the Wisconsin Center, historian Merle Curti, perhaps the University's most distinguished humanistic scholar, complained that Wisconsin's once path-breaking social studies programs had lost ground. "Our work, however competent, seems to be diffuse," he declared. "It is not comparable to our 'golden age' of 50 years ago," and it "appears to have no ordered guiding social purpose." The University of Wisconsin was

---

Ceremonies," ibid., October 3, 1956; "New Building Turned Over to the University," ibid., April 16, 1958; UW BOR Minutes, July 26, 1958.

[106]UW Foundation, "Progress Report," August 31, 1956. Series 5/101, UA.

[107]"New Center Is Dedicated to UW 'Idea,'" *Milwaukee Journal*, April 11, 1958.

no longer one of the best in the field, as it had been in the days of Van Hise and La Follette progressivism. Yet "only the social sciences and humanities can give us guidance in this world revolutionized by the natural sciences," Curti lamented.[108] Implicit if unspoken, was Professor Curti's disappointment that the Fred era, while impressive in many respects, had provided unbalanced leadership of the University by favoring the natural sciences and applied disciplines over the liberal arts. Curti's fear was that this narrow emphasis would increasingly hobble the institution's development during the coming years of inevitable expansion and change. He seemed to be calling for a new Van Hise.

---

[108]"Social Science Research Urged," *Wisconsin State Journal*, April 12, 1958.

3.

A Caretaker President

At the start of the 1956-57 academic year President E.B. Fred announced that by June 30, 1957, he would reach the University's mandatory retirement age of seventy. He went on to add that at the request of the Board of Regents he had agreed to stay on as president a year longer until June 30, 1958, to allow plenty of time to find a successor.[1] The president's announcement was hardly a bombshell; his retirement was predictable under well-established regent policy. What was surprising, however, was the board's decision to keep him in lame duck status for the better part of the next two years. The action no doubt reflected the regents' great satisfaction with Fred's leadership of the University since 1945 and their reluctance to launch a new presidential administration any sooner than necessary.

The Search for a New Leader

Whatever the board's reasoning, the hunt for the next UW president got under way slowly. Not until the following summer did the regents decide on the format of the search. The new president would be selected by the full board sitting as a committee of the whole, while a five-member steering or selection committee, chaired by Regent Charles D. Gelatt–at 40 one of the youngest but also most influential members of the board–would screen nominations, interview promising candidates, and prepare a short list. After prodding from the faculty's University Committee, administrative leaders, and even students, the regents authorized the Gelatt

---

[1]E.B. Fred, Presidential Address, UW BOR Minutes, September 8, 1956, UA.

Committee to solicit active input from two separate committees representing the faculty and the deans.[2] President Fred and his Administrative Committee decided the deans should be represented by the three most senior deans at Madison (Mark H. Ingraham of the College of Letters and Science, Rudolph K. Froker of the College of Agriculture, and Conrad A. Elvehjem of the Graduate School) and one at Milwaukee (Joseph G. Baier of the College of Letters and Science). The faculty decided to be represented by a committee consisting of one member each from the Madison and Milwaukee University Committees (Edwin Young, Madison, and Frederick Olson, Milwaukee), and a member named by each of the four faculty Divisional Executive Committees (James Crow, biological sciences; Murray Fowler, humanities; Gerard Rohlich, physical sciences; and Ralph Nafziger, social studies). Thus a total of ten of the University's most respected and influential faculty members were formally designated to assist with the search.[3] In practice the two groups often conferred together under the leadership of Ingraham and Young. Early on the members delegated Ingraham to advise Dean Elvehjem to stop attending their deliberations, since they considered him a prime inside candidate for the presidency.[4]

Regent Gelatt also called on UW alumni for advice and suggestions on how to meet a challenge he described as perhaps the greatest the board had ever confronted:

> The University today looks forward to one of the most critical eras in the nation's history of higher education. Tremendous increases in enrollment ahead are matched in magnitude by the continual expansion of mankind's knowledge. And to complicate these problems, the costs of operation and building seem to be increasing apace.

The committee, he said, planned to canvass leading educators around the country for expert advice on candidates best suited to guide the University

---

[2]Administrative Committee Minutes, July 23, 1957, Series 5/13, UA; *Daily Cardinal*, September 16, 1957.

[3]Administrative Committee Minutes, July 23 and August 13, 1957; UW Faculty Minutes, August 5, 1957, UA; *Daily Cardinal*, September 16, 1957; *WAM*, 59 (October, 1957), 15.

[4]Edwin Young recalled that at the first joint meeting with the Gelatt Committee, one of its members, Regent Carl E. Steiger, commented jokingly to his fellow regents, "Now, fellows, this time I think we ought to play it straight with the faculty." Young took this to mean that in 1945 the regents' consultation with faculty representatives had been pro forma because they had already settled on E.B. Fred as president. Edwin Young, comment to E. David Cronon, 1996. See also Mark H. Ingraham, oral history interview, 1974, UA.

in the difficult years ahead, but it would welcome nominations from any source. "The Regents have made no commitments," Gelatt promised. "They seek only the best president for Wisconsin."[5]

Although unlike the faculty the board did not authorize direct student consultation in the search, the *Daily Cardinal* nevertheless offered a thoughtful student perspective on the qualifications the regents should look for. The next president, the editors said, should:

> 1. Understand the traditions that had made the University great, especially its devotion to academic freedom as exemplified by the "sifting and winnowing" plaque.
> 2. Be closely acquainted with the main branches of scholarship–humanities, social studies, and the natural sciences–and be committed to a proper balance among them.
> 3. Be able to maintain an appropriate balance between the University's three major functions–instruction, research, and public service.
> 4. Possess good administrative skills but with the ability to keep larger objectives in view.

Finally, the *Cardinal* warned in what would become a recurring concern, that projected heavy enrollment growth in the immediate years ahead would require the new president "to decide how far the University can expand without sacrificing the quality of its instruction."[6]

Over the next several months the Gelatt Committee considered more than a hundred nominations and its members quietly interviewed a score of candidates from coast to coast. A student group promoted the candidacy of Adlai Stevenson, the twice-defeated recent Democratic presidential candidate, under the catchy slogan, S.O.S.–"Stevenson or Stagnation!" Ever alert to champion progressive causes, the Madison *Capital Times* promptly endorsed the suggestion.[7] A number of alumni followed up Regent Gelatt's call for assistance with a variety of suggestions, including several endorsements of the Stevenson nomination but also at least one expression of outrage at the campaign to turn over the University to a failed politician. Other alumni proposed various UW faculty members

---

[5]"The University of Wisconsin's Thirteenth President–Who Will He Be?" *WAM*, 59 (November, 1957), 8-9.

[6]*Daily Cardinal*, November 2, 1957. See also *WAM*, 59 (December, 1957), 5. The paper's list of presidential qualifications is paraphrased here.

[7]*Daily Cardinal*, February 24, March 15, 1956, July 19, 23, 26, 30, August 1, 20, 22, November 2, 1957; Fran Montgomery, "Campus Chronicle," *WAM*, 59 (October, 1957), 16. Stevenson declared himself honored by the nomination and did not withdraw his name from consideration.

and alumni, with several praising Graduate Dean Elvehjem's scientific qualifications and administrative experience. A Madison resident and 1948 graduate suggested another UW faculty member and rising campus administrator, Professor of History Fred Harvey Harrington.[8] Harrington's candidacy was also advanced less publicly but with more force by a number of faculty members including the Social Studies Divisional Executive Committee. The pro-Harrington group believed the Fred administration was substantially dominated by and had favored the natural science disciplines over the social sciences and humanities. A respected member of the Regent-Faculty Conference Committee and the Research Committee, Harrington had gained a campus reputation as an outspoken advocate of balanced research and program support for all parts of the University.[9] A similar concern was echoed in a thoughtful letter from John S. Lord, a prominent member of the Class of 1904. He proposed no candidates but cautioned: "At this time of international hysteria I fear that undue emphasis may be placed upon scientific achievement."[10]

Underlying Lord's concern was an event on the other side of the world that cast a long shadow over the deliberations of the Gelatt Committee. On October 4 the Soviet Union's news agency TASS announced that Soviet scientists had succeeded in lofting a small satellite–named Sputnik–into orbit around the earth. Sputnik's radio telemetry and even its visible course across the heavens could be monitored easily throughout the northern hemisphere. A month later on November 3 the Soviets launched Sputnik 2, which carried a small dog named Laika into orbit for seven days before it was parachuted back to earth.[11] These stunning achievements truly fascinated the entire world even as they demonstrated the Soviet Union's substantial lead over the United States in rocketry and space exploration.

For Americans this shocking Soviet triumph had ominous military implications. Coming at the height of the Cold War, the beeps and visible overhead presence of the two Sputniks set off a great national debate on the need to reform U.S. education and especially the urgency of bolstering American science and technology. "Not a Bird, Plane, But Sputnik; Students Not Too Concerned," declared a *Daily Cardinal* headline, but the editors reprinted in the same issue a *Christian Science Monitor* article soberly

---

[8]Ibid. (December, 1957), 2; (January, 1958), 4-7; (February, 1958), 6.
[9]Fred Harvey Harrington, oral history interviews, 1978, 1982, UA.
[10]*WAM*, 59 (January, 1958), 6. See also *Daily Cardinal*, January 9, 1958.
[11]*History of Space Exploration*, World Wide Web, http://nauts.com/histpace/-histpace.html.

predicting the satellites would bring new U.S. emphasis on scientific research and education.[12] In Wisconsin Dean Elvehjem agreed, warning that American universities must expand their basic research "if the nation is to continue to develop technologically."[13] The Soviet wake-up call was bound to be heard by the Gelatt Committee as its members pondered the qualifications needed for the next president, who would lead the University into the space age.

Although the screening committee made regular progress reports to the board, it succeeded in imposing strict secrecy on its deliberations. The predominant campus guess was that the regents would not be ready to choose a new president before March at the earliest, but on February 1, 1958, Regent Gelatt reported to the board that his committee had decided to recommend only a single candidate to succeed President Fred. The choice was no surprise: Dean Conrad A. Elvehjem of the UW Graduate School. The committee had also given a good deal of consideration to the other inside candidate, Fred Harrington, and concluded that both men were well qualified for the post. Gelatt said that earlier that morning the committee had met privately with Elvehjem at his Nakoma home, where he was confined with the Asian flu, and had received his acceptance of the appointment. "We are confident we have selected one of the nation's most outstanding educators, research men and scientists," Gelatt declared. The board quickly confirmed the selection unanimously, appointing the 56-year-old Elvehjem to be president effective July 1, at a salary of $23,000 annually.[14]

As a mark of their high regard for retiring President Fred, the regents took the unprecedented step of designating him professor emeritus of bacteriology and president emeritus, at a continuing half-salary of $13,000 and with the right to live rent-free in his longtime campus residence, the agriculture dean's house at 10 Babcock Drive. No previous UW president had been treated so generously. It was not revealed whether Fred had played any part in the selection of his successor, though he was clearly pleased with the choice of an insider and protégé. He had, after all, watched over the president-elect's career since Elvehjem's very first days at the University when Fred had served as his freshman adviser. "He

---

[12]*Daily Cardinal*, October 22, 1957.

[13]Ibid., December 7, 1957.

[14]UW BOR Minutes, February 1, 1958. Although this salary, which was $3,000 less than that paid outgoing President Fred, constituted a significant increase over Elvehjem's current dean's salary of $19,000, it actually amounted to a cut in his total income because the regents required him to resign his membership on several corporate boards.

is a fine and able man," the outgoing president declared, "and the regents have made an unquestionably wise selection." This was the general reaction. Economics Professor Edwin Young, the chairman of the faculty advisory committee, which had recommended both Elvehjem and Harrington, predicted the faculty would applaud the appointment. He pointed out that Elvehjem had the unanimous backing of both advisory committees and was held in "the greatest respect" on campus. "He will continue to give the kind of leadership that has made the University great," Young asserted.[15]

In acknowledging his selection Elvehjem pledged to carry on the program of retiring President Fred, who promised he would be available to help out the new administration as needed. Mindful of the significant faculty support for Harrington and the grumbling in some quarters that another scientist in Bascom Hall would mean continuing distortion in the allocation of University resources, the president-elect quickly assured the press and the campus community that he did not intend to emphasize the sciences at the expense of other disciplines. Rather, he promised to give impartial support to all fields. Indicating that the board was aware of this concern, Regent John D. Jones expressed confidence the new president would not be unduly influenced by his science background. "I'm satisfied he will be interested in promoting the social sciences and humanities, too," he declared. The Madison *Capital Times* gave qualified approval:

> There has been some uneasiness about the naming of a scientist to the presidency because of the fear that present trends in education may result in a one-sided emphasis on science to the neglect of other studies necessary to build well-rounded citizens. Dr. Elvehjem's words are reassuring.[16]

After the Elvehjem selection, President Fred told the regents there was one project he would like to work on in retirement–raising funds for a University art center and gallery.[17] Everyone, it seemed, wanted to reassure

---

[15]Ibid.; *Daily Cardinal*, February 5, 1958; "Conrad Arnold Elvehjem: 13th President of the University," *WAM*, 59 (March, 1958), 2-5. The special retirement provisions so generously arranged by the regents in 1958 for outgoing President Fred were in addition to his normal University retirement annuity and continued until his death in 1981 at the age of 93.

[16]*Daily Cardinal*, February 5, 19, and 27, 1958. For the next few months Elvehjem reiterated his determination to provide balanced leadership of the University. He made this a major and recurring theme in his fifty-minute inaugural address on October 9.

[17]"President Fred Will Get a New Title; Has a Project in Mind," *WAM*, 59 (March, 1958), 6.

the anxious humanities and social science faculty members they would not be neglected in the new administration.

An New/Old Administrative Team

Born in 1901 of Norwegian immigrant stock, Conrad Arnold Elvehjem grew up on a tobacco and dairy farm near McFarland, a few miles southeast of Madison. The family spoke mostly Norwegian at home. Young Conrad in fact did not learn English until he started school at the age of six, which was occasionally reflected in later years in his pronunciation and syntax. After graduating from Stoughton High School, his interest in the science of living things led him to the University, where he earned a bachelor of science degree in agriculture in 1923 and a Ph.D. in agricultural chemistry in 1927 under the supervision of Professor E.B. Hart, the long-time chairman of what was becoming the premier biochemistry department in the country and perhaps the world. Hart, who had a sharp eye for promising talent, recognized Elvehjem's quality and upon completion of his graduate study arranged a faculty appointment for him. Like Hart and most of the department, Elvehjem concentrated on nutritional research, gradually gaining recognition for his work on the role of such minerals as iron, cobalt, manganese, and boron in the diet. A post-doctoral year at Cambridge, England, led him into the study of enzymes, and he brought back a Barcroft respirometer, the first instrument of its kind in the United States for the study of respiratory enzymes.

Elvehjem's international stature was assured after he isolated nicotinic acid (niacin) in the late 1930s and discovered it could be used to cure pellagra, a debilitating dietary disease then common among poor people in the southern United States and other parts of the world. When Hart retired in 1944, Elvehjem at the age of 43 succeeded him as chairman of the biochemistry department. His scientific stature was already as high as that of his mentors and more senior colleagues, E.B. Hart and Harry Steenbock, and his contemporary, Karl Paul Link. Two years later he added the graduate deanship to his administrative responsibilities, holding both posts and running his active laboratory and graduate program up to his selection as president. By this time he had published more than 780 scientific papers on biochemistry and nutrition and was rightly regarded as one of the University's top scientists.

Modest and unassuming, shy to the point of often seeming cold and aloof on first meeting, but with a directness and work ethic inherited

Aaron Bohrod collage of President Conrad Elvehjem. UA, X25-3408.

from his rural Norwegian forbears, the new president possessed a number of the qualities of his predecessor. Both Fred and Elvehjem had spent nearly all of their professional lives at the University. They loved the institution and were dedicated to preserving and strengthening its quality. As hard-driving scientists who had earned distinguished scholarly reputations, each was accustomed to working long hours and weekends at his lab or desk. Both men, too, were confident that a scientist's tough-minded training and logical reasoning were ideally suited for solving difficult administrative problems. For more than a decade Elvehjem had successfully led a department that included several prickly prima donnas, while at the same time dealing with the more varied campus-wide problems of the Graduate School. He considered himself and was viewed by his associates as well-prepared for the challenges of the presidency.

There were also some significant differences between the two men. President Fred disliked public speaking, was not very good at it, and avoided formal speeches as much as possible, greatly preferring discussion in small groups or one-on-one conversation. He was a master of charming small talk and story-telling and often used them to control discussion so as to avoid dealing with issues he was not yet ready to confront. Elvehjem, too, was a good listener, and though not a compelling orator was a more effective communicator with groups of any size. Before his appointment he had often addressed service clubs locally and alumni gatherings around the country and he continued as president to maintain an active speaking schedule.

Fred was neither a glad-hander nor a joiner and restricted his memberships to a few professional and scientific societies and his social life to required University functions. Upon becoming president he had virtually ended his active scientific and professional life apart from service on a few national committees where he could influence policies affecting the University. Elvehjem, on the other hand, was considerably more involved with professional organizations and town-gown affairs. He was an active member of the First Congregational Church, two local literary societies, and the Madison Chamber of Commerce, and served on the boards of directors of the Wisconsin Alumni Association and the Downtown Rotary Club. Though he gave up his laboratory for the presidency, he continued his active involvement in national professional associations. Elvehjem and his warmly outgoing wife, the former Constance Waltz, UW '27 (like her husband known to her friends as "Connie"), were popular in the community and enjoyed a lively social life among Madison's upper crust. They belonged to two dance clubs and Conrad was a long-time member of the prestigious Town and Gown Dining Club.

President Fred thoroughly understood and enjoyed working with and through the complex and often ponderous faculty committee system. Elvehjem was more brusque and business-like in meetings, eager to get to the point and settle matters before moving on to the next problem; unlike Fred he often chafed at the slow-moving process of faculty government and disliked having to influence it. "I would never call him a patient soul," L&S Dean Mark Ingraham recalled:

> He was a man much more highly strung than Mr. Fred and found it hard to always curb his temper, but on the whole did it quite successfully. But you could see how stirred up he was on occasion.... I think he was just as devoted to the faculty control of educational policy as any of the other presidents, though perhaps more impatient with the slowness with which faculties reach decisions than some of the other presidents. He was a man whose natural instincts were to get things done fast, and he sometimes succeeded, and sometimes he merely succeeded in frustrating himself in trying to.[18]

Perhaps the greatest difference between Fred and Elvehjem was that the latter was much more willing to delegate authority and responsibility. President Fred tended to delay his decisions through endless consultation and then tried to stay involved in every step of their implementation. Things consequently often moved slowly, even glacially, during the Fred administration, but there was little that escaped the president's attention and involvement. Elvehjem was considerably less of a hands-on leader. While he may have lacked his predecessor's intimate knowledge of the University budget, the current state of the campus building program, or the individual interests, qualifications, and performance of recent faculty hires, he was more willing to bring issues to closure. He came into office, in fact, determined to change the pace of presidential decision-making. Conscious of the fact that E.B. Fred had preceded him as both graduate dean and president, Elvehjem was determined not to be thought of as simply Fred's protégé.[19]

---

[18]Ingraham, oral history interview.
[19]For contemporary views of President Elvehjem, see *Daily Cardinal*, February 5 and 27, 1958; October 9, 1958; July 27 and 31, 1962; *WAM*, 59 (March, 1958), 2-6, and 64 (October, 1962), 9-12. See also Fred Harvey Harrington, oral history interviews, 1983-84, UA.

The transition to the new Elvehjem administration on July 1 was uneventful, although the *Daily Cardinal* marked the day by recalling the disappointment in some quarters that the regents had passed over the other popular inside candidate, historian Fred Harvey Harrington. The paper summarized the unhappiness of the Harrington supporters with the perceptive comment: "The eternal struggle between the humanities and the natural sciences is being waged full force at the university."[20]

Harrington's rise to campus prominence stemmed from the fact that two years earlier President Fred had asked the outgoing chairman of the history department to join the campus administration on an informal part-time basis to provide advice and raise external funds for program and research support in the social sciences.[21] At first Harrington had neither title nor specific responsibilities (in correspondence he designated himself Coordinator of Social Science Research), but he was invited to attend the regular daily meetings of President Fred with his vice presidents and the bi-weekly meetings of the Administrative Committee, which included the vice presidents and deans. In both groups he participated in the discussion, offered his views and perspective, and took on special assignments. In the fall of 1957 the Board of Regents recognized Harrington's "kitchen cabinet" role by designating him Special Assistant to the President for Academic Planning. Harrington had increasing success in developing contacts with leaders of the major educational philanthropies and in the process attracted sizable grants from the Carnegie and Ford foundations for urban and foreign language and area studies. Indeed, it was almost entirely due to Harrington's initiative that the Ford Foundation gave the University its first million-dollar grant in 1959 to support a broad program of research and action on urban problems.[22] He also worked to develop the specialized research collections of the Memorial Library,

---

[20]*Daily Cardinal*, July 1, 1958.

[21]Harrington's appointment no doubt stemmed from a pessimistic report in 1956 by the Social Studies Divisional Executive Committee, which complained about the imbalance in University research support because of WARF's funding of the biological and physical sciences. The committee recommended the abolition of an ad hoc committee appointed earlier to review the status of UW social science research because it was "powerless to influence research and related educational policy except indirectly" and suggested these duties be assigned to "a new officer in the University's administrative structure who would have general responsibility for representing social science interests." Always alert for signs of faculty unrest, President Fred saw the Harrington appointment as a way of meeting this criticism. "Report to the President from the Executive Committee of the Faculty Division of the Social Studies," Series, 5/1/3, Box 7, UA.

[22]Joseph M. McDaniel, Jr., to Conrad A. Elvehjem, December 23, 1959, ibid., Box 43. See also below, pp. 199, 257, 310-14.

not a particularly high priority for either Fred or Elvehjem.[23] Shortly after Elvehjem's selection as president, Harrington arranged a grant from the Johnson Foundation of Racine and helped persuade Fred, Elvehjem, and the Board of Regents to create a UW Institute for Research in the Humanities, the first university enterprise of its kind in the country.[24]

Even before joining the Fred administration in 1956, Harrington was well-known to many of the regents through his election to the Regent-Faculty Conference Committee a decade earlier. His reputation there was as a forthright spokesman for the social sciences and humanities. As chairman of the special faculty Committee on Integration of Higher Education in Wisconsin in 1953, Harrington emerged as a leading Madison advocate of the development of the new University of Wisconsin-Milwaukee into a major urban campus.[25] Neither of these causes held a high priority for President Fred, but he recognized the public relations value of Harrington's presence in his administration.

So too did President Elvehjem. Six weeks after his appointment, the president-elect won regent approval for several administrative changes. The key one, announced shortly after Elvehjem took office, involved upgrading Harrington to be vice president for academic affairs, the number two campus administrative post. This necessitated bumping the current vice president, Fred's longtime associate Ira Baldwin, down to special assistant, resulting in an unusual exchange of positions by the two men. It will be remembered that Baldwin, like former President Fred a distinguished bacteriologist, had previously served as graduate dean and dean of agriculture before becoming vice president in 1948. That appointment, along with Elvehjem's as graduate dean two years earlier, typified President Fred's preference for agricultural scientists as his top associates. After a decade of highly creditable service as vice president, Baldwin's demotion in favor of a man considerably his junior in age and experience was awkward for all concerned. The switch raised faculty eyebrows, but it was popular in many parts of the campus and served to dilute the impression, so prominent in the Fred years, that the University was controlled by scientists from the College of Agriculture.[26]

[23]See, for example, Louis Kaplan, oral history interview, 1978, UA.

[24]Administrative Committee Minutes, January 7, 1958; UW BOR Minutes, May 3, 1958; *Daily Cardinal*, May 6, 7, 1958; September 19, 1959.

[25]UW Faculty Minutes, December 2, 1946; June 1 and October 5, 1953; June 7 and December 6, 1954; March 7 and June 6, 1955; Fred Harvey Harrington, oral history interview, 1978; see also below, pp. 529-31.

[26]*Daily Cardinal*, March 15, 18, 1958. The regents very likely had a hand in arranging this administrative switch in an effort to please both factions of the faculty.

Among insiders another development also caused comment. Besides continuing to live on campus in the agriculture dean's house, outgoing President Fred planned to stay active in University affairs and expected an office and secretarial help. Elvehjem offered him quarters in the new Wisconsin Center building where he could work on fund raising with the UW Foundation and the alumni association and serve as an official University greeter. Fred demurred, pointing out that he neither drove nor owned an automobile and would find the additional distance from his home difficult to manage. He insisted on staying in Bascom Hall and selected an office immediately below in the basement whose entrance was through the president's office. He continued to use the president's secretarial staff and office telephone line, sometimes answering before one of the secretaries could. Though he tried to stay out of his successor's way, it remained an awkward arrangement for all concerned and gave Elvehjem less freedom and independence than he would have liked.[27]

For several reasons President Elvehjem planned to continue the longstanding policy of having a scientist as dean of the Graduate School. The graduate dean chaired the powerful Research Committee that allocated the growing allotment of funds from the Wisconsin Alumni Research Foundation (WARF) each year. Although Elvehjem had never patented any of his own scientific discoveries, he appreciated the utility of the WARF

Harrington was subsequently told by Regent Wilbur Renk, the president of the board, that he could have had any of the other top campus administrative posts: vice president, dean of the College of Letters and Science, or graduate dean. Harrington was unclear whether Renk was speaking for the board or only himself. Harrington, oral history interview, 1982. Mark Ingraham also thought "Elvehjem was chosen with the understanding that he would ask Mr. Harrington to be vice-president, which happened." Ingraham, oral history interview, 1974. In his own oral history interviews in 1974-75 Baldwin likewise recorded his belief that the regents had dictated the elevation of Harrington:

> A bargain was made at the time Elvehjem became president. I think it's fair to say this was a bargain that the regents made both with Elvehjem and with Harrington. I wasn't in on it, but it was clear that Harrington would become vice-president and Elvehjem the president. It wasn't rivalry between two individuals as much as rivalry between the faculty groups that wanted to see each individual made president.

Ira L. Baldwin, *My Half Century at the University of Wisconsin* (Madison: Ira L. Baldwin, 1995), pp. 266-67.

[27]Reportedly, President Elvehjem once arrived at his office early one morning during the Medical School difficulties (see pp. 140-61) and discovered former President Fred–a legendary early riser–sitting at Elvehjem's desk going through his papers. He asked what Fred was doing, but the former president simply got up and left with no explanation. Thereafter Elvehjem wondered whether Fred might have been responsible for several news leaks about pending issues. See Fred Harvey Harrington, oral history interviews, 1983-84.

endowment derived from patented faculty research and shared President Fred's view that the WARF funds should be used primarily to support research in the natural sciences. He also thought it likely the great bulk of external research funds in the future would be designated for the natural sciences. Thus it seemed sound policy once again to select a prominent scientist as graduate dean. Elvehjem's first choice for the post was chemistry Professor William Johnson, but the faculty screening committee failed to nominate him. Instead, the president was obliged to accept another Letters and Science chemist, John Willard. Pressure from social scientists for representation in the Graduate School administration subsequently led Elvehjem and Dean Willard to agree to the appointment of Robert L. Clodius, a young agricultural economist, as associate dean.[28]

Otherwise, President Elvehjem was content to keep in place the administrative team he inherited from President Fred. He saw no need to replace any of the academic deans or the business staff, and he retained political science Professor William H. Young as the UW budget director and liaison with the executive and legislative branches of state government.[29] This continuity was hardly surprising; Elvehjem had known and worked closely with these campus administrators for years. Only as vacancies developed through normal attrition did the president make changes in the University's top administrative staff. Such was the appointment of H. Edwin Young as dean of the College of Letters and Science in September, 1961, to succeed retiring Dean Mark Ingraham. Young, a labor economist and chairman of the economics department,

---

[28]Ibid.; *Daily Cardinal*, May 6 and October 9, 1958. The regents approved Willard's appointment in the last few weeks of the Fred administration, but it was Elvehjem's call.

[29]Young, a specialist on state government, had served as executive assistant to Governor Oscar Rennebohm and remained close to him after Rennebohm left office and became a regent. Because of Young's contacts at the capitol and his expertise in state budgeting, President Fred saw him as a natural choice to help with the preparation and presentation of the University's budget. Although Young did not realize it at the time, he later concluded that one of Fred's characteristically indirect objectives was to use him as a foil to regain some of the lost presidential authority over UW budget and financial matters. During former President Dykstra's frequent absences in World War II, the regents had increasingly relied on A.W. Peterson, the University comptroller and later business affairs vice president, who encouraged the steady expansion of his authority and independence. Peterson resented Fred's bringing Young in as de facto budget director but could do little about it. Young assumed one reason Elvehjem kept him on as budget director during his administration was that Fred had briefed him on Young's usefulness vis-a-vis Peterson. William H. Young, oral history interview with E. David Cronon, August 28, 1996, UHP

was a widely respected faculty leader and a popular choice to head the University's largest academic unit.[30]

Continuity and Incremental Change

For the most part President Elvehjem adopted a reactive and laissez faire style of administration characterized by frugality and efficiency.[31] He believed he had inherited the leadership of a major research university with few internal problems needing presidential intervention. His major concern was to maintain the UW's scholarly eminence, particularly its impressive strength in the natural sciences. This explained his continuing interest as president in the operation of the Graduate School, especially its role in promoting faculty research. In Elvehjem's view the wise use of the WARF endowment was crucial for nurturing a cutting-edge research faculty that would in turn build a leading graduate school and assure the University its national stature. The value of WARF funds lay in their flexibility, for this made possible policies designed to stimulate faculty members to seek external research grants. An outstanding researcher himself, the president recognized the importance of a supportive campus scholarly environment in attracting and retaining top quality faculty. By the Elvehjem years the growing WARF endowment was generating about $1.5 million a year for support of faculty research, more than a ten-fold increase since the war and substantial enough to make a real difference in promoting the campus research environment.[32]

As graduate dean, Elvehjem had agreed with President Fred that the WARF funds should be reserved primarily for the hard sciences, especially the biological sciences from which the WARF endowment had originated. As the WARF grants to the University grew in amount after the war, Fred and Elvehjem were able to assign most of the smaller state appropriation for research to the social sciences and humanities. They were willing to make modest accommodations to the growing pressure from social scientists for access to WARF support, though at first only

[30]UW BOR Minutes, September 15, 1961; *Daily Cardinal*, September 16, 1961.

[31]Elvehjem regularly reminded the deans of the need to scrutinize expense accounts to be sure meals, lodging, and travel claims were held down and sought to reduce the number of courses and size and number of faculty committees. See Administrative Committee Minutes, July 8, August 12, December 9, 1958; January 27, February 18, June 30, July, 21, 28, December 15, 1959; January 5, 19, March 8, May 10, July 19, August 30, September 3, November 1, 1960; August 1, September 12, 1961; January 2, 1962.

[32]Graduate School Research Committee, Annual Reports to the WARF Trustees, 1958-62, UA.

for areas like experimental psychology that could be defined as "scientific." As president, Elvehjem expanded the recent practice of reserving a small part of the WARF grant each year for appropriate social science and humanities research. Well aware that the WARF trustees were mostly conservative businessmen who were skeptical of the value of research outside the natural sciences, each year he put together a small list of social science and humanities projects he thought they were likely to approve of and let the WARF board choose which ones to support. (This was in sharp contrast to requests from natural science faculty members, for which WARF funds were allocated by the faculty Research Committee and merely reported to the WARF trustees annually.)

President Elvehjem's expansion of WARF support for the social sciences and humanities was largely in response to a concerted and to some extent public drive by UW social scientists for access to WARF funds and a resulting greater interest by some members of the Board of Regents in more balanced research support across the University. The election of Democrat Gaylord Nelson as Wisconsin governor in 1958 brought to power a UW alumnus whose friends and political supporters included a number of prominent University social scientists. Both Nelson and his new regent, Arthur DeBardeleben of Park Falls, began to ask pointed questions about the role of the WARF endowment and the disposition of research support at the University.[33] Conceding that some social science and humanities departments had declined in stature in the inter-war years, and sensitive to complaints about the imbalance of funding for campus research activities, Elvehjem pledged: "I intend to make the continued improvement of the social sciences and humanities a major goal of my administration."[34]

---

[33]See UW BOR Minutes, July 8 and September 9-10, 1960. The following year the regents adopted a major policy statement entitled "The Future of the University of Wisconsin," which declared in part: "In all its research and scholarly effort the University should advance, *in balance*, the natural sciences, the social studies and the humanities. . . ." (Emphasis added) Ibid., March 10, 1961. Later that year the board's Educational Committee met with the University Research Committee to review the use of research funds, after which President Elvehjem pledged "strenuous efforts" to increase research funds for all major fields with special attention to such hard-pressed areas as the humanities. Ibid., July 20-21, 1961; *Daily Cardinal*, September 19, 1961. Perhaps responding to continuing pressure from some of the regents, especially Arthur DeBardeleben, only six weeks before his death Elvehjem discussed asking the legislature for an additional $750,000 of state research funds in the next biennial budget. Administrative Committee Minutes, June 12, 1962. See also below, pp. 244-46.

[34]Elvehjem, "The Question of Balance," *WAM*, 62 (November, 1960), 12.

Elvehjem in his biochemistry laboratory. UA, 2799-M.

Graduate Dean John Willard, President Elvehjem, and Preston
Hammer with new Sperry 1604 computer in Numerical Analysis
Laboratory, Sterling Hall, March 10, 1961. UA, 483-H-1.

Social Science Building under construction, October 27, 1961. UA, 5292-M.

Sellery Hall in Southeast Dormitory Area under construction, September 24, 1962. UA, 26/1.

Under Elvehjem, WARF funds provided modest support for faculty research in the anthropology, economics, geography, history, journalism, political science, psychology, sociology, and even English and several of the foreign language departments, in most cases for the first time. Beginning in 1959 WARF funds also helped establish and maintain the Survey Research Laboratory, a support unit primarily used by social science researchers. Under Vice President Harrington's further prodding, moreover, with Elvehjem's blessing WARF grants began to support faculty research at UW-Milwaukee, amounting by 1962 to 2 percent of the available WARF funds.[35] There may have been some faculty grumbling about this diversion of WARF money away from the Madison campus and from the hard sciences, but the steady growth of the WARF endowment and even more the increasing availability of federal support for scientific research helped to mute the opposition.

Improving Undergraduate Education

Apart from the Graduate School, President Elvehjem gave great latitude to his two vice presidents, Harrington in academic affairs and Peterson in business, and to the academic deans. He had little involvement with most of the curricular and program changes undertaken during his administration. An example was the creation of an undergraduate honors program in the College of Letters and Science in 1959. While Elvehjem approved of the undertaking, he neither played an active role in its development nor encouraged the other undergraduate schools to follow suit.

In a real sense the L&S Honors Program grew out of Sputnik-inspired student concern for educational reform. During the months after the Soviet space triumph a frenzied nationwide debate focused on the shortcomings and needs of American education at all levels. Much of the concern centered on whether American students were being challenged to develop their full intellectual potential. Congress quickly increased federal appropriations for education generally and late in 1958 passed the National Defense Education Act to channel federal funds into educational areas deemed important for the nation's defense. The major national foundations also responded by directing much of their resources to improving education; for example, the Ford Foundation made major

[35]Ibid.; Harrington, oral history interviews, 1978, 1982. Harrington believed President Elvehjem's tacit assumption was that he and Willard would be concerned with the natural sciences and Harrington would deal with the social sciences and humanities.

grants in 1959 to help the University upgrade teacher training and engineering education. Wisconsin Governor Vernon Thompson hosted a conference to stimulate citizen interest in the problems of higher education. The regents launched a study on the future development of the University. UW administrators and faculty began to discuss how the institution might do more for gifted students. The *Daily Cardinal* regularly featured news and editorials on educational topics, applauding the renewed interest in learning but also warning against narrow specialization. "We beseech the university to stand up for the humanities," the *Cardinal* urged, "despite the fact that 'the natural and physical sciences have the center stage'."[36] The paper also turned its attention to curricular details, scoffing at a 1935 Wisconsin law on teacher training that had the effect of requiring the School of Education to provide its graduates with as much preparation in conservation and agricultural cooperatives as in American history.[37]

UW student interest in educational reform climaxed on May 18, 1958, when a large group of upperclassmen presented outgoing President Fred with a respectful yet quietly eloquent petition addressed to the officers, regents, and faculty of the University. Signed by a diverse group of 172 student leaders, the manifesto lamented that the University of Wisconsin did not "hold the position of eminence it could enjoy in the world of education" because it "failed to challenge its students sufficiently":

> In many senses, it is too easy for thousands of students to "get by" and never learn to become critical, analytical thinkers or to achieve an understanding of the world around them. Students on all levels of attainment feel that they have not worked to the limits of their ability and time.
>
> The University must raise its standards. In some cases this means simply requiring more work; in many more it means emphasizing an improved quality of work and an intelligent, analytical approach to the subject matter.
>
> Students must extend themselves to achieve a deep and meaningful understanding of material. But this is possible only if the faculty seeks to help us by challenging us more fully.

Acknowledging that some students "failed to accept the academic challenge offered by the University," the petitioners pledged to work with the faculty for "a regeneration in excellence" that would "make the University of Wisconsin a great academic leader of the nation."[38]

---

[36]*Daily Cardinal*, May 7, 1958.
[37]Ibid., May 21, 1958.
[38]Ibid., May 28, 29, 1958. The petitioners included several future UW faculty

Less than a week after receipt of the petition the University Committee brought it to a general faculty meeting accompanied by a motion applauding the petitioners for their concern about academic standards. Quickly adopted by the faculty, the motion further requested the appointment of a special faculty committee to work with a counterpart student group to "explore plans to provide increased opportunity for gifted students and, in particular, to study the possibility of a general honors program in the College of Letters and Science," which enrolled most of the undergraduates. The special Student-Faculty Committee on Academic Standards, under the leadership of English Professor Helen C. White, met throughout the 1958-59 academic year, but the major recommendation of its final report was merely to suggest the appointment of another committee to study entrance and achievement examinations.[39]

Even though the faculty had already to some extent responded to the student petition before Conrad Elvehjem took office on July 1, one might have expected the new president to take public note of this remarkable student manifesto. If only for public relations purposes, he might have adopted it as a hallmark of his administration and launched a well-publicized campaign to raise University standards and move the institution to new heights of academic excellence. Elvehjem had not taught undergraduates for many years, however, and was not particularly interested in undergraduate education. He was far more concerned with the quality of specialized graduate education and the enhancement of faculty scholarship. The new president consequently neither discussed this thoughtful expression of undergraduate concern with his Administrative

---

members, Mary Lou Daniel, John E. Harriman, and William C. Thiesenhusen; the future publisher of the *Wisconsin State Journal*, James E. Burgess; a future UW administrator and Madison mayor, Joel C. Skornicka; and a future prominent historian, Gar Alperovitz. The Wisconsin Alumni Association subsequently asked Alperovitz, whom it had honored as WAA's outstanding junior the previous year, to expand further on the concerns of the petitioners. See Gar Alperovitz, "Toward a Regeneration in Excellence," *WAM*, 60 (November, 1958), 22-23, 36-37. Two weeks after the launch of the first Sputnik the *Daily Cardinal* had emphasized the need for higher standards in response to a University study predicting much higher enrollment over the next decade: "The University . . . at Madison should be changed radically to serve only those students who have shown an ability to do advanced work. Admission requirements should be based on college entrance examinations or high standing in accredited secondary schools. If this were done, the student population would remain substantially the same and could easily be controlled by applying higher standards." *Daily Cardinal*, October 19, 1957. See also ibid., January 7, March 4, November 11, 14, 17, 1959, and March 17, April 13, 1961.

[39]UW Faculty Minutes, June 2, 1958, January 5 and June 1, 1959; UW Faculty Documents 1331 and 1331A, January 5, 1959, and 1386, June 1, 1959, UA.

Committee nor mentioned it in his inaugural address the following October.[40] Instead, in presiding over his first meeting of the University faculty in the fall he merely called upon faculty members to give an extra hour a week for student contacts.[41] Going further, the *Daily Cardinal* suggested that students should cooperate "by spending a little more time on the books each week."[42]

It remained for Dean Ingraham and the faculty of the College of Letters and Science to develop a more specific response to the student petitioners and in the process produce the most significant educational reform of the Elvehjem presidency. Throughout much of the next academic year an L&S faculty committee developed plans for an ambitious four-year undergraduate honors program and two new baccalaureate honors degrees, which were approved by the L&S faculty and by the general faculty in April, 1959.[43] During the following year the L&S faculty Honors Committee under the leadership of English Professor Alvin Whitley fleshed out the administrative and programmatic details of the program and worked with departments to develop special honors courses. The Board of Regents gave its approval on April 9, 1960, and the new program went into effect for freshmen and sophomores in the 1960-61 academic year and for juniors and seniors thereafter.[44] "The prime purpose of a university is to offer

---

[40]It is instructive that in the first meeting of the president's administrative "cabinet"–the Administrative Committee–after Elvehjem took office, he handed out a list of twelve ways the University was aiding national defense, passed out reservation cards for the forthcoming meeting of the National Association of Land Grant Colleges, and distributed copies of a speech entitled "Who's in Charge Here?" and a research book, *Exploring the Unknown.* More substantive issues brought up by the president at the meeting included: appointment of a committee to consider the role and possible payment of the University band at commencement, appointment of 1958-59 divisional executive committee chairmen, how to reduce the size of various faculty committees, biennial budget requests and procedures, the parking committee's recommendation to build parking ramps near the Memorial Union and the Medical School, and the nature of the president's inaugural ceremony. There was no mention of either the recent student manifesto or undergraduate education in general. Administrative Committee Minutes, July 7, 1958.

[41]UW Faculty Minutes and UW Faculty Document 1344, October 6, 1958; *Daily Cardinal,* October 7, 1958. Nor did President Elvehjem endorse or associate himself with a subsequent request by student government leaders to the Board of Regents to "toughen" UW courses. *Daily Cardinal,* November 14, 1959.

[42]Ibid., October 9, 1958.

[43]UW Faculty Minutes, April 6, 1959; *Daily Cardinal,* April 8 and 11, 1959.

[44]UW BOR Minutes, April 9, 1960. The Honors Committee designed the purely voluntary program for students in roughly the upper ten percent of the L&S student body, and saw it as augmenting, not replacing, the regular curriculum. To qualify for an honors degree a student must have completed at least 40 credits in honors courses or work under honors procedures at a grade of B or better, with at least 10 of these credits outside the

a general public education," Whitley explained, "but a university should also offer a different kind of work for the mind that is capable of it. Without an honors program, you really don't have a general university."[45] The students whose petition started it all must surely have agreed.

The major and not insignificant cost of the program was in additional faculty time for staffing the new honors classes and for supervising senior honors theses and the extra honors work in regular courses. The Elvehjem administration and the Board of Regents sought special state funding for this work in 1960-61 but the legislature decided it should be absorbed as part of general instructional costs. Subsequent efforts to give the program recognized budget status were no more successful. This lack of specific funding to cover the very real additional costs of honors instruction remained a continuing problem, because it undermined the program's effectiveness and appeal to faculty members hard-pressed to handle their regular undergraduate and graduate teaching loads. Fortunately, the steady expansion of the faculty to meet surging enrollments over the next decade made it somewhat easier for departments to absorb the additional honors workload or at least for a time to obscure its extent. The lack of specific funding for honors instruction remained a continuing problem, however, and was a deterrent to providing honors work in other UW schools and colleges. Even so, the College of Letters and Science at UW-Milwaukee established a similar undergraduate honors program in the fall of 1959 and the School of Commerce in Madison followed suit in 1962.[46]

Another important development of the Elvehjem years was the growing internationalization of the University. Again, this reflected more the interest of Vice President Harrington, a specialist in American foreign relations, than of the president. The University had for many years attracted a sizable number of foreign students, but until the Second World War the curriculum and the interests of the faculty largely overlooked most of the world outside of Europe and North America. Only after the war, for example, did the history department begin offering courses in Asian and Latin American history, and not for another decade did it include Africa

---

major. The program also required a senior thesis or its equivalent culminating in a research project done under the supervision of a faculty member. While the plan awarded Sophomore Honors to students completing its requirements in the first two years, its design also permitted junior transfer students to earn an honors degree.

[45] "An Honors Program for Wisconsin," *WAM*, 61 (March, 1960), 14-15.

[46] UW Faculty Minutes, October 5, 1959; January 8, 1962. Not until 1969 did the Madison College of Agricultural and Life Sciences follow suit and provide an undergraduate honors program. Ibid., October 6, 1969.

as well. Other social science departments similarly lagged in offering related courses. By the mid-1950s UW faculty members were expanding the Wisconsin Idea to include service in the developing world, first to train engineering educators in India, and several years later economists in Indonesia.[47] President Fred had actively discouraged faculty members from accepting overseas assignments, believing they should focus their efforts on Wisconsin's needs, but Elvehjem was more open to international activities.[48]

The National Defense Education Act of 1958, which targeted federal funding for graduate study in subjects considered important for the national defense, provided a major stimulus for international education. Vice President Harrington was quick to exploit the act's potential for enhancing the University's work in foreign languages and area studies. Building on the fact that since 1931 Wisconsin was one of the very few U.S. institutions offering Portuguese language instruction, Harrington quickly set up a Center for Luso-Brazilian Studies in 1959 under the initial direction of Professor Lloyd Kasten, a prominent specialist on medieval Spanish but with knowledge of Portuguese as well. The center succeeded in obtaining one of the first NDEA area studies grants, which provided funds for Portuguese language instruction and graduate fellowships for Portuguese and Brazilian studies. In 1962 the center became part of a new and expanded NDEA-funded Language and Area Center for Latin American Studies.[49]

Similarly, Harrington quickly gathered together enough UW specialists on India to create a credible Indian studies center that qualified in the 1960 round of NDEA funding. Regularly renewed, the federal funds provided gradually increasing support for foreign language study in Hindi-Urdu, Telegu, Sanskrit, Tibetan, Marathi, Pali, and eventually Tamil, as well as Buddhist and other area studies. By 1961 the Indian Studies Program had become a regular academic department and the University was able to offer its expertise to train Peace Corps volunteers going to the Indian subcontinent. At the same time Harrington fostered the development of two other interdisciplinary programs to compete for NDEA funding in

[47]UW BOR Minutes, July 13, 1957; Administrative Committee Minutes, September 2, 1958, and August 14, 1959; *Daily Cardinal*, July 17, 1958.

[48]Baldwin, *My Half Century*, pp. 220-21, 264.

[49]"Luso-Brazilian Studies," *WAM*, 61 (December, 1959), 29; Lloyd Kasten, "The Luso-Brazilian Center," ibid. (February, 1960), 22-23; "Latin American Center," ibid., 64 (December, 1962), 8; Alyce Weeks, "The Area Studies Programs," ibid. (March, 1963), 13-15.

the future, one concerned with African and the other with Russian language and area studies. These benefitted from the vice president's success in 1962 in securing a five-year $1.2 million Ford Foundation grant for non-western international studies.[50]

The growing array of international studies and programs led to the selection of Harrington's colleague, history Professor Henry B. Hill, to coordinate them in 1961.[51] The following year, in collaboration with the University of Michigan, Hill launched the University's first junior-year-abroad program at the University of Aix-en-Provence, France.[52] Its success academically and its popularity among undergraduates inspired an impressive array of similar UW programs on four continents over the next several decades. Thus while President Elvehjem cannot be given major credit for extending the boundaries of the University from the state to the world–a large part of that distinction must go to Harrington and the faculty specialists he brought together for this purpose–the inter-nationalization of the University and its curriculum made major strides during the Elvehjem administration. The Board of Regents gave its blessing in a forward-looking policy statement. "The inter-dependence of the world's people, the ease of travel and communications, the rising importance of other cultures, and the quest for peace," declared the representatives of this once-isolationist state in 1961, "have tended to make the globe our campus. This trend we encourage."[53]

As academic vice president, Harrington with Elvehjem's blessing took the lead for the administration in pushing the University's opposition to the anticommunist provisions of the National Defense Education Act. Reflecting the lingering influence of McCarthyism and the continuing Cold War fear of the Soviet Union and the Peoples Republic of China, the framers of the legislation had included a requirement that recipients of NDEA funding must sign a loyalty oath and a disclaimer of membership in any subversive organization. Along with a number of other major universities, Wisconsin objected to this vaguely worded federal threat to academic freedom on the nation's campuses. Elvehjem's Administrative Committee initially feared the requirement would apply to all NDEA

---

[50]Administrative Committee Minutes, May 9, 1961; Weeks, "Area Studies Programs," 12-13, 16-18; "Huge Ford Grant Spurs UW Work in International Studies," ibid., 63 (June, 1962), 6; *Daily Cardinal*, May 9, 1959.

[51]Administrative Committee Minutes, October 3, 1961.

[52]"Students Heartily Endorse Junior Year in France," *WAM*, 64(June, 1963),10.

[53]"Report of the Committee on the Future Development of the University," UW BOR Minutes, March 10, 1961. Harrington very likely played a major role in drafting or at least influencing this report.

funding and be difficult to apply to foreign students and faculty members. An early Washington ruling limited the oath-affidavit provision to recipients of NDEA student loans and fellowships, leading the Administrative Committee to revise its objection.[54] Throughout, Elvehjem and Harrington and their administrative colleagues took a pragmatic view of the issue, even after the faculty University Committee proposed that the University should reject all NDEA funding until the requirement was removed. After considerable debate of the matter, the faculty agreed that the University could apply for NDEA funds while continuing to press for the elimination of the oath-affidavit provisions. Elvehjem appointed a special faculty committee, with Harrington as a prominent member, to study the matter, which succeeded in keeping the UW protest active while avoiding any damaging boycott of federal funds.[55]

In this cautious stance the UW administration agreed with the editors of the *Daily Cardinal*, who declared that while "loyalty oaths are repugnant and an unfortunate reflection of the culture," the issue really boiled down to "simple economics":

> Idealists on both sides may throw platitudes randomly about, and no doubt this will occur. However, we hold the view that if the University urgently needs the money, and its excellent student loan program will stand to be injured without it, the loyalty oath will have to be tolerated.[56]

As the campus debate over the loyalty oath simmered during the next year, the Student Senate also rejected a bill calling on the University to spurn NDEA funds while the offensive restrictions remained in effect. Asked about a *Capital Times* article predicting the University would quit the NDEA student loan plan, Harrington commented that it was "somewhat misleading" because UW intended to use NDEA funds while joining in a "united protest" with other universities. UW policy was best summarized in a *Cardinal* headline about a routine resolution adopted by the Board

---

[54] Administrative Committee Minutes, December 16, 30, 1958.
[55] Ibid., December 1, 15, 1959, January 5, 1960; UW Faculty Minutes, December 7, 1959, January 4, 1960; UW Faculty Document 1407, December 7, 1959, and 1409, January 4, 1960.
[56] *Daily Cardinal*, December 17, 1958. This pragmatism was strenuously rejected by a more idealistic undergraduate, David Obey, who would go on to serve in the Wisconsin Legislature and the U.S. Congress. He declared, "I oppose such an oath, not because I am disloyal . . . but because I happen to believe what Roger Williams (that nasty old radical) said, 'I humbly conceive that it is the express and absolute duty of the civil powers to proclaim an absolute freedom of conscience in all the world.'" Ibid.

of Regents in December, 1959, accepting an NDEA grant: "Regents hit loyalty oath, keep the money."[57]

The Changing Face of the Campus

As we have seen, one of the most serious problems confronting the University after the Second World War was the great need for more buildings–classrooms, laboratories, dormitories, recreational facilities, and the like–to accommodate the rapidly growing student body. As a stopgap solution, President Fred and his staff acquired a large number of surplus wartime temporary buildings to get through the immediate space crunch. Although the legislature provided some funds for regular construction in the years following the war, Fred and the regents had to fight hard for every dollar, and the amounts provided were never sufficient to meet all of the basic needs. An extreme but illustrative example of the problem was the decades-long campaign to obtain funds for a new library, a top faculty-student priority since the mid-1920s. Although state officials acknowledged that a new building was a pressing need, for various reasons construction of the Memorial Library was delayed for nearly a decade after the war.[58]

The availability of construction and remodeling funds had improved considerably by the time Conrad Elvehjem succeeded Fred as president. There were several reasons for this. By 1959 nearly 700 families were living in the University's Hill Farm real estate development, and the sale of residential and commercial lots had already generated about $3 million, which was more than sufficient for the acquisition and improvements at the much larger replacement Arlington Farm north of Madison.[59] President Elvehjem and the Board of Regents consequently were able to use some of the Hill Farm proceeds to meet other College of Agriculture building

---

[57]UW BOR Minutes, December 3, 1959; *Daily Cardinal*, November 19, 24, December 4, 16, 1959, January 12, February 10, 1960.

[58]See pp. 233-38 for more extended discussion of the efforts to get a new library building.

[59]UW BOR Minutes, October 24 and November 14, 1959. It will be recalled that when the Board of Regents was considering how to handle the sale of the Hill Farms complex, the highest bid from a private developer was about $1,000 per acre. By setting up a University-controlled corporation to handle the development, the regents eventually realized proceeds of about $3,500 an acre, plus continuing income from the Hilldale Shopping Center. The College of Agriculture was able to secure a replacement experimental farm at Arlington comprising about four times as much land as the lost Hill Farms acreage. Baldwin, *My Half Century*, p. 475. See also pp. 62, 177, 253-55.

needs in Madison. Another favorable development was the growth of the WARF endowment and the willingness of the WARF trustees to make occasional grants to help construct and equip campus research facilities, usually in the form of matching funds for such projects. The regents authorized the use of Hill Farm proceeds to construct a new veterinary science building in Madison, for example, augmented by a WARF grant of $1,375,000 for this project as well as for the Van Vleck mathematics building and a zoology research building for which federal grants were obtained.[60]

By this time, indeed, the growing availability of federal funds provided assistance for the construction of research, classroom, and even dormitory facilities. An example was Elvehjem's aggressive and successful effort to win a $1.5 million National Science Foundation grant in 1959 to construct a national biotron facility for research on the effects on living organisms of controlled environmental changes (in light, humidity, atmospheric pressure, and the like). A similar campaign brought construction and operating funds from the National Institutes of Health in 1961-62 for one of a planned network of national Regional Primate Centers supporting primate research, long a campus strength flowing from the pioneering work of psychology Professor Harry Harlow.[61] There was also growing recognition by state authorities that enrollments would inexorably rise sharply during the 1960s, at Madison and elsewhere around the state, as the post-war baby boomers reached college age. Additional facilities would be required to accommodate the growth, because this time there would be no ready supply of surplus temporary buildings for expansion. In fact, some of the temporary buildings still scattered around the campus were by now reaching the end of their useful life.[62] Making use of a combination of federal and program revenue funds, the Elvehjem administration constructed a number of student dormitories in these years: the Elm Drive commons and houses, a replacement Chadbourne Residence Hall, the first units of the sprawling Southeast Dormitory Area, and the continuing development of married student apartments at Eagle Heights west of Picnic Point.

---

[60]UW BOR Minutes, May 12, 1961.

[61]For the Biotron see *Daily Cardinal*, July 21, 1959; UW BOR Minutes, September 12, 1959; "Biotron," *WAM*, 61 (October, 1959), 9. For the Regional Primate Center see UW BOR Minutes, September 10, 1960, November 17, 1961, February 9 and July 13, 1962. See also below, pp. 247, 273.

[62]See, for example, UW BOR Minutes, October 24, 1959, and July 14, 1962.

Thus for a variety of reasons the Elvehjem years encompassed a lively construction boom. President Elvehjem and the Board of Regents regularly devoted as much as half or more of each monthly board meeting to physical plant matters: establishing building priorities, selecting sites, gaining necessary state and city approvals, securing funding, land acquisition, approving plans, specifications and cost estimates, and letting bids and contracts. The board continued to use its Wisconsin University Building Corporation to acquire and hold property and handle projects, such as dormitory financing, construction, or remodeling, for which there was a predictable revenue stream. State requirements made the construction process complicated, repetitive, and time-consuming. Often the regents delegated to their Executive Committee the authority to make timely decisions between board meetings. They also authorized President Elvehjem to raze obsolete buildings valued at less than $25,000, useful authority as UW acquired properties in the expansion area south of University Avenue in Madison or around the Kenwood campus in Milwaukee.[63]

The greater availability of science funding and the president's interest in strengthening the University's research base was reflected to some extent in campus construction priorities, as was federal assistance for dormitory construction. The more significant Madison building projects initiated or completed during Elvehjem's four years in office included: the first stage of the Social Science Building, the first stage of the Southeast Dormitory Area, Chadbourne Hall, the Elm Drive dormitory complex, Gym Unit 1 (the Natatorium) and planning for Gym Unit 2, the Hydrobiology (limnology) Laboratory, the Van Vleck Mathematics Building, the Mechanical Engineering Building, the Veterinary Science Building, the Genetics Building, the Psychology Building, the Zoology Research Building, the Extension Building and an Extension Services Building, the Mathews Chemistry Building, an addition to the Enzyme Institute, a High Energy Physics Laboratory, two cooperative scholarship dormitories (Susan Burdick Davis House and Henry Rust House), an addition to Slichter Hall, additional married student apartments in the growing Eagle Heights complex, and numerous Arlington Farm buildings. Also requiring a good deal of attention was the continued platting, street and sidewalk preparation, and sale of residential and commercial lots in the Hill Farm real estate development, as well as the construction and continuing legal actions over the Hilldale Shopping Center.[64]

---

[63]See UW BOR Minutes, October 24, 1959.
[64]On Hilldale Shopping Center developments, see pp. 135-37, 253-55.

Nearly as complex and time-consuming were the matters pertaining to UW branches outside of Madison. The most important of these was UW-Milwaukee, whose development remained controversial but was championed particularly by Vice President Harrington and several of the regents. The purchase of the Milwaukee Downer Seminary property in 1959 fueled the growth of the north-side Kenwood campus but also triggered ongoing discussion about what to do with the former Extension campus downtown. UWM construction projects in these years took place on the Kenwood campus and included: remodeling of the Main Building, a new Science Building, a new Fine Arts Building, an addition to the Student Union, expansion of the Heating Plant, a general classroom building and two temporary office/classroom buildings, and the acceptance of two nearby luxurious North Lake Drive mansions and grounds, one to be used as a conference center and the other as the residence of the Milwaukee provost.

Elsewhere, the growth of a network of permanent two-year Extension centers occupied a good deal of administrative staff and board time. Launched during the Depression mostly using local school buildings for evening and weekend instruction, these outlying Extension centers had largely closed during the war but were started up again and greatly expanded in 1945-46 to help accommodate the rapid enrollment growth of the immediate post-war years. By the mid-1950s most of the makeshift temporary centers had closed and the Extension Division, under the leadership of Dean Lorentz H. Adolfson, was seeking permanent facilities for the remaining centers located in Wisconsin cities without other higher education programs. The Board of Regents' post-war policy was to furnish Extension instructional staff for an appropriate array of freshman-sophomore credit courses if a county or city provided and maintained a dedicated classroom/laboratory/office building or campus for this purpose. The chance to acquire a branch of the University of Wisconsin by this means appealed to a number of communities.

Throughout the Elvehjem years Adolfson and his staff and the regents were consequently involved in numerous ongoing negotiations with local officials and county boards over the provision and funding of permanent two-year Extension centers in Kenosha, Racine, Sheboygan, Manitowoc, Menasha (Fox Valley), Green Bay, Marshfield, Marinette, Wausau, and for a time Wisconsin Rapids. By 1962 there were eight UW two-year centers, most of them in new buildings constructed by local governments for exclusive UW use. To facilitate the subsequent transfer of their students to the University, the curriculum of the centers was tied closely to the general education courses of the College of Letters and

Science in Madison. L&S departments helped select the center instructional staff and approved the curriculum and content of center courses. Since UW-Milwaukee was also being developed in close association with University authorities and faculty committees in Madison, during the Elvehjem years the Madison campus' direct instructional reach extended throughout much of the state. Although this expanding network was not yet designated as such, it clearly constituted a de facto University of Wisconsin system.[65]

Damping Down Inter-Institutional Rivalries

The expansion of University of Wisconsin campuses around the state occurred under the watchful eye of the new state Coordinating Committee for Higher Education (CCHE), created by the legislature in 1955 as a public watchdog over the University and its growing rival for state funding, the Wisconsin State College system operated by a separate board of regents.[66] During the Fred administration Vice President Ira Baldwin served as the principal University of Wisconsin liaison with the Coordinating Committee and as the CCHE staff co-director with President Eugene Kleinpell of River Falls State College. After Baldwin left the vice presidency, President Elvehjem asked him to continue these responsibilities and he did so for the next five years.

The weakness of the Coordinating Committee was implicit in its title; its functions were coordination and planning, not administration or management. The two rival state systems of higher education had equal representation of their regents on the committee and in its staff. CCHE had no independent budget, only the authority to draw on the resources of the University and the State Colleges as needed. The arrangement was a pale imitation of the merged single board of regents proposed periodically in the past and most recently by Governor Kohler in the mid-1950s. President Fred and the UW regents had opposed the Kohler initiative, and lobbying by UW officials and by both boards of regents had helped defeat it in the legislature. The effort persuaded the regents of both systems that some sort of coordination was probably inevitable, and Baldwin played

---

[65]The above account of regent involvement in physical plant issues is based on a review of UW BOR Minutes for the period of Elvehjem's presidency, 1958-62. See also L.H. Adolfson, "University of Wisconsin Centers, 1946-1972," *Wisconsin Academy Review*, 19 (1973), 27-28.
[66]See pp. 526-34.

a leading role in working out the details of the legislation establishing the CCHE in 1955.

Characteristically, President Elvehjem gave Baldwin a much freer hand in his CCHE work than had President Fred, asking only that he be kept informed about matters affecting the University. Elvehjem no doubt agreed with Baldwin that the CCHE represented an opportunity to demonstrate to Wisconsin political leaders that it was possible to achieve useful and cost-effective coordination without heavy-handed state control. Certainly within its structural limitations, CCHE accomplished a good deal during the Elvehjem-Baldwin years. It fostered inter-institutional contacts and collaboration, in many cases for the first time. Its staff and planning groups produced a number of useful studies detailing state educational needs. These examined the cost and adequacy of various educational programs, provided space utilization studies to evaluate building requests and determine funding priorities, and developed a phased closing of the two-year county normal schools. The committee even went so far as to put together a state master plan outlining the specialized fields of study each institution should offer and their relation to the programs of the vocational schools and the Extension centers. The most significant CCHE power lay in the statutory requirement that it review and recommend priorities for the operating and construction budget requests from the various higher education institutions before their submission to the governor and legislature. Nevertheless, during the Elvehjem years the original CCHE spirit of cooperation diminished significantly as UW leadership increasingly focused on opportunities for institutional growth and development.[67]

The Bowers Affair

By far the most serious difficulty confronting Elvehjem during what turned out to be his four-year presidency involved the Medical School, a long-running problem that surely contributed to his early death. It is worth examining in detail for what it reveals about President Elvehjem and his style of leadership.

In February, 1954, Dean William S. Middleton, who had headed the Medical School for two decades and been on its clinical staff since 1912, announced his impending retirement.[68] He subsequently left in mid-

---

[67]Baldwin, *My Half Century*, pp. 480-85, 530-33.

[68]Medical School Faculty Minutes, February 16, 1954, in 1954 Medical Dean Search Committee Papers, UA. There is some reason to think Middleton's decision was welcomed, even encouraged, by President Fred and Graduate Dean Elvehjem, who believed

year to advise the U.S. Veterans Administration on the operation of its system of hospitals. Under Dean Middleton's towering influence the school had developed a complementary mission–training and clinical treatment–with basic scientific research at most a secondary concern. To give greater emphasis to research and address a number of other problems in the school, President Fred and the Board of Regents decided to go outside for a successor. Their eventual choice was Dr. John Z. Bowers, a prominent internist and radiobiologist who was currently the Dean of the University of Utah College of Medicine.[69]

In keeping with President Fred's deliberative style, the search to replace Dean Middleton was thorough and wide-ranging, conducted by seven Medical School faculty members elected by their colleagues, and with advice from five physicians from around Wisconsin representing the State Medical Society. Both groups were under the overall leadership of a three-member regent search committee headed by a practicing physician, Dr. Raymond G. Arveson, himself a former president of the State Medical Society. The faculty search committee kept in close touch with the medical faculty, soliciting their colleagues' advice as to desirable qualifications and candidates. President Fred also played an active role in the search, assisted by Vice President Baldwin and Dean Elvehjem.[70]

---

the dean's emphasis on clinical work and training was outmoded and who wanted to see more basic scientific research at the Medical School.

[69]UW BOR Minutes, January 8 and February 12, 1955, UA; *WAM*, 56 (January 15, 1955), 6, 11.

[70]The medical faculty advisory subcommittee included seven members under the leadership of Professor D. Murray Angevine (pathology) and, ironically in view of later events, Associate Professor Anthony R. Curreri (surgery). Initially the members apparently thought they were to select the new dean or at least to propose a single name for consideration by the rest of the selection committee and the regents. President Fred and Vice President Baldwin met with them for "a very frank discussion" in which Fred bluntly told them:

> . . . the time has come for the Committee to report on two or three individuals they think qualified in order that he may proceed with the appointment of a dean. Both Mr. Fred and Mr. Baldwin assured the Committee that the selection of the Dean was determined by the Regents and that the Faculty might or might not be consulted. The function of the Committee was one of consultation and not one of appointment.

[Fred] Memorandum, November 1, 1954, Series, 4/16/1, Box 240, UA. During Bowers' second recruitment visit to Madison, accompanied by his wife, President Fred asked the Elvehjems to entertain and persuade them to come. Mrs. Elvehjem helped by discussing school opportunities for the Bowers' children. Fred also asked Professor Philip P. Cohen, the chairman of physiological chemistry, to make inquiries about Bowers from colleagues at Utah. Cohen reported positive endorsements. Philip P. Cohen, oral history interview,

Over the better part of a year the Search Committee screened 120 candidates and brought seven for campus interviews before recommending three, including the 41-year-old Bowers, to the president for the appointment.[71]

Bowers seemed an attractive choice because he was young, energetic, and promised to upgrade and modernize the school's curriculum, improve relations with the physicians of the state, and encourage more research by the medical faculty, all areas of concern to President Fred, Dean Elvehjem, and the Board of Regents.[72] Another consideration was the extent of inbreeding in the clinical departments and their greater emphasis on remunerative private practice than on teaching and research, especially basic research. Fred and the regents encouraged Bowers to raise the quality of the Medical School through judicious outside appointments and by finding ways to support his faculty in medical research as well as through clinical practice. The expectation was that the new dean should bring the teaching, research, and outreach activities of the Medical School to the level of other parts of the University. Still, at the time of Bowers' appointment President Fred acknowledged to the regents that there were disagreements within the medical faculty about the selection and its implications for the future of the school.[73]

Bowers quickly discovered that the state-funded base salaries in the Medical School, especially in the clinical departments, were relatively low compared with the income of private physicians in Madison and the

---

1980, UA.

[71]See Angevine to Fred, November 4, 1954; C.N. Woolsey to Fred, November 19, 1954, Series, 4/16/1, Box 240, UA. After President Elvehjem's death in 1962, Mrs. Elvehjem learned from sources at the University of Utah that Bowers had generated similar faculty opposition at his previous post and was being eased out when Wisconsin hired him in 1955. If true, this information was certainly not discovered by President Fred or the UW Search Committee. The papers of the Search Committee reveal nothing but praise for Bowers. President Fred did his own independent checking of the three recommended candidates and other possibilities. The Search Committee's secretary, Professor Clinton N. Woolsey, later recalled that Fred evidently was much influenced by the strong recommendation of Bowers he received from Allan Gregg of the Rockefeller Foundation. Woolsey to Robert E. Cooke, June 20, 1974, 1954 Medical Dean Search Committee Papers.

[72]See extract of letter from John Z. Bowers, July 1, 1954, Series 4/16/1, Box 240, UA; Bowers, "Modern Medical Training Emphasizes the Human Approach," *WAM*, 57 (February, 1956), 16-17, 29.

[73]In his usual elliptic style Fred explained: "The members of the Medical School staff are to be complimented for the fine spirit they have shown in aiding in the difficult task of selecting a new Dean. That differences of opinion exist among members of the faculty is nothing new. In fact, I think it would be most unfortunate to have on our staff persons who do not have different ideas and different interests." UW BOR Minutes, January 8, 1955.

state. Clinical faculty members were permitted to have a private practice, and some preferred to hold only part-time University appointments so they could devote more time to their private patients. Indeed, a number of the UW physicians generated most of their total income through their private practices. Dean Middleton had established a ceiling governing the extent to which such practice income could be used to increase salaries, but this was viewed as a gentleman's agreement and not strictly enforced. As a general rule the more private patient billings produced by a clinical faculty member, the higher his or her salary. Even when a clinical department pooled its private patient billings, the surplus remained under the control of the department rather than be used for general Medical School or hospital needs. Distribution of patient revenue across the Medical School was consequently quite uneven, with some "rich" departments like surgery, anesthesiology, or radiology generating and receiving much more of it than, for example, primarily instructional departments like anatomy or physiology. The system relieved the state and University of the need to put more tax funds into the hospital and Medical School, but it also provided a powerful incentive for the clinical faculty to emphasize patient treatment over teaching and scholarly research. It also was a source of continuing resentment among physicians in Madison and elsewhere in the state, who objected that University practitioners were charged only a small percentage of their billings for office and facilities use, far less than private physicians had to pay for their overhead costs.[74]

By the time Elvehjem took over the presidency in mid-1958, Dean Bowers was well along in his efforts to bring change to the Medical School. He created several new departments and specialties and set about expanding

---

[74]Along with his reform efforts, early in his tenure Dean Bowers may have rubbed President Fred the wrong way. Only a little over a year after his arrival, Bowers complained to the president that he thought he was underpaid and should have not only a higher salary but also an entertainment fund and a car for his personal use. The frugal Fred, who didn't own a car, entertained as little as possible, and walked everywhere on campus, responded that he thought it was unwise to ask for more money until Bowers "had demonstrated his ability as Dean of the University of Wisconsin Medical School." Fred also pointed out that Bowers had been away from Madison more than 90 days since his appointment; he said this was "too much time away," and was in fact "the same criticism which had been mentioned of Dean Bowers' work prior to coming to Wisconsin." In the president's customary third-person record of the conversation, he commented: "All in all, Dean Bowers seemed somewhat 'hurt' that Mr. Fred raised any question concerning Dean Bowers' administration of the Medical School. Mr. Fred tried to make clear that Dean Bowers' method of asking for additional funds was not in line with the usual procedure at Wisconsin. …" [Fred,] Memorandum of Conference with Dean John Z. Bowers, November 17, 1956, Series 4/16/1, Box 284, UA.

the size of the medical faculty, often through outside appointments of younger specialists to add new fields and reduce the level of inbreeding in the school. In structuring the appointments of new clinical faculty members, he sought to address the problem of low base salaries. As department chairmanships opened up, he sometimes filled them with outsiders who could bring fresh ideas and a new perspective.[75] He revitalized the medical teaching programs in a number of areas, expanded the roster of adjunct clinical faculty members from practicing physicians around the state, and established collaborative teaching relationships with several nearby community hospitals. Using his extensive national contacts, he brought in foundation and government grants for facilities, equipment, and specialized research. In an effort to reduce the isolation of most of the medical faculty from the rest of the University, he encouraged joint research activities with a number of related University departments outside the Medical School. In short, the dean seemed to be accomplishing exactly what the Board of Regents and the campus administration had laid out for him at the time of his appointment.[76]

Although it was not initially apparent, there were powerful countervailing forces building within the Medical School. From the beginning some of senior faculty members resented both the decision to bring in an outside dean and the reported criticism of the school advanced

---

[75]The 1954 Medical Dean Search Committee solicited comments from the medical faculty about the qualities needed in a new dean. One of the more insightful responses came from Associate Professor Robert W. McGilvery, who argued that the real problem of the Medical School was not arbitrary leadership but a lack of attention and assertiveness on the part of the faculty:

> The contrast between meetings of the medical faculty and of the general university faculty is striking. Some degree of *overt* dissension is an indication of alertness and health on the part of both the dean and the faculty, while confinement of expressions of disagreement to bitter huddles in the corridors and offices can only raise doubts about the integrity or courage of the participants. . . . Another contributing factor is the existence of *de facto* department heads rather than departmental chairmen, contrary to both the spirit and the letter of university regulations.

R.W. McGilvery to the Committee on the Medical Deanship, ca. April 30, 1954, 1954 Medical Dean Search Committee Papers.

[76]Cohen, oral history interview; James F. Crow, oral history interview, 1983, UA; Ralph Hawley, oral history interview, 1996, UHP; "Report of Survey of the University of Wisconsin Medical School," April 24-27, 1961, Series 4/17/1, Box 59, UA. Regarding curricular change, see UW Faculty Minutes, February 1, 1960, and UW BOR Minutes, February 20, 1960. For Bowers' view of his reform achievements, see his statement to the regents, Exhibit F, UW BOR Minutes, October 20, 1961.

as justification. The new dean was ambitious and hard-driving, sometimes devious and manipulative, and often impatient, abrasive, and insensitive to faculty concerns. Ominously, one of the more outspoken members of the Dean Search Committee, surgery Professor Anthony R. Curreri, had spelled out his somewhat limited view of a dean's role before Bowers' appointment:

> In the development of the Medical School policy, the executive committee should be given prior notice and provided with due and sufficient time for consideration and study of the problem. This individual should also discuss and accept the advice of members of the faculty through active committees in developing a program or appointing new men to key positions.[77]

Bowers' preference for outside faculty appointments, especially of new departmental chairmen, seemed to confirm a negative view of the Wisconsin Medical School, its faculty, its programs, and its achievements. The dean's indirect strategy of dealing with the clinical pay issue also backfired. Rather than confront this ticklish problem comprehensively, Bowers at first dealt with it piecemeal by setting the base salaries of new clinical faculty members considerably higher than those of current faculty. Even though the latter's total University income, including private practice, might be higher than the newcomers', the symbolism of setting their base salaries higher than those of longtime faculty rankled.

After Bowers brought in a new department chairman from outside at double the base salary of a senior full professor of long service who had himself sought the appointment, a storm of criticism erupted and its reverberations reached the president's office. Elvehjem suggested that Bowers make no additional faculty appointments until the school developed a comprehensive new salary plan governing clinical practice income. As part of this effort the president promised to provide additional state funds–eventually $100,000–to upgrade clinical base salaries if the faculty produced an acceptable plan reducing the emphasis on private practice.[78] The Bowers honeymoon was unraveling, with a growing division among the medical faculty over his methods and objectives, and with a normally standoffish president feeling the need to get involved.

---

[77]Anthony R. Curreri to Erwin R. Schmidt, April 6, 1954, 1954 Medical Dean Search Committee Papers.

[78][John Z. Bowers] "Problems of a Medical Dean," n.d., typed manuscript, pp. 24-25, Oral History Project files, UA.

Dean Bowers and a faculty committee began developing a new Clinical Pactice Plan in 1958 and it underwent several modifications before being presented to the clinical faculty the following year.[79] Although the plan was controversial, a majority of the faculty approved it in principle but asked for some modifications, most of which were in place by 1960. All new faculty members having private practice privileges were required to participate (after being recommended by their departmental chairmen and approved by the school's Medical Advisory Board). Membership was not compulsory for current clinical faculty but they might join by the same procedure. Once in the plan, participants were not permitted to resign from it without the approval of the Governing Committee, a group elected by plan members and chaired by the dean. Participants were permitted to supplement their official University salaries from private patient fees or consultation income on a fixed scale ranging up to 50 percent for instructors, 65 percent for assistant professors, 80 percent for associate professors, and 100 percent for professors. In addition to their allowable maximum salaries, the plan covered participants' malpractice insurance and various other specified overhead costs associated with their practice, including 5 percent of their billings paid to University Hospitals. Surplus receipts were to be deposited in a general Medical School fund administered by the plan Governing Committee and credited to the department generating them. For the first three years the generating department could initiate requests for their use; after three years the funds could be used generally across the school "for the purpose of furthering the research and educational potentialities of the Medical Center and its staff."[80] In short, the plan set limits on the private income of full-time clinical faculty members, extended the dean's control over surplus clinical earnings, and made possible the distribution of such revenue across the school.

Even with the modifications, several of the clinical departments were dissatisfied and held out against joining. One of the units most concerned about retaining control over its substantial income from private practice was the Department of Surgery. Although the UW surgeons typically had relatively low base salaries, with their practice income some of them were by far the highest paid faculty members anywhere in the University. The department was deeply suspicious of any effort to revise the existing salary plan, especially one that increased the dean's authority

---

[79]Administrative Committee Minutes, April 1, 30, June 3, 24, 1958; "The Consultation Practice Plan," March 16, 1960, Medical School Administrative Committee files, Series 12/1/2, Box 5, UA.
[80]Ibid.

as head of the plan's Governing Committee to control the use and distribution of the clinical practice income. The department's fight was led by Professor Anthony Curreri, a prominent thoracic surgeon and cancer specialist, who as medical chief of staff had spoken against the plan when Bowers first introduced it. Rather than base his opposition on a defense of the surgeons' high income from private practice, Dr. Curreri objected to what he considered inadequate coverage of overhead expenses, the lack of a provision for departments to support their younger faculty members and researchers who generated little or no practice income, the absence of any incentive to earn more than the plan maximums, and especially to the dean's chairing the Governing Committee that controlled the surplus clinic revenue.[81]

To break the stalemate with the surgeons, during 1960-61 Bowers decided to take advantage of the impending retirement of Dr. Erwin R. Schmidt, who had chaired the surgery department since its beginning in 1926. By recruiting an outside chairman as Schmidt's successor, the dean planned to introduce some new ideas and leadership. Although there were some excellent surgeons in the department, it was heavily inbred. There were complaints from students and surgical residents about indifferent teaching and from physicians around the state about the failure to introduce new procedures and programs. Even some surgery faculty members complained about the department's top-down style of governance and their inability to participate in program development or decision-making. Another consideration, certainly, was the dean's desire to end the department's boycott of the new Clinical Practice Plan.[82]

Dean Bowers' strategy was to by-pass the department and conduct the search for an outside chairman through an ad hoc selection committee consisting of himself and five chairmen of other Medical School departments. Dean Middleton had followed this procedure once in 1955 and Bowers had used it several times since without serious faculty objection. This time, however, the surgery faculty objected strongly and loudly both to the decision to recruit an outsider and to the department's exclusion from the search process. When the selection committee recommended Dr. John W. Cole of Western Reserve University as chairman, the surgery faculty retaliated by exercising its prerogative not to recommend his

[81]John Newhouse, "Medical School Splits on 'Outside Earnings'" *Wisconsin State Journal*, June 11, 1961. Newhouse, a prominent *State Journal* reporter and columnist, was a friend and former cancer patient of Curreri's who wrote a number of pro-Curreri pieces during the Bowers controversy.
[82]Bowers, "Problems of a Medical Dean," p. 10.

appointment to its faculty, even though the Biological Sciences Divisional Executive Committee informally agreed Cole was well-qualified for a UW faculty appointment. Instead, the department several times formally recommended Dr. Curreri as chairman. Curreri had been an intercollegiate boxer as a UW undergraduate and quickly showed he had lost none of his combative skills. He and the anti-Bowers faction took their case to the press and soon the row in the Medical School over Dean Bowers' leadership was front-page news.[83]

The dispute was more than a little ironic, because neither the Medical School nor the surgery department had previously been considered bastions of faculty democracy. Now, however, the surgeons pointed to the longstanding regents' policy mandating that departmental faculties be consulted annually on the appointment of their chairmen, a policy not previously followed anywhere in the Medical School. Indeed, the chairmen of some departments (like surgery's Dr. Erwin R. Schmidt) had often served for decades without reference to their colleagues. As the split deepened, the two Madison newspapers characteristically took opposing sides, with the *Capital Times* championing Dean Bowers and his forward-looking reforms and the *Wisconsin State Journal* defending Curreri and faculty rights.

Unlike former President Fred, whose hands-on style of presidential leadership would certainly have alerted him to impending trouble in the Medical School and very likely enabled him to head off the conflict before it became front-page news, President Elvehjem seems to have been blind-sided by the entrenched bitterness of the surgery department's revolt and the growing dissatisfaction with Dean Bowers' leadership within the school. Elvehjem had not only encouraged but mandated the dean's efforts to develop a new Clinical Practice Plan and he met at least once with Bowers and the surgeons to urge their support of it.[84]

The president had also endorsed the decision to recruit an outside surgery chairman. He gave enthusiastic backing to the selection of Cole, moreover, even offering to telephone him to personally offer the job. After Cole indicated his acceptance, Elvehjem authorized Bowers to present

---

[83]See *Capital Times*, November 21, 22, 23, 26, December 1, 1960; *Wisconsin State Journal*, November 21, 24, 1960; *Milwaukee Journal*, December 4, 1960; *Daily Cardinal*, December 6, 1960.

[84]*Wisconsin State Journal*, June 11, 1961. This presidential mediation foundered in part because the balance of the $100,000 fund Elvehjem had allocated to increase the state-funded portion of clinical faculty salaries was by this time insufficient to meet the needs of those not yet in the plan.

the appointment to the Board of Regents at its next meeting. Late that same night, however, he telephoned the dean and told him to hold up the Cole appointment. Dr. Curreri had gone to the president's home earlier that evening, and in an emotional meeting laid out the department's adamant refusal to accept Cole. Curreri had also delivered a withering indictment of Bowers' leadership in general, and to Elvehjem's great surprise asked to be named to replace him as dean. Given the Elvehjems' social friendship with the Curreris, this put the president in a painfully awkward position. Temporizing, he decided to hold up the Cole appointment. He permitted Bowers to present it to the regents at their December meeting, but without a recommendation so the board could defer a decision while the dean tried to put out the Medical School fires.[85] Publicly, if guardedly, Elvehjem expressed confidence the "people involved" would be able to solve their problems.[86]

This was overly optimistic. The press coverage of the dispute over the Cole appointment now expanded to include other issues, especially Bowers' controversial Clinical Pay Plan. An anonymous leaker, probably Curreri, explained to the *State Journal* that the surgeons' opposition was not based on any selfish desire to protect their high income, but rather their concern over how the dean would administer the plan's surplus revenue.[87] President Elvehjem met with Dean Bowers and the Medical School's Executive Committee on January 3 to consider how to damp down the dispute. Elvehjem advised the school to review and recodify its policies and procedures in line with general University faculty regulations, particularly with respect to departmental governance and the role of departmental chairmen.[88] In response, and in what the *Wisconsin*

[85]*Capital Times*, December 5, 1960; *Wisconsin State Journal*, December 6, 1960; Bowers, "Problems of a Medical Dean," pp. 10-16. Curreri also took his quest for the surgery chairmanship to the University Committee. See Curreri to University Committee, December 19, 1960, Series 5/96/2, Box 5, UA.

[86]Elvehjem, press statement, December 9, 1960, Medical School Controversy file, Series 12/00/07, UA. The University Committee also began to get involved behind the scenes at this time, meeting with Dean Bowers, with President Elvehjem, and with a number of medical faculty members. The committee declined to take a position on the surgery chairmanship issue but emphasized "that University rules be applied more regularly in Med School in future." Notes and final 1960-61 annual report, Series 5/96/2, Box 5, UA. One of the University Committee members was Professor James F. Crow, the chairman of the Department of Medical Genetics and thus a member of Bowers' Executive Committee, as well as an elected member of both the ad hoc committee and the Medical School Faculty Advisory Committee after its creation in the spring of 1961.

[87]*Wisconsin State Journal*, December 9, 1960.

[88]Medical School Executive Committee Minutes, January 5, 1961, Series 12/1/2,

Alumnus accurately described as "a most complex election," the increasingly divided medical faculty voted to elect a carefully structured ad hoc committee "'to review, define, interpret and codify' the procedures employed by the Faculty, Departmental Chairmen, Executive Committee and the Dean in the administration of the Medical School within the University by-laws or to suggest changes therein, with first consideration to be given to the manner of selecting departmental chairmen."[89] Elvehjem gave an optimistic progress report to the Board of Regents the following month, after which the regents declared their full satisfaction that the president had "energetically and effectively applied himself to making it possible for the Medical School faculty to resolve the problems confronting it . . . in the democratic way that is traditional to the University of Wisconsin."[90]

The members of the ad hoc committee were at first uncertain of the extent of their charge or how to proceed. After consulting with President Elvehjem, the University Committee, and various individuals, their most important recommendation was the creation of a permanent Medical School Faculty Advisory Committee. The new committee would come into being after the ad hoc committee completed its work. While its role was to be advisory, it would have broad authority to review actions and policies in any part or at any administrative level of the school whether or not specifically requested to do so. Its model seemed to be the University Committee–the executive committee of the general faculty–and the proponents acknowledged that no other UW school had such a committee. The easy approval by the medical faculty of this new watchdog committee was a further indication of Dean Bowers' deteriorating leadership position with respect to his colleagues.[91]

The ad hoc committee also dealt with the more immediate controversy over the selection of departmental chairmen. It recommended that the Medical School follow existing University policy, which provided

---

Box 5, UA.
[89]Medical School Executive Committee statement, January 16, 1961; Medical School Faculty Minutes, January 24, 1961, Medical School Administration, Series 12/1/1, Box 1, UA. See also Department of Medicine memorandum, January 13, 1961; Department of Surgery memorandum, January 13, 1961; Medical School Executive Committee Minutes, January 13 and 16, 1961, all in Series 12/1/2, Box 5; Elvehjem, press release, January 16, 1961, Medcial School Controversy, 1960-61 folder; *Wisconsin State Journal*, January 17, 1961; *Medical Alumni Newsletter*, April, 1961; *WAM*, 62 (April, 1961), 32.
[90]UW BOR Minutes, February 11, 1961.
[91]Medical School Faculty Agenda and Minutes, Series 12/1/1, Box 1, UA. See also Crow, oral history interview.

that the faculty members of each department were to be consulted annually on their preference for departmental chairman for the next year. Adding its own modification, the committee recommended that the resulting preference ballot be transmitted both to the dean and to the new Faculty Advisory Committee, which could "make any recommendations to the dean which it believes are in the best interest of the Medical School." After receiving the department's preference ballot and any additional advice from the Faculty Advisory Committee, the dean remained free to present whatever recommendation he chose to the president for approval. If the dean decided it was desirable to recruit an outside departmental chairman, he might use an ad hoc selection committee, but it "should include a representative of the department concerned." The ad hoc committee's proposal thus respected the traditional administrative authority assigned by the regents to the dean and the president, but it clearly aimed to bring more faculty oversight to the process. The Medical School faculty was of the same mind. It approved the measure easily, but not before defeating several amendments reflecting concern about the current dispute over the unsettled surgery chairmanship.[92]

While these policy changes were taking place in the spring of 1961, Dean Bowers arranged to have the Medical School undergo an accreditation review by the Association of American Medical Colleges and the American Medical Association. Bowers' associates believed he had a hand in determining both the timing and the composition of the five-member external review team that spent three days in Madison in late

---

[92]"Report of the Ad Hoc Committee on Medical School Procedures," April 4, 1961; Medical School Faculty Minutes, April 4, 1961, Series 12/1/1, box 1, UA. The deep divisions within the medical faculty were reflected in the voting on one of the amendments. Offered by Professor Philip P. Cohen, the chairman of physiological chemistry, it provided for an ad hoc selection committee to present a list of outstanding candidates if the departmental faculty and the dean disagreed over their preference for departmental chairman. The proposal was probably viewed as pro-Bowers, because its supporters said that representation from the department concerned on a selection committee was desirable "but not absolutely necessary." Spokesmen for the ad hoc committee noted that while their recommendation did not specifically provide for such a committee, neither was it excluded and thus was "implicitly included." In any event, the Cohen amendment failed by a vote of 41-44. The ad hoc committee provided further recommendations about the composition and functions of the Faculty Advisory Committee for consideration at the faculty meeting on June 2, 1961, a session by this time vastly overshadowed by Dean Bowers' threatened resignation. Rather than elect a new committee, the faculty constituted the members of the ad hoc committee as the Faculty Advisory Committee for the coming year. Medical Faculty Agenda and Minutes, June 2, 1961, Series 12/1/1, Box 1, UA.

April conducting a friendly examination.[93] Whether or not Bowers influenced the review or its timing, the report of the accreditation team could hardly have been more helpful to the beleaguered dean. It praised in considerable detail "the phenomenal progress. . . made in some areas in the past five years," particularly "the quality of the younger men who have been recently added to the staff in both clinical and preclinical areas." It congratulated Bowers and the faculty on the adoption of a "most far-sighted" consultation practice plan. At the same time the team viewed "with grave concern the unsettled succession to the Chairmanship in the Department of Surgery":

> A great unrest which pervades the entire faculty (and the medical center) as the result of the failure to resolve the dispute over the Chairmanship in Surgery has brought faculty morale to a low ebb and has provoked among the students a feeling that teaching is significantly hampered thereby. It has already caused comment on the national scene and will doubtless affect the recruitment and retention of faculty. It will surely disturb public confidence in the medical center. These factors when coupled with the apprehensive attitude of the faculty as to the future of the school make it imperative that the matter be concluded with all possible speed.[94]

Coupled with its high praise of Bowers' achievements, the team's "grave concern" seemed meant to be interpreted as criticism of President Elvehjem and the Board of Regents for failing to give the dean better support.

On May 10 nine Medical School departmental chairmen and the superintendent of University Hospitals met with President Elvehjem to express the group's unhappiness over the continuing surgery impasse and to urge an interim compromise. They stressed that any compromise ought to be structured so that no one could be seen as having won or lost. Above all, they argued, it was important not to undermine the authority and leadership role of the deanship. Elvehjem proposed that during the coming year the surgery department be administered by a committee of three, with the power to elect its chairman. He suggested a committee consisting of Drs. Curreri, Gale, and Price.[95] One of the delegation pointed out that this group would be considered pro-Curreri, and that permitting the committee to elect its own chairman could hardly be viewed as a

---

[93]Hawley, oral history interview.
[94]"Report of Survey of the University of Wisconsin Medical School," April 24-27, 1961, Series 4/17/1, Box 59, UA.
[95]The final composition of the committee replaced Price with Herman Wirka.

compromise. Elvehjem seemed to understand and agree. In closing, he remarked that he hoped Dean Bowers could sell the surgery faculty on this solution. The delegation remonstrated that it was important to maintain the dean's authority to *appoint* department chairmen. Bowers should therefore be in a position to *inform* the surgery department of his appointment of this Administrative Committee after consultation with the president.

Whether Elvehjem understood the group's concern for a true compromise and the need to preserve administrative authority is unclear. In any event he consulted with members of the surgery department prior to Bowers' meeting with the department, and he agreed to the department's insistence on the right of the three-member Administrative Committee to select its own chairman. The committee in fact elected Curreri as its head even before Bowers announced "his" compromise interim solution. It hardly required clairvoyance to determine who had won and lost, a question the newspapers quickly settled in their coverage of the outcome. The delegation of chairmen that had cautioned Elvehjem about the delicacy of the matter was outraged. They informed the president that the consequences of the botched compromise had seriously undermined administrative authority in the Medical School, including their own as departmental chairmen, and declared that the situation was thus "wholly unacceptable to us."[96]

Meanwhile, Dr. Cole informed reporters in Cleveland he would not "under any circumstances" accept the surgery chairmanship at Wisconsin. One of his colleagues at the Western Reserve University Medical School declared that Cole had been treated "rather shabbily," and said he doubted "whether Wisconsin could find any reputable surgeon from any place in the country to take that job now."[97] Worse, on May 24 President Elvehjem received a confidential letter from Dean Bowers stating: "I tender my resignation as Dean of the Medical School to become effective on a date to be determined."[98] News of Bowers' action soon reached the Madison press and was reported nationally by the wire services. Reportedly, the superintendent of University Hospitals, Edward J. Connors, and five Medical School departmental chairmen–all Bowers supporters–had

---

[96]Francis M. Forster, Ben H. Peckham, Robert Roessler, Edward J. Connors, P.E. Shideman, Nathan J. Smith, A.S. Evans, O.V. Seastone, and Philip P. Cohen to Elvehjem, May 19, 1961, Series 12/1/2, Box 5, UA.

[97]*Capital Times*, May 19, 1961.

[98]Quoted in "The President's Report on the Medical School," June 5, 1961, Medical School Controversy, 1960-61 folder.

submitted similar letters to take effect if Bowers' resignation was accepted. Although President Elvehjem declined comment, it appeared the dean had thrown down a large gauntlet. Rumors immediately fanned throughout the medical center and the campus that Bowers was planning to depart, taking with him an important part of the UW medical staff, perhaps to the new medical school being developed at the University of Arizona, which the dean had visited the previous week.[99] Most of the hospital interns and residents, and all four classes of the medical students, quickly mobilized behind Bowers. More than a hundred of them marched to the president's home and presented Elvehjem with a packet of signed petitions urging that the proffered resignations not be accepted and that the dispute in the Medical School be resolved. "We feel," warned one petition, "that the resignation of Dean Bowers and the concomitant resignations of those men supporting him in this impasse would result in irreparable damage to the Wisconsin University Medical Center."[100]

Bowers' strategy through his somewhat tentative resignation–"on a date to be determined"–was evidently to oblige the president to bring the issue to the Board of Regents for a decision, where he believed he had strong support. Worried about what the board might do, Elvehjem turned for advice to Vice President Harrington and to political science Professor William Young, his politically astute budget advisor. They were appalled that the dispute had gotten to this point, and warned that in any power contest between a dean and a president, if the dean won the president was effectively through. Consequently, whatever the merits of the Medical School issues, they believed Elvehjem and the presidency must be supported. They advised him to recommend acceptance of Bowers' resignation, then worked frantically behind the scenes to mobilize regent support for Elvehjem, finally warning Bowers that his resignation would be accepted if he did not withdraw it.[101]

The Harrington-Young script came off essentially as planned at the Board of Regents meeting on June 5-6, although discussion was intense (and the long-term results unclear) over two days and nearly eight hours

---

[99]*Capital Times*, May 27, 30, 1961; *Wisconsin State Journal*, May 28, 30, 1961; *Milwaukee Sentinel*, May 30, 1961.

[100]Group of signed petitions, May 29, 1961, Series 1/1/17, Box 22, UA; *Wisconsin State Journal*, June 1, 1961; *Capital Times*, June 1, 1961.

[101]Harrington later recalled that this was the first time Elvehjem had consulted him on anything to do with the natural sciences. Harrington, oral history interview, 1983-84; Young oral history interview.

of closed-door deliberations.[102] President Elvehjem began by recommending that Bowers' resignation be accepted effective June 30, that Associate Dean Otto A. Mortensen be named interim dean, and that hospitals Superintendent Connors also be appointed associate dean of the Medical School in charge of fiscal and budgetary affairs. The latter appointment would effectively detach Connors from the most influential group of Bowers supporters while providing balance to Mortensen, a Bowers critic. Elvehjem further recommended that the recently named three-member committee to administer the surgery department be replaced by an acting chairman other than Professor Curreri, and that a selection committee with one member from surgery be authorized to recruit two outside tenured faculty members, one for the surgery chairmanship. He emphasized that these recommendations had the full support of the Medical School's new Faculty Advisory Committee.[103]

The board was close to approving the president's recommendations when one of the regents suggested sleeping on the matter overnight. The next morning, again in executive session, the board listened to Dean Bowers and five of his departmental chairmen.[104] The regents did not call representatives of the Faculty Advisory Committee nor attempt any other sampling of faculty opinion. After further deliberation, Regent President Carl Steiger emerged to report that Dean Bowers had withdrawn his resignation. Steiger emphasized the regents' "support of the administration of the University" and their confidence that "with the cooperation of the Administration, the Dean of the Medical School, and the faculty" the parties could continue to improve the medical center and resolve "the differences which gave rise to the recent dispute."[105] The press headlined the result differently. "Med School Controversy Apparently Is Unresolved," trumpeted

[102]The newspapers had requested an advisory opinion from Attorney General John W. Reynolds as to the right of the press to be present, but the regents noted they had not asked for Reynolds' advice and had a legal right to consider personnel matters in executive session. UW BOR Minutes, June 5, 1961; *Capital Times*, June 6, 1961.

[103]"The President's Report on the Medical School," June 5, 1961, Medical School Controversy, 1960-61 folder.

[104]The chairmen accompanying Bowers included Drs. Francis M. Forster (neurology), Robert L. Roessler (psychiatry), Ben M. Peckham (obstetrics and gynecology), Nathan J. Smith (pediatrics), and John H. Flinn (director of the student health clinic), *Ashland Daily Press*, June 7, 1961. Bowers believed Governor Gaylord Nelson was behind the decision to give him and his supporters a hearing before the regents. Bowers, "Problems of a Medical Dean," p. 18.

[105]UW BOR Minutes, June 5-6, 1961; UW press release, June 6, 1961, Medical School Controversy, 1960-61 folder; "Medical School Debate Cools Off after a Bout of Fever," *WAM*, 62 (July, 1961), 38-39.

the *Capital Times* the next day; "Regents Give President Vote of No Confidence," concluded the *Wisconsin State Journal*.[106]

Unfortunately, the regents' spirit of cooperation did not suddenly infuse the Medical School. Within days Dr. William B. Youmans, the chairman of the physiology department, reported that 53 of the 102, or more than half of the tenured full and associate professors in the school had either by letter or petition expressed their dissatisfaction with Dean Bowers' administration and their desire for new leadership.[107] The *State Journal* chastised the regents editorially for ignoring faculty opinion before they decided not to accept Bowers' resignation in spite of Elvehjem's recommendation to the contrary.[108] During the next several months even some of Bowers' supporters concluded he could not bridge the differences within the medical faculty and provide it with effective leadership.[109] Over the summer Elvehjem and especially Young worked with Curreri and the surgery troika to make Bowers' Clinical Pay Plan acceptable to the surgeons. By September Elvehjem was able to tell the regents that all but two surgeons had joined the plan and Young predicted within a year it would cover 99 percent of the clinical faculty.[110] Dean Bowers seemed increasingly impotent and irrelevant.

So much so, in fact, that the Faculty Advisory Committee met with President Elvehjem and a group of regents on the evening of September 14, 1961, and recommended unanimously that Bowers be replaced as dean. The members of the committee agreed in general with Bowers' reform program, including the need for an outside surgery chairman, but said they had reluctantly concluded he was incapable of repairing the deep divisions within the medical faculty. The next day in executive session the board assured Elvehjem of its support in reorganizing the Medical School administration. Regents Steiger and Gelatt met with Elvehjem then with Bowers on the afternoon of September 20 and informed him

---

[106]*Capital Times* and *Wisconsin State Journal*, both June 7, 1961. The *State Journal* editorial began with a flat assertion: "The university regents on Tuesday gave President Elvehjem the strongest vote of 'no confidence' a university's chief executive has been handed since another board fired Glenn Frank in 1937."

[107]*Milwaukee Sentinel*, June 10, 1961.

[108]*Wisconsin State Journal*, June 22, 1961.

[109]Cohen, oral history interview; Crow, oral history interview. Cohen recalls that he and Crow, both of them departmental chairmen who had approved of Bowers' reforms and had supported him throughout the surgery dispute, concluded by this time he had lost his ability to accomplish anything and therefore went to him to urge that he resign.

[110]UW BOR Minutes, September 15, 1961.

of the general consensus that it would be in the best interest of both the University and Bowers if he sought another position. The dean strongly defended his record and asserted that his leaving would not solve all the problems of the Medical School. He also predicted it would be hard to find a replacement. The others agreed with his first point, but responded that they hoped a change would eliminate many difficulties. Although Regent Steiger warned that the press was following the Medical School controversy closely and might learn of this meeting, Bowers declined to reveal his intentions.[111]

After reflecting over the weekend, the dean decided not to resign or leave quietly. Like Glenn Frank before him, he retained legal counsel and formally requested a hearing by the full Board of Regents before any move to replace him.[112] As Steiger had feared, the matter became the subject of intense press scrutiny after the *Capital Times* broke the story on October 4 under the headline: "U. Regents Request Dean Bowers Quit." Elvehjem immediately provided less provocative clarification in a press release briefly summarizing the recent events, but it appeared the next session of the regents would be a stormy public replay of the board's lengthy deliberations the previous June.[113]

Dean Bowers explained his action at the next regular session of the Medical School Executive Committee before leaving the meeting and turning it over to Associate Dean Mortensen. By an 8-4 vote the committee then adopted a motion offered by Professor Philip Cohen, the chairman of physiological chemistry, expressing its "willingness and desire to meet with President Elvehjem and the Board of Regents to insure an adequate review of the administration of the Medical School."[114]

---

[111]Memorandum of Meeting Relating to the Medical School, September 20, 1961; Elvehjem, press release, October 4, 1961, both in Medical School Controversy, 1960-61 folder; Bowers, "Problems of a Medical Dean," pp. 18-21.

[112]Bowers retained three attorneys, thereby revealing both his combative nature and his political finesse: former Governor Philip F. La Follette (the voice of La Follette progressivism and father of the old Progressive Party), James E. Doyle (one of the architects of the reborn Democratic Party), and Edmund J. Hart (a prominent Republican). His choice of La Follette was ironic, given the latter's involvement in the regents' controversial firing of President Glenn Frank in 1937.

[113]*Capital Times*, October 4, 6, 12, 1961; *Wisconsin State Journal*, October 5, 6, 1961; *Milwaukee Sentinel*, October 5, 1961; *Daily Cardinal*, October 6, 7, 10, 13, 1961; Elvehjem, press release, October 4, 12, 1961.

[114]Medical School Executive Committee Minutes, October 6, 1961. At a subsequent meeting, on an 8-3 vote the committee adopted a motion offered by Professor Ben Peckham, a Bowers supporter, declaring "that it has supported and continues to support the administration of Dean John Z. Bowers on major policy matters including the selection

Meanwhile, the other UW deans were coming to view Bowers as a loose cannon who was threatening the structure and extent of University administrative authority. Under the leadership of Letters and Science Dean Mark Ingraham, the other Madison and UW-Milwaukee academic deans wrote to President Elvehjem emphasizing the important distinction between professorial and administrative service. To assure the academic freedom of teachers and scholars, society had established tenure protections:

> However, the scholar who assumes administrative duties as a dean should do so with the clear understanding that he has the right to voluntarily return to teaching, and the obligation to relinquish his academic post if in the opinion of the institution he should do so. Such a determination by the authorities of an institution is a matter of judgment and to be put into effect should not require either charges or a hearing thereon and except in very unusual circumstances should be recognized by the acquiescence of the individual through resignation as dean.
>
> The usefulness of a dean depends upon the confidence of his faculty and of the president of the institution. If either of these is lost to any substantial degree the dean's usefulness is seriously impaired. This impairment can reach the point where it is unwise for a dean to be continued in office. Again this is a matter of judgment, primarily on the part of the president whose recommendations normally should be followed.
>
> In addition to stating the above principles we wish at this time to express our respect for your leadership, our confidence in your administrative judgment, and our warm esteem for you as a colleague.[115]

Although Attorney General Reynolds issued an opinion on October 18 that the regents could dismiss an administrator without a public hearing, the board decided to deal with the issue in a regular public meeting. On the afternoon of October 20 Dean Bowers and his attorneys, along with assorted University administrators, interested faculty and students, and reporters from the print and broadcast media jammed into the crowded

---

of new departmental chairmen" and that "the Executive Committee shares with the Dean both the responsibilities for, and a justifiable pride in, the record of the past six years." Ibid., October 17, 1961.

[115]Mark H. Ingraham, John E. Willard, Erwin A. Gaumnitz, Lindley J. Stiles, R.K. Froker, George H. Young, A.H. Uhl, L.H. Adolfson, Joseph G. Baier, Kurt F. Wendt to Elvehjem, October 13, 1961, Medical School Controversy, 1960-61 folder. As a former president of the American Association of University Professors and a long-time advocate of faculty tenure, Ingraham's views carried great authority.

regents meeting room, where a previous board had dismissed UW President Glenn Frank twenty-seven years earlier. Reynolds was also there to provide advice to President Elvehjem and the regents. The board agreed at the start that Bowers, himself only, might have "appropriate time to make such statements on the matter as he chooses."

First President Elvehjem soberly summarized the events leading to his conclusion, which he stressed reflected the advice of the Medical School's Faculty Advisory Committee and a large segment of the medical faculty, that Dean Bowers had lost his capacity for effective leadership and should be relieved of his administrative post. Bowers next read a considerably longer statement reviewing the achievements of his administration. He recalled the charge President Fred and the regents had given him upon his appointment to reform the Medical School and quoted from the recent favorable accreditation review to demonstrate his successes in carrying it out. As for the complaint he had lost faculty support, he asserted: "It is impossible for a Dean to achieve this support if and when his President and Regents contribute to a situation in which the Dean's authority is clouded and his future is uncertain." This criticism, he made clear several paragraphs later, related to the issue of the surgery chairmanship, where the administration's temporizing had allowed an unresolved major question to create a variety of related and unrelated problems. "And then," he commented with more than a little sarcasm, "it is proposed that you rely on the resulting situation itself as the reason for proposing the removal of the Dean." Bowers closed by declaring: "If, after consideration, you wish to have my resignation as Dean of the Medical School, you may have it."

The regents so wished, and without extended discussion. The board promptly voted with one dissent to relieve Dean Bowers of his administrative responsibilities effective November 1, while continuing him as a professor of medicine at his current salary. "Not a question was asked," Bowers later recalled; "there was no sifting and no winnowing."[116] The lone dissenter, Regent Harold A. Konnak of Racine, explained his negative vote by stating he believed the dean had accomplished what he was hired to do. "His removal as Dean answers no questions for me concerning the problems of the Medical School," Konnak declared. "Right or wrong for me does not depend on popular majorities."[117]

---

[116]Bowers, "Problems of a Medical Dean," p. 17.

[117]UW BOR Minutes, October 20, 1961; "Medical School Dispute: Regents Dismiss Bowers," *Medical Alumni Newsletter*, October, 1961; "Medical School Crisis Comes to Head as Dean Bowers Is Dismissed," *WAM*, 63 (December, 1961), 18-20;

The dismissal of Dean Bowers, while hardly unexpected, provided no immediate solution to the problems and divisions within the Medical School. Indeed, two Bowers supporters, Dr. Robert Roessler, the psychiatry chairman, and Dr. John Flinn, the director of student health, promptly resigned their administrative positions in protest.[118] Elvehjem and his advisors believed they must move swiftly to start the healing process. Within hours of the regents' action, the following Saturday morning the president, along with Harrington and Young, met with the school's Executive Committee to discuss the procedures to be used in selecting an acting dean. With regard to the contentious surgery chairmanship, Elvehjem twice stated he intended to follow the recommendation of the Faculty Advisory Committee to recruit an outside surgery chairman and that Dr. Curreri would not be appointed to the position. Both Elvehjem and Harrington emphasized that the school's Administrative Committee, rather than the Faculty Advisory Committee, would continue to be the primary group advising the dean on "all normal operating procedures and functions."[119] Two days later Elvehjem met with the entire medical faculty to announce his appointment of a five-member screening committee, chaired by Dr. Ben Peckham, to develop a slate of suitable candidates to be acting dean. He said he was sorry about the regents' "necessary" action, but intended to move quickly in appointing a replacement. Any medical faculty member was eligible.[120] Meanwhile, a number of Wisconsin newspapers sharply criticized the Board of Regents and President Elvehjem both for their decision to dismiss Dean Bowers and their failure to justify it.[121]

By the end of October Elvehjem had persuaded Professor Philip P. Cohen, the chairman of the Department of Physiological Chemistry, to serve as acting dean. Cohen was quite reluctant to take the position,

---

Milwaukee Journal, October 21, 1961; *Daily Cardinal*, October 21, 26, 1961.

[118]*Capital Times*, October 21, 1961; Elvehjem, press statement, October 23, 1961, Medical School Controversy, 1960-61 folder. The *Capital Times* headlined its story: "U. Med School Men Resigning/Top Talent in Exodus." Contrary to the implications of the *Times* story, neither Flinn nor Roessler resigned his professorship.

[119]Medical School Executive Committee Minutes, October 21, 1961.

[120]Medical School Faculty Minutes, October 23, 1961, Series 12/1/1, Box 1, UA. The other members of the committee were James Crow (medical genetics), Ovid Meyer (medicine), O. Sidney Orth (anesthesia), and Van Potter (oncology). Peckham (obstetrics and gynecology) declined to chair the committee, so it was headed by Crow. University press release, October 23, 1961, Medical School Controversy, 1960-61 folder.

[121]See *Waukesha Daily Freeman*, October 23, 1961; *Racine Journal*, October 24, 1961, April 1, 1962; *Capital Times*, October 26, 31, November 1, 7, 1961; *Appleton Post-Crescent*, October 29, 1961; *Milwaukee Sentinel*, October 30, 1961; *Daily Cardinal*, October 26, November 1, 1961.

but he was a good choice.[122] He had supported Bowers and his reform program in the past but was not strongly identified with any faction. More recently he had urged the dean to resign in the belief he no longer had enough support within the medical faculty to accomplish anything. A scientist in a largely research department, Cohen had earned both an M.D. and a Ph.D. degree and thus possessed credentials recognized by both the clinical and the scholarly faculty. He was well-respected within the Medical School as a tough but fair-minded leader who could provide strong leadership while remaining sensitive to faculty prerogatives and opinion. As a biochemist he was personally and professionally close to Conrad Elvehjem and could work comfortably with the University president on what had become the campus administration's most difficult managerial problem.

Cohen agreed to take the deanship for a year but made clear he was not interested in the job on a permanent basis. Although he promptly set about trying to resolve the thorny issue of the surgery chairmanship, he and Elvehjem found it no easier than had Bowers to persuade the recalcitrant surgeons to accept an outside chairman. The dispute flared up publicly again in the spring of 1962 when members of the department appealed to the University Committee to support their right to nominate a chairman from within the department. "We settled that matter last October," commented one frustrate regent.[123] For a time Cohen even toyed with the idea of creating a new academic surgery department separate from the existing clinical surgery department. (Only one of the current UW surgeons–not Curreri–was a member of the Academic Surgeons, a prestigious national professional group.) Cohen gave up the idea when he recognized it would imply to the public that he thought the current surgery department was second-rate, when in fact it included some excellent surgeons. "They were belligerent, they were determined, they were mischievous, but they were not incompetent as surgeons," he recalled years later.[124]

---

[122]University press release, October 31, 1961, Medical School Controversy, 1960-61 folder; Cohen, oral history interview.

[123]Medical School Executive Committee Minutes, January 8, 1962; University Committee Minutes, April 4, 1962, Series 5/96/1, Box 1, UA; UW BOR Minutes, April 6, 1962; "Regents Review Some Problems," *WAM*, 63 (May, 1962), 24-25; *Wisconsin State Journal*, March 27, 1962; *Capital Times*, March 28, 30, 1962; *Daily Cardinal*, March 27, 29, April 7, 1962; *Beaver Dam Citizen*, March 29, 1962; *Racine Journal*, April 1, 1962.

[124]Cohen, oral history interview.

A Tragic Casualty

The impasse over the surgery chairmanship remained unresolved when on the morning of July 27, 1962, President Elvehjem collapsed in his office from a sudden coronary occlusion. He died less than two hours later with his wife Connie and son Robert at his hospital bedside.[125] Only 61, the president was the most tragic casualty of the effort to revitalize the UW Medical School.

While one cannot pinpoint the cause of a heart attack, it is difficult to avoid the conclusion that presidential stress shortened Elvehjem's life, that he literally gave his life to the University. Central to the strain, certainly, were his long-running difficulties with Dean Bowers and the medical faculty, some of the latter his close friends and a few his former students. A high-strung Type-A personality, Elvehjem must have realized from the first that his previous relatively low-key administrative service–as department chairman and graduate dean–had hardly prepared him for the high pressure rigors of the UW presidency. Indeed, his first episode of severe high blood pressure came on the very day he was appointed president. Scarcely a month after Dean Bowers' dismissal Elvehjem had to be hospitalized for several days of rest and treatment, following which he was on blood pressure medication until shortly before his death. The week he died the president and his wife had scheduled a weekend at their Door County vacation home. Anticipating it, she asked how much longer he planned to remain as president, pointing out he had now graduated a full four-year class of undergraduates. Elvehjem responded perhaps another four years, when he reached sixty-five. This, his wife agreed, was the outer limit, and she promised to hold him to it. Both had lost their zest for the presidential life.[126]

---

[125]*Daily Cardinal* extra, July 27, 1962.
[126]*Daily Cardinal*, November 30, December 1, 1961. Mrs. Elvehjem, Vice President Harrington, and other associates recalled that the blood pressure medication the president was taking sapped his energy and made him listless and easily tired.

4.

The Imperial President

The sudden death of President Elvehjem on July 27, 1962, created a major and unexpected emergency for the University and its Board of Regents. Vice President Fred Harvey Harrington, Elvehjem's close rival for the presidency four years earlier, had since that time made no secret of his ambition to move up to a university presidency when the right opportunity came along.[1] An experienced and hard-driving executive who was responsible for a number of the initiatives of the Elvehjem administration, just two months before Elvehjem's death Harrington had accepted the presidency of the University of Hawaii. There he could build on his longstanding professional interest in the Pacific Basin.[2] In fact, at the time of Elvehjem's death Harrington was teaching an American studies seminar in Kyoto, Japan, following which he was shortly scheduled to take up his new responsibilities in Hawaii.

To succeed Harrington as vice president for academic affairs, in June President Elvehjem and the regents had selected Robert L. Clodius, an agricultural economist who was scheduled to begin his new appointment September 1. The forty-one-year-old Clodius had been a popular member of the faculty since 1950, receiving the first Kiekhofer teaching award in 1953 and being elected to the prestigious University

---

[1]In 1960 Harrington was a disappointed finalist for the presidency of the University of Minnesota but afterward expressed appreciation for "the way in which people here have indicated that they want me to stay." Fred Harvey Harrington to J. Martin Klotsche, January 27, 1960, Series 5/1/3, Box 40, UA.

[2]Harrington had pioneered the study of American-Korean relations in his first book, *God, Mammon, and the Japanese: Dr. Horace N. Allen and Korean-American Relations, 1884-1905* (Madison: University of Wisconsin Press, 1944). In the summer of 1960 he had held a visiting appointment at the East-West Center of the University of Hawaii, where he met and developed a number of ongoing contacts with local university officials.

and Social Studies Divisional Executive Committees. He was currently chairing the Department of Agricultural Economics and serving as part-time associate dean of the Graduate School. Clodius' experience in campus-wide administration was relatively recent and limited, however, and few thought he was ready to take over the administrative leadership of the University. At a hastily called special meeting of the board following the Elvehjem funeral on July 31, the regents named Harrington, who had been summoned back from Japan, as acting president, and delegated authority to the board's Executive Committee to consider how to fill the vacant presidency.[3]

Even before the Elvehjem funeral and the regents meeting, there already was press speculation that Harrington might be offered the presidency.[4] In a four-hour closed meeting on the afternoon of July 31, the Executive Committee, its ranks augmented by most of the other regents, decided there was no need to conduct a regular presidential search if Harrington was willing to take the job and if the Hawaii Board of Regents could be persuaded to release him from his commitment. After consulting Harrington, just returned from Japan, and a telephone appeal to the Hawaii regents, the way was clear to move ahead with the appointment. Polling of the absent regents, the faculty's University Committee, and the leading deans that night and the next day revealed overwhelming support for the choice, which became general as the press reported the selection.[5] Regent Ellis Jensen of Janesville expressed gratification at the "unanimity" of campus support for Harrington, which had enabled the Executive Committee to "act with more dispatch than we had hoped for earlier." For his part, Harrington pledged to "carry on the traditions of this great institution and to help us move forward to a greater future," while, he added tactfully, continuing "the work of Conrad Elvehjem."[6] Regent President Jacob F. Friedrick

[3]UW BOR Minutes, July 31, 1962, UA.

[4]See *Capital Times*, July 28, 30, 1962; *Daily Cardinal*, July 31, 1962. The other Madison paper responded with an editorial declaring, "There is no need for haste, and every reason to avoid it." *Wisconsin State Journal*, July 31, 1962.

[5]*Capital Times*, August 1, 1962; *Milwaukee Sentinel*, August 1, 1962; *Milwaukee Journal*, August 1, 1962. In its annual report to the faculty, the University Committee noted that its members, including the two newly elected members for 1962-63, had discussed the selection of a successor to President Elvehjem with the regents. The board's choice, the committee reported, "coincided with the Committee's unanimous recommendation." UW Faculty Document 1565, "Annual Report of the University Committee," November 5, 1962, UA.

[6]UW BOR Executive Committee Minutes, August 1, 1962, UA.

likewise invoked the memory of the late president, describing Harrington's appointment as a mark of the regents' respect for Elvehjem, because the board had chosen "the man he designated as the person best qualified to administer the University in his absence."[7]

The full board made the appointment official on August 6, unanimously electing Harrington as the fourteenth president of the University of Wisconsin at an annual salary of $34,000, the same as he was scheduled to receive at Hawaii and identical to that of Elvehjem following a recent salary increase. In seconding the appointment, several of the regents commented on the board's good fortune at being able to respond so easily and quickly to the unexpected loss of President Elvehjem and with such impressive backing from the University community. Regents Gelatt and Werner stressed the board's satisfaction at again being able to fill the presidency from the ranks of the UW faculty, for the third time in a row. Board President Jacob Friedrick, a Milwaukee labor leader, noted that he represented a segment of the state's population that like himself had not had the benefit of a university education. "Nevertheless, I, and all of these people, have been served by this University in many ways" through its graduates: teachers, doctors, engineers, industrialists, even labor leaders. "All of us," he pointed out, "and, for that matter, those far beyond the boundaries of the state of Wisconsin, have the advantage of this University. I am quite sure that under the leadership of Dr. Harrington it will not only be continued, but extended."[8] A Milwaukee television station expressed the general sentiment when it exulted editorially that the board "couldn't have made a better choice in selecting a new president." Harrington, the station general manager explained, possessed "all the qualities of inspiring leadership needed to direct the growth of a great university." He was, moreover, known to be "a firm advocate of a rapid buildup" of the University of Wisconsin-Milwaukee.[9]

---

[7] UW News Service press release, August 1, 1962, Series 40/1/5/1, Box 5, UA.

[8] UW BOR Minutes, August 6, 1962; *Daily Cardinal*, July 31, August 2, 7, New Student Edition, 1962; "A Positive Force: The University's Fourteenth President, *WAM*, 64 (October, 1962), 13.

[9] WITI-TV (Channel 6) Editorial, broadcast twice on August 6, 1962, Series 4/18/1, Box 4, UA. Interestingly, the general manager of the station was Roger W. LeGrand, who had been appointed executive editor of the *Daily Cardinal* to pick up the pieces after the bitter 1938 strike. See E. David Cronon and John W. Jenkins, *The University of Wisconsin: A History*, vol. 3, *Politics, Depression, and War, 1925-1945* (Madison: University of Wisconsin Press, 1994), pp. 619, 634-40.

Tall and erect, self-assured, lean of frame and direct of speech, the new president was an impressive figure. At 6-feet, 4-inches in height, the 50-year-old Harrington dominated most gatherings not only with his imposing stature but also his quick grasp of issues and contagious assurance. One of his assistants, Donald Percy, later recalled that Harrington tended to monopolize staff meetings because he was "so smart and so bright":

> He was a very tall man and a singular presence, not only for his academic stature but his personal stature. He had this booming voice, and had this marvelous way of no matter where you were, he was talking down to you, even when you were seated opposite him. . . . Even when he was listening to you, he knew what you were going to say, and he already had figured out what the answer to the question was. . . . You always had the sense that he knew where he was going and he had a plan.

Percy noted, however, that Harrington's brilliant mind, encyclopedic knowledge, and especially his aloof reserve handicapped his interaction with some regents and legislators:

> Fred was not a person you ever got really close to personally. That was almost by design. . . . He was an awesome person in the legislature and made people–not by design, I don't think it was conscious–but you tended to feel small. And they were offended. He always had the answers; he was always on top, and he always knew best. A lot of people probably didn't trust him.[10]

One of Harrington's deans, who greatly admired his quick mind and encompassing academic vision, also noted this weakness:

> I saw his shortcomings in dealing with politicians. It was awfully hard for him not to be condescending and to talk down a little bit. It was very hard. Partly it was his stature, even, and his voice. It wasn't even his internal attitude. It was hard for him to not come off that way, when he's talking to a union leader from Kenosha who's five-foot-three, and he's trying to explain these words to [Assemblyman] Molinaro or somebody like that. It was sort of a comic scene, you know. He didn't have a common touch. Fred Harrington didn't know how to be the common man and turn a funny phrase, or whatever. He just couldn't do it.[11]

[10]Donald Percy, oral history interview, 1984, UA.
[11]Peter L. Eichman, oral history interview, 1988, UA.

President Harrington in his new Van Hise Hall office. UA, X25-3399.

The new president differed from his immediate predecessors, E.B. Fred and Conrad Elvehjem, in other respects as well. Perhaps most significant, he was not a scientist though he appreciated the traditionally important place of the natural sciences in the University. Any university president, Harrington declared pointedly after his appointment, "does not represent any single discipline. He represents them all."[12]

A nationally respected historian of American foreign relations, Harrington was not a Wisconsin native. Born in 1912 in Watertown, New York, he was educated at Cornell and New York University, where he earned a Ph.D. degree in history in 1937. That same year he accepted an instructorship at Wisconsin, where with the exception of a four-year interlude at the University of Arkansas between 1940 and 1944, he was to spend essentially the remainder of his life. Harrington returned from Arkansas in 1944 as an associate professor and was quickly promoted to full professor three years later. His sharp mind, unusually retentive memory, keen political sense, and remarkable organizational skills were not lost on his colleagues, who recommended him for the chairmanship of the history department between 1952 and 1955.[13] The following year, as we have seen, President Fred recruited him as a special assistant on matters involving the social science and humanities disciplines. It was this increasingly visible campus-level service that positioned and prepared him for the vice presidency and the presidency. As much as any UW president, Harrington accepted the challenges of high office eagerly, expectantly, and with supreme confidence.

"It Is Time to Be Bold"

The new president moved quickly to put his stamp on the University administration and to make clear he intended to provide dynamic leadership at all levels. Declining to accept the offered resignation of Robert Clodius, Elvehjem's choice for academic vice president, Harrington instead asked the regents to begin Clodius'

---

[12]UW BOR Minutes, August 6, 1962; *Daily Cardinal*, August 7, 1962.

[13]One of Harrington's great achievements in these years was to develop a remarkably effective placement service for the department's graduate students, especially those in American history. He spent most of his time at professional meetings nosing out the available jobs and deftly promoting the most attractive Wisconsin candidate for each position. He worked at all levels, moving established Wisconsin Ph.D.s into better, more senior positions and then acting quickly to place newly minted UW graduates into the vacancies he had helped to create. His success was awesome, so much so that the history profession came to refer to the Wisconsin placement activities as the Big Red Machine.

appointment immediately. He also recommended the promotion of Neil G. Cafferty from University business manager to vice president for business affairs, assuming some of A.W. Peterson's longstanding responsibilities for budget and fiscal matters.[14]

President Harrington used the first regular meeting of the Board of Regents following his appointment for an extended discussion of opportunities and goals. He pointed out that the biennial budget request previously prepared by the Elvehjem administration had emphasized the importance of the University's remaining a great institution and of keeping it strong. "Remaining" and "keeping" were defensive, static terms, he declared, hardly appropriate at a time when "we are in the greatest expansive period of American higher education." In view of the University of Wisconsin's tradition of innovative leadership–"one of the greatest in American higher education"–he said it was time to return to the commanding academic role Wisconsin had played in the nation during the early twentieth century. For the immediate future, Harrington emphasized, Wisconsin should aim to be "the leading University in the Midwest in every way"; the next challenge was to become "the greatest University in the country."

The new president recalled recent newspaper comment about the concentration of federal research grants on both coasts and the sharp decline of such spending in the middle west. While the University of Wisconsin had always promoted basic research, its tradition also included "the willingness to recognize that fundamental research has some application." Consequently, "Wisconsin could again be a leader in returning government research and defense contracts to the Midwest." What was required was not just money, but ideas, tradition, drive, and will. "We have that will," he promised, "and need to put it into a sustained drive for the next quarter of a century." These comments were not meant as criticism of his immediate predecessors,

---

[14]Peterson had over many years emerged as a powerful campus administrator in his current roles as trust officer and vice president for business and finance. The elevation of Cafferty, one of his staff, may simply have been a recognition of the growing complexity of University finances, or it may have been Harrington's not-so-subtle way of reducing the importance of Peterson, who had developed considerable independent influence with the Board of Regents. Peterson announced his impending retirement in September, 1965, and died the following month. Cafferty then replaced him as vice president for business and finance and trust officer and his former position was left vacant. In recognition of Peterson's long and distinguished service, in 1968 the Board of Regents named the new administration building after him. UW BOR Minutes, September 24, November 11, 1965, June 9, 1967, and June 14, 1968.

he hastened to add, for the University had made dramatic advances since World War II, especially in the life sciences. But with so many opportunities now open "it is time to be bold." In light of these challenges, he observed, "it must be agreed that the [Elvehjem] budget under consideration is an extremely modest budget."

In response to a regent query about a possible third four-year UW campus in southeastern Wisconsin, the president tactfully pointed out that the board had as yet taken no position on the matter. With this possibility in mind, however, and in association with the Coordinating Committee for Higher Education, he had asked Vice President Clodius to undertake a study of population trends, present educational services, and likely future needs of the region. There was little doubt what Harrington thought such a study would reveal, and if there should be a decision to establish a new four-year campus in the state, he intended the University to be ready to fill the need.

This initial board meeting was a veritable tour de force and at the same time a typical Harrington performance: well-prepared and organized remarks delivered extemporaneously, bold ideas with impressive command of detail, and overall, incisive upbeat leadership. The president's vision of a revitalized and dynamic University of Wisconsin was compelling. Indeed, he made it seem the institution was already fast on its way to new national leadership and greatness. It was, in short, a pep talk of a sort not heard by the regents in decades. The board responded by voting unanimously that the Elvehjem budget request "should be considered a rock bottom budget; and that the additional needs of the University, not provided in this budget, should be made evident to the Governor and the Legislature." No regent could have left this meeting unaware that a decisive new hand was at the helm.[15]

President Harrington spelled out his vision for a wider audience in an inaugural address on October 20. The occasion was a banquet at the Field House commemorating the centennial of the Morrill Land Grant Act. The hundreds of diners seated at tables crowded onto the basketball floor were served with impressive military precision by a staff of white-coated waiters from the Memorial Union. After dessert, Harrington recalled how at a dark time for the Union during the Civil War, Abraham Lincoln and the Congress had taken a long view of the nation's educational needs by adopting the Morrill Act, a far-sighted

---

[15]UW BOR Minutes, September 14, 1962.

plan to assist the states in developing a broadly based system of public higher education:

> Today, too, our nation is in danger. We face serious problems on the home front, and a permanent state of crisis in world affairs. But, taking our lead from Abraham Lincoln, we have every reason to think in long-range terms, to build for the long future, to think now of supporting the teaching and research that will help our State and nation in the long years before us.

The University of Wisconsin was only "a tiny and feeble institution" when Lincoln signed the Morrill Act in 1862, but it had since that time developed "into a very special place, one of the great universities of the modern world." This had been accomplished with broad-based support from the people of Wisconsin, federal grants, and private gifts. "In turn," the new president pointed out, "we–far more than other universities–have emphasized service to the State."

Harrington confidently predicted that in the future the University of Wisconsin would be a much bigger university, with overall enrollment growing from the present multi-campus total of 33,000 to more than 50,000 during the current decade and exceeding 100,000 by the turn of the century. Far from creating insoluble problems as many feared, this growth would result in a better institution, "better for instruction as well as for research and public service":

> We are not going to limit the growth of the University in Madison. We expect continuing growth and mounting distinction in Madison. But we also look for a great future for the University of Wisconsin-Milwaukee. The Center System, too, is expanding and improving rapidly, and is a vital element in our University structure. We expect further to have in the relatively near future a third four-year branch of the University in southeast Wisconsin. . . . There is no magic in numbers; but there is no poison either. . . . So we should and we will take the qualified young people gladly.

This bigger University of Wisconsin would "serve Wisconsin better than ever before." Continuing and expanding its century-old service to Wisconsin farmers, the University of the future would also turn its attention to the state's forests and recreation areas, the needs of commerce and industry, and the problems of the fast-growing cities. While UW faculty members would continue to engage in "basic, fundamental, theoretical research," their work would be "the basis for the practical applications of tomorrow," for "the theoretical scientist and scholar is the partner of the working engineer or administrator." In the years ahead Wisconsin industry, commerce, agriculture, and government would "depend more than ever before on the graduates of our University, and on the research done by our University staff."

The University was thus moving into an age of greater responsibility. "We will need support, a great deal of support," Harrington concluded, "but we are confident it will be forthcoming, and that we will be able to do our job in return."[16] Not since the visionary days of the great Van Hise had a UW leader offered such a broad and optimistic affirmation of the Wisconsin Idea of a service university. As the *Daily Cardinal* pointed out approvingly, here was "a new man with a new vision."[17]

Neither the man nor the vision was really new, of course, but both seemed ideally suited for the times. For one thing, Harrington recognized that demographics favored institutional growth. Over the next few years the post-war baby boom generation would reach college age, setting off an enrollment flood that would rival the GI inundation of the nation's colleges and universities after the Second World War. Higher education, especially the public institutions, would inevitably have to grow to meet the coming demand. Almost certainly there would be additional federal and state funding to provide new facilities, additional faculty, and perhaps even new institutions, to handle the boomer flood. Recent trends also suggested the likelihood of expanded federal and foundation support for applied research on social and health problems. The coming years thus offered the potential to be a golden age for those universities positioned to take advantage of it. Fred Harvey Harrington intended for the University of Wisconsin to be ready.

But there was more than simple opportunism behind the president's vision. Progressive in his political and social views, Harrington truly identified with the La Follette tradition in Wisconsin politics. Convinced the state had a special role to play in American higher education, he admired its citizens' longstanding commitment to education and their pride in the achievements and high quality of their University at Madison. Here, he recognized, the egalitarianism implicit in the Morrill Act's creation of a national system of low cost public uni-

---

[16]Fred Harvey Harrington, "The University and the State," *WAM*, 64 (November, 1962), 14-16.

[17]*Daily Cardinal*, October 20, 1962.

Harrington inaugural at Field House, October 20, 1962. UA, 5649-M.

Fred Harvey Harrington, Lee Iaccoca, Robert Clodius. UA, 6098-M.

versities had taken deep root. Frequently Harrington emphasized what a remarkable achievement it was for this state of only average size, population, and resources to have developed one of the major research universities of the world. Sharing the concern of most Wisconsin residents and political leaders, he was determined to keep higher education affordable and open to all academically qualified students, even if this involved expanding the University in Madison and creating other branch campuses. Above all, Harrington believed deeply in the Wisconsin Idea of a service university committed to helping the people of Wisconsin and their government solve problems of immediate and longer range concern. There was, he was convinced, no more promising place to apply his values to the task of academic leadership.

The new president moved quickly on several fronts to implement his ideas. For more than a decade he had worked to increase University support of the social sciences and humanities, partly through obtaining external foundation grants and partly through his lobbying of Presidents Fred and Elvehjem and the Board of Regents. He and other social scientists, notably UW sociologist William H. Sewell, had campaigned with some limited success to break the essential monopoly of the natural sciences over the growing research funds generated by the Wisconsin Alumni Research Foundation. Their efforts had prodded Presidents Fred and Elvehjem to overcome some of their considerable misgivings and expand the number of WARF grants supporting a limited range of faculty research projects in the social science and humanities disciplines. As president, Harrington quickly went further. At the first meeting of the WARF trustees following his appointment, he announced that henceforth the Graduate School would administer WARF funds on a merit basis across the entire University. Faculty members in all fields were now eligible to apply to the Graduate School Research Committee for WARF support and their proposals would be judged competitively on their merits. He noted that as in the past the committee's actions would be reported to the WARF trustees at the end of each year, but for their information and not their specific approval.[18]

Implicit in Harrington's vision of the future–and infusing most of his administrative actions in the years ahead–was his basic

[18]Fred Harvey Harrington, oral history interview, 1978, UA. Harrington recalled that the WARF trustees accepted this change without objection or comment, perhaps because they realized the awkward position Elvehjem had put them in by asking the WARF board to select the specific social science and humanities projects to be supported, but not grants in the natural sciences. See above, pp. 120.

assumption that the University of Wisconsin would continue to be a single, centrally managed institution with subordinate branch campuses and programs. This was not just Harrington's opinion, but a well-established UW faculty view that had been articulated most recently by the Ingraham Committee on University Functions and Policies in 1948 when it proposed combining all of Wisconsin public higher education.[19] In this view, as the University grew it might have an increasingly plural character, but it would not become a system of loosely related, more or less autonomous institutions. This single institution philosophy would prove more difficult to sustain as Harrington's "multiversity" developed over the decade, but it remained at the core of his administrative philosophy.[20]

In fact, the single institution policy was far easier to describe in the abstract than to apply to specifics. For example, the original University of Wisconsin in Madison[21] was recognized by the state and the federal governments as Wisconsin's land grant institution. It was consequently the regular recipient of substantial cooperative extension and other federal funding channeled to the federal land grant schools.

---

[19]Committee on University Functions and Policies, "First Report," October, 1948, pp. 65-73, UHP. The 1955 legislation establishing CCHE and UWM had implicitly adopted this view by stating that the new Milwaukee branch was to be an "integral" part of the University of Wisconsin.

[20]It should also be noted that Harrington was merely following the example of his predecessors, although to be sure they had headed a smaller and less complex institution than the one that emerged under his leadership in the 1960s. The Milwaukee Extension Center was established before World War I by the University Extension Division, as were the two-year centers elsewhere in the state beginning in the 1930s. Presidents Fred and Elvehjem took a very paternalistic view of the new UW-Milwaukee after 1955, exercising tight control over all aspects of its development as a branch of the University. Only gradually under President Harrington did UWM gain a measure of autonomy within the single institution framework, thus moving away from the unitary UW concept.

[21]The focus of this history, of course, is on the original University of Wisconsin and its various programs and activities on and off the Madison campus. This focus inevitably gets more diffuse as the University expanded its outreach and especially after it took on the responsibility for developing a branch university in Milwaukee, two new four-year collegiate institutions, and an array of two-year centers. Soon after its creation in 1955, the Milwaukee campus was referred to as the University of Wisconsin-Milwaukee, or UWM, but at first no such hyphenation or abbreviation was used for the Madison campus, which continued to be called the University of Wisconsin. President Harrington often used this term to embrace the entire UW system as well as the Madison campus alone. For clarity, this history will sometimes use the hyphenated name UW-Madison, although the term came into use only gradually after the adoption of the chancellor system in the mid-1960s and especially after the big merger of the 1970s.

As branch campuses developed, and especially after the creation of a separate extension unit in 1965, there was confusion and disagreement about whether UW-Madison or University Extension should hold the land grant designation and receive the federal funding related to it. The Madison campus also belonged to and in some cases was a founding member of such prestigious national academic organizations as the National Association of State Universities and Land Grant Colleges (NASULGC), the exclusive Association of American Universities (AAU), the Council of Graduate Schools, and the American Council on Education (ACE). Even after Harrington developed a separate Madison campus administration, he chose to continue the practice of his predecessors by representing UW-Madison at NASULGC, AAU, and other national meetings. He chaired the ACE Commission on Academic Affairs in 1962-65, after which he served on its board of directors. He held the NASULGC presidency in 1968-69, where he used his influence to install UW-Madison political scientist Ralph K. Huitt as the organization's executive director.[22]

There continued to exist a confusing overlap, if not in the president's mind, between his expanding central administration of a multi-campus system and the increasingly distinct UW-Madison leadership and administrative structure. The confusion extended to such small matters as who would host the monthly dinner for the regents whenever the board met in Madison. When the board held a meeting at one of the other campuses the local chancellor hosted such dinners; in Madison the president invariably took on this role, one that Harrington was reluctant to abandon or share. Similarly, he remained ambivalent about how much independence to allow the Madison and other chancellors in campus-oriented fund-raising or lobbying with the regents and state officials. Probably this ill-defined overlap of roles and authority was inevitable even with the best of intentions, but President Harrington's failure to address it made the Madison chancellor's position and authority ambiguous as the administrative structure was developing in the 1960s.

Early on Harrington showed his flexibility in modifying the single institution philosophy when it suited the circumstances. At a meeting of the regents in the fall of 1962 he raised the question of whether the Madison and Milwaukee campuses should be considered as one institution or separately when applying for external funds. He

---

[22]See "UW President Honored," *WAM*, 69 (December, 1967), 20.

pointed out that Congress in the National Defense Education Act had limited each institution to a maximum of $250,000 in student loan funds. Wisconsin would consequently gain more funding if Madison and Milwaukee each applied as separate institutions. On his recommendation the board approved a policy that the two universities could "be considered separate institutions for filing applications for federal and private foundation grants." Following this action the board minutes recorded an interesting exchange:

> Regent Werner inquired whether reference to the University did not usually mean the University at Madison. President Harrington replied that that was correct and, as an example, noted that the foundations usually send only one copy of material relating to the availability of grants, which copy is sent to the University at Madison. He stated that reference to the University means either the University at Madison or the entire University, including all its branches.

The minutes did not record whether this response clarified the terminology for Regent Werner and his board colleagues.[23]

Further evidence that the new president had big long-range plans came when the regents discussed the implications of a recent action by the Madison City Council annexing certain outlying University lands: University Bay creek and marsh, Picnic Point, University Houses and the Eagle Heights area, part of the Arboretum, and the Charmany and Rieder farms. Vice President Peterson explained that although the action came as a surprise and without notice, the University did not plan to protest because these were state-owned lands clearly under the control of the regents. He thought it was of no consequence in which municipality they were located. President Harrington interjected that the regents should understand the importance of the Charmany and Rieder farms, located south of Mineral Point Road adjacent to the Hill Farms residential development. "We must reach the conclusion that we are going to run out of space" on the central Madison campus, he warned, and these 200-300 acres "will be needed in the future for academic purposes." He suggested the regents might wish to ask the administration to consider the future possible use of these lands for instruction and research. The board promptly directed such a study.[24]

[23]UW BOR Minutes, November 9, 1962.
[24]UW BOR Minutes, October 5, 1962. Peterson's complacency about the Madison annexation proved unfounded when, again without notice, the city shortly

When late in 1962 the administration of out-going Democratic Governor Gaylord Nelson proposed holding down construction costs by limiting enrollment on the Madison campus, including a 20 percent ceiling on non-resident undergraduate enrollment, Harrington vigorously objected. He predicted, erroneously, that future enrollment growth would be slower at Madison than at UW-Milwaukee or the two-year University centers and in any event could be accommodated by developing academic facilities in the Charmany-Rieder farms area. Setting limits on University enrollment, he warned the regents, would simply result in shifting students to the rival State College system.[25]

In a subsequent discussion with the board, the president declared that he did not favor using the Charmany-Rieder area for a research park on the lines of the Science Park later developed there by the University in the 1980s. Applied research should be organized by interested corporations and not by the University, he argued. UW scientists could and should assist business in many ways–consulting, sharing facilities and equipment, training–but they must continue to concentrate on basic research and leave the applications to be developed by industry's own researchers.[26] The Harrington administration's thinking about the best use of the Charmany-Rieder farm acreage underwent a number of changes in the years ahead, but the president always kept open the option of developing additional academic facilities there.

Creating a Central Administration

Within the context of the single institution philosophy, Harrington steadily expanded the size and reach of what he called the Central Administration. As early as his second Board of Regents meeting he gave the regents a lengthy outline of his planned administrative expansion and reorganization. Among other things, the

---

afterward raised the tax assessments on the Charmany and Rieder farms and began taxing previously exempt University properties such as Picnic Point. Outraged, the regents launched a legal challenge and directed Harrington to seek relief from the state legislature. Ibid., February 8, 1963.

[25]UW BOR Minutes, December 7, 1962. Harrington succeeded in beating back this effort to establish enrollment limits, partly because the suggestion arose in the closing months of the Nelson administration. Nelson's successor, Democrat John W. Reynolds, was considerably more supportive of the University and of higher education in general.

[26]UW BOR Minutes, January 11, 1963.

president warned that a third four-year campus in southeastern Wisconsin would require its own provost and separate administration, as would the Madison campus in due course. Predicting the addition of as many as six more two-year University centers over the next few years, he suggested the centers probably should be separated from University Extension and placed under a separate administration. Though general in nature, his plans were sweeping and covered most of the administrative structure. The board was impressed: Regent Steiger applauded the proposed changes as long overdue and promised to back efforts to get the necessary funding; Regent DeBardeleben declared the president had presented "a very inspiring and important program."[27]

Harrington's administrative expansion involved both central and Madison campus administrative functions. As a separate Madison campus administration also developed, the distinction between the central and campus roles remained blurred. Departmental chairmen and individual faculty members sometimes sought funding or other support directly from the president or vice president rather than from their deans or other Madison campus administrators. If rebuffed at a lower level, they were often inclined to pursue their cause all the way to the top of the administrative ladder. In responding, Harrington and Vice President Clodius sometimes bypassed the campus administrative structure. Clodius had a special concern for Madison arts programs and on a number of occasions used his position to build up Madison's School of Music without prior discussion with campus administrators. Both Harrington and Clodius were interested in developing various Madison international programs. While this high level patronage was not unwelcome, UW-Madison administrators tried repeatedly but with only limited success to channel the central administration largesse to fit within their own priorities for the campus.[28]

Quiet, unassuming, and seemingly ego-free, Bob Clodius was not exactly the Harrington type, but the president got along well with his

---

[27]UW BOR Minutes, October 5, 1962.

[28]Not long after Chancellor Robben Fleming was appointed to head the Madison campus, one of his assistants called his attention to two unexpected allocations from Vice President Clodius for Madison campus activities: "You might want to mention to Bob," he suggested pointedly, "that we would like to have such requests referred to us before the allocation is made." What was even more annoying to Madison administrators was Harrington's and Clodius' tendency to make advance commitments against funds already earmarked for UW-Madison without consulting the campus administration. See Robert H. Atwell to Robben W. Fleming, August 27, 1965, Series 4/31/6-2, Boxes 1 and 2, UA.

inherited deputy and they complemented each other nicely. The vice president, in fact, was viewed by some as the only real link to the Elvehjem administration in the new Harrington structure. Unlike most of Harrington's immediate staff, moreover, Clodius had credible faculty and professional standing and good connections nationally with foundations and the federal government. As the president increasingly delegated responsibility for program and budget details to Clodius, the latter became his trusted colleague and alter ego, who had no personal ambition other than to help his chief build a great university system. Much of the success of the Harrington administration came through the quiet behind-the-scenes leadership and careful attention to detail provided by Vice President Clodius.

Ordinarily, Harrington sought more aggressive, confident, even brash younger associates who shared his expansive vision. Soon a number of hard-driving young presidential special assistants were scurrying around the campus and the state carrying out their leader's programs. One of these was Charles A. Engman, an engineer and administrator whom Harrington had met at the University of Hawaii and brought to Madison in 1963. Engman increasingly became the president's general troubleshooter and after 1965 held the position of vice president for administration. Another assistant was George Field, a hold-over Elvehjem assistant, whom Harrington assigned first as liaison with WARF and other foundations and after 1964 with state government. In 1967 Field was promoted to vice president for University development and state relations. One of the few admitted Republicans in the Harrington administration, Field was particularly useful as the primary UW lobbyist dealing with the GOP-controlled legislature throughout the decade and with the executive branch after Republican Warren Knowles was elected governor in 1964. Field's politics made him the target of good-natured kidding from his boss and other staff members, most of whom identified with the liberal wing of the state Democratic Party. Field became president of Wisconsin State University-River Falls in 1968, an indication of his successful legislative collaboration with Eugene McPhee, the director of the rival State University system, and his standing with the generally conservative WSU Board of Regents.

Harrington recruited Karl E. Krill from Ohio State University to coordinate UW responses to federal legislative and executive developments and funding opportunities. Subsequently he installed Krill as dean of the UW-Milwaukee Graduate School as it was evolving from direct Madison control in the mid-sixties. Two presidential assistants, Charles Vevier, a UW-Milwaukee faculty member, and Donald R. McNeil, had studied with Harrington while taking their Ph.D.'s in history at Madison in the 1950s. McNeil, previously the assistant director of the State Historical Society, was more recently a freelance writer with whom Harrington was working on a Carnegie Foundation study of adult education.[29] Charles J. Stathas, who had been recruited by A.W. Peterson in 1961 as the University's first full-time attorney handling primarily real estate transactions, became Harrington's legal advisor.[30] Another aide, Wallace L. Lemon, formerly director of the the Bureau of Management of the state Department of Administration, began working as a special assistant to Vice President Clodius in 1963. Within two years he was reporting directly to Harrington with initial responsibility for liaison with state programs and medical science developments and increasingly for coordinating University-wide facilities planning and construction. Clodius then recruited Donald E. Percy from the administrative staff of the UW-Madison College of Letters and Science to serve as his chief assistant. Percy subsequently began working for Harrington as well. By the early 1970s he had risen to be a senior vice president for budget and administration. Thus within a year of Harrington's assuming the presidency he was well-along in fleshing out an expanded and clearly designated Central Administration for the University.

Presidents Fred and Elvehjem had consulted extensively with a small cabinet of senior associates–the Administrative Committee–meeting frequently to consider any and all aspects of University activities. Harrington increased the size of his cabinet but cut back its meetings to one morning a week. He also gradually reserved a number of important decision/action areas for himself and his vice presidents

---

[29]Both Vevier and McNeil were ambitious and very much "on the make." Their style suited Harrington, who, as he once said, wanted staff members "with a great deal of push." Although McNeil had no previous academic administrative experience, he asked to be appointed a vice president. Harrington declined the request, but later commented quite accurately, "if a person was not on the make in those days, I tended to be rather suspicious of him." As he said in colloquial terms, Harrington sought to create an administration of "pushers," because he intended the University of Wisconsin to be very much "on the make." Harrington, oral history, 1985, UA.

[30]Harrington told Stathas early on that he realized he would be surrounded by people who would tell him only what they believed he wanted to hear, and he consequently counted on Stathas to advise him honestly concerning the letter and spirit of the law. "I may not always follow your advice," he promised, "but I'll never blame you if I get into trouble." Charles J. Stathas, conversation with E. David Cronon, 1998.

without reference to the larger administrative group. When McNeil warned in 1964 that the cabinet was "restless" under this more Spartan diet, the president responded: "I don't doubt that some of the troops are restless about the Cabinet meetings. But not all–by no means all–and the Cabinet is evolving in a direction that suits me." He promised further changes in the future, but observed shrewdly, "Changing a good many things at once maximizes opposition."[31]

Besides creating a new central administrative structure, Harrington also began reshaping the Madison campus administration. In the spring of 1963 he replaced Elvehjem's graduate dean, chemist John Willard, with the younger and more energetic Robert A. Alberty, also a chemist, who the president believed would be more aggressive in building federal research support.[32] Another Fred-Elvehjem holdover soon shunted aside was William H. Young, the canny political scientist who had served for nearly a decade as the University's budget director and occasional lobbyist with state government and the regents. Unlike Dean Willard, Young was replaced less precipitously but also less generously. The president gradually let Young know that he and Clodius intended to take care of the budget preparation and that they and George Field would handle the University's dealings with the governor's office

---

[31]Donald R. McNeil to Harrington, March 5, 1964; Harrington to McNeil, March 17, 1964, Series 4/18/1, Box 49, UA. President Harrington concluded his unusually long and frank response with a revealing postscript: "This is the kind of letter T.R. used to write to explain his actions. I have written almost none of these during my presidency, and perhaps I should not have written this one. But I'm glad I did."

[32]UW BOR Minutes, April 5, 1963; "Dean Willard to Return to Teaching," and "Dr. Alberty Named Graduate School Dean," *WAM*, 64 (May, June, 1963), 11, and 7; *Daily Cardinal*, May 11, 1963. Alberty's appointment continued the tradition of having a natural scientist as graduate dean. The mild-mannered 55-year-old Willard was a distinguished physical chemist who had leaned heavily on Elvehjem in administering the Graduate School. Alberty, only 41, had already demonstrated his administrative ambition and abilities as associate dean of the College of Letters and Science. Harrington smoothly handled the change by promoting Willard to one of the new prestigious Vilas research professorships, whose research responsibilities precluded any major administrative assignment. Alberty resigned in late 1966 to become dean of science at the Massachusetts Institute of Technology and was replaced as graduate dean by Robert M. Bock, a professor of biochemistry and prominent member of the University Research Committee. Under the evolving UW-Madison administrative structure both Chancellor Fleming and President Harrington were involved in Bock's selection. UW BOR Minutes, November 4, 1966, and January 13, 1967; *Daily Cardinal*, November 9, 1966; "Graduate School Dean Leaves for MIT Post," *WAM*, 68 (December, 1966), 18-19; "Graduate School Dean," ibid. (February, 1967), 15-16.

and the legislature.[33] Harrington also deftly promoted the genial Madison Dean of Students, LeRoy Luberg, to be dean for public services, a fancy title for a position as presidential assistant for general public relations and outreach services.[34] This enabled the president to move Martha Peterson, the able Madison Dean of Women, to the new central administration post of dean of student affairs for all UW campuses.[35] The president increasingly drew on the director of the University News Service, Robert Taylor, to advise on public relations matters and prepare press releases for the Central Administration. Taylor's effective shift to the Central Administration was made clear when Harrington promoted him to be vice president for public information in 1968.[36] To make sure Wisconsin shared in the burgeoning federal funding, the president assigned political science Professor Ralph Huitt to establish a University office in Washington through which he and Karl Krill could maintain close and regular contact with various government and private higher education offices.[37]

In the fall of 1963 President Harrington advised the Madison faculty that the growing administrative structure required the creation of a Madison provost position, distinct from the Central Administration, to handle the day-to-day administration of the campus. The post would be analogous to that of Provost J. Martin Klotsche as the leader of the University of Wisconsin-Milwaukee. Its purpose was to free Harrington and Clodius to concentrate on the larger multi-campus issues of the growing UW system.[38] Harrington and the regents designated Clodius as acting Madison provost while they considered candidates to fill the new position.[39] Their choice, described by the president as "the key

---

[33]William H. Young, oral history interview with E. David Cronon, August 28, 1996, UHP. In an informative letter to Madison Chancellor Robben Fleming discussing his administrative team, Harrington explained that Young no longer worked on the budget ("now shifted to Clodius") but still handled patents and patent policy for the central administration. Harrington to Fleming, March 30, 1965, Series 4/18/1, Box 82, UA.

[34]"LeRoy Luberg Named Dean for Public Services," *WAM*, 65 (November, 1963), 8.

[35]"The Change in Student Affairs," *WAM*, 65 (February, 1964), 8-11.

[36]UW BOR Minutes, October 4, 1968.

[37]*Daily Cardinal*, May 9, 1963.

[38]Klotsche, a UW history Ph.D., had headed the old Milwaukee State Teachers College when it was merged with the UW Milwaukee Extension Center and assigned to the UW Board of Regents as the University of Wisconsin-Milwaukee in 1955. He continued to head the new institution as its provost after the merger.

[39]UW Faculty Minutes, October 7, 1963, UA; *Daily Cardinal*, October 8,

appointment" in his administrative reorganization, was Robben W. Fleming, a University of Illinois law professor and specialist in labor relations. No stranger to Wisconsin, Fleming was a graduate of Beloit College and the UW Law School and had previously directed the UW Industrial Relations Center.[40]

With Fleming's appointment, Clodius was promoted from academic vice president to the unmodified title of vice president, and given responsibility for the budget and completion of the overall administrative reorganization. Harrington announced that he and Clodius would now be able to spend more time on the development of the Milwaukee branch of the University, where he had set up an office and apartment for their use when in Milwaukee.[41] The creation of the Madison provost position awakened student leaders to the possible dangers inherent in the new, more complex administrative structure. "The effect will be a 'leveling' of the Madison campus as a branch of the University," predicted the *Daily Cardinal* ominously:

> The University now faces two alternatives. We can follow the path to a centralized university, with our own campus declining in importance, and, we fear, in academic standards. Or, we can separate the [two] state universities, return each to individual autonomy, and provide universal higher education without a sacrifice to academic excellence.[42]

Evidently an option neither the *Cardinal* nor President Harrington considered was some sort of broad state-wide reorganization of Wisconsin higher education along the lines proposed by the Ingraham Committee a decade-and-a-half earlier.[43]

1963. Mindful of faculty sensibilities about such a major administrative change, Harrington was careful to touch bases with the major faculty governance organs on the Madison campus. He consulted the University Committee about the makeup of a search committee (two University Committee members, one from each of the four Divisional Executive Committees, and two academic deans). In the end he and Clodius made the selection from among the list of candidates provided by the committee.

[40]UW BOR Minutes, January 10, 1964; "Robben Fleming Named Provost at Madison," *WAM*, 65 (February, 1964), 5; *Daily Cardinal*, February 11 and September registration issue, 1964.

[41]"Clodius Named Vice President," *WAM*, 65 (June, 1964), 7; *Daily Cardinal*, January 15, May 9, 1964.

[42]*Daily Cardinal*, March 12, 1963. The reference is clearly to the Madison and Milwaukee branches of the University, since the Wisconsin State Colleges had not yet begun calling themselves universities.

[43]See pp. 80, 523-24, 596.

Provost Fleming arrived to take up his new post for the fall of 1964. A few months later Harrington persuaded the regents to revive the title of chancellor for Fleming and Klotsche, used for the first two heads of the University a century earlier.[44] Once in office, Fleming quickly recruited two young vice chancellors: James W. Cleary, a UW-Madison speech professor, for academic affairs, and Robert H. Atwell, a Washington, D.C., budget analyst and program planner, for financial and administrative matters. Another key Fleming appointment, especially as student protests developed, was that of Joseph F. Kauffman, formerly the director of training for the Peace Corps in Washington, as dean of students. The Fleming administration was relatively short-lived, notable primarily for beginning the development of a separate UW-Madison administration and for its gingerly handling of the first serious student demonstrations against U.S. involvement in the war in Vietnam.[45] Chancellor Fleming left in the summer of 1967 to become president of the University of Michigan. Kauffman, used up by his handling of student protests, departed the following year to become president of Rhode Island College. Cleary accepted the presidency of San Fernando Valley State College in 1969 and Atwell left the next year to become president of Pitzer College, both in California.[46]

Accustomed to thinking of their campus as *the* University of Wisconsin, the Madison faculty was increasingly uneasy over Harrington's administrative reorganization and especially the implication that the Madison faculty now represented but one branch of an expanding multi-campus institution. In Milwaukee the faculty was also beginning to chafe over its junior partner status vis-à-vis Madison. Accordingly, in the spring of 1963 the Madison faculty, in collaboration with its Milwaukee colleagues, recommended the effective separation of the two faculties administratively and the virtual autonomy of each in dealing with its own campus affairs. The two bodies continued to maintain some liaison and joint committees, but UWM was increasingly viewed as a separate and distinct unit.[47] For several years thereafter

---

[44]UW BOR Minutes, January 8, 1965; "Title of Chancellor Returns after 100 Years," *WAM*, 66 (February, 1965), 6.

[45]See below, pp. 455-621.

[46]"Chancellor Fleming Named U of Michigan President," *WAM*, 68 (April, 1967), 4; "Dean Kauffman Named President of Rhode Island College," *WAM*, 69 (February, 1968), 19; *Daily Cardinal*, February 6, 1968, March 7, 1969, June 19, 1970.

[47]UW Faculty Document 1586, April 1, 1963; UW Faculty Minutes, May 6, 1963; UW Faculty Document 1612, "Annual Report of the University Committee," November 4, 1963; UW BOR Minutes, May 10, 1963. Since 1942 the members of the

Madison political science Professor David Fellman, a constitutional law expert, chaired an ad hoc codification committee to redraft the University's Laws and Regulations to spell out the faculty's role in the evolving multi-campus UW system. A measure or at least a symbol of campus autonomy became even clearer in early 1965 when President Harrington announced that Fleming and Klotsche rather than he would henceforth preside over the meetings of their respective faculties.[48]

Modeled closely after the Madison faculty governance structure, by the mid-sixties the UWM faculty largely operated separately or as part of two new system-wide representative bodies, the University Faculty Assembly and the University Faculty Council. Based on proportional representation of the faculty of the several campuses and two-year centers, the assembly was chaired by President Harrington or Vice President Clodius and was designed as a legislative body for the entire faculty of the expanding UW system. It proved to be ineffective because there were few system-wide faculty governance issues requiring regular legislative attention. The Council, on the other hand, was modeled after the influential campus University Committees and thus had greater authority and influence as a smaller executive committee of the total UW faculty.[49]

---

four broad divisions of the Madison faculty—humanities, social studies, biological sciences, and physical sciences—had elected twelve-member Divisional Executive Committees to handle division business. Chief among their responsibilities was academic quality control by providing advice to the academic deans on the qualifications of faculty candidates for tenure as well as departmental proposals for new or modified courses or other curricular issues. The latter responsibility also sought to prevent unnecessary course duplication. After the University took over responsibility for the development of UW-Milwaukee in 1955, UWM gained elected representation on the Madison divisional committees, and the latter expanded their purview to include Milwaukee tenure cases and curricular proposals. While the 1963 faculty action created UWM divisional committees to provide advice on curricular matters, it also retained what were described as "All-University Divisional Committees," with Milwaukee membership, to review tenure recommendations. The legislation stipulated, however, that UWM members of these all-University committees "shall not participate in actions involving [Madison's] curriculum." In other words, Milwaukee was free to develop its own curriculum but needed a Madison faculty endorsement for its tenure cases. This awkward and implicitly insulting provision was soon abandoned, and apart from a few continuing joint committees the UWM faculty governance structure operated separately from Madison's.

[48]UW Faculty Minutes, January 4, 1965; *Daily Cardinal*, April 7, 1964.

[49]For example, the University Faculty Council held hearings and recommended the disciplinary action taken by the Board of Regents against four UWM faculty members charged with serious campus disruption during anti-war protests in May, 1970.

Regardless of the new system-wide faculty governance structure, Harrington, Clodius, and other central administrators continued to take a direct role in the affairs of individual campuses on occasion, notably in encouraging new instructional and research programs and facilities at Madison and Milwaukee. Their detailed oversight of established academic activities on the two campuses was increasingly pro forma, however. Clodius was not replaced in his original position as vice president for academic affairs, and his broader administrative responsibilities limited his close attention to academic matters on the several campuses. Correspondingly, this tended to strengthen the authority of Fleming and Cleary in Madison and their counterparts elsewhere in the system.

Of the two Madison vice chancellors, Cleary's responsibilities were more clearly defined, because the campus had a well-established tradition and structure for faculty and academic governance. Its various instructional programs, departments, schools, and colleges had long enjoyed considerable autonomy in handling their academic affairs. In contrast, Vice Chancellor Atwell's two major concerns, budget and administration of the Madison campus, lacked the established structure and focus of Vice Chancellor Cleary's academic responsibilities. The Central Administration was located on the Madison campus, at first mostly in Bascom Hall, later in the Peterson Administration Building, and by the latter 1960s partly in the towering new campus skyscraper, Van Hise Hall. Harrington's and Clodius' subordinates were accustomed to handling the business and administrative affairs of the Madison campus as well as those of the expanding UW system. Although distance obliged Vice President Cafferty to allow UW-Milwaukee to develop its own business office, he saw no need for a separate business office in Madison under the control of Fleming and Atwell. He regularly assured the two UW-Madison administrators that his staff could provide them with whatever data and fiscal information they needed. Even more than the president, Cafferty's views and behavior were solidly rooted in the single university concept guiding the Harrington administration as it developed a multi-campus system.

There was considerably more than abstract terminology behind this view. The Madison campus was both the oldest and by far the largest and most developed unit of President Harrington's expanding multiversity, and to the dismay of the president and the regents, students continued to prefer the Madison branch of Harrington's "single" University. With the arrival of the baby boom generation in the early

1960s, the growing Madison enrollment generated millions of dollars of additional tuition and enrollment funding. At the same time, Madison faculty members were attracting nearly all of the millions of dollars of external research and program funds flowing into Wisconsin. These came mostly from the federal government, which permitted generous overhead charges as high as 42 percent of the grant to cover underlying University expenses associated with the activity. Harrington and his immediate associates regarded the overhead funds as general University income to be dispensed entirely at their discretion.[50] Several years after leaving office President Harrington defended his tight control of the overhead funds:

> Well, it was totally University money–that is, the question of who controls the overhead is a question of whether it is in the president's office, or is it controlled by the campuses? Certainly it is my view that the president of the University and the Central Administration should have the say with reference to where one puts this. Obviously, a good deal of it goes back to the campuses that develop it, but it is a clear point, entirely obvious, that the problem of developing overhead, and the reason why overhead is given, is because of the administration of the University. That is, the business office has much more expenditure with reference to overhead than anybody else, and obviously the business office wants to control it.[51]

The question wasn't "entirely obvious" to UW-Madison faculty and administrators concerned about who decided where and for what purpose the millions of dollars of overhead funds being generated by Madison research and program grants should be spent. Suspicious Madison researchers, anxious to maximize the value of their grants, were apt to agree with Dr. Peter L. Eichman, dean of the Medical School between 1965 and 1970, that the overhead funds amounted to a giant "slush fund" for the president and chancellor. "It was outrageous," he declared in an oral history interview years later. "They were taking

---

[50] In 1965 Vice President Clodius responded to a questionnaire from the University of Minnesota asking how the University handled indirect cost (overhead) revenues, especially whether it had a formula for returning any portion of the overhead to the departments generating the grants or to units like the library and physical plant that were factored into the overhead rate. Clodius reported simply: "All indirect cost reimbursements on contracts and grants are budgeted as general income." Questionnaire response, Series 40/1/2-1, Box 3, UA.

[51] Harrington, oral history interview, 1985, UA.

$7 million a year out of this Medical School and probably not returning a million of it."[52]

Faced with meeting the substantial costs needed to develop UW-Milwaukee, additional two-year University centers, and after 1965 two new four-year campuses in the Fox Valley and southeastern Wisconsin, it is not surprising that Harrington, Clodius, and Cafferty viewed this substantial UW-Madison revenue stream as part of a single institutional budget embodying interchangeable resources. As the UW system grew, Madison administrators like Fleming and Atwell learned to be vigilant in trying to assure that their campus received an appropriate share of the sizable revenues it was producing.

The overhead funds were especially useful because they were non-lapsing and until near the end of Harrington's presidency largely escaped detailed state scrutiny. In Harrington's first year as president Madison overhead income amounted to more than $2 million; in 1965-66 the total reached $4.5 million, and by 1970 it exceeded $7 million.[53] Some of the overhead and other Madison revenues were budgeted in the President's Special Capital Fund and the President's Unassigned Fund to be used as Harrington directed, often at other campuses. In short, Harrington tended to view UW-Madison as a cash cow that could be milked for the general development of his expanding UW system. He once remarked to a concerned Atwell that the Madison campus was "rich" and could "lose $50,000 walking between buildings" without missing it.[54]

---

[52]Eichman, oral history interview.

[53]UW Financial Statement of Operation Appropriations, 1962-63 and 1965-66; UW Monthly Financial Management Report, 1969-70, both at UW System Office of Financial Management.

[54]Robert H. Atwell to Robben Fleming, August 23, 1966, Series 4/31/6-2, Box 2, UA. The occasion was Harrington's decision to purchase the site and equipment of the Midwest University Research Association near Stoughton after MURA lost out to Illinois and failed to win the federal contract to develop a new accelerator in the middle west. The complex became the present Physical Sciences Laboratory. Atwell was concerned lest UW-Madison have to absorb either the purchase or the future operating costs without having the opportunity to prioritize the project with other campus needs. He told Fleming: "I am less than completely happy with this arrangement. I suspect in one way or another we are going to have to fund some portion of the MURA costs in lieu of doing something else and we have had little opportunity to assess the priority of the MURA activity in relation to other alternatives. At this point, I think there is very little we can do but accept the course of action laid down by the President, but I thought you should know the latest developments and my reaction to them."

There was also income from certain discretionary University endowment and trust funds, unexpended tuition balances, and salary savings resulting from staff turnover. The income from various University endowment and trust funds was smaller than the overhead but it too came almost entirely from Madison campus sources. The largest of the trust funds was derived from the bequest of Kemper K. Knapp, who had bequeathed his estate to the University in 1944. By the time Harrington became president the Knapp Fund amounted to $4.3 million and was generating well over $200,000 in income each year. As an assistant to President Fred in 1956, Harrington had helped arrange Knapp funds for a lectures program at UW-Milwaukee; this support subsequently grew to include scholarships and regular visiting professorships. As vice president, Harrington established the practice of serving ex officio on the faculty committee making Knapp grants, a role continued by Vice President Clodius. Harrington also persuaded President Elvehjem to rule that UW-Milwaukee should have access to all University trust funds, though he cautioned UWM Provost Klotsche not to expect much initially until his institution was stronger academically.[55] As president, Harrington's single university policy validated Milwaukee's claim for regular support from Knapp and other Madison funds. UWM faculty members customarily served on the committee making Knapp grants and twice during the latter 1960s chaired it. By 1966 the Knapp Committee had established the practice of awarding a visiting professorship each year to the two Colleges of Letters and Science in Madison and Milwaukee and otherwise accepting UWM's equal access to Knapp support.[56]

---

[55]Harrington almost certainly was behind President Fred's decision in 1957 to create a high-level administrative committee chaired by L&S Dean Mark Ingraham and including UWM Provost Klotsche to review the possible use of University trust funds at Milwaukee. The committee recommended that general scholarship and fellowship funds should be used to support students on both the Madison and Milwaukee campuses and that other UW trust funds could also be used by either campus "except where they are explicitly given for work at one campus or the other or where by implication are more appropriately used on one campus than the other." Minutes of the Committee to Study the Use of University Trust Funds for Activities at the University of Wisconsin-Milwaukee, August 6, 1957, UHP. See also Harrington to Klotsche, October 17, 1961, Series 5/1/3, box 62, UA. This letter clearly illustrates how Harrington lobbied President Elvehjem and otherwise worked to expand UW-Milwaukee access to the Brittingham and Vilas funds controlled by outside trustees, including an effort to get Klotsche appointed to the University's Vilas Committee.

[56]Knapp Fund Committee minutes and annual reports, 1956-70, Series 5/1/3, Boxes 2, 10, Series 5/1/4, box 5, Series 40/1/2-1, Boxes 12, 37, 62, UA.

Similarly, the faculty committee administering the smaller Anonymous Trust Fund began making grants as early as 1958 to support UW-Milwaukee humanities and arts activities. The fund was based on the income from an anonymous gift of stock in 1944 intended to enhance the artistic and cultural life of the University. By the latter 1960s the Anonymous Fund Committee, traditionally chaired by the Madison L&S dean, was annually granting UW-Milwaukee $7,500, or a little more than a third of its budget. In 1964-65, in fact, the committee gave Milwaukee $7,000, while budgeting only $3,000 for Madison projects so it could build a contingency reserve for expenses associated with the future opening of the Elvehjem Art Center in Madison. In making this initial block grant the committee suggested that UWM should establish its own Anonymous Fund Committee to decide how to allocate these funds. UWM Vice Provost Vevier initially seemed to believe Milwaukee would henceforth have its own portion of the underlying trust fund, but the parent Madison committee retained control and merely made annual grants to its Milwaukee counterpart.[57] Harrington and Clodius regarded the Anonymous Fund as a general University resource, appointing the parent Madison committee and formally approving its grants.[58] They ignored the plain fact that the Knapp, Anonymous, and most other UW trust funds antedated the existence of UW-Milwaukee and other UW branch campuses and presumably were intended by their donors to benefit the Madison campus. Instead, the two top administrators' actions were predicated on the assumption that any funds given to the University of Wisconsin, broadly defined, might be used at any branch of the emerging UW system.[59]

---

[57]See Charles Vevier to members of the UWM Anonymous Funds Committee, June 4, 1964, Series 5/1/4, Box 31, UA. The Anonymous Fund was based on stock in the Simpson Timber Company, a closely held west coast lumbering firm. Because the Board of Regents believed the stock was significantly undervalued in view of the company's large holdings of old growth redwood forests, the University decided to retain the stock even though it produced only modest income. Eventually in the late 1970s the company bought out the University's stock for more than $3 million, in the process instantly turning the Anonymous Fund into one of the largest UW trust funds.

[58]This paragraph is based on Anonymous Fund Committee budgets and correspondence, Series 4/16/1, Box 323; Series 4/17/1, Box 52; Series 4/18/1, Box 41; Series 5/1/4, Box 31; Series 40/1/2-1, Box 106, UA.

[59]After Harrington resigned the UW presidency in 1970 he spent several years in India as a special representative of the Ford Foundation. On a trip back to Madison he asked one of the authors, E. David Cronon, then a member of the Madison University Committee, to brief him on campus developments in his absence. The state had recently

Three more specialized endowment funds were controlled by outside trustees who made grants for University purposes as recommended by the UW president. Here, too, Harrington considered all three open for use anywhere in the developing UW system. One was the Brittingham Family Trust, created in 1925 by the will of a wealthy Wisconsin lumberman and former regent and administered by members of the Brittingham family for open-ended support of University activities. Another was the Wisconsin Alumni Research Foundation, also created in 1925, which supported faculty research through the marketing of patents on University research and investment of the resulting income by an outside board of UW alumni trustees. Harrington saw the substantial WARF endowment as critically important for the development of UW-Milwaukee as a graduate and research university. At first the UW-Madison Research Committee reviewed requests submitted by faculty from UWM and the UW centers for WARF research grants, but by the latter 1960s Milwaukee had its own research committee and a separate WARF block grant.[60] A third, and rather different, outside source was the Vilas Trust Fund, created in 1908 but available to the University only in 1962 at the start of Harrington's presidency. The Vilas funds were controlled by outside trustees and could be spent only for certain specified purposes. These included

---

decided to merge UW and the State Univesity systems (see Chapter 9) and the issue now was how the merger would take place. Cronon explained that UW-Madison leaders were scrambling to regain control over Madison endowments, bequests, and other financial assets and fighting to establish the principle that funds generated by or intended for a particular campus in the merged system must be used for that campus only. Harrington expressed strong disagreement, arguing that this was "selfish." He rejected Cronon's counter-argument that Wisconsin did not have sufficient resources to fund a system of fourteen UW-Madisons and that the real challenge of the future would be to keep the state's major university strong for the leadership and associated benefits it could bring to the new system. An egalitarian policy would inevitably mean averaging UW-Madison down in breadth and quality if funding became tighter. Harrington's objections showed he was still committed to an expansive vision more appropriate for the early 1960s than for the realities of a decade later.

[60]Clay Schoenfeld, "The W.A.R.F. Story; The Wisconsin Alumni Research Foundation: Sixty Years of Research and Realization–1925-1985" (Madison: unpublished manuscript, 1986), pp. 87-88, Appendix D. The WARF trustees were uneasy over the diversion of WARF funds to UW-Milwaukee, believing the return on their investment would be much better in Madison. They readily agreed to phase out their UWM block grant beginning in 1974 after the Merger Implementation Act stipulated that gift and grant funds originating by or intended for a particular university of the new University of Wisconsin System should be reserved exclusively for use at that campus.

undergraduate scholarships and graduate fellowships and, most importantly, an unspecified number of Vilas research professorships designed by Colonel Vilas to equal the most prestigious chairs at any American university. In keeping with his single university philosophy and to speed UW-Milwaukee's development as a major research university, Harrington moved quickly to assign Vilas support to UWM.[61]

Political and Institutional Rivalry

Even as he was building a new administrative team, President Harrington was rethinking the overall structure of higher education in Wisconsin. A key element, of course, was the relationship between the evolving multi-campus University of Wisconsin and the system of nine former State Teachers Colleges, renamed Wisconsin State Colleges in 1951 and Wisconsin State Universities in 1964. Harrington could claim some responsibility for the decision to designate the state colleges as universities. At a meeting with WSC leaders called to improve relations between the two systems, the UW president asked what his counterparts most wanted for their institutions. They replied that some day they wanted their colleges to be called universities. Always less concerned with symbols than substance, Harrington airily replied that he personally had no objection to this. "We had been using up our fight in order to get the new campuses [Parkside and Green Bay]," he later explained.

> Besides that, it didn't seem to me to be all that important. ...I knew it was going to happen, and we were trying to be friendly and all that. . . . So that what I did there was to give them the green light, and I don't think they would have moved to use the term 'Wisconsin State University' if we had said we were bitterly opposed to that. I don't think they would have moved at that time.[62]

[61]Peterson, Memorandum of a Conference Attended by the Trustees of the William F. Vilas Trust and Members of the University of Wisconsin Vilas Committee, March 11, 1963, Series 40/1/2-1, Box 22; Clodius to University Vilas Committee, April 18, 1969, Series 4/21/1, Box 5; Ihab Hassan to Harrington, October 25, 1969, Series 40/1/1/1, Box 230; UW BOR Minutes, March 6, 1970, UA. See also pp. 252-53.

[62]Harrington, oral history interview, 1985. When the the WSC regents voted to change the name of their institutions to the Wisconsin State Universities in 1964, McPhee conceded that the title was intended to "raise WSC prestige and improve the system's competitive position vis-a-vis the University." Passively, the state Coordinating

Both systems had been created by separate state legislation over time and each was governed by its own board of regents. Harrington's approximate counterpart was Eugene R. McPhee, the long-time WSC/WSU executive director. Formerly a professor of education in charge of teacher training at Eau Claire State Teachers College, McPhee was named to the new position of Director of the State Teachers Colleges in 1949 by the then-named Board of Regents of Normal Schools. The post was defined as the chief administrative officer and educational advisor of the board with responsibility for coordinating "the needs of the colleges in dealing with State and Federal Agencies and with other institutions and facilities."[63] Although each of the State Colleges/Universities was headed by a president, these officials were by no means autonomous. McPhee, based in Madison and backed by an authoritarian board, exercised tight control over the system. While he lacked the academic stature and visibility of the UW president, he was a skillful and formidable politician, determined that his institutions would share in the development of higher education in the state.[64]

While the State Colleges/Universities continued to emphasize their traditional teacher training, by the early 1960s they were also moving into liberal arts and specialized professional education and were beginning to offer limited graduate studies at the master's degree level.

Committee for Higher Education concluded that the issue of institutional names was outside of its jurisdiction. CCHE Minutes, April 24 and June 12, 1964, Government Publications, SHSW; Gale Loudon Kelly, "The Politics of Higher Educational Coordination in Wisconsin, 1956-1969" (Ph.D. dissertation, University of Wisconsin-Madison, 1972), pp. 193-94. As Harrington recalled in his later oral history, neither he nor the UW regents chose to contest the name change, very likely recognizing the importance of not undermining the autonomy of the WSU Board of Regents.

[63]State Normal Schools, BOR Minutes, July 22, 1948, and July 6, 1949, Government Publications, SHSW.

[64]Donald Percy remembered the frustration of UW representatives because McPhee regularly managed to get them scheduled ahead of the state college system in budget hearings before the governor and the legislature's Joint Finance Committee. The University people invariably had to fight hard over several days and make painful trade-offs to salvage the most important parts of their budget request, especially the salary raise funds. McPhee would come in their wake and say humbly, "I'll take what they got," and thereby appear to be the soul of reason and restraint. Years later Percy declared, "it was just amazing." Percy, oral history interview. University lobbyists always requested a certain percentage increase for salaries, whereas McPhee shrewdly asked for the same dollar allotment as the University received. Since faculty salaries were lower in his system, this meant his staff got higher percentage increases than their UW counterparts. Harrington, oral history interview, 1985.

Though self-declared, their claim to university status was thus not mere academic puffery. Their enrollments were rising rapidly, moreover, and as a group by the mid-1950s they were attracting more undergraduates than the Madison campus and were growing at a faster rate. In 1965 the aggregate WSU undergraduate enrollment surpassed that of the UW combined campuses. Four years later the WSU system ranked fifth in the country in total enrollment, compared to eighth for the UW system.[65] Spread widely around the state, they constituted a broad political base that McPhee knew how to utilize effectively. President Harrington had good reason to be concerned about the rapid growth and political influence of this rival educational system.

The University likewise possessed significant political assets of its own. For many years UW spokesmen had boasted with a good deal of truth that the University's boundaries embraced the entire state. This was certainly true of extension programs, which for many years had brought a variety of credit and non-credit instruction to all corners of Wisconsin. Extension's AM-FM radio stations covered the state and its expanding television network reached the more populated urban centers. The two major UW campuses in Madison and Milwaukee were located in the state's largest and politically most influential cities. By 1962, moreover, the two-year centers, still expanding, had further extended the University's educational and political reach to eight smaller cities. UW alumni held influential posts in the legislature and were spread throughout the state where they could be mobilized by the Wisconsin Alumni Association to bring political pressure to bear. Like McPhee's multi-campus system, in short, Harrington's University was also in a position to generate significant political support.

As we have seen, the state government in 1955 created the Coordinating Committee for Higher Education (CCHE) to assure more effective overall management of Wisconsin higher education. Wary of another layer of state control, the two boards of regents had worked together to assure that their representatives would staff and largely control the new Coordinating Committee. Their only area of agreement

---

[65]"Proposal for the Distribution and Establishment of Two-Year University Centers and State College Branch Campuses," CCHE Working Paper #44, October, 1963; CCHE Working Paper #40, "A Ten Year Enrollment History in Wisconsin Public and Private Colleges," October, 1963; CCHE Working Paper #5, "Enrollment Projections 1964-1973: Wisconsin State Colleges and University of Wisconsin Campuses," January, 1964, Government Publications, SHSW; *Green Bay Press-Gazette*, August 16, 1966; "System Ranks 5th in Size in Nation," *Wisconsin State Universities Report*, January, 1969.

regarding the other major part of the 1955 higher education reform, the creation of a new university in Milwaukee, was that it should not be an autonomous institution; one of the two systems should have it. McPhee and his regents were not at all happy about losing their flagship campus to the University, whose leaders in turn had for decades resisted the creation of a rival public university in the state's largest city. Indeed, President Fred and his colleagues made sure UWM's development would be tightly controlled by its parent. Among Madison faculty and administrative leaders in 1955 and afterward only Fred Harvey Harrington spoke out strongly in favor of developing UW-Milwaukee as a major university.[66]

If the University may be said to have won the 1955 turf battle, in the process McPhee and Harrington both learned an important political lesson. In future expansion contests, the local community was likely to prefer a UW campus over affiliation with McPhee's less prestigious system.[67] For McPhee especially, political support among the public members of the Coordinating Committee and in the legislature was essential to advance his system's interests. Further competition became inevitable when the legislature in 1963 authorized the State Colleges, like the University, to establish two-year branch campuses in communities approved by the CCHE.[68]

During the Fred and Elvehjem years Vice President Ira Baldwin had served as the University's liaison with the Coordinating Committee and initially was one of its two co-directors. Having played a key role in drafting the CCHE legislation, Baldwin believed in demonstrating that CCHE's coordination role could be effective and useful to the state. Because this initial cooperative spirit had eroded considerably by 1962, Baldwin asked President Harrington to replace him, eventually with Professor Carlisle Runge of the Law School. Harrington's competitive instincts, combined with the combative style of UW Regent Arthur DeBardeleben as a CCHE member, served to undermine and sometimes

---

[66]Another part of the bargain was that Milwaukee State College President J. Martin Klotsche would head the new University of Wisconsin-Milwaukee. Harrington, oral history, 1985. To compensate the State College regents for losing their Milwaukee campus, the 1955 legislation brought Stout Institute into the WSC system and combined the Platteville School of Mines with the State College campus at Platteville. Ira L. Baldwin, *My Half Century at the University of Wisconsin* (Madison: Ira L. Baldwin, 1995), p. 481. See above, pp. 98-103, and below, p. 534.

[67]Harrington, oral history interview, 1985.

[68]Chapter 419, *Laws of Wisconsin*, 1963.

polarize the coordinating agency, which increasingly lost its effectiveness and public support in the 1960s.[69]

Developing UW-Milwaukee

High on the agenda of the Harrington administration from the very first was the rapid development of the University's Milwaukee branch. "We will move ahead at UW-M," Harrington promised a Milwaukee faculty meeting shortly after taking office, adding, "and soon and fast."[70] The president hoped to make UW-Milwaukee the prototype of a new-style urban university specializing in the study and solution of urban and inner city problems. Created through a complicated political compromise, UW-Milwaukee's administration was a blend of its original components. Provost (Chancellor after 1964) J. Martin Klotsche, for example, was a holdover from the former Milwaukee State Teachers College, which he had headed since 1946; his continuation in the top position was part of the bargain struck at the time of the merger. Joseph G. Baier, the first dean of UW-Milwaukee's core College of Letters and Science, was a biologist with a Milwaukee Extension background. Although Klotsche was a historian and a 1931 Madison Ph.D., he and the president were not close. Harrington considered him a genial social climber who, while well-connected with the Milwaukee community and the regents, was an indecisive temporizer who lacked the vision and drive to build the Milwaukee campus into a high quality and innovative urban university.[71]

This lack of confidence in Klotsche led Harrington increasingly to by-pass the provost/chancellor and turn for advice on Milwaukee matters to his former student, UWM Associate Professor of History Charles Vevier. To give official credence to this relationship, in the fall

---

[69]See below, pp. 537-53.

[70]See Robert L. Erdman to Harrington, October 12, 1962, and Harrington to Erdman, October 16, 1962, Series 4/18/1, Box 17, UA.

[71]Harrington knew Klotsche rather well, having collaborated with him on behalf of UW-Milwaukee even before assuming the presidency. He had mixed feelings about him, once describing him as "a gentleman–really a very nice person, a rather sweet person." As part of the restructuring of the UWM administration, Klotsche offered to resign but Harrington turned him down, later explaining, "Klotsche was not the kind of person you could dispose of easily, because he was very well tied-in to the Milwaukee community and extremely well tied-in to the regents . . . and a close friend of [Governor Gaylord] Nelson." It seemed easier to work around him. Harrington, oral history interview, 1985.

of 1962 Harrington offered Klotsche additional funding so both the provost and he could hire a UWM faculty member as a part-time special assistant: political scientist Donald Shea for Klotsche and Vevier for the president. In a joint announcement of these appointments, Harrington and Klotsche promised that their two new assistants would work closely together, with Shea seeking "outside foundation, government and private support for worthy projects" and Vevier giving "particular emphasis to studying the strength and potential of existing UWM programs and personnel, and to working with UWM faculty members and administrators in developing promising new projects." These assignments were designed to help UWM move ahead as rapidly as possible, the statement explained, and were "in fact, similar to those which President E.B. Fred gave to one of us (Fred Harrington) in 1956-58."[72] Vevier's job description made him seem suspiciously like a de facto deputy for academic affairs waiting for a higher title.

To some extent Vevier shared his mentor's commitment to social action and his belief that UW-Milwaukee should do more to identify and work on the city's racial and inner city problems. One of his early assignments was to explore how to strengthen the social work program at Milwaukee and give it a distinctively urban focus by separating it from the more general program in Madison.[73] The president's great enthusiasm for social action was soon evident in his correspondence with Vevier. Late in 1962, for example, as student interest in civil rights was building on the Madison and Milwaukee campuses, Harrington sent Vevier a *New York Times* clipping headed "Educators Spur Rights Teaching" and commented: "We should do something at UW-M about civil rights. But what?" On another occasion he wrote:

> This Negro business is really booming. I'm all for making the most of it at UW-M, (1) in teaching (why not more courses?); (2) in research (what better field?) and (3) action programs.
> Let's do all the thinking we can on this. Do we need

---

[72]Harrington and J.M. Klotsche to "Dear Colleague," December 10, 1962, Series 4/18/1, Box 17, UA; *UWM Post*, January 10, 1963. Shea, a political scientist, had formerly taught in the Milwaukee Extension Center beginning in 1949. Harrington also intended Vevier to be in charge of the presidential office he planned to establish for use when he or Clodius were in Milwaukee. See Vevier to Harrington, January 3, 1963, ibid.

[73]Charles Vevier to Harrington, November 1, 1962, ibid.

new appointments? Money for a survey? Or what? Let's talk about it.[74]

Characteristically, Provost Klotsche was neither copied on this correspondence nor a party to many of the other Harrington-Vevier discussions.

While still vice president, Harrington had obtained a large Ford Foundation grant–the University's first million dollar grant–to develop urban studies and urban extension activities.[75] After the Board of Regents approved a new department and graduate program in urban affairs for Milwaukee in December, 1962, the president continued to press for bold action in developing the field there. He was particularly upset a few months later at the national attention given in the press to a new urban affairs program at Rutgers University. "The Rutgers' urban folks are not nearly as good as we are," he complained in a letter addressed jointly to Klotsche and Vevier:

> But I do want to say that we have been successful in this urban field, quietly successful; but perhaps less adventurous in Milwaukee than we should have been. I don't care too much about the newspaper notice, for we may have overplayed that at the start. But I am concerned about our being at the forefront in action, experiments, and approaches that will yield something special in national notice, in ability to attract staff, in ways of helping our metropolis, in pointing toward state and national legislation. And I desperately want to get into the Negro question in Milwaukee.[76]

Harrington had already been more blunt in letting Klotsche know of his impatience over the slow pace of progress at UW-Milwaukee:

> The UW-M is a growing but still weak institution when it comes to research. In its development it will be able to get help from our central administration. But it must scramble for itself. It must push. It must go after things. . . . Now we will supply some help, but the major job must be done in Milwaukee. It has not been done by Milwaukee. As you

---

[74]Harrington to Vevier, December 4 and November 23, 1962, ibid.

[75]Joseph M. McDaniel, Jr., Secretary, Ford Foundation, to President Conrad A. Elvehjem, December 23, 1959; U.W. News Service release, January 5, 1960; "University of Wisconsin Negotiations with Ford Foundation on Urban Research Grant, undated memo, ca. January 13, 1960, all in Series 5/1/3, Box 43; Harrington, oral history interview, 1985; UW BOR Minutes, February 20, 1960. See also below, pp. 310-14.

[76]Harrington to Klotsche and Vevier, April 13, 1963, Series 4/18/11, Box 17, UA.

know, I am again and again distressed by the lack of vigor among many of the administrative and faculty people in Milwaukee, by the tendency to be defensive and to slow things down when suggestions come along, and by the opportunities we are missing. . . . I know that you have not had as much money for travel, etc. as you might have wanted; but you have all you want now, and you can have more by asking for it.

One solution, he suggested, was to give Klotsche more administrative help:

I suppose that what we ought to do is to move forward to a Vice Provost rather quickly, a person who could function as a promoter and driving force on the Milwaukee campus, much as I and now Bob have tried to do for the whole University. Let us talk about this soon.[77]

Having planted the suggestion, the president continued to press Klotsche that he needed a vice provost to help move UWM along. He also stressed this necessity a month later to a special regent study committee in laying out an elaborate development plan for UW-Milwaukee.[78] By July he had persuaded Klotsche and the regents not only to create the position but to appoint his protégé Vevier to the post.[79] Harrington intended to rely on Vevier rather than Klotsche as the major instrument for building UW-Milwaukee. "The UW-M has the green light, and must move ahead," he regularly reminded Klotsche, "much faster than it has gone to date (much faster than many of your administrators and faculty want to go)."[80] The president advised a newly recruited UWM administrator of the importance of getting to know Vevier rather than Klotsche:

Joe Klotsche was so loaded with inside and outside chores that he could not devote himself fully to the academic development of the UW-Milwaukee. Vevier now takes over that job, which includes budget control. He is the key to your

---

[77]Harrington to Klotsche, January 25, 1963, Series 4/18/1, Box 17, UA. Vice President Clodius received a marked copy of this carefully drafted letter, Vevier a blind copy.

[78]Harrington, "Preliminary Report for the February 7 Meeting of the Special Regent Committee on the Future of the University of Wisconsin-Milwaukee," ibid.

[79]*Daily Cardinal*, July 16, 1963.

[80]Harrington to Klotsche, July 8, 1963, Series 4/18/1, Box 50, UA.

hopes for real development, at Kenwood Hall and elsewhere. Bob Clodius and I will look to him for recommendations.[81]

With Vevier in a key position in the UWM administration, Harrington loosened the purse strings. During 1963-64 he funneled more than $278,000 from the President's Unassigned Fund and over $88,000 from the President's Special Capital Fund for special projects on the Milwaukee campus, or 37 percent of the total disbursements from these two discretionary funds. This was far more than UWM's previous share or, indeed, its "claim" to the overhead funds comprising these two accounts.[82] Vevier counted on the central administration to back him over Klotsche. After making his first budget allocations as vice provost in the summer of 1963, for example, Vevier cautioned Harrington and Clodius to "both stand guard at your end and prevent Joe Klotsche from making any more budget commitments or promises to the deans if he feels pressured to do so."[83] Clearly, Vevier intended, and was expected, to be Harrington's, not Klotsche's deputy. The inevitable result was that the Milwaukee administration was not a smooth-functioning, mutually-supportive team.

It gradually became evident, however, that Vevier was not entirely Harrington's man either. Headstrong, ambitious, status-conscious, once in power he tended to see himself as the de facto Milwaukee chancellor with an increasingly territorial UWM focus. Vice President Clodius expressed surprise to Harrington that Vevier had "picked, appointed and charged" two search and screen committees for the letters and science and graduate school deanships without checking with him:

> I hope you have been consulted at every step because I have not been. In many ways I consider these more important than Letters and Science and Education deanships in Madison. And, for the good of all, it must not appear to the UWM faculty that Charlie is picking the deans.[84]

When Vevier raised a question about Milwaukee's freedom to use the

---

[81]Harrington to Bernard J. James, July 31, 1963, ibid.

[82]UW Financial Statement of Operation Appropriations, 1963-64.

[83]Vevier to Harrington and Clodius, August 16, 1963, Series 4/18/1, Box 50, UA.

[84] Clodius to Harrington, October 7, 1965, Series 40/1/2-1, Box 109, UA.

supplementary institutional grants accompanying National Defense Education Act fellowships, Harrington cautioned Clodius:

> I have for some time wanted to take a look at all our institutional grants and related income. I think we use it badly, on our poorer individuals; and on routine work rather than good new projects. . . . Part of my desire is for central administration to have something to say about innovation at the University. . . . Naturally, I am sending no copy of this to Vevier or anyone else at Milwaukee. And to no one on the Madison campus.[85]

Both Harrington and Clodius remained ambivalent about how much autonomy and independence to allow the University's branches.

Harrington's growing disenchantment with Vevier and his dissatisfaction with Klotsche in fact led him to contemplate a more complete restructuring of the UWM administration. In the spring of 1966 he and Clodius evidently considered the possibility of recruiting a prominent University of California-Berkeley administrator and urban affairs specialist, Martin Meyerson, for the top administrative post at UWM. Meyerson had just been passed over for the Berkeley chancellor's position after serving as acting chancellor for a year. He was clearly open to recruitment for a top administrative position elsewhere (and would shortly accept the presidency of SUNY-Buffalo). Clodius was aware of Meyerson's availability through his close contacts at Berkeley, where he had done his graduate work. Harrington was intrigued by the Meyerson possibility, but told Clodius: "Although your Meyerson-Klotsche proposal has real merit, I fear it is unworkable. But let's think and talk about it."[86] Several months later the University news service reported that Klotsche would take an eighteen-month leave of absence to direct a study of higher education in Brazil for the U.S. Agency for International Development. The assignment obviously had Harrington's backing. Indeed, given his and Clodius' extensive Washington contacts, it may in fact have been arranged by them. By issuing a press release about the appointment before bringing it to the Board of Regents, the president may also have wanted to forestall any regent objections to this unusual leave.

A Milwaukee area editor was not alone in asking how important Klotsche's University job was, if he could abandon it for a year-and-a-

---

[85]Harrington to Clodius, February 8, 1966, ibid.
[86]Harrington to Clodius, April 5, 1966, ibid.

half.[87] Donald Slichter, the president of a major Milwaukee insurance company and the incoming head of the Wisconsin Alumni Association, hotly told a University administrator he considered the arrangement "an affront to the people of Milwaukee."[88] Although Harrington quickly stressed that Klotsche would continue as chancellor after his return from Brazil, there was considerable press speculation that the overseas appointment was intended to strengthen the Central Administration's role in UW-Milwaukee affairs. "UWM Will Be Run by Harrington's Men," headlined the *Milwaukee Journal* in a story raising questions about excessive presidential power.[89] The regents were enough concerned to demand a closed-door discussion of the Klotsche leave, during which Harrington was criticized for his handling of the matter. "Harrington Accused of Bypassing Regents," trumpeted the *Daily Cardinal*, suspecting the affair was really "a power play to rid the University administration of non-Harrington appointees."[90] The president was forced publicly to defend his aggressive leadership style and to promise an effective plan for governing UW-Milwaukee during its chancellor's lengthy absence.[91]

If Klotsche's Brazil assignment was in reality designed to strengthen the Central Administration's role at UW-Milwaukee, it was a misstep that backfired. The affair sparked the first serious, if muted, criticism of Harrington's leadership by the regents, the press, and key University supporters around the state. It also raised suspicions of the president among UWM faculty members and fortified their resolve for more campus autonomy and a stronger faculty role in campus governance. If Klotsche's absence in Brazil was intended to free the hand of Vice Chancellor Vevier to accelerate the president's plans for the campus, this too miscarried. By this time not only were Harrington and Clodius having second thoughts about Vevier as their chosen

---

[87]*Waukesha Daily Freeman*, September 12, 1966.

[88]L.E. Luberg to Harrington, September 23, 1966, 40/1/2-1, box 109, UA. Harrington responded: "The 'affront to the people of Milwaukee' comment is most interesting. As you know, leading people of Milwaukee (of whom Don is one) have until recently had almost zero interest in UWM. The decision to move toward major university status was ours–and was at first received with indifference or skepticism, even hostility by many of them. If they are now changing, and are interested–as some signs suggest–then we have reason to be pleased, even though this means criticism, too." Harrington to Luberg, September 27, 1966, ibid.

[89]*Milwaukee Journal*, September 4, 1966.

[90]*Daily Cardinal*, September 13, 1966. See also *Milwaukee Sentinel*, September 5, 10, 1966; *Wisconsin State Journal*, September 10, 1966.

[91]See *Milwaukee Journal*, September 11, 16, 17, 1966.

instrument to remake UWM, but so too were much of the Milwaukee faculty and staff, and not just because he was suspect as the agent of the Central Administration. Much of the Milwaukee criticism of the Klotsche leave in fact was based on widespread concern over Vevier's likely expanded role during the chancellor's absence. Although the vice chancellor had some of Harrington's qualities–a quick mind, drive, ambition, and decisiveness–he lacked the older man's experience, maturity, and deftness in handling people. Vevier impressed many of his UWM colleagues as stubborn, arrogant, manipulative, and power-hungry. His unpopularity was such that upon Klotsche's return to the campus in the fall of 1967 the chancellor took over many of Vevier's responsibilities, making clear that he, not the vice chancellor, was firmly in control.[92] With Vevier's wings clipped locally and no longer enjoying the Central Administration's favor, he resigned early in 1969 to take the presidency of Adelphi University in New York.[93]

The University of Wisconsin-Milwaukee grew substantially in enrollment, staff, and an expanded array of undergraduate and graduate programs during the 1960s. In a period of fierce competition for faculty it managed to recruit a few genuine academic stars. The institution did not, however, reach President Harrington's goal of becoming a leading university engaged in innovative research on urban problems and providing creative approaches to bring higher education to disadvantaged inner city residents. UWM's development would undoubtedly have proceeded more slowly without Harrington's interest and personal intervention. Yet it also might have gone further if the president had put together a campus administration more capable of realizing his dream.

Equally important, Harrington was counting on the continuing growth of federal funding for work on urban problems under President Lyndon Johnson's Great Society programs. As the Vietnam War grew in intensity and expense during the latter sixties, federal spending on

---

[92]Ibid., September 28, October 1, 1967. In an oral history interview years later Harrington commented on his indirect efforts to supply some "push" to Klotsche and the UW-Milwaukee administration: "And what I did was to use my assistants–my assistants like Engman, for example, and McNeil–and appointed a special assistant from the Milwaukee campus, Vevier–and ultimately Vevier became vice chancellor over there with those people–to push. The selection of Vevier was probably unfortunate because Vevier, while a pusher–just the kind of person McNeil was–was also a very difficult person to get along with, and caused all kinds of trouble and didn't work out." Harrington, oral history interview, 1985.

[93]*Milwaukee Sentinel*, February 15, 1969.

domestic programs was cut back. The war, rather than the cities, moved to center stage. Even a can-do optimist like Harrington understood that the state of Wisconsin by itself could not afford to develop another doctoral research university comparable in depth and quality to the original University of Wisconsin in Madison, no matter how important its specialized mission. By the time he left the presidency in 1970, Harrington had been forced to scale back his expectations for UW-Milwaukee, whose development proceeded thereafter much more slowly and modestly. For Harrington especially, this must have been a bitter disappointment.

Creating UW-Parkside and UW-Green Bay

Even before President Harrington took office there was talk of another four-year university in southeastern Wisconsin to help educate the post-war baby-boomers who would soon be reaching college age. The new president made clear at his first regents meeting that if a new campus were authorized he wanted it developed by the University. Harrington held to this position tenaciously thereafter, in part to broaden the University's political base vis-à-vis the rapidly growing State College system. Because southeastern Wisconsin was already served by Whitewater State College and two UW freshman-sophomore centers in Kenosha and Racine, there was some question about the need for another campus in that part of the state. In fact, as the prospects for creating another four-year university grew brighter, a number of Wisconsin communities expressed interest in acquiring it. Most of them assumed it should be a UW branch. During the next two years the UW regents also gave consideration to a possible branch in northeastern Wisconsin. Delegations from Racine, Kenosha, Sheboygan, and Green Bay lobbied the board, the Harrington administration, and the Coordinating Committee for Higher Education, each seeking to be chosen as the site for a new four-year branch. President Harrington was initially cool to the idea of developing two new universities, but eventually swung around to supporting a northeastern branch as well. He was no doubt influenced by political considerations. A Kenosha-area branch had strong Democratic support and a Fox Valley campus appealed to Republicans. Both campuses would strengthen the University's political base in two important population centers, each one traditionally aligned with one or the other of the state's major political parties.[94]

Meanwhile, Gene McPhee and his rival State College Board of Regents were not pleased with the prospect that the University might acquire one or perhaps two new four-year branches, each of them located not far from a WSC campus. They too began considering the expansion of their system at both the two- and four-year level. As the issue moved to legislative consideration, and rather late in the discussions about the need for one or more new universities, the WSC board adopted a resolution on May 22, 1964, requesting that any new four-year campuses be assigned to the State College system. This, the regents explained, would be in keeping with their system's historical development and mission focused on undergraduate education. McPhee stressed his board's belief "that any new institutions primarily offering undergraduate instruction plus some fifth-year study at the graduate level should come under the jurisdiction of the Board of Regents of State Colleges."[95] Though reflecting a certain logic, the resolution really represented McPhee's extreme bargaining stance; there were hints that a suitable compromise might be brokered involving the assignment of one of the new campuses to each system.

In the end it was the politicians who decided. George Molinaro, the powerful Democratic leader from Kenosha in the legislature, steadfastly pressed the case for a four-year UW branch in southeastern Wisconsin and helped secure the site for the new UW-Parkside in his mostly Democratic district. Not to be outdone, Republican politicians supported the proposed northeast university because it would be located in a traditional GOP area. McPhee and his regents made a special play for the latter campus, but were not able to overcome the preference of the Green Bay proponents for a UW branch. McPhee's influence was sufficient, however, to assure that UW-Green Bay was built on a site northeast of the city rather than on an alternative location in the more populous Fox River Valley south of Green Bay. If he could not win the battle over operating the new northeast university, then he wanted it located as far away as possible from his Oshkosh campus.

Harrington's choice to head and develop the new southeast campus, UW-Parkside, was 46-year-old Irvin G. Wyllie, currently the

---

[94]Harrington, oral history interview, 1985.

[95]WSC BOR Minutes, May 22 and July 15, 1964, Government Publications, SHSW; Harrington oral history interview, 1985.

chairman of the UW-Madison Department of History.[96] Like McNeil and Vevier, Wyllie had first come to Harrington's notice as an American history graduate student working on his doctorate in the late 1940s. Harrington subsequently helped bring him back to Madison from the University of Missouri in 1957 as an associate professor of history. Wyllie was a lot like the president: brash and cynical, supremely self-confident, and eager to use his departmental chairmanship as a launching pad for further administrative advancement. He was also smart, creative, hard-working, and politically astute. Chancellor Wyllie was committed to creating a branch university whose new buildings would possess architectural distinction and whose curricula would focus particularly on the industrial needs of the Racine-Kenosha area.

To lead the new northeast campus–quickly and logically named UW-Green Bay–Harrington and the regents appointed Edward W. Weidner, a 45-year-old political scientist currently directing the Center for Developmental Change at the University of Kentucky. Weidner had spent two years in graduate study at the University of Wisconsin during the Second World War, but Harrington was more familiar with his recent work as an Asian specialist and especially his service as vice chancellor of the East-West Center in Hawaii in 1962-65. Like Wyllie, Chancellor Weidner planned to set his new university apart from others in the state by organizing its curricula and structure along non-traditional lines and by taking advantage of the growing popularity of environmental studies. Beginning their work in 1966, over the next three years Chancellors Wyllie and Weidner worked many long hours supervising the design and construction of buildings, assembling a faculty and an administrative and support staff, and overseeing the

---

[96]UW BOR Minutes, May 6, 1966, UA; *Daily Cardinal*, May 7, 1966. Characteristically, President Harrington did not consult a faculty search-and-screen committee in selecting the chancellors of the two new campuses, arguing that there was as yet no appropriate faculty body from which to appoint such committees. One of Chancellor Wyllie's first decisions was to find a neutral name for his as yet paper institution so as not to offend the cities of Kenosha and Racine, each of which hoped to provide its name and site for the new campus. Since the property eventually selected, primarily by Harrington, was in western Kenosha County adjacent to Petrifying Springs State Park, Wyllie came up with the imaginative and certainly inoffensive name of UW-Parkside. His efforts were not entirely successful in mollifying Racine city and county politicians who had hoped the new campus would be located within their boundaries. On December 2, 1969, without prior notice or discussion with UW officials, the Racine City Council voted to cancel the lease and sell the building used by the UW Center in Racine, which Chancellor Wyllie was counting on for continued use as a freshman-sophomore branch of the Parkside campus. UW BOR Minutes, December 12, 1969.

design of curricula and planning of courses. Even with support from the regents and legislature and help from Harrington and the Central Administration, Wyllie's and Weidner's achievements in this brief period were remarkable. To the surprise of many who doubted it could be done, the first undergraduate students were able to enroll at the new branch universities in the fall of 1969.[97]

Before this, however, there were indications of continuing uncertainty about the nature of the two new campuses. Under mounting political pressure to control the state's rapidly expanding higher education structure and budget, the CCHE moved to slow the development of graduate programs at UW-Milwaukee and the State Colleges, now renamed Wisconsin State Universities. In the fall of 1968 it also decided tentatively that the Green Bay and Parkside campuses should have the same student-faculty ratio, teaching load, and faculty salary structure as the WSU system. Although it subsequently reversed this position under heavy UW pressure, Regent President Charles Gelatt, one of the most influential members of the UW board, used the initial CCHE decision to raise the question of whether the state's resources were sufficient to fund four Universities of Wisconsin, and whether "it might even be open to discussion as to whether these two institutions ought not to be part of the state university system rather than the University of Wisconsin system." Surprised and shocked that this previously settled issue might be revisited, President Harrington quickly offered a number of reasons why the two new campuses should be part of the UW system, closing with the hope that "President Gelatt's strong voice was a lone voice on this Board in suggesting that we may have been wrong in developing these new campuses." Gelatt pointed out the CCHE's increasing difficulty of distinguishing among the institutions under its jurisdiction, which "could result in merging the various institutions into one system." His concern, he emphasized, was to protect the essential greatness of the original University of Wisconsin in Madison. None of the other regents was willing to follow Gelatt's lead in reopening either the jurisdictional question or discussing the larger resource issue, so Gelatt concluded with a warning that the UW position "must be more forcefully brought before the Coordinating Council for Higher Education and the people of the state."[98] The exchange was an ominous indication that Harrington's expansionist vision was losing its allure for some University supporters. It also

---

[97]*Daily Cardinal*, September 16, 1969.
[98]UW BOR Minutes, October 4, 1968.

highlighted the president's reluctance to take the lead in seeking a more rational and sustainable structure for higher education in Wisconsin.

Completing the Reorganization

A major part of President Harrington's reorganization of the University involved the outreach and service activities pioneered by Wisconsin since the late nineteenth century. These included the agricultural outreach work of the Cooperative Extension Service of the College of Agriculture, probably the best such agency in the country, and the activities of the University Extension Division, which offered a wide variety of credit and non-credit educational programming to the general population of the state. UED services included evening and weekend courses in locations around the state, correspondence study, instruction over the WHA radio and television stations, and a network of freshman-sophomore University centers. Traditionally, there had not been much overlap or even contact between the two extension agencies, which were budgeted and staffed separately and quite differently.

Eager to improve adult education and the University's urban outreach, Harrington early concluded that the synergy resulting from a merger and redirection of the two extension services, along with WHA, would enable the University of Wisconsin once again to provide pioneering leadership in this field, as it had in the glory days of its great President Van Hise. He was convinced the expanding domestic agenda of the Kennedy and Johnson administrations in Washington and the parallel interest of the great national foundations would bring vastly increased support for urban extension activities. Just as Wisconsin and other land-grant universities had applied their expertise to the problems plaguing American farmers in the late nineteenth and early twentieth centuries, so they would now be called upon to work on the problems of urban America. The urban challenge needed a unified, coordinated approach involving all parts of the University.

A year into his presidency Harrington persuaded the Board of Regents that the eight two-year University centers should become an independent credit-granting instructional unit and that the two extension services and WHA be merged into another independent unit.[99] The board promptly voted in favor of the merger of all extension activities

---

[99]"Recommendation Concerning Organization of Adult Education and Extension Activities," unsigned statement, probably the basis for Harrington's remarks to the regents, September 3, 1963, Series 40/1/1/1, Box 6, UA.

and approved the creation of a UW Center System to administer resident instruction outside of Madison and Milwaukee. In addition to the existing eight two-year University centers and any others to be developed in the future, the new unit was given jurisdiction over whatever new junior-senior programs might subsequently be authorized outside of Madison and Milwaukee.[100]

The story of the ill-starred effort to merge and redirect the University's extension activities is discussed in greater detail later in this study.[101] Suffice to it note here, however, that the merger did not bring the revitalization of UW outreach Harrington had expected. Combining two units with different missions, experience, funding, and staffs proved much more difficult than the president anticipated. Nor did he foresee the long-term consequences for extension and the two-year centers of effectively severing their traditional ties to the parent academic departments in Madison. Neither was there the increase in federal and foundation support for new urban extension services he had counted on. Far from restoring the pioneering spirit of UW outreach, Harrington's extension merger both weakened the enterprise and undermined UW-Madison's historic role as the state's land-grant university.

The New Golden Age

The early Harrington years constituted a heady and exciting period, a veritable new golden age. The institution clearly had a president who thought big and exuded an air of can-do optimism that could not but inspire the UW community. Change was in the air and one need only look around to confirm this. The Madison campus was changing constantly, with new buildings sprouting every year and student enrollments growing inexorably, setting off an ongoing debate about the need for a second nearby campus and/or enrollment limits. The University budget was also rising rapidly, infused by the expanding enrollments and generous research, program, and construction support from the federal government and national foundations. Academic

---

[100]UW BOR Minutes, September 6, 1963. After it was clear the University would be authorized to develop new branch universities in Racine-Kenosha and Green Bay, the regents limited the jurisdiction of the Center System to the freshman-sophomore centers in order to allow the new four-year campuses to control their own academic development. UW BOR Minutes, November 4, 1966.

[101]See Chapter 9.

departments were doubling and tripling in size; older faculty members could not recall a time when it was so easy to get authorization to add staff and develop new fields of study. New programs, centers, research institutes, and even departments and schools appeared regularly. University news releases regularly reminded the state how UW researchers were exploring the frontiers of useful knowledge: developing satellites for more accurate weather forecasting, combating cancer, exploring the genetic code governing human development, studying the causes and alleviation of poverty, and the like. All this expanded activity enabled the Madison city airport to attract several national airlines, for UW administrators and faculty traveled extensively as they represented the University in Washington and elsewhere across the country and world. For a time President Harrington even acquired a small fleet of surplus passenger airplanes of various sizes for official UW use. It was a time to dream of new academic frontiers, for under Harrington's expansive leadership just about anything seemed possible.

A listing of some of the major buildings constructed at this time will give a sense of the rapidly changing face of the campus during the Harrington years: the Peterson Administration Building, completion of the Southeast Dormitory Area, Biotron, Alumni House addition to the Wisconsin Center, Natatorium, Nielsen Tennis Stadium, National Regional Primate Center, WARF Building, Middleton Medical Library, McCardle Laboratory for Cancer Research, University Health Service, Entomology-Plant Science Building (the Harry L. Russell Laboratories), Daniels Chemistry Building, Computer Science Building, Meteorology and Space Science Building, Van Hise Hall, Steenbock Memorial Library, the massive Humanities Building and Elvehjem Art Center complex, Engineering Research, Union South, Teacher Education, Educational Science, Helen C. White Hall and the Undergraduate Library, Noland Zoology Building, and Vilas Hall for the Communication Arts. A number of these new buildings were multi-story skyscrapers: Engineering Research, Space Science and Engineering, Russell Laboratories, WARF, Witte and Sellery Halls, and especially Van Hise Hall. The latter greatly altered the campus skyline by overshadowing Bascom Hall, the traditional headquarters of the University.

Never before had the University been able to expand its physical plant so extensively. A prominent symbol of the 1960s construction boom was the plywood fence erected around the Humanities-Elvehjem Art Center construction site along Park and State

UW Chancellors L.H. Adolfson (Center System), Martin Klotsche (UW-Milwaukee), Donald McNeil (University Extension), I.G. Wyllie (UW-Parkside) , Edward Weidner (UW-Green Bay), and EdwinYoung (UW-Madison). UA, X25-3407.

Humanities Building site with wall. UA, S-2594.

Excavating for Van Hise Hall. UA, X25-3374.

Van Hise Hall looming over Bascom Hall. UA, 7/3.

213

streets on the lower campus during the late 1960s. The fence quickly replaced the long-since demolished Kiekhofer Wall as a vehicle for student expression: slogans, notices of meetings and calls for rallies, cartoons and other art work, serious poetry and doggerel, and even light-hearted anonymous philosophizing. (Example: "Incest is best when kept in the family.") For several years the fence was the University's closely watched Democracy Wall, the forerunner of a more famous counterpart in Beijing, China, a decade later.

The Unraveling

President Harrington's difficulties in reorganizing and redirecting University outreach were only one sign of the changing times; another was the increasingly strident student comment on the Humanities Fence. Much of what had seemed a logical and feasible, if clearly ambitious, agenda for an activist president in the early 1960s turned out to be problematic and divisive only a few years later. Harrington's once-confident and compelling leadership itself came into question. For this the UW-Madison student body, reacting to national issues, bore some responsibility. The frequent, noisy, and eventually violent student protests of the latter sixties undermined public and legislative support for the University and its president.[102]

There was no small irony in this. Harrington was proud of the University's long tradition of student activism, personally identified and sympathized with most of the student concerns, was responsible for the recruitment of several faculty members who became icons of the more radical student protesters, and steadfastly resisted proposals to crack down on campus demonstrations. When Arlie Mucks, the director of the Wisconsin Alumni Association, warned after a student sit-in protest that "our image must change" if the University were to hold the support of its alumni and friends, Harrington responded:

> You say that if we want to hold our friends, "our image must change." "Our image," Arlie, is that we are one of the great universities, high in quality, strong (very strong) in freedom of expression, a university at which we crush neither students nor faculty; a university that has had many out-of-state students since Van Hise's day; a university that has always considered itself strong enough to tolerate some dissenters and non-conformists. This "image" is a reflection

---

[102]See Chapter 8.

of fact and tradition that long predates Bob Fleming and me.
It is a tradition of which we are all very proud. We could
hardly change the "image" without changing the institution.
Could we?[103]

Harrington's question posed what was to become an insoluble problem
for the increasingly embattled president.

Harrington's early interest in mobilizing University resources
to work on problems of racism and inner city poverty paralleled the
involvement of UW-Madison students in the civil rights movement of
the early 1960s. The president did not hesitate to align the University
and himself personally with the broad goals of the civil rights
movement. Early in his presidency he pointedly resigned from the
Madison Club after it blackballed two prominent Jewish residents for
membership.[104] He likewise declined to stay in clubs or use facilities in
other cities for alumni gatherings if they had restrictive membership
policies against women or minorities. Among university presidents
Harrington was a notable national leader in trying to alleviate inner-city
problems and extend a helping hand to improve southern black colleges.

By 1965, however, student activism in Madison and elsewhere
was shifting away from minority civil rights at home to opposition to
U.S. involvement in the war in Vietnam. On this issue Harrington
hesitated to follow the students' lead, even though he personally
sympathized with their opposition to the war. He did not agree,
however, with tactics designed to pressure the federal government by
spurning federal grants and contracts, barring war contractors from
holding employment interviews on campus, or shutting down the
University. He knew that neither the Board of Regents, state officials,
nor the general public would tolerate such disruptive protests.

Harrington ordinarily relied on his chancellors to deal with
student demonstrations on their campuses and did not directly involve
himself. Consequently, Chancellor Robben Fleming handled the first
significant Madison anti-war protest, a student sit-in demonstration at
the new administration building in late May, 1966. Organized by the

---

[103]Mucks was a colonel in the U.S. Air Force Reserve who felt strongly that
the anti-war protesters were unpatriotic. Arlie M. Mucks, Jr., to Robben Fleming,
February 24, 1967; Harrington to Mucks, March 6, 1967, Series 4/19/1, Box 57, UA.
Upon receiving a copy of Harrington's letter Fleming responded: "Thanks for your note
to Arlie. It is one of the things that I enjoy about working with you." Fleming to
Harrington, March 14, 1967, ibid.
[104]"President Harrington Resigns from Madison Club," *WAM*, 67 (November,
1965), 13-14; *Daily Cardinal*, October 15, 16, 28, 1965.

campus chapter of the radical Students for a Democratic Society (SDS), the protesters demanded that the University cease cooperating with the Selective Service Administration by providing draft boards with class rank and other academic information about UW students registered for the draft. Since the protesters were orderly and did not interfere with the offices in the building, Fleming permitted them to remain for five days before persuading them to withdraw, so as not to appear to be pressuring a faculty meeting called to consider the issue. The nearly 900 faculty members present in Music Hall on May 23 approved a compromise solution: the University should not give class-standing information directly to draft boards but it could provide it to individual students on request. While most observers applauded the peaceful outcome, predictably some student militants were dissatisfied. A few critics, on the other hand, thought Fleming and Harrington ought to have cracked down and ejected the demonstrators. The president told Chancellor Fleming, however, he was pleased with the result. He thought Fleming and Dean of Students Kauffman had averted a "catastrophe" and believed their deft handling of the protest had strengthened and validated the delegation of authority under the University's new chancellor system.[105]

Fleming drew more criticism when he provided $1,155 of personal funds to bail out some of the students arrested after another SDS-led demonstration that turned violent at the Engineering Building in February, 1967. The protesters were attempting to block job interviews by the Dow Chemical Company, the leading manufacturer of napalm for the Vietnam War. Fleming's purpose, he explained afterward, was to avoid creating martyrs and possibly escalating the protest to the point of mass arrests. Although the *Daily Cardinal* and many students were critical of SDS-sponsored violence, anti-war sentiment and protests were increasing in frequency and intensity. Harrington reminded the Board of Regents of the numerous student demonstrations elsewhere in the country and promised to continue upholding the University's long tradition of freedom of speech. The University, he said, must itself be neutral, but it should not be neutral on whether its students should be concerned about matters of public interest.[106]

When Chancellor Fleming left to become president of the University of Michigan in the late summer of 1967, Harrington's

---

[105]Harrington to Fleming, May 27, 1966, Series 4/19/1, Box 38, UA.
[106]UW BOR Minutes, March 10, 1967.

popular choice for a successor was Vilas Professor of Sociology William H. Sewell, a distinguished demographer largely responsible for building his nationally ranked department after World War II.[107] The two men knew each other well, for they had worked together in the 1950s to open up WARF funds for support of social science research. Sewell shared Fleming's and Harrington's private misgivings about the war and also their belief that the University must remain neutral on the issue. He was, he reminded the faculty, committed to follow its instructions to keep the University open and to hold job interviews on campus for all legal employers.

Sewell's tenure as chancellor was brief–less than a year–while he presided over a badly fractured campus. He never recovered from a second, more violent anti-war protest against further employment interviews by the Dow Chemical Company in the Commerce Building on October 18, 1967. With hundreds of demonstrators blocking the hallways and entrances to the building and their leaders unwilling to take responsibility or do more than issue ultimata, Sewell called for Madison police reinforcements to assist the badly outnumbered University police in restoring order. The city police–many of whom resented college students as a privileged class and especially had no love for what they saw as long-haired, draft-dodging hippies–used billy clubs to empty the building. When some of the protesters fought back, the police employed tear gas to clear the area. A number of students were arrested; 13 were suspended and 3 eventually were expelled after disciplinary review. The following day student leaders called a widely honored class strike to protest the use of force on campus. Dow II had brought the war home and in the process had radicalized many previously uncommitted students.

Chancellor Sewell postponed further Dow and other controversial employment interviews pending the report of a faculty-student committee charged with studying the issue in the aftermath of

---

[107]UW BOR Minutes, June 9, 1967. There is evidence to suggest that Sewell was Harrington's second choice for chancellor at this time. The president evidently preferred Edwin Young, the former dean of the College of Letters and Science, who had left the University in 1965 to become president of the University of Maine. Harrington subsequently told Professor James Villemonte, the chairman of the University Faculty Council, in confidence that Young "was on the Madison Chancellor list produced by your committee, and seemed to me the best name; but he was not then available because of commitments to his Maine trustees." Harrington to Villemonte, March 4, 1968, Series 40/1/1/1, Box 93. See also Tim Wyngaard, "Young Has No Plans to Be 'Policeman' in New UW Job," *Green Bay Press Gazette*, September 15, 1968.

the Dow riot. His decision angered a number of the regents, who believed the board had given a clear directive that job interviews were to continue to be held on campus regardless of objections by some students.[108] Clearly finding his administrative responsibilities distasteful, Sewell apparently offered more than once to resign in mid-year, but Harrington persuaded him to stay on. The chancellor made his resignation definite in late June, 1968.[109] Much of the campus community saw him as a victim of the war, a decent man who would have made a fine academic leader in normal times but who had no stomach for the role of chief campus policeman. The *Daily Cardinal* expressed regret over Sewell's personal suffering, but thought he was "certainly not the man for the job." Rather than liberal idealists like Sewell and Kauffman, the paper observed, the campus needed "shrewd

---

[108]UW BOR Minutes, February 16, 1968. Rarely has a high University administrator been chastised as bluntly as Chancellor Sewell was by several of the regents at this meeting for his decision to postpone further Dow interviews. Eventually President Harrington sought to defuse the matter by explaining that Sewell had consulted him and that he supported the decision, which he declared was within the chancellor's administrative discretion because the Dow interviews were only postponed, not canceled. Although the board took no action, only Regent DeBardeleben supported Sewell, with Regents Nellen, Renk, Ziegler, and Gelatt (for absent Regent Greenquist) expressing varying degrees of criticism.

[109]Sewell to Harrington, June 27, 1968; Harrington to Sewell, June 29, 1968, Series 40/1/1-1, Box 143, UA. Commiserating with Sewell, Charles Gelatt, the president of the Board of Regents, reminded him that it had been "a year in which no one could look particularly good, a year something like the one President Hoover lived through in 1932." Gelatt to Sewell, July 1, 1968, ibid. To a faculty critic Harrington denied that Sewell had been forced out:

> Public announcements are always misunderstood. But the fact is that Bill's resignation was entirely voluntary; that he was never asked to leave by anybody, and was more than once persuaded to stay. Ultimately, he chose teaching and research, as many do.

> Did Bill always have full support from me, from you, from the Board? The record will show strong support from the Regents, in the face of public pressures on the Board. . . .

> I know that the future is uncertain, and that the next chancellor will have trouble, as his predecessors did (perhaps more). In the situations that will arise, you may want to help him, if he is the sort of person you want for this job—and I feel that he will be.

Harrington to Anatole Beck, July 16, 1968, ibid. The *Daily Cardinal* headlined the news: "Sewell Resignation Caps Year of Trial," while the *Capital Times* eulogized Sewell as "the Victim of the Irrational Right and Left," both July 2, 1968.

manipulators" who could deal with a student demonstration "and not feel bad about it later."[110]

Sewell's successor as chancellor in September, 1968, was Edwin Young, currently one of Harrington's vice presidents and formerly president of the University of Maine. Young had come to Madison to work on a Ph.D. after World War II, following which he accepted a faculty appointment in the Department of Economics and the School for Workers. A labor relations specialist, he had been chairman of his department for a number of years and then dean of the College of Letters and Science between 1961 and 1965 before taking the presidency at Maine. Young retained his vice presidency in the Central Administration while heading UW-Madison.[111]

[110]*Daily Cardinal*, July 2, 1968.

[111]UW BOR Minutes, March 15, September 13, 1968; *Daily Cardinal*, March 19, 26, September 17, 1968. Young's availability was fortuitous, as he was an experienced administrator who knew the campus well. Harrington had apparently sought Young for the chancellorship at the time of Sewell's appointment in 1967, but he was not available then. After the outlook for higher education in Maine deteriorated in the spring of 1968, Harrington quickly arranged to bring Young back to a newly created but poorly defined vice presidency in the central administration. There is tantalizing evidence, although Young doubts it, that Harrington was stockpiling Young as a prospective Madison chancellor in the event the Sewell administration collapsed. One of the regents confirmed that Harrington had endorsed Young in a closed personnel session as well-qualified to fill either of the two top jobs at the University. See Matt Pommer, "Former Dean Young Returning to U.W.; Seen as Possible Heir to Harrington," *Capital Times*, March 16, 1968. Both Harrington and Young planned for the latter to be vice president for academic affairs, but the University Faculty Council balked at approving Young's appointment to what its members considered a line administrative position without going through a faculty search-and-screen process. Harrington argued that Young had already earned faculty tenure during his previous nineteen years at Wisconsin and had previously been approved by two rigorous UW search-and-screen committees for high administrative posts. To avoid any embarrassing delay he dropped the academic affairs modifier to make clear the new vice presidency for Young would be regarded as a staff rather than a line appointment. Young was presumably to work on federal relations, coordinate fund raising, and handle other administrative chores so Harrington could spend more time on the deteriorating UW public relations with state government and the press. To Young's dismay, it soon became apparent to him that Harrington and Clodius had no plans to delegate any meaningful responsibilities to him, perhaps because of the faculty concern about the position. The president may also have merely acted on an opportunity to acquire an able administrator while helping an old friend and former neighbor leave an unpromising situation. (Before Harrington's appointment as president the Youngs and the Harringtons had been neighbors on Ridge Road, known locally as Power Hill because of the number of University administrators living there.) Cronon, conversation with Edwin Young, Sepetmber 18, 1996, UHP; University Faculty Council Minutes, March 2, 1968, UA; Harrington to Villemonte, March 4, 1968, Series 40/1/1/1, Box 93, UA.

Student sit-in at Peterson Building, May, 1966. UA, X25-3392.

Mass rally on Bascom Hill, 1969. UA, 4766-1.

"Bascom Memorial Cemetary, Class of 1968," appeared in *Daily Cardinal*,
December 12, 1968, photo by Tieger. UA, X25-3375.

Leaving President Harrington's Van Hise Hall farewell party, September 17, 1970.
UA, 4349-J-1.

Chancellor Young had a number of opportunities to test his skills as a "shrewd manipulator," because over the next several years the campus was anything but tranquil. Student protests over the war and other issues mounted in frequency and intensity even after the new Nixon administration in 1969 began troop withdrawals from Vietnam, made selective service a one-year lottery, and reduced draft calls while undertaking peace negotiations with the North Vietnamese authorities. Twice Young and Harrington–in February, 1969, and again in May, 1970–found it necessary to ask Governor Knowles to send in national guard troops to maintain order on the campus. Knowles also had to call on the national guard to protect and maintain order at the state capitol in September, 1969, when a welfare sit-in protest turned violent in part because of substantial participation by UW students. Thus three times in little more than a year civil law and order broke down in Madison and had to be restored by the use of troops under state authority. By mid-1970 many windows on campus and on State Street were boarded over, the result of too-frequent trashing by student militants.

Regents, state political leaders, and probably a decisive majority of the faculty and student body applauded Chancellor Young's firmness and determination to keep the campus open and functioning in the frequent turmoil. On the other hand, President Harrington's seeming aloofness from the disturbances undermined his authority. The chancellor system he had established now made him appear uncaring, uninvolved, and ineffective at a time of genuine crisis. Harrington's known ambivalence about the war and how to deal with the war protesters, moreover, contributed to a growing belief that he was no longer up to the job.

By the spring of 1970 the president was aware he had lost the confidence of a number of influential members of the Board of Regents, now solidly Republican and skeptical of his liberal politics and expansive policies. Determined to leave under his own power, on May 8 Harrington presented his resignation to the board effective October 1, having first privately negotiated the terms of his departure with key regents.[112] The resignation came amidst the worst campus rioting yet, the explosive, almost despairing student reaction to the U.S. invasion of

---

[112]UW BOR Minutes, May 8, 1970. In accepting the resignation, the board appointed Harrington Vilas Research Professor of History with minimal instructional responsibilities. Subsequently, at Harrington's request his appointment was generalized to the UW System at large rather than solely at UW-Madison so he would be free to lecture on other campuses.

Cambodia and the shooting deaths of four young protesters at Kent State University by the Ohio National Guard.

Nothing so sharply highlighted the contrast between generations, and between the student radicals and anti-war liberals like Harrington and Sewell, as their differing view of the University in this national crisis. The radicals saw the University as an institution symbolizing and embodying much that was evil in American society. Like the society as a whole, they believed the University needed fundamental change before it could be worthy of their respect. For them it also was a power-base, easy and largely risk-free to manipulate, by which to generate publicity and challenge the national government. For Harrington, on the other hand, as well as for Fleming, Sewell, Young, and most of the faculty, the University was a fragile institution whose very nature required it to be intellectually open and neutral. Taking divisive stands on political issues in the University's name would not only compromise its integrity and academic freedom but almost certainly would jeopardize its public support. Harrington consequently did not speak out publicly and officially against the Vietnam War until the Cambodia-Kent State rioting in May, 1970. By that time he had decided to resign and had long since lost any ability to influence either the regents or most of the anti-war demonstrators.[113]

---

[113]Following the announcement of Harrington's resignation, he had an interesting exchange of letters with former Chancellor William Sewell, who left office in 1968 rather bitter over the president's failure to support him more strongly during his turbulent year as head of the Madison campus. Sewell expressed regret over Harrington's decision to step down and assured him:

> When calmer times return and your administration can be judged against the background of its accomplishments, I am sure you will be recognized as one of the truly great presidents in the history of the University. You came into office at a time when the University was in great need of forceful, imaginative, and creative leadership, and you gave it just what it needed. I am sorry that the forces of unreason both from the right and from the left have made it impossible for you to continue, but you can take great pride in what you have done for this University. . . . We may not have always agreed on everything, but we have never been very far apart in our aims for the University, for higher education, or in our political views. I hope that in the future we will have many opportunities to be together.

Obviously moved, Harrington responded that Sewell's gracious letter had "meant a great deal to me":

> It all began when you and I and a few others were pushing for an improvement in social science and humanities support inside the

President Harrington was still in office a few months later when an enormous bomb planted by four anti-war activists blew up much of Sterling Hall and its Mathematics Research Center, killing one researcher and injuring several others.[114] The enormity of the act seemed in a terrible perverse way to symbolize the national excesses of the 1960s. It was also a massive punctuation mark denoting the end of the most ambitious and activist administration in University history, one that, like the Sterling Hall bombers, had always planned and acted on a grand scale.

University. Out of that came all the rest and most of it has been good. And I take pride in the fact that the administration and the faculty have stuck together, quite in contrast with what has happened in many other universities. As for my work as president, I am satisfied with the record. When I took the job I decided to push and push hard, knowing that turn would come. It has come; as you know I have been considering pulling out for two years. The key point is the time at which one can no longer be sufficiently persuasive with Regents and politicians to help the University. In my case that time has come and I have chosen to pull out quietly because I am convinced by doing so I increase the chances of getting an academic successor. . . . You are right, our goals and views are very much alike; and the Harringtons value the friendship of the Sewells very much indeed.

Sewell to Harrington, May 14, 1970; Harrington to Sewell, June 5, 1970, Series 0/7/33/08, Box 2, UA.

[114]See below, pp. 515-19.

5.

The Academic Enterprise

Describing the University of Wisconsin faculty and students during the period 1925-45 in the third volume of this history, we highlighted their efforts to make the University an inclusive community. Our use of the word "community" in two chapter titles was no accidental figure of speech. From at least the end of the nineteenth century, UW leaders sought ways to lower and bridge the walls between departments and disciplines and to encourage interaction and socializing across the entire University. Characteristic was President Charles Van Hise's leadership in establishing a faculty-staff University Club in 1906, his vision of a similar student union, and his encouragement of a still-continuing network of small dining clubs to promote informal faculty interdisciplinary contact and town-gown relationships. Even earlier, the sharing of research equipment across disciplines was a well-established and financially essential University practice that stimulated intellectual collaboration and joint faculty research projects. Shared faculty appointments across department and even college lines were easy to arrange and relatively common, and it was not unknown for a faculty member to begin his UW career in one department and end it in another, occasionally even in another college. The creation of the four faculty divisions in 1942 was but a continuing manifestation of this effort to break down departmental isolation and facilitate interdisciplinary contact and activity. Throughout the first half of the twentieth century the Wisconsin faculty was noteworthy among the great research universities of the country for its University-wide esprit and its substantial role in institutional governance.[1]

[1]See E. David Cronon and John W. Jenkins, *The University of Wisconsin: A History*, Volume 3, *Politics, Depression, and War, 1925-1945* (Madison: University of Wisconsin Press, 1994), especially pp. 510-50.

Similarly, UW students of these years were proud to be part of an academic community of growing national stature and import. Frequently they came to the University's defense when it was criticized by Wisconsin newspapers and politicians. In 1931-32, for example, when an ambitious up-state editor sought to use attacks on the University to fuel his lagging gubernatorial campaign, students formed what would later be known as truth squads to trail the candidate around the state refuting his charges. This student-devised tactic was so successful in generating favorable publicity that for a number of years afterward the University administration provided travel funds to send student speakers throughout the state under the auspices of a student-run Public Relations Committee. Other examples of commitment to community were the major role played by students in raising funds for construction of the Memorial Union in the 1920s and the annual work days organized by student leaders in the 1940s to improve and beautify the campus.[2]

Unfortunately, the emphasis on community seems rather less appropriate for this volume. For a variety of reasons community spirit eroded considerably among faculty and students after the Second World War. By 1970 the faculty and student esprit so notable in earlier years had diminished considerably. Increasingly, the primary loyalty of many UW faculty members was to their professional disciplines and their departments (or even a departmental subset) and much less to their university. Student loyalty to the institution had similarly eroded, replaced by concern for national issues in which the University was seen as an impediment rather than an ally.

There were a number of reasons for this. One, certainly, was the great increase in the size and academic complexity of the University at Madison and the development of branch campuses elsewhere in the state. It was harder to identify with the University of Wisconsin as a unique scholarly community when the term meant both the increasingly large and less personal Madison campus as well as a developing multi-campus system. The explosive growth of knowledge, moreover, proliferated disciplines and sub-disciplines tending to divide departments and fragment the campus. Faculty generalists, who emphasized breadth over depth and gave students an over-arching integrative approach to learning, became an increasingly undervalued and endangered academic species. Their decline reduced the sense of common intellectual bonds tying together a mutually supportive academic community.

[2]Ibid., especially pp. 623-82.

Another divisive element was the growing availability of external research funds, coupled with a University policy that encouraged faculty members to look outside the institution for their research support. This fostered a healthy entrepreneurial spirit and greatly expanded the University's research budget by conserving internal funds for facilities and promising start-up projects. On the other hand, it also increasingly divided the faculty into haves and have-nots, for the external support was not universally available but largely concentrated on fields deemed of national importance. Faculty members who regularly generated part or all of their salaries and research support through outside grants understandably felt less allegiance to the institution housing them, for they knew they could easily move elsewhere with their grants and graduate students if they chose.

Undergraduates, too, found it more difficult to develop and maintain an inclusive community spirit as the University grew ever larger, more complex, and inevitably more formal and bureaucratic. Rebellious and suspicious of authority, the baby boomers of the 1960s adopted a much more narrow definition of community, one that for many adherents viewed the University as evil and considered its faculty and administrators as enemies rather than colleagues in a common enterprise. The anti-war trauma of the late 1960s divided faculty and students alike, from each other and from the University. A campus occupied by soldiers–as UW-Madison was twice during 1969-70–could hardly seem to its members to be a community, at least not the sort Van Hise had envisioned. By the end of our period the University had become more an enterprise–more accurately a multitude of specialized enterprises–than the embodiment of Van Hise's dream of a mutually reinforcing, well-integrated academic community.

Increasing Size and Complexity

The overwhelming growth of the University in the quarter century after World War II was far beyond anything previously experienced. We have seen how the deluge of veterans using their GI Bill benefits sorely strained the campus at the end of the war, when Madison enrollment more than doubled in one year between 1945 and 1946.[3] The bulk of the ex-GIs were gone by 1950, when the advent of the Korean War also put some constraints on enrollment. In the early 1950s student numbers hovered below 14,000 for several years before turning upward again in mid-decade.

---

[3]See Chapter 1.

By 1960 the student body exceeded the peak veteran years, after which there was a steady if less precipitous rise throughout the sixties as the post-war baby boom generation arrived on campus. The boomers numbered 35,549 at Madison in 1969-70, reflecting an unprecedented four-fold enrollment growth since 1945.[4] In no previous quarter century had the University expanded so rapidly and dramatically.

Increasing numbers of students required more staff, of course, so there was a similar growth of the faculty and especially of the support staff during the period. Between 1945 and 1971 the number of full-time equivalent (FTE) faculty grew from 809 to 2,324, or nearly three-fold, with the proportion of tenured faculty rising significantly, from 421 to 1,505. The use of graduate assistants in teaching and research also continued, increasing from 546 FTE in 1945-46 to 1,234 in 1970-71. There was an even sharper rise in the number of support staff over the period, from 290 to 1,531, reflecting the growing practice of employing non-faculty professional staff for many activities related to instruction, advising, and research, often paid from the growing volume of external grants.[5]

The expansion of the faculty occurred across the University, in response to both student pressures and program development. The large College of Letters and Science, which generated more than half of the total student credit hours and provided instruction in a number of basic subjects to all undergraduates, grew from 215 FTE faculty at the end of the war to 969 in 1970-71. The faculty rosters of the other major undergraduate units also increased significantly: Agriculture, from 247 to 308; Commerce/Business, from 15 to 72; Education, from 44 to 200; and Engineering, from 63 to 166. Even the larger graduate professional schools, which were in a better position to limit their enrollment to staffing capability, increased their faculty size substantially over the period as they added new specialties: the Law School, from 13 to 35; the Medical School, from 92 to 345. Much of this expansion took place during the boomer years of the 1960s. The period would later be remembered nostalgically by faculty members across the country as the "golden sixties." It sparked the longest and most extensive head-hunting season in history, when the nation-wide shortage of qualified faculty members drove up salaries and speeded promotion and tenuring as never before.

The unusual opportunity to add faculty in large numbers during this period enabled UW departments and their parent schools and colleges

---

[4]Enrollment figures are fall semester head counts, taken from tables prepared by L. Joseph Lins, "Fact Book for History of Madison Campus," notebook, 1983, UHP.
[5]Staffing data are from ibid.

to enrich their instructional and research activities considerably, adding fields and specialties not previously available at the University. A number of departments doubled, tripled, quadrupled and more in faculty size during these years. When seeking new colleagues to teach additional sections of popular courses overwhelmed by students, departments rarely sought to duplicate the skills and interests of existing faculty. Rather, they recruited scholars able both to meet the present need and add new fields and approaches. The result was an unprecedented enrichment of the curriculum and a proliferation of new instructional and research programs across the University. Some of these led to the creation of new departments, centers, institutes, and even schools.

As departments expanded, strengthened, and added new specialties, there was a tendency to spin off some of these sub-disciplines into new departments. The School of Education underwent the most extensive such reorganization during the 1960s, with activist Dean Lindley J. Stiles creating a number of new academic departments out of the original large Department of Education: Educational Psychology (1961), Educational Administration (1962), Curriculum and Instruction (1963), Educational Policy Studies (1964), Counseling and Guidance (1968), and Studies in Behavioral Disabilities (1968), the latter two being divided from an earlier single department during the administration of Dean Donald J. McCarty.[6]

Similar though usually less sweeping changes occurred elsewhere. The College of Letters and Science created a number of new academic departments as new or expanded faculty expertise developed. Sometimes existing departments were simply broken up into their component parts, as when Social Work (1946) and Anthropology (1958) were spun off from Sociology as separate units, and Communicative Disorders separated from Speech (subsequently renamed Communication Arts) in 1969. Other new departments growing out of largely new specialized faculty strength were: Meteorology (1946), History of Science (1947), Linguistics (1954), Hebrew and Semitic Studies (1955), Indian (later South Asian) Studies (1959), Statistics (1960), Urban and Regional Planning (1962), African Languages and Literature (1964), Computer Sciences (1965), and East Asian Languages and Literature (1967). The Department of Afro-American Studies, created after the black student strike in 1969,[7] was an exception to the general rule; it began de novo in response to a declared institutional need and developed its faculty and courses gradually thereafter. The college also

---

[6]Ibid., pp. 12-14.
[7]See below, pp. 478-86.

dropped its administrative oversight of the Pharmacy and Nursing programs, both of which became free-standing schools in 1950 and 1956 respectively.

There were a number of similar basic organizational changes in the College of Agriculture over the period as well as a considerable expansion and renaming of existing departments and programs. To stake out a broader mission, the college changed its name to Agricultural and Life Sciences (CALS) in 1967,[8] added a School of Natural Resources (1967), and new Departments of Forestry (1962), Landscape Architecture (1962), Food Science (1967), and Nutritional Sciences (1969), plus a related Food Research Institute (1966). It also changed the names of several units: the two Departments of Agricultural Bacteriology and Economic Entomology dropped the modifiers to their names (1951) Animal Husbandry became Meat and Animal Science (1962), the two Departments of Dairy Husbandry and Dairy Industry combined to form Dairy Science (1962), Poultry Husbandry became Poultry Science (1962), Wildlife Management became Wildlife Ecology (1967), and Soils became Soil Science (1969). The Department of Home Economics grew into the School of Family Resources and Consumer Sciences (1969), while continuing as part of CALS (subsequently renamed the School of Human Ecology as a free-standing unit). CALS continued to enhance its strength in basic science, especially in its well-established Departments of Bacteriology, Biochemistry, Genetics, and Plant Pathology.

The College of Engineering made fewer structural changes while expanding considerably in size and program complexity. It increased its outreach activity by developing an Engineering Experiment Station (1949), added new Departments of Nuclear Engineering (1958), Industrial Engineering (1969), and changed the names of the Departments of Drawing and Descriptive Geometry to Engineering Graphics (1965), Mechanics to Engineering Mechanics (1967), and Mining and Metallurgy to Metallurgical and Mineral Engineering (1970). As was the case with other schools and colleges, most of the programmatic changes occurred within existing engineering departments. The newly independent School of

---

[8]When this request came before the general UW-Madison faculty for approval, representatives of the Medical School strongly objected to the implication that the College of Agriculture could claim primacy over the life sciences. Surely, they said in arguing for delay and a broader study of the issue, the Medical School's claim was as good or better than Agriculture's. At a time of lightly attended faculty meetings, rather than in the later representative Faculty Senate, the medics failed to reckon with the political skills of always well-prepared Agriculture Dean Glenn S. Pound. With the votes of his well-organized faculty augmented by the many county agents brought to Madison for the occasion, Pound's measure carried easily. UW Faculty Minutes, December 4, 1967, UA.

Commerce moved into its own new building on the western slope of Bascom Hill in 1956 and changed its name to the School of Business a decade later.[9] While growing considerably in size, Business continued the practice of not organizing its faculty into separate departments, a practice followed by the smaller Schools of Law, Nursing, and Pharmacy.

Benefitting from growing clinical activities and the increasing flow of federal funds into bio-medical fields, the Medical School also expanded greatly in this period, even with the handicap of a succession of temporary deans following the controversial dismissal of Dean John Z. Bowers in 1961.[10] New departments or divisions created in this period reflected the increasing specialization of medical treatment and research: Preventive Medicine (1948), Oncology (1950), Neurology (1957), Anesthesiology (1962), Medical Genetics (1962), Neurophysiology (1962), Pediatrics (1964), History of Medicine (1969), Ophthalmology (1975), Human Oncology (1976), and Rehabilitation Medicine (1976). In addition, some existing departments changed names to reflect their developing missions more accurately: Medical Bacteriology became Medical Microbiology (1947), Neuropsychiatry became Psychiatry (1957), Obstetrics and Gynecology became Gynecology and Obstetrics (1959), and Pharmacology and Toxicology became simply Pharmacology (1965). Having long since outgrown its facilities in and around the University Hospital at the western foot of Bascom Hill, by the end of our period the Medical School and hospital staff were planning the development of a giant Clinical Sciences Center and new hospital adjacent to the Veterans Administration Hospital at the far western edge of the campus, a massive and continuing development that opened in 1979.

These structural changes suggest how much the University was expanding and changing during this quarter century. They do not, however, reveal much about the staffing and curricular changes occurring at the basic operating level within the academic departments, especially in the latter 1950s and 1960s. Departments typically took advantage of additional staffing opportunities made possible by the increasing student enrollments and growing research funds to add faculty with new and different specialties, thereby greatly expanding their coverage of their disciplines.

By no means unique, the changes in the Department of History illustrate how profoundly the post-war growth increased the University's

---

[9]Ibid., May 12, 1966.
[10]See above, pp. 140-61. It should be pointed out that Dr. Anthony R. Curreri, a key figure and issue in the Bowers controversy, finally succeeded in his aspiration to chair the Department of Surgery in 1968.

intellectual diversity. As was characteristic of most U.S. universities at the time, in 1945 the history department essentially focused on the historical development of the United States and Europe, and its coverage of the latter was primarily limited to Great Britain and western Europe. Professor Paul Knaplund, the long-time department chairman and a specialist on the British Empire, taught a popular lecture course and seminar on its history, but he tended to emphasize the self-governing dominions over the empire's third world parts; moreover, his Eurocentric focus stressed the beneficial results of British rule. With the return of Fred Harrington in 1944, the department added a course on the history of Latin America, but Harrington was a specialist on U.S. foreign policy and viewed Latin America from a North American perspective. Not until the GI boom years after World War II did the department add a trained Latin Americanist, Clifton Kroeber, along with its first specialist in the history of China, Eugene Boardman. With the appointments of Robert L. Wolff in 1946 and Michael B. Petrovich in 1950, the department expanded out of western Europe and began offering courses on the history of eastern Europe, Russia, and the Balkans.

Along with general institutional growth, history enrollments and staffing benefitted considerably from the University's imposition of an American History and Institutions requirement for all undergraduates in 1952 during the McCarthy red scare.[11] The resulting hiring boom brought new faculty expertise in hitherto ignored aspects of American and European history, the areas that continued to attract the most student interest. In addition, the department moved far beyond its traditional curriculum with the appointments of Philip D. Curtin, Jan Vansina, and Steven Feierman in African history, Alfred E. Senn in Soviet and Baltic history, Kemal Karpat in Turkish and Middle Eastern history, John B. Kelly on the Arab Middle East, Maurice J. Meisner and Yu-Sheng Lin in Chinese history, Harry Harootunian in Japanese history, Robert E. Frykenberg and John F. Richards in the history of India, Pekka K. Hamalainen in Scandinavian history, John L. Phelan, Thomas E. Skidmore, and Peter H. Smith in Latin American history, and John R.W. Smail in Southeast Asian history. By

---

[11] UW Faculty Document 1032, "American History Requirement (College Recommendations), 1951-52, " January 7, 1952; UW Faculty Minutes, January 7 and June 2, 1952, UA. The requirement was developed by the Fred administration and the faculty to head off possibly more drastic action by a conservative Board of Regents or the legislature. Although this considerable boost to history enrollments thereafter helped justify more faculty positions, by 1965, with a number of U.S. history courses swamped by indifferent students simply meeting the requirement, the department led a successful campaign to drop it. See, for example, UW Faculty Minutes, March 1 and December 6, 1965.

1970 the department numbered 61 regular faculty members, compared with only 11 in 1945; its courses and scholarship now literally spanned the globe.

Traditionally benefitting from a large captive enrollment in Freshman English, the faculty roster of the Department of English expanded from 28 to 70 between 1945 and 1970. Before World War II the department had emphasized the major authors and traditional canon of English and American literature. As its staff grew in number they were able to launch programs in creative writing and English linguistics. They also began offering courses on the work of lesser known English and American authors, including women writers, many of whom would scarcely have rated a mention in earlier years. Similarly, the department extended its purview to include Irish and American black literature. The result was a much broader, considerably richer, and more challenging array of courses for English majors and other interested students.

Similar growth in faculty numbers enriched the intellectual diversity of all departments. The Department of Mathematics grew from 18 faculty in 1945 to 84 in 1970, for example; Physics from 9 to 53; Political Science from 8 to 40; Philosophy from 8 to 28; Art History from 3 to 11; Comparative Literature from 2 to 11; Chemistry from 24 to 56; Botany from 11 to 27; Chemical Engineering from 7 to 21; Civil Engineering from 11 to 33; Electrical Engineering from 8 to 45; Biochemistry from 11 to 29; Bacteriology from 8 to 20; Entomology from 7 to 22. New departments created after 1945 also shared the expansion: African Languages and Literature had a faculty of 8 by 1970; Indian Studies 18; Communicative Disorders, 16; Computer Sciences, 34; History of Science, 11; Meteorology, 19; Statistics, 21; Urban and Regional Planning, 14. The Department of Sociology, Anthropology, and Social Work included a combined faculty of 22 in 1945. As separate units, the Sociology numbered 61 by 1970; Anthropology 18; and Social Work 44 (including clinical faculty). The sweeping expansion of the University's academic and intellectual horizons in such a short time was literally breath-taking.

Gaining the Memorial Library

For faculty members in the humanities and social science disciplines, no post-war University development was more welcome and noteworthy than the opening of the Memorial Library building in 1953. The new facility was seen as belated University recognition of and support for the research needs of these library-based disciplines. Under the heading "An Elusive Phantom," in the previous volume of this history we recounted the frustrating efforts over two decades to persuade the state to provide funds to relieve the severe space problems of the University's main library, then located in the north wing of the State Historical Society building on the lower campus.[12] By 1945 the overcrowding of the stacks and reading rooms in the historical library building had reached scandalous proportions and was endangering the collections, frustrating users, and contributing to an undesirable proliferation of auxiliary libraries and storage facilities around the campus. With good reason the general faculty identified a new library as the number one post-war University building priority.[13]

The story of how the administration of President E.B. Fred finally succeeded in getting a special $5.9 million appropriation in 1949 for the Memorial Library building is more complicated than can be recounted here.[14] Underlying it is the fact that neither President Fred nor Vice President Ira Baldwin, both bacteriologists, shared the same sense of urgency in resolving the library's space problems as did the humanities and social science faculty whose disciplines relied much more heavily on the library collections for teaching and research. Like other scientists, Fred's and Baldwin's research was laboratory-based; they primarily read journal articles rather than books and used the comprehensive branch library located in Agricultural Hall for their scholarly needs. When the legislature appropriated $8 million rather than the requested $12 million in 1945 for post-war University construction, Fred's and Baldwin's first reaction was to stretch the appropriation by retaining the Historical Society space and constructing a new library in phases over time, an approach viewed with horror by the proponents of a new library building. Because detailed plans for a new library building were not ready by 1948, President Fred worried the unspent funds might be recaptured by the legislature. He therefore decided to divert the library's share of the appropriation to construct the first phase of a new engineering building.[15] At a special meeting of the

---

[12]See Cronon and Jenkins, *University of Wisconsin*, pp. 685-700.

[13]See UW Faculty Minutes, December 7, 1936, and May 2, 23, 1949.

[14]See above, pp. 233-38.

[15]The delay seems to have been largely the fault of the state architect, Roger Kirchoff, who in 1945 had taken upon himself the preparation of the plans working with the University Library Construction Committee. Kirchhoff was relatively inexperienced in large building design, and in the end this turned out to be the largest state project since the completion of the state capitol in 1915. In 1949 Kirchhoff sought assistance from the Milwaukee architectural firm of Phillips and Ebele, primarily to help with drafting and detail work.

Crowded stacks at State Historical Society/UW library, 1945.
UA, X25-3383.

Professor Emeritus L.C. Burke carrying first book, Coverdale Bible,
into new Memorial Library; l-r: Mark Ingraham, Gilbert Doane,
Oscar Rennebohm, E.B. Fred, and Burke, July 27, 1953.
UA, X25-2029.

235

faculty the president explained the problem, and then shrewdly called upon L&S Dean Mark Ingraham, who had more standing with the library supporters, to announce the administration's decision to switch the funds to the engineering project.[16] Thus, in spite of the faculty's top priority ranking, a new library building was once again on hold.

What seemed a disaster at the time to many dismayed and even outraged faculty members, turned out to be a blessing in disguise. Aware that diverting the library funds to the College of Engineering had angered a considerable part of the Letters and Science faculty, President Fred made getting a new and more generous library appropriation a high priority. He persuaded Governor Oscar Rennebohm, a Madison businessman who was generally sympathetic to the University and whose administrative assistant, political science Professor William Young, was a strong library advocate, to include an appropriation for the library in the governor's $25 million state construction request to the 1949 legislature. At a special meeting called for the purpose in late May, the general faculty unanimously adopted a resolution proposed by history Professor Paul Knaplund, a leading library advocate, urging affirmative action by the legislature. The Knaplund resolution pointed out that the faculty had twice since 1936 voted that a new library was the University's top building need:

> During the last 20 years the University of Wisconsin Library has dropped behind those of institutions of similar rank in the Middle West and in the Nation, both in its collections and in facilities for using existing collections. This situation has reached a critical stage with the increased enrollment of upperclass undergraduate and graduate students–a large number of whom are greatly dependent upon Library facilities and equipment for their work. . . .
> The faculty of the University of Wisconsin is pleased to note that the Governor appreciates the needs of the University for a Library and respectfully urges the Legislature to approve his recommendation of an appropriation providing for the building of a Library at the University of Wisconsin.[17]

There came a black moment in early July when lobbying by the state Chamber of Commerce persuaded the Republican caucus in the state senate to delete the library project from the appropriation bill–described as a "slight but harmless reduction"–in order to hold down the size of any tax increase. A disheartened President Fred at first believed the library

[16]UW Faculty Minutes, October 5, 1948.
[17]Ibid., May 23, 1949.

was lost, but a small group of faculty and administrative staff members persuaded him to wage an all-out fight to reverse the action.

With strong support from the governor and intense lobbying by Fred and a few University staff members, enough senate votes were switched to restore the library project and work out an acceptable tax compromise. Using a pen once belonging to the revered UW President John Bascom, Governor Rennebohm triumphantly signed the $5.9 million UW library appropriation bill on August 3, 1949.[18] With considerably more money than would have been available under the 1945 appropriation, the University could now move ahead with the construction of a full-scale modern library building. Ground breaking and construction began the following year, marred initially by the embarrassing collapse of some of the underlying steel structure before it had been adequately bolted together. Although the large project required an additional appropriation before completion, by the fall of 1953 the University at last had adequate stack space for its main collections and a number of commodious reading rooms, studies, and carrels for its faculty and student users.[19]

Most of the University community rejoiced in the splendid new Memorial Library building, dedicated to Wisconsin residents who had fought in the nation's wars. Ironically, as President Fred surveyed the

---

[18]*Daily Cardinal*, August 4, 1949. Witnessing the signing were Frank J. Sensenbrenner, the president of the Board of Regents, L&S Dean Mark H. Ingraham, UW Vice President Ira Baldwin, UW Librarian Gilbert H. Doane, and Professor Paul Knaplund, the feisty chairman of the history department. A number of people deserve credit for their role in the fight to restore the library appropriation, but Knaplund's presence at the signing ceremony appropriately acknowledged his tireless advocacy of a new library. He was one of the most influential and persistent library champions, and there is little doubt that his nagging had helped mightily to keep President Fred focused on the project, especially in the dark days after the initial senate action deleting the appropriation. Knaplund's important role in the library fight was recognized by his being selected as the faculty spokesman at both the ground breaking ceremony in 1950 and the dedication of the completed structure three years later.

[19]For a discussion of the efforts to get the Memorial Library, see Campus Planning Commission Minutes, February 27, May 21, June 26, November 29, 1945; June 26, 1946; June 11, November 4, 1947; October 7, 1948; December 7, 13, 1949, Series 5/24, Box 1, UA; UW BOR Minutes, June 25, November 15, 1947; October 16, 1948; May 14, 24, July 16, 1949, UA; UW Faculty Minutes, October 5, 1948; May 2, 23, 1949; Scott Cutlip, oral history interview, 1977, UA; Fred Harvey Harrington, "Paul Knaplund and the University," in *Paul Knaplund* (Madison: State Historical Society of Wisconsin for the Department of History, 1967), pp. 61-63; Louis Kaplan, oral history interview, 1978, UA; Ira L. Baldwin, *My Half Century at the University of Wisconsin* (Madison: Ira L. Baldwin, 1995), pp. 207-9; "How the Badgers Got a Library . . . and Other Buildings," *WAM*, 51 (October, 1949), 4-6; "Wisconsin's Memorial Library; Four Tough Years," *WAM*, 22 (December, 1950), 12-13.

spacious new facility, his happiness was mixed. He now worried that the University had overbuilt, that he would be accused of extravagance for constructing a library whose stacks and reading rooms were not immediately used to full capacity. To forestall such criticism, he and Vice President Baldwin pressed Louis Kaplan, the associate director and effective head of the library, to share his space temporarily with other campus units; they suggested among others the Library School and the counseling service. Kaplan objected that such tenants would require expensive remodeling and he was skeptical how temporary their tenure would be. Having just gained relief of the library's longstanding space problems, including room for the future growth of the student body and the collections, Kaplan and his staff were understandably aghast at the prospect of sharing their new quarters simply to allay the president's public relations concerns. In the end Kaplan made a strategic compromise; he accepted the Extension Division's package library service, which sent out collections of books and related materials to discussion groups around the state. This unit could be accommodated in the basement without any remodeling and could easily be moved to another location in the future.[20] Kaplan's defensive stance was wiser than he probably realized at the time. Even with the construction of substantial new branch libraries for agriculture, engineering, and undergraduate use in the 1960s, the great growth of the student body and the main library research collections necessitated an addition to the Memorial Library by 1974.

Expanding WARF Support

By far the biggest change in the scholarly enterprise of the University during the quarter century after World War II was the massive infusion of external funds, primarily from the federal government but also from foundations, corporations, and other private sources. Nearly all of this external funding was use-specific and most of it supported specific kinds of research and training. The grants commonly provided salary support for faculty, fellowships and traineeships for students, support staff, equipment, and on occasion new facilities or even entire new buildings. Some external grants supplied funds for instructional staffing and programming, usually in fields not presently offered at the University. The external funding agencies thus helped to shape the instruction and research agendas of the University. If this involved the seduction of a

---

[20]Kaplan, oral history interview.

previously "free" academic community, as radical student critics at the time often claimed, it must be acknowledged that the alleged victim was an aggressive participant in the process. Indeed, it is hard to overemphasize either the eagerness with which the University sought outside funding after the war or its impact in shaping the nature and focus of the institution.

An especially convenient source of external private funding was the Wisconsin Alumni Research Foundation (WARF), the captive pioneering venture established in 1925 to manage and market patents based on UW faculty research discoveries.[21] WARF was predicated on a simple yet at the time revolutionary concept: to patent and market the results of faculty research and thereby generate income to support additional UW research. It was also a highly controversial undertaking, because at the time the common expectation was that a university ought to preserve, expand, and spread learning, not restrict and profit from it. Since UW researchers and their laboratories were taxpayer supported, moreover, it could be argued (and frequently was) that any resulting discoveries ought to belong to the public. To distance the University from charges of commercialism, WARF was incorporated as a legally independent private foundation, run by a board of trustees consisting of devoted UW alumni and supporters, whose stated corporate purpose was "to promote, encourage, and aid scientific investigation and research at the University of Wisconsin."[22]   The first of the WARF patents, and the reason for the foundation's creation, involved biochemistry Professor Harry Steenbock's process for irradiating certain foods with artificial ultraviolet light in order to enhance their vitamin D content. The discovery promised to arrest and even cure the then common bone disease of rickets. Steenbock had insisted on patenting his process in 1924 to make sure it was not used to undermine Wisconsin's dairy industry by improving the nutritional value of oleomargarine. He had no interest in handling the marketing and licensing of his patent, however; hence the creation of WARF for this purpose.[23]

---

[21]See Cronon and Jenkins, *University of Wisconsin*, pp. 68-70; Clay Schoenfeld, "The W.A.R.F. Story; The Wisconsin Alumni Research Foundation: Sixty Years of Research and Realization, 1925-1985" (Madison: unpublished manuscript, 1986).

[22]Schoenfeld, "W.A.R.F. Story," p. 12 and Appendix A. Over the years WARF also acquired substantial real estate for conservation purposes along the Wisconsin River at Wisconsin Dells, as well as a rustic center at Upham Woods and several farms. Although the foundation was sometimes criticized for these holdings, by restricting development WARF preserved the beauty of the upper dells, and generations of UW students have enjoyed weekend camp-outs at Upham Woods.

[23]WARF was for many years a highly controversial undertaking, regularly chastised by the Madison *Capital Times* as an evil corporate monopoly, even when its actions were

A later valuable WARF patent came from biochemistry Professor Karl Paul Link's discovery of the blood anti-coagulant dicumarol, which as the prescription drug coumadin became the standard treatment for the prevention of strokes and also the basis for WARF's highly effective and lucrative rat poison Warfarin.

A less happy WARF undertaking was the decision to patent the anti-cancer drugs 5-fluorouracil (5-FU) and 5-FUDR developed by oncology Professor Charles Heidelberger at the McArdle Laboratory for Cancer Research in the mid-1960s.[24] 5-FU turned out to be one of the most effective chemotherapy agents for treating some forms of cancer. WARF granted an exclusive license to the drug giant Hoffmann-LaRoche, which had helped fund Heidelberger's work, to manufacture and market 5-FU. Because Heidelberger's research had also been supported in part by grants from the U.S. Public Health Service and the American Cancer Society, the PHS objected to WARF's patents and its exclusive license to Hoffmann-LaRoche. Accusing WARF of restraining trade in violation of the federal anti-trust statutes, the agency claimed at least partial ownership of Heidelberger's research and threatened to cut off PHS and perhaps other federal funds to the University. Under prodding from UW President Harrington, the dispute was quietly settled in 1965 with WARF assigning a quarter interest in the five Heidelberger patents to the Public Health Service. The agency thereafter declined to grant exclusive rights to manufacture 5-FU, thus effectively placing the drug in the public domain. Following this dispute, WARF and University officials developed new WARF guidelines ending the practice of exclusive licenses and seeking

---

clearly in the public good, as when it acquired and held much of the river frontage around Wisconsin Dells in order to preserve its natural beauty from commercial development. There were many who disapproved of Steenbock's decision to control and indirectly profit from a major public health discovery developed in a publicly funded laboratory. Over Steenbock's strong objections that he wanted no payment for his discovery, the WARF trustees insisted that he receive 15 percent of any net licensing income. Otherwise, the trustees argued, other UW inventors would be unwilling to assign their rights to WARF. The action eventually made Steenbock a wealthy man, even though during the last 10 years before his patent expired in 1947 he quietly declined to accept more than $12,000 a year, leaving the balance to accumulate to nearly $1 million in a special WARF fund for scientific research under his direction. This special WARF Steenbock research fund is still supporting UW research. The lingering controversy over Steenbock's decision to patent his discovery may well have kept this distinguished scientist from a deserved election to the National Academy of Sciences.

[24]Charles Heidelberger, "A Rationale Approach to Chemotherapy," *The Cancer Bulletin, 29* (1969), 96-98. Ironically, 5-FU chemotherapy did not suffice to save Heidelberger from his own later attack of cancer.

to assure broad distribution of products or processes developed under WARF patents. In recognition of WARF's value in both supporting research and bringing out scientific discoveries, a subsequent agreement between the University and the federal Department of Health, Education, and Welfare–the parent agency for the Public Health Service–required HEW-funded researchers at the University to notify the granting agency of any inventions and to assign them to WARF for possible patenting and development.[25] Thus the 5-FU controversy ended on a more positive note for WARF and the University.

During its first half century WARF obtained about 250 patents on UW research, 42 of which yielded a profit in royalties. Three of these generated more than $1 million each, and nine produced between $100,000 and $1 million. The biggest winners were Steenbock's vitamin D irradiation patent, which yielded about $8 million in net royalty income by the time it expired in 1945, and Link's dicumarol-Warfarin patents, which netted over $11 million by 1956.[26]

The growth of the WARF endowment came much more from shrewd investing than from patent royalties, however. Guided in the early years by an astute financial manager and alumnus, Thomas E. Brittingham, Jr., the foundation built up its substantial endowment through a combination of patent licensing and informed investments in emerging growth companies. Brittingham believed in remaining fully invested at all times and unlike most institutional money managers at the time put the bulk of WARF's portfolio into common stocks. Beginning in 1928 WARF was in a position to begin making small grants ($1,200 the first year) to support faculty research at the University; these increased in number and scope as the foundation's endowment and income grew. In 1940 the WARF endowment was just under $5 million; over the next three decades it ballooned to well over $100 million, even as the trustees were making increasingly generous grants to support University research.[27]

---

[25]Jim Hougan, "WARF's Math and Cancer Drug Pacts," *Capital Times*, May 14, 1971; Edward B. Cohen, "The House That Vitamin D Built: The Wisconsin Alumni Research Foundation" (Center for a Responsive University, 1971, typescript); E.B. Fred, *The Role of the Wisconsin Alumni Research Foundation in the Support of Research at the University of Wisconsin* (Madison: WARF, 1973).

[26]E.B. Fred, *WARF: Fifty Years* (Madison: WARF, 1975).

[27]Thomas Brittingham, Jr., "Bold Investor: Taking Risks Has Paid Off One University Fund," *Barron's*, July 15, 1957; Edwin Young to John C. Weaver, January 20, 1971, Series 40/1/1/2-1, Box 17, UA. By the late 1960s federal tax laws required WARF to pay out its net earnings each year. Concerned to assure the continued growth of their endowment, the trustees invested in emerging growth companies whose capital gains could

Although an independent non-profit foundation, WARF was substantially under University influence. The first trustees were all prominent UW alumni and longtime supporters of the University who each put up $100 of their own funds to launch the venture, and who, like the first WARF presidents George Haight and Tom Brittingham, devoted much time and effort to the foundation's successful operation and growth. After WARF was in a position to make grants, typically the UW president and/or dean of the Graduate School met annually with the WARF trustees to request support for specific purposes and for an increasingly substantial block grant to fund the research of individual faculty members as determined on a competitive basis by the Graduate School Research Committee. This large, broadly based faculty committee generally gave priority to start-up requests from new or younger faculty members to help them become more competitive for other outside support. Between 1967 and 1977 the trustees also made more modest block grants to support faculty research at UW-Milwaukee as determined by its similar Research Committee. The WARF funds were entirely flexible at the discretion of the foundation's trustees and could therefore also be used as leverage for soliciting and augmenting grants from other sources.

During WARF's first three decades the trustees limited their support to the natural sciences in recognition of the initial source of the endowment. The trustees also believed, accurately, that this restrictive policy was more likely to generate further patentable discoveries than grants in the social sciences and humanities. Harry Steenbock, whose vitamin D research had led to WARF's creation, was regarded by the WARF trustees as an elder statesman and informal advisor, and he strongly opposed expanding WARF grants beyond the natural sciences. Not surprisingly, most UW scientists shared Steenbock's protective view, as did President E.B. Fred, Vice President Ira Baldwin, and Graduate Dean Conrad Elvehjem, all of them biological scientists. Indeed, President Fred sometimes asserted, inaccurately, that the WARF charter restricted the foundation's support to the natural sciences.

By the 1950s, however, UW social scientists were beginning to protest the great and growing distortion involved in the University's generous support of research in the natural sciences as contrasted with

be retained and reinvested. According to its 1968 tax return, for example, the foundation had a gross income of $11,088,298, of which $7,360,975 came from capital gains. The trustees contributed $3,884,227 to the University that year, and reinvested $6,462,386. WARF, 1968 990-A tax return, Series 40/1/2-1, Box 132, UA. See also Jim Hougan, "WARF Investments: Color Them Green," *Capital Times*, May 12, 1971.

its limited support for the social sciences and humanities. To call attention to the problem and promote social science research, in 1951 the Executive Committee of the faculty Social Studies Division persuaded President Fred to create a special Social Science Research Committee. Over the next several years the committee's achievements were modest, but they served to highlight what everyone knew–that the success of WARF had created a serious imbalance in the University's support of faculty research. After reviewing the situation again in 1956, the divisional Executive Committee recommended that this special committee be abolished and its duties "assigned to a new officer in the University's administrative structure who would have general responsibility for representing social science interests as a member of University administrative councils where major decisions on educational and research policies are made."[28]

Ever alert to head off any incipient faculty rebellion, President Fred accepted this recommendation and as we have seen asked Professor Fred Harvey Harrington, a respected faculty leader and the outgoing chairman of the history department, to join the campus administration on a part-time basis. At first Harrington had neither title nor specific responsibilities (in correspondence he called himself coordinator of social science research), but he regularly attended the cabinet meetings Fred held with his vice presidents and deans. Harrington also began an aggressive campaign to attract outside foundation and federal support for UW social science programs. The following year the Board of Regents acknowledged his new responsibilities by designating him special assistant to the president for academic planning.

No doubt partly in response to the growing unrest among UW social scientists, in 1956 WARF President Thomas E. Brittingham, Jr. offered $50,000 a year for up to five years from the Brittingham Family Trust to support professorships in the social sciences and humanities. President Fred may in fact have inspired the Brittingham gift to help reduce faculty concern in these fields in order to preserve the WARF money for the natural sciences. In one of the characteristic memoranda summarizing his conversations with Tom Brittingham about the gift, the president recorded that Brittingham wanted a public announcement of his gift to make clear it was offered because WARF funds were reserved for the natural sciences. Fred also noted that the outspokenly no-nonsense Brittingham had asked "the administration to see that no 'crack-pots' are

---

[28]"Report to the President of the University from Executive Committee of the Faculty Division of the Social Studies," March 28, 1956, Series 5/1/3, Box 7, UA.

appointed and supported through these funds."[29] In a University press release President Fred and Dean Elvehjem pointed out that the Brittingham gift would "encourage maintenance of a good balance between work in the social and the natural sciences at Wisconsin."[30] Faculty skeptics may have wondered just how their leaders defined a "good balance."

Because the Brittingham funds were limited and transitory, Fred and Elvehjem soon concluded it might be politic to open the WARF door a crack and spread the foundation's funds a bit more widely. In May, 1957, Dean Elvehjem proposed using $25,000 of the WARF block grant to support social science faculty engaged in mass communications and survey research. The grant launched what became the continuing Survey Research Laboratory, a means of conducting scientific polling for faculty researchers. Elvehjem justified the action by noting the federal National Science Foundation had recently decided that quantitative social studies qualified as scientific research. Consulted informally, Harry Steenbock agreed to this limited "experiment," and the WARF trustees raised no objection. It was a small but nevertheless genuine breech of WARF's traditional allocation policy, though hardly a major advance: $25,000 out of the more than $1.3 million WARF grant for 1957. There were further small WARF grants for specific social science and humanities research projects following Conrad Elvehjem's appointment to the UW presidency in 1958, especially after Democratic Governor Gaylord Nelson and his new outspoken regent, Arthur DeBardeleben, began openly questioning what they implied was a deliberate University policy of short-changing scholarship in the social sciences and humanities. A $500,000 increase in the state's appropriation for research made it easier to justify broadening WARF's focus.[31] The WARF policy shift was strongly encouraged by Fred Harrington, Elvehjem's vice president for academic affairs, who in addition persuaded the president to rule that UW-Milwaukee was eligible for support from WARF and various University trust funds.[32]

---

[29][E.B. Fred,] Memorandum of Discussion with Thomas E. Brittingham, Jr., May 17, 1956, Series 4/0/3, Box 87, UA.

[30]Press release, June 3, 1956, ibid.

[31]Edwin Young to John C. Weaver, January 20, 1971, Series 40/1/1/2-1, Box 17, UA; Schoenfeld, "W.A.R.F. Story," pp. 85-87.

[32]See Fred Harvey Harrington to J. Martin Klotsche, October 17, 1961, Series 5/1/3, Box 62, UA. Harrington's letter informed the UW-M provost President Elvehjem had ruled that Milwaukee was eligible to apply for Brittingham, Vilas, and Knapp Committee professorships. The WARF trustees remained uneasy about the diversion of their funds to UW-Milwaukee and Harrington's expansive, free-spending ways. Early in 1971 Vice President Clodius offered some telling advice to the new UW president, John C. Weaver:

In February, 1962, the Board of Regents received a report from a special committee on research needs drafted by its chairman, Regent DeBardeleben. The report decried the "serious imbalance favoring research and scholarly advancement in the natural (biological and physical) sciences as contrasted with similar activities in the social sciences and humanities," a situation DeBardeleben blamed on "the ear-marking by the state legislature, agencies of the federal government, and private foundations" of their research support. While acknowledging WARF's critically important support of UW natural scientists in the past, he called for a major reorientation in the foundation's allocation policies:

> During recent years while federal support of the natural sciences has been increasing at a rapid and massive rate, WARF funds have continued to be applied, exclusively until 1957 and overwhelmingly since that time, to research in the natural sciences. Because federal and state funds for research are allocated largely to the natural sciences, and sources available to the social sciences and humanities are relatively small and utterly inadequate, now and prospectively, to meet the pressing needs in those areas, the allotment of all or a major portion of WARF funds on an unrestricted basis to permit needed support of research in the social sciences and humanities is a crucial necessity.[33]

The regents responded with a resolution directing the University administration "to give even greater attention" to the problem of balance in "the support of scholarly inquiry in all disciplines, with increased emphasis on those areas of social studies and humanities which are currently receiving little or no federal support." The board recommended that "the foundations, in particular WARF, which exist for the purpose of assisting the University" should make their grants "on a wholly unrestricted basis."[34] Although the regents lacked the power to direct the WARF trustees, several

---

My best advice on the matter of a mechanism for dealing with the WARF Trustees is to proceed with caution. Most of the present Trustees harken back to E.B. Fred and Connie Elvehjem. They liked the intimate and direct dealing with the Dean of the Graduate School, each of whom subsequently became President. . . . Furthermore, while they tolerate WARF support at UWM, I suspect most believe it is a waste of funds. Also they are rather suspicious about WARF funds being used to balance budgets rather than for direct project research.
Clodius to Weaver, February 22, 1971, Series 40/1/1/2-1, Box 17, UA.
     [33]Arthur DeBardeleben, "Findings Concerning Research Needs," UW BOR Minutes, February 9, 1962.
     [34]Ibid., February 9, 1962.

months later Regent DeBardeleben drove the point home by amending a routine motion expressing the board's appreciation of WARF support and adding the words "by the provision of funds to the University for research on a wholly unrestricted basis."[35]

Elvehjem's untimely death in 1962 brought the social scientist Harrington to the presidency and with it an immediate presidential review of the use of WARF funds.[36] At his first meeting with the WARF trustees following his appointment, President Harrington announced, to no openly expressed objection, that WARF support would henceforth be open on a competitive basis to faculty researchers across the campus. The Graduate School would continue to report each year to the WARF trustees its use of the WARF block grant, but only for the trustees' information and not their approval, as had been done in recent years with respect to the grants outside the natural sciences.[37] Graduate Dean John Willard summarized the new policy in his 1962 report to the trustees:

> It is now the Research Committee's aim to distribute the research funds available to it on the basis of the quality of the programs proposed rather than on the basis of the fields in which they fall. As increasing federal support becomes available in certain areas and as the research programs in many fields at the University continue to grow, the funds which can be used as needed in strengthening the University without restriction to field assume increasing significance.[38]

In 1962 the Graduate School also began aggressively encouraging faculty members to apply for federal and other outside research funds, in order, as Dean Willard explained in his annual report, "to conserve for *facility* needs the funds made available by the WARF trustees and

---

[35]Ibid., June 5, 1962. DeBardeleben's heavy-handed motion was viewed by some of his colleagues as both gratuitous and controversial. It was adopted on a 5-3 vote only after considerable debate. One of the opponents, Regent Carl Steiger, argued strongly that a simple resolution of thanks ought not to contain an already expressed policy suggestion; he then voted against the amended motion.

[36]See above, p. 174.

[37]Fred Harvey Harrington, oral history interview, 1978, UA.

[38]Quoted in Schoenfeld, "W.A.R.F. Story," p. 88. Not surprisingly, there continued to exist among some WARF trustees a belief that the change in allocation policy violated the original purpose of WARF because their investment in research in the natural sciences brought a greater return in patentable discoveries for the foundation to market. In 1967 the WARF board asked for a thorough review of where WARF funds were being used, by whom, and for what. The University's response satisfied some but not all of the trustees, and the issue continued to trouble University-WARF relations for the next two decades. Ibid., p. 90.

the State."[39] Undoubtedly inspired by President Harrington, this strategy certainly paid off. During the 1960s the University nearly doubled its usable research space, with half of the new buildings receiving major WARF support for land acquisition, construction, or specialized facilities. Table 1 lists the WARF construction grants for this period, most of them in the form of matches to obtain other funds.

Table 1.
Major WARF Building Grants
1945-1971

1948	Enzyme Institute (entire)	$ 350,000
1957	Enzyme Institute Addition (part)	300,000
1950	Chemical Engineering Building (part)	500,000
1951	University Houses (entire)	2,710,839
1953	Primate Laboratory (entire)	160,462
1954	Biochemistry Building addition (part)	1,300,000
1955	Pine Bluff Observatory (entire)	200,000
1955	Birge Hall addition (part)	250,000
1956	Sterling Hall addition (part)	1,200,000
1956	Service Memorial Institutes addition (part)	750,000
1959	Chemistry Research Building (part)	1,454,000
1960	Genetics Laboratory (part)	850,000
1961	Van Vleck Hall (part)	150,000
1961	Zoology Research Building (part)	750,000
1961	Veterinary Science Research Building (part)	475,000
1963	Laboratory of Molecular Biology and Biophysics (part)	1,100,000
1965	Elvehjem Art Center (part)	400,000
1966	Engineering Research Building addition (part)	185,000
1967	Steenbock Agriculture Library (part)	1,207,900

In several instances WARF's value was indirect but no less important. The various external grants for the construction of the $4.8 million Biotron in 1966, for example, came to the University largely because

---

[39]Quoted in ibid., p. 106.

of WARF's longstanding support of research in the biological sciences.[40] In addition, at the suggestion of University officials, in 1969 the WARF trustees authorized construction of the 14-story WARF Building on two acres of land on Walnut Street at the western edge of the campus. The WARF administrative staff has since occupied the top two floors of the building, with the remainder rented to the University as "surge" space for programs and projects temporarily in need of additional space. After amortizing the construction cost through these rental payments, the building was scheduled to be presented to the University in 2001.[41]

Although this WARF construction assistance was substantial, the bulk of WARF grants to the University were administered competitively by the faculty Research Committee to support individual faculty research projects. WARF block grants for this purpose were averaging well over $3 million annually by 1971 and totaled more than $37 million in the quarter century after World War II.[42] WARF support constituted only a little over 4 percent of the total annual research budget of the University by the end of our period.[43] Yet because of WARF's long-time role in strengthening the natural sciences at Wisconsin as well as the usefulness of its flexible funds for obtaining matching grants, the Wisconsin Alumni Research Foundation is without doubt the single most important reason why the University was competitively positioned to gain access to the surging flow of federal and other external research support in the post-war years.

A Second Boot-Stapping Mechanism

Prior to World War II the University had rarely engaged in private fund-raising efforts. Most of its alumni and other supporters believed the State of Wisconsin had the primary obligation to meet University needs and that private gifts in any quantity might in fact encourage the legislature to shirk this responsibility. The Wisconsin Alumni Association supported itself through a dues structure, and while it encouraged graduates to remember their alma mater with bequests, the WAA otherwise did not see itself as a fund-raising arm of the institution. The major exception to this limited and passive view was the campaign after the First World

---

[40]See below, pp. 264-66.

[41]Schoenfeld, "W.A.R.F. Story," pp. 134-38.

[42]Ibid., Appendix D; Fred, *Role of Wisconsin Alumni Research Foundation*, p. 14. This figure includes the relatively small WARF research grant to UW-Milwaukee beginning in 1967.

[43]Fred, *WARF*, pp. 24-25.

War to raise private funds for the construction of the Memorial Union.[44] Surprisingly, the success of this first University capital campaign did not immediately suggest the need for an ongoing mechanism to undertake similar development efforts in the future.

It remained for President Fred in 1945 to suggest to the Board of Regents the need for more organized private support to help meet University needs in the post-war era. The result, as we have seen, was the creation of the tax-exempt University of Wisconsin Foundation (UWF) to solicit gifts for the University.[45] Like WARF, with which it has often been confused, UWF was organized as a legally separate, non-profit private corporation run by a large self-perpetuating board of directors consisting of alumni and supporters of the University. Its sole purpose was to raise and receive private funds to support University activities and, in essence, serve as the UW development office. Also like WARF, as a private organization, UWF activities were beyond state control; the trustees could threaten to withhold their support if it appeared the legislature was basing its appropriations for the University on what it assumed the foundation could provide.

One of the new foundation's first major gifts was for the establishment of the Frederick Jackson Turner professorship of history in 1947, matching the WARF-funded Charles Sumner Slichter professorship in science. The Turner chair was the University's first distinguished named professorship. It was awarded to history Professor Merle Curti, Turner's last student at Harvard, partly to hold him at Wisconsin in the face of an attractive offer from Berkeley. The Slichter chair was used to recruit Clinton N. Woolsey, a leading neurophysiologist, to the Medical School.

Under the leadership of a retired attorney and devoted UW alumnus, William J. Hagenah, the University of Wisconsin Foundation embarked on its first capital campaign to raise a $5 million Centennial Fund in part to construct the Wisconsin Center for continuing education. Hagenah was succeeded by Robert B. Rennebohm in 1955 who directed a second major UWF campaign in the 1960s to raise funds to build the Elvehjem Art Center (subsequently renamed the Elvehjem Museum of Art). Although like WARF the University of Wisconsin Foundation started slowly, by 1971 it had raised more than $10 million since its inception and was channeling more than $1 million a year to the University.[46]

---

[44]See Cronon and Jenkins, *University of Wisconsin*, pp. 589-605.

[45]See above, pp. 76-77.

[46]William H. Young, "The University's Supporting Resources, 1949-1974," in Allan G. Bogue and Robert Taylor, eds., *The University of Wisconsin: One Hundred*

Other External Funding

All of the UW presidents after World War II encouraged the pursuit of outside funds, but by far the most aggressive in this regard was Fred Harvey Harrington, first as E.B. Fred's special assistant, then as Elvehjem's vice president, and finally as UW president between 1962 and 1970. Harrington understood that his ambitious vision of an expanding service-oriented, multi-campus University system could not be achieved solely through the support provided by the State of Wisconsin. Nor could UW-Madison achieve his goal of becoming the leading research university of the middle west and perhaps the country without leveraging massive amounts of outside funding on top of the University's existing resource base.

Unlike his predecessors Fred and Elvehjem, Harrington was a gambler. A characteristic example was his willingness to allow some continuing salary commitments, e.g., for tenured faculty, to be made on so-called soft money from fixed-term external grants that might or might not be continued in the future. Few administrators at other universities, public or private, were prepared to make continuing salary commitments beyond the level of their "hard" (or reasonably assured) budget, lest a shortfall in the unpredictable outside funds leave them with salary obligations they could not meet. Harrington was confident the Madison faculty would be competitive enough to continue regularly drawing in outside grants containing salary support and flexible overhead money. Consequently, he was willing to permit some continuing soft money appointments. The result was a considerably larger and more diverse faculty than could be paid solely on the University's state-funded budget. By the end of the Harrington era, for example, about 20 percent of the faculty salaries in the College of Letters and Science were regularly being paid from soft external funds, as were the salaries of some continuing support staff. Had the L&S staff roster been built strictly within the limits of the college's state budget, and the soft external funds used only for temporary short-term appointees hired for the duration of the grants, L&S instructional and research programs would have had to be scaled back and staffed more modestly and less efficiently. Although risky, the strategy proved to be manageable. In effect, the faculty's research grants were helping to fund a far more diverse instructional staff and therefore a much richer curriculum

---

and Twenty-Five Years (Madison: University of Wisconsin Press, 1975), p. 83.

than Wisconsin citizens and students were paying for with their tax and tuition dollars.

Besides the Wisconsin Alumni Research Foundation, there were several other private sources either under University influence or its direct control. One of the former was the already mentioned Brittingham Family Trust, established in 1924 as a bequest by a former UW regent, Thomas E. Brittingham, Sr. The trust was a private entity under the control of the Brittingham family, but the will stipulated that its accumulated income was to be used for grants to the University for special purposes. Typically the family was guided by suggestions from the University administration in determining these allocations. Until his death in 1960 the dominant figure in managing the Brittingham Trust was Thomas E. Brittingham, Jr., also a founding WARF trustee and subsequently its president. In recognition of Brittingham's long selfless service to his alma mater, following his death the WARF board established a 25-year program of WARF Brittingham visiting professorships in his honor.[47]

Grants from the Brittingham Trust and other Brittingham family benefactions often supported projects in the social sciences, humanities, and arts, such as the special professorships mentioned above, a $1 million construction grant for the Elvehjem Museum of Art and subsequent support for purchase of works of art, music artist-in-residence appointments for the Pro Arte Quartet and the Viennese pianist Paul Badura-Skoda, seminars in art history, support for the East Asian Theater Program, and a long-running program of scholarships for foreign students. The Brittingham family's interests were eclectic. Among other things it provided $100,000 to purchase the Eagle Heights farm in 1951 for development of what became a sprawling married students housing complex, support for the construction of tennis courts, pediatrics, cancer, and superconductivity research, oceanography research and graduate training, and the development of a program in bio-engineering. By 1970, the Brittingham family, through its continuing trust and other benefactions, had given the University more than a hundred gifts since the elder Brittingham presented the Lincoln statue in 1908. These totaled well over $3 million, with most of the funds coming after World War II.[48]

---

[47]WARF Board of Trustees, Resolution on the Thomas Evans Brittingham, Jr. Professorships, November 18, 1960, Series 4/16/4, Box 13; UW BOR Minutes, December 9, 1960; University press release, December 9, 1960, Series 5/1/3, Box 62, UA; *Milwaukee Journal*, December 10, 1960.
[48]"Brittingham Family Gifts to the University of Wisconsin," September, 1970, Series 40/1/2/1, Box 108.

A similar University-dedicated fund under the control of outside trustees was the Vilas Trust, created in 1908 in the will of William F. Vilas, a pioneer Wisconsin lumberman, Civil War hero, U.S. senator and cabinet member, UW law professor, and UW regent. After taking care of the needs of Vilas' wife and daughter during their lifetimes, the Vilas trustees were charged with building up the estate to create an endowment of $30 million for certain specified uses by the University. The most significant of these was the establishment of a group of Vilas research professorships, carefully designed by Colonel Vilas to be the University's most prestigious chairs, plus a number of Vilas graduate fellowships and undergraduate scholarships. Although the estate was valued at $11.5 million at the time of Vilas' daughter's death in 1960, the trustees were free to begin making limited grants to the University while building the endowment up to the required $30 million level. Discussions between UW administrators and the trustees began almost immediately, but the trustees proceeded cautiously and declined to release funds to the University until 1962-63 at the start of the Harrington presidency.[49]

At an early meeting with the Vilas trustees President Harrington commented that the University might want to use some of its Vilas music allotment at UW-Milwaukee. Thus prompted, the trustees responded with a declaration that "all campuses of the University are eligible for support from the Vilas Fund as far as the conditions of the will are concerned."[50] Harrington and Clodius promptly moved to assign a Vilas research professorship to UW-Milwaukee as a faculty recruiting inducement. Only after a number of false starts and disappointments was Milwaukee successful in appointing Ihab Hassan as Vilas Professor of English and Comparative Literature for 1970-71. Meanwhile, there were already a dozen Vilas professors at UW-Madison, mostly in the social sciences and humanities disciplines.[51] The Vilas research professorships remain the

---

[49] A. W. Peterson, Memorandum of Conference - Vilas Trustees and University Vilas Estate Committee, May 31, 1961, ibid., Box 22.

[50] Peterson, Memorandum of a Conference Attended by the Trustees of the William F. Vilas Trust and Members of the University of Wisconsin Vilas Committee, March 11, 1963, ibid. Harrington very likely encouraged and probably inspired this broad interpretation of the scope of the Vilas Trust, as it fitted his concept of a single university whose branches shared common resources.

[51] Clodius to University Vilas Committee, April 18, 1969, Series 4/21/1, Box 5, UA; Ihab Hassan to Harrington, October 25, 1969, Series 40/1/1/1, Box 230, UA; UW BOR Minutes, March 6, 1970. Like the WARF trustees, the Vilas trustees decided to reserve their support for UW-Madison after the merger of the state's two systems of higher education in 1973.

University's most distinguished chairs, with their holders playing an important role in the selection of new appointees.

The largest of the University-controlled trust funds, the Kemper K. Knapp bequest, was smaller than these outside endowments, but by the 1960s was supporting two or three distinguished visiting professorships as well as a number of undergraduate and graduate scholarships and fellowships each year.[52] Until the WARF trustees broadened their restrictive allocation policies, the faculty Knapp Committee devoted a substantial portion of its fellowship funds to supporting graduate students in the social science and humanities departments.[53]

A new and unconventional source of unrestricted private funds for the University came from the Hilldale Shopping Center, located three miles west of the campus at the corner of Midvale Boulevard and University Avenue. Madison's first planned modern shopping mall, Hilldale was developed in the late 1950s on forty acres reserved by the Board of Regents for commercial development from the University's Hill Farms, then being sold off as residential lots for private housing. It had soon become apparent after the war that this large UW experimental farm complex, comprising more than 600 acres and some of it in use by the University since the late nineteenth century, was blocking the westward growth of the city, which was expanding westward on either side of the UW land. Accordingly, the state legislature authorized the regents to dispose of all UW farm land between University Avenue and Mineral Point Road and replace it with an experimental farm further away from Madison. As lots from the Hill Farms were sold after 1955 the College of Agriculture was able to acquire a large new farm with four times the acreage in the Arlington-Leeds area about fifteen miles north of Madison.

One of the regents, former Governor Oscar Rennebohm, a successful Madison businessman, persuaded his colleagues that the University should itself handle the sale and development of this valuable tract of land, both to maximize the return to the University and to exercise some control over the resulting Hill Farms residential development.

---

[52]By the latter 1960s the Knapp endowment amounted to more than $4 million and the Knapp Committee was spending more than $400,000 a year to support various activities, mostly in the humanities and social sciences.

[53]The Knapp Committee chairman, economics Professor James S. Earley, complained to President Harrington early in 1963 about WARF's discriminatory graduate fellowship policy in favor of the natural sciences, which resulted in his committee having to concentrate the Knapp funds on the social sciences and humanities. Harrington responded: "We hope to get a break through on this imbalance question soon." Earley to Harrington, January 21, 1963; Harrington to Earley, January 29, 1963, Series 5/1/4, Box 5, UA.

Rennebohm chaired a special board Committee on Agricultural Lands to supervise the large undertaking. The board established a captive private company, the University Park Corporation, to handle the real estate development and establish minimum building and design standards for construction and improvement of all properties in the area. It placed Professor Richard U. Ratcliff of the School of Commerce in charge of the project initially, and contracted with a number of consultants to develop a master plan and provide the necessary engineering and real estate services. The development was conceived to be a largely self-contained community, with a commercial area in the northeast corner buffered by apartments and park land from the more than 800 single family residential lots. To provide an appropriate mix of housing, in addition to six high rise apartment buildings adjacent to the commercial area, about 50 lots were set aside for smaller multi-family residences. The development was closely controlled so as to allow an orderly progression of streets and utilities and minimize the disruption of real estate land prices elsewhere in the city. Even so, demand for Hill Farms lots was so great that by the end of 1960 all but ten of the single family residential lots had been sold and 510 homes had been constructed. The University sold the Madison School Board twenty acres of land in the eastern part of the development at a reduced price for construction of an elementary and junior high school, named for Charles R. Van Hise, the great UW president of the early twentieth century. The school opened in the fall of 1957 with 526 students; within four years its enrollment had soared to 1,434 students and it had required two additions, making it the second largest elementary and junior high school in the city.[54]

Regent Rennebohm argued that the University, rather than some private developer, should profit from the operation of the Hilldale Shopping Center, planned as part of the commercial section of the development. Under Rennebohm's leadership the regents set up two private corporations: Kelab, Inc., a non-profit organization with the sole function of directing gifts and profits from its assets to the University for scholarships, research, and education; and Hilldale, Inc., a fully taxable company all of whose stock was held by the University of Wisconsin Foundation. Kelab, Inc., purchased a 34-acre tract for the shopping center in the commercial section of the development and rented it to Hilldale, Inc., to develop and operate the projected $12 million Hilldale shopping mall. The regents thus retained

[54]Madison City Plan Division, "Report on Plan for Development of University Hill Farms," January, 1954, *UHP*; "The Hill Farms Story," *WAM*, 62 (January, 1961), 13-21.

indirect UW control of the entire Hill Farms development, while refuting objections that the University as a tax-exempt public agency was engaging in unfair and socialistic competition. Even so, there were complaints about this convoluted and seemingly incestuous corporate structure. Private interests sued to block the shopping center development, arguing that the University was really engaging in business for and with itself. Eventually the Wisconsin Supreme Court ruled 6-1 in favor of Hilldale, and the U.S. Supreme Court declined in 1961 to review the favorable decision.

The mall opened with its first group of stores the following year. By the mid-1960s profit from Hilldale rental income was producing a modest but increasingly significant return to the University of Wisconsin Foundation and thence to the University. Like WARF before it, the Hilldale shopping mall was a controversial but creative bootstrapping mechanism to create a private endowment for the long-term support of University activities, eventually in the form of scholarly awards, lecture series, and distinguished professorships. Thanks to Regent Rennebohm's far-sighted vision and interest, this major University initiative during the fifties and sixties was one of the few instances where the board not only established a UW policy but played a direct role in implementing it.[55]

President Harrington aggressively sought other private funding sources outside the University, notably the Carnegie Corporation and the Rockefeller and Ford Foundations, among the largest philanthropic agencies in the country. Although Carnegie and Ford were disposed to favor the elite private universities, Harrington was determined Wisconsin should join this select group. The University received its first Ford funds in 1951-53: $465,000 under the foundation's Pre-Induction Scholarship Program to support the education of so-called Ford babies–young academically gifted high school male students advanced to college-level work so they could earn a baccalaureate degree before reaching draft age. Numerous

---

[55]See UW BOR Minutes, June 5, 1961, December 7, 1962, and November 4, 1966; "The Commercial Development" and "An Endowment for the City and the University," *WAM*, 62 (January, 1961), 18-19, 21; "Oscar Rennebohm Ends His Term as a Member of the Board of Regents," ibid. (July, 1961), 48; "Hilldale Shopping Center to Provide Major Support," ibid., 64 (January, 1963), 26-27; "Hilldale Makes Major Contribution to UW Projects," ibid., 68 (December, 1966), 19. A major problem in developing the Hilldale Shopping Center was coming up with construction funds before there was any rental income, since the WARF trustees declined to invest in the project. Among other sources, UW officials borrowed from the Anonymous Fund. The first sizable return from Hilldale in 1966–$50,000–was used to replenish this fund. Most of the proceeds from the sale of lots in the Hill Farm was used for the benefit of the College of Agriculture, particularly to acquire and equip a large replacement experimental farm at Arlington north of Madison. See also above, pp. 135-37, 177.

other Ford grants to the University followed: $100,000 in 1957 for Professor Merle Curti's multi-volume History of American Philanthropy, a series of grants beginning in 1957 and totaling more than $1.6 million by 1965 to help develop a modern program in economics at Gadjah Mada University in Indonesia, two grants in 1959 and 1962 totaling $1.125 million to improve teacher education, $1.2 million in 1962 for the development of international studies with another $1 million in 1966, $1.5 million in 1963 for research on reproductive biology, $1.7 million in 1963 for partial help constructing the Biotron, and just under $2 million in 1964 for a UW teacher training program in northern Nigeria. In 1966 Ford included the UW Graduate School with a small number of other leading doctoral institutions in a lavishly funded seven-year program aimed at speeding the completion of doctoral work in the social sciences and humanities, granting the University $1.725 million for the first phase. By the mid-sixties, the University was averaging several substantial Ford grants a year.[56]

To his considerable frustration, however, Harrington was never able to persuade the Ford Foundation to move Wisconsin into the top tier of Ford-favored institutions, with multi-million dollar grants as generous as those awarded to such private universities as Harvard, Columbia, and Chicago. Still, his standing with foundation officials was high. After Harrington resigned as president in 1970, his sympathetic Ford contacts

---

[56]Never was a foundation program so poorly conceived and timed as the seven-year program. Ford officials had correctly noted the growing length of time graduate students in humanities and social science disciplines were taking to complete their doctoral studies. This was a serious problem at a time when there was a national shortage of qualified faculty to teach the baby boomer generation. The Ford analysis was also correct in attributing part of the delay to the comparative lack of student financial support in these fields, as contrasted with the much more generous student support available in the natural sciences. As a result many graduate students in the humanities and social sciences found it necessary to take a reduced course load and work part-time. Ford's solution was to provide a generous amount of fellowship support to a few doctoral institutions, provided they restructured their doctoral programs to make it possible for full-time students to complete their Ph.D. work in five or at most six years. Someone at Ford had not done a careful demographic analysis, however. By the time this program to speed the production of new Ph.D.s expired, the boomer generation was moving on, college enrollments were declining, and the earlier faculty shortage had been replaced by a glut in most fields. Academia was entering a depressed job market that would extend over the next two decades.

For subsequent Ford support see, for example, Harrington, William H. Young, and Robert Taylor, "The University of Wisconsin and the Ford Foundation, 1951-1965: A Study of the Impact of Changing Resources on the Functions and Objectives of Higher Education," April 15, 1966, p. 15a, Series 4/0/3, Box 124, UA; Joseph M. McDaniel, Jr., to Harrington, October 18, 1966, Series 5/1/3, Box 43, UA; "International Studies Grant, First Annual Report to the Ford Foundation," September, 1968, UHP.

arranged a two-year appointment for him as a free-lance Ford representative in India with minimal day-to-day responsibilities, thereby providing him with the welcome opportunity for reflection, research, and intellectual regeneration far from the turmoil that had plagued the last years of his UW administration.

Harrington's pursuit of Ford dated back more than a decade to when he was vice president and successfully cultivated Ford officials in 1959-60 to obtain the University's first million dollar grant for the development of urban studies and urban extension activities. Harrington and Ford officials hoped the grant would among other things help Wisconsin expand and deploy its pioneering rural county agent system to address the problems of the cities.[57] In the University's proposal Harrington explained:

> As a great Land-Grant University, we have had nearly a century of practical experience in combining professional and fundamental research investigations with the application of research findings to specific problems, notably in agriculture. . . . With the transformation of the American economy, it is now logical for state universities, while continuing to serve agriculture, to give increasing attention to the city.[58]

Writing informally to his Ford contact the same day, Harrington gave another reason for wanting "to step boldly into this thing": "If we can, for example, effect a combination or close cooperation of General and Agricultural Extension, that alone is of tremendous importance to the state university system."[59] Already, it seems, Harrington was contemplating the possible merger of the two UW extension programs, a bold move that was to be a controversial highlight of his presidency.[60]

In a sense this first large Ford grant grew out of Tom Brittingham's 1956 offer, mentioned above, to provide $50,000 for up to five years from the Brittingham Trust to support social science research at the University. Accepting a recommendation from the Social Studies Divisional Executive Committee, President Fred decided to devote half of the Brittingham funds

---

[57]Joseph M. McDaniel, Jr., Secretary, Ford Foundation, to President Conrad A. Elvehjem, December 23, 1959; UW News Service release, January 5, 1960; "University of Wisconsin Negotiations with Ford Foundation on Urban Research Grant, undated memo, ca. January 13, 1960, all in Series 5/1/3, Box 43, UA; Harrington, oral history interview, 1985, UA; UW BOR Minutes, February 20, 1960. See also above, pp. 310-14.

[58]Harrington to Paul Ylvisaker, October 23, 1959, Series 5/1/3, Box 43, UA.

[59]Ibid.

[60]See Chapter 6.

to developing urban studies. In his new role as the president's social science advisor, Harrington shrewdly suggested the title Urban Research Program since, as he pointed out to Fred, "it stresses the research side."[61] The new undertaking was not just to meet urgent societal needs; a UW press release expressed the belief that "once started, the program will attract support from national foundations, government agencies and other sources."[62]

An early decision of the Urban Research Committee, chaired by Harrington, was to recruit Coleman Woodbury, a leading urban specialist, to head up the program as a professor of political science. Woodbury was an attractive choice, not least because he was a Ford Foundation advisor on urban issues and grants. Harrington soon decided Woodbury's approach was too scholarly and his outlook too conservative; he was more interested in commissioning broad scholarly background studies than in developing bold action programs that might appeal to outside funding agencies. The impatient vice president soon shunted Woodbury aside and himself took over the negotiations with Ford that in 1959 culminated in the $1 million urban studies grant stressing a combination of research, training, and ameliorative social action.[63]

Harrington gave the Ford grant a cute acronym: TRUE (Teaching, Research, Urban Extension). Under its impetus the UW administration set up an academic Department of Urban and Regional Planning at Madison and a similar Department of Urban Affairs at UW-Milwaukee.[64] Woodbury's more cautious long-term approach proved prescient. By the end of the five-year urban grant, Harrington, now president, found that his optimistic expectations had not been entirely TRUE. The University could show considerable progress in establishing teaching and research programs on urban issues at Madison and Milwaukee, but there had been much less success in developing collaborative urban extension activities and social action programs. In fact, the difficulty of coordinating the two UW extension units, strengthening their ties to relevant campus departments in Madison and Milwaukee, and redirecting their efforts to meeting urban problems convinced Harrington of the need to combine extension into a single agency under one administrator. In a report prepared for the Ford

[61]Harrington to Fred, August 26, 1956, Series 5/1/3, Box 7, UA.

[62]Undated press release, ca. September 8, 1956, ibid.

[63]See, for example, Harrington to members of the Regents Educational Committee, October 13, 1959; Harrington to Coleman Woodbury, October 25, 1959; Harrington to Ylvisaker, October 26, 1959, all in ibid., Box 43.

[64]See "The University of Wisconsin Teaching, Research, and Urban Extension Program, First Annual Progress Report to the Ford Foundation," February 28, 1961, Series 4/17/1, Box 28, UA; UW BOR Minutes, June 5 and December 7, 1962.

Foundation in 1966 reviewing its various grants to the University, Harrington commented: "But perhaps the most important side-effect of the Ford urban grant was the consolidation of extension activities of the University. There was no direct cause-and-effect but a number of factors, contributed by the Ford urban study, helped make this very difficult administrative reorganization possible."[65] Determining causation of complex events is always tricky, but at least the president assumed Ford officials would be gratified to believe they had played a part in merging the two UW extension units.

Smaller grants from other foundations also had a measurable effect on University activities. For example, the Carnegie Corporation provided a five-year grant totaling $70,000 in 1948 for the development of Scandinavian studies under the leadership of Professor Einar Haugen, thereby launching the University's first area studies program.[66] Carnegie funds in the amount of $371,000 also helped develop a program in Comparative Tropical History under the leadership of Professor Philip D. Curtin, to emphasize the comparative study of tropical America, Africa, South Asia, North Africa, and the Middle East. Ever alert to the possibility of foundation support, Vice President Harrington had pushed Curtin to apply for this grant. Years later, still with some amazement, Curtin recalled Harrington's expansionist zeal:

> It was really quite remarkable the way Fred operated in those days. He called me in–I was an assistant professor at the time or maybe a first-year associate professor, but I'd been here a very short time. He said that he'd heard me talking about what I thought ought to be done in history–that I had some ideas about teaching, about non-Western history. He pointed out that these ideas might be put into effect and profit not only the University but myself. And he said, for example, "Wouldn't you like to have every third year off for research? Wouldn't you like to have money for graduate students? Wouldn't you like to have money to hire other people with ideas? If you take this program to someone like the Carnegie Corporation or the Rockefeller Foundation you might get a substantial grant."

[65]Harrington, Young, and Taylor, "University of Wisconsin and the Ford Foundation, 1951-1965," p. xxiii. See also below, pp. 310-12.
[66]Einar Haugen to John W. Gardner, May 19, 1948, Series 7/1/8-2, Box 11, UA; UW BOR Minutes, August 28, 1948; "Scandinavian Study," *WAM*, 50 (December, 1950), 9.

I never knew about this at all. It was completely beyond anything I'd had to do with as a Ph.D. candidate.[67]

Curtin's tropical history initiative subsequently provided the faculty nucleus for a flourishing program in African history, one of the most distinguished in the country, and the nation's first Department of African Languages and Literature. After the Carnegie funding dried up, the program dropped its tropical focus as too restrictive and changed the name to Comparative World History.

On a larger scale, the Rockefeller Foundation had for many years provided a succession of grants to the University, mostly in support of bio-medical research. Significant Rockefeller research and program grants continued throughout this period in a variety of areas, notably $100,000 for equipment in the new Enzyme Institute in 1948, and $46,750 to launch a program in Indian Studies in 1959.[68] Two years later Carnegie funds enabled the latter program to add an undergraduate study abroad year in India, the first in the United States. In another humanities area, in 1955 the Wisconsin chapter of the American Jewish Committee provided a grant of $75,000 over five years to establish a professorship in Hebrew Studies. Its first incumbent, Meneham Mansoor, thereafter proceeded to develop a Department of Hebrew Studies (later Hebrew and Semitic Studies) offering instruction and research in Arabic, Hebrew, and related

---

[67]Philip D. Curtin, oral history interview, 1975, UA. Curtin, originally a Caribbeanist, had been recruited by the history department in 1956 partly to carry on Paul Knaplund's coverage of the British Empire. He soon expanded his interests to include west Africa, the source of most New World blacks, and partly as a way of attracting graduate students in 1959 persuaded the department to approve a general Ph.D. field in Comparative Tropical History. Under Harrington's prodding, Curtin applied to the Rockefeller Foundation for support, which correctly pointed out that the CTH program as yet lacked much in the way of either staff or students. Not deterred, Curtin had better luck with a revised proposal to the Carnegie Corporation. In 1960 Carnegie came through with a five-year grant totaling $215,000 for research and training in the history of tropical countries, and extended the grant in 1965 in the amount of $156,000. Curtin maintained tight control over the Carnegie funds and used them in part to build up a distinguished nucleus of African historians in the department. See Philip D. Curtin, Proposed Change in the Ph.D. Requirements in Non-Western History, October, 1959; Request for Support in Aid of the University of Wisconsin Program in Comparative Tropical History, to the Carnegie Corporation, March 25, 1960; Carnegie Corporation to Conrad A. Elvehjem, November 16, 1960, all in Series 5/1/3, Boxes 31 and 75, UA; Request for Extension of the Support for the Program in Comparative Tropical History, to the Carnegie Corporation, April 1, 1965; UW news release, May 10, 1965, Series 5/1/4, Box 48, UA.

[68]UW BOR Minutes, May 28, 1948; *Capital Times*, November 10, 1958; UW news release, November 11, 1958, May 4, 1959, Series 5/1/3, Box 18, UA.

biblical languages and literature.[69] A similar grant of $75,000 from the Johnson Foundation in 1958 established a distinguished visiting professorship at the new Institute for Research in the Humanities. By the 1950s foundation funds were shaping the University's instructional and research activities to a far greater extent than the *Capital Times* and other progressive critics had feared in 1925, when they blocked regent acceptance of a Rockefeller research grant to the Medical School.[70]

Opening the Federal Spigot

By far the largest source of external funds in this period, and with the greatest impact on University research and instruction, was the federal government. Before the war, in 1940-41, the University's total research budget amounted to less than $1 million, of which only $151,290 came from the federal government; by 1970-71 UW research funds had mushroomed to $64.8 million for the year–a 67-fold gain–of which well over half was from federal sources.[71] Federal funds also supported a considerable variety of undergraduate and graduate instructional programs, were a major source of graduate fellowships and traineeships, and helped fuel the construction boom that was remaking the campus landscape in these years. In the immediate post-war years the federal government massively expanded access to higher education through the GI Bill of Rights; in the 1950s and 1960s it played an increasingly significant role in reshaping the curricula and research activities of the nation's colleges and universities, including the University of Wisconsin.

The National Science Foundation

The growing role of the federal government in education and research after World War II was very much a product of cold war competition with the Soviet Union. In May, 1950, Congress created the National Science Foundation (NSF) to channel federal support for basic scientific research and maintain the country's lead in science and tech-

---

[69]UW BOR Minutes, March 12, 1955; Ira Baldwin to A.W. Peterson, July 12, 1955, Series 5/1/2, Box 65, UA. To steer clear of contemporary Arab-Israeli disputes, Mansour, an Egyptian-born Jew, wisely decided to build his department by emphasizing Biblical era studies.

[70]See Cronon and Jenkins, *University of Wisconsin*, pp. 124-28.

[71] Fred, *The Role of the Wisconsin Alumni Research Foundation in the Support of Research at the University of Wisconsin*, pp. 14, 24-25.

Atom smasher vacuum tank; Professors Willy Haerberli and Hugh T. Richards, July 31, 1959. UA, 4644-M.

Social Science Building, with additions stretching toward Lake Mendota, 1974. UA, 8110-H-1.

Harry and Margaret Harlow with two friends at Primate Laboratory, 1968, *Wisconsin State Journal* photo. UA, 3/1.

Melvin Laird, Dr. Harold Rusch, Dr. Kenneth Endicott, and President Harrington, with model of new McArdle Labs to be built for $2.5 million, October 13, 1962. UA, 5623-M.

nology. The enabling legislation was open-ended: "to promote the progress of science; to advance the national health, prosperity and welfare; to secure the national defense; and for other purposes."[72] Guided by a civilian National Science Board composed of famous scientists who were asked to determine foundation priorities, NSF also established a series of advisory panels staffed by prominent scientists to assure objective peer review of its grants. At the initial meeting of the National Science Board held in the White House on December 12, 1950, the board elected chemist James B. Conant, president of Harvard University, as its chairman, and UW President E.B. Fred as vice chairman.[73] Fred's successor as UW president, Conrad Elvehjem, was appointed to the NSB shortly before his death in 1962. Soon UW scientists were serving on NSF advisory panels and UW faculty members and graduate students were receiving NSF competitive grants. As early as 1954-55, for example, 9 UW faculty members were members of NSF advisory panels and 15 UW scientists received NSF grants. In addition, 46 of the NSF fellows chosen that year attended Wisconsin as graduate students and 13 as undergraduates. Especially in the biological sciences the University of Wisconsin was from the first recognized by NSF as a major national center for scientific research and training.[74]

What made the National Science Foundation unusual among federal agencies, most of which favored applied research on specific problems, was NSF's willingness to fund basic research exploring the frontiers of knowledge. In addition to grants to individual researchers and pre- and post-doctoral fellowships, the foundation also funded the improvement of facilities to promote high quality and costly scientific research.

An example was the University's Biotron, an unusual research facility constructed with NSF support in the mid-sixties. In this instance the initiative came from the foundation, and the experience revealed some of the uncertainties of federal funding. Unique in the world at the time, the Biotron had its origins in a study conducted by the Botanical Society of America for NSF in 1958-59. The study committee, chaired by a distinguished UW botanist, Folke C. Skoog, emphasized the need for a facility to enable scientists to conduct climate-controlled experiments

---

[72]National Science Foundation, *The First Annual Report of the National Science Foundation, 1950-51* (Washington: Government Printing Office, 1951), p. 1.

[73]Ibid., p. 1 and Appendix I, p. 23.

[74]National Science Foundation, *The Fourth Annual Report of the National Science Foundation: Fiscal Year 1954* (Washington: Government Printing Office, 1954), Appendix I, pp. 63-71, Appendix II, pp. 72-89, and Appendix IV, pp. 112-16.

with plants and animals under varying atmospheric and temperature conditions. After soliciting proposals from a number of universities, NSF awarded a grant of $1.5 million to the University of Wisconsin to construct the Biotron. The UW building committee, chaired by biochemist Robert H. Burris, selected a site off Observatory Drive on the far west campus and recruited a Canadian botanist, Harold A. Senn, as Biotron director to plan the facility's make-up and oversee its construction.[75]

Senn and his committee quickly discovered, however, that NSF's $1.5 million was not nearly enough to cover the cost of constructing such a unique facility, at least as originally conceived by NSF and the Skoog Committee. The initial goal had called for duplicating any climate on earth, including the extremes of the poles, and to accommodate even the largest animals. When this turned out to be prohibitively expensive, the committee cut back the climate extremes to the sub-arctic, ranging from central Canada to southern Argentina. By late 1961 it was clear that to realize the original vision of NSF would cost $5.3 million, and even under a reduced budget with all non-essentials removed, the Biotron could not be built for less than $4 million. Rapidly losing its enthusiasm, NSF approved a truncated building plan but declined to increase its $1.5 million grant, merely allowing the University to use it as a match to attract other funds.

Senn, Skoog, and UW scientists were by now committed to completing the project, and for the next two years they and UW officials aggressively sought other grants. In May, 1962, the National Institutes of Health contributed a $1 million matching grant, and in January, 1963, the Ford Foundation offered $1.7 million, enabling the Board of Regents to approve a $4.2 million construction budget in May, 1964. Maddeningly, the bids for the complex structure came in $775,000 over this budget. Senn immediately sought further help from Ford, NSF, and NASA, all of which declined put more money into the project. After the State Building Commission offered to match additional grants up to $500,000, NSF agreed to put up another $300,000 to match the state money. With some further tweaking of the building plans, the $4.8 million construction project finally got under way. When completed in 1967, nine years after Skoog's initial dream, the Biotron consisted of 48 climate-controlled laboratories of various sizes on two floors, with a third level containing the elaborate mechanical systems required to make the labs operational. Scientists from Wisconsin and around the world could now rent climate-controlled space for their experiments in this unique national facility. The Biotron was both a symbol

[75]UW BOR Minutes, July 11, September 12, 1959; Biotron Building Committee Minutes, June 22, 1960, Series 24/9/2, Box 12, UA.

and validation of the high reputation of the life sciences at the University, but it also illustrated the complications of trying to parlay federal support to maintain this status.[76]

The National Aeronautics and Space Administration

Another federal agency with a rapidly expanding R&D budget was the National Aeronautics and Space Administration (NASA), especially after President Kennedy's 1961 pledge to place an American astronaut on the moon by the end of the decade. UW Vice President Clodius alertly pointed out to interested faculty members and administrators that "NASA has loomed on the horizon as a major source of research support." Clodius was particularly intrigued by NASA's willingness to provide full-cost facilities grants—"bricks, mortar, and fixed equipment." He urged a study of campus space needs that might qualify for such NASA support.[77] Following a talk with NASA Director James Webb in April, 1963, President Harrington reported that Webb "thinks of us as a prime possibility for NASA in [the] future." Webb had stressed that NASA wanted a broadly based University-wide effort, with Harrington himself involved, and had invited a UW proposal. Harrington pressed his associates: "Can we get something together? Time is urgent. I think we should have a project in some preliminary shape to go in this spring. Can we get it?"[78] Clodius formalized the effort with the appointment of a high-level interdisciplinary faculty Committee on Space Sciences chaired by chemist Robert A. Alberty, the new graduate dean.[79] The Harrington-Webb conversation about the

[76]UW BOR Minutes, July 13, November 9, 1962, May 8, August 14, 1964; Jim Feldman, "Biotron," *The Buildings of the University of Wisconsin* (Madison: Jim Feldman, 1997), pp. 356-58.

[77]Robert L. Clodius to Arthur Code, Reid Bryson, and Joseph Hirschfelder, with copies to L&S Dean Edwin Young, Engineering Dean Kurt Wendt, and Graduate Dean John Willard, November 23, 1962, Series 6/1/2, Box 131, UA.

[78]Harrington, Memo on Call to James Webb (NASA), April 10, 1963, Series 40/1/2-1, Box 19, UA.

[79]The committee consisted initially of 9 UW-Madison members: Alberty (chemistry), Bryson (meteorology), Code (astronomy), Duffie (solar laboratory), Epstein (political science), Holt (economics), Potter (oncology), Richards (physics), and Singer (philosophy), and 2 from UW-Milwaukee: Smith (commerce), and Vevier (history). Subsequently two more Madison faculty members, Hirschfelder (chemistry) and Suomi (meteorology), were added to the committee. In appointing the committee Clodius noted: "It seems clear that the University will have a major role and responsibility in this field, and a faculty committee is needed to help define this role and to establish the policies as well as the programs to be pursued." Clodius to the Committee on Space Sciences,

possibility of a sizable institutional grant took place as NASA had already funded several large UW projects: Arthur Code's orbiting astronomical observatory experiment ($1.8 million thus far), another Code project to design instrumentation for measuring ultraviolet intensities ($564,000 to date), Verner Suomi's and R.J. Parent's work on meteorological satellite data processing ($459,000 to date), and $700,000 for support of Joseph Hirschfelder's Theoretical Chemistry Institute, formerly funded by the Office of Naval Research.[80]

By early July the Space Sciences Committee and UW officials were ready to submit a preliminary institutional grant request to NASA, which Clodius described to engineering Dean Wendt as "a formal presentation of an informal proposal" that "commits us to nothing except an interest and a hope."[81] After learning that NASA's budget for block grants had been reduced, however, UW officials decided to "split all projects that can go to NASA on their own out of the institutional request" and to urge the Space Sciences Committee to "think of some more new projects."[82] NASA reacted negatively to a relatively small building request from the meteorology department for $330,000, suggesting that the University should come up with something more substantial and "imaginative."[83] Quickly revving up the Space Science Committee's creative juices resulted in a $3 million bricks-and-mortar proposal for a Space Science and Engineering Center that could also meet meteorology's facility needs. Alberty's NASA contact advised him the agency "would choke on a $3.0 million request," but could swallow "about $1.5 million plus or minus $250,000."[84] Taking the hint, the University decided to apply for $1,750,000 for a Space Science and Engineering Center building, plus an institutional grant in the amount of $540,000.[85]

April 30, 1963, ibid.

[80]Proposal for NASA Research at the University of Wisconsin, in R.A. Alberty to Committee on Spaces Sciences, June 10, 1963, Series 6/1/2, Box 136, UA; T.L.K. Smull to John E. Willard, April 17, 1963; Harrington to Willard, April 23, 1963, Series 40/1/2-1, Box 19, UA. Between 1965 and 1971 NASA funding of Hirschfelder's Theoretical Chemistry Institute totaled $2.45 million. Office of University Affairs of the National Aeronautics and Space Administration, *NASA University Program, Quarterly Report of Active Grants and Research Contracts* (Washington: Government Printing Office, 1970).

[81]Clodius to Kurt Wendt, July 11, 1963, Series 5/1/4, Box 34, UA.

[82]Alberty to Space Science [sic] Committee, December 26, 1963, Series 6/1/2, Box 136, UA.

[83]Alberty to Harrington, June 12, 1964, Series 40/1/1/1, Box 15, UA.

[84]Alberty to Harrington, September 25, 1964, Series 6/1/2, Box 131, UA.

[85]Karl E. Krill to Harrington, December 9, 1964, Series 40/1/4/1-3, Box 32, UA. Krill, Harrington's special assistant for federal grants, commented to his chief: "NASA

When approved by NASA, the institutional grant was for $500,000 spread over three years. It might be extended at $250,000 a year thereafter "if the University can come up with sufficiently worthy projects," Dean Alberty cautioned UW scientists.[86] The larger NASA construction request for a Space Science and Engineering Center was more complicated, because UW officials hoped to combine it with the Department of Meteorology's building project, which already had commitments of NSF and state funding totaling $2.6 million. To increase NASA's interest in the project, Dean Alberty with regent approval created an umbrella Space Science and Engineering Center directed by meteorology Professor Suomi, so there would be an actual UW program seeking NASA's help in gaining some terrestrial space. Finally, after seemingly endless negotiations and two affirmative site visits, NASA came through with a construction grant of $1.7 million for its share of the combined Meteorology and Space Science Building.[87] Over several years University officials had gradually learned that NASA's pockets weren't as deep as they had originally thought, and more to the point, the agency was more interested in actual space-related research such as Suomi's and Code's satellite-based science than in broader, open-ended institutional assistance. Still, obtaining a new 15-story building to house the meteorological and space science programs made this effort in creative financing well worthwhile.

---

is an 'agency in a hurry' and seeks to put its money into items as close to an end product as possible. I have not encountered anyone from NASA who is at all apologetic about incompatibilities between NASA short-run goals and university long-run goals. Their position is pragmatic and simple: 'NASA has a job to do; if NASA money is bad for your campus, don't take it.' (This doesn't answer, however, another criticism voiced frequently, by scientists particularly: NASA's crash program is not in the long-run best interests of the *country*.)"

[86]Alberty, Memorandum to All Faculty in Physical and Biological Sciences, and Departments of Economics and Political Science - Madison & Milwaukee, May 14, 1965, Series 6/1/2, Box 131, UA. In practice, the Space Science Committee awarded these funds competitively in relatively small grants to support space-related research projects proposed by individual faculty members.

[87]UW BOR Minutes, December 11, 1964, August 20, 1965, February 4, April 1, September 9, and November 4, 1966. See also Robert A. Ragotzkie, Summary of the Revision of a Proposal for the Construction of a Meteorology Building, [October, 1966] Series 40/1/2-1, Box 50, UA; Request from the University of Wisconsin to NASA for Funds to Construct a Space Science and Engineering Center, December 30, 1964, Series 40/1/4/1-3, Box 23, UA; Alberty to Donald G. Holmes, February 2 and April 26, 1965, and R.W. Fleming to Holmes, April 19, 1965, all in Series 6/1/2, Box 157, UA; Harrington to Holmes, June 7, 1965, Series 40/1/2-1, Box 48, UA; Alberty to Fleming, June 10, 1965, Series 40/1/4/1-3, Box 23, UA; Fleming to Suomi, August 2, 1965, Series 40/1/2-1, Box 48, UA; Alberty to Holmes, March 23, 1966, Series 40/1/1/1, box 15, UA.

The Mathematics Research Center

Another research area benefitting greatly from external funding was mathematics, primarily represented by the three College of Letters and Science Departments of Mathematics, Statistics, and Computer Sciences. Besides research grants to individual faculty members from a variety of sources, these departments flourished because of their close association with a unique national resource hosted by the University, the Mathematics Research Center (MRC) funded by the U.S. Army. In the early 1950s army officials had convened a panel of distinguished mathematicians, including UW Professor Rudolf E. Langer, to consider how best to meet the army's needs for high level mathematical expertise. One of the recommendations of the panel was that the army should establish and finance a civilian research center at a major university, whose staff would have academic appointments and close association with other local mathematicians. To attract distinguished scholars, the center's visitors and permanent staff should be free to choose their research problems and to publish their findings in accordance with regular academic procedures. The army accepted this recommendation and solicited bids from a number of universities to host the center. Langer persuaded his colleagues and UW officials to put together the winning proposal. WARF then financed a $1.2 million addition to Sterling Hall (completed in 1959) to house the UW Mathematics Research Center, which had begun developing under Langer's direction in 1956.[88] J. Barkley Rosser, a distinguished mathematician and computer scientist and former president of the Society of Applied and Industrial Mathematics, was recruited to direct the center in 1964.

The Mathematics Research Center was administered as a regular research unit of the College of Letters and Science, although with some significant differences from other UW research centers and institutes. For one thing, the MRC director reported not only to the L&S dean but also through various army offices to the army's chief of research and development. The MRC budget came almost entirely from the army, averaging by 1969 about $1.3 million a year. To allow flexibility in setting MRC salaries and in paying for travel and relocation expenses free of the constraints of UW and state regulations, WARF was enlisted to act as the subcontractor-employer of MRC personnel. By the late 1960s the

---

[88]UW BOR Minutes, December 10, 1955. Because of its close association with the U.S. Army, its sponsor and continuing source of funding, the center was often referred to as the Army Mathematics Research Center (AMRC), especially by its critics.

MRC staff consisted of about 40 scientists, including 10 permanent members, each affiliated with a regular academic department, and a larger number of visitors appointed for a semester or longer, some from UW departments but most from other universities in the United States and abroad. The MRC permanent members were required by the contract to devote part of their time to consulting with army personnel about their mathematical problems either at MRC or in the field and to hold a U.S. security clearance at the secret level. Otherwise, MRC staff members did no classified work and were free to work on theoretical or applied problems of their own choosing and to publish their results. Typically the center hosted one or two major conferences a year on some special topic that drew distinguished mathematicians from around the world to Madison for a week. These conferences and even more the ongoing stream of MRC visitors were a source of faculty recruits for a number of UW departments in the Colleges of Letters and Science and Engineering.

The dominant University view was that in spite of its anomalies the Mathematics Research Center was a definite plus for the campus, buttressing the mathematical sciences in particular and the hard sciences generally. As the host of this unique and well-funded faculty think tank, the University of Wisconsin was the envy of the mathematicians around the world. And as other support for research plateaued in the late 1960s and faculty members found it more difficult to get grants from the National Science Foundation and other federal agencies, this relatively small R&D piece of the nation's defense budget seemed especially useful.

As campus opposition to the Vietnam War grew in extent and intensity, however, the army's sponsorship of MRC made the center an inevitable target. In vain Director Rosser and University officials pointed out the center's value to UW scientists, and futile were their assurances that the center was not engaged in secret research and that MRC staff members were as free as other UW faculty members to choose their research topics and publish their results. Rosser conceded that MRC permanent staff members occasionally consulted on mathematical problems at army installations, but he explained that any such work on classified projects was done off campus, as was the practice of UW faculty consultants in other fields. The MRC director estimated that in 1969 such off-campus consulting amounted to only about one-half of one percent of total MRC activity in the previous year, and only a small part of this involved classified discussions.[89] Radical anti-war students and faculty, led especially by

[89][J. Barkley Rosser] "Rowen Strikes Again," [ca. December 5, 1969], Series 4/21/1, Box 36, UA.

SDS activist and *Daily Cardinal* columnist James Rowen, took such denials as admissions that the University was hiding something and, worse, was guilty of collaborating with the bloody agents of U.S. imperialism.[90] The army-funded Mathematics Research Center remained a divisive issue until its "destruction" by a huge car bomb detonated outside Sterling Hall early in the morning of August 23, 1970. Ironically, because most MRC mathematicians needed little in the way of equipment beyond pencil and paper, the center was back in business at a new campus location within a few days.[91]

MRC symbolized for many the moral question of whether the University should accept federal funds for applied research that might support a government policy with which some members of the campus community strongly disagreed. The College of Agriculture's Land Tenure Center, financed by the U.S. Agency for International Development (AID) to study ways to bring about land reform in Latin America, was another such controversial symbol. UW officials sought to defuse at least some of the MRC concerns by lobbying the army to drop its consulting requirement and the need for security clearance of the permanent members. There was even consideration of trying to get the National Science Foundation or some other less objectionable federal agency to take over the funding of the center.[92] Even had such efforts been successful, it is doubtful the changes would have silenced the more extreme critics, who argued that in a proper people-oriented university MRC should be replaced by a "Center for the Study of the Rich" or a "Center for the Study of Imperialism."[93] One UW mathematician, himself the recipient of Department of Defense support although his research had no military applications,

---

[90]See Howard Halperin, James Rowen, David Siff, and Ed Zeidman, *The Case against the Army Math Research Center* (Madison: Students for a Democratic Society [1969]); also Rowen's series of anti-MRC articles in the *Daily Cardinal*, March 20, 28, May 14, 20, October 3, 15, 23, November 4, 13, 22, December 4, 9, 10, 1969; March 16 and April 8, 1970. One of the MRC members, statistics Professor Bernard Harris, whom Rowen had attacked for his consulting visits to army bases in 1968, publicly challenged Rowen's research: "In summary, of the three consulting trips cited by Mr. Rowen, one did not exist, and the remaining two resulted in open publications which are soon to be available in standard scientific periodicals." Bernard Harris, letter to the editor, *Daily Cardinal*, December 6, 1969.

[91]See below, pp. 515-19.

[92]See John A. Nohel and Seymour V. Parter to Stephen C. Kleene, October 24, 1969; J.B. Rosen to Rosser, October 30, 1969; Donald E. Percy to Vice Presidents Clodius and Engman, November 20, 1969, all in Series 4/21/1, Box 36, UA.

[93]Halperin, Rowen, Siff, and Zeidman, *The Case against the Army Math Research Center*, pp. 12-13.

later reminded his colleagues that morality offers no universal guidance on policy issues of this sort. "The money for MRC was federal tax money," Wolfgang Wasow commented wryly in 1988, "and the opponents of the military policy of the USA in 1970 should be pleased that a few dollars of the enormous defense budget were diverted from military use."[94]

The Atomic Energy Commission

Less controversial, perhaps because its grants were less visible to campus activists, was research support from the Atomic Energy Commission, created after the war to operate the nuclear processing facilities of the wartime Manhattan Project and to explore peace-time uses of this fantastic new source of energy. A number of UW faculty members–physicists, chemists, and mathematicians–had worked on various aspects of the Manhattan Project during the war, and it was natural for them to turn to the AEC for research support after they returned to the campus. UW faculty members served on AEC advisory panels, and as early as 1950 UW researchers held six AEC research grants (in physics and chemistry), more than were awarded that year to any other university.[95] Soon UW biologists and even a few social scientists were also competing successfully for AEC support.[96] By 1970 the Atomic Energy Commission

---

[94]Wolfgang Wasow, "My Two Years as Department Chairman, 1970-72," notes for a talk in 1988 celebrating the twenty-fifth anniversary of Van Vleck Hall, UHP. Wasow expressed surprise at the extent of the opposition to MRC among a non-negligible minority of his departmental colleagues, even though few of the critics "had professional interests close to applied mathematics." Some simply thought the center's presence over-emphasized this branch of the discipline within the department. In any event, Wasow emphasized, "no mathematicians who read the technical reports of MRC could fail to realize that all of the work was non-military." Much of his time as chairman, he recalled, "was spent in formal and informal discussions with my colleagues trying to rally as many of them as I could to my view that MRC was a very valuable asset at the University."

[95] *Seventh Semiannual Report of the Atomic Energy Commission, January 1950* (Washington: Government Printing Office, 1950), pp. 190-91, 212, 215.

[96]In 1954, for example, UW biologists received seven AEC research grants, equaled only by researchers at Johns Hopkins University, and one in biophysics. In addition, UW psychologists Harry F. Harlow and P.H. Settlage received support under the medicine category for their primate brain research. *Fifteenth Semiannual Report of the Atomic Energy Commission* (Washington: Government Printing Office, 1954), pp. 126-34. The following AEC report featured an article describing the AEC-funded research of UW limnologist Arthur D. Hasler using radioisotope tracer techniques to measure the uptake of mineral nutrients by plants, fish, and aquatic insects in Wisconsin lakes. *Sixteenth Semiannual Report of the Atomic Energy Commission* (Washington: Government Printing Office, 1954), pp. 58-59.

was providing more than $3 million a year to fund scientific research at the University, ranking it tenth in the country among the 191 institutions receiving AEC support that year. In addition, the agency had supplied and was supporting the physics department's nuclear reactor as well as fusion research in the Department of Nuclear Engineering of College of Engineering.[97]

The National Institutes of Health

In addition to the U.S. Public Health Service mentioned above in connection with the 5-FU chemotherapy controversy, there were a number of other federal agencies supporting bio-medical research. Chief among these was the National Institute of Health and a number of smaller national institutes located together at Bethesda, Maryland: Allergy and Infectious Diseases, Arthritis and Metabolic Diseases, Cancer, Dental Research, Heart, Mental Health, and Neurological Disease and Blindness. These federal institutes, administered by the Department of Health, Education, and Welfare, frequently funded UW researchers, increasingly as their budgets grew under Lyndon Johnson's Great Society initiative. For example, NIH regularly supported research projects in the psychology department's well-known Primate Laboratory. Indeed, psychology Professor Harry Harlow's longstanding research on monkeys led NIH officials to select the University as the site for one of the Regional Primate Centers established in the early 1960s to provide national facilities for primate research. NIH awarded a construction grant of $1.29 million to the University in June, 1961, and the Primate Center opened in 1964.[98] Each of the two UW primate facilities, both directed by Harlow until his retirement, had its own separate monkey colony because the Primate Laboratory emphasized psychological research and the Primate Center provided facilities and animals for broader bio-medical research. In time, part of the Primate Center's large monkey colony was housed in a University-constructed monkey house at the Madison zoo, used both as a holding and observation facility as well as for breeding. The UW monkeys quickly became one of the zoo's most popular attractions, though few zoo visitors were aware of this unusual town-gown connection.[99]

---

[97] Atomic Energy Commission, *1970 Financial Report* (Washington: Government Printing Office, 1970), p. 46.

[98] See UW BOR Minutes, September 10, 1960, June 6, November 17, 1961, February 9, March 9, July 13, September 14, 1962, April 5, May 10, June 10, 1963.

[99] Regrettably, in 1997-98 the University felt obliged to transfer the Vilas Zoo

A prominent user of the Primate Center was pediatrics Professor Harry Waisman, whose pioneering research on mental retardation in children was recognized with one of twelve federally funded regional centers proposed by NIH to investigate the causes and treatment of mental retardation. With education Professor Richard Heber, Waisman prepared a UW proposal for such a center, which in 1966 was funded with a $4.6 million grant from NIH and the Public Health Service, augmented subsequently by additional funds from the state, the federal government, and the Joseph P. Kennedy Foundation. Construction of the $7.2 million complex, located off Marsh Lane north of the Veterans Administration Hospital, began in 1971 and was completed two years later. The regents named the center for Waisman, who tragically died in 1971 just as construction was getting under way.[100]

The various National Institutes of Health and the Public Health Service were thus an increasingly important source of support for the University's already strong programs in the life sciences during the fifties and sixties. Their grants embraced researchers in most departments in the College of Agriculture, the Medical, Pharmacy, and Education Schools, the Enzyme Institute, the McCardle Cancer Laboratory, and such diverse L&S departments as anthropology, botany, chemistry, psychology, social work, sociology, and zoology. Like the National Science Foundation, NIH grants supported not only specific research projects but also provided funds for facilities and equipment, graduate and post-graduate training, and support staff. The national health agencies were very much a part of the enormous expansion of federal support of higher education at Wisconsin and elsewhere in these years.

Meteorology–From Nothing to National Stature

One could cite many examples of how UW departments flourished as a result of this revolutionary change in the University's funding base. One will have to suffice: the Department of Meteorology (later renamed Atmospheric and Oceanic Sciences). The UW meteorology program did not exist as a functioning unit at the end of World War II, yet it became a major beneficiary of federal largesse over the next several decades. The

monkeys to another regional primate center after NIH withdrew its financial support of the zoo colony following a campaign by animal rights activists to block the use of any of the zoo monkeys for invasive bio-medical research.

[100]Ibid., November 12, 1965, March 10, 1967, July 25, 1969, April 10, August 14, 1970, February 2, 1971; Feldman, *Buildings of the University of Wisconsin*, pp. 432-33.

roots of the modern department actually reached back to 1853, when Professor John W. Sterling established the first meteorological station in Madison on the roof of North Hall. His observations were discontinued during the Civil War, but resumed in 1869 under Professor W.W. Daniels and incorporated into the network of the newly established national Weather Bureau. In 1883 the staff of the Washburn Observatory took over responsibility for the observations. Two decades later the U.S. Weather Bureau re-established a Madison station in space provided by the University in North Hall. Instruction in meteorology and climatology began in the 1880s and continued under tutelage of Weather Bureau staff until 1944 when Eric R. Miller, the federal employee in charge of the North Hall weather station, retired. By then Miller also held the UW title of lecturer and was listed in the University catalog as chairman of a meteorology "department" consisting of himself and geography Professors Glenn Trewartha and Verner Finch.[101]

Miller's retirement left a vacancy that L&S Dean Mark Ingraham filled in 1946 with the appointment of Reid A. Bryson, a Ph.D. candidate at the University of Chicago, as assistant professor of geography and geology. During the war Bryson had served as a young meteorologist in the Army Air Corps on Guam, where with a colleague he had discovered what later came to be called the jet stream while predicting weather for bombing raids over Japan. Ambitious and entrepreneurial but concerned that his interest in climatology put him on a collision course with his senior colleague in the geography department, Glenn Trewartha, in 1948 Bryson persuaded Dean Ingraham to offer an assistant professorship to Verner E. Suomi, a classmate friend from his Chicago days, and to create a new Department of Meteorology with Bryson as its chairman.[102] The fledgling department began with a $9,500 WARF grant for research supplies and equipment, some of which Bryson and Suomi constructed themselves and some they acquired as surplus electronic gear from the Truax air base. Their first research project involved detailed measurements of the heat and water budget of the Marsh Farm along University Bay, work that required the development of sensitive radiation instruments. This experiment was a forerunner of Suomi's much more ambitious later efforts to measure

---

[101]Gisela Kutzbach, *125 Years of Meteorlogy at the University of Wisconsin, 1853-1978* (Madison: Department of Meteorology, 1978), pp. 2-4.

[102]Interestingly, Bryson had not yet completed his Ph.D. work when he was appointed chairman of the new department. He had written a thesis during the war but upon his return to graduate work had difficulty getting his peripatetic Chicago major professor to approve one of several drafts. See Reid A. Bryson to Mark H. Ingraham, January 27, 1948, Series 7/1/2-3, Box 5; Bryson, oral history interview, 1986, UA.

Meteorology Professors Reid Bryson and Verner Suomi with electronic temperature and wind speed instrument, January, 1949. UA, 199-M.

Meteorology and Space Science Center; Union South under construction at upper left. UA, 3913-J-1.

the heat budget of the earth from space satellites. Bryson and Suomi were both strong-willed personalities who soon clashed, eventually concluding it was better not to work on common research projects. Within a year Suomi was exploring the use of a surplus radar unit atop North Hall to study weather patterns and Bryson was analyzing lake currents on Lake Mendota, testing and expanding Birge's decades-old lake heat budget research.[103]

The meteorology department grew slowly at first, then much more rapidly in the late 1950s and 1960s, encouraged by a series of supportive L&S deans (Ingraham, Edwin Young from 1961 to 1965, and Leon D. Epstein from 1965 to 1969). The department was able to appoint twenty faculty members between 1956 and 1969, and its growing staff was able to attract sizable external research grants. Heinz Lettau got a major grant from the U.S. Army to study the structure of air flow near the earth's surface; Reid Bryson's and Robert Ragotzkie's lake research drew support from the Office of Naval Research beginning in 1957; Verner Suomi, with Weather Bureau and NASA support, designed a radiation experiment to measure the earth's energy budget that was successfully launched on the satellite Explorer VII in 1959; Lyle Horn obtained Weather Bureau funding to study atmospheric energetics; and Bryson's work paid off with the department's first NSF grant in 1963 to establish a Center for Climatic Research for interdisciplinary research on climatology. By 1968 the department's research grants were totaling more than $1 million annually, and three of its faculty members were directing well-funded research centers: Bryson (Center for Climatic Research), Suomi (the Space Science and Engineering Center), and Ragotzkie (the Marine Studies Center).

---

[103]Bryson, "Report to the Meteorological Steering Committee," December 6, 1948, Series 7/1/8-2, Box 10; Kutzbach, *125 Years of Meteorology*, pp. 5-6; Bryson, oral history interview. Active researchers and stimulating teachers, both Bryson and Suomi were recommended for promotion to the rank of associate professor with tenure in 1950. Since the Department of Meteorology belonged to the Physical Sciences Divisional Committee, Dean Ingraham referred the tenure issue to its Executive Committee, which advised against promotion at this time. Because Suomi also had a half-time appointment in the College of Agriculture, Dean Rodolph Froker had also referred his case to the Executive Committee of the Biological Sciences Division, which recommended his promotion and tenure. Embarrassed and perplexed, the two deans conferred with representatives of the two divisional committees and with President Fred and then decided to proceed with the promotion of both men, the first time a Letters and Science tenure decision had been made differing from the advice of any of the divisional committees. Bryson's geography nemesis, Glenn Trewartha, was an influential member of the Physical Sciences Divisional Committee at this time. See Ingraham to G.T. Trewartha, September 29, 1950, Series 7/1/2-3, Box 6, UA.

Ragotzkie was also instrumental in having Wisconsin designated as a national Sea Grant College in 1968 and was appointed to direct the program. Soon after his appointment in 1946 with the mission to develop a modern program in meteorology, Bryson developed courses in oceanography and paleoclimatology. Suomi's arrival in 1948 introduced additional courses on micro-climatology and meteorological measurements, including sophisticated air-mass analysis and the use of radar for storm detection. After the department awarded its first Ph.D. degree in 1953, the graduate program grew steadily, until by 1970 it was considered one of the best in the country and a leading source of new Ph.D.s in meteorology. Its faculty–now numbering 19–was recognized internationally for its expertise in meteorology, climatology, oceanography, atmospherics, and satellite observations.

Continuing his interest in interdisciplinary approaches, Bryson took a leading part in the growing interest in environmental issues on campus. He chaired a special interdisciplinary Committee on Environmental Studies in the mid-sixties that led to the creation of a research-oriented Institute of Environmental Studies (IES) in the Graduate School. The continuing interest in the environment led to a decision in 1969-70 to broaden the institute's mission to include instruction as well as research and give it quasi-school status operating directly under the chancellor. Bryson was the logical choice to be the first director of this expanded IES and he thereafter played a leading role in its development.[104]

In 1963-64 the rapidly growing meteorology department sought funds from the National Science Foundation to provide more suitable facilities in order to maintain what President Harrington described as "the momentum of this significant contribution to the national scientific effort."[105] NSF officials shared this positive assessment and agreed to

---

[104]Chancellor Fleming created the Special Committee on Environmental Studies in 1965 to try to sort out a "turf" contest over where environmental studies should be located. He wanted advice on how to deal with two proposals from the College of Agriculture, one of which eventually led to the creation of a School of Natural Resources in the college. Environmental scientists elsewhere on campus objected to any development that might imply that the College of Agriculture had control over this field. Bryson shared this concern and led his committee to recommend an institute in a neutral location, a policy reaffirmed when IES was given its broader mission in 1970. See R.W. Fleming to Bryson and other members of the Special Committee on Environmental Studies, November 22, 1965; "Recommendations on the Administration of Environmental Studies Activities at the University of Wisconsin," committee draft report, November 15, 1966, Small Series 37; "A Proposal for the Institute of Environmental Studies," draft, December 19, 1969, Series 4/21/1, Box 30, UA.

[105]Harrington to Howard E. Page, July 26, 1963, Series 5/1/4, Box 30, UA.

provide substantial construction funds for a new facility. As noted earlier, between 1966 and 1968 using a combination of NSF, NASA, and state funds, the University constructed an impressive 15-story Meteorology and Space Science Building on Dayton Street near the southwest edge of the campus. The new building was a suitable monument to the remarkable progress of this department and especially the quality of its staffing decisions over two decades.

Embracing the World

The substantial growth of the faculty and the massive infusion of outside money produced a variety of instructional developments in this period. Meteorology was by no means the only field that prospered. New and revised courses and curricula proliferated year by year. Changing technologies also played a significant role in enriching course content. In laboratories across the campus scientific equipment used for teaching and research grew ever more complex, precise, and expensive, and a University objective was to see that students as well as faculty were able to use it. Improved sound equipment made feasible the construction of larger classrooms equipped for audio-visual enhancement of amplified lectures. One of the first to explore these possibilities was a young history professor, Michael Petrovich, who in the 1950s developed a Russian history course systematically using projected images and recorded music to reinforce his lectures. Recognizing the promise of this multi-media approach, the School of Education equipped a special experimental classroom for Petrovich and others to use. Rapidly growing computing needs in instruction, research, and administration were mostly met through a centralized Madison Academic Computing Center (MACC) housing a succession of large expensive mainframe computers. Once-common punch cards became obsolete, surpassed by faster and more efficient electronic data compilation and manipulation. By the end of this period smaller and cheaper mini-computers were beginning to threaten the centralized campus computing monopoly, a trend accelerated by the development of still cheaper personal computers during the next decade.

Harrington asked for $1,872,337 of NSF funds, promising the University would provide the balance of the proposed $4,031,773 project budget. A revised proposal the following year for a $2.6 million project scaled back the NSF request to $1,356,650. Robert A. Ragotzkie to Charles Engman, Summary of the Revision of a Proposal to NSF for the Construction of a Meteorology Building [October, 1964], ibid., Box 50; UA.

Similarly, during the sixties xerographic copy machines began to revolutionize clerical work in support of teaching and research.

University Extension experimented with group and individualized credit instruction across the state using radio and telephone linkages between instructor and students. Its effort to develop more effective distance instruction using the new technologies, dubbed Articulated Instructional Media (AIM), seemed promising enough to attract a large Ford Foundation grant for a time. Though not yet much in use in campus instruction, a few faculty members were beginning to explore television as a promising instructional tool. More common was the University radio network's continuing practice of broadcasting University lectures and entire courses for the enlightenment of its statewide listening audience.

One of the most significant developments was the growing internationalization of the University's activities, accelerated by foundation and federal grants reflecting Cold War competition with the Soviet Union and the communist world. In the late 1950s, for example, the Ford Foundation began funding a multi-year consulting and training program by the UW Department of Economics to assist Gadjah Mada University in Jogjakarta, Indonesia, in developing a modern graduate program in economics. The program was intended to provide the experts needed to guide Indonesia's economic development and help assure that it would be a buffer against further communist expansion in Southeast Asia. Ford and U.S. Agency for International Development (AID) grants funded similar training programs by the College of Engineering in India and Indonesia and a teacher training program conducted by the School of Education in northern Nigeria. The College of Agriculture's AID-funded Land Tenure Center provided training on land reform to Latin American academics and government officials. Out of these international outreach efforts grew the UW Center for Development, also funded by grants from the Ford Foundation, which offered practical graduate training to career officials from developing countries around the world. Unique among American universities, the center's eighteen-month master's degree program combined theory courses in public administration and development economics with the study of real life third-world development problems.

These Ford- and AID-funded outreach training programs for Asia, Africa, and Latin America had a spill-over effect in raising awareness of international issues in regular UW courses. As faculty members in Agriculture, Education, Engineering, and Letters and Science returned from overseas assignments in third world countries, their varied experience served to enrich their teaching and expand the content of their courses.

The same was true of UW recipients of Fulbright grants for lecturing and research abroad. The Cold War influenced the curriculum more directly, of course. A number of departments–anthropology, economics, geography, history, political science, sociology–introduced courses dealing with aspects of the Soviet Union, the People's Republic of China, and the communist goal of world revolution.

External funding also stimulated the development of foreign language instruction and interdepartmental area studies programs dealing with remote parts of the world hitherto ignored in University classes. A Rockefeller Foundation grant launched the UW Indian Studies program in 1959 and two years later Carnegie funds enabled the program to undertake the first undergraduate study abroad program on the Indian subcontinent. Carnegie funds laid the basis for a flourishing African Studies Program offering instruction in a number of sub-Saharan African languages. The UW Department of African Languages and Literature, created in 1964, was the first in the country and the first to offer a Ph.D. degree in that field. During the 1960s federal National Defense Education Act (NDEA) funds began to underwrite a limited number of area studies centers with multi-year grants awarded competitively. Several UW programs quickly qualified for this valuable and prestigious support: South Asian Area Studies (1960), Latin-American Area Studies (1962), and African Area Studies (1965). By 1970 the University was regularly offering instruction in 54 foreign languages, most of them added to the curriculum during this period. It was also sponsoring 10 undergraduate study abroad programs in 7 countries.

Curricular Reform

There were several broader developments in curricular reform in this period. The first built on the legacy of Alexander Meiklejohn's short-lived Experimental College between 1927 and 1932. Meiklejohn had developed a unified liberal arts curriculum for a select group of freshman-sophomore men involving the intensive study of ancient Greece in the first year and a comparative study of nineteenth century America in the second. Steadily falling enrollments doomed the experiment in the depth of the Great Depression, but its vision of a broadly unified liberal arts curriculum remained appealing to many.[106]

---

[106]See Cronon and Jenkins, *University of Wisconsin*, pp. 143-211.

Shortly after the Second World War there was a successful move by a small group of L&S faculty to recreate another integrated freshman-sophomore curriculum embodying some of the Meiklejohn ideas. Led by English and educational methods Professor Robert C. Pooley, the director of Freshman English, the group included one member of the old Experimental College faculty, classics Professor Walter R. Agard. The new program, called Curriculum B or more popularly Integrated Liberal Studies, created a number of new courses designed to bring together the materials of many subjects into a pattern revealing the heritage of western civilization.[107] Opened to an initial class of 300 freshmen in the fall of 1948, ILS students were expected to enroll in several common ILS courses each semester, plus some electives, for the first two years of their University studies. Although the planners retained a course on ancient Greece, they carefully avoided one of the major deficiencies of the old Meiklejohn curriculum by featuring a required integrated science course each semester.[108] ILS flourished initially, but by the sixties student interest was waning and the program was running into the staffing problems common to interdisciplinary instructional programs having to draw their faculty from a number of departments. The initial ILS faculty had consisted mostly of enthusiastic senior generalists who welcomed a team-taught comparative and integrated approach to learning. As they retired or moved on to other interests, it proved difficult to find successors with the same broad interests and commitment. By the end of our period it was increasingly evident the program needed rethinking and rejuvenation.

As student and faculty interest in the ILS program was declining, however, another effort at undergraduate curricular integration emerged among campus biologists. Reflecting their development over many decades, the UW biological sciences were scattered over a number of departments in three large units, the Medical School and the two Colleges of Agriculture and Letters and Science. The rapid, even explosive advances in genetics, molecular biology, and biochemistry after World War II led a number

---

[107]UW Faculty Document 806, Curriculum B Committee, "A Program of Integrated Liberal Studies, Part I," and UW Faculty Minutes, May 5, 1947, UA; *Daily Cardinal*, May 9, 1947, July 2, September 26, 1948. Besides Pooley and Agard, the initial ILS faculty included James S. Earley (economics), Arch C. Gerlach and Richard Hartshorne (geography), W.W. Howells (anthropology), C. Leonard Huskins (botany), Aaron J. Ihde (chemistry), Paul MacKendrick (classics), Llewellyn Pfankuchen (political science), Gaines Post and Robert L. Reynolds (history).

[108]"Curriculum," *WAM*, 49 (November, 1947), 6; "New Integrated Course Will Add Human Touch to Curriculum as Well," ibid. (April, 1948), 17; "Curriculum B," ibid. (August, 1948), 21-23.

of UW scientists to question the utility of this fragmented organizational structure, which they believed inhibited the development of integrated and coordinated biology courses and curricula, especially at the undergraduate level. Responding to this concern, on November 11, 1964, Provost Robben Fleming appointed a Biology Curriculum Committee, chaired by bacteriology Professor Joe B. Wilson, to consider "a more broadly based biology curriculum."[109]

Joe Wilson proved to be an astute politician in confronting the delicate task of assessing and correcting the weaknesses the undergraduate biology curriculum. Before tackling the problem of what to include in a core curriculum that would give undergraduates a well-rounded preparation to major in one of the biological sciences, he arranged for the committee to meet with representatives of the nearly two dozen biology departments on campus. The members then spent considerable time examining the introductory courses currently offered by the Departments of Zoology, Botany, Genetics, Biochemistry, and Bacteriology, as well as analyzing the courses actually taken by a number of current and past students majoring in some aspect of biology. They also reviewed recent curricular developments at other major universities before debating various proposed integrated curricula in basic biology that also included appropriate preparation in chemistry, physics, and mathematics.[110]

The Wilson Committee's report, given to Fleming on June 9, 1965, called for sweeping changes in the preparation of undergraduate biology majors. Departments would continue to be free to determine the requirements for their own majors, but they were encouraged to support a new biology core curriculum, quickly dubbed Bio-Core, which would henceforth "constitute part of the undergraduate training of every biologist." The core curriculum consisted of a sequence of integrated courses broadly covering the various biological sciences and coordinated with related instruction in mathematics, physics, and chemistry. The report called for the program to have a faculty director, its own classroom and laboratory space, and be supervised by a faculty council that would also work with the various biology departments "to achieve the most effective upper division instruction in light of changes brought by introduction of the core

---

[109]Robben W. Fleming to Biology Curriculum Committee, November 11, 1964, Series 4/20/1, Box 5, UA. Besides Wilson, the committee included Donald H. Bucklin (zoology), Warren H. Gabelman (horticulture), Gerald C. Mueller (Medical School), Eldon H. Newcomb (botany), William G. Reeder (zoology), Folke Skoog (botany), William H. Stone (genetics), Frank M. Strong (biochemistry), Dean Glenn S. Pound (Agriculture), and Dean H. Edwin Young (Letters and Science).

[110]Wilson to Fleming, January 27, 1965, ibid.

curriculum."[111] Recognizing the existence of some faculty resentment over the Wilson Committee's criticism of existing introductory biology courses and complaints of inadequate departmental representation on the committee, Fleming moved cautiously in order, as he told Vice President Clodius, to "minimize any departmental opposition that may be lurking in the weeds."[112]

Most UW biologists welcomed the Wilson Committee recommendations, however. Planning for the new Biology Core Curriculum got under in the fall of 1966 and the first Bio-Core courses were launched the following year under the supervision of a faculty committee chaired by radiology Associate Professor Kelly H. Clifton. To emphasize that Bio-Core was a University-wide undergraduate program though assigned administratively to the College of Letters and Science, the chancellor appointed the Bio-Core faculty director and committee and secured pledges of financial and staffing support from the three deans of Agriculture, Letters and Science, and Medicine.[113] This bifurcated and informal support structure would generate problems in the future, but in the late sixties the creation of an integrated biology curriculum was a major advance. Along with the earlier Integrated Liberal Studies program, it demonstrated a UW faculty commitment to find ways to improve undergraduate education, especially at the introductory level.

Another important curricular development of these years involved a more general effort to increase the rigor of undergraduate education. This was the development of the University's first general honors program and two new honors degrees in the College of Letters and Science, a response to a remarkable student initiative requesting more demanding courses and greater intellectual challenges following the Soviet Union's Sputnik triumph in 1957. The School of Commerce developed an honors

---

[111]"Report of the University of Wisconsin Biological Curriculum Committee," June 4, 1965; Wilson to Fleming, June 9, 1965, ibid.

[112]Fleming to Clodius, September 7, 1965, ibid. The most vocal concern was expressed by the Department of Zoology, which objected to the Wilson Committee's "blanket condemnation of biology teaching at the University," and thought the new core curriculum ought to be managed primarily by the L&S Departments of Botany and Zoology. Fleming thought the zoology department's hostile reaction "was influenced by the controversy over the location of their [new] building." The complaint was, in any event, the only significant negative reaction to an otherwise well-received report. Lemuel A. Fraser to H. Edwin Young, October 8, 1965; Fleming to Leon D. Epstein, December 10, 1965. See also Philip P. Cohen, March 23, 1965, all in ibid.

[113]"The Biology Core Curriculum," March 19, 1968; Faculty Division of the Biological Sciences, Executive Committee Minutes, February 23, 1968, ibid.

program in 1962, but other Madison undergraduate units were slower to follow suit.[114]

Other curricular changes deserve at least brief mention. In 1947-48 the University established an Industrial Relations Center under the leadership of Robben W. Fleming, a 1941 UW law graduate with experience in mediating industrial disputes. The new center aimed to draw together the University's considerable faculty expertise scattered across several departments and stimulate the cross-disciplinary study of labor-management issues, while at the same time pioneering in the development of a strong interdisciplinary graduate program in the field. Operating directly under President Fred initially, the center was assigned to the College of Letters and Science in 1957 and changed its name to the Industrial Relations Research Institute in 1965, though it continued to combine graduate instruction with research.

The industrial relations program had strong ties to the Department of Economics, which since the days of Richard T. Ely and John R. Commons was known nationally for its institutionalist approach. By the 1950s institutionalism was becoming passé among economists and the department badly needed a renaissance that would bring more balanced coverage of the field. The process began under the leadership of Professor H. Edwin Young, chairman from 1952 until his appointment as L&S dean in 1961 and himself an institutional labor economist. The turning point in rebuilding the department came in 1958 when Young, with the help of one of his new faculty recruits, Peter O. Steiner, managed to attract Harvard economist Guy H. Orcutt, a rising young theorist and econometrician. Orcutt was appointed as Brittingham Professor of Economics with support from a $100,000 WARF research grant, which enabled him to establish Wisconsin's Social Systems Research Institute.[115] Orcutt helped to recruit other strong faculty members with similar

[114]See above, pp. 127-31.

[115]Young later explained that the $100,000 WARF grant was crucial in attracting Orcutt, but with an unusual twist. Young had persuaded the Graduate School to provide the grant as a research inducement for recruiting Orcutt. President Fred, Vice President Baldwin, and Graduate Dean Elvehjem were all well-acquainted with Harvard economist Sumner Slichter, who had grown up in Madison and had a family cottage on Lake Mendota. Slichter apparently assured the UW administrators their WARF money was not at risk, because it was inconceivable a tenured Harvard economist would ever leave Cambridge for Madison. David B. Johnson, "Edwin Young," in Robert J. Lampman, ed., *Economists at Wisconsin: 1892-1992* (Madison: Department of Economics, 1993), p. 142. At its peak the Social Systems Research Institute had faculty members from eleven departments who by 1965 attracted nearly $1 million in external research grants to the institute. Ibid., p. 145.

interests–Arthur S. Goldberger, Martin H. David, Charles C. Holt, Richard H. Day, and Harold W. Watts–and to greatly strengthen the department's graduate program before he departed for the World Bank in 1970.

As part of a major reorganization under Dean Glenn S. Pound in the mid-sixties, the College of Agriculture not only changed its name to Agricultural and Life Sciences but expanded its purview as well. In 1966 it created a School of Natural Resources to respond to the growing national concern with environmental and ecological issues. Pound also increased the college's faculty expertise and courses on rural land use and planning. CALS could make a good case that it contained much of the UW faculty expertise on natural resource subjects, but despite disclaimers to the contrary faculty members with environmental interests in other campus programs viewed the move as a bold attempt to preempt the field.[116] Their concern over "turf" issues eventually led Chancellor Young to appoint an ad hoc committee under the leadership of Joe Wilson, by now an associate dean of the Graduate School, to consider the appropriate organization of environmental studies at the University. The result was the creation of the Institute for Environmental Studies in 1970 under the direction of Reid Bryson designed to be a cross-campus unit coordinating instruction and research in this growing interdisciplinary field.[117]

Change Via Student Activism

During the 1960s student activists increasingly questioned University policies and authority. At first their criticism focused on regulations governing student life–housing, women's hours, student activities, and the like–and, as student opposition to the war in Vietnam

---

[116]UW (Madison Campus) Faculty Document 52, "Report of the College of Agriculture on the Organization of Natural Resources Program," March 7, 1966. The College of Agriculture report to the Madison faculty about the new school, submitted by a committee chaired by agricultural journalism Professor Bryant E. Kearl, contained a number of disclaimers, e.g.: "We neither claim nor seek for the College any kind of monopoly on this area of study. At the same time, the large concentration within the College of people who have long been working on issues of this kind suggests that the College has at this time the most important single concentration of natural resource activities in the University." Interested faculty elsewhere on campus were not reassured by the committee's suggestion that the new agriculture unit would need additional facilities that might be shared with other related programs, though such "sharing of facilities need not require the administrative absorption of such units."

[117]UW BOR Minutes, March 12, 1971.

mounted, challenges to alleged University complicity in the war effort. By the latter sixties student concerns included academic matters as well. Indeed, the University's decision to create the Institute for Environmental Studies owed much to steadily growing student pressure for more attention to ecology issues, culminating in the first Earth Day celebration in the spring of 1970.

A different sort of student issue was agitation over the University's conventional A-F grading policy, a system that had been unchanged for decades other than the shift in 1949 from a three- to a four-point valuation for calculating grade point averages.[118] Student radicals argued that grading student performance was demeaning and coercive, that it undermined student-faculty relations and constituted a barrier to learning for its own sake. They also objected to the University's reporting male students' academic performance and status to their draft boards. Some professors and teaching assistants shared the idealistic view; others were troubled about the role grades had come to play in determining student draft status during the Vietnam War.

Under pressure from student radicals and other reformers during 1968-69 a few faculty members and TAs experimented unilaterally with alternative grading systems. Most of the changes involved giving A grades to all or nearly all of the students in a course, thus effectively moving to a modified pass-fail system. The faculty of at least two departments–history and sociology–intervened to halt such unauthorized experimentation, which the majority feared would accelerate grade inflation and make problematic the use of grade point averages to compare student performance. The grading experimentation and demands for change led the University Committee in the fall of 1968 to appoint a faculty-student committee, chaired by mathematics Professor R. Creighton Buck, to review faculty legislation and practice in grading and to recommend any desirable changes.[119]

The Buck Committee held hearings, studied national developments, and conducted an extensive review of campus grading practices, finally

---

[118]UW Faculty Minutes, March 7, 1949; *Daily Cardinal*, March 8, 1949. There were some variations within the general grading policy. The Law School was authorized to use a different system, for example, and the Graduate School required a passing grade of B or better in graduate level courses.

[119]Besides Professor Buck, the committee included Professors Robert Ammerman (philosophy), Leonard Berkowitz (psychology), R. Byron Bird (chemical engineering), Gerald Gerloff (botany), Robert Kauffman (animal science), Edward Miller (physics), Valters Nollendorfs (German), Charles Perrow (sociology), and students Sue Ohlson, Greg Schultz, Monroe Sprague, and Barry White.

presenting its report in February, 1971. In a prologue it noted some reasons for the recent student concern over grades and grading, especially the relationship between class performance and the military draft, quoting a statement by Carl Davidson, a national leader of the Students for a Democratic Society:

> The abolition of the grade system is a demand that cannot be met by the administration without radically altering the shape and purpose of our educational system. Since education would have to take place through personal contact between the student and his professor, classes would necessarily be limited in size. Evaluation of a student's work would not have to be temporally regulated and standardized. Finally, the Selective Service would have a hell of a time ranking us.[120]

As finally approved by the UW-Madison Faculty Senate over three contentious meetings in the spring of 1971, the Buck Committee's lengthy deliberations resulted in only minor changes to the status quo. Both the committee and the senate reaffirmed the value of a terminal course grade and agreed to broaden the pass-fail option. The senate also approved the committee's proposal to incorporate additional flexibility into the existing A-F grading system by introducing three new grades: AA, AB, and BC, and substituting the N grade denoting "no credit" or "not satisfactory" for the old D and F grades. It declined, however, to approve committee recommendations to cease calculating general grade point averages and to include on a student's public transcript only those courses for which credit was earned. Without debate the senate agreed to recommend creation of a permanent Committee on Undergraduate Education to encourage and support innovative teaching. The entire exercise demonstrated that the general faculty was considerably more resistant to radical change in academic matters than were some students and younger faculty members, mostly in the College of Letters and Science and School of Education.[121]

Demands for student power and control over academic policy sharpened as a consequence of a three-week student strike in February, 1969, led by black students whose thirteen "non-negotiable" demands included a black studies department and baccalaureate degree program in which black students would have co-equal authority with the faculty.

---

[120]UW (Madison campus) Faculty Document 27, "Report of the Committee on the Grading System," February 8, 1971.

[121]Ibid.; UW Faculty Minutes, March 1, 29, and April 5, 1971. See also below, pp. 471-77.

Although blacks were a small but cohesive minority of the student body, their strike demands attracted broad support from white students eager to promote student power while demonstrating their support for an historically oppressed minority. Some of the early rallies and marches drew as many as 8,000-10,000 participants, overwhelming University and Madison police. For the first time in history, on February 12 Governor Warren Knowles responded to a request from University and city officials and sent in national guard troops to maintain order in the campus area. The last of the state force was not withdrawn from the campus until February 21. The faculty was badly shaken and divided by this ugly expression of student discontent, which threatened violence to achieve student power over academic affairs, traditionally a faculty responsibility. Over the course of several tense mass meetings, the faculty approved the creation of a new Department of Afro-American Studies, though significantly the faculty refused the demand for equal or even substantial student authority in the governance of the new department.[122]

A similar but more general objective of some student activists, especially in the large College of Letters and Science, was to reduce or eliminate degree requirements. In addition to the one or two semesters of Freshman English required of all undergraduates, the two main L&S baccalaureate degrees–the Bachelor of Arts and Bachelor of Science–both required varying amounts of work in mathematics, foreign languages, science, social science, and humanities, as well as a major field of concentration. As in most liberal arts colleges across the country, the faculty intent for these traditional degrees was to assure that L&S graduates had received exposure to the broad fields of learning and had mastered at least one subject in sufficient depth to appreciate its complexity and understand how knowledge builds on knowledge. The rebels rejected such logic and structure. They argued that students were tuition-paying consumers, who should be able to choose their courses freely and develop their own degree programs. They demanded a general studies degree with no breadth or other requirements beyond the 120 credits needed for the regular L&S baccalaureate degrees.

To respond to these demands, in November, 1969, the L&S faculty voted to request the appointment of a special committee to review the college's degree requirements.[123] The new L&S dean, Stephen C. Kleene, a distinguished mathematician,[124] appointed a faculty-student committee

---

[122]See below, pp. 482-84.

[123]L&S Faculty Minutes, November 24, 1969, UA.

[124]Kleene replaced Dean Leon D. Epstein, who resigned in the summer after

for this purpose the following January, asking it to conduct a broad review of the L&S curriculum and degree requirements. Chaired by history Professor E. David Cronon, the Curriculum Review Committee consisted of eight faculty members and five students.[125] Meeting weekly for more than a year, the committee first conducted a series of open hearings during the spring of 1970 to allow interested students, teaching assistants, and faculty members to express their views and offer suggestions for improving undergraduate education in the college. While some of these ideas were thoughtful and helpful, others were impractical, contradictory, or self-serving. A common theme expressed by many students as well as some faculty members was for greater flexibility and student choice.

Even before the committee got under way, the Department of English dropped an unwelcome bombshell on the campus. Explaining that entering freshmen were now better-prepared in their writing skills, the department abolished English 102 and 181, the advanced Freshman English courses, and turned English 101 into a remedial course for what it estimated would be only a small percentage of entering freshmen needing additional work in composition. To cushion the shock of abandoning courses heretofore required of all first-year UW students, the department offered to create a Writing Laboratory to help students improve their writing skills on a voluntary basis.[126]

While there was indeed some evidence that student writing had been improving over the previous decade, the unstated reason for the

---

four years in the post. See UW BOR Minutes, June 13 and August 22, 1969; "L&S Dean Epstein Resigns, to Teach, *WAM*, 70 (July, 1969), 17-18, and "S.C. Kleene Named Dean of L&S," ibid. (August, 1969), 16-17; *Daily Cardinal*, August 12, September 16, October 2, 1969.

[125]Explaining that he hoped the Curriculum Review Committee would accomplish the most significant work of his deanship, Kleene appointed himself as a voting member of the committee. Besides Cronon and Kleene, the other faculty members were: Reid A. Bryson (meteorology, geography, and environmental studies), Dennis L. Dresang (political science), Robert J. Lampman (economics), John. J. Magnuson (zoology), Eldon H. Newcomb (botany), and J. Thomas Shaw (Slavic languages). Kleene selected the five student members with advice from the L&S student academic affairs staff: Jean E. Dunwiddie (LS 3), Douglas F. Hager (LS 3), Jeffrey R.M. Kunz (LS 3), Mark H. Stepner (LS 2), and Curtis V. Trinko (LS 3).

[126]See L&S Faculty Document 156, "Report of the Curriculum Review Committee," April 19, 1971. Just how much interest most of the English faculty had in the department's offer to create a Writing Laboratory is unclear and perhaps suspect. It was evident that dropping English 102 and 181 and sharply reducing the number of English 101 sections would cost the department a major share of its teaching assistantships, the primary support of most English graduate students. The Writing Laboratory would presumably offer a means of replacing some of these lost positions.

surprise action was that senior members of the department believed they had lost control of the Freshman English courses to the largely radicalized junior faculty and TAs staffing the numerous sections of English 101, 102, and 181. Most of the tenured majority of the English faculty objected to unauthorized grading experiments and indications that many freshmen were getting more exposure to Karl Marx and Che Guevara than to the writers and poets from the traditional canon specified in the departmentally approved reading lists. Rather than offer courses whose content and standards the department could neither control nor wished to stand behind, the faculty simply voted to stop offering them.

Because of its significance for the entire campus, the English department's action had to be considered by the Curriculum Review Committee before it had time to share ideas about an ideal liberal arts education, let alone consider specific degree requirements. English TAs and junior faculty members, seeing their jobs at risk, denounced their department's action and promptly appealed to the committee to reverse it. Believing the committee lacked such authority and in any event also skeptical of the quality of the current Freshman English program, committee members declined to get involved in a departmental fight. They agreed, however, that development of communication skills was an essential part of a quality liberal arts education. But if courses designed to achieve this were not offered and staffed by the English department, then by whom? The question was being asked in all of the undergraduate schools and colleges on campus, since all of them required one or two semesters of Freshman English for graduation. Given the University's long tradition of the virtual autonomy of a department in determining its curriculum, there seemed no way to force the English department to offer courses it declared were not needed, and whose doubts about their current quality some of its leaders were willing to concede privately.

To learn what students thought of the Freshman English program the Curriculum Review Committee commissioned a random survey of current second-semester freshmen and seniors conducted by the UW Survey Research Laboratory. Although the response rate may have been affected by an inopportune postal strike, a total of 322 students (58 percent of the freshmen and 52 percent of the seniors) returned their questionnaires. A clear majority of the respondents said they were dissatisfied or very dissatisfied with the effectiveness of the freshman composition courses. Yet over two-thirds of the freshmen and half the seniors expressed support for some course, either required or voluntary, on writing improvement. More than a quarter of the seniors recommended writing experience in the context of other courses through papers, essay exams, and the like. A sizable majority (72 percent of the freshmen and 62 percent of the seniors) thought an ideal composition course should "develop writing skills," as contrasted with approximately 10 percent favoring "critical thinking," the current buzzword of radical activists.[127] Students, it seemed, agreed with the English department's assessment of its Freshman English program, but not with its solution.

Nor did the members of the Curriculum Review Committee. To buy time while developing a longer-term solution, the committee recommended, and the college faculty approved on May 18, 1970, that the L&S English composition requirement be changed to one semester with the possibility of exemption. Other campus units quickly followed suit. This acknowledged the English department's fait accompli without endorsing it or precluding other action in the future. In its final report the committee commented acidly on the department's behavior: "Irrespective of the merits of this action, the Committee believes that the proper way to seek to change a degree requirement is to recommend a change in the requirement, not to act unilaterally to abolish the courses which satisfy it."[128]

The committee proposed one other interim change before completing its review. On November 23, 1970, the L&S faculty approved its recommendation to extend the option of independent study to qualified freshmen and sophomore students, a privilege previously offered only to upperclassmen. This was in keeping with the widespread support for more flexibility and opportunities for individual study.

The Curriculum Review Committee worked throughout the spring of 1970 and much of the next academic year before reporting to the L&S faculty in April, 1971.[129] While retaining the goals and much of the content

---

[127]L&S Curriculum Review Committee Minutes, April 8, 1970, UA.

[128]"Report of the Curriculum Review Committee," p. 2.

[129]It is worth recording here that one of the committee's regular evening meetings came during the rioting over the entry of U.S. troops into Cambodia and the subsequent shooting of a number of student demonstrators by the Ohio National Guard on the campus of Kent State University in May, 1970. Chairman Cronon received a telephone call from Dean Kleene late that afternoon informing him that Chancellor Young had imposed a 6:00 p.m. curfew on the campus to be enforced by the national guard troops then patrolling the area. Kleene asked whether Cronon thought the committee would be aware of this cancellation of its meeting. Cronon said he thought the faculty members were likely to hear of the curfew, but doubted all of the student members would. He said he would go to the scheduled meeting room in case any of the committee showed up. To his surprise, all five of the student members came, having talked their way into the locked Humanities Building past the national guard sentries. They clearly wanted to talk less that night about

of the traditional liberal arts degrees, the committee's lengthy and complex report introduced a number of curricular changes and provided for considerably more student choice. The report rejected a no-requirements general studies degree, but offered students the option of devising their own individual inter-departmental major under the sponsorship of a faculty adviser. It increased the distinction between the B.A. and B.S degrees, while retaining but modifying the breadth requirements for both degrees. Similarly, it changed the unpopular foreign language requirement for both degrees, reducing its extent and providing it could be met by previous work in high school and by a combination of work in two foreign languages.[130]

More problematic was the committee's attempt to deal with the loss of English 102 and 181, previously required of several thousand UW freshmen each year. Declaring that attainment of communication skills was an essential part of a liberal education, the report recommended that L&S departments henceforth be required to certify before graduation that their baccalaureate majors had achieved a satisfactory level of verbal and written communication appropriate for the particular major. Although committee members had little expectation this shift from an entering to an exit requirement would bring revolutionary changes in either student performance or faculty teaching practices, they hoped it would encourage departments to hold students to higher standards of communication. To assure ongoing faculty attention to curricular issues, the report also called for a standing L&S curriculum committee to provide advice to the college's Student Academic Affairs staff in interpreting and approving adjustments to the new degree requirements. Surprisingly, considering the ferment of the times, the L&S faculty approved the new curricular requirements

---

curricular issues than about the troubles nationally and on campus, which were clearly evident from the sounds of street demonstrations and sirens, along with tear gas seeping into the room. Cronon asked why they had decided to come that night rather than join the marchers outside. The response was heartening to a faculty member feeling increasingly beleaguered. All five said they considered the curricular review they were engaged in was important for the long-term interests of UW students and their University than any street demonstrations over U.S. foreign policy.

[130]Retention of a significant foreign language requirement for both the B.A. and B.S. degrees was one of the more controversial recommendations in the eyes of many students and some faculty members. The provision permitting a combination of work in two languages was aimed at protecting Latin instruction in the minority of Wisconsin high schools still offering it, inasmuch as few offered more than two years of work. Throughout its deliberations the committee was well aware of the University's indirect influence over secondary education in the state through its entrance and degree requirements.

on April 28 with only one minor change.[131] The recently established Madison Faculty Senate gave its endorsement the following month.[132]

Although radicals denounced the L&S curricular changes as too conservative and mostly cosmetic, many students welcomed the increased options and greater flexibility now offered them. Some of the reforms were subsequently adopted by other Madison undergraduate schools and colleges. While L&S faculty members may have differed on specific requirements, most applauded the retention of the traditional goals of a loosely structured but nevertheless broad undergraduate liberal arts education. The L&S undertaking was the most significant large-scale curricular reform of the period, affecting in some ways all undergraduates. It was also largely a response to the dominant mood of the sixties, student pressures for change.

---

[131]The amendment retained the existing requirement of six credits of literature within the twelve-credit humanities breadth requirement. The committee had argued that most students were likely to take some literature courses in satisfying the requirement and should be encouraged to consider other options such as art and music history, classics, history, philosophy, and the like. Whether they were also concerned about the possible loss of enrollment, the English and foreign language faculty made an impassioned plea for the centrality of literature in a liberal arts education.

[132]UW (Madison Campus) Faculty Document 60 and Minutes, May 17, 1971; *Daily Cardinal*, April 21, 22, 28, May 17, 1971; *Badger Herald*, April 22, 1971. Although there was consideration of creating a Madison faculty senate as early as 1965, the increasing frequency of large and sometimes unruly general faculty meetings gave new impetus to the idea in the late sixties. By late 1969 the faculty was ready to move on the idea, and it approved the creation of a smaller, and presumably more representative senate in January, 1970. The new body held its first meeting on October 5, 1970. See UW Faculty Minutes, November 1, 1965, February 5, 1968, December 1, 1969, January 12 and 19, April 6, and May 4, 1970, October 5, 1970; also UW (Madison campus) Faculty Document 295, January 19, 1970.

6.

Reshaping the Wisconsin Idea

A key element of President Fred Harvey Harrington's reorganization of the University of Wisconsin during the 1960s involved restructuring the institution's highly regarded public service activities. Two major campus units handled most of this function, widely known as the Wisconsin Idea since early in the century. The first of these was the extension program of the College of Agriculture, probably the best in the country, which provided up-to-date applied knowledge to the farmers and rural families of the state through non-credit short courses, institutes, farm days, and the like. The agricultural or "co-op" extension program, formally named the Cooperative Extension Service, received funding from local, state, and especially federal sources. Its extensive network of county agricultural, home economics, and youth agents effectively set the national standard. Parallel with and separate from co-op extension was the outreach program of the University Extension Division, which linked the rest of the University to the state. UED offered credit and non-credit educational programming through evening and weekend off-campus classes, correspondence study, a network of freshman-sophomore University centers, via the University's radio and television services, which comprised yet a third outreach unit. Unlike CES, UED was funded mostly by state appropriations and user fees, the latter generally providing between one-half and two-thirds of the division's annual budget. President Harrington sought to merge these two units, along with WHA radio and television, in a stunning effort to shape a cutting-edge public service, social action agency that truly would be more than the sum of its already highly distinguished parts.[1]

[1]Much of the research for this chapter was conducted by Susan O. Haswell.

Cooperative Extension

In 1952 UW Agriculture Dean and Director Rudolph K. Froker appointed agronomy Professor Henry L. Ahlgren associate director of the Cooperative Extension Service. Froker remained formally in charge as CES director, but his associate director would, as was customary at the college, actually run the program. Hank Ahlgren had already spent twenty-five productive years at the University, first as an undergraduate, then as a graduate student in agronomy and soils, and finally as a faculty leader in his department and college. Ahlgren possessed an acute and broadly absorbent mind. Early in his career, for example, he helped organize a faculty dining club, "Our Group," that encouraged interdisciplinary collaboration among its members. He also strove to reshape the undergraduate study of agronomy by emphasizing the "why" of things over the traditional focus on "how." His text and laboratory books (particularly those co-authored with colleagues L.F. Graber and Richard Deloret) embodied this perspective and became the standard throughout the United States and beyond. Ahlgren's research accomplishments on pasture and forage crops were equally innovative. Thus in 1949 Dean Froker had appointed him chairman of the agronomy department.[1]

Ahlgren at first resisted Froker's offer of the associate directorship. He was comfortable with his departmental role, respected and productive as a researcher, and proud of his many students who increasingly were populating the field both as scholar-teachers and as practitioners.[2] The wooing took several months.[3] During this time

---

Two publications by knowledgeable University staff members discuss some of the material covered here: James W. Gooch, *Transplanting Extension: A New Look at the "Wisconsin Idea"* (Madison: Office of Outreach Development, 1995) and Grace Witter White, *Cooperative Extension in Wisconsin: 1962-1982* (Dubuque, Iowa: Kendall/Hunt, 1985). A detailed and comprehensive history of the University of Wisconsin Extension remains to be written.

[1]Ahlgren earned his B.S. degree in 1931 with majors in agronomy and soils. He received M.S. and Ph.D. degrees in 1933 and 1935, with major emphasis in agronomy and soils and minor work in plant physiology. On his textbooks, see L.F. Graber and H.L. Ahlgren, *Agronomy: Principles and Practices* (Dubuque, Iowa: William C. Brown, 1946); Richard J. Deloret and Henry L. Ahlgren, *Crop Production: Principles and Practices* (New York: Prentice-Hall, 1953). See also Henry L. Ahlgren, oral history interview, 1980, UA; Ahlgren biographical materials, UA; Henry (Hank) Ahlgren, *Someone is Knocking On the Door: My Joyful Journey* (Madison: Henry Ahlgren, June, 1997).

[2]As Ahlgren recalled it: "My goal was to train a person in each of our land grant universities in this country who did the same work that I was doing here. I made

Ahlgren reflected on current agricultural extension programming at Wisconsin and the possibilities for its future. As a long-time faculty member and chairman, he appreciated the College of Agriculture's enduring allegiance to maintaining an interrelated program of teaching, research, and public service within each of its academic departments. He had himself participated in extension work around the state and through a weekly WHA radio program with agronomy extension specialist Vic Burcalow. Yet while Ahlgren recognized the value of the current co-op extension program, he also believed some major changes were needed. In his view, America was rapidly becoming more urban than rural, and the college needed to assist with this fundamental transition. Ahlgren thus warmed to the challenge and agreed to accept the position, provided he could try to make some basic reforms.[4]

Associate Director Ahlgren early set out to improve the quality and prestige of his CES staff. Most of the department-based extension specialists in the college possessed only a baccalaureate, or possibly a master's, degree while their colleagues by this time generally had Ph.D.s. This severely limited their informal standing in the departments as well as their ability to climb up through the faculty ranks. Similarly, the typical county-based extension agent held a bachelor's degree in some technical aspect of agriculture but lacked formal instruction in the more directly educational aspects of the job. Ahlgren thus was concerned for the ability of his field force to deal effectively with the complex organizational and interpersonal challenges to come. As of 1952, the only training programs specifically designed for extension agents were three-week summer in-service courses offered at the University and two other American agriculture colleges.[5]

---

some progress but not all. I got along pretty well." Ahlgren, oral history interview

[3]Froker approached Ahlgren in February or March of 1952, and Ahlgren at first demurred. "In fact," he recalled later, "if he [Froker] had not been as persistent as he was, and he sort of kept coming back all during the spring and summer and finally by late fall of 1952 I decided that maybe I should accept his invitation." Ibid.

[4]In recommending Ahlgren for the associate directorship, Dean Froker argued, "There is no doubt but that Professor Ahlgren has more balanced support [throughout the college] than any of the other three nominated for this position." The other candidates were Robert C. Clark, rural sociology professor and state 4-H leader; Robert J. Muckenhirn, soils professor and assistant director of the UW Agricultural Experiment Station; and Arlie Mucks, assistant director of Agricultural Extension. The dean also noted, "Professor Ahlgren has not sought the position of Associate Director but is willing to accept it. Professor Mucks is very anxious to have the position." Froker to E.B. Fred, August 7, 1952, Series 4/16/1, Box 161, UA.

[5]Besides UW, only Cornell University and Colorado State University at Fort

To correct this situation, Ahlgren persuaded Dean Froker and others that the college's Department of Agricultural Education should provide a more substantial curriculum for aspiring county agents to augment their technical studies. This resulted in a return to the department's original name, Agricultural and Extension Education in 1954. Ahlgren also encouraged the department-based extension specialists to take leaves of absence and work toward advanced degrees, which he stressed was requisite for progress along the tenure track.[6] He eventually used the county agent training program to justify more tightly structured job titles to support specialized career lines where none had existed before.[7] As this process developed, more of the county staff earned advanced degrees. Eventually Ahlgren was able to ask the Door County Agricultural Committee if they would care to employ Wisconsin's first agent with a Ph.D. "If he's all right otherwise," was the reply![8]

During a meeting of the National Association of State Universities and Land Grant Colleges (NASULGC) shortly after his appointment, Ahlgren made a similar pitch to his fellow extension directors. What, someone had asked, was the one action that would most improve cooperative extension? Ahlgren replied that most needed was advanced-degree training of middle and top extension managers. But no such program existed. The Extension Committee on Organization and Policy (ECOP)–the directors' governing board–thereupon voted unanimously to support the establishment of one. Ahlgren was soon courting the Kellogg Foundation of Battle Creek, Michigan, to fund the effort. He then arranged to have the new National Agricultural Extension Center for Advanced Study established on the UW campus in Madison and

---

Collins offered these short programs. Ahlgren, oral history interview.

[6] Ibid.

[7] Prior to Ahlgren's initiative, people generally were classified as agricultural agents, home economics agents, or assistant agricultural or home economics agents. A 4-H agent would probably be an assistant agent. Ahlgren's effort produced such titles as county 4-H agent, farm management agent, resource development agent, and so on. ". . . we established the principle," reflected Ahlgren, "which I think has born great fruit, in that you could make a career in every one of those positions, that you wouldn't have to hold one position and seek another one in order to come out financially and otherwise better. I think this was one of the real changes that we were able to initiate here and I'm awfully glad to say that it's one of the real significant changes that occurred here and it was comforting for me to know that what happened here [was] followed very rapidly nationally thereafter." Ibid.

[8] Commented Ahlgren about this response: "There was still an element of suspicion you see among people of these, what they call book learning professors. . . . I think we don't have it anymore but we had it then." Ibid.

obtained additional support from state and federal sources. In September, 1955, the center began offering degree work to graduate students from across the United States, Canada, and Puerto Rico. The center finally closed its doors in 1968, as originally planned, after its graduates had spread out across the landscape and started local advanced-degree training programs of their own. During the thirteen years of its existence, the center received over $1.6 million from Kellogg and granted 94 M.S. and 92 Ph.D. degrees through the UW Graduate School. In 1961 Ahlgren also had a hand in founding the professionally oriented *Journal of Extension*, published initially by the center.[9]

Another Ahlgren objective was to modernize the agricultural extension service program itself. Over the decades since the formal organization of CES in 1914, a list of more than three dozen activities had accrued requiring annual reports to federal authorities. This resulted in wasted time, increasingly fragmented service, and confusion about the purpose and focus of co-op extension programming. After Ahlgren's fellow directors in the north-central region elected him their representative to ECOP in 1954, he concluded that the programming problem was a national one.[10] Thus when he became ECOP chairman in 1957, he proposed modernizing the national CES program to take account of the changing composition and needs of the American public. He chaired the resulting study committee, whose 1958 report, "A Statement of Scope and Responsibility: The Cooperative Extension Service Today," proved to be a watershed document.[11]

The "Scope Report," as it generally became known, was the first of three collaborative efforts that helped redefine the role of

---

[9]UW BOR Minutes, May 7, 1955, UA; Ahlgren, oral history interview. For an early overview of the center's activity, see "Second Annual Report of the National Agricultural Extension Center for Advanced Study, Including Program Plans for 1957-58," (Madison: University of Wisconsin, July, 1957), Series 4/16/1, Box 273, UA; John W. Jenkins, *A Centennial History: A History of the College of Agricultural and Life Sciences at the University of Wisconsin-Madison* (Madison: College of Agricultural and Life Sciences, 1991), pp. 138-39, 141-42, 147; E.R. McIntyre, *Fifty Years of Cooperative Extension at Wisconsin, 1912-1962*, Circular 602 (Madison: University of Wisconsin Extension Service, 1962), pp. 162-63.

[10]In June of 1956 Assistant Secretary of Agriculture E.L. Peterson addressed ECOP and called for the development of a "modern charter" for extension. "Report of Subcommittee on Implementation of the Scope Effort," November, 1960, Series 9/4/21-2, Box 8, UA.

[11]Originally entitled "The Cooperative Extension Service Today: An Outline of Major Responsibilities," the report was drafted by a subcommittee and submitted to ECOP on November 9, 1957. Ibid.

modern cooperative extension programming in Wisconsin. The report explicitly reaffirmed the original mandate of the federal Smith-Lever Act, "to aid in diffusing among the people of the United States useful and practical information on the subjects relating to agriculture and home economics, and to encourage the application of the same." It also noted the "rapidly changing scene" that called for the shifting of "programs and methods to meet ever-changing conditions and demands." Accordingly, the "Scope Report" recommended nine "areas of program emphasis": (1) efficiency in agricultural production; (2) efficiency in marketing, distribution, and utilization; (3) conservation, development, and use of natural resources; (4) management on the farm and in the home; (5) family living; (6) youth development; (7) leadership development; (8) community improvement and resource development; and (9) public affairs. Furthermore, while its focus remained on the farm and rural non-farm population, the "Scope Report" also explicitly included "urban residents" among co-op extension's potential clienteles. Cooperative extension had identified a new frontier.

Chairman Ahlgren and his ECOP colleagues intended the "Scope Report" to serve as "but one of a series of steps in a program of modernizing the work of our service." Accordingly, in January,1958, ECOP named seventy-five extension leaders from around the country to nine task forces charged with "indicating how Extension can accomplish its objectives in each program area." The groups set to work. In July Ahlgren hosted them at a meeting at UW-Madison that produced "A Guide to Extension Programs for the Future," which ECOP formally approved on May 1, 1959. It now fell to the individual state services, including Wisconsin's, to reshape their programs in light of the "Scope Report" and the "Guide." Perhaps not surprisingly, Wisconsin's was completed in late 1960, one of the first in the nation. Thus eight years into his tenure as associate director, Henry Ahlgren had been largely instrumental in modernizing cooperative extension, both at home and to a great extent throughout the nation.[12]

Finally, in addition to his early national leadership activities, Ahlgren throughout his tenure with CES involved himself with a broad range of programs and agencies directly related to the work of cooperative extension in Wisconsin. These included the Wisconsin State Soil

---

[12]"Report of Subcommittee on Implementation of the Scope Effort." This committee consisted of six members drawn from various parts of the United States, with Ahlgren serving as chairman. "Report of Subcommittee on Implementation of the Scope Effort." Ahlgren biographical materials, UHP.

and Water Conservation Committee, Wisconsin Farm Progress Days, the Wisconsin Rural Development Committee, the University of Wisconsin Upham Woods Committee, the Agricultural Records Cooperative, the Wisconsin Exposition Council, the Farm Museum Committee of the State Historical Society, the World Food and Agricultural Foundation, and the Wisconsin Agricultural Savings Bond Committee. Ahlgren was far from a passive member of these organizations, and in at least one case was instrumental in forming a new and important group, the Wisconsin Association of Agricultural and Extension Committees of County Boards. This grew out of his successful effort during the early 1960s to obtain state-level legislation to implement the programming changes recommended in the Wisconsin program guide. Overall, Ahlgren's involvement with many of these organizations extended from the early 1950s through the mid-1970s, indicating his ability to work closely and cordially with a wide variety of individuals and interests.[13]

The University Extension Division

Hank Ahlgren's counterpart at the University Extension Division was political science Professor Lorentz H. Adolfson. Placed in charge of UED in 1944, Adolfson served in this role for nearly twenty years.[14] When he was offered the position, Adolfson was in the process of completing his Ph.D. studies at Madison, and was not in any way contemplating an extension career. He therefore was reluctant to accept the assignment. But his graduate mentor, Professor John Gaus, persuaded UW President Clarence A. Dykstra to ignore Adolfson's protests, and the diffident candidate soon found himself setting out on a new and unanticipated profession. No self-promoter or empire builder, Adolfson freely delegated responsibility to such lieutenants as Wilbur M. Hanley (in charge of the freshman-sophomore centers) and Theodore J. Shannon (who handled the remainder of general extension programming); they consequently tended to become the visible public spokesmen for their units.[15] Quietly efficient and unobtrusive, the Adolfson

---

[13]Ahlgren, oral history interview and biographical materials. Ahlgren also served on numerous UW-Madison faculty committees. His membership on the Public Functions Committee spanned twenty-eight years.

[14]The regents first appointed Adolfson acting associate director on February 12, 1944, and removed the "acting" qualifier on January 9, 1945. UW BOR Minutes.

[15]Fred Harvey Harrington, oral history interview, 1985, UA.

Agricultural extension agent in the field, 1951. UA, X25-3381.

University Extension Division leaders Clay Schoenfeld and Theodore "Ted" Shannon with plant pathologist Riksh Syamananda (center) noting extension sites, August 4, 1953. UA, 25-3400.

administration earned respect across the campus, including from Hank Ahlgren and his CES staff. Indeed, by 1958 when the Board of Regents were deciding on a successor to UW President E.B. Fred, the search-and-screen committee included Adolfson as one of its four nominees.[16]

During Adolfson's tenure, most of it as director, UED expanded from a unit focusing largely on correspondence study to include a wide variety of credit and non-credit in-service adult education programming. This included sponsorship of a growing number of high quality institutes and conferences in professional and liberal arts fields.[17] A total of 229 such programs attracted nearly thirty thousand participants in 1953. The opening of the Wisconsin Center in 1958 was a culmination of this effort.[18] As late as the 1990s, UED veterans recalled the Adolfson era as a kind of golden age for innovative programming. A major handicap, however, was the legislature's steadfast refusal to increase significantly the UED appropriation to match its expanding activities. Thus in 1954 Adolfson explained to the regents: "There is a ceiling of fees beyond which you will jeopardize programs. We may have reached that ceiling in correspondence study fees, which, in state institutions, are the highest in the nation. The Extension Division, outside of day classes, is about two-thirds self-supporting." Associate Director Ahlgren, on the other hand, had little reason to complain, because his agency was able to provide its services without charge to most recipients due to the substantial financial support it received at both the county and federal levels.[19]

For Director Adolfson and his UED colleagues, the legislature's self-support mandate for general extension encouraged the expansion of correspondence programming as a means of producing revenue to pay for other public service work. Thus, when the University of Chicago decided to close down its highly regarded program of leisure-time correspondence courses, Adolfson acquired and transferred the program to Madison. Similarly, UED gained financially from its continuing arrangement as administrative home of the United States Armed Forces Institute (USAFI), housed in downtown Madison near the campus. The USAFI partnership was mostly amicable and productive,

---

[16]Ibid. The other nominees were Conrad Elvehjem, Harrington, and Kurt Wendt.

[17]Lorentz H. Adolfson, oral history interview, 1983, UA.

[18]*The 50-Year Story of the Wisconsin Idea in Education* (Madison: University Extension Division, 1956), p. 36.

[19]UW BOR Minutes, January 9, 1954; *50-Year Story*, p. 30.

and by the 1950s UED staff members were grading over 25,000 USAFI papers a month.[20] At the height of the Cold War, however, the staunch UW commitment to academic freedom collided with the anti-communist concerns of the Department of Defense, which sought to arrange a contract to give it control over whom the University could employ to produce and grade the USAFI correspondence courses. The resulting dispute assumed national proportions as UW President E.B. Fred, backed by the Board of Regents, led a country-wide resistance to this controversial federal effort.[21]

During the 1950s Adolfson tried to improve the association between his faculty and their counterparts in the campus academic departments, particularly in the College of Letters and Science but also in Engineering and Commerce. He took this initiative at the urging of President Fred, whose background in the College of Agriculture had stressed the value of integrating extension with other academic departmental functions. Unlike co-op extension, the UED lacked this tradition. Because of budget limitations and the strong tendency of prior leaders to organize its teaching staff separate from the resident departments, the University Extension Division attracted neither the expertise of the University's ablest scholars nor their interest and allegiance. President Fred deplored this situation, which he viewed as intrinsically unproductive, and he encouraged Adolfson to counter it. He did this whenever possible by arranging joint faculty appointments, usually for the UED faculty member in charge of each disciplinary or subject field, thus gaining at least a foothold in a number of campus departments. By 1953 twenty-three units enjoyed continuing formal ties to their counterpart campus departments. Adolfson viewed this as one of his major accomplishments as director.[22]

---

[20]As a pioneer of correspondence study, UED had advised the U.S. Navy on developing an off-duty educational program before World War I. Shortly after American entry into World War II, the War Department authorized the establishment of an army correspondence study program. This resulted, in April, 1942, in the establishment of the U.S. Army Institute in Madison, originally administered by the army with UED staff handling the instruction. The following September the program was opened to navy personnel. In February, 1943, the program was renamed the U.S. Armed Forces Institute. The original core of 64 technical-vocational courses quickly expanded in breadth and were offered at both the high school and college level. Ibid.

[21]Summary of Adolfson's oral report to the regents on UED organization and activities, UW BOR Minutes, January 9, 1954.

[22]Included among the fields were: art education, chemistry, commerce, economics/sociology/anthropology, education, engineering, English, French-Italian, geography, German, history, journalism, law, library methods, mathematics, music,

Adolfson also quietly supervised a fundamental transition in the two-year University centers. During the immediate post-war years, he and his UED colleagues scrambled to make University instructional resources available throughout the state to returning GIs and traditional college-age youngsters the crowded University in Madison could not accommodate. If a locality could demonstrate adequate student demand and furnish classroom or laboratory space, general extension would provide the instruction. At one point during the latter 1940s, general extension was operating over thirty such centers. These arrangements, however, were explicitly temporary.[23] As the post-war rush began to subside, a number of local communities began lobbying for permanent freshman-sophomore centers, even agreeing to supply permanent facilities for this purpose. By 1953 UW centers were in continuing operation at Green Bay, Kenosha, Manitowoc, Marinette, Menasha, Racine, Sheboygan, and Wausau.[24] Director Adolfson was responsible for administering them, while the Madison resident departments ordinarily handled faculty appointments and associated academic matters. The University centers were thus evolving into a new sort of collegiate agency, neither fully an extension unit, nor a degree-granting school, but nevertheless an effective and popular provider of University instructional services. The challenges associated with this development increasingly fascinated Adolfson, and in 1964 he agreed to President Harrington's request that he become the first chancellor of the newly independent University Center System.[25]

In a separate category was the Milwaukee Extension Center, created before the First World War to provide non-credit in-service instruction to residents of the state's largest city. After the war the Milwaukee Extension Center began offering credit courses to returning veterans and thereafter became the first permanent UW outpost. It did this with its own resident faculty providing freshman-sophomore level courses in a dedicated downtown facility. As we have seen in Chapter

---

pharmacy, photography, physical education, political science, psychology, Spanish, and speech. *50-Year Story*, p. 35. For their part, the resident departments welcomed the association as a chance to provide the staff and determine the content of the extension courses offered for credit by correspondence and at the two-year extension centers to make sure it dovetailed with their own courses.

[23] *50-Year Story*, p. 38.

[24] Ibid., p. 36.

[25] Harrington, oral history interview. According to Harrington, Hanley handled the "politicking around the state" while Adolfson administered the educational activity. "He handled this very well." See also pp. 171, 210.

2 of this study, the center was combined in 1955 with the Wisconsin State College at Milwaukee to form the University of Wisconsin-Milwaukee.[26]

UED also maintained several other types of educational service units. These included: the Bureau of Information and Program Services, which ran a "package library" program; the Bureau of Lectures and Concerts that organized "lyceum" offerings for schools and civic groups; the School for Workers offering summer institutes, classes, and short courses for laboring people; and the Industrial Management Institute furnishing analogous instruction for a business clientele. The two Bureaus of Community Development and of Government conducted regional development projects, consultations, and specialized research.[27] Under Director Adolfson's leadership, the University Extension Division made available a broad and multi-faceted program of credit and non-credit instruction for the general population of the state. In 1956 the division published a pamphlet celebrating its first half-century of service to the state: *The 50-Year Story of the Wisconsin Idea in Education*. Most of the document reviewed past and present UED programs in highly glowing terms. A final section pointed out that the majority of the Wisconsin population now resided in urban centers and over 82 percent of the people were engaged in urban occupations. "This means,"observed the anonymous author, "that general extension has increasingly heavier responsibilities than agricultural extension in Wisconsin. . . . The new need in Wisconsin is for a general extension service equipped to serve the modern urban population."[28]

---

[26]There are several sources on the historical background of the University Extension Center in Milwaukee. Among the most prominent, see: Merle Curti and Vernon Carstensen, *The University of Wisconsin: A History*, 1848-1925, vol. 2 (Madison: University of Wisconsin Press, 1949), pp. 221, 577; E. David Cronon and John W. Jenkins, *The University of Wisconsin: A History*, vol. 3., *Politics, Depression, and War, 1925-1945* (Madison: University of Wisconsin Press, 1994), pp. 803-815; Elisabeth Holmes, The Urban Mission Anticipated: A Biography of the UW Extension Center in Milwaukee (Milwaukee: University of Wisconsin-Milwaukee Foundation, 1976); and *50-Year Story*, pp 19, 25, 36.

[27]Ibid., pp. 37-38.

[28]Ibid, p. 42. Adolfson had hinted at this new urban mission early in 1954, vaguely referring to prior efforts on campus and nationally to develop cooperative arrangements with agricultural extension: "The line is blurring between urban and rural communities in terms of educational services for the people. We are exploring here and in the other land grant institutions how the two extension services can be brought together to best serve all of the people, both rural and urban." BOR Minutes, January 9, 1954.

WHA Radio and Television

A third major outreach unit was organized around the University's pioneering radio station, WHA, which also dated from the time of World War I. Subsequently, under the leadership of Harold B. McCarty, WHA developed a variety of instructional programming ranging from the elementary school to the college level. In 1947 McCarty supervised the first broadcasts of WHA-FM, later renamed WERN, designed by Glenn Koehler and Jack Stiehl. During the late 1940s and early 1950s McCarty presided over a considerable expansion of the state's radio network to include not only AM station WHA in Madison but also FM stations WERN, WHAD, WHKW, WHWC, WHLA, WHHI, and WHSA broadcasting across the state. In 1954 WHA television began broadcasting from improvised studios in the old Chemical Engineering Building near Lake Mendota, with William Harley serving as station manager from 1954 to 1960. Adolfson told the Board of Regents in 1954:

> Educational television is going to reshape and influence extension as a whole. . . . Within the next decade educational television will be worked into the whole of the Extension program. The Extension Division has no particular concern as to who operates the television facilities, but is concerned with the basic programming of educational TV.[29]

WHA's Division of Radio Education was loosely supervised by a faculty oversight committee involving members from co-op extension, general extension, and the resident academic departments. This committee worked with McCarty on programming ranging from regular University lecture courses, to farm and homemaker hours to musical entertainment to the Wisconsin Idea Theater. In 1965 WHA launched an Educational Teleconference Network (ETN) linking 200 sites across Wisconsin through two-way audio connections. Four years later 26 of these locations formed the Statewide Extension Education Network (SEEN), employing both audio and new freeze-frame video technology. ETN and SEEN made possible highly effective refresher courses for thousands of Wisconsin engineers, social workers, health professionals, business people, and farmers. By the early 1960s pressures were building to change WHA from a largely informal instruction-oriented agency to a more professional public broadcasting enterprise. The

---

[29]UW BOR Minutes, January 9, 1954.

change was exemplified by the recruitment in 1962 of the hard-driving and creative Lee Sherman Dreyfus from Ball State University as WHA-TV station manager.[30] In 1969 WHA-TV became the first educational television station in the country to win a prestigious Emmy award from the National Academy of Television Arts and Sciences for its week-long documentary series, "The Inner Core: City within a City."[31]

Meanwhile, Harold McCarty retired in 1966 after a thirty-five year career with WHA. He was succeeded by Ellis James Robertson, a Madison native and former National Educational Television executive, who had received his first broadcasting experience at WHA as a UW student. McCarty's consultation with his staff about policy was always minimal, and there were few organized constituencies within the state he needed to cultivate. He was, nevertheless, an adept politician who knew how to ingratiate himself with legislators and who participated prominently in community affairs through membership in such key civic organizations as Madison's Downtown Rotary Club. He had strong supporters in Henry Ahlgren and speech Professor Fred Haberman, both of them influential members of the faculty Radio-Television Committee, which shared oversight responsibility over WHA with the Wisconsin State Radio Council.[32]

---

[30]Dreyfus served as a highly visible station manager for three years, after which he left to become president of Wisconsin State University-Stevens Point.

[31]*Wisconsin Public Broadcasting: Seventy-Five Years of Service, 1917-1992* (n.p., n.d.), UHP; Wisconsin Legislative Council, "University of Wisconsin Policies: Committee Report," submitted to the Governor and Legislature December 1, 1954, insert to *WAM*, 56 (January 15, 1955), p. 20; "Highlight History of Extension in Wisconsin, 1862-1989," Chancellor's Office, UW-Extension, January, 1989, UA; University Extension Division, Department File, series 18, UA; James Gooch to John W. Jenkins, February 17, 1998; *The Extension Story: University of Wisconsin-Extension* (University of Wisconsin-Extension, September, 1972), pp. 5-6; "UW Extension Pushes Concept of Lifelong Learning," *Milwaukee Journal*, July 12, 1970; "Extension Stresses Problem Solving," ibid., July 13, 1970; "Extension Teachers 'Travel' by Phone, Radio, Tapes," ibid., July 14, 1970.

Among the most popular radio programs during the 1960s were: the "Weather Round-Up," reported by the various transmitter engineers; "Accent on Living," formerly "Homemakers Program," with Jean Fewster; "Chapter A Day," with Karl Schmidt; "Views of the News," "University Roundtable," and "Roundtable," moderated by Roy Vogelman and often featuring prominent UW scholars and a guest panel of politicians and journalists; "Etcetera," with Jim Collins; and a variety of classical music selected by Cliff Roberts and often introduced by veteran announcer Ken Ohst. See Arthur Hove, "WHA: Not so Much a Radio Station as a Way of Life," *Wisconsin Tales and Trails*, 8 (Spring, 1967), 32-35.

[32]Ahlgren, oral history interview; Harrington, oral history interview.

UW speech class using WHA-TV equipment, 1957. UA, X25-2874.

Geography Professor Loyal Durand's classroom lecture broadcast over WHA-Radio.
UA, X25-3379.

Harrington and the Foundations

The entry of history Professor Fred Harvey Harrington into campus-level administration, first in 1956 as President Fred's special assistant, after 1958 as vice president in the Conrad Elvehjem administration, and finally as president after 1962, assured a bold rethinking of the University's relations with the state. As a social scientist, Harrington was well aware of the implications of the shift to a more urban society. We have already seen how his early campus responsibilities led him to pursue outside foundation support for social science research, especially in urban studies. With Brittingham funds he led the recruitment of Coleman Woodbury as professor of political science and director of urban research in an ambitious undertaking to establish the University as a leading center of modern urban studies.[33] In 1959 Harrington learned the Ford Foundation would soon award several $1 million grants to institutions of higher education for the intensive study of urban affairs.[34] He promptly obtained President Elvehjem's blessing to move ahead with this opportunity, and Coleman Woodbury, who previously had served as Ford's key advisor on urban affairs, took charge of the negotiations.[35]

Impatient with Woodbury's deliberate approach, Harrington soon short-circuited the process by unilaterally writing and submitting the University's grant application. He explained to Woodbury and his colleagues that he had unexpectedly received word from Ford program

---

[33]The UW Urban Research Committee, with Harrington as its chairman, "generally agreed that the University emphasis should be on research and training (without, however, neglecting the service angle)." Urban Research Committee Minutes, November 12, 1956, Series 5/1/3, Box 7, UA. See also above, pp. 256-57.

[34]As early as December, 1956, Harrington had spoken with Ford Foundation officials about the possibility of obtaining a grant for the University. "I think that we can get their support for a project if we get going," he reported. Harrington to Norman N. Gill, December 28, 1956, 5/1/3, Box 7, UA. Ford subsequently provided $35,000 to support Coleman Woodbury's early work in Milwaukee and anticipated providing much more substantial support. Harrington to Elvehjem, May 15, 1959, ibid., Box 43.

[35]According to Harrington's later recollection, Paul Ylvisaker, a Ford Foundation official, visited Bascom Hall to inquire of President Elvehjem if the University was interested in one of these grants. Elvehjem turned to Harrington, who responded, "Of course we should do this, and this should be a grant not only for the Madison campus, but for Milwaukee as well." Harrington, oral history interview. Harrington subsequently told Elvehjem, "Coleman Woodbury has handled most of the negotiations; and has set this up as a start toward a much larger grant." Harrington to Elvehjem, May 15, 1959, Series 5/1/3, Box 43, UA.

director Paul Ylvisaker that the UW application was needed immediately or Wisconsin would have no chance of being funded. With no time for consultations, Harrington had simply been forced to complete the task himself. What he did not so readily admit was that Woodbury's heavily academic approach to urban studies did not address what the Ford trustees, not to mention Harrington himself, had in mind for a UW urban initiative.[36] Rather than merely studying urban problems, they wished to mount projects to alleviate them. Thus Ylvisaker's advice to Harrington was not only to get the UW proposal to Ford quickly, but also to emphasize the UW land-grant tradition of using agricultural extension agents as activists in promoting social change.[37] This is what

[36]Ironically, one of the considerations in recruiting Coleman Woodbury to Wisconsin in 1957 was his role, in Harrington's words, as "the major adviser of the Ford Foundation on urban studies." Harrington to Fred, January 10, 1957. See also "Urban Research Program," January 26, 1957, both in ibid., Box 7. This report discusses the role envisioned for Coleman Woodbury at Wisconsin: "It should be stressed . . . that we will concentrate on fundamental research on urban problems, and not duplicate work being done by taxpayers' organizations, or state, county or city agencies. Our desire is to contribute to basic knowledge; and thus provide assistance in tackling the tremendous problems which city growth has given our state and nation." Woodbury downplayed the extension role in a Ford-funded program. Coleman Woodbury to Urban Studies Advisory Committee and Henry J. Schmandt, Associate Director, Center for Urban Studies, October 12, 1959, ibid., Box 43.

[37]Ford's approach was well known to Harrington. For example, he clipped and saved a July 22, 1959, *New York Times* article headed, "Rutgers Gets $750,000 Grant To Set Up Urban Aid Service." It reading in part: "The Ford Foundation announced yesterday a five-year grant of $750,000 to Rutgers University to establish an experimental extension program on urban research in New Jersey. . . . Dr. [Mason W.] Gross [Rutgers president] discussed his hope of initiating . . . a program, similar to the Agricultural Extension Service, which helps solve farm problems." The proposal called for an urban research and extension center and for research liaison agents to be placed in selected urban communities or regions to survey research needs and report and advise the Rutgers faculty on long-range research programming. The grant proposal Harrington submitted to Ford was very similar, promising that the grant would "help us improve and expand our research-training-action program in urban affairs." About $400,000 would be spent on "Extension-Demonstration Experiments, probably one in a metropolitan setting, the Milwaukee area, and one in a small-city cluster. . . . In many respects, the Extension-Demonstration Experiments represent the key to this application. . . . By pooling the experience of General Extension and Agricultural Extension, we would like to develop the concept of urban agents, notably in the small-city cluster. . . . The urban agents should also be able to help in the training of urban specialists . . . by giving on-the-ground experience." Harrington to Ylvisaker, October 23, 1959. In a more personal letter that day Harrington told Ylvisaker: "We feel . . . that we ought to step boldly into this thing. If we can, for example, effect a combination or close cooperation of General and Agricultural Extension, that alone is of tremendous importance to the state university system." Justifying his hasty application to UWM Provost Klotsche,

Harrington proposed, and what the Ford Foundation readily assented to.[38] "It was my feeling what the Ford Foundation wanted," he later acknowledged, "and what I wanted, was that you should get into action right away."[39]

To implement the urban agent feature of the Ford grant, Harrington put UED Dean Adolfson in charge of the oversight committee.[40] We must speculate as to the vice president's reasons for this choice. Obviously, Adolfson's practical orientation and administrative experience made him more suitable than Professor Woodbury or one of his faculty colleagues, who favored developing a scholarly research base before starting any action programs. But why not turn to CES Associate Director Ahlgren, whose agricultural extension service had helped to set the standard in Wisconsin and the country for organizing and operating a network of problem-solving field agents? Even though Ahlgren's "Scope Report" and other initiatives had demonstrated his awareness of urban problems, Harrington probably believed Ahlgren was primarily interested in rural and agricultural issues. His strong personality and conservative political allegiances, moreover, did not mesh well with Harrington's and Ford's more liberal political orientation or Harrington's tendency to assert his influence. Adolfson's University Extension Division already had a substantial base in Milwaukee, the focal point of Ford's interest, although it functioned quite autonomously and more as an academic than an action agency. UED thus had the foothold for building a force of action-oriented urban agents. Finally, Adolfson, with his amenable personality, could be expected to accept direction willingly from Harrington as the program evolved.[41]

Harrington explained: "My statement features extension, partly because of Ylvisaker's preoccupation with the land-grant approach, partly because this does offer us a rather special opportunity to do something special in Milwaukee and the Fox River Valley and the whole University." Harrington to J. Martin Klotsche, October 24, 1959. All in ibid.

[38]Joseph M. McDaniel, Jr., Secretary, Ford Foundation, to Elvehjem, December 23, 1959; News release, UW News Service, January 4, 1960, Ibid.

[39]Harrington, oral history interview.

[40]Harrington to A.D. Telfer, January 26, 1960, Series 5/1/3, Box 43, UA.

[41]Harrington, oral history interview. Harrington explained: "And therefore we were interested in this, obviously–using the agricultural mode–but of course that didn't mean we'd use the agriculture people to do this kind of thing." And further: "But of course, even though they called it Cooperative Extension, you take these farm people and put them in the cities, who in the cities is going to pay attention to them? The mayor certainly isn't going to say, 'You county agents are the ones who can tell us what to do.' It didn't seem right to me, and the University Extension, anyway, seemed to be the better

Shortly after the University obtained the Ford grant, in 1960 Harrington agreed to conduct a national study of adult education. The project originated with Sandy Liveright, the director of the Center for the Liberal Education of Adults at the University of Chicago. He approached John Gardner, the head of the Carnegie Corporation, about funding the study. Liveright's proposal, which focused on adult liberal education, struck Gardner as too narrow, because it ignored the more applied aspects of university outreach as developed by the state universities and land grant colleges. It was in this context that Fred Harrington came to Gardner's mind. The two had recently become acquainted on Harrington's initiative when the UW vice president had sought out Gardner as a sounding board to discuss some of his evolving ideas about improving urban adult education. Thus as Gardner considered Liveright's idea of a national study of adult education, he naturally thought of Harrington as a respected and influential intellect who appreciated the importance of the subject but at the same time was not a member of the adult education establishment. Harrington considered the opportunity intriguing, but agreed to accept it only if the study covered agricultural as well as general extension. This was fine with Gardner, who funded the project via Liveright's center at Chicago.

After assuming the UW presidency in the summer of 1962, Harrington was simply in no position to devote much time to the adult education project. Consequently late that year he recruited Donald R. McNeil to help carry the load the load. McNeil had earned a purple heart during his World War II military service, and afterwards had studied for the M.A. and Ph.D. degrees in the Madison history department, where Harrington got to know him. During his graduate work McNeil had directed some outreach programming for the State Historical Society of Wisconsin and later served briefly as its acting director. Smart, energetic, and most especially glib, McNeil had left the society to try to establish himself as a freelance writer in Arizona.[42] He accepted Harrington's offer on a half-time basis and began traveling the country collecting data and making contacts with a large number of outreach professionals. Within a year McNeil decided to abandon his free lance writing career and joined the UW administration full-time as special assistant to the president.[43]

channel for this kind of thing."

[42]McNeil to Harrington, October 7, 1960, Series 5/1/3, Box 60, UA.

[43]"Study of the Role of the University in Adult Education," October 26, 1960, ibid.; UW News Service press release, June 23, 1963; Harrington to McNeil, June 25,

Harrington meanwhile circulated among the national adult education leadership, becoming an instant celebrity on the circuit. Seemingly everyone wished to discuss the Carnegie study with him and to share experiences and insights. Harrington accordingly was thrust to the forefront of the adult education movement.[44] This experience, combined with his key role in the Ford project, convinced Harrington that the University should become a major player as the nation moved to address the problems of its cities. The question was whether the University's outreach mechanisms were up to the challenge. He thought not. In remarks to a national meeting of cooperative extension administrators at Madison in the spring of 1962 Harrington mixed praise with blunt criticism. Although conceding he was "bowled over by your accomplishments," he nevertheless warned, "you are doing less than you can, less than you should do." Cooperative extension provided "the chief example of a successful adult education movement," but "you are not now in the forefront in planning for the future at most of our universities." At a time when America was much involved with the world, extension staff members were largely ignoring the international frontier. It was clear they needed to draw on the intellectual resources of the entire university, Harrington emphasized, yet "I am distressed to find so little cooperation and so much distrust between Cooperative and General Extension."[45]

Merger and Separation

One of Harrington's early objectives as president was to obtain increased federal funding to support a massively strengthened urban

---

1963, Series 4/18/1, Box 16, UA.

[44]Harrington, oral history interview. He explained: "And as I wrote the book, I got more and more involved because I went for meetings of adult educators–the university extension adult educators, the agricultural extension people, the radio and television people. I ended by attending these meetings and giving speeches at these meetings and hearing what these people had to say. So obviously I was something of an expert, one might say, on this area–perhaps with views that didn't agree with everybody, but at least I was very active in this area–so active in it, in fact, that I was known to the adult educators around the country." The book was not published until 1977. Fred Harvey Harrington, *The Future of Adult Education: New Responsibilities of Colleges and Universities* (San Francisco: Jossey-Bass Publishers, 1977).

[45]Fred Harvey Harrington, "Role of Cooperative Extension in the Land-Grant System," *Directing the Cooperative Extension Service: Selected Papers Presented at Seventh National Cooperative Extension Administrative Seminar, Madison, Wisconsin, April 30-May 4, 1962*, pp. 35-39, Series 4/18/1, Box 33, UA.

outreach mission for the University.[46] Toward this end, he maneuvered to have himself appointed chairman of the Legislative Committee of the National Association of State Universities and Land Grant Colleges. This gave him cachet to mount an energetic lobbying campaign to expand the federal mandate and direct the land grant institutions to address urban as well as agricultural problems. Not until after the assassination of President Kennedy late in 1963 was Congress willing to consider this change, however. In the wake of the national mourning of its fallen leader, President Lyndon Johnson undertook a broad program of social reform to create a "Great Society." Johnson was receptive to the NASULGC initiative. In an address at the new Irvine campus of the University of California in 1964, he advocated the federal funding of urban extension agents.[47] Title I of the Higher Education Act of 1965 authorized this expansion of federally supported extension activity. Although Harrington had hoped for federal support equivalent to the $60 million going annually to agricultural extension, Title I initially authorized only $25 million and the final appropriation turned out to be only $10 million. Distributed across the United States, these funds were far from sufficient to support what Harrington and his fellow academic social action advocates had in mind. Still, congressional approval of Title I's vision of a federal urban extension program kept the hopes of its proponents alive.[48]

President Harrington was convinced the urban challenge demanded a unified, coordinated strategy involving all parts of the University. Thus, well before the passage of Title I, he began positioning UW to obtain a major portion of the expected new funding. A year into his presidency he brought two important recommendations before the regents. The first proposed to separate the freshman-sophomore centers from the University Extension Division and establish them as an independent credit-granting unit administered by a provost who would report directly to the UW president. Regent approval of this recommendation paved the way for passage of the second: "That the Regents approve in principle the establishment of an Extension Division to

[46]Harrington recalled much later: "At that time, of course, I was over-optimistic about the future of getting money from the federal government to enable us to build up campuses, to do research and extension activities. Then that money began to dry up about that time." Harrington, oral history interview.

[47]Ibid.

[48]Ibid. Unlike the Cooperative Extension Service, which was administered by the Department of Agriculture, Title I was administered through the Department of Health, Education, and Welfare.

include agricultural and general extension and radio and television, and that the administration be authorized to develop the organizational structure of such an Extension Division, and report to the Regents." Harrington explained the need for the reorganization:

> The new demands of the cities, the need to link University research with industrial growth, the continuing problems of agriculture and the special needs of northern Wisconsin all point toward substantial University activity in the adult education and extension field. With changing times, . . . there is reason to combine our activities.[49]

The president's timing was fortuitous. The current agricultural representative on the board was Gilbert Rohde, president of the National Farmers Union, a Democratic-leaning organization of smaller farmers. Rohde had recently been appointed to the regents by Democratic Governor Gaylord Nelson. The NFU believed the agriculture colleges of the country and their extension programs catered to the interests of large commercial farms typically represented by the rival GOP-leaning Farm Bureau Federation. Often in the past the agriculture seat on the Board of Regents had been filled by a representative of the Wisconsin Farm Bureau Federation, who might be expected to view with alarm any threat to CES independence. Rohde's support for an extension merger carried a good deal of weight with his fellow Democratic regents, both to diminish Farm Bureau influence and to direct greater University attention to urban areas, where Democratic political support was based. Politics aside, the entire board lined up behind the new and energetic president, who far more than most of his predecessors was articulating a bold vision for a revitalized University and a new version of the Wisconsin Idea.[50]

---

[49]UW BOR Minutes, September 6, 1963; "Recommendation Concerning Organization of University Center System," September 3, 1963, Series 4/18/1, Box 40, UA; "Recommendation Concerning Organization of Adult Education and Extension Activities," September 3, 1963, Series 40/1/1/1, Box 6, UA; Press Release, UW News Service, September 6, 1963, Series 4/18/1, Box 40, UA. For Harrington's recollection of these events, see his oral history interview, 1985.

[50]Harrington recalled later: "I was at that time setting up a program for the University, and the new campuses were one part of it. The more vigorous style in moving into the legislature was another, and this merger was another part of my program for the University, and the regents tended to support me. Thus the regents approved merger without dissent. . . . Obviously, what I was doing was taking hold and pushing this. There was no immediate outcry; there was no statewide protest at this being done." Ibid.

Harrington had managed the preliminary steps cleverly, consulting only to the extent necessary and then moving quickly to obtain regent approval. By-passing the affected extension staffs almost entirely, he spoke only with their top leaders, informing them of his plan rather than soliciting their advice. Neither Ahlgren nor Adolfson seemed pleased with the prospect, but each was "willing to try."[51] WHA's McCarty was generally indifferent, apparently not considering the institutional home of his agency a matter of importance. He would go on doing the same things regardless of the larger administrative structure. This was not the view of the College of Agriculture, however, whose departments were likely to be disrupted if it lost control of its longstanding outreach arm. Fortunately for Harrington, Agriculture Dean Froker was both a passive leader and in declining health. Once Froker recognized its significance, he apparently tried to resist the move, but his late efforts were ineffectual.[52]

With regent approval in principle, on November 16, 1963, President Harrington appointed a special committee, chaired by UW political science Professor Ralph Huitt, "to recommend a plan for combining the extension activities of the University in one service."[53]

---

[51]Ibid. As Harrington recalled it, he knew Ahlgren had more clout nationally and locally than Adolfson and was pleased he chose not to resist, perhaps because he and Harrington were friends or because he wished to limit the power of the agriculture dean over cooperative extension. Ahlgren also may have thought he was a logical choice to be put in charge of the merged unit. Ahlgren's later recollections of the initial reactions to the proposed extension merger were a little different: "everybody wasn't in favor of this. In fact as far as I know there were very few people in either Agricultural Cooperative Extension or in the University Extension Division or perhaps even in the radio and television section that were sure at that time that this was a desirable development." Ahlgren recalled that Adolfson "did not object strongly to the merger. . . . He was neutral pretty much." Ahlgren, oral history interview.

[52]Harrington, oral history interview; John Ross, oral history interview with John W. Jenkins, 1991, UHP. Froker's successor, Glenn Pound, would eventually become a major critic of this reorganization. But at the time of his interview for the deanship, President Harrington told him he must accept the decision and he agreed. Harrington, oral history interview; Glenn S. Pound, "Changes in Cooperative Extension at the University of Wisconsin, 1965-1979," 1979, Series 90/80, UA; Harrington conceded: "Pound, of course, was a man of great vigor and a fighter, and had he been dean when this first came up, he would have made all kinds of a fuss. So that merger was effected in part because of the personnel, I suppose. It was possible to move it through because of that."

[53]See Glenn S. Pound, "Changes in Cooperative Extension," p. 2; "Individuals to attend meeting Saturday, November 16, 1963, President's Office . . . to discuss establishment of program in Extension–University-wide." Listed were Harrington, Clodius, Robert Dick, Ralph Huitt, Quentin Schenk, John A. Schoenemann, Theodore

Huitt had recently headed a UW lobbying office in Washington, where, among other things, he had sought without success to persuade Congress to provide funds for general extension work in the states.[54] Earlier, he had been involved with UW outreach activity while serving on Adolfson's UED Committee on General Education for Adults.[55] In addition to Chairman Huitt, the new Committee on the Reorganization of Adult Education and Extension Activities had seven members, three from the College of Agriculture, one from the School of Commerce, one from UWM, and two from University Extension Division administration.[56]

As its first step the Huitt Committee received reports from Ahlgren and Adolfson detailing the work of agricultural and general extension in Wisconsin.[57] Next Harrington's special assistant, Donald McNeil, appeared before the committee to discuss the "findings" of the ongoing Carnegie adult education study and their "implications for the work of our committee."[58] Over a number of meetings the committee interviewed UED and CES extension leaders in Madison and Milwaukee and met with President Harrington to get his perspective. It also arranged a session with Dean C. Bryce Ratchford of the University of Missouri Extension Service, whose recent administrative merger particularly intrigued President Harrington. After this the committee convened without guests "to take a bearing,"[59] and Huitt reported to Harrington: "Ratchford came and was worth the money. . . . Our

---

Shannon, Dorothy Strong, George B. Strother, and Gale VandeBerg. Series 40/1/1/1, Box 6, UA.

[54]"Extension Bill in House," Harrington memo to Adolfson, William Young, Clodius, and Ralph Huitt, October 19, 1962, Series 5/1/4, Box 7, UA. This was one of a long succession of similarly unsuccessful bills reaching back at least into the 1950s.

[55]"WHA-TV begins political course: 'The National Government,'" *Daily Cardinal*, October 2, 1956; Adolfson to Policy Committee on General Education for Adults nominees, September 8, 1959, Series 5/1/3, Box 29, UA.

[56]The members and their affiliations were: Director Robert N. Dick (UED field services), Prof. Huitt (L&S political science), Prof. Quentin Schenk (UWM), Prof. John Schoenemann (Agriculture horticulture), Dean Theodore Shannon (UED administration), Prof. Dorothy Strong (Agriculture home economics), Prof. George Strother (UED commerce), and Prof. Gale VandeBerg (Agriculture Cooperative Extension Service administration). Clodius to Dear Colleagues, November 19, 1963, Series 40/1/1/1, Box 6, UA.

[57]See Huitt to Extension Reorganization Committee, November 19, and December 11, 1963, ibid.

[58]Huitt to Extension Reorganization Committee, January 8, 1964, ibid.

[59]Huitt to Extension Reorganization Committee, April 21, 1964, ibid.

Committee is about through with its education. By the beginning of summer I think we will be getting down to cases."[60]

Chairman Huitt realized his committee might have trouble reaching agreement on its controversial assignment, so he began by asking his colleagues "to frame the problems the Committee must solve and establish priorities among them," with each member preparing a short narrative for internal circulation to "give the whole Committee a chance to discover whatever latent consensus there may be."[61] By late fall, the committee had divided into drafting subcommittees, with which Huitt met individually. In November, he alerted President Harrington and Vice President Clodius to the thinking of the subcommittees "to make sure that the full Committee would not be considering something which the Administration did not want."[62] Work continued within this context, until Huitt was able to advise President Harrington to expect the final report toward the end of April, 1965. "It is our hope," he added, "that you will not have to make it public until the middle of May at the earliest."[63]

Huitt's latter comment referred to a campaign then under way to cultivate support for the report. The chairman had scheduled informational meetings to explain things to the Associated Press and state newspaper editors as well as to the College of Agriculture faculty. "Other members of the Committee are making similar plans," he noted. Robert Dick, for example, planned to confer with three members of the Marinette County Agricultural Committee and several local extension staffers there. Dick subsequently reported that "no opposition" seemed likely. The officials did, however, raise a number of questions about funding, staffing, and programming that President Harrington should, in Dick's opinion, be prepared to answer when talking about the

---

[60]Huitt to Harrington, April 30, 1964, ibid. During May and June, the committee heard testimony from several more individuals, some of whom had responded to a general invitation circulated by the group. These included: Charles McDougal, Federal Extension Service; Commerce Dean Erwin A. Gaumnitz; Agriculture Dean Rudolph K. Froker; Professor Carlisle Runge, special assistant to President Harrington and co-director of CCHE; Bernard James, director of the Center for Advanced Study in Organization Science; Professor Gerald Rohlich, associate dean of UW Graduate School; Professor Robert C. Clark, director of National Agricultural Extension Center; Pharmacy Dean Arthur H. Uhl; and Kathryn F. Clarenbach, project associate to UW Dean of Women. See Huitt to Extension Reorganization Committee, May 5 and 20, and June 2, 1964, ibid.

[61]Huitt to Extension Reorganization Committee, June 17, 1964, ibid.

[62]McNeil to Harrington, November 23, 1964, Series 4/18/1, Box 84, UA.

[63]Huitt to Harrington, April 22, 1965, Series 40/1/1/1, Box 6, UA.

reorganization with county boards around the state.[64] The Huitt Committee report was released on May 12. Its thoughtful recommendations for a complicated merger of UW extension activities were a tribute to the chairman's patient and astute leadership. Committee member George B. Strother congratulated Huitt on his "wise and witty" leadership. "When I chair my next committee," he observed, "I can say I took my post-graduate work under one of the masters of the art."[65]

The report began by referring to the committee's assignment: to "recommend a plan for combining the extension activities of the University in one service." The issue, in other words, was not *whether,* but *how.* The committee members, each of whom represented one outreach agency or another, had been careful to think exclusively in terms of the University of Wisconsin as a whole: "our loyalty has been to it and to the idea and values of continuing education." Although no member was satisfied with every detail of the study, "we are unanimous in our belief that extension education has an even more vital role to play in the life of Wisconsin in the future than it has now or in the past, when so much was achieved." The body of the report consisted of three narrative sections and an appendix containing several models of possible administrative organization.[66]

While acknowledging the proud and diverse achievements of UW outreach, the committee stressed that "we want a single educational unit to marshal the resources of the University to meet the many needs for continuing education of our State's people, rural, urban and suburban." Without prescribing a detailed structure, the report called for "one statewide administrative unit for extension functions of the University," on a par with the Madison and Milwaukee campuses and the new University Center System. As with these three other major units, University Extension should be administered by a chancellor reporting directly to the president. Further, the extension chancellor would control "all Federal titles associated with the spending and accounting for money provided for the support of extension activities by

---

[64]Robert N. Dick to Huitt, May 27, 1965, ibid. Huitt later forwarded this letter to Harrington, characterizing the Marinette visit as "part of our program to get acceptance of the extension merger. I think it will be useful to you when you and Bob [Clodius] prepare to meet with the county board chairmen." Huitt to Harrington, June 9, 1965, ibid.

[65]George B. Strother to Huitt, May 28, 1965, ibid.

[66]"Report and Recommendations of the Extension Reorganization Committee to the President of the University of Wisconsin," May 12, 1965, Series 1/1/3, Box 111 and Series 40/1/1/1, Box 6, UA.

the Federal government." This provision served notice that no longer would the agriculture dean at Madison designated Director of Cooperative Extension, a title associated with his office since inception of the service prior to World War I. In sum, "the Chancellor of Extension should have responsibility for extending the resources of all the University to the State without regard to the geographic boundaries associated with campuses."

Another set of proposals defined the new University Extension internally, describing a complex, free-standing, non-degree-granting institution of higher education whose campus would be the entire state of Wisconsin. Teaching and research faculty would be grouped by departments within school- or college-like "academic units." Some departments would function as before in an "integrated" manner with a corresponding resident campus department in such fields as agriculture and medicine. Here the agricultural extension model would prevail. On the other hand, "autonomous" departments would mimic the traditional University Extension Division organization, which maintained its own separate departments, some members of which might have joint appointments in corresponding resident units. A second type of administrative arrangement, with appropriate sub-units, would provide instructional support. This would contain such important agencies as public radio and television, as well as county, inter-county, and area or regional extension offices. The latter were a basic feature of cooperative extension, but now were to be expanded to support any subject matter or program content. Another section of the report discussed personnel policy: staff titles, career paths, training, promotion, tenure, and the like. A final section dealt briefly with the role of UW radio and television in the new University Extension.

It remained for President Harrington to select and recommend to the Board of Regents the first University Extension chancellor. By this time it had become established University practice for a faculty search-and-screen committee to provide advice on high administrative appointments. Harrington, however, chose not to follow this uncertain path. On August 10 he wrote to Ralph Huitt:

> Will your committee (or such members as are in town this summer) supply me with six or more names of persons now in the University whom we should consider seriously for the Extension Chancellorship? They need not be given in priority rank. . . . If you want to add any possibly suitable outside names, they will be welcome. But Wisconsin has

been such a leader in general and cooperative extension that I feel no great urge to go outside.[67]

Huitt canvassed his committee by telephone and shortly submitted a confidential list of ten names for Harrington's consideration.[68]

The slate was comprehensive and included the most obvious inside contenders. Lorentz Adolfson, the former UED dean, led the group from general extension, along with his successor, Theodore J. Shannon, and Wilson B. Thiede, a respected adult education leader now teaching in Madison's School of Education. From the CES, there were agriculture Dean and Acting CES Director Glenn Pound, whom Harrington had selected to succeed the ailing Froker in 1964, Associate Director Ahlgren, and three other prominent agriculture faculty-administrators, Bryant E. Kearl, George W. Sledge, and Gale L. VandeBerg, the latter a Huitt Committee member. Historian and extension administrator Frederick I. Olson represented UWM. Don McNeil, Harrington's special assistant and collaborator on the Carnegie adult education study, probably made the list at the president's informal suggestion, since he had no significant extension, administrative, or UW experience.

Harrington weighed his options for nearly two months. His request of Huitt indicated he favored an inside candidate, but otherwise he kept his counsel while he and Clodius touched base with various of the University's interested constituencies, explaining the proposed new extension system and fielding recommendations for chancellor. As might be expected, farm spokesmen tended to favor agriculture and the status quo, frequently nominating Hank Ahlgren. Those more interested in general extension boosted Ted Shannon. UED and CES staffers offered similar views and recommendations. In mid-October the president informed at least one partisan faculty delegation he was leaning toward appointing a chancellor with a neutral background as a means of minimizing conflict between the two sides. Shortly thereafter,

---

[67]Harrington to Huitt, August 10, 1965, ibid. By-passing a formal search could be justified on the grounds that extension at UW had always operated outside the faculty governance context and that time was of the essence. The Huitt Committee, moreover, consisted of a number of highly qualified individuals who had spent the past year studying the problems of merger. Harrington also felt comfortable with Chairman Huitt's judgment. He surely agreed with the latter's observation, reported in the *Wisconsin State Journal* on February 23, that the extension chancellor must be "aggressive, militant, and dedicated," since these were the qualities Harrington always sought in his staff.

[68]Huitt to Harrington, August 17, 1965, 40/1/1/1, box 6, UA; Harrington, oral history interview.

in advance of the board's next meeting, Harrington sent a confidential memorandum to the regents informing them he intended to propose Dr. Donald McNeil, his co-author on the as yet unfinished adult education study, as the new extension chancellor.[69]

McNeil was the clear compromise candidate on the list, and from President Harrington's point of view he was also the best choice. More than anyone at the University he had worked with Harrington to obtain passage of Title I as well as foundation support for urban-oriented action programming. Harrington had designated him as the administration's point man in charge of the University's expanding civil rights and anti-poverty efforts. This included shaping a number of early UW affirmative action initiatives, overseeing a succession of federally sponsored Great Society training programs, and keeping tabs on several inner core projects for the underprivileged in Milwaukee.[70] It was precisely this sort of activity that Harrington expected his reorganized University Extension to undertake. Even taking into account McNeil's lack of administrative experience, in the president's eyes he was not just adequately qualified for the chancellorship, he was ideally qualified.

McNeil himself had for some time taken steps to make sure his patron reached this conclusion. Even before returning to Madison from Arizona to join the Harrington administration, he sent the UW president a copy of his advice to a gathering of national extension leaders: "Adult educators must gear their programs and thoughts more to meeting the social needs of the area and clientele they serve. This means heavy emphasis on tying adult education to action programs."[71] He also urged Harrington to find an extension chancellor "who has some experience in both Ag and General Extension who might lead this program into some sort of cooperation and consolidation, not just at the top as in Missouri, but all the way down the line"[72]

[69]Charles S. Bridgman to Harrington, October 18, 1965; Harrington to Each Regent, October 19, 1965, 40/1/1/1, box 6, UA.

[70]See, for example, "Blueprint for Action, Designed by Delegates to the Second Inter-University Conference on the Negro," February 17, 1964, Series 4/18/1, Box 49, UA. This report distilled the ideas, including concrete steps for institutions of higher education, discussed at a conference on improving Negro education held at Wingspread, Racine, Wisconsin. McNeil chaired the reporting committee. See McNeil to Harrington, June 2, 1964, for a list of programs for the disadvantaged with which McNeil was involved. Ibid.

[71]Donald R. McNeil, "Future Fields of Emphasis in University Extension," in *Proceedings of the Forty-Seventh Annual Meeting of the National University Extension Association*, 60 (1962), p. 20.

[72]McNeil to Harrington, October 26, 1962, Series 4/18/1, Box 16, UA.

UW President Harrington and U.S. President Johnson. UA, 3/7, 100.

Black faculty exchange program, 1964; from left clockwise: John S. Lash, Texas Southern U.; Cecil Patterson, North Carolina College; Chester Ruedisili; Donald McNeil; Glenn Rankin, Agricultural and Technical College of North Carolina; Jack Barbash; photo by Gary Schulz. UA, 6211-M.

Once back in Madison, McNeil threw himself into his UW assignments, which included the adult education study and fund raising and cultivation of the national foundations. And he made sure his boss knew he retained an interest in extension. As the Huitt Committee got under way, the president responded to some unsolicited advice from his young assistant: "your point is sound (we should merge with general Extension)," but "this happens, however, to be a sensitive area (Froker, Clark, Clodius, etc.). We'll go at it slowly."[73] McNeil reported frequently on his numerous contacts and accomplishments, in one case proudly noting that a Ford Foundation official "has asked me to get six or eight good people together to meet him in New York to talk about 'action programs for Negroes.'"[74] Acting as the eyes and ears of the president, McNeil discussed the work of the Huitt Committee over lunch with its chairman and then reported in detail to Harrington on what was said.[75]

Nor was McNeil shy about evaluating potential extension chancellors for the president. In late 1964, for example, he described a recent meeting with Ford's Paul Ylvisaker, who suggested two outside possibilities. McNeil dismissed them by observing, "I got the idea that Ylvisaker thinks more in terms of city planning types and urban research people in connection with such a job."[76] He also undermined Henry Ahlgren, whom many thought by far the ablest and most experienced of likely inside contenders. McNeil reported recent conversations in which the associate CES director had threatened to oppose the reorganization if basic features of the cooperative extension model were disturbed. "I said there seemed to be no problem here." McNeil commented on Ahlgren's apparent "cunning" and his seeming inability to "get at the guts of the matter" under discussion. "I was most surprised with his lack of knowledge of general extension, and his really rather narrow view of extension and the University."[77]

On several occasions McNeil forcefully offered his own views on extension reorganization. One instance grew out of Harrington's refusal to approve McNeil's request that UED be designated to administer a series of federal anti-poverty action grants. "The essence

---

[73]Harrington to McNeil, November 27, 1963, ibid., Box 49.

[74]McNeil to Clodius, March 6, 1964, ibid.

[75]McNeil to Harrington, November 23, 1964, ibid., Box 84.

[76]McNeil, "Field Trip/New York, N. Y., and Washington, D. C./December 7, 8, and 9, 1964," ibid.

[77]McNeil, "Field Trip/Milwaukee, Wisconsin/December 21, 1964," ibid.

of the problem is the concept of Extension in this University," responded McNeil:

> If the Extension Division cannot handle research and training grants by utilizing the resources of the various departments, then Extension is not what I think it to be. ... I know that the split between residence departments and Extension is deeply embedded in this University (though less so than in many institutions across the country), but resident faculty, administrators, and Extension people are all beginning to deplore this "we and thee" concept. We want to break down that idea. Extension is an integral part of the University and is successful only to the degree that it can enjoy the confidence and respect of residence departments. . . . In my mind our three traditional functions–research, training, and extension–have equal value and validity and each must be assumed to be of equal trustworthiness and competence. If they are not in fact that, then we should make them so.

"At some point," declared the undeclared candidate, "I'd appreciate the chance to talk out this Extension business with you and Bob [Clodius]."[78]

Early in 1965 McNeil made sure Harrington was aware he had declined to be considered for a vice presidency at Hofstra University because of his growing regard for the "'Wisconsin Idea.'" "Perhaps I am being presumptuous (or naive)," he explained, "but under this administration, with these traditions and these talents and resources lying all about, I feel that all of us here may take part eventually in transforming the very nature of the modern university."[79] A month later he reported on a meeting with high officials of the U.S. Office of Economic Opportunity: "I believe we have now established a line between the directors of the various programs and the University at a high enough level that when an individual proposal gets in trouble we can bring some force to bear on it. . . . I think I should try to stay on top of everything we are proposing to them."[80] The primary UW action program agency and the aspiring UW action program manager were approaching intersection. In May McNeil announced the award to UW of a new

---

[78]McNeil to Harrington, December 23, 1964, ibid.

[79]McNeil to Clifford L. Lord, January 5, 1965, blind copy to Harrington. Harrington responded on January 8: "I'm glad you are not taking the Hofstra job–and are staying with us." Both in ibid.

[80]McNeil to Harrington, February 17, 1965, ibid. OEO programs mentioned included the Job Corps, VISTA, and the Community Action Program.

$220,000 OEO training grant, adding, "A few more like this and we may balance the Extension budget."[81] That September, in sending a reappointment letter to his special assistant, Harrington apologized for McNeil's modest salary increase, but added suggestively, "A change in administrative assignment would of course enable us to make a further adjustment."[82] The adjustment came on October 22, 1965, when the regents accepted the president's recommendation and appointed Donald R. McNeil as the first chancellor of the new University Extension.[83]

Regent President Arthur DeBardeleben announced the appointment, effective immediately, and called on President Harrington for a statement. Noting the University of Wisconsin was the "outstanding" American public service university, Harrington declared "we are right now at very much of a crossroads with the enormous urban problems of our civilization calling for our entering into a new era in our outreach to the social problems of the cities":

> We have substantial federal support for extension and we are going to have much more. The passage of the Technical Services Act and the Higher Education Act and the Arts Foundation Act all point toward the obvious conclusion that the federal government is going to come in strong with money to provide additional services, and for adult education as well as for education for the young. This combined extension will enable us to make an all-out attack on these problems of our State, and in areas in which we are interested beyond the State, so that we are going to be entering into a period of cooperation such as we have never had before.

Although Chancellor McNeil came neither from agricultural extension, nor general extension, nor radio and television, he nevertheless "has had exposure to all of them." "We have confidence in him," the president concluded. "We think this University and this State have had great leadership in this area, and . . . we want to continue to expand that leadership."[84] Years later Harrington explained: "I was choosing a

---

[81]McNeil to Harrington and Clodius, May 4, 1965, ibid. He emphasized that the grant was obviously beneficial to extension, because it involved "Social Work, the School for Workers, Ag Extension, the Institute of Governmental Affairs, Commerce, and the Cooperative Training Center."

[82]Harrington to McNeil, September 3, 1965, Series 40/1/1/1, Box 13, UA.

[83]McNeil's salary for 1965-66 as special assistant was $20,400; he received $24,000 as chancellor.

[84]UW BOR Minutes, October 22, 1965.

person who had to move into something and build it," and McNeil was "very much on the make." In short, "I chose McNeil because he was a pusher."[85]

"The Year of the Merger"

A year passed, however, before the new University Extension really got going. In a 1967 report on "The Year of the Merger," Chancellor McNeil observed, "by October of 1966 we could humorously claim a chart which had not changed for a month and seriously cite evidence for a real merger at the operational level."[86] Well aware that he was embarking on a controversial undertaking, McNeil tried to consult as widely as possible on nearly every step along the way. He knew that his appointment was itself controversial, in that it had not been reviewed or recommended by a faculty search-and-screen committee.[87] The challenges were many and complex for the inexperienced new leader. "There were times in March and April," recalled McNeil, "when I didn't think anything was going right in this job."[88]

Only two days after his appointment, McNeil addressed a "brief note" to every extension staff member "to tell you how much I welcome the opportunity to work with you" and promising "that no precipitous

[85]Harrington, oral history interview. Henry Ahlgren was no doubt disappointed at being passed over, but later was able to view the rebuff philosophically: "I think the president found himself in the position where he wouldn't be able to pick someone from either Ag Extension or University Extension and get the kind of support that one would have to have to make this work, especially if there was quite a bit of suspicion to begin with. And so it's not surprising, for example, that the number one person, first person selected would be someone who was not presently in one of the two organizations, and that turned out, then, to be Don McNeil in this case." Ahlgren, oral history interview.

[86]Donald R. McNeil, "The Year of the Merger," *The Spectator*, Bulletin of the National University Extension Association (January, 1967), reprint, p. 1, UHP.

[87]On November 8, 1965, extension psychologist Charles S. Bridgman informed law Professor August G. Eckhardt, chairman of the Madison University Committee that "members of the Extension Division Faculty Executive Committee and other Extension faculty members have decided to ask the University Committee to consider exploring the question of . . . procedures preceding administrative appointments. . . . fuller consultation on the part of the Administration with those concerned and affected would have been desirable in the case of the recent appointment of a Chancellor of Extension. Such consultation seems to be a well established procedure in appointment of academic deans, through the functioning of a search committee." Series 40/1/1/1, Box 6, UA.

[88]Quoted in Jeff Smoller, "University Extension Plan Still Faces Problems," *Milwaukee Journal*, October 23, 1966, ibid.

upheaval is planned."[89] He hoped to start on a positive note and counter the low morale in extension ranks.[90] "I plan to work with the existing personnel in setting up the program," he told a reporter. "I am going to rely heavily on their judgment in bringing about the integration of the Extension services of the University."[91] A *Milwaukee Journal* article suggested that McNeil's goals lay beyond the traditional scope of extension in the relatively new area of federally funded social action programming. "I guess I'd like to lay an emphasis on this," he confided, "but certainly not at the expense of what we do for business and labor." In fact, "it may be that we can be most innovative there. . . . I can't be too specific yet, but we've really got some hot ideas to try in Milwaukee."[92] Alarmed, the *Wisconsin State Journal* farm reporter, Robert Bjorklund, asked McNeil to explain his apparent downgrading of cooperative extension. "I have a responsibility to all citizens of the state," McNeil responded. "The urban people are my concern because they make up the bulk of the population, but I still have a concern for agriculture and rural people."[93]

The new chancellor promptly set up an Administrative Committee to help plan the merger and began conferring with supportive colleagues and fellow UW leaders. One of these was Clay Schoenfeld, the well-connected University publicist and long-time Adolfson protégé, who offered a shrewd thought on how to approach the reorganization, or "Shotgun Wedding," as he called it. Schoenfeld proposed a "'steering committee,' composed largely of faculty members, some second-echelon administrators, and maybe some off-campus representation" to address important policy questions. "The chairman of this Committee is critical," he stressed. "I'd recommend Wils Thiede. . . . Some carry-over from the Huitt Committee would probably be desirable." The advice was welcome; on December 21 McNeil formed

---

[89]McNeil to Dear Colleagues, October 25, 1965, ibid.

[90]"From what I'm hearing around the campus," reported presidential assistant Robert Taylor to his chief in the summer of 1965, "the morale situation in both general extension and agricultural extension is not good. More than the consolidation, extension people, I hear, are bothered by the uncertainty. I'm told there's particular unrest among those without tenure." Taylor to Harrington, August 31, 1965, ibid.

[91]Matt Pommer, "Extension Chief Visions New Adult Schooling Era," *Capital Times*, October 30, 1965.

[92]David F. Behrendt, "Challenge Confronts UW Extension Chief," *Milwaukee Journal*, October 31, 1965, 40/1/1/1, 6, UA.

[93]Robert C. Bjorklund, "McNeil–Man on a Tightrope," *Wisconsin State Journal*, November 8, 1965, ibid.

a "special advisory committee on organization and structure," chaired by School of Education Associate Dean Wilson Thiede, a widely respected former UED administrator. The membership also followed Schoenfeld's suggestion, including representatives from CES (Patrick Boyle and Gale VandeBerg), UED (Robert Dick, Harold W. Montross, and George Strother), WHA (Karl Schmidt), and UW-Milwaukee (Bernard J. James). McNeil later added Harland Klagos, a former College of Agriculture administrator and more recently his special assistant for administrative affairs.[94]

As the Thiede Committee focused on the problem of organizational structure, Chancellor McNeil hosted a major conference in April, 1966, on the seemingly unlimited possibilities for University Extension and for social action programming in Wisconsin under President Johnson's War on Poverty. Wisconsin Republican Governor Warren Knowles offered his vote of confidence by declaring that McNeil's new unit would be responsible for administering programs funded under the federal Technical Services Act and Title I of the Higher Education Act.[95] The conferees discussed additional opportunities associated with the Economic Redevelopment Act and the Economic Opportunity Act, under which McNeil had already established an OEO-funded Center for Action on Poverty that would coordinate the Wisconsin phase of the War on Poverty.[96] President Harrington best captured the essence of the

---

[94]McNeil's initial Administrative Committee consisted of Henry Ahlgren, Robert Dick, Harland R. Klagos, Harold B. McCarty, Harold W. Montross, Frederick I. Olson, T.J. Shannon, and Gale L. VandeBerg. According to McNeil's early plans for this group, it first met on January 4, 1966, and weekly thereafter Beginning in mid-July, 1966, the committee consisted of the chancellor, the assistant chancellors, the deans, and the directors. Extension Administrative Committee Minutes, July 15, 1966, ibid. See also Clay [Schoenfeld] to Don [McNeil], n.d., ibid., Box 14. UW News Service release, December 10, 1965, ibid., box 6; McNeil to Robert Dick, December 21, 1965; Thiede to McNeil, December 24, 1965; White, *Cooperative Extension in Wisconsin*, pp. 13-15. A committee roster from January, 1966, included McNeil and John F. Meggers also as members. Meggers, an administrative assistant in the UW-Madison School of Education, evidently provided staff support to the committee. "Special Advisory Committee on Organization and Structure for University Extension," date stamped January 24, 1966, Series 41/1/1/1, Box 14, UA.
[95]"Governor Knowles speaks on State Problems and Solutions," *Daily Cardinal*, April 20, 1966; McNeil to All Extension Faculty and Staff, December 20, 1966, Series 41/1/1/1, Box 11, UA.
[96]Job Corps and VISTA were two of the programs involved. "'U' Extension Gets Grant to Found Poverty Center," *Daily Cardinal*, March 12, 1966. "The University Extension operation illustrates the university's effort to coordinate public service activities and to work with individuals and agencies in fighting poverty," McNeil

bright new world unfolding: "We are now in the middle of the problem-solving revolution, and of the major trends in higher education, it is difficult to state one more important."[97]

Chancellor McNeil soon began circulating a draft organization chart, entitled "Proposed structure, University Extension," which he and his top advisors had prepared. On May 25 Chairman Thiede wrote McNeil conveying his committee's unanimous endorsement of the chart or "plan," as then envisioned and including a set of guidelines "which help to interpret our feeling about your chart."[98] The draft chart and guidelines represented an important milestone in the reorganization. Two assistant chancellors would report to McNeil, one responsible for subject matter divisions and the other for field and support service units, including the numerous county and area offices currently dotting the state. Taken together, these two large sections would include essentially all substantial operations of the original UED, CES, and WHA. Another set of assistant chancellors–apparently in a "staff" rather than a "line" or operations relationship to the chancellor–would provide administrative and coordinating services at locations outside Madison with significant faculty resources, such as UWM and the new campuses under development at Green Bay and Kenosha-Racine (UW-Parkside). A limited number of special assistants, also reporting directly to the chancellor, were to supervise special new program areas such as international programs and Title I. Not surprisingly, these were fields of particular concern to the Chancellor McNeil and President Harrington.[99] An auxiliary services unit would house the business office and associated internal support agencies. The guidelines clarified some of the details of this organizational chart. More important, they reaffirmed the original philosophical underpinnings of the reorganization by

---

explained. "One of our directives from University President Fred Harvey Harrington is to help solve some of society's problems, and poverty has high priority." *Community Action Program: Center for Action on Poverty* (Madison: Center for Action on Poverty, September-December, 1966), Series 40/1/1/1, Box 128, UA; *Center for Action on Poverty: Design and Objectives*, newsletter, February, 1967, ibid., Box 11.

[97]McNeil, "The Year of the Merger," p. 2.

[98]Thiede to McNeil, May 25, 1966; McNeil to Thiede, June 15, 1996; McNeil to Boyle, Dick, James, Klagos, Montross, Schmidt, Strother, and VandeBerg, December 12, 1966, all in Series 41/1/1/1, Box 14, UA. Although McNeil would not officially discharge the Thiede Committee until December, its work was essentially completed at this point.

[99]Harrington thought Chancellor McNeil should give Title I activity his "personal attention." Harrington to McNeil, August 18, 1966, Series 40/1/1/1, Box 60, UA; "McNeil to Direct Title I Program," *Wisconsin State Journal*, August 18, 1966.

emphasizing the "problem" orientation of the new Extension structure, functioning on a University-wide basis in a statewide context.[100]

McNeil now moved to obtain approval of the proposed organization chart from the key constituent units. The process was essentially pro forma with radio and television and general extension, whose staffs already were largely independent of the campus academic departments and therefore unlikely to suffer major disruptions over changes in their administrative homes.[101] It was considerably more of an issue, however, with the UWM campus administration, which increasingly defined itself as heading a separate and distinct collegiate institution, a stand that contradicted the official all-University extension perspective.[102] The reorganization structure also seemed to threaten the College of Agriculture, whose Cooperative Extension Service had traditionally been based on a close integration with its campus academic departments, an arrangement neither portrayed in the chart nor clearly protected by the guidelines.

The Milwaukee case was handled by UWM Vice Chancellor Charles Vevier–like McNeil a Harrington history protégé. Although Vevier's arguments were couched in friendly language, he clearly objected to the proposed unitary structure. Rather than a staff-level Extension assistant chancellor stationed at UWM and reporting to McNeil, Vevier proposed an assistant chancellor with UWM status and authority equal to the assistant chancellors for programs and support. This "assistant chancellor of UWM-University Extension," as Vevier

---

[100]"Proposed Structure, University Extension," May 11, 1966; "Guidelines for the Organization of University Extension," May 26, 1966, both in Series 41/1/1/1, Box 14, UA. One of the early guidelines noted: "The nature of community problems and the complexity of the University Extension probably preclude a single rationale for structure." As Clay Schoenfeld had commented several months earlier: "Our objective is not to devise a neat chart but to produce action on the ground. A combination of approaches may suggest itself, particularly when we remember that our real job is finding happy homes for key people." Clay to Don [McNeil], undated, ibid.

[101]See, for example, Frederick I. Olson to Shannon, April 25, 1966, Series 41/3/12-6, Box 2, UA. Reporting on a recent meeting between Thiede and the Milwaukee Extension Division staff, Olson said, "Since this was a hearing rather than a formal meeting, no actions were taken, but I believe I am entitled to conclude that there was no serious dissent from the general structure proposed."

[102]During a discussion of the "Milwaukee relationship" by Chancellor McNeil's Administrative Committee, someone pointed out the irony that initially UWM had sought to model itself after the University in Madison; now under Harrington it had switched to a policy of developing into a "strong, different, urban university." Extension Administrative Committee Minutes, March 15, 1966.

called the position, would have responsibility "for all extension functions and programs related to the UWM campus and the general Milwaukee area." Equally important, he or she would also hold a half-time assistant chancellor appointment in the UWM campus administration, reporting to the UWM chancellor as well as to McNeil. Notwithstanding Vevier's claim to "understand and respect" McNeil's concern for the state-wide coordinating responsibilities of Extension, Vevier in essence was proposing a separate and largely independent UWM extension operation that would control all outreach activity (including "program" and "support," as Vevier's amended chart portrayed it) for the entire Milwaukee area.[103]

Agriculture Dean Glenn Pound also had concerns and had discussed the proposed structure with McNeil on April 7. President Harrington had made clear to Pound at the time of his appointment as dean that the extension merger was a settled issue. Thus in previous conversations with McNeil Pound had politely supported the general idea of reorganization. Now, with McNeil's organizational chart in hand, he was alarmed to see that he and his department chairmen were included nowhere in the structure, even though agricultural extension had always functioned within that administrative context. As Pound explained in a note to McNeil:

> Since subject matter departments are integral units of the College, it would follow that the lines of communication and administrative control between them and the Chancellor of Extension would be via their department chairmen and the dean of the College. I do not see how we can maintain an integration of extension and residence activities otherwise.[104]

Pound set his department faculties to work analyzing the draft chart and guidelines. Reiterating in various ways their dean's view of the problem, many saw the proposed reorganization as threatening to emasculate their agricultural extension activities and disrupting

---

[103]Vevier to McNeil, June 7, 1966, Series 40/1/1/1, Box 6, UA. None of this was a surprise to McNeil. For example, Fred Olson had reported to the Extension Administrative Committee on May 10 that a UWM committee had developed a separate "proposal for an inner core facility." Series 41/1/1/1, Box 12, UA.

[104]Pound to McNeil, April 7, 1966, Pound Files, Box 15, UA. On April 12, 1966, McNeil shared this letter with his Administrative Committee. VandeBerg interpreted Pound's position: "Concept of 'shared power' is implicit here, with Pound sharing authority with Extension program deans. . . ." A week earlier, on April 8, while discussing this same issue, McNeil had asserted he "must have ultimate authority." Extension Administrative Committee Minutes, April 8 and 12, 1966.

departmental and college operations. Instead, the favored options were to retain college authority over the extension specialists housed there, by explicitly including the department chairmen and college dean in the formal organizational structure, or to call off the reorganization altogether in favor of voluntary cooperation across schools, colleges, and campuses.[105]

Perhaps hoping a wider viewing might attract more support, on May 13 McNeil wrote to Pound requesting that he present "the proposed Table of Organization of University Extension to part or all of the College of Agriculture faculty." The chancellor claimed to share allegiance to the integrated department concept even as he declined to revise the plan or modify his asserted authority over all Extension personnel. "No chart can possibly explain the intricate arrangements and relationships of all the persons involved in a complicated mechanism such as University Extension," observed McNeil. "I would guess that, in fact, our proposed organization will have a great deal of movement sideways. . . . The point is that key decisions and policies will pass through your College of Agriculture structure." To reassure Pound, McNeil promised that personnel decisions would be initiated at the department level and then "handled through the regular channels up to your office and hence to me through proper Extension administrators." Furthermore, "After a period of trial, I am perfectly willing to review the structure and make whatever changes may be necessary to ensure a high-level, effective operation."[106] With these assurances, on May 18

---

[105]Appendix 6 of Glenn Pound's "Changes in Cooperative Extension at the University of Wisconsin, 1965-1979" contains copies of several letters from department chairmen. W.H. Gabelman, chairman of horticulture, reported: "We do not think that an administrative structure which bypasses the Dean of the College of Agriculture is in the best interests of coordination of research, teaching and extension. . . . In evaluating the position the specialist finds himself in, if he is not answerable to the Dean of the College of Agriculture, then he is not truly in the College of Agriculture. In fact, he is not in any college." After offering a similar analysis, Chairman John R. Schmidt of agricultural economics concluded: "I share the Department's concern that the proposed organization will have a splintering rather than an integrating impact." Dairy science Chairman R.P. Niedermeier told Henry Ahlgren: "We have concern that in the proposed structure extension specialists may not remain an integral part of the College of Agriculture. We would prefer that resident and extension faculty function under the direction of the Dean of the College of Agriculture. Only by functioning under one Dean can we avoid segmentation and the development of departmental cliques."

[106]McNeil to Pound, May 13, 1966. Appendix 6 in ibid. McNeil had earlier reported to his Administrative Committee that he had met with the Agriculture dean and was "willing to make special arrangement w/Pound, but DRM [McNeil] must have ultimate authority." Extension Administrative Committee Minutes, April 8, 1966.

Dean Pound convened a meeting of his department chairmen. After a long and largely skeptical discussion–with Henry Ahlgren recommending approval only by explicit reference to McNeil's qualifying letter and Pound urging passage on the assumption that the plan could later be reconsidered–the group voted to bring the question before the general college faculty. This occurred on May 26, with the assembly voting unanimously in favor after the college administration reiterated its qualified support of the plan.[107]

McNeil was well aware that this affirmation from the College of Agriculture was grudging and tentative. Both Pound and Ahlgren were well-known as tenacious defenders of College of Agriculture interests. Thus throughout the early months of 1966 Pound and Ahlgren had engaged in a quiet but enduring debate with McNeil over the ultimate disposition of agricultural extension. Ahlgren had warned McNeil:

> Before we can fully support this Codification proposal, we need to know more about the causes and effects that will develop between the Madison Campus and University Extension. . . . To us the Codification Committee proposal appears to provide the machinery for a clear separation of the Extension function from the research and teaching functions. If this is correct, we will be destroying something which we have spent many years in building in the College of Agriculture. We would need more evidence than is available now and more proof that separation is better than integration before we would be willing to approve this type of arrangement.[108]

---

[107]Departmental Chairman's Meeting, May 18, 1966, Pound, "Changes in Cooperative Extension," appendix 6; Called Meeting of the Faculty of the College of Agriculture, May 26, 1966, Series 40/1/1/1, Box and 14, UA. See also "Ag College Approves New Extension Setup," *Wisconsin State Journal*, May 28, 1966; Matt Pommer, "Move to Expand U. Extension Setup," *Capital Times*, May 27, 1966; "Extension Faculty Approved Historic Merger, *WAM, 67* (June, 1966), 12-13; UW News service release, May 27, 1966, Series 40/1/1/1, Box 6, UA.

[108]Ahlgren to McNeil, February 21, 1966. McNeil replied to Ahlgren on March 1. After discussing several possible scenarios, he concluded: "This leads me to the conclusion that each unit must decide what constitutes its faculty." McNeil assured Pound on February 10: "I want to repeat that I am anxious to expand services, not reduce them. In this light, I see Cooperative Extension being broader than the College of Agriculture. We do want specialists in other disciplines on other campuses. This would in no way disrupt our present operations with the College of Agriculture." All in ibid.

Why, then, did Pound and Ahlgren throw their support behind the McNeil reorganization plan? It seems unlikely they really favored it. Perhaps they believed the merger would collapse without their having explicitly to oppose it and thereby place themselves at serious cross purposes with President Harrington. Probably they also thought their Farm Bureau and USDA allies would block Harrington's plan to have McNeil designated by the Department of Agriculture as the head of the Cooperative Extension Service in Wisconsin.[109] Without this federal approval, Pound and Ahlgren would effectively remain in charge of agricultural extension and would control its federal funds regardless of the formal organizational structure of University Extension. According to Pound's subsequent recollection, Ahlgren had assured him that Washington would never approve the transfer because McNeil would then be the first state CES director with no experience in agriculture. Ahlgren and Pound were well aware of strong objections to the merger being expressed to the U.S. Department of Agriculture by some of the rural Wisconsin county boards and farm leaders.[110] But they badly

---

[109]Harrington had told Vice President Clodius on April 12: "I have been thinking over the federal Extension appointment, and have decided that this is in fact a critical test of strength in University-federal relations. Victory here is a must for us, and for all the other universities that want to combine general and agricultural extension. Some will want to put an agricultural man on top; but they must not be forced to do this. And anyway, agriculture stands to gain by merger. Hence I am not disposed to compromise. We must and will appoint McNeil; and they should be persuaded to accept this." Series 41/1/1/1, Box 17, UA.

[110]See, for example: "We have learned from a number of our County Extension agents that University of Wisconsin authorities are now negotiating with your office to transfer the Federal Extension appointment from the College of Agriculture to the office of the Chancellor. If such is accomplished, direction and administration will be placed in the hands of an individual who has no training, knowledge or background of experience in agriculture and home economics. . . . we would expect an erosion of educational services in the traditional areas served by the Agricultural Extension Service under such an arrangement even though we have been told that such will not be the case. . . . we are unalterably opposed to the transfer of all administrative authority and control of Agricultural Extension from its present position in the College of Agriculture to the new University Extension." Lloyd Owens, Waukesha, and other representatives of the Agricultural Committees of County Boards to Orville Freeman, Secretary of Agriculture, May 9, 1966, Series 40/1/1/1, Box 6, UA.

Owens eventually received a reply that dismissed his concerns: "You indicate in your letter that you feel the person who has the final responsibility to the USDA and whose appointment as Director is concurred in by the Secretary should be trained and experienced in Agriculture. We agree that this is highly desirable. However, to maintain this as a requirement would seem to eliminate some highly qualified leadership candidates and we feel that more important is a man's total knowledge and experience,

underestimated Harrington's and especially UW Vice President Clodius' influence with Democratic Party officials in Washington. Thus on June 10, 1966, shortly after the College of Agriculture faculty endorsed McNeil's reorganization scheme, President Harrington announced federal approval of the transfer of authority over cooperative extension to McNeil.[111]

Two days later the UW regents also sanctioned the transfer, received the chancellor's reorganization progress report, and voted to accept McNeil's recommendations for the two major assistant chancellors. One, George Strother, had served as chairman of the UED commerce department since its inception in 1963 and had been a supportive member of the Huitt and Thiede committees. He was to administer the programming divisions. To no one's surprise, Henry Ahlgren was appointed the other assistant chancellor, responsible for the field and support divisions.[112]

his capacity, his breadth, his sense of responsibility and his dedication." Mehren to Owens, June 13, 1966, ibid.

[111]See Pound, "Changes in Cooperative Extension," p. 4 and Appendix 3; McNeil to Clodius, March 8, 1966. In McNeil to Robben W. Fleming, March 15, 1966, McNeil explained: "The basic change will be to place the Cooperative Extension Service in University Extension, rather than in the College of Agriculture on the Madison campus." Draft Memorandum of Understanding Between the University of Wisconsin and the United States Department of Agriculture on Cooperative Extension Work in Agriculture and Home Economics, March 16, 1966, outlined the proposed changes; Clodius to John Schnittker, Under-Secretary of Agriculture, March 16, 1966; the federal CES administrator declared McNeil qualified for the CES directorship in Lloyd H. Davis, Administrator, Federal Extension Service, to George L. Mehren, Assistant Secretary, May 17, 1966, approval signature by Mehren dated May 26, 1966; Lloyd H. Davis, USDA, Washington, to Harrington, telegram, May 27, 1966; Lloyd H. Davis, Administrator, USDA Federal Extension Service, Washington, to Harrington, June 2, 1966; UW BOR Minutes, June 10, 1966; UW Statewide Communications Service news release, June 10, 1966; Clarke Smith, Secretary of the Regents, to Harrington, June 14, 1966; McNeil to Harrington, June 22, 1966, all correspondence in Series 40/1/1/1, Box 6, UA; White, *Cooperative Extension in Wisconsin*, p. 17. According to Harrington, Clodius was instrumental in obtaining the transfer by persuading his former major professor at the University of California at Berkeley, now the assistant secretary of agriculture, to grant the Wisconsin request. Harrington, oral history interview.

[112]"Extension Appointments" and "Extension Reorganization," UW Statewide Communications Service news releases, June 10, 196, Series 40/1/1/1, Box 6, UA; "Top U. Extension Aides Appointed/Education Dean Named," *Capital Times*, June 11, 1966. UED Dean Shannon's acceptance of a two-year assignment to serve as a higher education advisor to the Ford Foundation in the Middle East had paved the way for Strother's appointment. Shannon to Clodius, May 31, 1966; "Shannon Leave," UW Statewide Communications Service news release, June 19, 1966. An unidentified newspaper clipping ("Dr. Shannon to Start Two-Year Near East Work," July 2, 1966)

McNeil shortly filled out the rest of his top administration by filling three deanships under Strother: Harold Montross (Liberal and Professional Education), formerly a UED associate dean; Gale Vande-Berg (Economic and Environmental Development), previously assistant director at CES; and Glen C. Pulver (Human Resource Development); and two directors under Ahlgren: Charles A. Wedemeyer (Methods and Media), a UED educational methodologist; and Robert N. Dick (Community Programs), McNeil's special assistant for community programs. WHA's Harold McCarty, who recently had announced his intention to retire, temporarily retained the third directorship.[113] McNeil also expanded Harland Klagos's duties to include Administrative Services,[114] put Patrick Boyle, formerly of CES, in charge of Staff Training and Development,[115] and continued Frederick Olson as assistant dean or chief administrative officer for University Extension in Milwaukee. Along with Alice Weck, assistant to the chancellor and coordinator of public information, this group now constituted McNeil's expanded Administrative Committee.[116]

Only the Olson appointment had been a problem. UWM Chancellor J. Martin Klotsche, perhaps prompted by his aggressive Vice Chancellor Vevier, had written to McNeil on June 17 about his surprise at reading a University Extension newsletter implying that the regents

---

noted that Shannon was about to depart for Beirut, Lebanon, the original home of both of his parents. Series 40/1/1/1, Box 60. President Harrington wrote Ahlgren on June 24, "I am very glad that you are taking on the Assistant Chancellorship. . . . This is one more service you are rendering the University, and may be the most important of all." Harrington addressed this note familiarly to "Henry," although Ahlgren was generally known to his intimates as Hank. Series 41/1/1/1, Box 11, UA.

[113]McNeil to McCarty, May 3, 1966, Series 40/1/1/1, Box 6. On September 28, 1966, Alice Weck directed a memo to McNeil mentioning a "'Mac Wants Out' story" that the chancellor might want to discuss at the next Administrative Committee meeting. Series 41/1/1/1, Box 12, UA.

[114]Extension Administrative Committee Minutes, July 15, 1966.

[115]On September 27, 1966, McNeil informed his Administrative Committee that, after checking with the Thiede Committee and receiving no objections, he was appointing Boyle director of staff training and development and having him report directly to the chancellor. "It is understood he will work closely with the deans and directors in developing programs and identifying training needs, and that each dean and director will have training as a part of his responsibility." Series 41/1/1/1, Box 12, UA.

[116]UW BOR Minutes, July 13, 1966; "Personnel," news release, UW Statewide Communications Service, July 13, 1966, Series 40/1/1/1, Box 60; McNeil, "The Year of the Merger," pp. 3-4; White, *Cooperative Extension in Wisconsin*, pp. 15-16. Alice Weck assumed new duties as special assistant to the chancellor in mid-July, 1966. Extension Administrative Committee Minutes, July 15, 1966.

had approved McNeil's proposed extension structure. In fact, Klotsche accurately pointed out, the board had only acted on the Strother and Ahlgren appointments. Since "the Milwaukee question" was neither resolved nor discussed Friday, "I do not see how we can assume that a plan has been approved although your newsletter certainly gives that impression." Klotsche was further astonished to learn that McNeil's plan assigned only coordinative responsibilities to Olson's position:

> This I consider a gross underestimation of his responsibilities and does not give the position the authority that it must have. In all of our discussions with you, we in Milwaukee have certainly thought of this person as more than a coordinator. . . . There will be considerable unhappiness on this campus unless there is an early review of this matter with a clarification of the role of the assistant chancellor-Milwaukee on the UWM campus and his organizational and policy relationships to the other assistant chancellors and to your office and to mine. It would also be unfortunate if your people as a result of the newsletter concluded that the Milwaukee matter is already settled.[117]

McNeil was unmoved. In September, merely to complete his organizational chart, he reaffirmed Olson's old appointment as associate dean and allowed the larger turf battle between Extension and UW-Milwaukee to remain unsettled.[118]

The final part of the year-long reorganization was the most difficult. First came the allocation of departments and operating units to the various divisions arrayed under Assistant Chancellors Strother and Ahlgren. McNeil had outlined the process on June 2: "Our plan is to begin implementation at the top, with appointment of assistant chancellors first. Once they are appointed they will join in the selection

---

[117]Klotsche to McNeil, June 17, 1966, Series 40/1/1/1, Box 6, UA.

[118]A few days after Klotsche's complaint, McNeil received a letter from Orville H. Palmer, acting chairman of the UED commerce department in Milwaukee, strongly supporting Olson. McNeil forwarded it to Harrington and Clodius with these observations: "There is a great restlessness in Milwaukee among the Extension staff, of course, and I suppose I'll be getting more of these. I'll not send them all on to you, but I thought you'd like to see at least one person's version of how things have operated at UW-M." Palmer to McNeil, June 23, 1966; McNeil to Harrington and Clodius, June 19, 1966, ibid. For a time in early September McNeil's thought was to create a position of dean for international programs and appoint Olson to it. This would leave room for a new "chief administrative office at Milwaukee" filled by someone with a UWM faculty appointment but budgeted 100 percent by Extension. Extension Administrative Committee Minutes, September 6, 1966.

of the next level of administrators, who will, in turn, work with department chairmen in establishing where they fit best. To assure maximum faculty consultation, appointments will come first through an ad hoc committee on faculty organization."[119] The effort resulted in ninety-four sub-agencies. On Assistant Chancellor Strother's side, the great bulk of the old UED academic departments were placed under Dean Montross, while most CES biological science departments went to Dean VandeBerg,[120] and a mixture of UED and CES social studies departments, including the Center for Action on Poverty and a number of individual social action programs, were assigned to Dean Pulver.[121] The problem was less complicated for Assistant Chancellor Ahlgren's area, which broke down into "community services" or off-campus staffing, instructional media, and radio and television. Directors Boyle and Klagos reported directly to the chancellor.[122] As McNeil was fond of reminding people, the reorganization had directly affected more than a thousand full- and part-time employees and nearly fifteen hundred ad hoc appointees.[123]

---

[119]McNeil to Clodius, June 2, 1966, Series 40/1/1/1, Box 6, UA. See, for example, C.S. Bridgman for the Extension Organization Committee, "Summary of Responses Concerning University Extension Structure from University Extension Division Sub-units (up to 6/29/66)," Series 4/1/1/1-2, Box 16, UA.

[120]Dean VandeBerg also supervised the Geological and Natural History Survey, which, somewhat to McNeil's surprise, had joined Extension in January of 1966. See McNeil to Clodius, January 24, 1966, Series 40/1/1/1, Box 6, UA; Extension Administrative Committee Minutes, August 1, 1966.

[121]Strother to McNeil, Ahlgren, Montross, Pulver, VandeBerg, Dick, Wedemeyer, and Klagos regarding Departmental Allocations, list attached, Series 41/1/1/1, Box 21, UA; Untitled typed text and allocation list [ca. September 1, 1966], Series 41/1/1/1-2, Box 16, UA; Extension Administrative Committee Minutes, September 6 and 12, 1966; Strother to Montross, Pulver, and VandeBerg, Re Summary–Departmental Allocations, September 21, 1966, Series 41/1/1/1, Box 21, UA.

[122]Klagos's duties included supervising the business offices, Extension Duplicating, and the Wisconsin Center; obtaining office space for Madison-based staff; developing and presenting the annual budgets; and overseeing the staff benefit operation. He also was responsible for merging into a single budget office those units from the former UED, CES, WHA, and the State Geologist. *People in University Extension*, newsletter, February 28, 1967, Series 41/1/1/1, Box 11, UA.

[123]McNeil proudly informed his fellow chancellors (Adolfson, Fleming, Klotsche, Wyllie) and the Central Administration (Harrington, Clodius, et al.) on September 29, 1966: "It took almost a year, but here is the chart with the units finally allocated to the respective deans and directors of University Extension. . . . the lines of responsibility are now clear, and while we may reorganize the units under each dean and director in the months ahead, every person in Extension for the moment knows where he fits." Series 40/1/1/1, Boxes 21 and 60. See also McNeil, "The Year of the Merger,"

"The New Outreach of the University"

University Extension held its first all-staff meeting in Madison on October 11-14, 1966, a conference optimistically titled "The New Outreach of the University." Program chairman Patrick Boyle described the purpose as designed "to help all University Extension faculty better understand the new University Extension organization, its policies and procedures and its commitment to a statewide University Extension structure."[124] A key part of the program was Chancellor McNeil's "State of the Union" address. "At no time in the year–and we're eleven days short of a year for the merger," he observed, "has anyone acted in any way disgracefully, or tried to undo the merger; this is really splendid." New lines of responsibility and new operations were in place and "new working procedures" soon would follow. These achievements had occurred even in the face of "great dissent over the problem of the integrated department versus the autonomous department" because, and here he exaggerated a bit, "men of good will sat down at the table and came to agreement." McNeil declared that the USDA transfer of federal cooperative extension responsibility from the College of Agriculture to University Extension would bring a "strengthened" county staff structure better able to further the basic mission of getting "at the problems of society."[125]

McNeil's social action goals were evident in his review of the accomplishments of University Extension during the past year. Only a week earlier, Extension and UWM had rented space in the Milwaukee inner core, from which "we hope to mount new programs." Extension had trained participants in the Rural Community Action Program, VISTA (Volunteers In Service To America), and the Job Corps as part of the Johnson Administration's Great Society initiative. He listed "some new bridges to other state agencies," including the Wisconsin Department of Economic Development, the Department of Public Instruction, and the Wisconsin State University system. Shrewdly, he also praised Extension's "ongoing services," acknowledging that some long-time staffers "must look somewhat askance at the relative

---

pp. 3-4; *McNeil to Dear Colleagues*, newsletter, September 27, 1996, Series 41/1/1/1, Box 11, UA.

[124]Patrick G. Boyle, "Introduction," Annual University Extension Faculty Conference, "The New Outreach of the University," October 11-14, 1966, *Proceedings and Report*, ibid., Box 16.

[125]McNeil, "The New University Extension," in ibid..

newcomers who enter the field and start bragging of the great new things in University Extension when the veterans have been at it for years." Still, there was Pat Boyle's new retraining program, "which all of us are going to have to undergo," as well as a possible new National University Extension Training Center to pass along to the entire nation the unique lessons soon to be learned by Extension.[126] In the future there would be "even greater expansion of services to the counties," involving "people from different disciplines who can be close at hand and help make this system work." Continual "restructuring of the units" would be necessary as programming was increasingly shifted "off the regular campuses" and Extension tried to "get ahead of the problems instead of always having to react to them." Extension should develop plans for fighting poverty, for conservation, for economic development, and more. "I feel strongly that the university, and especially the University of Wisconsin, is an agency for social change and that we're an integral part of that agency for social change."

Also addressing the assembled Extension staff members was President Harrington, who predicted that "because the modern university is increasingly a public service-extension university, we may see the time when a faculty member must explain why he isn't involved in some service activities, extension activities, adult education activities, and social action work." It was this last category that appealed to the president. He recalled that Van Hise, "unquestionably our greatest president," had "actually said social welfare was one of the activities of extension, perhaps the fundamental activity of extension." Now, through such legislation as Title I (everyone present was aware of Harrington's key role in its passage) the federal government was planning "to use universities in assisting communities in community action programs." The time was not far off when it would no longer be possible "to say there is a difference between action programs and adult education."[127]

---

[126]McNeil and Boyle had visited the Kellogg Foundation seeking funding for this venture. See Extension Administrative Committee Minutes, October 6, 1967.

[127]Harrington, "The University and the State," in Annual University Extension Faculty Conference, October 11-14, 1966. Harrington's comments received considerable press coverage. Professor Elizabeth Brandeis Raushenbush, the daughter of the late Supreme Court Justice Louis Brandeis and a prominent progressive in the Madison economics department, applauded Harrington's vision: "I must write to tell you that what the papers quoted you as saying about Extension was music to my ears. It surely needs saying these days! It reminded me of Ed Witte's reply when (very shortly before his retirement) he was asked why he didn't refuse a request to go somewhere up in the State to make a speech. 'But,' said Ed, 'they asked me to come.' Who on the Faculty to-

Notwithstanding this inspirational rhetoric, the assembled Extension troops were confused and of many minds. This became evident when the assemblage divided into twenty-four small groups to consider a number of issues posed by the organizers. It was a curious exercise, partly because the merger itself begged at least one of the key questions while informed responses required considerably more knowledge than the great majority of those present possessed. At most, the small group discussion might best be described as part of the socialization process. Later, after reviewing the rather mixed responses, Bob Dick over-sanguinely reported : "There is an improvement in attitudes and a willingness to look ahead and adapt to a unified adminis-tration."[128]

The most tangible result of the conference came at the Memo-rial Union Theater on October 13, when Chancellor McNeil called to order the first-ever University Extension faculty meeting. The minutes described this as an "important and necessary" event because the assembly not only formed a "governing body" but also helped to create a belief "within the faculty that they are a part of the process." The gathering approved a University Extension Faculty Government plan developed by an eight-person organizing committee appointed earlier by the chancellor. Committee chairman Robert Rieck led discussion of the proposal, which precisely defined the Extension faculty and created a Faculty Senate, Committee on Nominations, and University Commit-tee–Extension. The governance plan received unanimous consent. Rieck also reported that Extension would send seven representatives to President Harrington's new all-University Faculty Assembly and maintain one member on the all-University Faculty Council.[129]

McNeil professed great satisfaction with the all-staff confer-ence. He told Assistant Chancellor Ahlgren, "you have what they call 'audience contact.'" He was especially effusive to conference organizer Pat Boyle:

---

day would feel that obligation?" Raushenbush to Harrington, October 17, 1966, Series 41/1/1/1, Box 16, UA.

[128]"Comments from Seminar Groups," ca. October 13, 1966, ibid.; Jeff Smoller, "UW Extension Plan Still Faces Problems," *Milwaukee Journal*, October 23, 1966.

[129]Besides Rieck, members of the organizing committee included Norman C. Allhiser, Charles S. Bridgman, Irving Brotslaw, Robert W. Finley, Milo V. Johansen, Karl F. Schmidt, and Louise A. Young. University Extension Faculty Minutes, October 13, 1966; "University Extension Faculty Government," October 10, 1966, both in Series 41/1/1/1, Box 16, UA.

I'm really terribly pleased at how these three days were handled. The workshops will produce a great deal. The preliminary sessions were just fine. The performances all-round were great, and I think that we have a new spirit abroad in University Extension. In fact I noticed the change from the first day to the third; it was quite striking. So many of the county staff especially, but even some of the specialists and the people from Milwaukee, were raving about the results.

WHA television's Lee Dreyfus, a skillful politician who later would be elected governor of Wisconsin, also congratulated Boyle: "One of the few such meetings I've ever found meaningful–excellent job."[130] But the question was still open whether the reorganized University Extension could produce such impressive "results" in its day-to-day programming.

Educational Communications

One of the goals of the McNeil administration was the modernization of educational communications in the state. This was envisioned to include not only the professionalization of public radio and television but also significant advances in instructional mediation. In a sense, the extension merger was premised on the assumption that a state-wide outreach agency must develop the technological and organizational capability to connect the University with the wider public off campus. As Charles Wedemeyer, the director of instructional media, put it, "The use of media is not frosting on the cake. We're trying to build a different cake."[131] One achievement was the Educational Teleconference Network, which became fully operational during 1966. ETN made possible interactive audio communication among dozens of sites across the Wisconsin in support of instructional and administrative activity.[132] More significant was the consolidation of Wedemeyer's unit with WHA radio and television to form a new Division of Educational Communica-

---

[130]Ibid.

[131]*People in University Extension*, No. 1, January 20, 1967, Series 40/1/1/1, Box 60, UA.

[132]UW News and Publications Service release, January 17, 1967, ibid.; "Extension Lectures Nurses throughout State by Phone," *Daily Cardinal*, February 21, 1967; A.R. Allen, Chairman, Extension Law Dept., to Dean Harold W. Montross, November 8, 1967, Series 40/1/1/1, Box 90, UA.

tions under Lee Dreyfus's successor, Ellis James Robertson.[133] Soon McNeil was able to report to President Harrington that Jim Robertson had "succeeded in shaking up WHA," primarily by recruiting full-time professional staff to replace what he referred to condescendingly as Harold McCarty's part-timers.[134] The resulting 1968 television series, "The Inner Core: City Within a City," produced WHA's first Emmy award, indeed the first ever awarded to a public television program.[135] The restructuring culminated in the summer of 1968 with the appointment of Luke F. Lamb, formerly the director of educational media for the Oregon State System of Higher Education, as permanent director of the increasingly wide-ranging media division, freeing Robertson to concentrate on radio and television programming.[136]

The McNeil soon discovered that media professionalism cost money, lots of it. As Jim Robertson told him in mid-1967, "Because of the dismal outlook for 'new funds' during 1967-68, I am revising the budget request of the Division of Radio and Television and channeling it into a single outstanding program project."[137] The WHA budgetary situation continued to deteriorate to such an extent that by the spring of

---

[133]BOR Minutes, December 9, 1966. See also *What's New in University Extension*, No. 2, December 21, 1966, ibid., Box 60; Extension Administrative Committee Minutes, February 5, 1968. Dreyfus had resigned his WHA post and his UW-Madison faculty appointment to accept the presidency of Wisconsin State University-Stevens Point.

[134]McNeil declared: "Jim Robertson has succeeded in shaking up WHA, and the only way he has been able to do it is to get some professional staff in. One of Jim's problems is that he can't attract new money to do things because he feels that the staff is of low quality. . . . he's done away with McCarty's old part-time concept, and he's hiring real professionals to come in and handle it like a professional station. . . . much of our budget deficit this year is because Jim has moved rather rapidly to add staff and improve all of his programming. . . . We diverted some carryover funds from USDA (on the grounds of disseminating Cooperative Extension Programs), and we used some of the money yielded by our other units to subsidize him. . . . in going over the budgeting at this time, it became apparent that if the merger had been only Co-op Extension and General Extension, we would have been on a much more stable financial base. The reason . . . is that we have not been able to plow any new money, except from income, into the program. . . . I will be coming back [from Africa] in April with a special appeal for funds to honor our commitment to Radio and Television." McNeil to Harrington, March 4, 1968, Series 40/1/1/1, Box 90, UA. McNeil overstated his criticism of WHA under Harold McCarty. For another view see Arthur Hove, "WHA–Not So Much a Radio Station as a Way of Life," *Wisconsin Tails and Trails*, 8 (Spring, 1967), 32-36.

[135]"WHA: Higher and Higher," *WAM*, 70 (May, 1969), 15, 19.

[136]News release, Extension Office of Public Information, June 3, 1968, Series 40/1/1/1, Box 90, UA; Extension Administrative Committee Minutes, June 10, 1968.

[137]Robertson to McNeil, May 23, 1967, Series 40/1/1/1, Box 90, UA.

1968, even as McNeil was praising Robertson's accomplishments to Harrington, the chancellor had reluctantly reached a startling conclusion: He now thought it had probably been a mistake to include WHA in the Extension reorganization, because educational communications was draining precious resources from the other divisions! Indeed, the budgetary problems were becoming so severe that Robertson's "shake-up" at WHA now seemed in jeopardy. Appealing for more financial support, McNeil told Harrington: "As for Radio and Television, we simply have to tool up to be the best so that the Educational Communications Board will use us for production for the network."[138]

Social Action Programming

Chancellor McNeil confidently expected his administration to be particularly noted for its social action work, and he eagerly sought to have University Extension involved in the Great Society programs being established by Congress and the Johnson administration. This participation led directly to McNeil's creation of the University Extension Center for Action on Poverty in March, 1966, and his recruitment of Glen Pulver and Helen M. Sheirbeck, formerly a consultant to the federal Office of Economic Opportunity. Subsequently McNeil hired Marshall H. Colston as a specialist on anti-poverty programs and traditionally black institutions of higher education.[139] Scheirbeck soon was able to report to McNeil's Administrative Committee on the major Wisconsin programs funded by OEO for the upcoming year and beyond. These included the poverty center itself, the Rural Community Action Programs Training Center, the VISTA Training Program, and Indian Home Management and Community Development Project. She also listed several "special" and "potential" programs she predicted eventually would receive OEO support through the center.[140]

---

[138]McNeil to Harrington, May 15, 1968, ibid.

[139]"Supplementary Personnel Items for Consideration by the Educational Committee of the Board of Regents," January 7, 1966; News release, UW News Service, January 7, 1966, ibid., box 6. For a photo of Helen M. Scheirbeck, the director of Center for Action on Poverty following Pulver, see *Community Action Program*, p. 10. UW News Service release, March 9, 1966, Series 40/1/1/1, Box 6, UA. The release explained that "Colston's new duties include serving as administrative secretary to the University committee on cooperation with predominantly Negro universities, including his own alma mater." For a progress report on Colston's activities, see *People in University Extension*, February 28, 1967, Series 41/1/1/1, Box 11, UA.

[140]The special projects included: Summer Orientation Community Action

This rosy forecast notwithstanding, the rising cost of the Vietnam War was killing the Great Society. Soon McNeil and Pulver felt obliged to cancel a planned transfer of the poverty center from Madison to Milwaukee, but also to move quickly to hire more "good people" to staff the unit, "so that when Federal funds diminish, we still have an effective University agency to carry on our own war against poverty."[141] As funding prospects began to dim, Extension issued a glowing account of the early successes of the center. Its report, *Community Action Program: Center for Action on Poverty*, issued in late 1966, was a slick publication describing the VISTA program at Camp Olympia near Hurley, and the Extension-RCA Job Corps training program at Camp McCoy near Sparta, where the skills taught would be "applicable to labor market demands in urban communities."[142] Subsequent reports emphasized that "University Extension is already heavily committed to a direct attack on the problems faced by economically and culturally deprived persons in Wisconsin, and especially in Milwaukee."[143] In spite of these upbeat assessments, by 1966-67

Program in Health, Manpower, Neighborhood Centers and Education; Literacy Training Projects; Migrant Literacy Education; Forest County Indian Literacy Education; and Spanish-speaking People in Milwaukee Literacy Education. Potential projects being explored included: Indian Technical Assistants, Tri-State Arts and Crafts Cooperative, National American Indian Institute, and Population Survey of American Indians. Extension Administrative Committee Minutes, July 5, 1966. See also other social action programming listed in "Wisconsin Extension Pioneered in Work as a State Problem," *Wisconsin State Journal*, February 26, 1967.

[141]McNeil to Vevier, October 6, 1966, Series 41/1/1/1, Box 12, UA. Like McNeil, whose comment to Vevier betrayed a reluctance to face budgetary realities, President Harrington also found it hard to believe the federal War on Poverty might slacken. Two years later he told a New York reporter: "Even in Wisconsin, where university involvement throughout the state is a tradition, the problems are so overwhelming that the thrust into urban action must come in large part from the Federal Government." Quoted in Fred M. Hechinger, "The Urban University," *New York Times*, May 3, 1968.

[142]*Community Action Program* (September-December, 1966), Series 40/1/1/1, Box 128, UA. See also *McNeil to Dear Colleagues*, newsletter, July 8, 1966, ibid., Box 6; Ellen Checota to McNeil, "A Highlight of the University Extension's VISTA Training Schedule for the First of Two Six-week Sessions," July 11, 1966, ibid., Box 60; McNeil to Clodius, July 29, 1966, ibid.

[143]See "University Extension Services to Minority Groups (A Compendium of Divisional Reports)," April 13, 1967; McNeil to Stephen T. Boyle, Office of the Wisconsin Governor, August 21, 1967, both in ibid., Box 90. The quotation is from the latter. A description of several University Extension programs in the Milwaukee inner core appeared in "Urban Problems and State Actions: A Report to the People of Wisconsin by Governor Warren P. Knowles," mimeographed, ca. September, 1967, ibid.

President Johnson's anti-poverty initiative had already seen its best days. University Extension would continue to receive occasional OEO program dollars but never at the level anticipated by President Harrington and Chancellor McNeil as they set out to accomplish the extension merger.[144]

Nor was Title I of the 1965 Higher Education Act, on which Harrington and McNeil had placed such high hopes for support of urban extension initiatives, any more productive. Because Wisconsin had been the major institutional proponent of the Title I social action strategy, Chancellor McNeil was the logical choice to head a NASULGC committee to monitor the crucial appropriation phase of the legislative process.[145] This committee quickly discovered that President Johnson had budgeted a terribly disappointing total of only $20 million for fiscal year 1967 and the House of Representatives had already cut that figure in half. Restoration became the committee's most pressing, if ultimately illusory, objective.[146] Worse still, the senate began to balk at even a $10 million total appropriation.[147] With the amount of funding uncertain, McNeil nevertheless had to put together a required state-wide plan spelling out the use of whatever Title I money did eventually become available. This plan and some creative maneuvering in Washington ultimately led to the funding of twenty short-term projects for Wisconsin in January of 1966, half of them to be run directly through McNeil's

---

[144]In November, 1967, the Ford Foundation announced anti-poverty grants totaling $10.8 million to the University of Chicago, Harvard, MIT, and Columbia. McNeil was devastated and told Harrington: "This is one of the most distressing things I've seen in a long time–four very elitist universities getting ten million dollars to do things that are primarily research-oriented. While I subscribe to the research idea, think what one-tenth of this amount of money would do for demonstration purposes in a place like Milwaukee! . . . we simply haven't told our story as to what an institution like ours can do in the action field; this grant only shows how little the Ford people know about what urban programs should and could be. For some reason, these big private universities have an inside line to Ford. Though I know this has always been their orientation, why can't we get into the mainstream?" McNeil to Harrington, December 6, 1967, ibid. See also "$10.8 Million Grant to Aid Urban Studies," *Milwaukee Journal*, November 30, 1967.

[145]As the NASULGC executive director explained to McNeil in his letter of appointment, "since our Association played a major role in initiating and pressing for the kind of legislation represented by Title I, we should continue as an Association to concern ourselves with its development." Russell I. Thackrey, executive director, National Association of State Universities and Land-Grant Colleges, to McNeil and committee, April 11, 1966, Series 40/1/1/1, Box 6, UA.

[146]McNeil to Pres. David Henry, University of Illinois, May 6, 1966, ibid.

[147]Extension Administrative Committee Minutes, October 3, 1966.

University Extension.[148] While this was good news for the social action advocates, it was increasingly evident that federal Title I funding would never be able to support the urban agent thrust at the heart of University Extension as originally envisioned by McNeil and President Harrington.

Community Programs

Chancellor McNeil planned for his new corps of Title I-funded urban agents to operate under the Division of Community Programs. Here they would augment cooperative extension's impressive system of rural agents and general extension's less numerous group of continuing education coordinators located in several offices throughout Wisconsin. Soon after his appointment as chancellor McNeil had promised a gathering of Green County 4-H leaders that "the county agent soon will have the lines of contact to tie together people with the total university."[149] Emphasizing the importance of field work in the reorganized University Extension, he and Community Programs Director Robert Dick pledged to visit each of the seventy-two county offices in an effort to educate and energize the field staff.[150]

Too little money and too ambitious programming objectives combined to produce a thorny set of problems. Realistically, the inadequate Title I appropriations meant there would be no new urban agent system in Wisconsin. Any fundamental changes would have to occur through the old cooperative extension county agent system. But

---

[148]The programs included a continuing education program for deaf adults (in Milwaukee, Racine, Kenosha, Waukesha, Madison, Fox River Valley, and Delavan); sponsoring of clinics for school board members around the state; some post-graduate instruction for physicians; a residential seminar for Milwaukee-area government administrators; the establishment of an experimental family financial counseling center in Milwaukee; an experimental program with Milwaukee clergy doing urban problem involvement; the sponsoring of children's drama programs in ten small northern Wisconsin communities; the continuation of the Paint Box Art Center in the Hillside Housing Project of Milwaukee; the development of an extension course for library aids; and the study of community service and continuing education programs run by Wisconsin institutions of higher education. See *McNeil to Dear Colleagues*, newsletter, July 8, 1966, Series 40/1/1/1, Box 6, UA.

[149]"McNeil Sees New Services, Extension System Will Be Continued," *Wisconsin State Journal*, December 19, 1965.

[150]White, *Cooperative Extension in Wisconsin*, pp. 23-24; Harrington, oral history interview. By late December, 1966, McNeil and Dick had visited 49 county offices, leaving but 23 to complete the circuit. *What's New In University Extension*, newsletter, December 21, 1966, Series 41/1/1/1, Box 11, UA.

USDA officials were quick to remind Assistant Chancellor Ahlgren, if he needed any prompting, that federal cooperative extension funds must be used exclusively for cooperative extension programming.[151] Yet thanks primarily to Ahlgren's "Scope Report"-related initiatives during the late 1950s and early 1960s, some modest program flexibility was available, along with a small amount of unanticipated USDA money.[152] Still, McNeil had to depend for the most part on existing field staff members, who were expected to perform their old activities and undertake new ones as well. Most of them, however, lacked the time, knowledge, and skills to do everything well, and few additional agents could be hired to ease the burden.[153] "That's where the shoe really pinched in and that's where it still pinches," Ahlgren commented in 1980. "Basically it's a matter of staffing–funding to provide staff that can take on the added responsibilities as an overall University-wide type of Extension, to offer the people of the state."[154]

---

[151]USDA CES Administrator Lloyd H. Davis insisted that the budgeting of county staff be adjusted when "they become involved in non-Cooperative Extension programs." Davis to Ahlgren, August 11, 1967, ibid., Box 17. In an earlier communication to Ahlgren, Davis hinted at a related problem he hoped to avoid: "As organizational and other changes are made which affect the Wisconsin Cooperative Extension Service, we want to be assured that for purposes of reporting and in all relationships with the public, officials and employees of the organization clearly identify Cooperative Extension as such. In future audits, such identification will be carefully reviewed." Davis to Ahlgren, August 25, 1966, ibid.

[152]In October, 1966, Ahlgren raised a question never asked at UED: how to spend $70,000 in carryover federal funds and a fresh $94,988 that had become available the previous July. McNeil thought USDA would be interested in this decision, particularly with regard to the recent agreement by USDA to transfer the state directorship from the college to McNeil, who believed Extension would thereby be in a better position to offer a broader spectrum of service out in the field. See Extension Administrative Committee Minutes, October 8, 1966. This may have been behind McNeil's note the following January: "Could you give me some idea of where we stand on the 'new type' of county staff. I would like to know what counties, and on what time schedule, we are beginning to introduce the new types of county staff." McNeil to Ahlgren, January 3, 1967, ibid., Box 11.

[153]One of the few examples of new hiring was the appointment of Lee C. Hansen in early 1967 as the Milwaukee county beautification agent, a new position unique in the nation, funded two-thirds by federal money and one-third by the county. A newspaper report of the new agent's appointment explained: "Hansen said he hoped to attack ugliness anywhere it was found in the city, although special emphasis would be given to the problems of the inner city." "Expert Starts in Unusual Post as County Beautification Agent," unidentified newspaper clipping, ca. March 26, 1967, ibid., Box 16.

[154]Ahlgren, oral history interview.

University Extension Chancellor Donald McNeil and
UW Center System Chancellor Lorentz Adolfson,
photo by Gary Shulz. UA, X25-3411.

New University of Wisconsin Extension Building, February 20, 1962.
UA, X25-3412.

The McNeil administration tried in several ways to solve this staffing question. To some extent the chancellor attributed the problem to a bad attitude on the part of the field staff, derived from the resistance to merger in the College of Agriculture. This no doubt was behind his early decision to visit all of the county offices to energize their staffs. He told Ahlgren: "We simply cannot let either the Division of Community Programs or our Extension departments plead that they are already overloaded."[155] More realistically, McNeil recognized the need formally to reorient the staff. He thus included a Division of Staff Training and Development in the new Extension structure, and it was no accident that he chose Patrick Boyle of the College of Agriculture to direct it. As McNeil reminded the first all-staff conference, "We can't operate an extension service unless extension is understood by those who are running it."[156] In December, 1966, Boyle unveiled his training plan for the division. In light of the confusion and ignorance displayed during the seminar phase of the recent staff conference, most of the initial training dealt with the preparation of a directory of all of the University Extension divisions, sub-units, and programs, and the basic orientation of the field personnel.[157] Boyle's effectiveness with the county agents was severely limited, however, by the lack of adequate training funds and the intractable nature of the problem.[158] He probably did as well as possible under the circumstances. Meanwhile, Community Programs Director Robert Dick reorganized his division in mid-1967 to provide more supervision of his field staff, which included district directors, program area chairmen, continuing education agents, and the county-based agents. The new arrangement expanded the

---

[155]McNeil to Ahlgren, August 25, 1967, Series 41/1/1/1, Box 17, UA.

[156]In October, 1966, McNeil invited his deans and directors to submit names for a division oversight committee. On December 9, he announced the ten-person committee, and six days later Director Boyle submitted his plan for the work of his division to the Administrative Committee. Members of the Advisory Committee on Staff Training and Development were William L. Blockstein, Lawrence Blum, Boyle, Elizabeth A. Elliott, George Hagglund, Donald L. Kirkpatrick, Robert Najem, Lowell Pierce, Donald J. Voegeli, and Leo M. Walsh. Extension Administrative Committee Minutes, October 3, 1966; McNeil to Administrative Committee, December 9, 1966, Series 41/1/1/1, Box 12, UA.

[157]"Staff Training and Development in University Extension," December, 1966; Boyle to Administrative Committee, December 15, 1966, ibid., Box 12.

[158]Whatever the limitations of his Wisconsin training program, in early 1967 Boyle was appointed chairman of the new ECOP Subcommittee on Extension Education and Training. *What's New in University Extension*, newsletter, February 28, 1967, ibid., box 11.

supervisory structure from four to seven geographic districts and added a supervisor for "special projects."[159]

The general extension program also had serious problems. Less than a week after the all-staff conference, McNeil told his Administrative Committee, "The financial situation of the Extension Division operation does not look good." He therefore announced a freeze on new appointments "until there is a better reading on the financial outlook."[160] The difficulty stemmed primarily from the longstanding state policy of funding only about a third of the cost of general extension programming. This meant, as we have seen, that user fees were needed for most services. Such charges made sense for correspondence study, certain conferences and institutes, and the summer School for Workers. Extension was now committed, however, to making the intellectual resources of the entire University available for problem-solving at the local or county level, essentially on the same basis as co-op extension's traditionally tax-supported agricultural services, including home economics and 4-H clubs. Adequate funding of Title I would have solved this problem for general extension work. Instead, McNeil and his colleagues had to wrestle with difficult questions concerning which programs should be offered free, which for a fee, how much, and who should collect the receipts.[161] The chancellor told a Milwaukee reporter: "If we're going to do the job expected of us we need more money, no matter where it comes from—state, federal or county tills. . . . I don't mind using the ability to pay concept, but I worry a great deal when financing becomes the all-important factor in academic planning."[162]

---

[159]Extension Administrative Committee Minutes, June 26, 1967.

[160]Ibid., October 19, 1966. McNeil had hinted at the general extension funding problem during his keynote address at the all-Extension conference: "We need more money. . . . There will be more Federal money, especially when the Viet Nam war is over. But, getting Federal money is not the real problem. The problem is getting State money."

[161]The Extension Administrative Committee recognized the problem in discussing Bob Dick's proposal to reorganize his Division of Community Programs: "This led to discussion of what role Community Programs people in the counties should have in arranging and collecting fees for University Extension programs that are not part of Cooperative Extension Programs." McNeil decided he would appoint a task force to look into this problem. Extension Administrative Committee Minutes, June 26, 1967. See also McNeil and Pound to All Extension Specialists and Department Chairmen in the College of Agriculture, July 24, 1967, Series 41/1/1/1, Box 14, UA.

[162]Jeff Smoller, "UW Extension Plan Still Faces Problems," *Milwaukee Journal*, October 23, 1966. Months earlier McNeil had lamented the state-mandated two-thirds self-support requirement for general extension programming. Robert C.

As University Extension's fiscal woes mounted, McNeil began seeking alternatives to the user fee and other ways to address his budget problems. In September, 1967, he recruited Thomas Cook from Northern Michigan University as a fund raiser to develop "higher levels of extramural support for Extension-sponsored projects."[163] He subsequently directed Dean Gale VandeBerg to establish an Office of Conferences, Institutes, and Short Courses (OCISC). VandeBerg placed agricultural journalism Professor Maurice White in charge of this unit, which unfortunately never managed to overcome the structural impediments involved.[164] Thus in spite of these and other initiatives the community programs effort of the new University Extension remained a fundamentally under-funded and highly stressed operation throughout the entire McNeil administration. Indeed, most remarkable was the ability of a dedicated support and field staff somehow to maintain the pre-merger quality of programming and on occasion by sheer force of will and personal commitment even to surpass it.

Troubled Relations with UWM

As the Community Programs unit struggled to fulfill McNeil's and Harrington's UW Extension vision, the administration at UWM was largely unwilling to help. Vice Chancellor Vevier wanted his campus to control all extension work in Milwaukee. He stubbornly declined to call University Extension by its official name and submitted UWM's Title I grant proposals directly to Washington without going through McNeil as University policy required.[165] Given Vevier's previous opposition to the proposed organizational structure, his continued failure to cooperate

Bjorklund, "County Extension Change Seen/New Look at Ag Committees Urged," *Wisconsin State Journal*, January 28, 1966.

[163]Extension Administrative Committee Minutes, May 29, 1967.

[164]White, *Cooperative Extension in Wisconsin*, pp. 20-21; Administrative Committee Minutes, May 6, 1968.

[165]On the name problem, see McNeil to Harrington, January 10, 1966, Series 40/1/1/1, Box 6, UA, although McNeil neglected to say what name Vevier wanted. On Vevier and Title I, see Extension Administrative Committee Minutes, October 3, 1966; McNeil to Clodius, April 24, 1967, Series 40/1/1/1, box 60, UA. In October, 1966, McNeil apparently thought he had blocked UWM from obtaining its own Title I grants, or engaging in "'projectitis,'" as he called it, by persuading President Harrington to promulgate a policy that all Title I funds must pass through University Extension. This proved to be a temporary expedient. Extension Administrative Committee Minutes, October 10, 1966.

came as no surprise to McNeil and his colleagues. What was more frustrating to them, however, was President Harrington's unwillingness to give McNeil clear and unambiguous authority over all outreach activity in Milwaukee. Evidently the president hoped both UWM and Extension would reach out to the surrounding community. In the summer of 1966 Harrington instructed McNeil to undertake a strong extension initiative in the city, and the chancellor told his Administrative Committee to spend more time there.[166] McNeil commented publicly that fall that "the apparent confusion over what UW divisions should work in the inner core area" was an example of issues needing to be settled before the extension reorganization would be complete.[167] There was, of course, no confusion at all; University Extension and UWM were in head-to-head competition for limited federal dollars and control over what programs there were. About all that McNeil and Vevier could agree on was that substantially more funds were needed before either side could provide a meaningful extension base in Milwaukee's inner core.[168]

While conversations continued intermittently between the chancellors' offices at Extension and UWM, McNeil's staff worked tacitly on the assumption that they would ultimately prevail. Assistant Chancellor Strother and his deans held a series of talks with UWM-based University Extension staffers Roy Francis, Ed Weber, and Karl Krill about "how to carry out the principle of a statewide system of University Extension rather than having a separate system grow out of the resources of UW-M, and what the machinery should be for establishing a chief administrator for Extension at Milwaukee."[169] This led to a meeting between McNeil and the Milwaukee area Extension faculty at which he expressed his opposition to Klotsche's and Vevier's goal of a "separate UWM Extension." His audience responded by complaining about problems relating to the Madison-based Extension deans and directors and "how much control they wish to exercise in Milwaukee." The group finally passed a resolution asking McNeil to appoint a committee of Milwaukee area Extension faculty to consult with their colleagues and report on UWM-Extension relations. The chancellor hesitantly agreed on the condition that any recommendations

---

[166]Ibid., July 15, 1966.

[167]Jeff Smoller, "UW Extension Plan Still Faces Problems," *Milwaukee Journal*, October 23, 1966.

[168]McNeil to Harrington, September 16, 1966, Series 40/1/1/1, Box 60, UA.

[169]Extension Administrative Committee Minutes, October 3, 1966.

would be advisory, not binding.[170] McNeil appointed this committee the next day, requesting a report by December 1 and offering four alternatives for consideration:

> (1) To maintain the status-quo. (2) To have a high-level appointment on a joint basis with UW-M. (3) To have a high-level 100 percent Extension appointment. (4) To have no academic administrator for the region, but direct ties between the department chairmen and our Deans and Directors.[171]

The advisory committee based its report on twenty-eight hours of deliberations, including hearings at which several high-level Extension and UWM administrators testified.[172] The committee also received and considered the views of a large number of Milwaukee-area Extension staff members. After listing pros and cons of the four alternative administrative arrangements specified by McNeil, the committee recommended adoption of the third: "To have a high-level 100 percent Extension appointment." This selection affirmed the importance, prestige, and uniqueness of the Milwaukee-area Extension operation and its metropolitan context, provided for substantial administrative and liaison support, and avoided involvement in potential conflicts of interest between the Extension and UWM administrations. Indicating the significance of this appointment, the committee recommended the title of Assistant Chancellor, although it said Dean also was acceptable.[173] McNeil's Administrative Committee reviewed the report favorably and left it to McNeil to specify the exact title and duties.[174] Interestingly, Patrick Boyle supported the third option, as opposed to Chancellor Klotsche's preference for the second, arguing that the

---

[170]Meeting of Milwaukee Area Extension Faculty, Minutes, October 26, 1966, Series 41/1/1/1, Box 12, UA.

[171]McNeil to A. Clarke Hagensick, October 27, 1966, ibid. The committee consisted of Hagensick (chairman), Willard Brandt, Gordon Bivens, Donald Kirkpatrick, Miss Anne Minahan, and Mrs. Barbara Rice. See also Extension Administrative Committee Minutes, October 31, 1966, which indicate Strother accompanied McNeil to this meeting of 75 Milwaukee area extension workers.

[172]Appearing for Extension were Strother, Dick, Montross, Pulver, VandeBerg, Olson, and Stanley Ryearson; for UWM were Klotsche, Vevier, Quentin Schenk, and Donald Shea.

[173]Hagensick to McNeil, December 1, 1966; "Report of the Faculty Committee on Milwaukee Extension Administration to the Chancellor of University Extension," December 1, 1966, ibid.

[174]McNeil to Administrative Committee, December 13, 1966, ibid.

College of Agriculture, where Dean Pound was still criticizing the reorganization plan, "could logically request similar treatment."[175]

Early in 1967 McNeil decided to name a dean at Milwaukee, thus minimizing as much as possible the stature of UWM in Extension work throughout the metropolitan area. He subsequently appointed a search-and-screen committee and discussed with his Administrative Committee where to place this official on the organizational chart.[176] With no agreement in sight between McNeil and the Klotsche administration in Milwaukee, the Extension chancellor asked President Harrington to transfer control of the Institute of Human Relations and the Milwaukee inner core Community Center Project from UWM to Extension.[177] Neither chancellor had budged from his original position, and neither would do so during McNeil's tenure. Nor was the president interested in resolving the conflict.[178] McNeil tried to deal with the standoff as constructively as possible, telling Chancellor Klotsche: "If you will instruct your Deans, as I will instruct mine, to work together and to make sure that there is agreement and coordination with all the programs going on . . . in the Milwaukee area, I think we will have come a long way toward providing joint program planning and implementation."[179] Maintaining the status quo constituted at least a partial victory

---

[175]Boyle to McNeil, December 14, 1966, ibid.

[176]For a time McNeil hoped to appoint Professor Hamilton Stilwell of Wayne State University dean at Milwaukee, but this appointment fell through. Strother to Harrington, May 24, 1967, Series 40/1/1/1, Box 60, UA. After a long search, Lynn Eley, dean of continuing education at Washington University in St. Louis, was appointed and took up duties in Milwaukee on August 1, 1968. McNeil to Administrative Committee, April 24, 1968, Series 41/1/1/1, Box 45, UA; Extension Administrative Committee Minutes, June 10, 1968.

[177]Ibid., May 15 and 19, 1967.

[178]Harrington, oral history interview. Taking a detached view in later life about a structural problem he was unwilling to resolve while president, Harrington commented that Vevier was "just the kind of person McNeil was. . . . Vevier pushed very hard for Milwaukee Extension as against Extension being run from Madison. That never was solved–hasn't been solved to this day, except by virtual autonomy or independence now."

[179]McNeil to Klotsche, June 5, 1967, Series 40/1/1/1, Box 90, UA. McNeil kept his sense of humor about relations with Milwaukee. In the summer of 1967 he told Harrington aide Chuck Engman, with copies to the president and others, "Things seem to be working out very well in Milwaukee, and maybe that's because Vevier and I both have been on vacation." Ibid. In early 1968, an arrangement was made transferring certain "Public Service" funds used for Upward Bound programming from UWM to Extension. In this instance UWM Chancellor Klotsche agreed to the transfer, but in negotiations with Vice President Clodius and not McNeil. McNeil to Harrington,

for UWM, as its administration sought to establish the institution on a relatively independent basis vis-à-vis University officials in Madison. McNeil's University Extension failed to prevail, but in the absence of meaningful Title I funding the defeat was of minimal significance.

An "Independent Agency"

Even as Chancellor McNeil was struggling against UWM's effort to obtain the greatest possible institutional independence, he was following the same course for his own agency. He thus made every possible use of his public relations machinery to build up an autonomous image for University Extension. In the summer of 1967, for example, he instructed Program Information Coordinator William N. Robersen to print 20,000 copies of Alice Weck's pamphlet, *University Extension Makes a Difference in Wisconsin*, and distribute it to numerous "target audiences" around the state.[180] Another set of initiatives tended to put Extension somewhat at odds with the larger University of Wisconsin and especially the parent Madison campus. Seeking to create a separate but equal institution, McNeil orchestrated the organization of an Extension Faculty Senate, a series of Extension faculty committees, and even an Extension League (for female faculty members and female spouses), all of which duplicated arrangements on the Madison campus while discouraging cooperative and collegial arrangements between the two faculties.[181] McNeil opposed the University policy of annual departmental faculty advisory ballots for Extension chairmen, on the grounds that "though conformity among

February 2, 1968, ibid.

[180]Robersen's targets were daily and weekly newspapers, radio, television, the legislature, the governor and staff, state constitutional officers, U.S. senators and congressmen, state and federal agencies, the Madison campus, the state universities, the UW Center System, Wisconsin city officials, business leaders, and foundations. See Robersen to the Administrative Committee, August 1, 1967, Series 41/1/1/1, Box 12, UA.

[181]See White, *Cooperative Extension in Wisconsin*, p. 13; McNeil to Harrington, October 18, 1966, Series 40/1/1/1, Boxes 16 and 60. McNeil forwarded the University Extension Faculty Government proposal dated October 10, 1966, which he characterized as the first document adopted at the first Extension faculty meeting, on October 13, 1966. See also Extension Administrative Committee Minutes, October 10, 1966. In October of 1967, Extension ran a second Annual Conference during which a University Extension Faculty Meeting was held. See University Extension Faculty Minutes, October 18, 1967, attached to David W. Stewart to All University Extension Faculty Members, October 20, 1967, ibid., box 90.

University units is desirable, each unit must have some flexibility."[182] He told the first all-staff meeting: "Unless there are Extension criteria on which to base salary increases and promotion, we shall never do anything really significant. . . . We must have our own structure and our own mechanism for judging our own people." He conceded that this was "a rather sticky point with the resident campuses."[183] Such pronouncements and actions eventually led President Harrington's office to reign in McNeil by requiring consultations with Central Administration and the Madison University Committee before any significant proposed Extension organizational or policy change could be taken to the regents. The stipulation was later extended to other program areas.[184]

Amid the mounting budgetary uncertainty, Chancellor McNeil tinkered with the formal structure of his unit, hoping for greater efficiency and accountability. He developed a close working relationship with Assistant Chancellors Strother and Ahlgren, and in 1967 promoted them to the title of vice chancellor, responsible between them for all eight Extension operating divisions. Also reporting to the chancellor/vice chancellors were the associate dean at Milwaukee, the secretary of the Extension faculty, the Title I office, and the public information officer. McNeil obtained regent blessing for the new administrative structure on October 13, describing it "as part of a full-

[182]Extension Administrative Committee Minutes, October 31, 1966.

[183]At the same time, McNeil also declared that Extension needed to strengthen "ties with the resident campuses at the departmental level, the deans' level, the college level and the campus level." Clearly, he did not view such "ties" as significantly limiting to Extension independence. A difficult and largely unresolved issue involved tenure decisions for persons holding joint appointments between Extension and a UW-Madison academic department. The Madison faculty divisional committees generally did not give much weight to public service in comparison with teaching and research in evaluating tenure qualifications. McNeil told Harrington, "We simply can't accept the advice of another unit's Divisional Committee without ours being accepted." See Strother to Charles S. Bridgman, July 20, 1967, and McNeil to Harrington, July 24, 1967, Series 40/1/1/1, Box 90.

[184]Extension Administrative Committee Minutes, May 15, 1967. In September, 1967, for example, Vice President Clodius wrote to McNeil: "You may assume that the principles of organization into the 5 Divisions and the use of joint and separate departments have been accepted by the Central Administration and the Regents." Clodius to McNeil, September 22, 1967, Series 40/1/1/1, Box 90. Similarly, the appointment of a Rank, Tenure, and Title Committee was delayed due to "further study by central administration." Administrative Committee Minutes, June 10, 1968. In January, 1968, Harrington instructed Clodius to "tell Don that his people should check in with Fan [Taylor of the UW-Madison Memorial Union] in this area." Handwritten comment by Harrington on McNeil to Wallace L. Lemon, January 9, 1968, ibid.

scale review of University Extension."[185] The structure continued to evolve, and by mid-1968, the original series of departments had been augmented by a new group of functional "sections" as well.[186]

McNeil's determination to establish University Extension as an independent unit controlling all UW outreach activities inevitably brought him into conflict with other University administrators. In addition to his continuing problems with UW-Milwaukee, McNeil's relations with Agriculture Dean Pound were uneasy at best. At first the two leaders squabbled over personnel and program policy and even custody of the employment records of extension specialists working in the college. The debate involved a fundamental disagreement over the extent of the reorganization and the college's long history of integrated departments. Rather than trying to resolve the underlying question, however, McNeil simply retained possession of the disputed materials and declared the matter closed.[187] Following instructions from Central Administration to cooperate, McNeil invited Dean Pound to sit on the Extension Administrative Committee. In July, 1967, McNeil and Pound worked out a revised arrangement that located Extension administrators Richard Vilstrup and Robert Rieck in Agricultural Hall near the dean's office as a means of nurturing "good communication and coordination."[188] While this reform noticeably improved working conditions at Agriculture, Extension officials remained unwilling to delegate any significant decision-making authority to Dean Pound and his colleagues.[189]

---

[185]Extension Administrative Committee Minutes, June 26, 1967. The reorganization followed "along the lines" of Chart No. 3, which was appended to the committee minutes of May 15, 1967. The eight divisions included: Professional and Liberal Education, Human Resource Development, Economic and Environmental Development, Radio and Television, Community Programs, Administrative Services, and Staff Training and Development. See also UW BOR Minutes, October 13, 1967; Clarke Smith to Ahlgren, October 16, 1967, Series 41/1/1/1, Box 11, UA.

[186]UW BOR Minutes, June 14, 1968; VandeBerg to McNeil, August 14, 1968, with attachment "1968-69 Sectional, Departmental, and Functional Unit Chairmen, Division of Economic and Environmental Development, n.d., Series 41/1/1/1, Box 45, UA.

[187]McNeil to Pound, October 28, 1966, ibid., box 12; Pound to McNeil, November 9 and 30, 1966; McNeil to Pound, November 25, 1966, ibid., Box 8.

[188]McNeil and Pound to All Extension Specialists and Department Chairmen in the College of Agriculture, July 24, 1967, ibid., Box 14.

[189]Pound declared in his "Changes in Cooperative Extension," p. 7: "As an example of excessive administration, on January 21, 1968, Pound, Rieck, Vilstrup, James Gilligan, and VandeBerg spent one hour discussing a request of a specialist to

McNeil's insensitivity to tradition and long-held views in the College of Agriculture extended to the Madison campus as a whole. On February 5, 1968, for example, he received a controversial report from his Extension Research Committee. McNeil had formed this group, chaired by Associate Dean E. Robert Marshall of the UW-Madison College of Engineering, to look into the question of designating research as a basic component of the Extension mission. This was, of course, a questionable role for an outreach agency, and was an issue guaranteed to raise eyebrows if not outright opposition from the campus academic departments and faculty. The Marshall Committee report, which characterized Extension as an "independent agency," endorsed the research mission idea and advocated granting Extension faculty members access to research support from the Wisconsin Alumni Research Foundation. Even more than McNeil's previous distancing of Extension from the UW-Madison academic community and its governance structure, such a proposal, if seriously pursued, would seriously upset and alienate the Madison faculty, already uneasy about Harrington's diversion of WARF funds to Milwaukee. Betraying his ignorance about the Madison faculty's proprietary feelings toward WARF and its importance to the research mission of the campus, McNeil initially embraced the idea. Luckily, he asked his Administrative Committee to review the Marshall Committee recommendations at a meeting he could not attend. McNeil's lieutenants easily agreed the report was not quite ready for action, and it never was presented to the Extension Faculty Senate for endorsement.[190]

Chancellor McNeil's concern for independence extended to a vision for a separate Extension campus. In March, 1968, he distributed a study from Director Harland Klagos reporting that the University Extension Space Committee had recommended consideration of "an

---

make an out of state trip. Three of us had already had a conversation with the chairman involved. We terminated the January 21 meeting with still another meeting to be held on the matter."

[190]The chancellor was en route to Africa at the time of this meeting, thereby perhaps encouraging a higher level of candor than usual among the members. The discussion is summarized in the minutes: "Dean Pound and others criticized the Extension Research Committee report, indicating that any attempt at implementation would place Extension on a collision course with the Madison Campus Chancellor." Administrative Committee Minutes, March 4, 1968; White, *Cooperative Extension in Wisconsin*, pp. 18-19. Upon his return to Madison, McNeil reiterated his strong backing of the report and its recommendations. Administrative Committee Minutes, April 1, 1968.

Extension Campus in a location separated from, but near the main University Campus." Klagos explained that his data "supports the need for new University Extension facilities and would apply to any site selected."[191] President Harrington shot down the scheme as both impractical and likely to damage UW-Madison's building prospects.[192] McNeil persisted, however, even though Harrington recognized the futility of the effort.[193] Always pushing independence, McNeil advocated changing the Central Administration's policy on overhead funds so Extension could have exclusive use of the overhead money associated with AID funding of Extension international programs. In this case, Vice President Clodius had to explain that the request was against UW policy, was impractical, and would harm Extension in the long run.[194]

Bailing Out

As we have seen, Chancellor McNeil's struggle to transform Extension into a new urban social action agency were repeatedly thwarted by funding problems stemming in large part from American involvement in the Vietnam War, with its resulting slowdown in domestic spending. Within Wisconsin, too, skeptical agricultural interests had worked quietly to resist McNeil's initiatives and protect their constituencies on the local level.[195] On December 4, 1967, Harley Klagos reported that Extension must brace itself for an anticipated $530,480 deficit by the end of the fiscal year on June 30. The challenge now was "to work out a program of decreased expenditure in all

[191]University Extension Administrative Services Space Services, "Analyses of Existing Space and Programs and Projected Space Needs to Fall 1972," March, 1968, Series 40/1/1/1, Box 90, UA.

[192]Harrington wrote in the margin: "I want to help Ex. but don't want to sacrifice other bldgs to help Ex. if they can't get anything. . . . FH"; Wallace Lemon, director of planning and facilities, to McNeil, March 19, 1968, ibid. McNeil, however, continued to press his case. McNeil to Lemon, April 10, 1968, ibid.

[193]McNeil to Harrington, September 16, 1968, ibid., Box 156.

[194]Clodius to McNeil, September 23, 1968 ibid.

[195]During the legislative session of 1967, for example, the Wisconsin legislature adopted Chapter 240 of Laws of 1967, which repealed a previous law allowing each county to establish a Committee on Agriculture and Extension Education. Such committees were important to Extension as it tried to expand the services available at the county level. The new law allowed the continued appointment of a Committee on Agriculture as before the reorganization. "The new law may have adverse effects on the University Extension effort in the counties, according to Mr. Ahlgren." Extension Administrative Committee Minutes, April 1, 1968.

divisions."[196] McNeil shortly increased the projected deficit to "over $600,000" and described the situation as a "budget crisis." A few days after that he received notification from Washington that major "retrenchment" was in the offing for agricultural extension funding.[197] As the budget problems worsened, McNeil's Administrative Committee characterized the situation as "a severe budget crisis," and concluded that "present budgetary reports and controls are inadequate," budgeting and spending practices must be reviewed and changed, and "at least a partial budget 'subsidy' must be requested from University Administration."[198] When McNeil announced that "no additional monies" would be forthcoming, he set off crises among the poverty programs and within WHA radio and television.[199] Operating expenditures and new hiring were severely curtailed, and the annual all-staff conference was postponed.[200]

Meanwhile, University Extension leadership was distracted by having to fend off press criticism of some of its social action initiatives. During 1967 there was a good deal of negative publicity about the anti-poverty training programs, as charges were made that a VISTA volunteer was "interfering" in the private lives of client Indians on Wisconsin reservations. Later there was a riot and a "near riot" by

---

[196]Ibid., December 4, 1967.

[197]Lloyd H. Davis to Director of Extension, December 20, 1967, Series 40/1/1/1, Box 90, UA. On January 2, 1968, UW Associate Vice President for Business and Finance Reuben H. Lorenz advised McNeil, "The Legislative Budget [1968-69] precludes any substantial deviation from this year's operation, and we may have some serious carryover problems." Ibid.

[198]McNeil to Administrative Committee, December 7, 1967, Series 41/1/1/1, Box 12, UA. Planning for the coming 1969-71 biennium was cautious and explicitly avoided optimism regarding future state support. Strother to Administrative Committee regarding Biennial Budget, 1969-71, March 25, 1968, ibid., Box 45; Extension Administrative Committee Minutes, April 1, 1968.

[199]Gordon Behling provided McNeil and Klagos with an overview of funding sources, staffing, and program areas for 1967-69. Memo, June 12, 1968, Series 41/1/1/1, Box 45, UA. McNeil told Harrington on May 15, "we are in desperate straits regarding the continuation of our poverty program, especially in the inner core and in continuing the momentum we have started in the shakeup in Radio and Television. . . . we have put great pressure on the departments to seek outside funding." Grants had increased, but some ongoing programs had not been funded at their former levels. "OEO has pulled back, FES has cut us, and one or two HEW grants were not renewed." Series 40/1/1/1, Box 90, UA. The following November McNeil reported more bad news to his Administrative Committee concerning recent CCHE actions on the UW biennial budget request. Extension Administrative Committee Minutes, November 4, 1968.

[200]Extension Administrative Committee Minutes, January 8, 1968.

disadvantaged enrollees at Job Corps sites at La Crosse and Camp McCoy. McNeil disclaimed responsibility for the VISTA disturbance, arguing that although the alleged offender had been trained by Extension, she currently was employed by the Office of Economic Opportunity.[201]

Considerably more serious and damaging was the controversy surrounding the distribution of a *Voices of Protest* pamphlet to a thousand youthful Wisconsin 4-H Club members at their annual meeting in Madison in June, 1968. Edited by rural sociologist Jay S. Johnson and published by University Extension, "Voices of Protest" consisted of statements by six unidentified "young adult" participants in the Dow anti-war protest on the Madison campus in October, 1967. Much of the material was inflammatory and some of the reported "facts" were untrue. Robert C. Bjorklund, the widely respected farm reporter for the *Wisconsin State Journal*, broke the story on June 19, characterizing *Voices* as "a total denunciation of the American system." The next day McNeil heard from Arlie Mucks, the executive director of the Wisconsin Alumni Association, requesting an explanation of why such material should be given to "our 4-H youngsters," and from UW Vice President Robert Taylor, who expressed Central Administration concern about the incident. Rural members from both houses of the Wisconsin Legislature also were critical. Extension's Department of Youth Development issued a statement rather weakly contending that "youth must learn basic democratic values and become aware of values that differ from their own." "The important point here," explained McNeil to President Harrington, "is that, as Extension tries to teach in a truly academic way, we will be getting mixed up more and more with problems such as this, and I would defend the statement of the Department [of Youth Development] to the extreme." Harrington thought otherwise: "If we are going to get young people involved, we must take care not to get into situations such as those."[202]

[201]McNeil to Harrington, March 2 and May 5, 1967; Pulver to McNeil, June 16, 1967, Series 40/1/1/1, Box 60, UA.

[202]*Voices of Protest: Summary of a Young Adult Workshop, The Clearing, Ellison Bay, Wisconsin, October 27-29, 1967*, ed. Jay S. Johnson; Taylor to McNeil, June 19 and 26, 1968; Mucks to McNeil, June 20, 1968; Taylor to Harrington, June 21, 1968; "Statement of the Faculty of the Department of Youth Development, University Extension, University of Wisconsin," June 24, 1968; McNeil to Harrington, June 24 and 26, 1968; McNeil to Mucks, June 24, 1968, all in ibid., Box 156; Bjorklund, "4-H Delegates Hear UW 'Voices of Protest'/Resource Material for 48th Annual Meeting Here," *Wisconsin State Journal*, June 19, 1968; "4-H Use of 'Protest' Ex-

Throughout 1968 situations like the *Voices* controversy abounded as Madison campus anti-war demonstrations increased in frequency and intensity. They generated a public backlash that spilled over to all parts of the University. For whatever reason, Chancellor McNeil began distancing himself from his unit. During a crucial phase of the budget-making process in the spring of 1968, for example, he spent several weeks on a trip to Africa and the Middle East that seemed to have only marginal value for his programs.[203] He also quietly entered the job market, pursuing at least three potentially serious openings.[204] He soon was successful. On December 13, 1968, a UW news release announced that McNeil, a "distinguished historian and a University of Wisconsin chancellor since 1965," had been named the first chancellor of the new "state-wide University of Maine."[205] In lieu of convening his postponed all-Extension staff meeting, McNeil offered an evaluation of the Extension merger:

> Each and everyone of us agrees that this was a positive action. . . . The merger has allowed the University of Wisconsin to more quickly and effectively bring the resources of the University to the people. That is our goal. Not only do we feel we are reaching the objective, but a group of our Extension peers has judged us, in a yet-unpublished report, as the best University Extension in the country. This does not mean everything is at its zenith. We still have problems, serious problems involving our budget, or lack of it.

Overall, he concluded, the merger had been a resounding success, and he planned on taking the lessons he had learned at University Extension with him as he moved on to his new assignment in Maine.[206]

---

plained/Exposure to Differing 'Values,'" ibid., June 23, 1968.

[203]Strother to McNeil, Ahlgren, and David Stewart, February 21, 1968, Series 41/1/1/1, Box 45, UA; Administrative Committee Minutes, April 1, 1968.

[204]Corbett to McNeil, February 20, 1968; McNeil to Harrington, February 23, 1968, Series 40/1/1/1, Box 90, UA.

[205]News release, UW Statewide Communications Service, December 13, 1968, ibid., Box 156; "McNeil appointed U. of Maine System Chief executive," *Daily Cardinal*, December 14, 1968; "U. of Maine Names Official," *New York Times*, December 13, 1968.

[206]"Statement of Donald R. McNeil to the Faculty of University Extension," January 28, 1969," Series 40/1/1/1, Box 156, UA. See also "Chancellor McNeil Goes to Maine," *WAM*, 70 (March, 1969), 19. There was no small irony in the fact that the development taking McNeil from Wisconsin–the creation of a merged system of higher education in Maine–was also responsible for bringing the head of the flagship campus

Chancellor Ahlgren

McNeil's impending departure soon produced hard questioning of the Extension merger. Not surprisingly, of course, Wisconsin agricultural interests were quick to express their critical views. Stated one prominent commercial farmer to President Harrington:

> I don't like to see. . . important farm oriented programs downgraded by misplaced emphasis on bargaining and co-ops, a poverty program, or attempts to deal with the problems of the cities. Let's keep the agricultural extension for agriculture and let the various and multiple other agencies deal with the other problems. Besides, why do we want our good Extension Service wasting its energies and stubbing its toe trying to solve these problems that nobody else has quite solved either. The Extension Service has enough to do working with agriculture without trying to build a kingdom to solve all of the woes of the world.[207]

That these were not isolated views was made clear by UW Vice President Charles Engman a while later, as he pressured McNeil to complete a paper "which will be useful in answering some of the questions about . . . Extension which are expected from the agricultural sector in the next couple of weeks."[208] Among other things, Engman was preparing for trouble at the upcoming regents meeting on January 10, 1969. As Chapter 4 of this volume makes clear, President Harrington by this time was in serious, perhaps irredeemable, trouble with an increasingly conservative board, which objected to his handling of anti-war student demonstrations and more generally questioned his politically liberal, social activist policies. University Extension, of course, was an explicit manifestation of the latter. Even though the president had already appointed a search-and-screen committee to recommend McNeil's successor, the regents set up a special committee of their own to oversee and participate in the search. The action was a striking indication of the distrust that was building in the top floors of the new Van Hise Hall.[209]

---

of the new system, former UW L&S Dean Edwin Young, back to Madison. Young had no desire to spend the next few years guarding his already insufficient campus budget within an underfunded merged system.

[207]Robert E. Tracy, Tracy and Son Farms, Janesville, to Harrington, December 23, 1968, Series 40/1/1/1, Box 156, UA.

[208]Engman to McNeil, December 30, 1968, ibid.

[209]On Harrington's search-and-screen committee see: Harrington to appointees,

The traditionally dominant Republican wing of the Wisconsin agriculture community wasted no time in mounting a campaign both critical of McNeil's University Extension and in favor of Henry Ahlgren as his successor. William KasaKaitas, the Wisconsin Farm Bureau Federation legislative lobbyist, wrote to the two search committees, stating his organization's case for Ahlgren. He blamed McNeil for a growing chasm between the University and the farm population of the state, deteriorating agricultural services combined with new programming incompetently handled, and "wavering" local support for Extension. KasaKaitas' solution was the appointment of Ahlgren. "He has the qualities of leadership and statesmanship, as well as an abundance of experience, needed to restore confidence in Extension. We trust that he would develop new dimensions and breathe new vitality into the Extension program."[210] Farm Bureau President Percy S. Hardiman was even more direct, reminding Harrington of the "considerable criticism" of Extension among the more than 26,000 members of his organization. He complained that county agents were "spending much time trying to serve in a capacity in which they are not trained. There is an intense feeling this must be corrected; and if it is not, I am positive there will be an organized movement to divide up Extension." After stating his support for Ahlgren, Hardiman concluded with a blunt threat: "I felt I should convey my thoughts to you, as well as those of others I have heard from. I hope you do not think we are brash, but we may be drawn into the turmoil if actions are not taken to provide some rectification of the problems."[211]

On the evening of January 27, Agriculture Dean Glenn Pound delivered an invited address to more than two hundred Extension faculty members at the Loraine Hotel in Madison. Earlier that day he had shared his text with Henry Ahlgren and believed he had obtained the vice chancellor's approval of it. Pound began by agreeing that the basic

---

January 2, 1969; News release, UW Statewide Communications Service, January 3, 1969, ibid. Harrington's search committee was chaired by Adlowe Larson, and included: William Blockstein, Priscilla Hargraves, Bernard James, Elizabeth Regan, Harold Reinecke, E. James Robertson, Gale VandeBerg, and Raymond Vlasin. The regent committee consisted of Regent President Gelatt and Regents Renk and Ziegler. Before setting up the regent search and screen committee, the board accepted McNeil's resignation, effective February 28, 1969. UW BOR Minutes, January 10, 1969; Clarke Smith to McNeil, January 15, 1969, ibid.

[210] William KasaKaitas to Adlowe Larson, January 16, 1969, Series 40/1/1/1, Box 156, UA.

[211] Hardiman to Harrington, January 22, 1969, ibid.

thrust of a merged Extension was "sound," and that the current five operational divisions made sense.[212] His quarrel was with "the structure and the administrative philosophy" that had evolved under Chancellor McNeil. This included the tendency toward a separate Extension identity that found expression, for example, in McNeil's desire to construct a distinct Extension campus near Picnic Point in Madison. Of related but even more concern to Pound was the current dual administrative structure governing extension work within the College of Agriculture (and within the other professional schools and colleges). Pound reported that his worst fears expressed during the 1966 reorganization had been realized, and he called for the return of all budgetary and administrative control over agricultural extension to his office. According to Pound's later recollection of this speech and related events, he had publicly criticized the McNeil administration as part of his support of Ahlgren's candidacy and with the latter's explicit assurance that as chancellor he would undertake the needed changes.[213]

A few days later, on January 30, President Harrington's search-and-screen committee reported to him. It listed ten criteria the members believed a new chancellor should meet:

> 1. Visionary capacity; 2. Organizational and administrative skills; 3. Courage; 4. Rapport with colleagues; 5. Ability to delegate; 6. Consultative sensitivity; 7. Stature with outside groups . . . ; 8. Academic tenure; 9. Skill with granting agencies; 10. Concern with Extension, upgrading and specialization.

The committee offered seven unranked candidates for the president's consideration, agreed to unanimously and listed alphabetically: Henry L. Ahlgren, Bernard J. James, Harold W. Montross, Glen C. Pulver,

---

[212]These were the Division of Liberal and Professional Studies, Division of Human Resource Development, Division of Economic and Environmental Development, Division of Community Affairs, and Division of Educational Communications.

[213]See "Statement by Glenn S. Pound at Annual Meeting of Epsilon Sigma Phi," January 27, 1969, typed manuscript; "Dean Pound Raps Extension Setup," *Wisconsin State Journal*, January 28, 1969; and Glenn S. Pound, "Changes in Cooperative Extension at the University of Wisconsin, 1965-1979," July, 1979. All Pound Files, Box 15, UA; White, *Cooperative Extension in Wisconsin*, pp. 19-20. Pound was not the only prominent UW-Madison critic of McNeil and his separate University Extension. See Spencer L. Kimball, dean of UW Law School, to Harrington, February 6, 1969. Vice President Clodius characterized Kimball's letter as "expressing a point of view that is typical of the professional schools and agriculture." Clodius to Ahlgren, February 21, 1969, Series 40/1/1/1, Box 156, UA.

Theodore J. Shannon, George B. Strother, and Gale VandeBerg. Curiously, nominees James and VandeBerg were members of the committee and both signed its report.[214]

Unlike his delay in selecting McNeil, two weeks later Harrington recommended that the Board of Regents appoint Ahlgren as the next chancellor of University Extension. He remarked later that he believed Ahlgren was a better choice than Shannon, who remained the favored candidate among many on the general extension side, but also conceded that his decision was politically expedient. Republican Governor Warren Knowles had recently appointed Walter Renk, a prominent Wisconsin corporate farmer and Farm Bureau activist, to the regents. Renk clearly favored Ahlgren, whose well-known Republican leanings made him attractive to other Knowles-appointed regents as well. The board quickly accepted Harrington's recommendation.[215] "Henry Ahlgren is known in every county of Wisconsin as a man who understands this state, its people, and its needs," declared the president. "We are happy that Henry Ahlgren is accepting this higher responsibility, and I know his appointment will be well received by the people of Wisconsin."[216]

Seeking to address the serious criticism leveled against University Extension since McNeil's resignation, President Harrington immediately assigned Chancellor Ahlgren the task of evaluating, as the *Wisconsin State Journal* reported it, "the Extension organization and its progress since its merger three years ago."[217] Ahlgren evidently did not regard this as a high priority, however, because he waited until October to name a committee of Extension administrators to conduct the investigation. Its members, Directors Patrick Boyle and Luke Lamb and Dean Harold Montross, received a brief but wide-ranging charge:

1) Examine the present organization of University Extension as it has evolved since the time of the merger,
2) Identify present concerns which are a result of organization and,

---

[214]Extension Chancellor Search and Screen Committee to Harrington, January 30, 1969, ibid.

[215]Harrington, oral history interview.

[216]News release, UW Statewide Communications Service, February 14, 1969, Series 40/1/1/1, Box 156, UA. See also "H.S. Ahlgren '31 Succeeds McNeil," *WAM*, 70 (April, 1969), 5.

[217]"Regents Name Ahlgren Extension's Chancellor," *Wisconsin State Journal*, February 15, 1969.

3) Suggest or recommend changes within our statewide framework which you believe would improve or correct the situation.

Ahlgren recommended that the committee consult with each UW chancellor and requested a report by December 15, 1969.[218] Reflecting his continuing interest in the issue, President Harrington assigned Donald Percy to oversee the exercise from the Central Administration.[219]

The committee apparently failed to meet Ahlgren's timetable. Chairman Boyle told Percy in February, 1970, about a recent committee meeting with President Harrington at which the members offered an informal report on three important topics. First, the committee had "obtained no evidence that indicated the merger should be reversed to the prior situation. In fact, we obtained strong endorsement of the merger." Second, the members had concluded they could not recommend a specific form of extension leadership at UWM except to encourage as much cooperation as possible. Third, and in the same flexible vein, the committee favored taking different approaches to extension work at each of the four degree-granting UW institutions (now including Green Bay and Parkside as well as Madison and UWM).[220]

Meanwhile, Chancellor Ahlgren's honeymoon at his new job was brief. In April, 1970, he was obliged to respond publicly to a report issued by the Kellett Commission, a blue-ribbon study group established by Governor Knowles, which recommended forming a "University School" combining all of the state's higher education extension agencies, including WHA television and radio. Major impetus for the Kellett proposal came from continuing concern among state officials and taxpayer groups over the skyrocketing cost and seemingly overlapping services of the public institutions of higher education in Wisconsin. The Kellett Commission may also have been influenced by recent criticism of WHA radio and television for some of its programming that seemed overly supportive of disruptive anti-war protesters at UW-Madison. Whatever the case, Chancellor Ahlgren felt compelled to

[218]Ahlgren to P.G. Boyle, L.F. Lamb, and H.W. Montross, October 21, 1969, Series 40/1/1/1, Box 229, UA.

[219]Ahlgren to Harrington, October 28, 1969; Ahlgren to L.H. Adolfson, October 28, 1969; Harrington to Ahlgren, November 3, 1969, ibid.

[220]Boyle to Percy, February 12, 1970, ibid. Ahlgren was listed as receiving a copy of this document.

speak out against the "University School" recommendation, as well as one opposing any state subsidy of University Extension programming. This he called "a shortsighted public policy that bases knowledge transfer on ability to pay."[221]

For Ahlgren, the final straw came suddenly on August 15, 1970, at a meeting of the Board of Regents, which three months earlier had accepted President Harrington's resignation effective the following October. The business at hand this day was the preparation of the University's biennial budget request. The several UW chancellors were expected to discuss the new program needs of their units. Ahlgren realized the prospects for additional state aid were bleak, so he proposed only a single new program directed at improving services to small businesses throughout the Wisconsin. Largely because of the strong opposition of a single regent, the board summarily refused to include this program in the UW budget proposal. Almost exactly at this moment, an aide informed Ahlgren that a USDA official in Washington was on the telephone and needed to speak with him immediately. He left the meeting room to take the call, which brought an invitation to serve as Deputy Undersecretary of Agriculture for Rural Development.[222] Furious with the regents, the Extension chancellor accepted the appointment on the spot and returned to inform Harrington of his decision. The lame duck president responded, "I don't blame you."[223]

Ahlgren viewed the Washington assignment as temporary and accordingly obtained a leave from his Extension post. During his absence Vice Chancellor George Strother served as acting chancellor. Strother proved to be a good stand-in, careful and accurate in his work, and possessing an upbeat personality and sense of humor. He kept Extension on track while occasionally offering his own views about the agency's purposes and future.[224] In Washington Ahlgren eventually found himself at cross purposes with the Nixon administration after he

---

[221]News from University Extension, press release with lead: "Henry L. Ahlgren . . . both praised and criticized a preliminary report by the Governor's Commission on Education Friday," April 3, 1970, UHP.

[222]Ahlgren considered his work as the acknowledged leading national advocate for rural development as one of his most significant contributions, later stating: "I was truly proud of that part of my mission [in Washington]. In fact, I was often referred to as President Nixon's 'Billy Graham' of Rural Development." Henry Ahlgren, *Someone Is Knocking on the Door,* p. 60.

[223]Ahlgren, oral history interview.

[224]See, for example, George B. Strother, "The Road Ahead," remarks to the UWEX Annual Conference, November 18, 1970, UHP.

insisted on interceding with the president about a revenue sharing plan that would severely damage agricultural extension in Wisconsin. While he managed to win on this issue, in the process he incurred the enmity of Chief-of-Staff H.R. Haldeman, who declared him persona non grata at the White House. Recognizing that he was unlikely thereafter to accomplish much in Washington, Ahlgren returned to Wisconsin in October, 1971, to resume his duties as Extension chancellor.

Here he encountered a massive new challenge. Democratic Governor Patrick Lucey was overseeing the legislated merger of the two systems of public higher education in the state, the University of Wisconsin and the Wisconsin State Universities. There naturally was considerable uncertainty and turmoil as the various academic communities worried about their futures. This included University Extension, of course, which now faced the daunting prospect of deciding how to incorporate an additional nine degree-granting campuses and other assorted specialized outreach agencies into its activities. This challenge, and those already facing his agency, largely occupied the remainder of Ahlgren's administration until his retirement in 1974.[225]

---

[225]In 1997, with the perspective of nearly three decades, Henry Ahlgren commented in his memoirs on the problems of University Extension, which he declared "continues to be a flawed organization that is not working and contributing to outreach as it could and should. It almost seems to me that trying to effectively use the resources of each of these four [pre-merger] units in a coordinated way is like trying to find a common denominator on how grapefruit, strawberries, sweet potatoes and elephants can best be used in planning and implementing a health program. The central need for what we have is to establish better coordination and integration of our resources without weakening or destroying control. The need for this important component of University resources is greater than ever before and will continue to become more important as we move farther into the age of science and technology. My hope and prayer is that the University Central Administration and its Board of Regents will study and find ways to make this important resource serve the needs of the people that it is fully capable of providing. The reorganization of Extension within the University system that I became a part of almost 30 years ago is not working and delivering as it should." Ahlgren, *Someone Is Knocking on the Door*, pp. 63-64.

"Freshman Forum" broadcast over WHA-Radio direct from UW classroom.
UA, X25-3416.

UW Vice President Ira Baldwin, Regents A. Matt Werner, W.J. Campbell, R.G.
Arveson, John D. Jones, Leonard J. Kleczka, and Thomas Brittingham, at map
of Eagle Heights tract (Brittingham family gift to UW). UA, 26/9.

373

Panty raider encouraged by residents at Alpha Phi
sorority house, 1952. UA, X25-3405.

Registration line at old Administration Building, corner of State and
Park streets, late 1940s. UA, X25-2003.

Barbara Bousel and Louise Insheivitz sweep off Lincoln Statue,
1959. UA, X25-3396.

Broom hockey during Winter Carnival on lower campus, ca. 1950.
UA, X25-3406.

UW Heisman Trophy Winner Alan "the Horse" Ameche, 1955.
UA, 24/1/1.

Gov. Walter J. Kohler, Jr., leads students singing "Varsity" at
state capitol after UW received Rose Bowl bid, November 24,
1952. UA, X25-3401.

Application of first Tartan Turf at Camp Randall Stadium. UA, X25-3398.

Badger quarterback Ron VanderKelen, (#15) in UW vs. USC Rose Bowl, 1963, photo by Carl Stapel. X25-3380.

377

Memorial Union Terrace, summer, 1962. UA, 1038-H-1.

Experimental bridge over Park Street to Memorial Union, 1966, photo by Ed Stein. UA, X25-3410

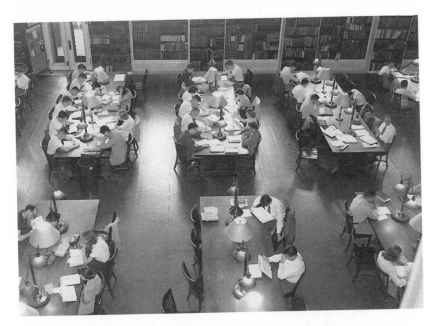

State Historical Society library reading room, June, 1950. UA, X25-697.

Helen C. White Hall library reading room, late 1960s. UA, X25-3389.

379

West side of campus, late 1960s. UA, X25-3415.

Lower campus, Humanities and Elvehjem, undergraduate library under construction, 1970. UA, 3913-J-1.

Ogg Hall and Gordon Commons of Southeast Dormitory Area. UA, 26/1.

Between classes on Bascom Hill, September 15, 1969, *Capital Times* photo by Bruce M. Fritz. UA, X25-2965.

UW Presidents Harrington, Weaver, and Fred, March 22, 1972, photo by Norman Lenburg. UA, X25-3397.

Edwin Young and Donald Percy. UA, 7374-J-1.

7.

The Rise of Student Power

During the 1960s students throughout the world clamored for self-determination, what they called "student power." To be sure, college students have traditionally chafed at rules, tested limits, and generally used their learning experience away from home as an important part of the maturation process. In the sixties, however, this phenomenon both nurtured and interacted with larger social movements seeking to address perceived national problems in a number of countries. In Madison, as in the United States generally, student participation and leadership of the anti-war and black power movements combined to produce an unprecedented period of campus idealism combined with acrimony, disruption, and violence. The following chapter, entitled "From Rights to Revolution," describes some of the more extreme and volatile manifestations of the drive for student power in Madison. This chapter seeks to identify the more important underlying elements involved in the growth of student power at the University, from its stirrings immediately after World War II to its formal acknowledgment and acceptance by a special University faculty committee in 1968.

The Returning Veterans

As we saw in Chapter 1, World War II veterans dominated University life throughout the latter 1940s. Older, more experienced and worldly than typical undergraduates, a considerable number of the ex-GIs were married with family responsibilities while they attended school. The veterans consequently brought a new kind of student culture to the campus. They were eager to make up for lost time and get on with their lives and careers. Thanks to the GI Bill, many were the first in their families to attend college and had few preconceptions about the experience. They believed the University's primary responsibility was to provide them with the opportunity to get an education and earn a degree, not to manage their lives. That it should resume its traditional pre-war role of surrogate parent, or *in loco parentis*, made little sense to most of the ex-GIs. This was obvious to UW faculty and administrators as well, and during the GI years the University quietly desisted from enforcing some of the regulations traditionally governing student conduct, at least with regard to these older students. UW officials viewed the period 1945-49 more as a continuation of the wartime emergency than a return to normal times.

Many of the veterans displayed a strong idealistic streak tempered with understandable war-weary cynicism. Most declined to join the established World War I veterans organizations–the American Legion and the Veterans of Foreign Wars–though some formed a UW chapter of the new American Veterans Committee (AVC). The AVC, locally and nationally, supported an internationalist foreign policy and a liberal view of domestic issues, including opposition to a veterans bonus and to racial or other forms of discrimination. Many veterans were skeptical of the developing Cold War with the Soviet Union, concerned that it might turn hot. While few were pacifists and their previous military service minimized the risk of their being recalled to active duty, some veterans joined other student critics in opposing ROTC and the draft as manifestations of unhealthy militarism. For most veterans, the overriding goal was to get started on a civilian career in a world at peace.

While many of the veterans concentrated on completing their University studies, some ex-GIs played a leading role in the creation of the U.S. National Student Association in 1947.[1] The organizing convention was held on the Madison campus just before the start of the 1947-48 academic year, and NSA was headquartered briefly in Madison before moving to Chicago. The preface of the NSA constitution stated the organization's purpose:

> We, the students of the United States of America, desiring to maintain freedom and student rights, to stimulate and improve democratic student governments, to develop better

---

[1]NSA was an American offshoot of the World Student Congress held in Prague, Czechoslovakia, during August of 1946.

educational standards, facilities, and teaching methods, to improve student cultural, social, and physical welfare, to promote international understanding and fellowship, to guarantee to all people, because of their inherent dignity as individuals, equal rights and possibilities for primary, secondary, and higher education regardless of sex, race, religion, political belief or economic circumstance, to foster the recognition of the rights and responsibilities of students to the school, the community, humanity, and God, and to preserve the interests and integrity of the government and Constitution of the United States of America, do hereby establish this Constitution of the United States National Student Association.[2]

The University of Wisconsin chapter of NSA made these purposes its own and often after 1947 provided leadership of the national organization. Over the next two decades and more, UW students would support local student initiatives in such areas as human and civil rights, academic freedom, and the regulation of extracurricular student life. These were the main concerns and issues that provided the underpinnings of the eventual student power movement.

Human Rights

Before the war UW students had, on a number of occasions, opposed anti-Semitism and racial discrimination when encountered on campus and in the city of Madison. This usually involved housing. The *Daily Cardinal* and student leaders were quick to object when Jewish or Negro students were turned away from local rooming houses.[3] After the war this concern gradually expanded to include the longstanding practice of racial discrimination in fraternity and sorority membership. There were increasing exchanges between the Student Board (the elected student government), UW President Fred's office, the Board of Regents, and numerous individual faculty members, but at first few substantive changes. Regardless of their inclination–usually to maintain the status quo–the local Greek chapters claimed to be bound by the

[2]United States National Student Association, *Report of the Constitutional Convention, Including A History, the Constitution and By-Laws and Summarized Panel Reports Which Outline the Program of the USNSA*, (Madison, Wisconsin: Constitutional Convention, 1947-1948), Series 19/2/3-2, Box 7, UA.

[3]See E. David Cronon and John W. Jenkins, *The University of Wisconsin: A History*, vol. 3, *Politics, Depression, and War, 1925-1945* (Madison: University of Wisconsin Press, 1994), especially pp. 542-49, 673-82.

membership policies of their national charters. The issue came to a head in 1949, when Dean of Students Paul L. Trump, acting for the Committee on Student Life and Interests (SLIC), presented the faculty with a "Report and Recommendations Concerning University Policies on Human Rights of Students."[4] The SLIC report launched a long-term effort by the University administration and faculty to combat racial discrimination in the campus community. While the rate of progress never entirely satisfied successive waves of student activists, changes were evident by the end of the 1950s. By that time, however, the student focus was shifting to the national civil rights movement and its more confrontational perspective and tactics.

The 1949 SLIC report, also known as Faculty Document 914, came in response to a formal complaint from the Student Board's Committee Against Discrimination (CAD), included as part of the SLIC report. It explained that the student committee had been formed in November of 1948 "to ameliorate ethnic relations and to eliminate discrimination practices . . . especially in the campus area." CAD was concerned primarily with "solving Negro problems," and sought "to promulgate the doctrine that all human beings should be treated alike regardless of creed or color." The student group objected that the University Housing Bureau was passively supporting discrimination by failing to require the operators of approved off-campus housing not to discriminate in renting their rooms. The University had considerable leverage over private landlords because undergraduate women were permitted to live off-campus only in UW approved housing. University officials had concluded, however, that they lacked legal authority to tell the private houses whom they must admit. CAD disagreed, and offered five recommendations: (1) require a non-discrimination policy for rental property owners, (2) remove discriminating houses from the approved rental list, (3) stop directing students to houses that discriminate, (4) stop requiring race and religious information in room application forms, and (5) establish a student-faculty committee to investigate reports of discrimination. Students had offered the first four suggestions in 1943 with no results; the fifth was new.[5]

---

[4]UW Faculty Document 914, "I. Report and Recommendations of the Committee on Student Life and Interests Concerning University Policies on Human Rights of Students; II. Minority Report; III. Report of the Student Board Committee Against Discrimination," October 3, 1949, UA.

[5]"Report of the Student Board Housing Committee: Student Housing and Discrimination," submitted to the Student Board of the University of Wisconsin, March

The CAD report also discussed conditions on campus in light of a public statement made by President Fred in November, 1947, about residence halls policy. "No consideration is given to race and color or creed," the president asserted. "This policy reflects the Wisconsin policy in all such matters. This shall be our policy in the future." A CAD survey had found some evidence to the contrary, however, with respect to the placement of both Negro and Jewish students. After noting the Wisconsin Legislature had recently mandated a non-segregated Wisconsin National Guard, CAD declared: "We believe in equal rights for all; that is, the right to be treated as an individual member of the human race, with no sub-divisions to this race. This does not mean equal but separate rights, as the Residence Halls would have us believe." The committee reported an instance when the director of the School of Nursing tried to dissuade a Negro student from moving into the Nurses Dormitory so she would not be resented and feel "discomfort and embarrassment." Stated the report, "We only ask that equal treatment be accorded all persons and that stress be laid on individual, not group, qualifications." CAD claimed that both Negroes and Jews suffered discrimination in employment with the University. "We hope for no special rights but only for treatment as an individual to be afforded all members of the human race." The Memorial Union, for example, should hire student workers "solely on the basis of individual qualifications." A final CAD recommendation was "that no photograph or information concerning race, religion, national origin or mother's maiden name be required on any application blank of the University. Too often such information is used for discriminatory purposes."

A second part of the SLIC report, issued on July 23, consisted of SLIC's defense of the University against the CAD charges, plus a few recommendations for change. On the whole, the committee believed the University "treats all students upon their qualifications and merits as individuals" and "now enjoys a high degree of democratic living." Instances of discriminatory treatment of course should be corrected immediately. At the same time, SLIC noted "the right of students of a given race or religious faith, if they so wish, to be employed, or to be housed together. We believe, however, that a higher purpose will be served if students do not exercise this right of self segregation." With respect to "approved" rental listings, current UW policy did not "imply

---

22, 1943, Series 4/15/1, Box 105, UA.

that the University approves or condones every action or attitude of operators." Besides, it would be impracticable to monitor and discipline every case of alleged discrimination. The wiser approach would be for the University to provide better "leadership" by encouraging owners not to discriminate or to refuse to list those who declare they do. To avoid misunderstandings, the term "approved" needed to be changed to something like, "privately supervised houses, certified as to physical facilities." Finally, SLIC endorsed the establishment of a student-faculty committee to serve the two-fold purpose of determining ways "of extending the democratic spirit and way of life upon our campus" and encouraging owners and employers to respect the human rights of all individuals.

Finally, Faculty Document 914 contained a "Minority Report" submitted by Summer Student Board President Lyle Miller and journalism Professor Henry Ladd Smith. The minority report rejected SLIC's sanguine view of the current situation. A "positive policy of non-discrimination" in rental housing, for example, would not consider a simple change in nomenclature from "approved" to "physical" as adequate. Similarly, UW dormitories should cease making same-race placements based on the assumption residents would object to mixed assignments. The minority report was pleased the School of Nursing had agreed to "drop its method of advice." On the other hand, it objected to SLIC's referral back to a study committee of a recommendation that discriminating passages in the national constitutions of local fraternities and sororities must be abolished, perhaps by September, 1952. Similarly, new or reactivated organizations should be required to select members "solely upon their individual qualifications." More generally, the University must do everything in its power to achieve "one-hundred per cent eradication of discrimination against students," or the "aims and methods of a liberal educational institution" would not be fulfilled. To be sure, "private, personal opinion cannot be legislated out of existence. But discrimination *can* be ruled out, and by so doing, prejudice will tend to disintegrate." The minority concluded with a strong exhortation: "The University already has the necessary policy; all that needs doing is to *implement* this policy."

The full three-part SLIC report expressed in a nutshell one of the emerging enigmas of post-war American life. On the one hand, both tradition and principle asserted the right of choice in private, individual relationships. On the other, those suffering discrimination on the basis of race or some other ascribed characteristic, objected that their access to employment, accommodations, or association was unjustly denied. As a public agency, the University found itself in the middle, declaring its adherence to a policy of non-discrimination while feeling obliged to tolerate if not actually cooperate in occasional behavior to the contrary. Sometimes the meaning of UW actions was open to interpretation. Thus, at the University faculty meeting of October 3, 1949, well-respected professors Richard H. Bruck, Walter R. Agard, and William G. Rice declared the arguments and recommendations brought forward by SLIC were not yet agreed to, and they convinced their colleagues to refer Faculty Document 914 back to the University Committee for additional study.[6]

It would take over three years and several important steps to settle things. On February 6, 1950, the University faculty amended and adopted Faculty Document 933, the "University Committee Report on Human Rights for Students." Faculty Document 933 began by making the "case for a positive, vigorous, and continuing program against prejudice, discrimination and segregation at the University and by the University." The University, the committee declared, was "doing considerably less than its full duty in this area." Several matters required attention. First, the University Committee recommended the creation of a joint student-faculty Committee on Human Relations to "work continuously on human relations problems." The committee would have responsibility to:

> (1) Follow up instances of discrimination seeking by education and persuasion to prevent their occurrence and recurrence;
> (2) Encourage extra-curricular education in this field;
> (3) Cooperate with interested groups on the campus and similar groups in the city and state;
> (4) Provide appropriate recognition for outstanding achievements in improving human relations;
> (5) Promote suitable research in techniques for dealing with prejudice and discrimination;
> (6) Keep the faculty informed as to progress made and when necessary recommend action to the faculty.

This was the major recommendation of Faculty Document 933.

The University Committee also identified "certain University practices" that "should be modified." The administration of the campus

---

[6]UW Faculty Minutes, October 3, 1949, UA. For a student perspective on this event see "Faculty Votes Study of Bias Reports," *Daily Cardinal*, October 4, 1949.

residence halls, for example, should cease all "segregation of Negroes" via "roommate pairings" either on its own initiative or when requested. Furthermore, "the University's responsibility to combat discrimination extends also to private housing for students," some of which received the institution's "affirmative stamp of approval." While the committee said "we agree with the Student Report that operation of an approved house is a privilege and not a right," it did not suggest precisely what this implied because "administrative problems in the way of accomplishing the objectives of this report vary from one type of housing to another." Requests for approved status by "rooming houses that persist in discrimination and segregation," should be denied, however.

The University Committee report acknowledged problems associated with "obsolete" national charter provisions of local fraternities and sororities, and recommended: (1) no approval of new organizations with discriminatory charters, (2) approval of continuing organizations on condition that "reasonable efforts" were being made to eliminate "undesirable restrictions," (3) required annual reporting to the Human Relations Committee, and (4) a mandatory evaluation of and report on "the situation" in 1953 by the Human Relations Committee. "It is understood," added the report, "that no action here recommended in any way abridges fraternities' freedom to select individual members as such." Concluded Faculty Document 933: "Human relations among students is in large measure a problem for students themselves. We think the students deserve high praise for taking the initiative in this field."

After endorsement by the University faculty, Faculty Document 933 moved to the Board of Regents for approval. Sensitive to political considerations and troubled by some of the analysis contained in the report, the regents requested that faculty representatives confer with them about the recommendations. The University Committee did so in June, 1950, and received a number of suggested wording changes for Faculty Document 933. Most, but not all, were largely uncontroversial (such as substituting the phrase "students of all races living" for "interracial living"). More substantive was the board's proposal for an added provision: "Any person who feels that he has suffered an injury as a result of any decision of the Committee [on Human Relations] shall have an appeal to the President of the University." The regents also called for deleting two assertions: (1) "We agree with the Student Board that operation of an approved house is a privilege and not a right" and (2) "Students and others have not infrequently gained the impression that certain [Housing] Bureau personnel is positively favorable to segregation. This is a situation that needs correcting." The University Committee agreed to the suggested amendments and recommended that the faculty approve them, which it did on October 2, 1950.[7]

This was not the end of the story, however. A few weeks later at its November meeting, the Board of Regents stunned the University community by rejecting the amended version of Faculty Document 933. Regent Daniel Grady, for decades a prominent progressive on the board, moved passage of a much more general resolution:

> The Regents commend the spirit which prompted the students and faculty in recommending the protection and preservation of human rights in the University of Wisconsin.
>
> The Regents are unanimous in their belief that the faculty and officers of the University of Wisconsin, throughout the long years of its history, have made an outstanding record in the safeguarding of human rights. Our University has historically served, regardless of race or creed, all who have sought its instruction. Its students now include members of all groups and segments of society, accepting each other and learning together. The Regents are proud of the ability of any student on our campus to gain recognition upon his or her individual merits, and are pleased with the growth in understanding upon our campus—an understanding so sorely needed in America and in the world.
>
> THEREFORE, BE IT RESOLVED, That the University of Wisconsin shall in all its branches and activities maintain the fullest respect and protection of the Constitutional rights of all citizens and students regardless of race, color, sect, or creed; and any violation thereof shall immediately be reported to the administration and the Regents for appropriate action to the end that any such violation of Constitutional rights shall be promptly and fully corrected, and future violations prevented.[8]

The resolution made no mention of Faculty Document 933, nor of the proposed Committee on Human Relations.

Before adopting Grady's resolution, several of the regents expressed their displeasure with Faculty Document 933. Regent William J. Campbell, an Oshkosh lumberman and one of the more conservative members of the board, complained that the University Committee had not adhered to its alleged agreement to remove from the report any

---

[7]Faculty Minutes, October 2, 1950.
[8]UW BOR Minutes, November 11, 1950, UA.

"statement that the University had discriminated against negroes." He further "objected to the report demanding that private housing be not recognized unless private owners agreed to take student roomers regardless of race, color, or creed, because he believed that the Regents shouldn't try to take fundamental rights away from individual property owners." Regent Grady expressed the more moderate conclusion that Faculty Document 933 was not entirely accurate with respect to the conditions it purported to describe. Grady's resolution, on the other hand, was "all inclusive" as a policy statement, "except with respect to the recitals" of undocumented facts. The board voted down a proposal to make some kind of reference to Faculty Document 933 and approved the original Grady resolution.

"It is a pity," observed economics Professor Harold Groves, a prominent social activist, "that the regents missed an opportunity to show that the elders are at least as sensitive to moral issues as the students."[9] The *Daily Cardinal* described the regents' action as "inadequate, narrow and antiquated. They have passed a resolution, which, on its own, will be totally ineffective. They have provided nothing but words, failing completely to implement their policy with a program of action."[10] Smarting from the board's rebuff, the University Committee promptly tried to reclaim the initiative by offering a resolution at the December faculty meeting "to implement" the regents' policy declaration:

> That a Committee on Human Rights be established, consisting of three faculty members and two students (panel of students to be nominated by the Student Board) appointed annually by the President, with the following duties: (1) by fact-finding and education to work toward elimination of racial and religious discrimination against members of the University community; (2) to keep the Faculty informed by occasional reports regarding the status of the human rights problem in the university community and make recommendations on matters of policy connected therewith; (3) to consider alleged violations of the human rights of members of the University community, and to report its findings to the University's administrative officers.[11]

[9]Quoted in "'Missed Opportunity'," *Daily Cardinal*, November 14, 1950.
[10]Ed., *Daily Cardinal*, November 14, 1950.
[11]UW Faculty Document 982, "University Committee Recommendation to Implement Resolution on Human Rights Passed by Regents Nov. 11, 1950," December 4, 1950; UW Faculty Minutes, December 4, 1950.

The faculty adopted the resolution, presented as Faculty Document 982, without dissent on December 4. Evidently not wanting to get into a further confrontation over the issue, five days later the Board of Regents unanimously approved a "statement concurring in the action of the Faculty."[12] There now would be a standing committee to study the problem, with its name upgraded from "relations" to "rights."

Seeking to move campus concern beyond the regents' rather cavalier treatment of the discrimination issue, President Fred quickly established the Committee on Human Rights, announcing its initial membership on January 2, 1951. His three faculty appointees were V.W. Meloche (chemistry), Walter R. Agard (classics), and Clifford S. Liddle (education). They were joined by students Lyle Miller (law) and Joy Newburger (L&S senior), both nominated by the Student Board.[13] President Fred designated Professor Meloche as chairman, seeking an establishment figure who could be counted on to keep a level head. Meloche convened the first meeting of the committee on Tuesday, January 9, promising it was "ready for anything the students want to bring up."[14] Almost immediately the committee heard its first case, a complaint from a white German exchange student, Helga Koenig, who claimed she had been evicted from her rented room at 522 State Street for entertaining a male Negro graduate student there. After investigating the matter, on February 16 the committee recommended "no action" because Miss Koenig was not a regular UW student, and her room was "not listed as an approved dwelling for women by the university." Therefore, announced Chairman Meloche, the case was unfortunately outside the committee's "jurisdiction." It had, however, been reported to the University administration.[15]

---

[12]UW BOR Minutes, December 9, 1950; UW Faculty Document 982. For reports on this monumental action, see "Regents Approve Human Rights Proposal," *Daily Cardinal*, December 12, 1950; "Regents Okay Proposal to Foster Fact-Finding on Human Rights," *WAM*, 52 (January, 1951), 20; "Human Rights of Students," *School and Society*, 73(January 6, 1951), 12.

[13]"Fred Appoints Human Rights Committee; To Work Toward End of Discrimination" and "On Dr. Fred's Newly-Appointed 'Rights' Group," ed., *Daily Cardinal*, January 3, 1951. Agard, Newburger, and Miller had served on an emergency student-faculty committee set up following the Board of Regents' refusal to approve Faculty Document 933. The other three members of this group were Professors Harold Groves and Henry Ladd Smith and Student Board President Karl Stieghorst.

[14]"Meloche Appointed Chairman of Human Rights Committe," *Daily Cardinal*, January 6, 1951.

[15]"Human Rights Group Gets First Case Today," *Daily Cardinal*, January 9, 1951; "Why Hide the Real Issue of Discrimination," ibid., January 16, 1951; "Ask No

Following the inconclusive Koenig case, the Committee on Human Rights evidently received no further reports of alleged discrimination and was largely inactive throughout the remainder of 1951. In December a controversy arose over a discriminatory clause in the national constitution of the campus legal fraternity, Delta Theta Phi, which had tried and failed to have the charter amended. The law student association had decided against punishing the local chapter, because of its good-faith reform effort. A group of dissatisfied students had then asked the Law School faculty to look into the case, and Chairman Meloche let it be known his committee also was available for consultation.[16] The faculty decided to pass the case over to the Committee on Human Rights, an action coinciding with a new complaint of racial discrimination involving an Enzyme Institute post-doctoral scientist who had sublet a room in his apartment to a Negro School of Commerce graduate student. Both the staff member and the student had been notified they were being evicted. Human Rights Committee member Agard declared he would present this incident to his group. The committee met in closed session on February 14 to consider both cases, but did not immediately make its findings public. Meanwhile, the Joint Council on Human Rights, a coalition of student political and religious groups, urged the Committee on Human Rights to take "appropriate action" in both matters.[17]

One reason for the committee's hesitation was uncertainty about its authority. Its mandate was clouded by the fact that the regents had declined to act on Faculty Document 933 when it was presented to the board in November of 1950. Described by its adherents and the *Daily Cardinal* as "a plan for outlawing and checking campus discrimination," students had unsuccessfully sought Faculty Document 933's approval by the regents in the past year. Now law Professor J.H. Beuscher, in a memorandum regarding the Delta Theta Phi case, told the Committee on Human Rights that because the regents had not formally rejected

Action by University for Evicted Girl," ibid., February 17, 1951.

[16]"Law Faculty to Consider Discrimination Complaint" and "Human Rights Group Is Best Place to Handle Bias Cases," *Daily Cardinal*, December 20, 1951; "Law Fraternity Discrimination Action Deferred," ibid., December 21, 1951; "Discrimination Case Remains Unsettled: Faculty Committee Proposal Awaited by Law Fraternity," ibid., January 18, 1952.

[17]"'U' Scientist Faces Eviction for Subletting to Negro" and "'U' Rights Body to Probe Bias in Legal Frat," ibid., February 12, 1952; "Human Rights Body Hears Eviction Case" and "Rights Council Urges Action on Bias Cases," ibid., February 15, 1952.

Faculty Document 933, it might in fact have become official UW policy by default.[18] Several student groups and the local chapter of the National Association for the Advancement of Colored People also urged the committee or the University faculty to establish a clear-cut and effective policy. The faculty responded in May by scheduling a special meeting to consider Faculty Document 1041, "Report of the Committee on Human Rights," which declared Faculty Document 933 official faculty policy and sought to expand its purview. Whether faculty approval of Faculty Document 1041 would require regent concurrence to establish its authority remained an open question.[19]

At a special University faculty meeting on May 19, Chairman Meloche presented the report, which noted that the committee had "functioned under the directives" of Faculty Document 982, which the regents had approved, and had "been influenced by principles outlined" in Faculty Document 933, which, it will be recalled, the board had specifically not approved. The committee pointed to a problem of achieving "regular improvement and campus-wide application of healthy principles of human relations" caused by the constant turnover of students. The committee therefore proposed that the regents' statement of human rights policy, repeated in Faculty Document 982, should be brought before the University community each year through letters to the Greek organizations and rooming houses and by publication in the *Daily Cardinal* and the freshman handbook. The committee praised campus dormitory and employment service officials, who had taken positive steps to inform their clients of the University's non-discrimination policy. The UW Housing Bureau had removed all references to race, color, or creed from its forms and lists, as had many private landlords.

The truly substantive part of Faculty Document 1041 involved its section on "Social and Professional Fraternities and Sororities." Here the committee requested formal approval of three new policies:

> That no new organization with charter provisions discriminating against candidates for membership because of race or color be approved by the University. . . .

[18]"Document 933 May be," ibid., February 19, 1952.

[19]"Faculty Votes to Hold Special 'Rights' Meeting," ibid., May 6, 1952; "Faculty to Meet May 19 on Human Rights Issue," ibid., May 9, 1952; " Board Asks OK of Rights Report," ibid., May 14, 1952; "Faculty to Consider 'Rights' Proposals" and "Faculty Should Adopt Report of Human Rights Committee," ibid., May 15, 1952.

That organizations now on the campus which have such a provision be required to counsel annually with the Committee on Human Rights. That continued approval of such organizations be conditioned upon a determined effort on their part to secure amendments to their respective constitutions eliminating such restrictions. . . .

That no such organization which has in its national or local constitution or pledge instructions a discriminatory clause shall be approved by the University after July 1, 1960.

After delaying consideration of several proposals on "Private Housing and Employment" from the Student Board and the Joint Council on Human Rights, the faculty voted approval of Faculty Document 1041 and these important new enforcement provisions.[20]

While the faculty vote was welcomed in many parts of the University, immediate discussion of its implications was largely overshadowed by a massive panty raid on Langdon Street that led to fines and suspensions for some of the student offenders. Later, as might be expected, the Inter-Fraternity Council passed a resolution opposing what already was becoming known as the "1960 clause." The council argued "that the most desirable and effective method for the removal of restrictive clauses is the action of the individual fraternity without any coercive threat."[21] In contrast, a *Daily Cardinal* editorial on May 21 praised the faculty action as a "positive step forward." This time the Board of Regents, having experienced considerable turnover in its membership since 1950, voted on August 9 by a 5-3 margin to endorse Faculty Document 1041, which included the substance of Faculty Document 933. "The action of the regents reaffirms the stand of a free university," declared a *Daily Cardinal* editorial; "it also makes of the words a force. Only this complement of principle and action can bring to reality a living expression of ideals. We hope this decision is the prophet of a new era in human relations, as well as the death knell of an aged university epoch."[22]

---

[20]UW Faculty Minutes, May 19, 1952; UW Faculty Document 1041, "Report of the Committee on Human Rights," May 19, 1952.

[21]Quoted in "Regents to Consider Faculty Proposals on Human Rights," *Daily Cardinal*, August 7, 1952.

[22]The regents voting in favor of approving Faculty Document 1041 were R.G. Arveson, Charles D. Gelatt, Mrs. Melvin Laird, Oscar Rennebohm, and George Watson; voting against were John D. Jones, Leonard J. Kleczka, and A. Matt. Werner. UW BOR Minutes, August 9, 1952; "Discriminatory Clauses Out! Regents Rule Against Clauses After 1960" and "Fraternities, Sororities Should Take Offensive In Human Relations," ed., *Daily Cardinal*, August 12, 1952.

Still remaining was a set of recommendations from the Student Board and Joint Council on "Private Housing and Employment," embodied in Faculty Document 1041A. The faculty referred this document back to the Committee on Human Rights in October, 1952, to evaluate in terms of the provisions of Faculty Document 1041. The committee spent most of the semester on the assignment, returning to the faculty on January 5, 1953, with its report, Faculty Document 1068. While the committee agreed with the students that racial discrimination in housing and employment should be eliminated, it disagreed on strategy. The students, for example, had proposed that all landlords wishing to list rental units with the UW Housing Bureau should be required to "pledge a policy of non-discrimination." If the pledge were violated, the housing "shall be removed from all University housing lists after a due notice and a fair hearing." The committee found these and similar provisions objectionable because of its "belief that the success of the Committee's work rests not upon preestablished rules, but upon investigation of the facts of each case, and the determination of suitable action." The faculty agreed with the committee's more flexible and less prescriptive approach and approved its report and recommendations, thereby rejecting the student proposals in Faculty Document 1041A.[23] After years of debate, the University finally had a clearly identified mechanism for combating racial discrimination and a coherent, if largely reactive, set of policies for guiding the effort.

The Human Rights Committee remained active throughout the 1950s. Much of its time and energy was spent investigating complaints of alleged racial discrimination in off-campus housing. These averaged from two to sixteen cases annually. Typical resolutions ranged from the ending of discrimination on a mutually agreeable basis at one extreme, to an owner's refusal to comply and being removed from the University rental lists at the other. Sometimes the committee simply could not determine whether discrimination had occurred. The committee also looked into new areas of concern, such as the issue of restrictive scholarships brought to it in 1955 by the faculty Committee on Loans and Undergraduate Scholarships. The committee's non-binding policy recommendation was:

> In those instances where it is possible to do so, the University should try to persuade persons and groups to give

---

[23]UW Faculty Minutes, January 5, 1953; UW Faculty Document 1068, "Report of the Committee on Human Rights," January 5, 1953.

scholarships that are open to all qualified students irrespective of religious or racial background. However, with regard to scholarships limited only to whites, or others which work to the disadvantage of minorities, the Committee believes that these should not be accepted in the future.[24]

In 1956 the committee "informally" considered the so-called Jewish houses, open exclusively to Jewish students but not for religious purposes, and concluded, "if a formal claim is ever made that an individual has been refused housing in such a house, and discrimination is found, the usual sanctions will be applied."[25] The most emotional issue during the decade involved student initiatives, beginning in 1955, to get the University to prevent students from living in rental units that discriminated. University authorities were reluctant to take such a step, however, owing to a tight off-campus housing market, especially for women, and concern over the constitutional rights of private property owners.[26]

The major continuing issue for the Committee on Human Rights involved the 1960 clause. In mid-1954 the committee reported that 14 of the 75 campus social and professional fraternal organizations had discriminatory clauses in their national constitutions.[27] During 1954-55, the committee participated in a Human Relations Conference at Camp Ankijig devoted entirely to this problem. Thirty-three Greek and 8 other student organizations participated, and a resolution requesting an extension of the deadline to 1965 resulted. By the end of the academic year, 12 offending clauses remained.[28] One clause fell during 1955-56.[29]

---

[24]UW Faculty Document 1181, "Annual Report of the Committee on Human Rights," June 6, 1955. The faculty voted to file this report and the policy recommendation it contained. UW Faculty Minutes, June 6, 1955.

[25]UW Faculty Document 1230, "Annual Report of the Committee on Human Rights," June 4, 1956.

[26]"With 4,036 single women and 8,211 single men on campus, there are simply not enough accommodations to deny occupancy on the basis of discrimination." "Staff Siftings: In Criticism of SLIC Bias Policy," *Daily Cardinal*, June 1, 1956. In March of 1958 a consensus among University officials resulted in an official letter to landlords explaining regent, faculty, and student policy on racial discrimination and warning that discrimination would lead to delisting. "'U' Discrimination Policy Set After Ten Months of Delay" and "Bias Letter Written," ibid., March 5, 1958.

[27]UW Faculty Document 1138, "Report of the Committee on Human Rights," June 7, 1954.

[28]UW Faculty Document 1181.

[29]UW Faculty Document 1230, "Annual Report of Committee on Human Rights," June 4, 1956.

The following year the committee received requests from two Greek organizations to accept their revised national constitutions. Each of these now included "vague" provisions for judging candidates as to their "socially acceptable" status. Suspicious of the motives involved, the committee brought the issue before the faculty in a report that reaffirmed Faculty Document 1041 and noted that it was important that Greek organizations "not be controlled and bound by legislation or compulsory interference from outside by national or regional groups or officers in their choice of fellows, and particularly they should not be asked to discriminate on the grounds of race, color, creed or other such criteria." The faculty affirmed this report and the committee granted provisional approval to the two groups involved.[30]

By the end of 1958, the deadline of June, 1960, was looming ominously, and seven organizations remained with objectionable clauses. When the Gamma Lambda chapter of Sigma Nu formally requested a five-year extension, Human Rights Committee Chairman Sieghardt M. Riegel, an associate professor of German and assistant dean in the College of Letters and Science, sought advice from UW President Conrad Elvehjem's Administrative Committee about the matter. Noting that between four and seven fraternities might be forced to close if the rule were not modified or rescinded, Riegel's committee proposed that the University grant a three-month extension to September 1, 1960. This would allow for action at the summer conventions of the national Greek organizations. The Administrative Committee advised Riegel to take up the issue with the University faculty, which eventually approved a recommendation to grant the three-month extension. In the process, the faculty rejected an appeal from the Inter-Fraternity Council for a more substantial extension in cases where "a local chapter can show that it is exerting a real and determined effort." The regents also affirmed the three month delay. Commented a *Daily Cardinal* editorial, "Wisconsin's plan is one which other universities have copied in their attempts to solve the discrimination problem. It is now our task to carry out the spirit of the 1960 clause and to remove actual discrimination from our sorority and fraternity rushing."[31] The

---

[30]UW Faculty Minutes, May 6 and June 3, 1957; Faculty Document 1271, "Special Report of the Committee on Human Rights (revised)," May 6, 1957; UW Faculty Document 1276, "Annual Report of the Committee on Human Rights," June 3, 1957.

[31]UW Faculty Minutes, March 2, 1959; "Report and Recommendations of the Committee on Human Rights Concerning University Faculty Document 1041," March

1959 actions of the faculty and regents were far from definitive in solving the discrimination issue in fraternity and sorority membership practices. The problem would continue, even as it was superseded in the minds of most participants by the increasingly contentious and wide-ranging campus involvement in the national civil rights and anti-war movements of the next decade.

Academic Freedom and the Cold War

The first post-war issue at the University genuinely involving academic freedom occurred in 1947.[32] During the spring of that year, campus Young Republicans called for the banning of a radical and allegedly Communist-affiliated student organization, the American Youth for Democracy (AYD). University policy traditionally allowed any student group not violating federal or state laws to register with SLIC and use University facilities while functioning openly on campus.[33] AYD had registered and was complying with University policies, so President Fred declined to act, partly because he believed it was better to keep subversives out in the open where their activities could be monitored more readily. In December, however, Fred refused to allow AYD to sponsor campus lectures by two known Communists, Gerhard Eisler and Carl Marzani. The president based his decision on the fact that one was under indictment for a federal crime and the other was free on bail pending the appeal of his conviction on similar charges. The *Daily Cardinal* backed President Fred editorially, but the Student Board interpreted the ban as undemocratic and "an insult to student intelligence."[34] As the Cold War's grip on the nation tightened, the University's free registration policy for student organizations and its

---

2, 1959, with ibid.; "Faculty Upholds '60 Clause," *Daily Cardinal*, March 3, 1959; "We Really Mean It," ibid., March 10, 1959. As of March, 1959, the affected fraternities included: Alpha Tau Omega, Pi Kappa Alpha, Sigma Chi, and Sigma Nu, social; and Delta Theta Phi, professional law fraternities.

[32]The Howard McMurray controversy of 1945-1946, triggered when the regents refused to employ a University Extension Division faculty member between his several runs for political office, was interpreted by many as an academic freedom case, but this requires an excessively broad definition. See "The Howard McMurray Case," in George C. Sellery, *Some Ferments at Wisconsin, 1901-1947: Memories and Reflections* (Madison: University of Wisconsin Press for the University of Wisconsin Library, 1960), pp. 112-24.

[33]See overview article, "Campus Communists," *WAM*, 48 (April, 1947), 18-19.

[34]"The State of the University," ibid., 49 (January, 1948), 37.

only slightly more restrictive policy on outside speakers would become increasingly controversial.

The broader issue of academic freedom as a central component of the University's educational mission also increasingly troubled many Wisconsin residents. So intense did the debate become by the fall of 1949 that the Board of Regents, known at that time for its conservative leanings, decided to restate UW's traditional policy in contemporary terms:

> In the present world-wide discussion of the future of human society, we believe that the University of Wisconsin, and all other institutions of higher learning, have a unique opportunity and responsibility. An opportunity critically to study the proposals and claims of systems alien to our own is the intellectual right of every student. And freedom to explore and discuss the issues in the field of his special competence is the right of every teacher. But to teach the foundations of "our American way of life," economic, political, and social, and the entire cultural life it makes possible, is the inescapable obligation of the University to its students. We believe this is best done through fair-minded, scholarly teachers working in many different fields of learning, and that it is now being done in this University.

When it came to core principles, evidently no compromise was possible.[35]

This regent declaration might have laid the academic freedom question at Wisconsin to rest had it not been for the United States' leadership role in the Korean War, beginning in the summer of 1950, and the rise of "McCarthyism" at home. Both encouraged patriotism and fear of communist subversion. Even before the North Korean attack, on May 11, 1950, nineteen UW students paraded with anti-military banners at the annual ROTC review at Camp Randall. The faculty Committee on Student Conduct subsequently placed the protesters on academic probation while simultaneously affirming "the right of students to free speech, free assembly and the right to express protest through peaceful picketing." The committee justified its disciplinary action by asserting "such rights do not extend to interference with regularly scheduled University classes or with officially authorized public exercises or ceremonies."[36] There was little campus support for the ROTC protest-

---

[35]UW BOR Minutes, March 8, 1952, referred to and once again quoted the BOR statement of October 15, 1949.

[36]Quoted in "How's Academic Freedom at Wisconsin?" *WAM*, 52 (February,

ers, nor, indeed, for the formation of a new Communist "front" student organization, the Labor Youth League (LYL). As with the AYD before it, LYL was and would remain controversial both in Madison and throughout Wisconsin and the country.[37]

As Cold War tensions mounted, the outside speaker issue continued to produce controversy. In May of 1951 two very different individuals were invited to speak on campus by student groups. One was Max Lerner, considered by many a liberal humanitarian but by some a "fellow traveler."[38] The other was Wisconsin's junior U.S. Senator, Joseph R. McCarthy, whose name was becoming synonymous with anti-communism. Eight hundred students and faculty members heard Lerner demand "complete freedom for competition of thought." In contrast, McCarthy's audience impolitely laughed him off the stage in response to what some considered his preposterous charges and incoherent rhetoric. The *Daily Cardinal* commented editorially, "We can have no fear for the future of America as long as students continue to demonstrate support for men like Max Lerner and their corresponding deep scorn for those like Joe McCarthy." Some readers viewed the matter differently: "We were thoroughly disgusted with your editorial of childish contempt regarding Senator McCarthy's speech at the Union," one critic told the paper. "You would be the first to cry 'Reactionary' if someone booed a 'liberal' speaker; the participants would be 'intolerant of free expression.'"[39]

While Senator McCarthy's appearance brought out the University's rudest audience in recent memory, campus passions increased the following year. UW students campaigned energetically for and against the senator's reelection in 1952, arguing over both the man and his shifting claims of national subversion and betrayal. Time and again in numerous connections, the issue of academic freedom was intensely

1951), 11.

[37]"Campus Group Labeled 'Front'," *Daily Cardinal*, March 14, 1950.

[38]UW Faculty Document 1001, "Report of the University Committee on Kemper K. Knapp Bequest," May 7, 1951; UW Faculty Document 1029, "Report of the Committee on Union Forum Committee on the Controversy Regarding the Appearance of Mr. Max Lerner," December 3, 1951.

[39]"The Laughs Were Appropriate for Joe McCarthy" and "Lerner Warns of Intolerance," *Daily Cardinal*, May 15, 1951; "Don't Praise Rude Audience," letter to the editor, ibid., May 22, 1954. On the long controversy leading to Lerner's appearance on campus, see UW Faculty Document 1001; UW Faculty Document 1029, "Report of the Committee on Union Forum Committee on the Controversy Regarding the Appearance of Mr. Max Lerner," December 3, 1951; "Highlights of the Year in Picture Review—Pickets, Football and Senator McCarthy," *Daily Cardinal*, December 3, 1951.

debated. Reflecting the times, the Board of Regents approved an American History and Institutions degree requirement it hoped would bolster student patriotism and deflect criticism of the campus.[40] Even so, it was increasingly evident to UW leaders that many Wisconsin residents were developing doubts about their University.

For some, the last straw came when the student Union Forum Committee invited Owen Lattimore to speak on March 16, 1952. Lattimore, an Asia specialist and foreign policy expert at the Johns Hopkins University, had been one of Joe McCarthy's favorite targets for two years.[41] McCarthy repeatedly charged that Lattimore, if not an actual card-carrying Communist, had none the less facilitated the Communist takeover of China while serving as a State Department adviser. Lattimore's invitation to speak at Wisconsin generated an immediate objection from those who accepted McCarthy's charges. One UW alumnus predicted that his appearance would add "further fuel in the dangerously raging fire of indignation of Wisconsin taxpayers who are increasingly being convinced that our tax-supported university is rapidly becoming a sounding board for communistic ideologies."[42]

"But, comrade, we called a mass meeting!"

---

[40] See above, p. 232.

[41] "Lattimore's appearance . . . will be the first time the John Hopkins professor has spoken in Wisconsin since he became the chief target of Communist charges by Sen. Joseph R. McCarthy more than two years ago." "Lattimore Talk Draws Interest," *Daily Cardinal*, March 15, 1952.

[42] Quoted in "Protest Lattimore Appearance Here," *Daily Cardinal*, March 8, 1952.

President Fred decided the University must again take a stand, albeit in a low key routine way. Accordingly, he read a statement to the regents on March 8 noting that "from time to time" the administration was asked about its guest speaker policy. It was "important that the purpose and policy of the University regarding these meetings be clearly understood," he declared. "True to its time-honored traditions, the University of Wisconsin provides a forum for the free exchange of ideas and viewpoints upon current events and issues." Referring to the regents' October, 1949, reaffirmation of academic freedom, the president quoted that statement and then listed the wide range of speakers invited to campus by the Union Forum Committee and other student groups, including Senator McCarthy himself. The regents then voted to incorporate Fred's statement into their minutes and to indicate "that this Board approves of the sentiments expressed in the statement by the President."[43] The Lattimore talk went off on schedule and with no untoward effects.[44]

The years 1952 and 1953 marked the high point of McCarthyism in the U.S. and Wisconsin. The period was extremely trying for the Fred administration, which steadfastly sought to defend basic academic principles while characteristically avoiding combative or antagonistic rhetoric and tactics, particularly in dealing with the state's political leaders. The president occasionally resorted to the politic caution he had displayed in 1947 when he found a reason to block the appearance of Eisler and Marzani on campus. The administration used a similar strategy in the spring of 1952 when, as the *Daily Cardinal* complained, SLIC delayed the registration of two new student organizations, one advocating "big power negotiations" and the other intending to sponsor a national conference in Madison on "academic freedom, equality and peace." SLIC officials evidently suspected the motives and intent of

---

[43]UW BOR Minutes, March 8, 1952; "Regents Defend Free Idea Forum," *WAM*, 53 (April, 1952), 13; "Lattimore March 16 Talk Defended by 'U' Regents," *Daily Cardinal*, March 11, 1952; "Scholar, Not Lobbyist/ Smear, Slander but No Proof Against Lattimore," ibid., March 14, 1952. The *Cardinal* declared editorially: ". . . there is no more important responsibility of a university to its students than that which guarantees a right to hear the current issues of the day discussed in an untrammeled atmosphere of free inquiry. The university first committed itself to such a policy in a regent statement of 1894. It is significant that it has reaffirmed its stand in 1952." "University Stands Firm on Policy of Freedom," ibid., March 11, 1952.

[44]"Lesson of Lattimore Has Vast Meaning for Academic Study," ibid., March 18. 1952.

some of the student organizers.[45] The committee eventually recognized the second group but disallowed its convention on the ground that control of the event was being exercised by persons outside the University. Although well-reasoned and within SLIC's purview, this and similar controversial decisions during the period tended to persuade some students that the University was overstepping its parental role by seeking to guide the political limits of their extracurricular lives.[46]

The 1952 national and state elections were especially contentious on campus. Pro- and anti-McCarthy groups mobilized to support or bash Wisconsin's controversial junior senator, while numerous campus "soap-box" programs and other forums offered all manner of views ranging from the far left to the far right. After the sweeping Republican victory in Wisconsin and nationally in November, rumors circulated that the UW Young Republicans were encouraging certain legislators to present a bill banning "subversive" groups from using University facilities.[47] At the same time, the University administration and the regents were braced for a budget battle in the legislature threatening to be the most difficult in two decades. Faced with these looming challenges, President Fred began thinking of ways he might deflect public attention from academic freedom controversies that damaged University relations with state political leaders and absorbed enormous amounts of his time.

In January, 1953, another academic freedom controversy erupted, this time amid newspaper reports that a congressional committee was preparing to investigate communism in the nation's universities, including, of course, UW.[48] The immediate issue was a campus speaking invitation by the local chapter of the Labor Youth League to Abner Berry, the Negro affairs editor of the Communist *Daily Worker*.[49]

---

[45]"But when officials take the added prerogative of scrutinizing political backgrounds of members, comparing their own personal views with the purposes of a group in question, or judging whether it would be a 'good thing' to have such a group on the campus, they are out-stepping their bounds." ibid., April 10, 1952.

[46]"SLIC Follows Student Board in Freedom-Restricting Action," ibid., April 18, 1952.

[47]"No 'subversive' meetings on Campus?" ibid., December 4, 1952.

[48]Administrative Committee Minutes, January 6, 1953, Series 5/13, UA.

[49]"Statement by University of Wisconsin Pres. E.B. Fred," January 14, 1953, Series 4/0/3, Box 19, UA. University policy did not provide blanket authority for any and every outside speaker to appear on campus. The appearance had to be sponsored by a recognized student group and be approved by the president, usually a pro forma matter Less than a month after the Berry affair, for example, the president, on the advice of his administrative committee and Professor William S. Stokes of the political science

Publicity surrounding the invitation raised again the University's free policy on student-sponsored outside speakers. A concerned Indiana woman wrote the president:

> In my opinion the entire situation boils down to one simple question: "If educators like yourself, who should be leaders of youth and moulders of character, allow these subversive organizations the freedom of your campus, then why are our young men being sent half way across the world to suffer and die fighting the same evil? Is it your opinion that these organizations should be allowed to grow until they actually attempt the overthrow of the government before anything is done to stop them? If you found termites in your home, would you allow them "freedom" until the house began to tumble before you took steps to stop them?

The essence of President Fred's reply was terse and defensive: "We agree that our country has much at stake. We differ on ways to combat the menace."[50]

This sort of response was not satisfactory to some in the state capitol. On March 12, 1953, at the urging of State Senator Gordon A. Bubolz, a conservative Appleton Republican and McCarthy backer, the Wisconsin Legislative Council adopted a resolution instructing the University "to reexamine its policy with regard to student organizations and to take appropriate action and report back to the council." Later in the session both houses of the legislature approved a resolution establishing "a joint interim committee" of three senators, five assemblymen and three citizen members "for the purpose of making a study of the fundamental and long-range policies of the state university and the subordinate agencies under its jurisdiction." As noted in Chapter 2 of this volume, UW Vice President Ira Baldwin brilliantly orchestrated the University's response to this potentially serious threat by broadening the study to evaluate sympathetically the full range of campus activities. With respect to academic freedom, the joint committee's report, issued in December of 1954, declared supportively: "In general, the University should continue its present policy of placing no restrictions on freedom

---

department, declined to allow another student group, with far less radical inclinations than LYL, to sponsor a talk by a woman convicted of subversion in Puerto Rico. The precedent of the Eisler-Marzani cases controlled in this case. Administrative Committee Minutes, February 13, 1953.

[50]Agnes L. Alt, Hammond, Indiana, to Fred, March 17, 1953; Fred to Alt, March 24, 1953, Series 4/0/3, Box 19, UA.

of speech or assembly beyond those established by State or Federal law."[51]

Meanwhile, the Bubolz resolution led President Fred and his administrative colleagues to review the issue of student organizations and guest speakers. Fred first asked the Student Life and Interests Committee to study the matter.[52] SLIC's response, written primarily by geography Professor Richard Hartshorne, was an eloquent five-page document modestly entitled, "Review of Policy and Regulations Applying to the Registration of Student Organizations."[53] Hartshorne's words were staunchly and unapologetically in the University's "sifting and winnowing" tradition. "The specific issue raised at this time," the SLIC report explained, "results from the presence on the campus of a student organization which advocates Marxist objectives, is affiliated with a national organization designated as communist and subversive, . . . and which on occasion has brought communists as guest speakers to address students." The report noted the two federal regulations defining "subversive" organizations: Executive Order #9835 of 1947, and Title I, "Subversive Activities Control," of the Internal Security Act of 1950. The first provided for a list of subversive organizations and the other for their registration, but neither banned them. As for the sole controversial UW student organization (out of 342), "Under the laws of the United States, this group is not illegal."[54]

The SLIC review noted that UW "student organizations are considered part of the educational process," their activities properly including the sponsorship of guest speakers, except those "who are under indictment in the courts or who are free pending appeal after conviction." This campus policy was based on the "celebrated" Board of Regents "sifting and winnowing" statement of 1894 and a 1922 board resolution explicitly making that policy "'applicable to teaching in the

[51]The statement explained: "We are trying to develop self-directing mature citizens capable of making their own evaluation of truth and falsehood. A more dogmatic policy might shield the individual student so much that he would be deprived of this essential educational experience. We believe in freedom of discussion and that continued emphasis on the privileges and benefits of our government and our system of free enterprise will make the youth of Wisconsin better citizens." Wisconsin Legislative Council, "University of Wisconsin Policies: Committee Report," submitted to the Governor and Legislature December 1, 1954, insert to *WAM*, 56 (January 15, 1955), 5. See also above, pp. 89-90.

[52]*Daily Cardinal*, March 14, 17, 1953.

[53]Included with Administrative Committee Minutes, September 22, 1953.

[54]LYL had fulfilled UW registration requirements on April 18, 1950, originally claiming 25 members and currently reporting 17.

classroom and to the use of University halls for public addresses.'"[55] The report recalled that the regents had asserted in October, 1949, that "an opportunity critically to study the proposals and claims of systems alien to our own is the intellectual right of every student." This both implied and expected "that almost all shades of opinion would be represented on this campus under a system of free registration."

SLIC offered two recommendations. First, the committee took what it called "the conservative position of urging that no drastic change" be made in UW policies or in the practice of "freely" registering any student organization that "does not violate either the letter or the spirit of present state or federal law." Second, it offered what might be called a beware-of-the-consequences resolution: "The University recognizes its responsibility to be concerned with the student's knowledge of the possible consequences of joining an organization designated, pursuant to law, as subversive. . . . Whatever steps are necessary and appropriate will be taken to fulfill this responsibility." The report gave several reasons in support of continued free registration of student organizations. First, the UW policy was supporting national security by allowing so-called subversive groups to operate openly.[56] It was also providing practical education and experience with the principles of democracy, especially "the rights of freedom of assembly and freedom of expression." SLIC strongly affirmed "the principles of academic freedom, a way of life that encourages independent thinking based upon untrammeled inquiry." Far from too much freedom and independence, the report declared, "the prevailing difficulty today is that students through fear are avoiding participation in discussion of controversial ideas."[57]

After considering the SLIC review and recommendations, on March 31 the Administrative Committee agreed with President Fred's

---

[55]For emphasis, SLIC quoted the most celebrated part the 1894 statement: "Whatever may be the limitations which trammel inquiry elsewhere, we believe that the Great State University of Wisconsin should ever encourage that continual and fearless sifting and winnowing by which alone the truth can be found."

[56]Explained SLIC: "J. Edgar Hoover has stated that any action which tends to drive the subversive organizations underground will complicate the work of his bureau."

[57]The SLIC review concluded eloquently: "Faith in freedom, not fear of freedom, is our heritage. the founders of this republic though faced with uncertainty and danger, created a free society with full allowance for divergent views. The early leaders of this University, when freedom was challenged, made untrammeled inquiry the guiding spirit for a great university. We propose that the wisdom of this heritage be applied to the problems of today."

suggestion that he appoint an ad hoc committee to look into possible ways his ultimate authority over guest speakers might be delegated.[58] Three months later, on June 30, this committee submitted its report, "Suggestions on Off-Campus Speakers Sponsored by Student Groups."[59] It concluded that the current procedure, with the president deciding questionable cases and occasionally seeking administrative or faculty advice, was adequate. A majority of the ad hoc committee recommended, however, that the guidelines used by the president to deny permission for certain outside speakers be expanded to include:

> persons who are known to be active participants in Communist or Communist-front organizations, or other organizations responsibly identified as subversive or as advocating, abetting, teaching or advising the desirability or propriety of overthrowing or destroying any government in the United States by force or violence.

As with the UW ban on indicted or convicted felons, these transgressions also carried "'moral implications.'" Professor Edwin Witte, a committee member, later explained the majority view: "Our objections . . . do not concern freedom of speech, but merely the fact that these propagandists 'play the university for a sucker.'"[60]

Two members of the ad hoc committee, Letters and Science Dean Mark H. Ingraham and geography Professor Richard Hartshorne, issued a separate minority report objecting to broadening the criteria for banning off-campus speakers.[61] They offered five reasons for this stand, which "demonstrate the grave dangers that arise when considerations of educational policy are dominated by concern for public relations." Ingraham and Hartshorne noted that under the current policy there had been few serious problems since 1922, and when they occurred "public concern tended to bring the question directly to" the president, who usually consulted his Administrative Committee for advice and made decisions on that basis. This was how the ban on convicted felons had

---

[58]Administrative Committee Minutes, March 31, 1953.

[59]Attached to Administrative Committee Minutes, September 22, 1953. Committee members included: Henry L. Ahlgren, A.S. Barr, Charles C. Center, Ben G. Elliott, Richard Hartshorne, Mark H. Ingraham, Kenneth Little (chairman), Edwin E. Witte, and George H. Young.

[60]Edwin E. Witte to Kenneth Little, August 31, 1953, included with Administrative Committee Minutes, September 22, 1953.

[61]Ingraham and Hartshorne, "Report of Minority Members of President's Committee on Off-Campus Speakers Sponsored by Student Groups," August 19, 1953. Included with ibid.

developed. "As a continuing practice we believe this is not an appropriate function of this committee," they declared. More appropriate would be involvement by the Student Life and Interests Committee, the "faculty body which is constantly engaged in supervising the activities of student organizations, under the direction of the Faculty." Ingraham and Hartshorne therefore proposed that SLIC be assigned "initial responsibility for formulation of policies and procedures on the sponsoring of outside speakers by student organizations," an arrangement that might "reduce the exaggerated importance attached to such problems by the public."

President Fred welcomed this advice and at the September 22, 1953, meeting of his Administrative Committee distributed a "suggested letter" to SLIC. His associates agreed on revisions and recommended that he send the document, which contained several new SLIC assignments.[62] The committee was given responsibility "to see that our students have 'knowledge of the possible consequences of joining organizations designated, pursuant to law, as subversive.'" Henceforth SLIC would "act for" the president "in granting student groups permission to use University facilities for student meetings to be addressed by outside speakers." In meeting this responsibility SLIC would make sure its "regulations governing the granting of permission" for guest speakers conformed with regent policy that UW facilities "'are operated for the express and sole purpose of assisting the University in effectively performing its general educational function.'" The president cautioned that "while keeping in mind our historic tradition of free inquiry, we must exercise great care that the freedoms we grant students are not abused by those who seek to exploit students and the University for their own purposes." SLIC must also make clear to all involved that "restrictions imposed by the laws of our state and nation on free speech" would apply in these cases.[63] "I am sure," Fred concluded, "that we all realize the University action and attitude in this matter is of greatest importance to University welfare. I shall be very grateful for your continued careful study and responsible action upon this question."

[62]Fred to Dean T.W. Zillman, chairman, SLIC, September 14, 1953, included with Administrative Committee Minutes, September 22, 1953.

[63]The letter then quoted from federal law that provided severe penalties for any person who "knowingly or wilfully advocates, abets, advises or teaches the duty necessity, desirability or propriety of overthrowing or destroying the government of the United States or the government of any state, territory, district or possession thereof, or the government of any political subdivision therein, by force or violence."

This was the situation when early in 1956 Commander G.E. Sipple of the Wisconsin American Legion mounted what turned out to be the last serious assault against the University's outside speakers policy in the period. In a letter addressed to President Fred, Sipple and his colleagues demanded to know: (1) Would the University ban LYL? (2) Would the University deny its facilities to communist or otherwise subversive speakers? and (3) Would the University send a list of subversive literature held in the library to federal authorities? President Fred declined to act and released his written explanation to the public, along with supporting documentation. The controversy generated a good deal of press coverage, only this time the University's stand was defended by some prominent members and leaders of Sipple's own organization. One of these was Christ J. Seraphim, a UW alumnus and former judge advocate of the Wisconsin American Legion. Explaining that the Wisconsin Legion had "a fine community program" and was damaged only "when some super-patriots seek headlines and go off on programs they are not professionally qualified to carry out," Seraphim promised that if Sipple "persists in attacking the university we will start a grassroots movement" to end the assault.[64] Lacking support even within his organization, Sipple grudgingly curtailed his effort to clean out the campus radicals.

Extra-Curricular Student Life

While human rights and academic freedom were issues of great importance at the University and throughout the country during the 1950s, they interested the student body as a whole intermittently and only a small fraction of the students ever got involved. The central focus of student life remained on academic and extracurricular activities. As UW President Charles Kendall Adams had appreciated before the turn of the century, it was probably intercollegiate athletics that most galvanized the student body (and, for that matter, the public), particularly in such rare instances as when the success of the 1952-53 Badger football team led to a post-season appearance in the Rose Bowl.

---

[64]Quoted in "Former Legion Official In State Defends UW Youth Group Policies," *Appleton Post-Crescent*, February 8, 1956. See also, for example, Fred to Sipple, January 31, 1956, with three enclosures: Fred to Sipple, January 31, 1956; Zillman and Hartshorne, Memorandum on Behalf of the Committee on Student Life and Interests, n.d.; and Memorandum on Behalf of the Library Committee, undated, all at Series 19/2/3-5, Box 1, UA.

Notwithstanding the criticism of the Committee on Human Rights and the pressure of the faculty's 1960 anti-discrimination clause, the Greek-letter fraternities and sororities, now concentrated along Langdon Street, flourished during the post-war period. For the non-Greek majority of the student body, the Memorial Union and State Street area provided rich and open opportunities, both culturally and socially, for University night life.

One expression of what might be termed student spirit was displayed in the occasional panty raid and water fight. Reminiscent of the inter-war period, one of the more notable incidents occurred in May of 1952 in conjunction with similar assaults on other American campuses. An estimated fifteen hundred male students were involved in the UW panty raid against Langdon Street women's houses. A *Daily Cardinal* editorial termed the fracas "an immature act," and University authorities also condemned it, suspending nineteen participants. An emotional campus debate followed, including the creation of a fund to pay the victimized coeds for their losses. Later it transpired that more than a few women had acted as "ringleaders in encouraging raiders."[65] Not everyone agreed with the punishments meted out to the participants. Complained one student editor of the *Cardinal*: "The strained and abnormal frame of mind which turned many normally law abiding citizens into thoughtless law-breakers has been dealt with in the same frame of mind by the university administration."[66] SLIC stalwart Richard Hartshorne sternly characterized the raid as "a break-down of law and order . . . intolerable in a civilized society." For Hartshorne, punishment, even including expulsion, must first and foremost "discourage any repetition by later students."[67]

The affair led the editors of the *Daily Cardinal* to "look deeper" into what they called "a glaring paradox in the way student conduct is practiced and preached at the university":

---

[65]"Cases of Langdon Women Pending," *Daily Cardinal*, June 3, 1952.

[66]Alan Seltz, "On the Soapbox: Conduct Committee Missed Corrective End in Suspension," ibid., May 28, 1952.

[67]Hartshorne did acknowledge, however, that a less extreme penalty might meet this same objective. "Those who make this assertion," he concluded, "are obligated to state what lesser penalties would be adequate for that purpose." Richard Hartshorne, "On the Soapbox: Penalty Must Discourage Repetition of Riot," ibid., May 28, 1952. Replying to Professor Hartshorne and the University's treatment of the offenders in general, one student correspondent later noted: "How can they help but become cynical?" Earl Yaillen, "On the Soapbox: Monday Night Raids May Yield All-New Sociological Theory," ibid., June 4, 1952.

It is common knowledge that regulations in the student handbook governing student conduct are flagrantly and frequently broken in letter and in spirit. Women in fraternity houses after 12:30 a.m. is not a rare sight, nor are co-eds in undergraduate men's apartments or rooming houses. The bars on Langdon street and hotels which serve liquor to students under 21 are known to all, and women's hours are a triviality easily gotten around. . . .

Rather than to charge our present generation with a grave breach of morality we believe that the laws governing student conduct are stifling and inadequate. The laws do not meet the needs of the student body living in 1952. They barely serve as regulations for a 19th century university operating under the iron-handed morality of American puritanism.[68]

The *Cardinal* editors were moving, and not very tentatively, toward the student power perspective of the latter 1960s.

"I'll trade you my bag of hydrogen bomb secrets for your sorority pass keys."

---

[68]"On Student Conduct," ibid., June 3, 1952.

Meanwhile, the springtime "riots" became a perennial concern for Wisconsin officials throughout the fifties, even though in most years they did not actually occur. Campus police were put on "alert" in May of 1953, for example, but UW students had to settle for reports from other campuses, including Harvard and the University of Illinois.[69] The 1956 season was enlivened only by the efforts of 150 Adams Hall dormitory residents, whose water fight was not nearly as noteworthy as their housefellows' failed efforts to keep it secret.[70] Things did break loose the following year, with a combined panty raid and water fight that attracted an estimated two thousand students to the corner of Langdon and Henry streets. At one point, Dean of Men Theodore Zillman warned, "Put down your buckets, or the policemen will start taking names." Not only did the dean thereby become a target, but also drenched were nearby police officers and a number of top-down convertible cars. Two arrests for disorderly conduct resulted during the mostly good-humored fracas. Declared one frustrated Madison police lieutenant, "I have psychologists and sociologists on my force who don't know why these things happen." Dean Zillman termed the student conduct "thoughtless, heedless, and irresponsible."[71]

The next day President Fred addressed a message "To the Students of the University of Wisconsin" on the front page of the *Daily Cardinal*. He expressed his "concern over the mob activities" of the previous night, though fortunately the "disgraceful behavior of a few students" had not caused any serious personal or property damage. "A primary goal of the university is to develop intelligent and responsible citizens," the president pointed out; students were not "set apart as privileged, to flaunt the obligations" of the general public. "Rather, they have a responsibility to show through their actions their gratitude for the special advantages they receive." Fred said University authorities would not act further on this matter until the Student Senate had taken it up. He concluded by expressing appreciation to "the residents of Madison who welcome you to their city and to their representatives, the police, who last evening handled admirably a difficult situation."[72]

---

[69]"University Police alerted for Repetition of '52 Raid," ibid., May 14, 1953; "'Spring Fever' Hits College Campuses," ibid., May 20, 1953.

[70]"150 Dormitory Residents Riot in Adams Living Unit," ibid., May 15 1956; "Housefellows Wrong In Trying to Silence Riot Story," ed., ibid., May 16, 1956; "Housefellows Defend Riot Incident," ibid., May 22, 1956.

[71]"Langdon St. Riot Scene," ibid., May 9, 1957.

[72]"Pres. Fred Expresses Concern Over Action in Water Fight," ibid., May 10, 1957.

As on other occasions subsequent issues of the *Daily Cardinal* overflowed with comments about the disruption. Interpretations varied, ranging from a periodic manifestation of "spring fever" to a serious breakdown of public order. Erwin A. Gaumnitz, the commerce dean and acting chairman of the faculty Committee on Student Conduct and Appeals, observed: "One of our biggest concerns is to have the student body realize the seriousness of participation in a riot or other mob activity." He supported a suggestion that the matter be turned over to the Wisconsin Student Association and the Student Court for action.[73] A *Cardinal* editorial concurred: "No one is sure yet if this will set a precedent for the future," but the prospect was hopeful.[74] Considerably less sanguine was David Trubek, a student editor and member of the SLIC subcommittee on publications. He complained that the *Cardinal* had failed to report the passage of a Student Senate resolution declaring "the fault for such incidents lies not only with the students but is also the responsibility of those who make the rules under which the students must live."[75] Indicative of at least some student sentiment was this open letter to Dean Zillman: "You showed yourself completely unaware of the life, problems, and thoughts of young people. Sir, I don't know if you make mountains out of mole-hills, but I have heard you make a malicious mob out of a happy crowd, a death-dealing riot out of an over-grown water fight."[76]

Viewed in isolation, such anti-establishment pronouncements might be interpreted merely as sour grapes on the part of a few disaffected students. In fact, however, they appear to have been indicative of rising tension between University authority in non-academic areas, sometimes referred to as *in loco parentis*, and evolving student sentiment against such constraints. One example was growing student concern about the campus police department. Initially the complaints focused on Officer Joe Hammersley, whose no-nonsense and unforgiving attitude had infuriated generations of UW students. In the spring of 1950, while breaking up the small student protest at the Camp Randall ROTC review noted earlier, Hammersley was asked what regulations were being violated. He reportedly replied, "I am the law:

---

[73]"Faculty Committee Accepts Students Officers' Proposal," *ibid.*, May 14, 1957.

[74]"Water Riot Incident," ibid., May 14, 1957.

[75]Dave Trubek to the Editor, ibid., May 15, 1957.

[76]Concluded the anonymous writer, "I leave this letter unsigned not because I fear punishment, but rather your punishment," ibid., May 16, 1957.

I make the rules."[77] Although the *Cardinal* conceded that "the stories have reached magnified and distorted proportions," student distrust of Hammersley was widespread and of long standing.[78]

"But Mr. Hammersley, we're engaged."

Hammersley's injudicious handling of the 1950 ROTC protest generated a reaction on campus, and soon the administration was considering reorganizing the UW police force. The *Cardinal* observed editorially: "The police department of the university should not be simply a carbon copy of the downtown constabulary. Its procedures should not be a prowl car, paddy wagon routing, but should reflect the standards and influences of a progressive educational system."[79] The following March students circulated a petition asserting: "It is our conviction that the present department is unfit, by training or experience to occupy the position of trust, confidence, and great responsibility which it now holds. We can no longer accept the often discourteous and illegal treatment to which members of the student body are subjected." Over a thousand students signed, resulting in the creation of a special student-faculty advisory committee to look into the complaints.[80] The committee's report called for the campus police force (consisting of

---

[77]"Pickets Stand," ibid., letter to editor, May 18, 1950. See also above, p. 401.
[78]"Hammersley's Destiny," ibid., April 30, 1947.
[79]"Police Policy a Job for Faculty and Students," ed., ibid., October 3, 1950.
[80]Quoted from "Students Urge Revision of 'Unfit' Police Force," ibid., March 7, 1952. See also " Three Students Offer to Testify Against 'U' Police Dept Abuses," March 8, 1952; "Student Cases Reveal Campus Police Conduct," March 13, 1952; "Police to Testify Today In Probe of Behavior," March 15, 1952; "Report on Police Expected Today: Committee Ends Session, May Advise Police Shakeup," March 20, 1952, all in ibid.

three patrolmen and investigator Hammersley) to be removed from the Department of Building and Grounds and either be placed under the direction of a full-time director reporting to the campus administration or simply be abolished in favor of city police services.[81]

In June, 1952, the regents approved President Fred's proposal to establish a free-standing Department of Protection and Security, whose director would be selected through civil-service competition.[82] Officer Hammersley lost all supervisory duties and was reassigned to investigative work under Vice President A.W. Peterson. Exulted the *Cardinal*: "We have waited a long time for a change in the police setup. The administration was not given a mandate just to reorganize. . . . Let's carry through on reorganization until police can be regarded as the responsible servants of the university community."[83] The next October the UW named 30-year-old Albert D. Hamann to head P&S. He had earned a baccalaureate degree in police science and administration at Michigan State College and subsequently was employed at the Wisconsin State Crime Laboratory adjacent to the campus.[84] As the result of a complaint against two department officers, the following year the regents adopted a code of rules and regulations for guiding P&S activities.[85] Over the next few years the new campus police department managed to avoid serious controversy, with most complaints occurring during large disruptions like water fights and panty raids or after the rare major football victory.[86] Even the unpopular Joe Hammersley managed to keep largely out of the limelight until the summer of 1959, when he was acquitted of charges of being "drunk and disorderly" while on duty. He died two months later in an automobile accident.[87]

---

[81]"Report Asks New Police Set-Up," March 21, 1952, ibid.; "Police Report Is Inadequate," ed., March 25, 1952; "Board Urges Correcting Future 'Abusive' Policing," March 26, 1952; "Students Skeptical on Police Report," [March 22] misdated March 29, 1952, ibid; and "Separate Police Force Is Advised," *WAM*, 53 (April, 1952), 14.

[82]"Regents Alter Police Set-Up," *Daily Cardinal*, June 27, 1952. For budgetary purposes, P&S remained with the Department of Building and Grounds.

[83]"Reorganization Is But First Step to Success," ed., ibid., July 1, 1952.

[84]"Albert Hamann To Head University Police Force," ibid., October 18, 1952.

[85]UW BOR Minutes, May 9, 1953; "Regents to Vote on Police Rules," *Daily Cardinal*, May 9, 1953; "Approve New Rules for University Police," ibid., May 12, 1953; "Regents Must Assure State of Integrity of 'U' Police," ed., ibid., May 13, 1953.

[86]"More on Water, War Police Tactics," letter to ed., ibid., April 26, 1958; "'U' Student Opinion Opposes Police Tactics After Game," ibid, October 21, 1959.

[87]"Hammersley Is Back On Force After Acquittal," ibid., July 9, 1959. The charges may have been a "frame-up." "Hammersley's Acquittal ... Good News To All,"

Vague stirrings of the later women's liberation movement were discernable during the 1950s. Although women were slow to regain their wartime leadership of student organizations like the *Daily Cardinal*, the paper regularly gave favorable publicity to the frequent announcements of higher grade point averages earned by the co-eds compared with their male counterparts.[88] A poll of 50 men at the Memorial Union in 1949 found 40 of them favoring continued access for women to the formerly male-only Rathskeller (a change made during the war and essentially unchallenged as permanent policy thereafter).[89] That same year the *Cardinal* announced the retirement of botany Professor George Smith Bryan, the "last known teacher to separate boys from girls in the classroom."[90] Further progress came in 1951: Governor Walter J. Kohler, Jr., named Mrs. Helen Laird to the Board of Regents (the first such appointment in fifteen years), Jean Matheson became the fourth female editor-in-chief in the *Cardinal*'s history, and the regents appointed Genevieve Dohse as the University's first female police officer.[91] By 1959 the *Cardinal* could proudly announce:

> Today there are more women in all extra-curricular activities than men. At present the *Cardinal* editor is Bonnie Barstow, the *Badger* Editor-elect is Sue Cech, and the Wisconsin Student Association president is Ann Olsen. A woman was Union president last year and

---

ed., ibid., July 9, 1959; "Crash Kills Cop Hammersley," ibid., September 15, 1959.

[88]"Badger Fair Sex Outranks Male Species," ibid., October 7, 1948; "Co-eds Outdo Men in Commerce, Education and Pharmacy Studies," ibid., December 5, 1951; "Once Again: Women Get Best Grades," ibid., September 25, 1952; "Women Students Top Men in Average Grade-Point Standings," ibid., September, 1953.

[89]"Nearly All Badger Men Want Women . . . In the Rathskeller," ibid., December 3, 1949. Prior to the war, women had first been allowed in the Rathskeller in 1936 for movie screenings. They gained more general use of the facility during the summer of 1937; in 1941 the Union Council authorized their access year-round after 2:30 p.m. daily. Mary Waters, "Der Rathskeller: It's Wunderbar," *WAM*, 54 (February, 1953), 22-24.

[90]"'Sex Segregation' Ends as Prof. Bryan Retires," *Daily Cardinal*, February 25, 1949. For some reason, the *Cardinal* neglected to mention the longstanding practice of Professor William H. Kiekhofer before his retirement in 1951 to seat the men and women in his popular introductory economics class on either side of the auditorium in Music Hall. See the illustration on p. 421.

[91]"The Governor and Womanhood," ibid., February 6, 1951. Matheson was a junior in journalism from Elkhorn, Wisconsin. "Matheson, Marcus to Head Daily Cardinal," ibid., March 29, 1951. On Genevieve Dohse, see "Regents Appoint 1st Policewoman," ibid., October 9, 1950

another girl has just completed her term as Independent Student Association president.[92]

As female students were assuming more leadership positions, there was growing contention over University regulation of women's housing. Undergraduate co-eds were required to live in University-approved housing subject to strict hours and visitation policies established by the Women's Self-Government Association (WSGA) under the guidance of the Dean of Women. In 1949 an informal referendum among UW co-eds supported the status quo.[93] Some, like Rita Torgerson, did not. "Out of my classes, in my social life," she complained, "I find I must be incarcerated in my dormitory at 10:30 weeknights, and 12:30 weekends. Obviously either my intelligence or morals are found lacking. And as a woman, I resent such assumptions."[94] The following year two women students explained: "We do not object to the fact of hours because we want to stay out later, but we do object on principle. We feel that girls who are old enough to come to college should be able to take care of themselves, and if they can't living under regulations here won't teach them."[95] Dean of Women Louise Troxell viewed the issue rather differently, stating that WSGA would "study the hour situation not only from the point of view of the students but of their parents and housemothers as well."[96] A fresh advisory referendum called for extending weekend closing hours from 12:30 to 1 a.m., but a subsequent polling of all campus women and housemothers by WSGA President Armina Bedrosian found to the contrary.[97] Finally, on September 28, WSGA representatives voted unanimously to extend the key privilege for upperclass women, permitting them to stay out after hours on a limited basis, but refused (68-3) to challenge the hours structure itself. Any change in the latter, Dean Troxell noted, would require approval from SLIC before going into effect. She left the impression that SLIC should not be troubled over trivial issues such as this.[98]

---

[92]"Our Women Over the Years," ibid., April 15, 1959.

[93]"John's First Column Draws Reader Fire," ibid., April 29, 1949.

[94]Rita Torgerson, letter to editor, ibid., April 30, 1949.

[95]Ivy Koskell and Mary John Hull, letter to editor, ibid., March 3, 1950.

[96]"Troxell: Hours Are No Injustice," ibid., March 25, 1950.

[97]"Referenda Win By Landslide," ibid., April 7, 1950; Armina Bedrosian, "WSGA President Explains Women's Hours," ibid., August 3, 1950; "Housemothers Veto Later Hours," ibid., September 23, 1950.

[98]"Co-eds Win Extra Key Privileges: Motions for Later Closing Hours Defeated by Big Majority Vote," ibid., September 29, 1950.

Joe Hammersley with UW's first female police officer, Genevieve Dohse, October 22, 1951. UA, 2363-M.

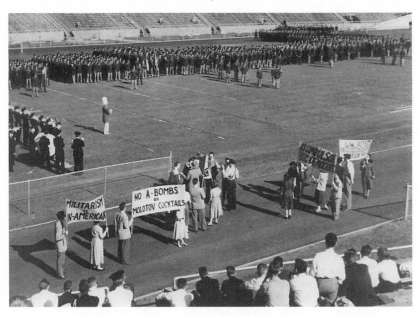

Protest against ROTC review, Camp Randall Stadium, January 29, 1951. UA, X25-3390.

Professor William H. "Wild Bill" Kiekhofer's economics class in Music Hall [ca. late 1940s]. Note gender segregated seating. UA, 629-M.

Rathskeller, spring, 1952. X25-470.

During the spring semester of 1952 *Cardinal* Editor Jean Matheson and her colleagues directed their attention to WSGA, which they argued should function under the Student Board rather than independently, because the latter meant the dean of women really was in charge. "It would not be too harsh, we believe, to say that WSGA has often been downright autocratic in its rule-making and rule-enforcing powers," the *Cardinal* declared. "WSGA could well be abolished in favor of a woman's affairs commission to operate clearly within the jurisdiction of the board. Its present legislating and judicial functions could be lodged in student board and student court."[99] The editors subsequently called for the abolition of WSGA and tried to counter the argument that a poll of coeds the previous fall against extended hours accurately represented UW women's sentiments: "Our own guess on the matter is that, rather than preferring no changes in existing rules, the co-eds have actually come to the slow conclusion that what they say in the matter will have little relevance to what WSGA will do."[100]

The next fall the *Cardinal* published a series of articles by Judy Rosenbloom, a senior history major and member of the so-called Gregg Commission, consisting of students, faculty, and parents, that recently had completed a study of campus social regulations.[101] Rosenbloom began by noting that some progress had recently been made at UW in the social regulation of female students. She then contrasted the situation in European universities, where students "are treated as adults and act as such," with conditions in the United States:

> As long as this idea is prevalent here that the school takes over where the family left off, social freedom for students, especially students of a state university, will be relatively limited. Schools have been given (or have taken) on responsibility not just for academic education, but for a watchdog protectiveness which once resided only in the family.

According to Rosenbloom, this accounted for the "extreme sensitivity" of the administration to "parent disapproval." A recent survey of parents

---

[99]"WSGA, WMA Serve No Need On Campus," ed., ibid., February 22, 1952. The editors also called for abolishing the Wisconsin Men's Association.

[100]"WSGA: Its Record of Unresponsiveness," ed., ibid., March 5, 1952. For a defense of WSGA, see "Judicial Officers Stand Up for WSGA," ibid.

[101]The committee chairman was education Professor Russell T. Gregg. Gregg to Dear Parents, April 2, 1952; "Report and Recommendations to the Committee on Student Life and Interests by the Special Committee Appointed to Study Social Regulations," June 10, 1952, Series 19/5/3/4-6, Box 1, UA.

indicated they believed "their children are not yet really mature enough for . . . independence." Thus they rejected by a two-to-one margin the idea that undergraduate women should be allowed to rent off-campus apartments on their own authority. Students, on the other hand, responded three-to-one in favor. Concluded Rosenbloom, "One can't help wondering how today's students as tomorrow's parents might vote in some hypothetical future survey."[102]

Rosenbloom's also discussed recent changes in regulations adopted by SLIC on the Gregg Commission's recommendation. One allowed co-eds to visit specified areas of men's residence halls and fraternities to work on school projects or as guests, at specified times and "under proper chaperonage." Another change allowed senior women with written parental consent to "live in a University-approved graduate house for women." The possibility of simply allowing senior women to rent anywhere off campus had been discussed at hearings and rejected on the grounds that someone still must be responsible for them and these off-campus facilities might be used improperly by other coeds. Rosenbloom noted, "The final solution was that senior women should have freedom of hours, but not of place of residence." Because of a severe housing shortage, few such rentals were available at the moment, but this limited opportunity "could be a beginning of raising the maturity status of senior women. Its significance will be in its potential."[103] Rosenbloom returned to the visitation regulations in her final essay. Perhaps most notable was her reminder that coeds still were precluded from calling on the majority of male students, who resided in private apartments and rooming houses not included in the new regulation. She concluded: "The principle of the school acting as a substitute for the family . . . can be seen operating in this instance . . . . These particular regulations are the attempt to satisfy student social needs at the same time they recognize parent-citizen pressure."[104] Her solution was that if UW coeds wished to change their hours regulations, they should work through WSGA to develop a request to SLIC; "they must let it be known."[105] Discussion continued over the next few years

[102]Judy Rosenbloom, "'U' Social Changes Senstive to Public Approval," ibid., September 30, 1952.

[103]Rosenbloom, "Rule Changes: Senior Women Get More Independence," ibid., October 1, 1952.

[104]Judy Rosenbloom, "Frats and Dorms: "New Rules Allow Women in Men's Houses," ibid., October 2, 1952.

[105]Judy Rosenbloom, "Rules Revision: Women Must Act to Change House," ibid., October 3, 1952.

about extending hours and even allowing undergraduate women 21 and older to live in unapproved off-campus housing. A few UW women argued they should be entirely free to arrange for their living arrangements without University interference, just like the men. Nevertheless, housing rules and regulations remained largely unchanged.

Reformers were similarly disheartened by the Athletic Board's decision in 1954 to abolish female cheerleading, following a three-year trial period. The *Daily Cardinal*'s front-page report noted, "Champions of girl sophistication and the old 'traditionalists' cheered, while football players and feminists groaned last night about the recent decision." Alan Ameche, the team's star fullback, no doubt spoke for many when he declared that it was the male cheerleaders who should go. More significant for this discussion was the comment of Dean of Women Troxell: "I think it's an immature activity that belongs to the lower levels of High School." Her counterpart, Dean Zillman, agreed: "Girls are too sophisticated to enter into the spirit of the game the way a good man cheerleader can." Eileen Simonis, a 1953 UW cheerleader, responded, "This is a co-educational school and girls should be able to participate more."[106] Perhaps, but not yet.

A fresh outlook came in 1956 when Dean Troxell retired and was succeeded by Martha E. Peterson. A native of Kansas, Peterson held a baccalaureate degree from the University of Kansas, where she had served as dean of women since 1952. On the day of her appointment at Wisconsin, she passed her oral preliminary examinations for a Ph.D. degree in guidance and counseling. Regarding "student problems," Peterson brought a more modern view of *in loco parentis*: "We haven't much choice these days at eighteen or nineteen but to grow up. College students should be treated as mature people." As dean, she believed "whole-heartedly in consulting people in a given area of concern," demanding, according to the *Cardinal*'s paraphrase, "equal responsibility from students and faculty in resolving disagreements."[107] Although never publicly contrasting her views with those of her predecessor, Peterson soon let it be known she favored reinstating "girl cheerleaders"

---

[106]"Girl Cheerleaders Abolished," ibid., May 21, 1954.

[107]U.W. News Release," March 10, 1956; "Martha Peterson New Dean of Women," *Wisconsin State Journal*, March 11, 1956; "New Women's Dean Is a Phi Beta Kappa," *Milwaukee Journal*, March 11, 1956; "New Dean May Act to Abolish Race Bars in Co-Ed Housing," *Capital Times*, March 12, 1956, all on file Peterson Biographical File, UA; "New Dean of Women Begins Residency Here," *Daily Cardinal*, July 3, 1956; Martha E. Peterson, "From Kansas to Oz: My Life as I Remember It" (Unpublished manuscript, July 9, 1996), UHP.

and generally hoped women would begin using their "majority power" better to influence American politics.[108]

It was in this context that a SLIC subcommittee the following May recommended lowering from 23 to 21 the age at which undergraduate women might rent their own apartments without UW restrictions. "The university is finally moving toward a more realistic policy," the *Cardinal* applauded editorially:

> There is no reason why the university should set itself up in the role of a guiding parent and attempt to control a woman's life, especially after she has reached the legal age. . . . Some people argue that the age at which women may live in apartments was set in the past, and should not be changed now. There must have been a good reason for it, they argue; but they can't remember the reason. A university needs to be continually re-evaluating its policy in the light of changing times.

SLIC promptly affirmed the subcommittee recommendation, which took effect when school opened for the 1957-58 academic year. The committee explained that there seemed to be "no moral justification" for regulating the lives of adults over 21, and besides there was "apparent strong student support" for the change.[109]

The authority of the Student Life and Interests Committee over many aspects of student extra-curricular affairs grew increasingly unpopular during the 1950s. Indeed, SLIC sometimes seemed to go out of its way to antagonize students, as when it established rules for the wearing of shorts and swimming suits on campus,[110] censored the *Octopus* humor magazine,[111] and imposed a long delay before approving a Folk Arts club and then made it difficult for Folk Arts and other

---

[108]"Peterson Charms Reporter During Informal Union Reception," *Daily Cardinal*, August 7, 1956; "Dean Peterson Encourages Women to Use 'Majority Power'," ibid., December 5, 1956. Female cheerleaders did return in 1956.

[109]"More Realistic Policy: Women's Housing," ed., ibid., May 22, 1957. "Associated Women Students Has Many Functions: Gals May Now Have Apartments If 21, Says SLIC," ibid., September 16, 1957. In the spring of 1953 WSGA had been renamed Associated Women Students, which was thought to be more fitting. "AWS Is Voice of Women Students," ibid., August 28, 1953.

[110]"Shorts, Sex Mags are Taboo in Dorms," ibid., October 16, 1953; "Terrace Rules: On Swimming Suits," ed., ibid., July 3, 1956..

[111]"SLIC Withdraws Octy Censorship," ibid., March 12, 1954; "Octy Publication Halted for Censorship Review" and "On Octy and SLIC," ed., ibid., May 19, 1955; "Octy Will Publish Its May Issue With 1 Stipulation," ibid., May 20, 1955.

groups to schedule public events for admission.[112] Students complained of being treated "like children," with the Student Life and Interests Committee operating as the campus "boss."[113] In 1957 the *Cardinal* likened SLIC to "an absolute dictator in terms of the functions of government."[114] The next year SLIC and the editors of the *Cardinal* came to loggerheads over a new policy closing all SLIC meetings to the public unless otherwise specified. Proclaiming the students' "right to know," the editors reported the policy had been adopted by a split vote, with three of the four student members opposing secrecy and only three of the eleven faculty members, including Dean Peterson, supporting it.[115]

One troublesome issue involved the regulation of women's visits to men's living accommodations.[116] In 1958 *Cardinal* reporter Jack Holzhueter ran a front page exposé of "illegal" apartment parties. His article included a photo of a man and woman kissing while she sat on his lap with cigarette in hand; he was holding a drink. Holzhueter called the parties "a definite part of life at Wisconsin." Dean of Men Zillman was upset:

> When we don't like a law, we live with it until we can get the thing changed. . . . Disregard for the present rules stems from lack of understanding of the kind of pressure put on other single people in other communities. They think the university regulations are silly, even when Mother or Dad would insist that, when at home, students maintain even stricter hours.

Zillman's administrative superior, Dean of Students LeRoy Luberg,

[112]"Dangerous Precedent Established by SLIC in Decision on Concerts," ed., ibid., July 15, 1952; "SLIC Should Act: Folk Arts Recognition," ed., ibid., March 15, 1956; "Monopolies: Study Needed," ed., ibid., November 13, 1957; Frank Peterson, "On the Soapbox: SLIC Must Remove Monopolies" and "Monopoly Regulation," ed., ibid., January 11, 1958; "SLIC Revises Monopoly Code" and "SLIC Liberal Decision: Pleasing," ed., ibid., May 13, 1958.

[113]Alan G. MacDiarmid, letter to editor, "Students Treated 'Like Children'," ibid., October 4, 1952; "SLIC is Campus 'Boss' Ruling On All Activities," ibid., February 2, 1955.

[114]"Study Needed: On the Nature of SLIC," ed., ibid., January 16, 1957.

[115]"We Oppose SLIC's Secrecy" and "Students Did Swell Job!," ed., ibid., April 17, 1958; SLIC Minutes of Special Meeting and Luberg to Meyer, June 4, 1958, Luberg to SLIC, June 10, 1958, Series 19/5/3-1, Box 4, UA.

[116]See "Just What Is SLIC: A Rundown On the Committee That Controls Student Life," *Daily Cardinal*, March 1, 1957; "SLIC Se-Up: Pretty Confusing," ibid., ed., March 6, 1957.

took a more practical stance: "Personally, I feel that a change in the rules would be advisable."[117]

Responding to the Holzhueter article and the considerable discussion it engendered in Madison and beyond, SLIC agreed to study the broad question of "social regulation," the first such exercise since the Gregg Commission of 1952.[118] The student-faculty study group began its work in the fall of 1958 under the leadership of sociology Professor Burton R. Fisher, who was soon succeeded by education Professor H. Clifton Hutchins.[119] In February Hutchins reported that the committee was "just about ready to start crystalizing thinking" on two key issues: "How far does the university's 'parental' responsibility extend?" and "What is the relation between the responsibility of the university and of the city and state authorities [in such areas as gambling]?"[120] The first question was of particular interest to the student body. A *Cardinal* editorial, for example, reported that the average age of UW undergraduates was 21.25, the average graduate student was 27.97, undergraduate men averaged 21.78, and undergraduate women averaged 20.15:

> Thus most students are of legal age. They can vote, drink, get married, and, in the eyes of the state, do anything that they'll ever be able to (except be elected President or Congressman). Yet the university prohibits them from attending unchaperoned parties or even being in the living quarters of students of the opposite sex without a chaperone. Closing hours apply to all women, regardless of age.

---

[117]Jack Holzhueter, "Official, Students Agree; Need Rules Change," ibid., March 8, 1958.

[118]SLIC Minutes, May 12, 1958, Series 19/5/3-1, Box 4; "Social Regulation: Study, Evaluation Needed, ed., *Daily Cardinal*, March 11, 1958, "Social Regulations: Politicians Want Study, ed., ibid., March 19, 1958; "Study of Illegal Parties Recommended: Apartment Parties Under Scrutiny By SLIC Group," ibid., March 25, 1958; "Apartment Party Study Will Begin: Deans Approve Rule Book Survey," ibid., May 22, 1958. For a review of the lurid and widespread treatment of Holzhueter's article at the hands of the commercial press, see "Sensational Story: Unfortunate Overtones," ed., ibid., May 20, 1958.

[119]Student members were Judy VanderMeulen, Mark Kisslow, Pat Wolfe, Nancy Hooper, Dick Brewere, and Judy O'Brien. Besides Fisher, faculty and administrators included Deans Peterson and Zillman, Kathryn Beach, H. Clifton Hutchins, and George Gurda. "Apartment Study 'Not Stalling'," ibid., November 22, 1958.

[120]"Social Rules Committee: Making Progress, But Must Do More," ibid., February 25, 1959.

Professor Richard Hartshorne in his Science Hall office, January, 1951. UA, 2076-M.

Panty raid at Alpha Phi sorority house on Langdon Street, May 22, 1952. UA, 23/14, 288.

Daily Cardinal "illegal" apartment parties expose,
March 8, 1958. UA, X25-3417.

State Street at night, November 13, 1965, photo by Del Deger.
UA, X25-3377.

The editors' recommendation was either to "apply the chaperonage rules" only to students whose parents request it or "let the immature children attend some other institution where they can be closely watched, and leave the university students with the freedom they want and deserve."[121]

In May, 1959, SLIC received and approved the recommendations of the Hutchins Committee abolishing most University chaperoning requirements. Students instead would now be liable for punishment when their actions "endanger the moral integrity of another" or damage the "good name of the university." In other words, reported the *Cardinal*, "the restriction on visits of women to men's living quarters would be repealed." Chairman Hutchins explained that chaperones would still be required for large social events because "a different psychology" applied there. Among the several "principles" that guided the Hutchins Committee, two were especially notable:

> * The individual member of the university community, whatever his age, is responsible for his own acts.
> * The individual member of the university community is further responsible for the conduct at gatherings of which he is a part and may be held personally liable for such conduct.[122]

The *Cardinal* applauded the long-desired change in an editorial entitled "Oh, Happy Day!":

> The SLIC recommendation will make standards of conduct more specific. If approved by the faculty, it will provide for punishment on the basis of action, not of location. . . . We hope that the faculty will recognize the reality of campus social patterns, respect the work done by the special committee during the past year, and approve the SLIC recommendation.[123]

The faculty, however, referred the SLIC recommendations back to the committee for "further study." According to Dean of Students LeRoy Luberg, faculty members thought the recommendation should specify exactly what changes would be made and which regulations would be modified. They also wanted to know more about the current housing

---

[121]"Who Are the Students: Adults or Children?" ed., ibid., February 26, 1959.
[122]"SLIC Asks Rules Change: Two Chaperoning Repeals Proposed," ibid., May 21, 1959.
[123]"SLIC Recommendation: Oh, Happy Day!" ed., ibid., May 22, 1959.

situation.[124] This set off another round of discussion involving University authorities and the student body, which lasted for another year.

A year later the faculty considered a revised SLIC chaperone recommendation, embodied in Faculty Document 1430. During the course of debate, four amendments were proposed but failed, one of them suggesting that any action be deferred until a new committee could study the entire question of *in loco parentis* at Wisconsin. Most notable in the revised recommendation, which called for dropping any apartment chaperone requirements, was a provision prohibiting all unmarried undergraduate students from living in apartments. This requirement, of course, already applied to undergraduate women, but now was being extended for the first time to undergraduate men. One of the failed amendments had sought to remove this prohibition. The faculty approved the SLIC recommendations by a substantial margin, thereby granting the students the letter, but hardly the spirit, of their longstanding request. Managing *Cardinal* editor John Kellogg commented acidly, "All we can do now is wake up to the fact that the faculty is not only ignorant of our best interests, but delights in going directly against them when they find out what they are."[125]

Transitions

The successful launching of the Soviet satellite Sputnik in the fall of 1957 changed not only relations between the United States and the Soviet Union but many aspects of American life as well. As we have seen in previous chapters of this volume, for higher education one result was the National Defense Education Act of 1958, which greatly expanded federal support of University research and training in fields deemed important for national defense (though the act's affidavit-loyalty oath requirement was a troubling reminder of lingering McCarthyism). The growing federal presence and influence at the University was increasingly apparent to students in the years ahead. At

[124]UW Faculty Minutes, June 1, 1959; UW Faculty Document 1387, "Report of the Student Life and Interests Committee," June 1, 1959; "Faculty Send Back Revision of Housing Rules to SLIC," *Daily Cardinal*, Summer Registration Issue, 1959.
[125]Faculty Minutes, May 9, 1960; UW Faculty Document 1430, "Recommendations for Changes in Social Regulations Governing University of Wisconsin Students On the Madison Campus," May 9, 1960; "Faculty OKs Apartment Parties: Age Restriction For Housing Set," *Daily Cardinal*, May 10, 1960; "Apartment Rule Details Not Set: Report on SLIC Study Due May 24," ibid., May 11, 1960; John Kellogg, "A Minority Editorial: Apartment Rules," ibid., May 12, 1960.

the same time, their suspicion of government was fed by repression of the black civil rights movement, the bungled Bay of Pigs invasion, the resulting Cuban missile crisis, unresolved conspiracy theories about the Kennedy assassination, and by the mid-1960s mounting concern over the undeclared but major war in Vietnam. For young people in particular the sixties was a time of growing doubt about the trustworthiness of constituted authority.

Simultaneously, an unprecedented mass youth culture was emerging, grounded demographically in the post-war baby boom generation that soon would reach the nation's colleges and universities. The boomers were relatively affluent, mobile, well-schooled, and sometimes alienated. As a generation they enjoyed unprecedented resources and the leisure to ponder what some of them found to be the nation's fundamental faults and failures. All across America they sought meaning on the road with Jack Kerouac, rocked around the clock with Bill Haley and His Comets, identified with rebel-without-a-cause James Dean, and joined Pete Seeger in making fun of their parents' "little boxes," the suburban tract houses in which many of them had grown up. Troubling doubts about the expanding U.S. military involvement in Southeast Asia led growing numbers of young people to question the American dream, however defined. In Madison, scrawny young Robert Zimmerman (Bob Dylan) visited The Pad on State Street,[126] singing his folk songs of generational revolution and proclaiming, "If God's on our side, He'll stop the next war."

With their long history of opposition to discrimination, UW students welcomed the national civil rights movement of the late 1950s. Soon the *Cardinal* was publishing first-hand reports from UW students who had spent their summer vacations fighting segregation throughout the American South.[127] UW involvement in the movement reached its peak during the so-called Mississippi Freedom Summer of 1964 and the bloody march from Selma to Montgomery the following year. Not only did the accounts of UW participants encourage broadened enthusiasm for correcting local manifestations of prejudice and discrimination, but they also introduced new tactics, especially the sit-in, for galvanizing

---

[126]See "Ginsberg's Death Brings Back Memories of Madison's Pad," *Wisconsin State Journal*, April 13, 1997.

[127]See, for example, Keith S. Brown, Jr., "Yankee Report on South: Whites Love Negroes," letter to ed., *Daily Cardinal*, June 30, 1960; "Students Lead Southern Civil Rights Drive, 'U' Law Student Back from South Observes," ibid., April 14, 1961; "Freedom Rider Describes Three-Week Prison Term," ibid., July 6, 1961.

support and winning immediate objectives.[128] As in the past, University student groups provided forums for numerous visiting civil rights activists. In the span of a single week during the spring of 1962, for instance, the campus hosted civil rights leader Martin Luther King, Jr., and black nationalist Malcolm X. The Committee on Human Rights continued its oversight of the Greek charter problem and asserted ever more stringent requirements on apartment and rooming house owners who wished to list their properties at the University. The civil rights movement seemed to demonstrate the validity of using the tactics of active protest, including physical coercion, to right societal wrongs.

At the same time, UW students continued to encounter a frustratingly recalcitrant faculty as they strove ever more aggressively to assume control over their extra-curricular lives. In the spring of 1963 the *Cardinal* pointed out that in contrast with past campus elections where national and international issues had often been discussed, "this campaign is exclusively concentrating on issues on the campus: in loco parentis, the liberalization of women's hours and student social freedom in general." The SCOPE party favored "'an immediate and significant increase in student rights vis a vis the University administration.'" The Social Action party advocated reducing SLIC's power, particularly its ability to veto Student Senate decisions. It also opposed "'all University policy based solely on paternalism.'" Concluded the *Cardinal*, "Both platforms thus support a program to lessen the control of the University over student affairs."[129] On the eve of the election, a *Cardinal* editorial proclaimed: "The time has come for students to declare their refusal to tolerate any dictation in their social life. . . . Both slates have concentrated on this primary issue–the complete liberation of the student from any control of the University other than academic."[130] Thanks to a well-organized campaign, SCOPE candidates prevailed in the election and looked forward to making important gains for student rights in the year ahead.[131]

---

[128]See "'Sit-ins' Herald New Day in South," reprint from *The Nation*, March 12, 1960, *Daily Cardinal*, March 18, 1960; "Student Gets First-Hand News of Sit-Ins," ibid., March 30, 1960; "Students Plan Second Chain Store Picketing," ibid., April 7, 1960; "Campus Newspapers Across the Nation Praise Sit-In Strikes, Attack South," ibid., April 13, 1960; "Apathy and Action: Bright Spots," ed., ibid., May 12, 1962.

[129]"Slates Urge 'Student Freedom'," ibid., April 6, 1963. For complete platform statements of the several student parties, see "The WSA Candidates and Platforms," ibid., April 9, 1963.

[130]"The Only Real Issue In Today's Election," ed., ibid., April 9, 1963.

[131]"Organize Now, Changes Later, Says Campbell," ibid., April 11, 1963.

UW freedom marchers Ralph Bear and Marty Goldstein. UA, X25-3414.

Civil rights bus at Memorial Union preparing to depart for Washington, D.C.,
August 28, 1963. UA, 5878-M.

The Remington Committee

A month after the 1963 student election, the faculty adopted a resolution requesting President Harrington to appoint a special Committee on Non-Curricular Life of Students. Its charge was "to make a broad study" of University policies and procedures in light of expected enrollment increases. The baby boomers were on the way, and UW authorities were concerned that their numbers might leave many students largely on their own in their extracurricular lives. The faculty also was responding to recent Student Senate decisions and the spring WSA campaign against the University's *in loco parentis* regulations.[132] Bob Dylan had warned the "mothers and fathers throughout the land" that "your sons and your daughters are beyond your command." University officials were not so sure of this, but the faculty realized someone had better look into the matter.

Law Professor Frank Remington was named to head a seven-member panel, which set out upon a two-year study of student life. The Remington Committee's existence helped to embolden student leaders to push for more changes, while SLIC and other campus authorities largely held the line pending the committee's report. On August 12, 1965, the Remington Committee submitted a preliminary "Report of the Non-Curricular Life of Students Committee." It included 56 pages of narrative and a lengthy appendix with supporting documentation, constituting an unprecedented and revealing overview of the University's handling of student "misconduct" since the early 1950s.[133] The committee's primary sources were UW faculty members and administrators responsible for the agencies dealing with student extracurricular life, such as Protection and Security, the Dean of Students and the Deans of Men and Women, SLIC, residence halls, and the faculty Committee on Student Conduct and Appeals. The committee reported that the primary faculty approach was "educational" (as opposed to "legalistic") in most student matters. This had led, for instance, to a highly controversial decision in 1963 that students not be allowed legal counsel at disciplinary hearings. There also seemed to be a tendency for University authorities to emphasize how an alleged miscreant's behavior

---

[132]"Report of the Non Curricular Life of Students Committee," Frank J. Remington, Chairman, August 12, 1965, p. 9, Series 5/196, Box 1, UA.

[133]Membership of the committee included Frank Remington (chairman), R. Wray Strowig, Donald Novotny, Lee Dreyfus, Seymour Halleck, M.D., Douglas Marshall, and E. E. LeMasters.

might affect the "image" of the University over its implications for the student personally. Apparently even as late as 1965 the institution was referring students to UW psychiatrists for "evaluation of antisocial behavior," with "intervention" sometimes recommended. While failing to address the *in loco parentis* issue directly, the Remington Committee nevertheless had uncovered and presented considerable relevant and sometimes shocking information.

For the next eight months the Remington Committee's preliminary report circulated among the faculty and administration, with students paying essentially no attention to its revelations. On April 4, 1966, the University faculty received a three-page "Report and Recommendations of the Committee to Study Non-Curricular Life of Students, 1963-1966."[134] The document summarized the lengthy preliminary report and appendix, and some of its observations were striking. Criticizing the vague disciplinary guidelines currently in force, the committee declared the University needed to determine "the kinds of student conduct which are considered to be misconduct" and to communicate this to the student body. The report complained that "important questions of policy relating to student misconduct are decided by the default of the Faculty and Administration." The Department of Protection and Security, for example, was operating "without guidelines" from the faculty and academic administration. The University should establish "standards of conduct," and these "must be constantly evaluated as circumstances change to prevent vagueness of interpretation from producing arbitrary and inconsistent action." At the same time, "the University should recognize the limitations of its power to create 'responsible members of society.' It is only one of the institutions which help to shape the lives of students, and shares this responsibility with the family, the home town, the church and other institutions."

The Remington Committee offered several specific recommendations for remedial action:

> More precisely, the Committee suggests that the University's concern be directed toward conduct which: 1) threatens the safety of the members of the University community; 2) threatens the property of the University; 3) threatens the integrity of the educational process.

---

[134]UW Faculty Document 57, "Report and Recommendations of the Committee to Study Non-Curricular Life of Students, 1963-1966," April 4, 1966.

In light of the problems uncovered by the committee, "continuing study" should be given to:

> 1) clarification of the authority of the Department of Protection and Security; 2) clarification of the relations between the University administration and the law enforcement authorities in Madison and Dane County; 3) clarification of the roles of counseling and discipline in dealing with student misconduct; 4) development of appropriate sanctions for misconduct, other than social probation and suspension.

Thus in essence the Remington Committee recognized and acknowledged that the University had lost track of its place in the evolving culture of student life and needed to reorient its policies accordingly. With other pressing issues before it, however, the University faculty merely filed the report, thereby tacitly deciding to do nothing for the time being.

The Student Power Initiatives

A year passed without any systematic action on the Remington Committee recommendations. Then, over the course of several weeks of deliberation in April, 1967, the Student Senate of the Wisconsin Student Association began adopting legislation soon known collectively as the Student Power Bills. The first of these, Bill 15-SS-25, "Basic Policy Declaration of the Wisconsin Student Association, 1967-68," was central.[135] After stating that "students should govern themselves and regulate their lives and interests democratically through WSA," the Student Senate declared it "an infringement of those rights" for UW authorities "to impose rules, regulations, or restrictions on students without their consent, in solely student areas of concern." It further asserted the "basic right of students to coordinate student activities and organizations and to establish those regulations over student life which affect none other than students through the student government."

The University's "responsibility," on the other hand, was to "recognize" those rights by taking "appropriate actions and measures to withdraw the operations and cease the exercising of power by the University . . . , particularly through the Student Life and Interests Committee, in opposition to the policies herewithin expressed." Instead, the senate declared that WSA "henceforth assumes exclusive power to

---

[135]Student Senate Minutes, April 20, 27, 1967, Series 19/2/3-7, Box 16, UA.

define eligibility requirements for participation in all phases of student activity, to regulate undergraduate social traffic and to counsel student organizations and groups." Furthermore, "the WSA and only the WSA will establish all policies, rules and regulations governing student social and group life." Student power extended beyond WSA to all duly constituted student organizations: "The Student Senate . . . recognizes that, insofar as it is consistent with the interests of the student body, students in their various self-governing groups should be autonomous in their roles as members of such groups." Bill 15-SS-25 concluded by calling for an "all-campus referendum" on May 3 to determine if WSA were "to communicate this Basic Policy Declaration to appropriate individuals and organizations and work to implement the principles this Declaration asserts."

At the regularly scheduled faculty meeting on May 1, two days before the special campus-wide student referendum, Madison Chancellor Robben Fleming called attention to two faculty documents, 140 and 141, that had been distributed at the door. The first was a "Report by the University Committee Regarding Student Senate Bill 15-SS-25." The second was an explanatory letter from WSA President Michael Fullwood. Chancellor Fleming also noted that Fullwood had asked to appear before the faculty to discuss 15-SS-25. A motion to this effect failed on a vote of 54-76, and the chancellor announced that Faculty Documents 140 and 141 would be sent out with the minutes of the meeting.[136]

While declaring it "entirely acceptable" that students might govern themselves in areas not encroaching on University prerogatives, the University Committee report rejected as "clearly illegal" under state statutes that the any segment of the University community could "'assume' power unilaterally." The Student Senate's "ultimatum" was thus "contrary to the spirit of cooperation" traditionally operating at Wisconsin and sought to preclude deliberate and well-considered reforms. Although the immediate issue was the recent Student Senate action, the members of the University Committee also had "a much broader concern" regarding events and trends of the past two years. "It is becoming evident that the present University structure and regulations were designed without reference to such situations and problems," they noted, "and are proving ineffective as a framework within which to operate." The committee therefore was:

---

[136]UW Faculty Minutes, May 1, 1967.

considering the advisability of sponsoring a study, in depth, of the role of student government with reference to University regulations and procedures. We are taking an open-minded attitude in this regard and thus are receptive to suggestions as to goals, procedures, and scope. There are real advantages to working through established channels.[137]

WSA President Fullwood evidently was not so sure of the advantages of University channels. He began his letter to the faculty by bluntly declaring: "Bill 15-SS-25 is in effect a Declaration of Student Rights. It enunciates the concept that students possess the intrinsic and basic right to regulate their own affairs in matters of solely-student concern through their student government." Those rights were infringed when, as stated in the bill, "an organ" of the University imposed "rules, regulations, or restrictions on students without their consent in solely-student areas of concern." To be sure, "cooperation" had operated in the past but not adequately, particularly with regard to recent SLIC actions. Therefore, "the Student Senate determined in this case to enunciate what it considered basic principles of student rights, and not ask that they be given to the students to exercise, but indicated that they would be exercised." The students, then, were requesting "recognition" and not the granting of their rights. From the students' point of view, the University consisted of scholars and teachers on the one hand and students on the other. Students were prepared to "recognize" the faculty's "responsibility and right" to superintend "learning in selected disciplines," but the students asked "in return the recognition of the faculty that the students hold the intrinsic right to regulate their own affairs through their student government." If the May 3 referendum should pass, "I will respectfully request the faculty to come together in special session to consider this resolution to give their approval for the principles expressed therein."[138]

The May 3 referendum did pass by a substantial margin of 6,146 to 3,906. On May 17 the Student Senate adopted Bill 15-SS-65, a "Special Resolution," outlining five new Student Life Committees

---

[137]UW Faculty Document 140 "Report to the Faculty of the Madison Campus by the University Committee Regarding Student Senate Bill 15-SS-25," May 1, 1967. The University Committee membership at this time consisted of Eugene N. Cameron (geology and geophysics), August G. Eckhardt (law), John D. Ferry (chemistry), Douglas G. Marshall (rural sociology), William H. Sewell (sociology), and James R. Villemonte (civil engineering), chairman.

[138]UW Faculty Document 141, "Michael Fullwood, President of the Wisconsin Student Association, to Members of the Faculty," May 1, 1967.

intended to supersede SLIC and its subcommittees. Each committee would consist of five voting student members and three non-voting faculty advisers. The Student Court would be responsible for settling most student life disputes and appeals from student governmental decisions, and a new Student Life and Interests Appeal Board, composed of five students and five faculty members would handle appeals from decisions of the Student Court. Finally a position of Student Attorney would be established. All of this would "go into effect upon either Faculty approval of the principles of 15-SS-25 or by a majority vote of the entire Senate should the Faculty reject the same."[139]

Anticipating a looming student showdown with the University faculty, the WSA Summer Board fleshed out and to some extent softened the assertions of the two student power bills and the WSA constitution. The result was a report, adopted by the Summer Board on August 7 as Bill 15-SS-35. "The university student of today is an adult," proclaimed the report's preface, and students expected the University to function as "an academic and educational institution." All other "additional functions . . . must be stripped away. . . . Thus the interference in the non-academic lives of the students . . . will have to end." The day of the University's social control of students through "hour regulations, visitation restrictions, and a host of other 'don't'" rules had passed. "It is the right of the students to govern themselves through their student government," and the faculty should delegate "authority to regulate in such matters to the students":

> This report seeks to delineate what matters fall in this realm in the eyes of the Student Senate. It seeks to answer questions that have justifiably been raised by both administrators and members of the faculty. It seeks to put in context and expand in particulars the principles passed by the Student Senate.[140]

Specifically, the report asked "that the faculty adopt policies in two areas: (1) Areas of individual liberties and areas coming under civil law . . . and (2) areas of solely student concern where the WSA would be allowed to legislate." In the first instance, the University simply would desist; "the status of a student shall be effected [sic] only by his

---

[139]"6146 to 3906," *Daily Cardinal*, May 4, 1967; Student Senate Minutes, May 17, 1967, Series 19/2/3-7, Box 16, UA.

[140]WSA Summer Board, "Recommendations to Student Senate," adopted unanimously August 7, 1967 as 15-SS-35, Series 5/111, Box 2, UA.

ability to participate in classroom activities." The University's "right to counsel a student" would remain in effect, however. In the second category, "areas of solely student concern should be . . . defined and placed within the jurisdiction of WSA and other autonomous student governing bodies." (These were the areas of SLIC's current responsibility.) The new WSA constitution would delegate control over "internal affairs" of student organizations to various "autonomous" student groups. But WSA "would set up guidelines within the areas of solely student concern which would protect the individual liberties of students under WSA regulations and the rules of other student organizations." WSA also would "set the minimum standards of supervised and approved housing and designate whom must live therein."

The WSA Summer Board report concluded by identifying and explaining needed organizational and legal changes. A Student Life Appeals Board would settle disputes over activities involving "areas of solely student concern." Membership would include two law faculty members, two law students, one faculty member-at-large, one undergraduate student, and an assistant dean of the Law School, who would serve as chairman. This legalistic approach continued in the report's treatment of Student Senate responsibilities, which the writers interpreted as analogous to the faculty's role in University governance. It therefore outlined in considerable detail the responsibilities of seven proposed Senate Legislative Committees that would supervise areas currently under SLIC jurisdiction. As to those agencies that "presently carry out the regulations," such as the University's Department of Protection and Security, they henceforth would operate according to the "legislative authority" of "the students themselves."

Similarly, the Student Court and various "autonomous" student courts, would manage the day-to-day "judiciary function." While the new WSA constitution would "delegate legislative and judicial jurisdiction to the various autonomous student governmental groups on campus," WSA would nevertheless "set the standard" for such important areas as "supervised housing." Thus no "separate hours for men and women" would be allowed because this would violate "a basic concept that there should be no discrimination by race, religion, or sex." On the other hand, such issues as "rushing, pledging, initiation membership and social regulation in the fraternity and sorority system would be considered an internal affair of the Interfraternity Council and Pan Hellenic Association." The report also laid out plans for the Wisconsin Union, the *Daily Cardinal*, and the Student Activities

Reserve Fund. It concluded by presenting a new draft WSA constitution embodying these changes.

The regular WSA Student Senate held a marathon meeting on October 12, 1967, finally voting approval of the Summer Board's recommendations. This was a two-part process, the first involving the board's "Report," which was slightly amended and adopted as Bill 15-SS-105. The proposed new WSA Constitution, also slightly amended, was approved as Bill 15-SS-139. WSA ultimately issued this legislation in the form of a recommendation to the faculty entitled "Student Power Report, 1967."[141] Coinciding, however, with preparations for a second major campus protest against recruiters from the Dow Chemical Company, this final senate action on the student power initiative was quickly overtaken by events.

The Crow Report

Meanwhile, as a direct response to the student power bills, in August, 1967, the University Committee had appointed an ad hoc Committee on the Roles of Students in the Government of the University. Chaired by genetics Professor James F. Crow, the committee included eight other prominent faculty members.[142] The committee was charged with three "tasks": to study past and present student involvement in University governance; to "formulate principles" for making decisions about enhanced student participation that would support high quality education and are "consistent with the obligations" of the University to "the people of the State"; and finally to recommend "relevant structural changes, that may be necessary to implement the formulated principles in the context of the times in which we live." Under the circumstances, the challenge was formidable.[143]

---

[141]Student Senate Minutes, October 12, 1967, Series 19/2/3-7, Box 16, UA; "Student Senate Report, 1967, Adopted October 12, 1967 as Bill 15-SS-105, Bill 15-SS-139," Series 5/111, Box 2, UA.

[142]Besides Crow, a former acting dean of the Medical School who held membership in three academic departments (genetics, medical genetics, and zoology), the committee included: William W. Beeman (physics), Kenneth M. Dolbeare (political science), William H. Hay (philosophy), Robert J. Lampman (economics), Peter L. Monkmeyer (civil engineering), George L. Mosse (history), Clara Penniman (political science), and Walter B. Raushenbush (law).

[143]UW Faculty Document 219, "Report of the Ad Hoc Committee on the Role of Students in the Government of the University, hereafter referred to as the Crow Report," letter of transmittal dated February 6, 1968, considered and filed with minutes

The Crow Committee cast a wide net in its deliberations. Most directly, of course, it took into account the various student government legislative actions, including those of the WSA Summer Board in August, and especially the WSA "Student Power Report, 1967." It studied similar developments at other institutions, especially at Cornell, New York University, and the University of California, Berkeley. It "received numerous suggestions from students in and out of Student Senate." It held public hearings, corresponded with and interviewed many individuals, and consulted a few additional outside sources. Assuming that its final report would be detailed and extensive, the committee initially focused on issues that seemed to beg for quick resolution. Ultimately, it believed its work was only the beginning of an ongoing student-faculty effort to address all questions centering on the role of students at the University.

Professor Crow submitted a 54-page report to the University Committee on February 6, 1968. Denying that its recommendations were "revolutionary," the committee nevertheless acknowledged that "they do represent distinct acceleration of established trends and, in some respects, tentative new departures which we hope will become trends in the future." The members claimed to have come away from the exercise with "a sense of opportunity and hope, inspired by the thought that fuller realization of the ideals of education is ultimately consistent with all of those interests and goals." Time would tell.

The Crow recommendations embraced four categories. First, the committee called for "practically complete withdrawal by the University from its *in loco parentis* activities." University representatives should cease all regulation of students' off-campus personal lives and of "nonacademic" matters on-campus, such "as hours regulation." Students over 20 years of age should be allowed to live off campus, in housing of their choice, as should all married students and any student with parental consent. These recommendations effectively called for the end of UW housing regulations as developed by SLIC's living conditions and hygiene subcommittee, approved by SLIC, and formally endorsed by the faculty. Because various other campus units also issued regulations about student housing, the Crow Committee recommended the creation of a student-faculty Campus Student Housing Committee to act comprehensively in this area.[142]

---

of the Special Madison Campus Faculty Meeting of May 13, 1968. The quotations are from page 2.

    [142]"Crow Report," pp. 33-37.

The committee called for "broader student participation in various forms in practically all areas of University government." A single exclusion was "direct student participation in decisions on faculty appointments, promotions, and salaries." Not only did the committee offer suggestions for expanding student involvement on numerous campus committees,[143] it also proposed a new method by which student government might bring issues directly before the faculty.[144] The committee recommended that the Divisional Student-Faculty Conference Committees, established by faculty action in May of 1965, be retained and reviewed after another two or three years.[145]

"We advocate greater student self-governing authority," the report declared, with correspondingly reduced University supervision. This implied the abolition of the controversial Student Life and Interests Committee. Its powers should be distributed among the student government and "smaller, joint student-faculty committees with limited jurisdictions." A new Committee on Student Organizations should be established to act as an arbiter between and among the various student governing agencies, such as the Student Court, the faculty, the administration, and the regents. Voting members would include four teaching members of the faculty (one of them serving as chairman) appointed by the chancellor, and the presidents (or alternates) of WSA, the Wisconsin Union, and the Senior Class. The chancellor also would appoint one person from the Dean of Students staff as a non-voting member. Anticipating the possibility that WSA or other student members might refuse to participate, the committee declared that "the faculty members shall continue to serve as an appellate body overseeing activities having to do with student organizations."[146]

---

[143] Ibid., pp. 42-46.

[144] Ibid., pp. 39-41.

[145] Ibid., p. 46. See also UW Faculty Document 20, " Recommendations of the Student-Faculty Conference Committee," May 3, 1965; UW Faculty Minutes, May 3, 1965.

[146] SLIC operated with five subcommittees: Forensics, Dramatics, and Music; Fraternal Societies and Social Life; General Student Organizations and Politics; Living Conditions and Hygiene; and Publications. Members included five faculty members (each serving as chairman of one of the subcommittees), three staff members from the Division of Student Affairs, and six students (presidents of WSA, Associated Women Students, the Wisconsin Union, and three students nominated by WSA, one of whom must be a graduate student). The committee noted SLIC's "jurisdiction" was limited and listed other student agencies and activities that operated under their own charters: the Wisconsin Union, *Daily Cardinal*, athletics, student health services, University residence halls, and lectures and convocations. Thus the name Student Life and Interests

Finally, and increasingly pertinent, the committee proposed restructuring, limiting, and clarifying all "University disciplinary procedures" according to the principles enunciated in the 1966 report of the Remington Committee. While it appeared that in practice University authorities were already generally following the Remington Committee's guidelines, the 1967-68 *Student Handbook* continued to present outdated policy. In any event, the University should no longer, with a very few exceptions, duplicate civil law penalties. It should retain only a limited number of disciplinary powers, to be exercised by student-faculty panels and faculty appeals committees without the participation of administrative officials as judge or jury. New student conduct policies should be established by a new joint-committee of three students and six faculty members.[147]

Although not included among its recommendations, the committee recognized the potential conflict between its proposals and the Board of Regents' human rights policy, which stated:

> The University of Wisconsin shall in all its branches and activities maintain the fullest respect and protection of the Constitutional rights of all citizens and students regardless of race, color, sect, or creed; and any violation thereof shall immediately be reported to the administration and the Regents for appropriate action to the end that any such violation of Constitutional rights shall be promptly and full corrected, and future violations prevented.

The committee supported "vigilant enforcement of the principle" by all members of the University community, and declared, "we do not favor changing the operation or responsibility of the Human Rights Committee, which seems to us to be doing an exemplary job."[148]

In the midst of the continuing campus turmoil over the war in Vietnam, the faculty held a special meeting to discuss the Crow Committee report on May 13, 1968. The document was filed without much comment, debate, or any formal action on its recommendations.

Committee was "misleading." "Crow Report," p. 47.

[147]Ibid., pp. 12-19, contained a long, detailed, and sometimes conceptually difficult discussion of recommended methods for identifying student behavior potentially liable for University disciplinary action. The report, pp. 20-32, went on to discuss current UW disciplinary agencies (the Student Court, SLIC, and Dean of Student Affairs and related administrators) and to recommend new ones (Committee for Student Conduct Hearings, Committee for Student Conduct Appeals, and Committee on Student Conduct Policy).

[148]Ibid., p. 7.

This would come subsequently in piecemeal fashion. Still, the die had been cast. The general concept of student power had been acknowledged and supported by a duly constituted committee of respected senior University faculty members. In the spirit of Bob Dylan's popular anthem, the times they were indeed a-changin'.

8.

From Rights to Revolution

During the latter half of the 1960s, UW students, like those on campuses all across the country, were engaged in an increasingly bitter and sometimes violent protest against their government's involvement in a bloody civil war in Southeast Asia. Their suspicion of the promises of politicians and their rejection of seemingly bankrupt leadership in Washington led to a growing distrust of any authority, including that of the faculty, administrators, and regents charged with operating the University of Wisconsin. This fed the drive for student power and a determination to take charge of the educational process as part of the larger goal of building a better, and for some radicals a socialist, world. The latter sixties were among the most turbulent years in the University's history, a time when students received much of their education, along with a fair amount of misinformation and cynicism, outside the classroom and in the streets.

If anti-war protests exemplified and even dominated this period, one should nevertheless remember that they did not entirely replace traditional student activities and high jinks. In October, 1969, for example, after the Badger football team's first victory in 23 games, there was a joyful student victory march down State Street to the capitol, parading past boarded-up windows trashed in anti-war protests.[1] Similarly, hormonally challenged male students, egged on by their female victims, mounted a traditional panty raid on the women's southeast dorms less than a month after the tragic Sterling Hall bombing in 1970.[2] Paradoxically, even during the most violent episodes, when Madison police, sheriff's deputies, and national guardsmen had to be

---

[1] *Daily Cardinal*, October 15, 1969.
[2] Ibid., September 23, 1970.

called in to restore order, there were large areas of the sprawling campus largely unaffected and uninvolved. The battle zone tended to be concentrated in the Bascom Hill-Lower Campus-Library Mall area, with the rest of the campus often ignored by the protesters.

The Vietnam Trauma

By the mid-1960s student activists at the University were shifting their emphasis from the civil rights movement at home to foreign affairs, particularly the growing United States military involvement in southeast Asia. Following the Second World War, France had sought to regain control over its former colony, French Indo-China, which had been occupied by Japanese forces in 1940 and held throughout the war. Of the three major Indo-Chinese states–Vietnam, Cambodia, and Laos–the more numerous Vietnamese led the resistance to the reimposition of French rule. Under the leadership of Ho Chi Minh, a charismatic French-educated Vietnamese patriot and communist, the former colonists first launched guerrilla attacks and eventually pitched military battles against French troops sent to subdue them. Well aware of the United States' anti-colonial origins and its action in 1946 freeing the Philippines, the major American Asian colony, Ho Chi Minh expected the U.S. government to view his independence movement favorably. Instead, the Truman and Eisenhower administrations were preoccupied in the 1940s and 1950s with rebuilding the shattered nations of western Europe and creating an anti-communist military alliance against the Soviet Union. After 1949 their anti-communist concern included the new Peoples Republic of China. The United States therefore provided arms and military equipment to the French and permitted their use in Indo-China. The Vietnamese rebels in turn received arms and other assistance from the two major communist states, the Soviet Union and China.

Despite superior armament, France was unable to win a colonial war that was increasingly unpopular at home. After suffering a major military defeat at Dien Bien Phu in 1954, the French government reluctantly decided to pull its forces out of Vietnam. Rather than see Ho Chi Minh's communist forces take over the entire country, an international conference in Geneva divided Vietnam temporarily into two sectors at the seventeenth parallel pending unification after national elections. The northern half was under Ho Chi Minh's anti-colonial but communist-led regime based in Hanoi. The southern part, swollen by thousands of Roman Catholic refugees from the north, was under a hastily organized western-oriented Vietnamese government in Saigon. Both sides claimed to represent the Vietnamese people and aspired to rule the entire country. Following the French withdrawal, President Eisenhower approved the continuation of U.S. military aid to the anti-communist Saigon regime and sent American military advisors to train the fledgling army of the so-called Republic of Vietnam in the south. Still arguing over the "loss" of China to Mao Zedong's communist regime, American politicians and policy makers feared a "domino effect" throughout southeast Asia if Vietnam and the rest of Indo-China were also to go communist.

Viewing the lingering French influence and American support of the Saigon regime as proof of continuing western colonialism, the Hanoi regime sought to expand its rule to the south. Supplied and encouraged by the Soviet Union and China, Ho Chi Minh mounted a combination of hit-run attacks by local Vietcong guerrillas and increasingly an all-out military campaign by the North Vietnamese army. In response the Kennedy administration increased military aid to the Saigon regime and dispatched more military advisors and eventually U.S. combat forces to assist in the defense of South Vietnam. Following Kennedy's assassination in late 1963, President Lyndon Johnson reluctantly stepped up the American military support of South Vietnam, trapped by his concern not to be the first American president to lose a war–in this instance the undeclared war to contain communism in southeast Asia.

Under President Eisenhower, American involvement in Vietnam had been limited to a few hundred military advisors. President Kennedy had increased these to about 16,500 by the time of his death in 1963. Feeling locked into an interventionist policy not of his making or wish, President Johnson none the less began a rapid and ever more extensive expansion of U.S. forces and warfare in Vietnam, though never as much as his generals believed necessary for a decisive victory. The effort was seemingly ineffective in a country where much of the largely peasant population had little concern for the domino theory or interest in helping westerners defend their land against other Vietnamese. American forces numbered 185,300 by the end of 1965 and 485,600 the following year, reaching a peak of 542,400 in January, 1969.[3] By this time the United

---

[3]Lt. Gen. Joseph M. Heiser, Jr., *Vietnam Studies: Logistic Support* (Washington: Department of the Army, 1974), p. 14; see also the Annual Reports of the Secretary

States had dropped more bombs on Vietnamese targets than the Allies had delivered in all of World War II. Between 1964 and 1973, when the last U.S. soldier left Vietnam, about 27 million young men of what might be termed the Vietnam generation reached draft age. Of these about 11 million served for a time in the armed forces and more than 58,000 died in what turned out to be the country's longest war.[4] It was hardly surprising that by the late 1960s the war in Vietnam had become the most contentious and divisive issue in Madison and the nation.

The Rise of the New Left

The University of Wisconsin had for many decades attracted and encouraged an activist student body, which since the 1920s regularly included a sizable bloc of matriculants from eastern states. Many of these easterners were children of parents of varying leftist political persuasions and degrees of activism. These non-resident students, many of them Jewish, tended to be disproportionately active in campus politics and extracurricular affairs and more liberal-to-radical in their views than the great bulk of Wisconsin students. They helped give the University its worldly atmosphere, lively extracurricular life, and activist reputation.[5] They also played a leading part in developing and shaping the anti-war movement on campus in the latter sixties.

As we have seen in the previous chapter, during the early post-war years UW student activists were concerned mainly with defending and expanding individual rights, including self-determination for students locally. They opposed racial and religious discrimination in local housing, campaigned against compulsory ROTC, scoffed at McCarthyism and red scare tactics, and in the early 1960s provided support for the burgeoning Negro civil rights movement in the south. UW students participated in the historic 1963 March on Washington, the Mississippi Freedom Summer voter registration project in 1964, and the Selma to Montgomery march the following year that generated

---

of Defense for the period.

[4]George Donelson Moss, *Vietnam: An American Ordeal* (Englewood Cliffs, N.J.: Prentice Hall, 1990), pp.226-29; Christian C. Appy, *Working-Class War: American Combat Soldiers and Vietnam* (Chapel Hill: University of North Carolina Press, 1993), pp. 26-37.

[5]See E. David Cronon and John W. Jenkins, *The University of Wisconsin: A History*, Vol. 3, *Politics, Depression, and War, 1925-1945* (Madison: University of Wisconsin Press, 1994), especially pp. 551-682.

massive public support for the Voting Rights Act of 1965. The interest in individual rights elsewhere in the country helped to fuel a successful campaign against restrictive University policies governing student life and extracurricular activities in Madison.

This focus on domestic concerns was reflected in the columns of the *Daily Cardinal* and the agendas of the student organizations of the period. An example was the Students for a Democratic Society (SDS), which came to epitomize the so-called New Left of the 1960s. SDS grew out of the old socialist Student League for Industrial Democracy in 1960 and was initially concerned with such domestic issues as Negro civil rights, union organizing, disarmament, anti-poverty programs, and conversion of defense industries to peace-oriented production. SDS leaders were critical of what they saw as the sterile factionalism of the old-line leftist groups—what they called the Old Left—and sought to build a new activist student movement to reform and democratize American society at all levels. Especially in its early years the group attracted a number of talented graduate students, mostly in the social sciences and humanities, who produced some thoughtful critiques of societal problems. Although SDS leaders emphasized full participatory debate and collective decision-making, by the late sixties the organization had fallen victim to the very factionalism it sought to avoid. When SDS nationally was slow to adopt an active anti-war stance, local chapters and members were more militant in opposing the U.S. intervention in Vietnam as the single most important issue facing the country. By the latter 1960s some SDS members, especially the so-called Weathermen nationally and the Mother Jones Revolutionary League in Madison, were moving from protest to violent resistance and insurgency.

A small Madison SDS chapter was launched in 1962-63 under the leadership of a mathematics graduate student, C. Clark Kissinger. One of Kissinger's early projects was mobilizing UW student support for striking auto mechanics at the Bruns Garage and Volkswagen dealership in Madison.[6] The UW chapter continued to grow slowly, attracting mostly graduate students and meeting regularly for discussion of societal problems. During 1964-65 Kissinger served as the national SDS secretary in Chicago. The Madison SDS chapter was by then only one of several leftist student organizations on campus, overshadowed at

---

[6]C. Clark Kissinger, "Students Get Back into Labor (on the Ground Floor)," undated unpublished report [October, 1963], SDS Collection, Series 2B, Box 15, SHSW Archives; *Daily Cardinal*, July 11, 1963.

first by the older and more visible communist DuBois Club, the Young Socialist Alliance, and by the more broadly based Committee to End the War in Vietnam (CEWV) following its formation in the spring of 1965. As concern about the war deepened, UW students also took an active role in the statewide Wisconsin Draft Resisters Union (WDRU), which counseled young men about the selective service system and helped some objectors flee the country to avoid it.[7]

Other activist groups had a more fleeting life, forming and fading in response to specific objectives and issues. The names of some of these mostly ephemeral groups recapture the protest fervor of the latter 1960s: the Committee on the University and the Draft, the Committee for Student Rights, the Committee against Army Recruitment, the Anti-Dow Coordinating Committee, the Committee for Direct Action, the Committee to Liberate the Southeast Area Dorms, the Committee to Defend Individual Rights, the University of Michigan-Berkeley Solidarity rally, the "C.I.A., Why? - Speak Out Teach-In," the "March against State Interference," the "Women Say **Yes** to Men Who Say **No**" march, and the United Campus Action political party. Though never the largest activist group, SDS came to symbolize the New Left at the University and to provide some of the more reasoned position papers and much of the leadership of a number of the more notable demonstrations. A favored gathering place for campus radicals in these years was the Rathskeller of the Memorial Union. Often they used the front steps of the Union as the starting point for their rallies and demonstrations. Other radical hangouts were the campus YMCA and the Nitty Gritty bar on Johnson Street.[8]

---

[7]UW student WDRU members gained considerable attention in 1969 when they organized a symbolic sanctuary for draft resister Ken Vogel in the First Congregational Church adjacent to the campus. Dozens of students joined Vogel in his vigil, all wearing name tags saying "My name is Ken Vogel," to frustrate any attempt by FBI agents to arrest him. Although supporting Vogel's anti-war stand, the church's moderator, William Bradford Smith, resigned in protest over the church ministers' open-door policy and the alleged immoral conduct of some of the overnight protesters. The congregation, however, voted to back the vigil. After more than two weeks Vogel was arrested for draft evasion. *Daily Cardinal*, September 17, 18, 23, 25, 26, 30, October 4, 11, 1969.

[8]An unintended consequence of the heavy use of the Memorial Union by activists and counter-culture advocates was a corresponding decline in use by more traditional students, faculty, and townspeople. Historically, profits from food sales had helped to subsidize much of the Union's other programming, but by the end of the decade the reduction in food service patronage was seriously affecting the Union's overall budget. The opening of Union South in 1970 further aggravated the problem,

During 1965-66 the Madison SDS chapter became more active under the leadership of Martin Tandler, a history graduate student, sending speakers into the dormitories to generate opposition to the war in Vietnam.[9] Moving from talk to action, SDS members played the leading role in organizing a week-long peaceful sit-in demonstration at the new administration building in May, 1966, to protest the military draft. It was the first student occupation of a building in the University's history.

The rising student concern about the draft followed President Johnson's decision not to order a general call-up of Army reserves or national guard units for service in Vietnam. This necessitated growing reliance on the selective service system to produce ever-larger monthly draft calls to meet the Army's expanding Vietnam manpower needs. In 1965 President Johnson doubled the monthly draft calls from 17,000 to 35,000, and the figure later rose to 50,000 new draftees a month. The philosophy behind the selective service system was embodied in its name; the law was premised on a form of social engineering that exempted or deferred certain groups from being drafted because their current employment or studies were deemed more important to the nation than military service. Full-time students in good academic standing, for example, were at first automatically granted 2-S deferments while in school. UW administrators braced for trouble, but at first hoped the situation would follow the pattern of the Korean War when students had accepted the draft without incident. "I guess we really won't meet any trouble," UW Student Affairs Dean Martha Peterson told Joe Kauffman, her Madison campus counterpart, in late 1965, "unless there are inconsistences in the application of draft calls."[10]

Indeed, most UW-Madison students initially supported the U.S. defense of Vietnam, which the *Daily Cardinal* called "a dirty, necessary war."[11] A poll conducted by the UW Survey Research Laboratory late in 1965 revealed that 72 percent of the student body gave unreserved support to American participation in the war and only 16 percent

---

because it attracted the more conservative nearby agriculture, engineering, and meteorology students and faculty.

[9][James O'Brien] "An Informal History of Madison SDS, or 'Gee, Grandpa, I Bet You've Been Fighting for Progressive Causes Longer Than Anybody!'" unpublished draft article, SDS Collection, box 43, SHSW.

[10]Martha Peterson to Joseph Kauffman, November 29, 1965, Dean Joseph F. Kauffman Papers, UHP.

[11]*Daily Cardinal*, September 29, 1965.

expressed disagreement.[12] Student opinion began to shift, however, as the buildup and the fighting expanded and as draft calls increased. Since draft boards took older men in the 18-26 age pool first, graduate students were the most threatened if they lacked a student deferment, and were the most capable of organizing a resistance movement on campus. For UW student advisers, counseling male students about rapidly changing draft policies and regulations was once again a job requirement.

SDS leaders early recognized the value of the draft in expanding their base of student support. An internal SDS position paper noted in 1964 that the recent three-year congressional reauthorization of selective service provided a significant organizing opportunity:

> Of all the issues which ought to allow for successful campus organizing programs, the issue of Selective Service would seem to have the widest possible base. Although Selective Service does not select college students, it selects large numbers of former college students, and it is a major problem confronted by all college males. . . .
>
> The average American student has used all kinds of evasionary tactics to express his unhappiness with the draft and to keep out of the service. These anti-social tactics have had the net impact of causing the burden of conscription to fall on less educated groups. For the average fraternity guy to get into a movement to abolish the draft would be a recognition that the problem is social, not personal.[13]

The rising draft calls seemed to underscore the validity of this organizing approach.

Campus concerns about the draft accelerated after selective service officials in Washington moved to tighten requirements for 2-S student deferments by reinstating the Korean War era College Qualification Test and requiring applicants to provide their local draft boards with official proof of their academic status and class rank. The intent was to reserve student deferments for more serious and committed students. Widespread concern over these announced changes enabled Madison SDS leaders to mount a protest and sit-in demonstration at the new administration building on May 16-20, 1966, two days after the first draft qualification test was offered on campus. Disciplined, orderly,

---

[12]Ibid., January 26 and July 19, 1966.
[13]SDS Peace Research and Education Project, "Toward an Effective Peace Program on Campus," draft ms., SDS Collection, box 33, SHSW.

and peaceful, the sit-in protesters did not interfere with the employees or offices of the building. They simply demanded that the University "positively refuse to cooperate with the Selective Service Administration in any way" and "issue a statement condemning the use of grades, class rank, and other academic criteria in determining acceptability of young men for the draft."[14] As SDS leaders had foreseen, by making opposition to the draft a societal and not a personal issue, they succeeded in attracting broad campus support for a demonstration they shrewdly allowed to proceed under the leadership of the more inclusive ad hoc Committee on the University and the Draft.[15]

Endorsed by the *Daily Cardinal*, the Student Senate, and the Inter-Fraternity Council, the anti-draft protest also drew considerable faculty support. Working closely with President Harrington, Chancellor Fleming and his staff handled the protesters deftly, permitting them to occupy the building for five days as long as the sit-in remained peaceful and non-obstructive. After 27 faculty members petitioned for a general faculty meeting to discuss UW draft policy, Fleming promised a mass rally of students on Bascom Hill he would recommend that their representatives be permitted to address the faculty. "There are serious questions involved," he acknowledged, "and it will be useful for faculty and students to take a fresh look at them together."[16] He persuaded the sit-in demonstrators to withdraw over the weekend so as not to appear to be pressuring the Monday faculty meeting when it considered the issue.[17]

---

[14]Undated leaflet, "Why We Protest–Why You Should Join Us"; Committee on the University and the Draft to President Harrington, undated, both in Series 4/19/1, Box 38, UA.

[15]Conscious of the need to project an image of broad campus support, the committee protested to Chancellor Fleming about the negative coverage of its activities by the local Madison press, declaring that it resented such "smear tactics." "The use by these papers of photographs of bearded students, etc., and the disproportionate identification of *out-of-state students* misrepresents the university-wide student support for the movement, clearly indicated by the Wisconsin Student Association and the Inter-Fraternity Council's support of the movement." Richard Stone to Fleming, May 19, 1966, Kauffman Papers, UHP.

[16]Remarks by Chancellor Robben W. Fleming, Lincoln Terrace, May 18, 1966, UW press release, UHP. At the rally campus area ministers read a statement signed by 15 of their colleagues endorsing the protest and commending the Student Senate for calling upon the University "to adjure any intermediary relationship between students and the Selective Service System." Statement, May 18, 1966, Kauffman Papers, UHP.

[17]President Harrington's old department–history–played a large role in the anti-draft protest. Six of the nine protest leaders identified confidentially by Dean of Students Joseph F. Kauffman after the sit-in were history graduate or undergraduate

Much to the dismay of more militant students who called it a "betrayal," the nearly 900 faculty members present decided that while information about class standing should not be given directly to draft boards, it "should be available to the individual student on request." The meeting also authorized Fleming to cooperate with the Wisconsin Student Association in appointing a student-faculty committee to study University draft policy.[18] A subsequent faculty meeting to consider this committee's report reaffirmed the decision to provide academic information to students on request rather than directly to draft boards and endorsed the current flexible system of deferments under a non-universal military draft.[19] President Harrington also wrote President Johnson and the Wisconsin congressional delegation in Washington expressing his concern, and that of the larger University community, over inequities in the selective service system.[20]

Among the faculty supporters of the protest, several senior history professors deserve mention because of their growing influence over student radicals in the next few years. One was William Appleman Williams, a World War II Annapolis graduate and navy pilot, who had studied U.S. foreign relations under Harrington after the war and replaced him in the department after Harrington moved into campus administration. Williams shared his mentor's emphasis on economic determinism in foreign policy, an approach appealing to young

---

students; several history faculty members addressed the protesters sympathetically or used class time to discuss draft issues. Of the 27 faculty who signed the call for the special faculty meeting on May 23, 12 were members of the history department. The meeting was originally scheduled for the Social Science Building, but was moved to Music Hall to accommodate the 892 who attended. The proceedings were broadcast to the Great Hall of the Memorial Union for a large student audience. Both practices–ad hoc mass faculty meetings called on demand and broadcast proceedings for the benefit of student protesters–became increasingly common over the next several years. See Kauffman to Fleming, June 2, 1966, Series 4/19/1, Box 38, UA.

[18]UW Faculty Minutes, May 23, 1966, UA. It should be emphasized that in spite of the widespread campus support for the 1966 anti-draft demonstration, not all students agreed with the protesters. At the height of the protest one male student wrote Chancellor Fleming that the issue was not whether the University had the right to release information about grades and class rank to draft boards, but whether it had the right to deny him the privilege of having his information released, a view also expressed by a number of regents. See Elliott M. Friedman to Fleming, May 19, 1966, Kauffman Papers, UHP.

[19]UW Faculty Minutes, November 17, 1966.

[20]Harrington to President Lyndon B. Johnson, June 23, 1966, Series 4/19/1, Box 38, UA. An identical letter was sent to each member of the Wisconsin congressional delegation.

Marxists. Although not a pacifist, Williams was outspokenly critical of American involvement in what he considered a Vietnam civil war and was supportive of peaceful anti-war protests. Even more popular with student radicals was Harvey Goldberg, like Williams a UW history Ph.D. An unabashed Marxist, Goldberg was fascinated by leftist revolutions; students sometimes joked that no matter what the title of his popular lecture courses on social history he always featured violent uprisings and revolutions approvingly. A third history professor popular with student activists was George L. Mosse, a distinguished German-born expert on European cultural history. Mosse's and Goldberg's classes regularly attracted hundreds of students and filled the largest lecture halls on campus. Although Mosse was critical of the war, unlike Goldberg he stressed democratic values and opposed violence. By the end of the decade Goldberg had won the popularity contest with hardcore student radicals. It was to prove more than a little ironic that Harrington's protégés in his old department helped to nourish the student demonstrations that eventually brought down his presidency.

There was widespread public approval of Harrington's and Fleming's peaceful handling of the 1966 anti-draft protest. A few critics complained that University authorities should have forcibly ejected the demonstrators, and some protest leaders and faculty continued to condemn any University cooperation—even indirect—with the selective service authorities. Most, however, agreed with the *Milwaukee Journal*'s assessment that the demonstration had ended peacefully because of "the good sense of the administrators and of the overwhelming majority of the students."

> President Harrington and Chancellor Fleming, upholding the UW's long tradition of free assembly and dissent, kept cool, stated the university's position firmly but calmly, listened to the protesters' case and provided an honest airing of the dispute. The faculty has now backed the administration. Policies governing draft and selective service procedures will remain essentially unaltered.
>
> The UW seems to have shown the nation that a student protest can be a legitimate exercise in democracy, not a disruptive episode in bitterness.[21]

---

[21]*Milwaukee Journal*, May 26, 1966. The *Wisconsin State Journal* was similarly impressed that Harrington and Fleming had "showed the stuff that college leaders need today," and added: "Madison's police force may have felt frustrated, standing on the sidelines; but in their Monday morning quarterbacking they will have to admit that this was the university's game, and that the university played it well."

The Board of Regents shared this positive view, though several members questioned whether the administration's decision not to report class rank directly to the selective service authorities might not disadvantage some students in the draft.[22] For himself, President Harrington credited the good judgment and coolness under fire of Chancellor Fleming and Dean of Students Joseph F. Kauffman with having averted a potential "catastrophe." The whole affair, he told Fleming, had strengthened the new chancellorship system, which was "now firmly established."[23] As for Fleming, he told the faculty on May 23 that the key and unresolved issue was "whether we can maintain this University's great reputation for protest without coercion. So far we–and by 'we' I mean faculty, students, and Administration–have been almost alone among the great universities in our mutual willingness to tolerate strong differences of opinion among us without resorting to the kind of coercion which destroys a free society."[24] It was a good question, with the answer unclear but soon forthcoming.

Because the University continued to cooperate indirectly with selective service authorities, the more militant anti-war protest leaders considered the outcome of the draft sit-in a defeat. Over the next few months they stepped up their agitation against the Vietnam War. In October a few militants broke up a Democratic Party rally at the Stock Pavilion and prevented U.S. Senator Edward Kennedy from speaking over their constant shouts and catcalls. The heckling of Senator Kennedy may have succeeded in its goal of publicizing the anti-war movement, but it was mostly negative publicity. The action was almost universally condemned on campus and around the state and nation. The Student Senate even voted to place the offending Committee to End the War in Viet Nam on provisional status and to monitor its actions in the future. With the example of the escalating Free Speech Movement at Berkeley very much on his mind, Fleming chose not to make martyrs of any of the protesters, though he recognized the stakes were rising. He warned the faculty:

> There are some students who apparently believe that they alone have the truth, and that this justifies them in insisting that all others speak on their terms. A few such students

Wisconsin State Journal, May 25, 1966.
[22]UW BOR Minutes, June 10, 1966, UA.
[23]Harrington to Fleming, May 27, 1966, Series 4/19/1, Box 38, UA.
[24]Press release, Remarks of Chancellor R.W. Fleming to a Meeting of the Madison Campus Faculty, May 23, 1966, Series 4/19/1, Box 38, UA.

seem determined to bring about a confrontation which will result in disciplinary action. Nevertheless, our tactics and our actions must not be geared to theirs.[25]

Increasingly, UW administrators and the student protesters were acting on different premises and talking past each other.

On February 21, 1967, the Madison SDS chapter organized a march of about a hundred students to the Commerce and Chemistry buildings to protest job recruiting by the Dow Chemical Company, the leading manufacturer of napalm (jellied gasoline) bombs for the war. With the support of the faculty University Committee, Chancellor Fleming had previously warned against any obstruction of buildings or interview rooms by the demonstrators:

> The University Administration has consistently taken the position that freedom on the campus is not divisible. If students who wish to interview a prospective employer can be prevented from doing so, they can also be prevented from hearing a speaker to whom some persons object. However, idealistic the motive, neither tactic is permissible on a campus which cherishes freedom.
>
> The proposed action, if taken, will constitute an attack upon the University and will be treated as such.[26]

The ensuing melee resulted in the arrest of two of the SDS leaders, both graduate students.

The following day several hundred protesters undertook an anti-Dow sit-in demonstration at the Engineering Building; University police arrested seventeen students when they refused to leave the Engineering Placement Office at the end of the day. The arrests mobilized additional student support for the protest, which Chancellor Fleming helped to defuse by announcing to a late-night campus rally that he had personally provided $1,155 in bail money for eleven of the arrested students who lacked funds to secure their release from jail. Fleming's action was roundly criticized by some who favored a tougher law-and-order stance, but was, he explained afterward, designed to blunt the force of the protest and head off its escalation to the point of mass arrests. Besides, he thought it unfair for some of those arrested, several of them in his

---

[25]Fleming, "Report to the Faculty on the Senator Edward Kennedy Incident," Madison Faculty Document 96, November 7, 1966. See also Fleming to John J. Walsh," November 10, 1966, ibid., box 58.

[26]Fleming, prepared statement, February 20, 1967; James R. Villamonte to University Committee members, February 20, 1967, Kauffman Papers, UHP.

view unsophisticated young undergraduates, to remain in jail when their wealthier fellows were able to make bail. "We've been close to another Berkeley," Fleming soberly told a large special faculty meeting the next day, which after discussion voted to endorse existing student conduct rules but to consider employment interview policy at a later meeting.[27] In a subsequent report to the faculty the chancellor said he was guided by his assumption "that the faculty wants to preserve dissent, but without anarchy, and that it wants order, but without repression."[28]

The anti-war protesters clearly did not speak for the entire campus. The disapproving *Daily Cardinal* thought SDS and its noisy followers should "shut up, go home, grow up, and come back when they are able to deal effectively with the very real problems that the University faces."[29] A hastily formed We Want No Berkeley Here Committee mounted a rally against the SDS protesters that drew 800 students to the Bascom Theater. "This is the first time I haven't felt lonely in a crowd in days," Fleming told them. For deliberately mounting an obstructive and violent protest, the Student Senate voted 19-11 to decertify the SDS chapter as a UW-Madison student organization. The action was subsequently enjoined by the Student Court, thereby creating a constitutional impasse and no penalty, but SDS leaders decided they needed to build more student support before attempting other mass actions.[30]

Privately, Chancellor Fleming boasted about his "pillow" strategy to handle the demonstrators: "students can punch the pillow but it moves over without greatly observable changes!"[31] President Harrington reminded the Board of Regents of similar demonstrations at many other universities and declared his intention to continue the University's long tradition of defending freedom of speech "even if the results are distasteful." While the University must itself be neutral, he cautioned, "it should not be neutral in the belief that young students should be involved in questions of public interest."[32] Perhaps because the more committed students believed such views patronized their deep anti-war convictions, tensions continued to mount during the remainder

---

[27] UW Faculty Minutes, February 23, 1967.
[28] UW Faculty Document 122, Fleming, "The Enforcement of Chapter 11 of the Laws and Regulations Governing the University of Wisconsin," March 6, 1967, UA.
[29] "SDS Protesters Negate Own Cause," *Daily Cardinal*, February 24, 1967.
[30] For a comprehensive day-by-day review of these events, see "Students Challenge Administration in Vietnam War Protest," *WAM*, 68 (March, 1967), 18-20.
[31] Fleming to Otto A. Silha, March 1, 1967, Series 4/19/1, Box 57, UA.
[32] UW BOR Minutes, March 10, 1967.

of the spring semester. There was another large anti-war demonstration against job interviewing by the Central Intelligence Agency, protests against the University's trial pedestrian bridge across Park Street at the Memorial Union, and finally a mass blocking of west-bound University Avenue on the afternoon of May 17 to protest the city's installation of a wrong-way east-bound bus lane, followed the next night by sporadic trashing of the windows of State Street businesses.[33] The unrelated character of these demonstrations suggested that for some students, including increasing numbers of undergraduates, confrontation and mass action were becoming a preferred form of public discourse.

Chancellor Sewell's Turbulent Year

Robben Fleming departed for his new post as president of the University of Michigan in the late summer of 1967. He was succeeded as chancellor by Vilas Professor of Sociology William H. Sewell.[34] To most of the faculty Sewell seemed an ideal choice. Largely responsible for building his nationally ranked department, he had been at the University since 1946 and was widely respected for his scholarship and his leadership of the campaign to open WARF research support to all segments of the faculty. He had, in fact, just been elected as chairman of the faculty's prestigious University Committee. A distinguished demographer, he hoped to continue his active research program during his administrative service. Like Fleming and Harrington, Sewell was personally opposed to the U.S. intervention in Vietnam and like them was committed to maintaining an open campus. He argued that individuals but not universities were free to take a moral stand against the war. The editors of the *Daily Cardinal* were inclined to give Sewell the benefit of the doubt. Paul Soglin, a self-styled radical columnist for the paper, applauded Sewell's anti-war views and pointed out approvingly that on the University Committee he was "the one professor most sympathetic and responsive to the needs of the students."[35] As the new

---

[33]The demonstration against the wrong-way bus lane on University Avenue followed a tragic accident in which a UW senior, Donna Schueler, lost her leg after stepping accidentally into the path of a city bus traveling east on the otherwise one-way west-bound thoroughfare. City authorities eventually agreed that east-bound buses, like other traffic, would have to use one-way east-bound Johnson Street, a block to the south, despite some inconvenience to their University passengers. *Daily Cardinal*, March 3, May 6, 16, 17, 18, 19, 20, 23, 1967.

[34]UW BOR Minutes, June 9, 1967.

[35]*Daily Cardinal*, June 23, 1967. See also ibid., July 14, 1967. A native of

chancellor prepared to take office, however, comments by members of the Board of Regents suggested that a vocal minority of the governing board was becoming impatient over the campus disorders and the apparent inability or unwillingness of the University administration to control the demonstrations and to discipline student and faculty offenders.[36]

However promising its beginning, the Sewell administration lasted less than a year until the chancellor resigned on June 27, 1968, over his failure to restore order to an increasingly fractured and tumultuous campus.[37] Things unraveled quickly during and following a second and more militant protest on October 18 against the return of the Dow Chemical Company for employment interviews. The Sewell administration had unwisely scheduled these in the Commerce Building in the heart of the campus. More numerous and more militant this time, the anti-Dow demonstrators crowded into the halls, disrupting classes as well as blocking access to the interview rooms. With University police unable to control the situation, Sewell authorized a call for reinforcements from the Madison city police, who used their billy clubs to remove the demonstrators from the building and eventually employed tear gas to clear the area. The action radicalized some previously uncommitted students and triggered a class strike the following day that was honored by large numbers of undergraduates and teaching assistants, especially in the College of Letters and Science and the School of Education. Harrington and Sewell suspended 13 demonstrators pending court action and disciplinary review; eventually a number of these served jail sentences and three were expelled. Responding to faculty concern about the handling of the Dow riot, the University Committee put together an ad hoc student-faculty committee chaired by law Professor Samuel Mermin to review the handling of obstructive demonstrations and campus employment interview policy.[38] Such

---

Chicago, Soglin was currently a WSA senator and history graduate student. Over the next several years he took an increasingly prominent role in the campus anti-war movement. While a law student he was elected to the Madison common council, and during the 1970s and again in the 1990s he twice served as Madison's mayor.

[36] See the extended discussion in UW BOR Minutes, June 9, 1967.

[37] Sewell to Harrington, June 27, 1968; Harrington to Sewell, June 29, 1968, Series 40/1/1-1, Box 143, UA.

[38] Besides Mermin, the committee consisted of Professors J. Ray Bowen (chemical engineering), E. David Cronon (history), Haskell Fain (philosophy), Stephen C. Kleene (mathematics), Hugh T. Richards (physics), and Norman B. Ryder (sociology), all appointed by the University Committee; and an equal number of students

temporizing drew only sarcastic contempt from the more militant protesters:

> Today the university faculty passed a momentous piece of legislation. In the wake of student disruption of the university's status quo and the riot squad's attack on the students, the faculty has taken decisive action. It has called for a committee. A committee to "draft recommendations" and review all the facts. . . . The faculty was unflinching in its seizure of power from the administration.[39]

Much to the unhappiness of some regents, who believed the board had given a clear directive to continue on-campus job interviews, the chancellor postponed several other controversial interviews pending the report of the Mermin Committee. This headed off further anti-Dow (though not other) demonstrations during the year but probably fatally undermined Sewell's standing with an increasingly hard-line faction on the Board of Regents. Indeed, President Harrington felt obliged to defend Sewell before the angry regents after this action.[40]

Sewell also demonstrated independence from his old friend and patron, the president. When Harrington announced publicly he intended to recommend that the Board of Regents summarily fire Robert Cohen, a philosophy teaching assistant, for his obstructive conduct in the Dow protest, Sewell courageously rebuked the president. The regents, he declared in a press release the next day, should "not prejudge a person's guilt pending the final determination of his case." Cohen was entitled to full due process before any action was taken on his University employment, he said.

---

selected by the Wisconsin Student Association: Gary L. Baran (LS 5, sociology), Andrew H. Good (BA 4, history), Roland Liebert (LS 5, sociology), James F. Marty (Bus 4, actuarial science), Wendy K. Rifkin (BA 3, history), Joel Samoff (LS 5, political science), and Toni L. Walter (Bus 4, marketing).

[39]"Pre History," undated, unsigned leaflet handed out October 23, 1967, Kauffman Papers, UHP. See also other assorted anti-Dow leaflets, ibid. Following what came to be known as Dow II, the Teaching Assistants Association published a thoughtful 61-page pamphlet, *Strike*, providing a detailed review and analysis of the major UW anti-war protests beginning with the 1966 anti-draft sit-in. It should be consulted for its useful time-line of the background events leading up to the obstruction of the Commerce Building on October 18, as well as its critical analysis of administration and faculty response. For a contemporary summary and some interesting photographs from an official University perspective, see "Day of Obstruction–The Dow Protest," *WAM*, 69 (November, 1967), 4-9.

[40]UW BOR Minutes, February 16, 1968.

The beginning of the Dow II protest, October 18, 1967. UA, X25-3384.

The end of the DOW II protest, *Capital Times* photo, UA, X25-3176.

I see no great danger to this University if Mr. Cohen continues performing his duties as a teaching assistant; if his rights are violated, however, this threatens all of us and the integrity of our institution. . . .

Thus I must affirm as a person, as a teacher, and as chancellor of this campus, that I find the recommendation that Mr. Cohen be dismissed before completion of due process unacceptable, and I intend to recommend to the regents that they avoid such actions that will damage the credibility, integrity and reputation of this fine University. Whatever the legal powers of the regents may be in this matter, they can best serve the University and our society by demonstrating to all a sense of wisdom and fairness in the heat of controversy.[41]

The discomfited Harrington promptly issued a follow-up press release explaining rather lamely that of course he intended to recommend that the regents give Cohen "full opportunity for due processes in connection with the recommendation for his dismissal."[42]

The president was obviously finding it difficult to respond to the demands of the University's many constituencies on and off campus, while also delegating authority (and responsibility) under the new chancellor administrative structure. One of his concerns was a bill introduced in the legislature two days after what was quickly called Dow II responding to the widespread perception that out-of-state activists were responsible for the recent violence. The bill proposed to limit non-residents to 15 percent of the total enrollment at any public university in Wisconsin and to establish certain priorities for their admission. It also noted gratuitously that "the faculties of the public university systems in this state are heavily dominated by persons not natives of this state," a veiled suggestion that perhaps legislation might be needed to deal with this problem, too.[43] The State Senate quickly set

---

[41]UW News and Publications Service, Sewell press release, November 17, 1967, Series 4/20/1, Box 21, UA.

[42]UW News and Publication Service, Harrington press release, November 17, 1967, ibid.. Cohen subsequently refused to attend his disciplinary hearing and was dropped as both a teaching assistant and a student.

[43]Assembly Bill 1040, October 24, 1967, Kauffman Papers, UHP. The threat of legislative quotas on non-resident enrollment set off a flurry of expressions of concern and intense lobbying by University administrators, faculty, and the state Coordinating Committee for Higher Education. For the fall of 1967, 29.6 percent of UW-Madison's undergraduates and 67.6 percent of its graduate students were non-residents. A 15 percent limit on non-resident students would have reduced their numbers by 8,203 and would have cut the University's income by $9 million. Such a limit would be especially

up a select committee under the chairmanship of Republican Lieutenant Governor Jack B. Olson to investigate "the riotous and unlawful activities of the week of October 16, 1967, occurring on the Madison campus of the University of Wisconsin."[44]

For the most part, Harrington was content to let Sewell and his aides handle the growing student unrest on the Madison campus, which the president saw as the first real test of his chancellor system. From Harrington's perspective, one of the advantages of the new layered administrative structure was that he could be somewhat insulated from the more controversial happenings on the campuses. The difficulty was that he and the regents never spelled out the extent of the chancellors' authority, and the board and the public held the president ultimately responsible for everything that happened in Harrington's "single" university. Thus as Madison Vice Chancellor Atwell once shrewdly commented, "because survival is Fred's dominant instinct and because he is an innately aggressive administrator, he will frequently intervene in the grossest kind of way if it suits him. I guess that is the Admiral's privilege."[45]

The Crow Committee to consider how to respond to the WSA student power demands and the Mermin Committee to investigate the DOW riot reported late in the spring of 1968 after working simultaneously during much of the year and to some extent considering related and over-lapping issues. Although anti-war and especially anti-draft agitation had continued after Dow II, the existence of these two important student-faculty groups may have had a calming effect on the student body. So too did Chancellor Sewell's quick response to the assassination of the widely respected black civil rights leader Martin Luther King in the spring of 1968. Sewell promptly suspended classes for a campus-wide memorial service, launched a program of scholarships for disadvantaged minority students, and appointed a committee under the experienced leadership of education Professor Wilson B. Thiede to consider how to improve race relations at the University and

---

damaging to the Madison Graduate School, which was indisputably a national, even international, resource and whose programs attracted students from all across the country and around the world. See CCHE #80, Informational Item, November, 1967, ibid.

[44]Senate Resolution 13m, Senate Sub. Amendment 1 (1967). Student activists promptly filed suit in federal court to block this investigation on the ground that it would violate the first amendment of the U.S. Constitution. See *Connections*, November 27, 1967.

[45]Atwell to Chancellor H. Edwin Young, September 17, 1968, Series 4/21/1, Box 1, UA.

increase its minority enrollment, course content, and services.[46] These actions, coupled with the relatively small number of black students and the preoccupation of most student activists with the Vietnam War, helped head off the rioting that occurred elsewhere in the country after the King assassination. The most ominous event of the spring term was the firebombing of South Hall, the headquarters of the College of Letters and Science, in the early morning hours of May 19. The quick alarm sounded by an after-hours janitor confined the blaze to one room and limited the destruction to its furnishings and some student academic records. No group claimed responsibility and the crime was never solved, but the event suggested that some activists were moving well beyond rallies and picketing.[47]

Although the faculty and eventually the regents accepted most of the recommendations of the Crow Committee on the student power question,[48] neither the University Committee, the Madison faculty in a highly charged three-hour meeting, nor ultimately the Board of Regents accepted the major recommendation of the badly split Mermin Committee created to review the Dow riot. By a primarily student majority, the committee sought to assure University neutrality in the present highly charged atmosphere through "a moratorium on all employment and recruitment interviews on campus by outside agencies." The decision as to when to lift the moratorium would be left up to the Wisconsin Student Association.[49] The Mermin Committee consisted of seven

---

[46]Sewell to Bernard C. Cohen, E. David Cronon, Philip D. Curtin, Burton R. Fisher, Sterling Fishman, G.W. Foster, A.O. Haller, Robert J. Lampman, Michael Lipsky, Martin B. Loeb. Russell Middleton, Robert J. Miller, Walter B. Rideout, and Wilson B. Thiede, May 15, 1968; UW press release, May 16, 1968, ibid., box 18. It should be pointed out that one of the authors of this volume, E. David Cronon, was an appointed faculty member of the Mermin and Thiede Committees. He was also an elected member of the University Committee in 1969-72.

[47]*Daily Cardinal*, May 21, 1968. One can only speculate as to the motivation behind the South Hall firebombing. The tactic had been used by black rioters in racial uprisings in Watts in 1965 and Detroit and Newark in 1967 and in many U.S. cities following the King assassination in 1968. The firebomb or "molotov cocktail" was also regarded by white student leftists as a cheap and easily manufactured weapon of proletarian revolution.

[48]See above, pp. 442-46.

[49]UW Faculty Document 191, "Report of UW-Madison the Ad Hoc Committee on Mode of Response to Obstruction, Interview Policy, and Related Matters," March 13, 1968. The proposed moratorium may have had quiet backing from the chancellor. Sewell's sociology department colleague, Norman B. Ryder, a Canadian citizen, was the chief faculty proponent of the moratorium within the Mermin Committee and privately kept Sewell informed of the committee's deliberations. See "Norm" to

faculty members appointed by the University Committee and, in an unprecedented concession to the student power demands, seven students appointed by the WSA President and Student Senate. The latter group lacked a campus-wide perspective; 5 of the 7 students were from the College of Letters and Science, the campus unit with the least developed undergraduate placement services. The recommendation for the moratorium on employment interviews was adopted 8-6, with the majority consisting of 5 students and 3 faculty members. The remaining 4 faculty and 2 students submitted a lengthy minority report arguing that this important service to the student body should be continued. Michael Fullwood, the WSA president and a strong proponent of student power, applauded the Mermin minority's support of continued University job placement services. "I must emphatically reject the Majority Report," he wrote the University Committee. "It seems most clear to me that a majority of the student body favors the maintenance of the University Placement Service on the University campus. I do not think the rights and wishes of this majority can be ignored."[50]

Dow recruiters returned unmolested in the spring of 1968, but with Chancellor Sewell's resignation in late June the campus braced for more uncertainty and likely trouble in the coming year. To a friend, Sewell explained, "The events of the year convinced me that I was the wrong man for the times and the situation at Madison."[51] The editors of the *Daily Cardinal* regretted any personal anguish the chancellor might

---

"Bill," February 28, 1968, with Sewell's notation, "Discussed with Ryder, 2-29-68," ibid. In any event, Sewell had ample reason to know the Board of Regents was quite unlikely to accept any full or partial moratorium on campus placement interviews, since he had been brutally criticized by some of the regents for postponing controversial interviews after the Dow riot the previous October. See UW BOR Minutes, February 16, 1968.

[50]Michael D. Fullwood to Eugene Cameron, March 11, 1968, Series 4/20/1, Box 7, UA.

[51]Sewell to William Bevan, January 14, 1969, Series 7/33/8, Box 1, UA. When a friend at UCLA inquired whether Sewell might be open to another administrative post elsewhere, his response was enlightening: "I am not interested in any administrative job in any university at the moment. If I were ever to be tempted again, it would be as President of a university with a good Board of Regents and at a place where there was real campus autonomy so that I would have no administrator above me. The California, Wisconsin and New York mega-universities, with Presidents second-guessing Chancellors, are no place for men with independent spirits. It is bad enough to have to deal with students, regents, alumni, legislators, and the general public without having to do it according to someone else's dictates and style." Sewell to Richard T. Morris, July 29, 1968, ibid., Box 3.

have suffered during his year of turmoil, but agreed he was "certainly not the man for the job."

> The kind of administrators which are needed on this campus are not liberal idealists–like Sewell or the also-retiring Dean of Student Affairs Joseph Kauffman. What we need here are shrewd manipulators.
> Both Sewell and Kauffman deplored the nature of their positions in that they were required to act more as policemen than educators. . . . A considerable number of students consider the administrators' hands stained with blood, although these two suffered as much as any one else on that day.
> What is needed is a chancellor who can do that kind of thing and not feel bad about it later. Or even better, one who can outwit the students as much as possible.[52]

New Leadership, Strategies, Problems

Sewell was succeeded as chancellor in September, 1968, by economics Professor Edwin Young, a labor relations specialist, long-time department chairman, and former dean of the College of Letters and Science between 1961 and 1965, when he resigned to become president of the University of Maine.[53] Chancellor Young took office as student radicals adopted a major change in strategy. Discouraged by their inability to win support from a majority of the general faculty for University-wide action against the war, SDS leaders decided to abandon their efforts to build a student-faculty coalition. Believing that "militant confrontations are absolutely indispensable for building the movement on campus," though also recognizing that such tactics undermined "the delicate work of laying the groundwork for a movement in the community," they decided to concentrate on organizing undergraduates at the department level. The Madison SDS newsletter explained the new goal:

> Beginning with the Dow demonstration of February 1967 and the subsequent Student Power debate, those segments of the faculty who had earlier expressed sympathy with the student movement cautiously began dissociating themselves from what they termed the new tactical and programmatic "extremes." Most student activists, however,

---

[52]"Educators in Administration," *Daily Cardinal*, July 2, 1968.
[53]UW BOR Minutes, March 15, September 13, 1968; *Daily Cardinal*, March 19, 26, September 17, 1968. See above, pp. 217, 219.

refused to recognize this turn of events. The splash of cold water (for many, though not all) came during and after the "Great Dow War" in October 1967, when the faculty–including "our friends"–repudiated the student movement and exposed themselves as bankrupt, i.e. adamantly liberal.

The October events clearly demonstrated that the student movement has left the faculty far behind, both in regard to program and willingness–"guts"–to fight. If the movement is to grow further, and if it is to grow in the right direction, it must completely abandon the old illusions about a common faculty-student movement. Indeed, it must recognize that the faculty, as presently constituted ideologically, are not only not on our side, but are our direct enemies. The student movement must turn away from the professors and concern itself with the only real campus constituency with a radical potential: other students, and in particular the undergraduates. . . . And to reach the masses of undergraduates, it is necessary to push the contradiction most relevant to their daily routine, the contradiction between student and faculty.[54]

Reflecting on the short-lived student strike after Dow II, another leftist analysis circulated widely on campus had similarly concluded:

Students as workers must first reach a certain stage of critical consciousness which understands in a fairly complete fashion the nature of repression in our educational factory and the necessary measures for freedom. . . . A real student strike would seek to *change the basis of power* in the university and society. UW strikers only pleaded with existing power for a fair deal. But given the conflict of interest between us and the irrational established power, there will never be freedom from fear and anxiety and force until strikers actively take over the means of established power or destroy that power through disruption of or withdrawal from the university.[55]

During the summer and fall of 1968 SDS formed student associations in a number of academic departments, mostly in the

---

[54]Abner Spence, "On the Correct Handling of Contradictions among the People or We've Got to Reach Our Own People," *The* [Madison SDS] *Call*, vol. 2, no. 6 (April 5, 1968), 1-4, SDS collection, box 43, SHSW. See also *Connections*, February 5, 1969.

[55]"The Activist Role," *Strike* (Madison: Teaching Assistants Association, 1967?), p. 30.

College of Letters and Science and the School of Education.[56] In addition to their anti-war activities, the new student groups issued sweeping demands for curricular change in their respective departments, including abolition or at least modification of the grading system and major changes in course content, requirements, and teaching methodology. Above all, they insisted on a co-equal voice for students in shaping the new academic enterprise. Whether regarded as a natural extension of the student power movement or merely a clever tactic to alienate more undergraduates from the faculty, the effort was clearly intended more for building a revolutionary undergraduate base than for accomplishing serious academic reform. The trick, one of the student activists noted, was to steer a course between academic reforms "which the university can co-opt" and the larger and more important goal of developing "a radical consciousness which insists on the necessity of building a revolutionary movement to destroy imperialism and racism."[57]

A large-scale survey of UW-Madison graduate student opinion in the fall of 1968 revealed considerable support for protest activity and student power, though the latter was most commonly defined as greater student influence over the curriculum, grading policies, and University governance. The survey revealed little interest in outright student control, or in the hiring of faculty and administrators or service on departmental committees. While the respondents believed some of the student agitation should be directed against the UW administration, most thought the targets should be off campus–the U.S. government and society in general. Few had a negative view of the faculty and in fact most believed the faculty should have the most important role in setting University policy. Most viewed student demonstrations positively, though less than half had ever participated in any kind of student protest, and 71 percent agreed the recent demonstrations had not disrupted their education. Support for various protest tactics varied considerably. More than 90 percent approved of circulating petitions and participating in rallies and over 70 percent supported picketing. Less than half supported class boycotts and only a quarter approved of

---

[56]The SDS chapter sought to radicalize freshmen and other new students through a 36-page *Student Handbook*, published in 1968 and sold for 10¢, which offered a critical analysis of the University and stressed the "powerlessness" of UW students. It also introduced newcomers to the activities of various left-wing campus groups.

[57]Jeff Herf, "Schizophrenia and Revolution," *HSA Newsletter*, undated [fall, 1968], 2, UHP.

sit-ins. While about half condoned non-violent civil disobedience, the respondents overwhelmingly opposed violence and thought students who disobeyed UW regulations should be punished by the University. Interestingly in view of the numerous campus demonstrations against job recruiters, more than half supported this University service. While most respondents opposed both the draft and classified military research at the University, about three-fourths favored voluntary ROTC.[58] Although there are no comparable data about the views of UW undergraduates at this time, the survey suggested that SDS activists had their work cut out for them.

As SDS leaders had anticipated, even in departments where there was a good deal of faculty sympathy for student anti-war activities, most faculty members were unwilling to relinquish control over instruction, grading, and related academic matters. Over the next few months a number of departments made good faith (and usually short-lived) efforts to create mechanisms to provide for a greater voice for their students in departmental deliberations, but these were derided by SDS as meaningless and insulting tokenism. The noisy campaign for greater student involvement in departmental affairs had an effect, however. Increasingly in the eyes of many undergraduates, the faculty now joined the administration as the enemy, unwilling either to confront the evil of the Vietnam War or to join with students in reforming the University.

The first of the departmental student groups, and the prototype for those following in other departments, was the History Students Association (HSA), formed over the spring and summer of 1968. By the end of the year there were more than a score of these departmental student associations. Besides the HSA, among the more active student associations were those in the Departments of Economics, English, Political Science, Psychology, Sociology, and the School of Education. There was also an association of radical science students. As the first and most ambitious of the new student groups, the experience of the History Students Association is worth detailing here. The history department provided fertile ground for SDS-sponsored academic reform in 1968-69, as it had experienced explosive enrollment growth during

---

[58]Vice Chancellor Bryant Kearl to Edwin Young, undated, enclosing UW Survey Research Laboratory, Graduate Student Survey, Fall, 1968, Series 4/21/1, Box 42, UA. The survey involved 556 graduate students in the humanities and social sciences in the College of Letters and Science: 338 non-residents (U.S. but not Wisconsin) and 218 Wisconsin residents.

the 1960s. By this time the department was overwhelmed with more than 650 graduate and 900 undergraduate majors, by far the largest number of any department in the University. Especially at the undergraduate level these numbers were more than the over-worked and under-manned history faculty could handle well. SDS activists correctly assumed these potentially disaffected students were ripe for organizing against their increasingly factory-like educational experience. The department faculty also included several political radicals and a larger number of liberals, at least some of whom the student activists presumed would be supportive of SDS objectives.

Comprised initially of less than a half-dozen SDS members, HSA made its presence felt at the very first history faculty meeting of the 1968-69 academic year. History chairman E. David Cronon had called a special meeting on short notice in order to advise the faculty of a confidential report passed on by Chancellor Young warning that radical students were apparently planning to disrupt some classes–including perhaps in history–the following Monday, the first day of the new term. Young thought the faculty should be alerted to this possibility. Cronon preferred to pass on the information verbally rather than by memo so his colleagues could discuss various options. When the faculty members arrived for the meeting, scheduled in a vacant departmental classroom, they found a small group of students present. Cronon informed them the room was about to be used for a faculty meeting. Responding that they represented the new History Students Association, the students declared their intention of participating in all faculty meetings. Their chief spokesman, Malcolm Sylvers, one of Harvey Goldberg's leftist graduate students, declared that inasmuch as they and the faculty alike were students of history, the student members of the department now demanded co-equal status in determining department policy. Not wanting either to establish a meeting precedent or discuss the rumored class disruption in front of the students, Cronon declined to call the faculty meeting to order as long as students were present. After some fiery speeches and a ten-minute standoff, the student group departed, vowing to return for future faculty meetings.[59]

---

[59]Besides Sylvers, the student group included undergraduates Mark Rosenberg, Billy Kaplan, and Francesca Freedman. Sylvers had very likely been informed of the unscheduled meeting by his major professor, Harvey Goldberg, the most radical of the senior history faculty. Goldberg had not alerted Cronon to the planned HSA intrusion, so it was ironic that his was the only history class to be disrupted by radical students the following week. For the HSA account of this confrontation, see Francesca Freedman,

This set the pattern for the rest of the year, with HSA students, most of them SDS members or sympathizers, attending departmental faculty meetings and noisily attempting to inject themselves into the discussion. In response, the department developed a rule that only faculty members could speak at department meetings unless one of the faculty present requested permission and received unanimous consent from the group for a limited student presentation. Because the HSA activists in reality constituted only a small proportion of the history majors, a more moderate rival group calling itself the History Students for Reform (HSR) soon organized. HSR students rejected SDS-style confrontation and violence but shared a number of the HSA goals for reforming the department and enlarging student participation in its affairs. The difference between the two groups was more one of style and tactics than of substance.[60]

Billy Kaplan, and Mark Rosenberg, "On Masters and Slaves–or Who Is the History Department," *HSA Newsletter*, undated [fall, 1968], UHP. See also *Daily Cardinal*, September 17, 18, 19, 1968, and a rather garbled and inaccurate account in Roger Rapoport and Laurence J. Kirshbaum, Jr., *Is the Library Burning? A Report on American Students, Student Unrest and Student Power* (New York: Random House Vintage Books, 1969), pp. 53-61.

[60]The announced goals of the History Students Association were: (1) governance of the University by students and faculty, including within the history department "equal authority of students and faculty"; (2) elimination of "the coercive tool of grading by abolishing the grading system" and substitution of "a mutual evaluation process"; (3) freeing students "from the coercive condition of financial insecurity by providing support for all students for the duration of their education"; (4) establishing "the primacy of teaching in the University by eliminating the pressure to publish and instituting a policy of hiring and firing teaching faculty on the basis of their teaching"; (5) making learning "a cooperative experience by instituting the teaching contract option, by which students and teachers decide on what they want to learn and teach, and by what means"; (6) abandoning survey courses to "allow students to take an active role by exercising their intellects on historical problems"; (7) changing the relationship of the University to society by increasing enrollment of minority and poor and working class students, using University resources for progressive ends such as expanding the School for Workers, providing aid for "those underdeveloped countries striving for independence from imperialism," and severing University connections with the defense establishment. History Students Association, *Critique and Program* (Madison: History Students Association, September, September, 1968), pp. 32-40. See also History Students Association, *Up against the Blackboard* (Madison: History Students Association, December, 1968), both in UHP.

The program of the rival History Students for Reform was less overarching but similar in some concerns: (1) student voting rights in department meetings and committees; (2) a student voice in faculty hiring, promotion, and firing; (3) emphasis on teaching rather than research; (4) a student bill of rights; (5) the right of students to determine with the instructor the structure and requirements of a course; (6) review of

To facilitate more orderly student input into department policy, Cronon and the history faculty created two student-faculty committees, one with three elected graduate student majors and the other with three elected undergraduate majors. To assure the widest possible student participation in the election, the department organized and paid for a mail ballot to choose the student representatives, confident the SDS-sponsored History Students Association did not speak for most of the history majors. The more moderate HSR slate swept the balloting, with an HSA representative winning only one of the six seats.[61] This rebuff did not end HSA efforts to participate in and disrupt department meetings, however, since the SDS goal was to radicalize the student body. In an attempt to maintain order, the frustrated history faculty eventually decided by a vote of 24-16 to permit only the elected student representatives to attend faculty meetings, a policy abandoned a year later after a court case involving the English department questioned the legality of closed faculty meetings.[62]

The English department in fact experienced even greater turmoil during the latter sixties than did the history department. Because all undergraduates were required to take at least one and sometimes two semesters of Freshman English, the department needed a large staff of teaching assistants and junior faculty to teach the many sections of

---

the present grading system and consideration of alternatives; (7) use of graduate students to teach new courses desired by students; (8) review of the department's policies for financial support and teaching assistantships; (9) recruitment and support of minority students; (10) formation of an active organization of history majors, which would produce a handbook describing and evaluating history courses; (11) initiation of a History Department Newsletter; (12) a history student-faculty lounge. HSR leaders explained that their organization was open to all students "who want change in the History Department but reject the idea that reform can only be achieved by rash actions or disruption of classes" in contrast with "history student associations whose commitment extends to chimerical schemes of revolutionizing society by radical techniques." History Students for Reform, "Program of Action," undated [October, 1968], UHP.

[61]*Daily Cardinal*, October 25, 1968. The lone HSA undergraduate representative was SDS activist William "Billy" Kaplan. The two student-faculty committees functioned with increasing difficulty for several years, but then lapsed because students found it difficult to recruit representatives willing or able to devote any substantial time to departmental administrative matters. The department then followed the practice of adding one or more students to ad hoc faculty committees dealing with issues of particular interest to its student majors.

[62]"In their attempt to resist the flow of social change," unhappy HSA leaders declared after the history department's ban, "the history department has . . . clearly acted ahistorically." *Daily Cardinal*, March 7, 1969. See also ibid., March 12, 14, 20, 25, April 1, 1969, February 14, 1970.

English 101 and 102. As the anti-war and student power protests mounted, department meetings grew increasingly tense and noisy, with students joining untenured junior faculty members in challenging the leadership of the senior faculty. A substantial part of the Freshman English staff became disaffected and radicalized, to the point where in 1970 the department's faculty majority concluded they had lost control of these two courses. They thereupon voted to abolish English 102 and to restructure English 101 into a remedial course to be taken by a small minority of entering freshmen clearly needing to improve their writing skills. This set off a curricular crisis outside the department that is discussed in Chapter 5.[63]

One of the demands by student activists in history, sociology, English, and a number of other departments was for a revision of the grading system, which the radicals claimed was coercive and constituted a barrier to true learning for its own sake. A few faculty members agreed with this basic proposition; others were troubled by the role grades had come to play in determining student draft status during the Vietnam War. For a variety of reasons, therefore, under student pressure a small number of faculty members across the University unilaterally adopted different grading policies during 1968-69. The history department, for example, discovered that several of its more radical faculty members were giving mostly A grades, thus essentially converting the regular grading system into an unauthorized pass-fail system. Because grade point averages played a significant role in awarding departmental honors, fellowships, and graduate assistantships, such unilateral experimentation had ramifications far beyond the particular course. In a stormy department meeting, a majority of the history faculty voted that any future deviation from the established University faculty-approved grading system must have prior departmental approval. The department also decided to annotate the transcripts of students in one history course offered the previous semester to explain

---

[63]See above, pp. 289-94. Two of the more militant campus protest leaders were English junior faculty: Assistant Professors David Siff and Francis Bataglia, both of whom were eventually let go by the department. The deep split among the English faculty was reflected in the annual vote for department chairman in 1970, several months after Siff had been notified that his appointment would not be renewed. After five ballots the result was: Charles Scott, 31; David Siff, 16; Robert Kimbrough (put forward as a compromise candidate), 14; abstention, 1. Inasmuch as Siff was effectively ineligible to serve as chairman, the Siff voters were simply showing their disdain for their elders. *Daily Cardinal*, April 22, 1970.

that it had not been graded on the regular basis and all students had received the passing grade of A.[64]

Assistant Professor Michael A. Faia of the Department of Sociology was a prominent faculty leader in promoting the grading revolution. Faia's refusal to use the conventional grading system led his senior colleagues to take over the grading of his courses in the summer of 1968 and was a factor in their decision not to renew his appointment a few months later, an action bitterly protested by the radical Sociology Student Association.[65] The rampant grading experimentation during 1968-69 led the University Committee to appoint an ad hoc committee on grading, which eventually recommended increased flexibility but continuation of the existing letter grade system.[66] A lingering consequence, at Wisconsin and elsewhere in the country, was the general inflation of grades and decline in grading standards during the latter sixties. This was more pronounced in the humanities and social sciences than in the more scientific and technical fields.[67]

Variations of the history department's often traumatic experience in dealing with its newly energized graduate and undergraduate students occurred in a number of departments during 1968-69, but

---

[64]Ibid., October 24, 1968, and February 5, 8, 1969.

[65]Ibid., October 15, 1968, January 9, 28, February 6, 25, May 24, 1969, April 10, 1970; "Faia'd," *Rhubarb: The Sociology Student Newsletter*, No. 7, February 3, 1969; Michael A. Faia, *Dunce Cages, Hickory Sticks, and Public Evaluation: the Structure of Academic Authoritarianism* (Madison: various student groups [1968?]), UHP.

[66]UW Faculty Minutes, November 4, 1968; UW Faculty Document 276 and Faculty Minutes, October 6, 1969; *Daily Cardinal*, November 15, 16, 19, December 12, 1968, May 24, October 7, 8, November 21, 1969. See also above, pp. 287-88.

[67]It is difficult to determine the extent to which grading standards changed during the quarter century covered by this volume, though there was a widespread feeling on the part of faculty members that both faculty expectations and their grading standards had declined. During this period the campus shifted from a 3 to a 4 point grading system and introduced several modifications that make it impossible to compare average student performance over time. One of the concerns about the grading changes introduced by the Buck Committee in 1971 was that the new intermediate grades of AB and BC, far from increasing precision in grading, would merely add another inflationary element. An ad hoc committee on grading in the College of Letters and Science commented: "Our intuitive judgment suggests that the trend toward 'easier grading,' where the C is treated as the D now is, the BC as the C, etc., is possible. In this committee's judgment, grading standards have already eroded too much. However, we cannot impose standards and we doubt that any grading system, no matter what symbols are employed, can solve the problem. Obviously this issue deserves further attention." Preliminary Report of the College of Letters and Science Committee on Implementation of the New Grading System, undated [1971], Series 4/31/5, Box 15, UA.

generally over shorter periods and usually with less confrontation and bitterness. For many UW faculty members the year was one of unprecedented student unrest. The assertions of student power at the department as well as the campus level was a challenging and often unpleasant experience with which they were quite unaccustomed. From New York, where he was a visiting scholar at the Russell Sage Foundation for the year, former Chancellor Sewell watched with dismay, telling an Arizona sociologist in the fall of 1968:

> I am particularly troubled by what is happening at the department level. I have always advocated student participation in university decision making. However, I do not think our students should have the major voice in department policy. Our students have been organizing and making the most unrealistic demands on the department. They not only want to be heard on curricular matters, a position which I share with them, but they are also demanding equal determination of budget and promotions to tenure. While I, of course, know that they are demanding much more than they expect to get, I find their tactics outlandish. I doubt that those of us who have grown up in the gentlemanly tradition, which has governed universities in modern times, will be able to adapt very readily to the new style of student faculty relations.[68]

Meanwhile, anti-war demonstrations of an increasingly disorderly nature continued. Ralph Hanson, the UW police chief, reported 20 arrests in November, 1968, up to that time "an all-time high" in the number of students arrested by his force in any month. "This seems to me," he told his supervisor, "a sad reflection on our changing campus environment and certainly a matter for increased concern."[69]

The Black Student Strike

The widespread agitation for academic reform during the fall of 1968 prepared the way for broad support by white students of a strike by black student activists early in the second semester. After growing agitation throughout the fall, leaders of the student Black Peoples Alliance issued first eight and then thirteen "non-negotiable" demands, including greatly expanded recruitment of minority students, faculty,

---

[68]Sewell to Raymond V. Bowers, October 1, 1968, Series 7/33/8, Box 1, UA.
[69]Ralph E. Hanson to A.F. Ahearn, January 16, 1969, Series 4/21/1, Box 21, UA.

and administrators, more black-run minority support services, and most important the creation of a black studies department in which black students would have co-equal responsibility for curriculum and staffing. The strike followed immediately on the heels of a student-organized symposium on the Black Revolution at which some of the speakers had advocated violent protest.[70]

The strike reflected both the growing militance of blacks nationally, including strikes by black students on a number of other campuses, and the impatience of some Madison black students with the progress of the Thiede Committee, appointed by Chancellor Sewell to deal with such issues after the assassination of Martin Luther King the previous spring. Ironically, the success of the strike, itself a manifestation of the growing movement for black separatism and black power, depended on substantial support from the predominantly white student body. This was provided by an unlikely coalition of disaffected groups: liberals concerned with righting America's lingering legacy of slavery and racist oppression, academic reformers, anti-war and anti-draft activists, the newly energized Teaching Assistants Association reacting to a current legislative proposal to end the remission of non-resident tuition for graduate assistants, and a number of influential undergraduate organizations including the WSA Student Senate and the *Daily Cardinal*.

Disruption of classes and growing violence by the strikers and their supporters, estimated to number at times as many as eight to ten thousand demonstrators, soon overwhelmed the UW police force, Madison city policemen, and county sheriff's deputies attempting to keep order on and around the campus. At the request of President Harrington, Chancellor Young, and Madison Mayor Otto Festge, Governor Warren P. Knowles took the unprecedented step on February

---

[70]*Daily Cardinal*, November 22, 26, 27, December 3, 5, 1968, and February 4, 1969; *Connections*, February 5, 1969; Black Students undated strike flyer [1969], SDS Collection, Box 43, SHSW. One of the saddest of the demands, yet symptomatic of the black power movement, was for the replacement of Ruth Doyle as the head of the so-called Five Year Program of academic and financial assistance for disadvantaged minority students. Mrs. Doyle had started the program in 1966 and had since worked primarily with black students to help assure their academic success. Although black militants agreed she was "a beautiful person," they demanded her replacement simply because she was white. In the face of this opposition she resigned the directorship of a program the Ford Foundation had described as one of the three best in the nation. *Daily Cardinal*, May 10, September 21, November 7, December 3, 11, 1968, February 4, 1969.

Chancellor Edwin Young meeting with demonstrators during the black strike, February, 1969. UA, 3512-J-1.

National Guard troops on Bascom Hill, 1969. UA, X25-2062.

12 of calling out the state national guard to keep the University open and functioning. The initial 900 guardsmen were subsequently augmented by another 1,000, and some of this state force remained on campus until February 21.[71] The legislature reacted angrily to the turmoil at the other end of State Street. With little opposition the assembly adopted a resolution calling for the expulsion of any student blocking access to a University building, while the senate passed a bill by an overwhelming 29-1 margin denying state financial aid for two years to any one convicted of offenses during campus demonstrations.[72]

The strike and resulting turmoil exceeded the wildest dreams of student revolutionaries. At a press conference Chancellor Young promised that the University would remain open, emphasizing that "the state of Wisconsin is more powerful than the demonstrators." The *Daily Cardinal* rejoined: "This University moved closer to self-annihilation Thursday, as its withered soul continued to be bartered away for dollars and votes, by an ignorant, self-serving governor and legislature, an unmoving chancellor, and a silent president."[73] Even after the national guard was withdrawn, a substantial police presence remained in the campus area. Altogether during the turmoil, 36 students were arrested and 3 suspended by order of the Board of Regents. Much to the disappointment of student demonstrators who had misjudged the support from some younger and more radical faculty members, an impressive 1,372 faculty signed a quickly circulated petition backing the University administration's "refusal to surrender to mob pressures."[74]

---

[71]See, for example, "Chronology of Activity Regarding Black Students," November 15, 1968 - March 25, 1969, Series 4/21/1, Box 20, UA; John Newhouse, "Black Leader at UW Seeks End to Injustice," *Wisconsin State Journal*, April 1, 1969; *Daily Cardinal*, February 13, 1969.

[72]Ibid., February 14, 1969.

[73]Ibid., February 14, 1969.

[74]"Unhappy First for Wisconsin," "As Students Reported It," and "The Blacks' Demands and the Chancellor's Reponse," *WAM*, 70 (March, 1969), 4-7, 9, 14-15, 24, 27; *Daily Cardinal*, February 18, 1969. Reacting against the turmoil in their department during the year, a substantial number of history professors signed the petition. This led *Connections*, a lively New Left campus periodical edited by several history graduate students to complain that the department was emotionally invested in appearances and lacked proper scholarly detachment from the strike. "What the vast majority of history faculty apparently cannot understand," the paper declared, "is the essentially historical nature of the crisis which grips us, and the futility of expecting the development of that crisis to conform to its preconceived notions of social assimilation." *Connections*, February 25, 1969. Eventually U.S. District Judge James Doyle, whose wife Ruth directed the University's program for disadvantaged minority students, reinstated the three suspended students on the ground the regents had not provided adequate due

This impression of faculty unity was misleading, however. At a tumultuous mass faculty meeting called by petition on February 19 to discuss the strike and the black student demands, by a vote of 518-524 the faculty only narrowly defeated a motion calling on the administration to reverse its decision not to admit three black students expelled from Wisconsin State University at Oshkosh for participating in a violent demonstration there.[75]

The black strike put great pressure on the student-faculty Thiede Committee on Studies and Instruction in Race Relations to finish its final recommendations on ways to improve University services to minority students. The key unsettled question was the strikers' demand for an autonomous black studies department in which students would have an equal vote with the faculty on curriculum and staffing. After extended debate the committee was unable to reconcile its differences on this issue. A narrow majority recommended creating a new Department of Afro-American Studies with its students having a substantial,

---

process. President Harrington quickly deplored this limit on campus disciplinary authority: "We are seriously handicapped by Judge Doyle's ruling in our efforts to take quick and decisive action to protect the university and its community from those who would disrupt or destroy it." *Daily Cardinal*, March 19, 1969.

[75]The admission of the expelled Oshkosh students was one of the thirteen demands of the striking black students. Indicative of the great faculty concern about the campus turmoil and the presence of the national guard, this unprecedented meeting drew about 1,300 faculty members to the Memorial Union Theater with another 150 participating by closed circuit television in the Wisconsin Center dining room. Students could listen to the proceedings in rooms B-10 Commerce and 6210 Social Science. Another indication of the importance of the meeting was the unusual presence of President Harrington, who thanked the faculty for its petition supporting the administration in opposing disruption and obstruction, declaring that "there had perhaps been no comparable expression of faculty opinion in the history of the University." The president explained that he and Chancellor Young had agreed it was necessary to call in the national guard and promised that the University would remain open. Those who disrupted its activities would "be punished under University and Wisconsin regulations with all proper protection under due process procedures." The University's tradition of faculty power was being threatened, he warned, and he called on the faculty "to live up to its responsibilities, to listen to students, but not allow them to take over control of the University, or force the Regents or Legislature to punish the University by financial reprisals or by reducing faculty power." UW Faculty Minutes, February 19, 1969; *Daily Cardinal*, February 20, 1969. Actually, the decision not to admit the expelled Oshkosh students was made by Harrington, not Young, though the latter may have agreed with it. The president realized, far better than the black students or their faculty supporters, that neither the regents, the legislature, nor the public would tolerate UW-Madison's admitting students simply because they were black if they had been expelled for violent conduct at another Wisconsin university.

though not controlling, voice in its affairs. The minority filed a dissenting report, arguing it would be wiser policy and in keeping with traditional practice to start with an inter-departmental academic program using an initial nucleus of existing faculty and courses and under regular faculty control. Such a program might begin immediately and could evolve into an academic department as it matured and gained experience and strength.[76]

Following further campus disruptions, the general faculty took up the Thiede Committee's recommendations on March 3 at another tense mass meeting in the Union Theater, with an overflow group participating by closed circuit television from the Wisconsin Center auditorium. On the key issue of whether to create an interdepartmental black studies program or a new academic department, either one offering a black studies undergraduate major, the faculty eventually voted 540-414 in favor of starting a new department, one in which students would have a representative but not co-equal voice.[77] Because students would not have equal authority in the new department, many of the demonstrators agreed with the *Daily Cardinal* that the Thiede proposals were "utterly unacceptable," "an insulting compromise," and "only token efforts" toward a needed broader reform of the curriculum. Mixing metaphors with hyperbole, the paper likened the faculty to "a flock of lemmings" marching blindly to the sea, "morally bankrupt, politically impotent, and intellectually emasculated. . . . But the sea is advancing to meet us–the tide is coming in," the *Cardinal* warned.[78] The black strike thus managed to combine black power with broader student power concerns, and its aftermath brought the further radicalization and estrangement of a sizable part of the student body. As it turned out, the

---

[76]UW Faculty Document 260, "Report of the Committee on Studies and Instruction in Race Relations," March 3, 1969.

[77]UW Faculty Minutes, March 3, 1969. There was a preliminary indication that some faculty members planned to amend the majority Thiede Committee recommendation to accept the black student demand for co-equal authority in the affairs of the new department. Chairman Thiede headed off this move by quietly letting it be known he would then change his vote and lead the opposition to his committee's narrow majority recommendation for a new department, throwing his support behind the minority recommendation for a more traditional interdepartmental program. With the outcome of the debate so much in doubt, proponents shelved their amendment. As finally approved, the new department was to be organized initially by a steering committee consisting of seven faculty members and two students appointed by the chancellor after consultation with the dean of the College of Letters and Science where the department would be located administratively. UW Faculty Document 260a, March 3, 1969.

[78]*Daily Cardinal*, February 20, 27, 1969.

faculty's refusal to grant equal or even substantial student authority in organizing the new Department of Afro-American Studies was a major factor in the subsequent development of a strong program of black studies at Wisconsin, sooner than at universities like Harvard where at about the same time the faculty capitulated to similar black power student demands.[79]

Another outcome of the black strike was as predictable as it was unwelcome to University administrators and faculty members. Increasingly convinced that much of the student unrest was imported, that non-Wisconsin students were playing a disproportionate role in campus protests, some members of the Board of Regents moved to set further limits on out-of-state enrollment. One of the regent hardliners, Dr. James Nellen of Green Bay, demanded information on the geographical distribution of out-of-state applications the previous fall, and especially the percentage of successful applicants from Illinois, New York, and New Jersey. The prospect of such enrollment restrictions, also being discussed in the legislature, was deeply disturbing not only to student leaders but also to the faculty. If applied to the Graduate School, such restrictions would devastate most UW graduate programs, which drew students from across the country. Thirty-six concerned L&S departmental chairmen promptly wrote Dean Leon Epstein, warning that curtailment of out-of-state enrollment would seriously damage the University and their academic programs:

> Given the context of our times, and the absence of any serious attempt to defend the proposal to restrict nonresident students on its merits, we can only conclude that this is a punitive response directed at radical and activist students, if not at the University community itself. If this be the motivation, it is misdirected, for it punishes the vast majority of responsible students and many innocent youth who aspire to attend the University of Wisconsin without altering the probability of student activism. While we strongly favor the application of appropriate discipline to those who violate University regulations, the proposal to limit out-of-state enrollment does not effectively address itself to this problem.[80]

[79]See Roger Rosenblatt, *Coming Apart: a Memoir of the Harvard Wars of 1969* (Boston: Little Brown, 1997).

[80]36 L&S chairmen to Leon D. Epstein, March 12, 1969, quoted in Judith S. Craig, "Graduate Student Unionism: the Teaching Assistants Association at the University of Wisconsin-Madison, 1970-1980," (Ph.D. dissertation, University of Wisconsin-Madison, 1986), p. 52. See also *Daily Cardinal*, March 6, 8, 12, 18, 20,

The state legislature also reacted to the recent campus violence and vandalism, with the senate launching a formal investigation. To the dismay of the editors of the *Daily Cardinal*, an early casualty was the University's biennial budget request. Speaker Harold Froehlich, the conservative leader of the Republican-controlled assembly, introduced five bills intended to forestall future disruption. The measures provided that (1) any student convicted of a crime arising out of a campus disruption at a state institution was ineligible for readmission for a year; (2) anyone using amplified sound equipment on a campus, if its effect was disruptive, could be punished by a fine of $100 or 30 days imprisonment; (3) university chancellors and presidents could designate periods when a campus and its facilities were closed to people other than students and staff; (4) any student convicted of a crime involving obstructive behavior, or who had been expelled or suspended, would be guilty of a misdemeanor if he returned to the campus; (5) the conduct of any member of the academic staff of a state institution of higher learning who was convicted of a crime involving obstructive behavior must be reviewed by the appropriate board of regents, which might dismiss the offender, who thereafter could not be rehired without the express permission of the board.

Testifying before the legislature's Joint Education Committee, President Harrington endorsed all five assembly bills, explaining that the new legislation was needed in view of calls for renewed campus violence. "We at the University have given a great deal of leeway to people who want to protest certain policies," the president declared, "but we have always opposed violence and actions which interfere with the rights of others." Having made this tactical move to the right, Harrington urged the legislators not to enact proposed drastic curbs on non-resident enrollment, leaving that determination to the Board of Regents and the state Coordinating Committee for Higher Education.[81] Governor Warren Knowles, with significant legislative assistance from his brother, state Senator Robert P. Knowles, managed to head off the most damaging anti-University bills. Still, the recurring turmoil, reflected in a violent block party in the Mifflin-Bassett Street student ghetto over the weekend of May 3-4, was undermining support for the University and its leaders in the legislature and around the state.

The black strike was the largest mass student action yet, involving at times over three weeks as many as eight to ten thousand

1969.

[81]Ibid., March 6, 1969.

demonstrators and considerable property destruction on and off campus. Student radicals were surely satisfied at this tangible evidence of their influence. James Rowen, a columnist for the increasingly leftist *Daily Cardinal*, cautioned, however, that the upheaval did not constitute a true revolutionary movement. "The strike was broken not by the Guard and the cops," he pointed out, "but by the lack of strikers' solidarity and especially the professors' refusal to join."[82] The latter was a continuing problem for the radicals, because violent protests eroded faculty support. Nor was it clear that the ambitious SDS effort to radicalize and organize students at the department level was building a lasting revolutionary movement. James O'Brien, an SDS organizer and UW history graduate student, gave a frank appraisal of the departmental organizing campaign to a national SDS leader in the spring of 1969. "I'm not sure what all this adds up to," O'Brien concluded. "It's next fall that will determine whether the department organizing will be permanent and if so whether it's a viable tactic for radicals. I'm much less optimistic than I was."[83]

Violent Revolution

In the year ahead student activists redoubled their efforts and came closer to achieving their goal, if not of triggering a full-blown revolution, at least of destabilizing the University and the larger society. Ending the Vietnam War became the overriding objective of increasing numbers of students in Madison and around the nation, and they grew more and more disillusioned with the seeming unresponsiveness of political and campus leaders. At the same time, student radicals fragmented into competing groups differing over anti-war tactics and their wider goals. While the war and the draft were unifying themes, otherwise there was wide disagreement over whether the solution required a thorough-going revolution and what its nature should be. In Madison, Students for a Democratic Society largely abandoned the departmental organizing campaign of the previous year, concluding that its results were mixed and too limited. The campus SDS chapter suffered from the same divisions that shattered its parent national organization following the street violence at the 1968 national Democratic convention in Chicago. Some UW SDS members shared the

[82]Jim Rowen, "No Sale / The Movement Isn't Yet," ibid., March 8, 1969.
[83]James P. O'Brien to Carl Davidson, April 26, 1969, SDS Papers, Box 43, SHSW.

violent outlook of the national SDS Weatherman faction and began calling themselves the Mother Jones Revolutionary League. They often helped spark the window-smashing and trashing that increasingly accompanied anti-war rallies and protest marches during 1969-70. Whereas such tactics had earlier been condemned by the editors of the *Daily Cardinal* and other student leaders, now they were more and more accepted as legitimate weapons against the agents and symbols of U.S. imperialist oppression.

Indeed, what distinguished the Madison protests in 1969-70 was their often violent and disruptive character and the justification, if not active participation, by many students and by the increasingly radical *Daily Cardinal*. "Tear up the country," Rennie Davis, an SDS leader and chairman of the National Mobilization Committee to End the War in Vietnam, urged 1,300 freshmen at an SDS-sponsored "unorientation" meeting in the Union Theater at the start of the fall semester in 1969.[84] New Left groups played a major role in planning UW activities in connection with a national anti-war moratorium on October 15, 1969, designed to build support for a march on Washington a month later. Chancellor Young rejected an ultimatum issued by local SDS leaders demanding that the University terminate its ROTC programs and the Land Tenure and Mathematics Research Centers.[85] The Land Tenure Center of the College of Agriculture studied the effect of land ownership policies in developing countries. Since it received funding from the U.S. Agency for International Development, it was viewed by student radicals as an instrument of American imperialism. The Mathematics Research Center had regularly been funded by an ongoing contract with the U.S. Army since its establishment in 1956. Its permanent faculty sometimes consulted at Army installations but most of their research was highly theoretical and unclassified. Like any pure mathematical work, it might have military or other applications, however. James Rowen, a radical *Daily Cardinal* columnist, published a series of polemical articles attacking the center as part of his larger condemnation—labeled "Profit Motive 101"—of the University's alleged support of the U.S. military-industrial complex.[86]

---

[84]*Badger Herald*, September 18, 1969.

[85]*Daily Cardinal*, October 16, 1969; *Badger Herald*, October 17, 1969.

[86]*Daily Cardinal*, March 11, 12, 13, 14, 18, 19, 20, 21, 28, May 14, 20, 22, August 5, 15, October 3, 12, 15, 1969. Rowen's anti-MRC research was summarized in a lengthy pamphlet distributed by SDS at campus rallies supporting the moratorium. Howard Halperin, James Rowen, David Siff, and Ed Zeidman, *The Case against the*

The day before the Vietnam Moratorium two women students–both SDS members–were arrested after disrupting an international MRC seminar on graph theory at the Wisconsin Center. They had thrown red paint at the speakers and participants to symbolize their indirect support of the war.[87] More than fifty meetings took place on campus on Moratorium day, and some faculty and teaching assistants devoted their classes to a discussion of the war. The event culminated with the largest campus rally yet, a packed Field House crowd estimated at 15,000. Among other speakers Jim Rowen denounced the myth of a neutral university: "It is up to you–the people–in this community, primarily the students and faculty, each and every day to militantly confront the warmakers and their cohorts on this campus."[88] Rowen's editors agreed, with the *Cardinal* going so far as to declare that the continuing presence of ROTC and the Land Tenure and Mathematics Research Centers on campus was not only "reprehensible" but "intolerable."[89] Another *Cardinal* staffer, Leo Burt, rejected the complaint of cynics that leftists had been co-opted by allowing WSA, peace groups, and other liberals to take over the leadership of the October moratorium. He called for 10,000 Madisonians to join the November anti-war march on Washington, "a brand new opportunity for the left to assume its responsibilities and make its presence felt . . . to demand the US out of Vietnam and an end to Empire."[90]

The largely peaceful nature of the October Moratorium and declining campus interest in the November Washington march stimulated some activists to take more direct action. In late November 300-500 students joined a noisy march around the campus waving North Vietnam flags and denouncing ROTC and University military research. SDS leader Billy Kaplan termed the action "the beginning of building

Army Math Research Center, Series 4/2/11, Box 36, UA.

[87]*Daily Cardinal*, October 15, 21, 1969. The two students, Margo Levine and Linda Stern, withdrew rather than face University disciplinary charges, but the Board of Regents nevertheless decided to sue them for $5,000 damages to Wisconsin Center furnishings. Ibid., November 12, 1969.

[88]Ibid., October 23, 1969. Following the Field House rally a large part of the crowd marched silently in the rain down State Street to the state capitol to conclude their anti-war protest.

[89]Ibid., October 17, 1969. The paper subsequently denounced campus administrators for not negotiating with SDS over its ultimatum and declared that the University's silence was "another proof of the invaluable role Universities play in maintaining American foreign and domestic policy." Ibid., October 28, 1969.

[90]Ibid., October 21, 1969.

a movement."[91] A smaller SDS group, disdained by some activists as crazies, charged into several UW offices wearing Army fatigues and brandishing toy machine guns. In early December SDS teams entered some of the larger lecture classes to mobilize students against the evils of American imperialism. Three SDS members were arrested after failing to leave and allow Professor Stanley Payne to teach his freshman European history survey course.[92] On Friday, December 12, a larger SDS march smashed windows in scattered campus buildings and attempted unsuccessfully to firebomb T-16, a well-guarded building housing the Air Force ROTC program, after which they seized thousands of student identification cards in the Peterson Building.[93] An SDS leaflet announcing the rally had promised, "The War Is Coming Home."

Also moved to take direct action was a 25-year-old Madisonian and sometime UW student named Karleton Armstrong, who had been a participant in the T-16 march. When Armstrong had enrolled in the University in 1964 he was a thoroughly square young freshman, warned by his eastside father to shun campus politics. He signed up for Air Force ROTC, went out for crew, and enrolled in courses for an intended major in nuclear engineering. An indifferent student, however, he was soon on academic probation. He changed his major several times and twice dropped out while continuing to live in the student ghetto and maintaining his campus associations. Armstrong was increasingly radicalized by contacts with Rathskeller Marxists and active participation in the anti-war movement. Something of a loner, he had concluded by late 1969 that marches and rallies would never suffice to persuade the U.S. authorities to end the war. What was needed was more forceful action to cripple the American war machine.[94]

After the campus emptied for the Christmas break, Armstrong returned alone to T-16 at 4:00 a.m. on Sunday morning, December 28, carrying two gallon jugs filled with gasoline. He smashed a window in the rear of the building, tossed in the jugs, and threw in a match. An alert agriculture student hurrying to work at the milking barn heard the

[91]Ibid., November 20, 1969.

[92]Ibid., December 10, 11, 12, 1969. Payne's teaching assistant, Brian Peterson, was reassigned after calling the professor "a pig" for using the campus police to restore order, and the University promptly secured a restraining order against further SDS disruption of classes.

[93]Ibid., December 13, 1969.

[94]Tom Bates, *Rads: The 1970 Bombing of the Army Math Research Center at the University of Wisconsin and Its Aftermath* (New York: Harper Collins, 1992), especially pp. 59-176.

glass break, noticed the flames, and turned in a fire alarm. By the time the fire trucks arrived the flames had mostly died out after scorching the cement floor and damaging some furniture. Using a pay phone, Armstrong alerted the new underground newspaper *Madison Kaleido-scope* and claimed the firebombing as the work of what he called the Vanguard of the Revolution.[95]

Armstrong's next move three days later was far more daring. On New Year's Eve he persuaded his younger brother Dwight to steal a small airplane from the Morey Airport in nearby Middleton and help him bomb the Badger Ordnance plant at Baraboo, which was manufac-turing gun powder for the Vietnam War. It was a risky and harebrained scheme, because a snowstorm was developing and Dwight had never soloed before, let alone flown at night. Still, they managed to reach the plant and drop Karl's homemade bombs–three large mayonnaise jars filled with a mixture of ammonium nitrate fertilizer and kerosene. The bombs failed to explode because Armstrong had not realized they needed an explosive ignition device. The two brothers then managed to land safely at the deserted Sauk Prairie airport, where Karl's girl friend Lynn Schultz was waiting with her car's headlights illuminating the darkened runway. This time Karl attributed the bombing attempt to a mysterious New Year's Gang. It was not until after the somewhat skeptical *Kaleidoscope* printed a story about the attack that police and Badger officials discovered the unexploded ANFO bombs.[96]

Frustrated that his anti-war campaign had gained little attention or results, early on Saturday morning January 3, Armstrong tossed a gallon vinegar jar filled with gasoline through a window in the old Red Gym on Langdon Street. Used primarily for recreational sports, the building also housed the Army ROTC program. The jar shattered against a brick wall inside, and the gasoline easily ignited when he

---

[95]Ibid., pp. 154-56; *Madison Kaleidoscope*, January, 1970. Mark Knops, the editor of *Kaleidoscope*, quoted the unidentified caller as warning: "The policy of our group is to increase the level of violence against both on-campus and off-campus institutions of repression. On the campus, our activity will escalate until the University administration accedes to the demands of SDS and other student power-oriented groups. The level of violence will be raised until either these demands are met or the University physical plant is destroyed and the institution shut down."

[96]Bates, *Rads*, pp. 156-66; *Kaleidoscope*, January, 1970. Because his bombs had not exploded, Karl had trouble convincing the press that the bombing attempt had actually taken place. Eventually after several anonymous telephone calls he persuaded *Kaleidoscope* to publish a report of the attack. Only then did the police and employees at the Badger Ordnance plant discover his makeshift bombs.

tossed in a flaming newspaper. This time Karl succeeded in setting off a major conflagration in the historic building, which burned unnoticed for two hours before a security guard reported what quickly became a three-alarm fire involving eleven fire engines before the blaze was extinguished. The arson attack was featured news around the state, though ironically the ROTC offices in the rear of the building escaped the flames. The following night Armstrong attempted to firebomb the unmarked selective service headquarters on Capitol Court but mistakenly hit the nearby UW Primate Laboratory instead. Researchers working inside quickly turned in an alarm and the fire was extinguished with minimal damage. Shaken by this miscue, Armstrong decided to call a halt to what he called his winter offensive against the war.[97]

When students returned for classes after the Christmas break, the recent firebombings dominated campus discussion. Notable was the reaction of the *Daily Cardinal*, which abandoned its past stance against violence and in an editorial titled "The End of the Road" applauded the unknown bombers:

> There are some, perhaps many in the movement who see one and only one way of renewing and strengthening the fight for change. Several of those people, whoever they are, were responsible for the firebombings of the Red Gym, the Primate Lab and the State Selective Service headquarters in the last four days. They call themselves the Vanguard of the Revolution. They are indeed. They have chosen to initiate direct action. They have chosen to show to those both in and outside the movement that the immobile and repressive position taken by this nation can only be countered head on in the streets with bombs and guns.
>
> It is a new phenomenon on this campus, that the very men who have passed the repressive laws, called in the National Guard, summoned Dane County Sheriffs and refused to listen at all to calls for change, are now very much against the wall, trembling not only for the safety of their institution but for their own safety as well. We can have no sympathy for them. They are receiving the inevitable product of their actions.
>
> If acts as those committed in the last few days are needed to strike fear into the bodies of once fearless men and rid this campus once and for all of repressive and deadly ideas and institutions then so be it.[98]

[97]Bates, *Rads*, pp. 170-76; *Kaleidoscope*, January, 1970; "Bad Days for Old Red," *WAM*, 71 (February, 1970), 6-8.

[98]*Daily Cardinal*, January 6, 1970.

This endorsement of terrorism, the first in the country by a college student newspaper, received national press attention and condemnation. The president of the Board of Regents thought the board should consider ejecting the paper from the campus.[99] The upstart *Badger Herald*, the new weekly student paper created the previous fall as a conservative response to the increasingly leftist *Cardinal*, soberly warned that firebombing was "dangerous business," because of the likelihood that people could be hurt even if the bombers' intent was only to attack property.[100] Most Madison peace organizations, the officers of the Wisconsin Student Association, and even the radical Young Socialist Alliance also denounced the bombings. An exception was SDS, whose members voted to endorse the recent violence as "a blow against the day-to-day terror perpetuated around the globe by the ruling class system of American imperialism."[101] The radical *Kaleidoscope* likewise applauded the New Year's Gang, even publishing a cartoon showing how to make a molotov cocktail. "The bombings were PROPAGANDA BY THE DEED," the paper declared, "acts of resistance designed to create a mass movement."[102]

Early in the second semester a fragmented SDS, supported by the *Daily Cardinal*, began organizing against the General Electric Company, a war contractor some of whose workers were currently engaged in a strike marred by violence. Other campus leftists and peace groups joined to support a February 12 rally against the visit of GE recruiters.[103] "G.E. Off Campus," proclaimed the *Cardinal*:

> We urge all students to attend the rally. It will be a unique and important opportunity to confront what in a symbolic sense may . . . be your next employer. It will be a crucial time to say no to the dissemination of a destructive technology, to say no to the worker and consumer abuse, to say no to exploitation of blacks and women and people of the third world.[104]

[99]UW BOR Minutes, January 16, 1970; *Daily Cardinal*, registration issue, February, 1970.
[100]"Firebombings–Dangerous Business," *Badger Herald*, registration issue, January, 1970, p. 4.
[101]Bates, *Rads*, p. 184; *Daily Cardinal*, January 9, 1970. One SDS member explained, "These were revolutionary acts, and I never thought I'd see the day when the *Daily Cardinal* would be more revolutionary than SDS."
[102]*Kaleidoscope*, January 14, 1970.
[103]"Confront GE," *Daily Cardinal*, February 7, 10, 11, 1970.
[104]Ibid., February 12, 1970.

Repulsed by tear gas employed by police guarding the engineering placement office, hundreds of anti-GE protesters then went on an unprecedented destructive rampage across the campus and up State Street, smashing windows and spray painting leftist graffiti such as the slogan "New Year's Gang–Live Like Them!" scrawled on the campus YMCA building. Later that night someone firebombed the Kroger's supermarket on University Avenue, the largest grocery store in the immediate campus area.[105] *Cardinal* columnist Jim Rowen exulted over this evidence of developing revolutionary spirit:

> The students successfully integrated G.E., ROTC, AMRC, Krogers', Devine and others into the one system which they constitute. Combining understanding and action, students hit their precisely defined oppressors harder and longer than ever before in this city–and that is revolutionary.[106]

Karleton Armstrong was likewise inspired by the anti-GE violence in Madison, which had occurred while he was hiding out at his uncle's home in Minneapolis. He decided to return and mount another attack against the Badger Ordnance gunpowder plant. This time he would cut off its electric power by dynamiting one of the generators at the Wisconsin Power and Light Company's nearby Prairie du Sac hydroelectric substation on the Wisconsin River. Unaware of Badger's emergency backup generators, he fashioned a crude bomb of thirteen sticks of dynamite and blasting caps purchased in Minneapolis. His girl friend Lynn Schultz drove him to the power plant a little before midnight on Sunday, February 23. Placing the bomb proved more difficult than Armstrong had anticipated, because the generators area was both lighted and protected by a high barbed wire fence. Cutting his hand getting over the fence, he succeeded in placing the dynamite under a transformer, but had not yet connected it to a twelve volt automobile battery when he realized he had been observed by a plant watchman. Unnerved, he hastily scrambled over the fence and into Lynn's waiting car, leaving his disabled bomb and battery behind where they were quickly discovered by WPL employees. It was another Armstrong

---

[105]Ibid., February 13, 1970; *Kaleidoscope*, February 19, 1970; "Anti-GE Demonstration Becomes Riot," *WAM*, 71 (March, 1970), 6-7.

[106]*Daily Cardinal*, February 14, 1970. See also Leo Burt, "G.E. Thursday in Perspective," ibid., February 17, 1970. Rowen was subsequently arrested and jailed for his activities on GE Day. Ibid., February 25, 1970.

fiasco, but Madison leftists were heartened by news of the return of the New Year's Gang, the Vanguard of the Revolution.[107]

The TAA Strike

While his physical plant staff was busy replacing broken windows and watching for more firebombs, Chancellor Young was trying to head off a threatened walkout by many of the University's graduate teaching assistants. Organized by a small group of TAs in late June of 1966 in the aftermath of the anti-draft sit-in, the initial stated goals of the Teaching Assistants Association (TAA) were mostly of the bread-and-butter variety designed to improve the pay and working conditions of UW teaching assistants.[108] Although there was some radical rhetoric and talk of using the strike weapon, the group's first president, philosophy graduate student Warren Kessler, discounted such tactics at least initially, warning "there are scads of students who need our jobs." Later the TAA emphasized its origin in the anti-war and anti-draft protests and its concern for educational reform.[109] The TAA at first attracted little support among graduate students because of its peculiar blend of traditional trade unionism and leftist social action.

TAA membership soared, however, after Representative John C. Shabaz, the assembly's Republican majority leader, introduced a bill during the black strike to terminate the traditional remission of non-resident tuition for out-of-state graduate students holding assistantships. The bill was part of a larger conservative effort to reduce the number of non-resident students at the University, who were believed to be responsible for much of the campus unrest.[110] In response, the TAA sent

---

[107]Ibid., February 24, 1970; Bates, *Rads*, pp. 200-206. Armstrong left behind some valuable evidence if he were ever apprehended--human hair on the tape holding the dynamite together and a bloody thumb print. The bomb's components were commonly available, however, and the technology did not yet exist for a general search of fingerprints on file, let alone DNA analysis of hair fibers.

[108]By far the best account of the early history of the TAA is Craig, "Graduate Student Unionism."

[109]*Daily Cardinal*, June 30, 1966; Teaching Assistants Association, *TAA Handbook*, August, 1974.

[110]*Daily Cardinal*, February 5, 7, 8, 12, 13, 20, 21, 1969; *Connections*, February 5, 1969, supplement, p. 3, February 25, 1969. Shortly after the introduction of the Shabaz bill, the Republican-dominated Board of Regents voted to reduce the level of out-of-state freshmen students to 15 percent of the total by 1971-72, from the current limit of 25 percent. Faculty concern helped prevent the restriction from applying to graduate enrollment, which was about two-thirds from outside Wisconsin. As things

membership cards to all 1,900 TAs promising to fight the Shabaz bill and proposing that the organization be designated as the exclusive bargaining agent for campus teaching assistants. Although faculty members told their graduate students the bill had little chance of passage and they believed University administrators had been assured in any event that Governor Knowles would veto it, within a few weeks the union claimed to have signed up approximately 1,100 members.

Emboldened by the new strength of their organization, TAA leaders demanded that the University engage in collective bargaining and negotiate what would be the first employment contract with unionized graduate assistants in the country. At first Chancellor Young refused, citing the absence of legislative authorization. When a strike over the issue seemed likely in the spring of 1969, Young agreed to begin bargaining provided the TAA's claim of majority support was confirmed in an election supervised by the Wisconsin Employment Relations Commission. The chancellor, whose academic specialty was labor relations, was later criticized severely by many faculty members for taking this action on his own authority, but his background had conditioned him to the belief that labor disputes ought to be channeled through an orderly negotiating process.[111] The union subsequently won 77 percent of the WERC-supervised balloting on May 15-16, gaining majority approval in 52 of the 81 campus departments employing teaching assistants.[112] Collective bargaining thereupon began under a

---

turned out, sharply higher non-resident tuition rates thereafter had an even greater effect on cutting out-of-state enrollment. See especially UW BOR Minutes, March 14, 1969.

[111]Young later came to believe that in view of the unstable radical union the TAA became, his decision to recognize and bargain with it was probably a mistake. "We gave in too much," he acknowledged to a group of labor relations scholars in 1980. In a subsequent oral history interview he noted his concern not to let his difficulties with the teaching assistants undermine the University's traditionally strong support from the state's organized labor movement, which might not identify with the TAA but would support the right of any group of employees to form a union. "I wasn't concerned about the TAs," he said. "I was concerned about our continued relation with the rest of the labor movement. . . . So that was the game all along—not to let our TA thing damage our relationship with bona fide trade unions." Craig, "Graduate Student Unionism," pp. 118-19.

[112]There were 1,835 teaching assistants eligible to vote across the University; of these 1,209 valid ballots were counted, with 931 voting for the TAA and 278 for "No Union." Although the TAA needed to win only a majority of the votes cast, it also won a narrow majority of the total eligible voters. In 21 of the 52 departments voting for the TAA, however, affiliation was decided by a minority of the department TAs. Ibid., pp. 124-25 and Appendix B, pp. 454-55; Andrew Hamilton, "Wisconsin: Teaching Assistants' Strike Ends in Contract Signing," *Symposium* (Logan, Utah: Utah State

path-breaking Structure Agreement under which the University agreed to recognize and negotiate with a union of graduate students.

Bargaining proved more difficult than Chancellor Young and the University's bargainers anticipated, owing largely to the inexperience, suspicion, anti-establishment ideology, and transitory character of the TAA team. The University team was headed by Neil Bucklew, a recent industrial relations graduate, who had been hired after the faculty members and administrators involved in developing the Structure Agreement realized how time-consuming the bargaining process was likely to be.[113] Because the TAA prided itself on participatory democracy, it declined to name a permanent bargaining team. Instead, team membership shifted constantly, regularly necessitating a review of past discussion and decisions. The union also encouraged its members to attend and observe the bargaining, sometimes leaving the UW bargainers wondering just who constituted the TAA team. A confidential TAA memo distributed to its bargainers and stewards after the first negotiating session laid down the union's strategy for the negotiations:

> 1. Convince yourselves that nothing new or significant will be forthcoming from the other side of the table.
> 2. Members of the bargaining team, stewards and other TAs should understand that because this process is a new undertaking for the TAA and because it is necessary for you to be aggressive at the table, some mistakes will be made along the line.
> 3. Convince yourself also that the guys on the other side of the table may be nice guys when they're at home with their families, but as representatives of the managements of this University, they're real bastards who are out to screw you.
> 4. Distinguish clearly between what is meant by tentative agreement on an item by item basis and package bargaining.

University Graduate Student Association, May 1970), p. iii.

[113]Bucklew was assisted by a large policy committee, also called the Committee of Thirty, consisting of a representative from each department employing fifteen or more TAs in the spring of 1969. A smaller and more manageable Council of Ten provided a core of bargainers drawn from the largest TA-using departments in the College of Letters and Science (chemistry, economics, English, history, mathematics, psychology, speech, and zoology), plus a member each from the School of Education and the College of Engineering, and three ex officio associate deans (two from L&S and one from the Graduate School, who also as faculty members represented English, German, and Spanish and Portuguese, all heavy TA-employing departments). Craig, "Graduate Student Unionism," pp. 137-39.

5. When they make bullshit proposals, you ought to make it clear to them that you consider them so.

6. Probably the biggest thing you have going for you is the fact that you're assumed to be radical graduate students, knowing little about the bargaining process and very skeptical that it works at all in meeting your needs. . . . Take advantage of the skills you've learned in the University environment: be extremely skeptical of anything they suggest, break down everything they suggest into small components that are easy to understand and can be criticized, question their assumptions, make them explain why they are interested in some item or reject another. . . . Save the rhetoric for times when either reporters are present, or someone from the central administration is present, or when you want them to believe that they are causing the negotiations are breaking down [sic].[114]

Gaining agreement with the TAA over the terms of an employment contract also proved elusive because of the union's broad agenda, which mixed traditional bread-and-butter demands with more ideological academic and human rights issues. The TAA sought to gain greater job security for its members through a guarantee of renewed appointments during the duration of an individual's graduate career up to ten years, a limit on the number of students in TA-taught courses, sick leave, and health benefits. It proposed that the performance of TAs be evaluated by department committees consisting of one-third students, one-third teaching assistants, and one-third faculty, rather than by the existing departmental faculty committees. TAA members argued this new approach would be a suitable model for the evaluation of faculty members as well. Recognizing that job security depended on funding, the union demanded to be involved in deciding on legislative requests, resource allocation, and budgeting. Some of the demands raised faculty

---

[114]"Confidential. For Distribution to TAA Stewards and Bargaining Team Members Only. Comments on the TAA-University Administration Bargaining Sessions–May 28, 1969," quoted in Craig, "Graduate Student Unionism," pp. 140–41. Craig speculates that the memo was written by James Marketti, a TAA leader and industrial relations graduate student, one of the few union members with a background in collective bargaining. Her review of the notes for thirty-three bargaining sessions showed thirty-five different individuals identified as representing the TAA, of whom eighteen attended only one session. Another twenty-nine TAA representatives were not identified by name in the notes. Although four TAA bargainers participated in twenty-seven or more sessions, under the circumstances it was difficult for the University bargainers to build a sense of rapport with their constantly shifting opposite numbers. Ibid., p. 139.

eyebrows, such as the union's proposed environmental standards specifying the size and form of TA office space and furnishings, including lighting levels, color, upholstery, leg clearance for desks, and atmospheric and acoustic requirements. Faculty members who typically shared typewriters and cramped office space in buildings some of which dated back to the early years of the University could only shake their heads in amused disbelief. Adding up all of the TAA demands, John Schmitt, the skeptical president of the state AFL-CIO, concluded the money "just wasn't there."[115]

More contentious was the TAA's emphasis on several human rights and educational planning issues designed at least in part to win support from undergraduate and graduate students outside the union. Arguing that "much of the structure and content of University education reflects and perpetuates an inequitable society through forms of explicit and de facto discrimination," the TAA demanded that the University and the union work to end discrimination "through hiring, admission and education policies," areas traditionally considered the faculty's domain. Even more controversial was the demand that each academic department engage in collective bargaining with the TAA to establish mechanisms giving students and teaching assistants a decision-making role in the educational planning of all courses employing TAs.[116]

These ideological issues threatened faculty authority over departmental staffing and instruction and consequently undermined support for the TAA among most UW faculty members and even within the traditional labor movement. In fact, Schmitt, the head of the state AFL-CIO, recommended dropping the educational planning demand on the ground that it was not a proper union issue.[117] TAA leaders responded that their organization was different. "If America is to be changed, it should be obvious that our generation is going to have to do the changing," declared a TAA newsletter. "What a parody of progress it would be for us to march backward eating bread and dusty butter as

[115]"Teacher Aides Press Participation Demands," *Milwaukee Journal*, March 13, 1970, in ibid., p. 120.

[116]Hamilton, "Wisconsin: Teaching Assistants Strike," pp. ii-iii.

[117]*Daily Cardinal*, March 13, 1970. The *Cardinal* cautioned the TAA not to yield on educational planning. "If they sacrifice the educational reform demand, if they get 'realistic' as Schmitt says they must, they are a bread and butter union. If they are a bread and butter union those of us who are committed to real change in this society, those of us who want control over the lives we lead so that we may begin to attack some of the vital problems this country is ignoring, those of us who have supported them thusfar, must withdraw our support and move on our own." Ibid., March 14, 1970.

we drag the polluted and competitive present into a lost socialist and democratic future."[118] Equally important, the educational planning issue was also an important means for the union to mobilize undergraduate support. Although University negotiators at one point put forward an educational planning clause, faculty opposition forced its withdrawal.

By early 1970 the bargaining was at an impasse. The TAA directed its team to conclude bargaining by January 8, after which, failing settlement, the union would take unspecified action. It eventually set a strike deadline for March 15. There was a flurry of further bargaining from March 11 through the late hours of March 15, until TAA leaders announced that the membership had rejected the University's latest contract proposal and were now on strike. Before this, the University administration had taken steps to prepare the campus for the first strike by any of its instructional staff in its 121-year history. L&S Dean Stephen Kleene, whose college employed most of the campus teaching assistants and where TAA membership was strongest, wrote his department chairmen on March 10 reminding them of the faculty's obligation to continue teaching and setting down procedures for determining which TAs were not teaching and should be removed from the payroll.

> . . . I have been quite amazed that queries came to me from TAs and faculty whether they would forfeit pay by going out on strike. The Chancellor has spoken on this; but it shouldn't have been necessary. No employee in a labor union–that is, any ordinary labor union–expects to be paid by his employer when he is out on strike, nor does he expect it to be concealed from his employer that he is striking. Which brings me to the even more astonishing circumstance that there are those–TAs and even faculty–who have suggested that they would regard as provocative such steps as the University needs to take to determine which of its employees are working during a strike.[119]

Aware that the by-now thoroughly radical *Daily Cardinal* was unreservedly supporting a strike,[120] the campus administration relied on

---

[118]Hamilton, "Teaching Assistants' Strike," p. iv.

[119]Stephen C. Kleene, Memorandum to Department Chairmen in the College of Letters and Science, March 10, 1970, quoted in Craig, "Graduate Student Unionism," p. 155. See also *Daily Cardinal*, March 12, 1970.

[120]On March 7 a *Cardinal* staff member explained why students should support a TAA walkout: "The TAA strike is the one chance that we have, as graduate and undergraduate students together, to gain the power which would allow us to control a

the University news service's *Campus Report* to inform students and staff of the University's side of the dispute. In a "Special Issue on the TAA Strike" on March 10, Chancellor Young appealed to the TAA leadership to reconsider. The head of the University bargaining team, Neil Bucklew, explained "What's It All About?" by reviewing the areas of disagreement and discussing the positions taken by the two sides.[121] A major communications problem was that few students saw Bucklew's report; most got their information about the strike issues from their teaching assistants and the *Daily Cardinal*. And now the TAA's emphasis on mandatory participation by TAs and students in educational planning and departmental staffing paid off in mobilizing undergraduate support for a strike.

"On Strike" headlined the *Cardinal* on Monday morning, March 16, 1970, promising, "Today we are going to close this University down." In response Chancellor Young denounced the strike as both illegal under state law and in violation of the TAA's own commitment at the start of its bargaining with the University. He pointed out that state labor leaders had declared the University reasonable and responsible in its negotiations with the TAA and noted that Local 171 representing UW blue collar workers had told its members to ignore the strike and report to work as usual. Young's lengthy statement was carried both by the *Cardinal* and the new tabloid *Campus Digest* launched by the campus administration to disseminate official University statements and reports about the dispute. The staff of the *Daily Cardinal* (whose press was now owned by the University and which printed *Campus Report*) objected to printing what it saw as a rival strike-breaking paper. The University therefore used the state printing division to produce *Campus*

---

few facets of our own lives. . . . We must strike both the demands and the principle; we must not accept any halfway compromises. We learned from the moratorium that a one-day strike proves nothing; to be effective, we must shut this place down. The success of this strike could set a greater precedent than most of us realize–we have before us our one chance to prove to the nation that we are determined to have control over our own lives." Three days later, in an editorial entitled "Why Undergraduates Should Strike," the paper declared: "The longer we wait, the harder it becomes to even begin. There is a long battle still ahead. Together we can win it. The strike is, in more ways than one, our best chance within the University yet." On March 11, with bargaining still going on, the *Cardinal* called for massive student support: "The TAA intends to picket every classroom building 12 hours a day. They cannot carry out such massive picketing on their own. They will need undergraduate, graduate student, and other support. . . .We must face the fact that the time for fooling around has stopped. Under the leadership of the TAA, we are going to try to close this University down."

[121]*Campus Report*, vol. 6, no. 3 (March, 1970).

Digest for free distribution to students and staff.[122] Young also established a telephone rumor center to provide prompt and authoritative information about the issues and impact of the strike.

The strike was most effective in reducing class attendance in the College of Letters and Science and the School of Education, most of whose instruction was centered on and around Bascom Hill where the picketing was heaviest. Although the University did not collect figures on attendance, the Space Management Office conducted surveys on the use of assigned classrooms. Throughout Tuesday, March 17, 157 of 406 assigned classrooms were in use in Van Hise Hall (where most of the foreign language classes were taught), 63 of 157 in Bascom Hall (English and the social studies), 73 of 182 in the Humanities Building (primarily history, speech, music, and art), and 52 of 78 in chemistry. The numbers were slightly higher but similar the next day.[123] Because the Teamsters Union initially honored TAA picket lines, the strikers also blocked food service deliveries to the dormitories and the Memorial Union, liquid nitrogen service to chemistry labs, and halted the campus bus service. There was little disruption of classes in the Colleges of Agriculture and Engineering, where the TAA had limited support.

Aware that it would be difficult to sustain a protracted strike, on March 18 the TAA sought the involvement of Professor Nathan P. Feinsinger, director of the Law School's mediation center. Feinsinger readily agreed, delighted to participate in such an historic dispute.[124] He began informal discussions with the two sides–informal, because the University administration had broken off bargaining at the start of what it regarded as an illegal strike. The University also sought a court injunction against the strike, arguing that it was irreparably harming the ability of students to get the education they had contracted for.[125] Student support of the strike varied considerably, with many students honoring and even participating in TAA picket lines. It was difficult to measure the true impact of the strike, however, because some students

[122]*Daily Cardinal*, March 17, 18, 19, 1970; *Badger Herald*, March 20, 1970.

[123]Craig, "Graduate Student Unionism," p. 162.

[124]"We were always looking around for fresh case studies," Feinsinger explained later. "This was ideal." Feinsinger, oral history interview, 1976-77, UA, quoted in Craig, "Graduate Student Unionism," p. 163. The chancellor was not overjoyed at this development. "I see no reason for another form of interaction," commented Chancellor Young. "We're not bargaining with the TAA, but we will listen to Mr. Feinsinger." *Daily Cardinal*, March 20, 21, 1970.

[125]*Daily Cardinal*, March 17, 19, 20, 1970; *Badger Herald*, March 20, 1970; *Capital Times*, March 19, 1970; *Wisconsin State Journal*, March 20, 1970.

marched on picket lines while also attending their classes and some strikers (and sympathetic faculty members) arranged to continue teaching their classes off campus.

For the most part the strike was orderly and non-violent, a development applauded as "a rare treat" by the conservative *Badger Herald*.[126] Not all strike supporters were committed to peaceful action, however. Someone purporting to represent the New Year's Gang threatened to begin bombing campus buildings if the University did not accept the TAA demands within a week. The Mother Jones Revolutionary League added its militance to picket lines, concentrating especially on the Mathematics Research Center. Some strikers welcomed this SDS support; other more moderate picketers left when the hard-core leftists joined the lines and sought to expand the protest beyond the union demands.[127] As the strike wore on, tempers and tactics escalated. On March 24 TAA President Robert Muehlenkamp and three others were arrested for blocking delivery to Gordon Commons, the kitchen and dining facility for the southeast dormitories complex. Later in the day another striker was arrested for blocking deliveries at the Social Science Building.[128]

The increased militancy may have been intended to show the strikers' resolve as the campus prepared for the ten-day spring recess beginning March 27. The TAA announced its intention to continue picketing delivery areas during the break and set a general membership meeting for Sunday night, April 5, just before the resumption of classes. But by this time pressures were mounting on the strikers to reach a settlement. Teamsters Local 695, which had previously honored TAA picket lines, reluctantly allowed the campus buses to resume operation. "The drivers have a limit as to how much they can stand," explained Donald Eaton, the secretary-treasurer of the union.[129] The University revealed that 318 striking teaching assistants would receive reduced pay checks on April 1, with another 167 adjustments possible after further review.[130] On April 3 Circuit Judge William Sachjten handed down his ruling on the attorney general's petition for an injunction against the

---

[126]*Badger Herald*, March 20, 1970.

[127]*Daily Cardinal*, March 16, 18, 1970; *Badger Herald*, March 20, 1970; *Wisconsin State Journal*, March 13, 18, 1970.

[128]*Daily Cardinal*, March 25, 1970; *Wisconsin State Journal*, March 25, 1970.

[129]*Capital Times*, March 30, 1970.

[130]Ibid., April 1, 1970. Most of the assistants whose pay was docked taught in the College of Letters and Science (302 out of nearly 1,400 total TAs).

strike, declaring it illegal and ordering the striking assistants back to work.

With the resumption of face-to-face bargaining during the break, it was quickly evident the TAA's educational planning demand was the most significant barrier to a settlement. For many teaching assistants this was an important ideological objective, essential for reforming education at the University; indeed, some were supporting the strike largely or only for this reason. TAA leaders recognized the issue was also critical in holding the allegiance of the union's undergraduate supporters. For a large majority of the faculty, on the other hand, retaining control over course content and instruction had become a bottom line matter. "They could close this university down until September and we still wouldn't give an inch," declared chemistry Professor Alex Kotch, a member of the University bargaining team.[131] The 1969 Structure Agreement, which laid down the scope and framework of collective bargaining with the TAA, had agreed there should be mechanisms in each department enabling a teaching assistant "to participate in a meaningful way in the educational planning for courses in which he shares a responsibility," and that these mechanisms were "a proper subject for collective bargaining."[132] University bargainers had come to believe, however, this contentious issue could more productively be dealt with outside of contractual language; consequently, their latest proposal omitted any mention of educational planning.[133]

TAA members voted at their April 5 meeting to reject the latest University offer and continue their strike, defying the injunction—"this unethical and repressive judgment of the courts."[134] The impasse was essentially decided at two mass faculty meetings on April 6-7. After heated and protracted debate, rather than endorse bargaining on educational planning and stipulate how students and teaching assistants were to be involved, the faculty adopted the following resolution:

---

[131]*Milwaukee Journal*, March 26, 1970; *Capital Times*, March 26, 27, 1970.

[132]University of Wisconsin-Madison and Teaching Assistants Association, *Structure Agreement*, "Procedure for Obtaining Recognition and Structure for Collective Bargaining," April 26, 1969, Section 8, UA.

[133]*Capital Times*, March 27, 1970.

[134]*Daily Cardinal*, April 7, 1970; Craig, "Graduate Student Unionism," p. 181. Before the strike ended the University provided the names of 29 striking TAs to the attorney general for defying Judge Sachjten's injunction. Sachten found 21 in contempt on April 23, and sentenced each to a fine of $250 or thirty days in jail. The sentence was appealed over the next several years but eventually the fines were paid in 1973.

> It is in the interest of the University community to insure that there are mechanisms in each Department that give students and Teaching Assistants an opportunity to participate in a meaningful way in educational planning. Such department mechanisms shall be developed by each department on the Madison campus in collaboration with the students and Teaching Assistants involved in the courses offered by that Department. Such mechanisms, however, shall not infringe on the ultimate responsibility of the faculty for curriculum and course content.[135]

The first two sentences, acknowledging the language of the Structure Agreement that had provided the framework for bargaining, were moved by Professor E.R. Mulvihill, the chairman of the Department of Spanish and Portuguese, on behalf of the Council of Ten. They were adopted by a vote of 531-140. The final and rather contradictory sentence emphasizing faculty rights was offered as an amendment from the floor by history Professor Theodore S. Hamerow, a hardline faculty rights proponent. It also carried, 530-256. On this student power issue there was obviously little give from a substantial part of the faculty.

With support for the strike waning, the next day the TAA membership turned down a motion to escalate the strike and instead voted 534-348 to accept the University's April 7 contract offer. TAA President Muehlenkamp lauded the results of the struggle:

> This strike has built a union. Members who thought they would never strike, who thought they would never last a week, who thought they couldn't stay out after Easter, now find they can do a lot more. They know we need to do more. This union will be back next year–and the struggle will be different.[136]

The strike, he said, had taught students and teaching assistants who their real enemy was:

> We're talking about individual faculty members. . . . We have a few protections and mechanisms and we're going to run every goddam complaint through the grievance procedure. We're going to bust the asses of those professors and going to go through the courts.

---

[135]UW Faculty Minutes, April 7, 1970.
[136]*Wisconsin State Journal*, April 10, 1970.

TAA Vice President Henry Haslach told the membership their task was now to form an alliance with the campus blue collar workers, including research assistants, specialists, and secretaries. "I don't know about you people," he said, "but I'm going to use my energy to organize against this motherf---king University for next time."[137] Regardless of the rhetoric, the TAA had won a great deal: union recognition and exclusive representation, bargaining rights, and a contract providing UW-Madison teaching assistants with greater job security and a more carefully delineated grievance procedure. Time would tell whether the gains came at the cost of a more formal and confrontational relationship with their academic departments and teachers.

Like the TAA leadership, the *Daily Cardinal* was also uncertain who had won what it described as "the first annual TA strike," since "the contract was so pitiful it is hard to find words to describe it." But the editors thought the student movement had achieved much. "One thing is certain, if winning is defined as the dynamic of learning which we will in turn apply to the next struggle we face, then we have gained from this strike."[138] Chancellor Young pointed out that the TAA had gained nothing that had not been offered by the University before the strike. With the benefit of hindsight and minimizing his own role in the outcome, he later complained that the strikers had really been beaten but were bailed out by some of the faculty and University bargainers who belonged to the "Nate Feinsinger settle at-any-cost school."[139]

After protracted debate, an unhappy Board of Regents approved the contract on April 10 by an 8-2 vote, first rejecting as untimely an amendment declaring that any TAA strike in the future would bring automatic withdrawal of recognition and an end to collective bargaining with the union.[140] The legislature's powerful Joint Committee on Finance voted 12-1 to ask state Attorney General Robert W. Warren to rule on the legality of the TAA contract and by a narrower 7-6 margin urged the regents to rescind it. A number of unhappy legislators argued that the University had no authority to make some of the commitments

---

[137]*Daily Cardinal*, April 10, 1970.

[138]Ibid., April 10, 1970. In another editorial the paper blamed the faculty for taking "the onus of crushing the strike away from the chancellor's office. . . . They are old men possessing and trying to preserve a dying institution. They can and do play their great games oblivious to our needs. They cannot do this for long. They are the past and will be overrun." Ibid., April 7, 1970.

[139]Quoted in Craig, "Graduate Student Unionism," p. 185.

[140]UW BOR Minutes, April 10, 1970. The discussion lasted more than two hours and occupied an unprecedented nineteen single-spaced pages of the minutes.

embodied in the contract, and blamed the strike and what they regarded as a give-away settlement on the general permissiveness of the Harrington administration. The critics were neither mollified nor reassured when Warren eventually ruled the contract legal.[141] Behind the considerable misgivings of many regents, legislators, and faculty members was the realization the University had embarked on a new and uncharted path in dealing with its graduate students, one bound to have an effect on instruction at both the undergraduate and graduate levels. Some faculty, in fact, were bitter the administration had agreed to recognize and enter into a collective bargaining contract with the TAA without formal involvement and approval by the faculty governance structure, except on the limited issue of educational planning. Only the high regard generally felt for Chancellor Young kept this criticism from open expression.[142]

Climaxing a Tumultuous Semester

Like many campuses around the country, UW-Madison was a tinderbox of student rebellion in the spring of 1970. The seemingly endless war in Southeast Asia remained the primary corrosive influence, even though the Nixon administration had lowered draft calls and begun troop withdrawals from Vietnam. Selective service was now on a lottery basis, moreover, so that student deferments were a thing of the past and no longer occasioned feelings of guilt. Still, by 1970 many students in

---

[141]Craig, "Graduate Student Unionism," pp. 189-90, 194-95. In response to the Joint Finance query whether the contract could bind future Boards of Regents, Warren ruled that the contract was valid and binding only for its duration; future boards were free not to continue recognition of the TAA and not to enter into another agreement. Similarly, while the legislature could not impair the present legally binding contract, it was free to direct what the Board of Regents might do in the future.

[142]Chancellor Young argued that the faculty did not approve the collective bargaining contracts with other UW unionized employees and in any event had been represented informally by the Committee of Thirty, Council of Ten, and by several faculty members on the bargaining team. His critics responded that the comparison with the University's blue collar unions was fallacious. Teaching assistants were much more closely and directly involved with the faculty's primary responsibility for the University's instructional program, both as junior teaching staff and as graduate students; hence the faculty as a body ought to have a major role in developing and approving any new institutional arrangements involving them. Young's faculty critics believed his labor mediation background had led him to minimize the likely problems of working with a hybrid union of immature and transient graduate students who had no long term stake in either their jobs or the institution.

Madison and elsewhere no longer trusted their national government and institutions, or by extension authority at any level of society. Far from the traditional student tendency to view the future with hope and optimism, the mood of the boomer generation had grown deeply pessimistic that necessary reform could be achieved without fundamental change, perhaps even revolution. Youthful idealism had been replaced by dark suspicion and despair.

The 24-day TAA strike, coupled with the earlier firebombings and the destructive anti-GE protest, suggested that the alienation might produce the most disruptive semester yet. More trouble was to come. Shortly after the end of the strike the *Daily Cardinal* staff elected the paper's top management for the coming year. Named as editor-in-chief was Rena Steinzor, who had allied herself with Jim Rowen during the year to turn the paper into a leftist collective operating by consensus and ending the role of the Cardinal Board in appointing the editors. Something of a mother hen to the staff, Steinzor was alternately aggressive and profane yet solicitous of her colleagues' well-being and safety, regularly reminding the paper's reporters to carry gas masks to campus demonstrations. Steinzor was a hard-core radical, proud that her grandfather was a Russian-born New York garment-cutter and union activist, and a card-carrying member of the Communist Party. In her opening editorial she predicted: "That revolution we are always talking about is, in many ways, starting for us right here."[143] On April 17 the *Cardinal* urged its readers "To the Streets" in what the organizers predicted might be the biggest anti-war march yet. During the rally at the capitol a so-called Revolutionary Contingent of several hundred radicals went on an hour-long rampage around the square and down State Street, smashing $100,000 worth of plate glass store-front windows before being dispersed by police with clubs and tear gas who tore down the demonstrators' street barricades in the Mifflin-Bassett area.[144] The *Cardinal* applauded some though not all of the trashers' actions and targets, but cautioned: "The moment must be chosen carefully. This Saturday was not the moment." In a separate signed editorial Steinzor distanced herself slightly from her colleagues and supported the trashing, which she attributed to the Mother Jones faction

---

[143]*Daily Cardinal*, April 14, 1970.

[144]Ibid., April 21, 1970. One of the *Cardinal* reporters covering the rally was its SDS expert, Leo F. Burt, later recruited for the New Year's Gang as a participant in the August, 1970, MRC bombing.

of SDS as "not an expression of youthful frustration but a highly political reaction to a growing crisis."[145]

On April 30 President Nixon dispatched U.S. forces into Cambodia to destroy the supply routes used by the North Vietnamese for their forces in the south. UW students had just voted overwhelmingly (3,327 to 890) in a campus referendum calling for an immediate American withdrawal from Vietnam.[146] Campus protests, some of them violent, immediately erupted all over the United States against this expansion of the war. In an editorial headed "Time of Reckoning" the *Daily Cardinal* warned ominously:

> Nixon had better begin arming for a new kind of war in this country, civil war. He has lied, he has cheated, he has escalated. And the time of reckoning is about here.[147]

In Ohio, Governor Rhodes sent the national guard onto the campus of Kent State University to keep order. In a tragic standoff against taunting student demonstrators, the troopers lost control and fired, killing four protesters and wounding eleven others. UW activists mobilized the campus to join in a nationwide strike against the Cambodian incursion and the bloody repression at Kent State. In a front-page editorial headed "Survival," the *Cardinal* declared:

> How many more deaths will occur in this country over the next few days is an open question. The stakes are very high now in the United States of America. . . . Each of us is involved not only in the human machines of war, such as the draft, but in an institution which is essential to waging such wars. We must strike and strike hard—into the community and on our campus to turn the tide now raging so viciously against us.[148]

The resulting protest strike involved thousands of UW students and quickly erupted into sporadic but continuing violence over the next

---

[145]Ibid., April 21, 22, 1970. One reader responded: "The next time you want to throw some rocks, why don't you stand in a circle and throw them at each other. You'll be doing everyone working for peace a big favor." Another wrote: "As for Saturday's 'revolutionary contingent,' I can't think of any very sound advice on the way to foment or 'catalyze' the revolution. But I can tell them that the Mickey Mouse crap they engaged in Saturday sure as hell isn't it." Ibid., April 22, 1970.
[146]*Badger Herald*, May 1, 1970.
[147]*Daily Cardinal*, May 2, 1970.
[148]Ibid., May 5, 1970.

week or so. On the evening of May 5 rioting demonstrators began firebombing a number of buildings on and near the campus. The Kroger's supermarket on University Avenue, set afire in an earlier demonstration although it was the most convenient source of groceries for students and other nearby residents, this time was totally destroyed by the flames. Roving "affinity groups" even tossed firebombs into the homes of six faculty members, including UW emeritus President E.B. Fred (apparently believing it to be President Harrington's residence) and Colonel Joseph T. Meserow, professor of aerospace and head of the UW Air Force ROTC program. Fortunately, none caused serious damage. Warning that the University was "in danger," a shaken Chancellor Young declared a state of emergency and joined Madison Mayor William Dyke in requesting Governor Knowles once again to send the national guard to assist the hard-pressed UW and city police in maintaining order. Asked at a press conference if the University might close, Young responded wearily: "I hope not. It is my intention to continue the operation of the campus and to make it possible for students to attend class."[149]

As the rioting continued, the chancellor designated Monday, May 11, as a Day of Concern and urged departments to hold open hearings with faculty and students for "an examination of the critical issues facing the nation."[150] At the regular meeting of the Board of Regents on May 8 President Harrington, as always controlled and urbane, announced his resignation effective October 1. The president had contemplated this move for several months, recognizing that his support from regents, legislators, and the public was crumbling. He had in fact worked out the terms of his departure with key regents in advance of the meeting. Under the circumstances, however, it appeared Harrington had been forced out by the rioters, as in a larger sense he had.[151]

The *Daily Cardinal* termed Harrington's departure "predictable," and applauded the widespread firebombing:

> All over the nation, hundreds of thousands of students are bringing that fire on home. For it long ago became obvious that the power elite which runs this country just was not going to listen to peaceful marches and refused unilaterally to stop not only their genocidal actions on the Southeast

[149]Ibid., May 5, 6, 8, 1970.
[150]Ibid., May 12, 1970.
[151]UW BOR Minutes, May 8, 1970.

Asian people but their police state tactics on dissenters at home. . . . The police and the Guard are a wedge between the powers that run the capitalist system and the people. The Guard, for example, is composed to a large extent of men attempting to avoid the draft. We must learn to move around them. Some of our members did exactly that. . . when fires broke out in several business establishments notably Kroger's.[152]

There were 44 arrests by the second night of rioting and for a time the campus area seemed to be approaching anarchy. Editor Steinzor preferred to call it "a highly disciplined fight against institutions and ideologies which are repulsive and fatal to the way of life we want to lead."[153] Although sorely tempted, the Board of Regents took no action to censor or suppress the *Cardinal*, but several regents declared themselves "appalled" at its calculated efforts to whip up student violence. Regent Bernard Ziegler, chairman of the board's Study Committee on Student Newspapers, described the paper as "not much more than a revolutionary instruction sheet."[154]

Although the great majority of students continued to attend their classes, on the eastern part of the campus around Bascom Hill normal academic life was difficult to impossible to maintain amid roving bands of protesters, accompanying police and guardsmen, intermittent sirens, and occasional clouds of tear gas. By the end of several days of rioting the first-floor windows of most University buildings and along State Street had been smashed and were boarded up. In an effort to control high school students and others drawn to the disorders, Chancellor Young ordered University buildings locked at 5:00 p.m. and the campus closed to all persons without valid UW identification. Faculty in a number of departments decided to suspend classes or devote them to a discussion of the war and thus in effect to support the student strikers by winding up the semester early. There was such variation in the announced plans of individual faculty members that the campus administration instructed the separate schools and colleges to decide how to grade students on their academic work during this tumultuous and truncated semester. The largest undergraduate college, Letters and Science, gave students three options: regular final exams and letter grades, taking an incomplete and making up the missing work subse-

---

[152]*Daily Cardinal*, May 6, 9, 1970.

[153]Rena Steinzor, "Anarchist Journalism," ibid., May 8, 1970.

[154]UW BOR Minutes, May 8, 1970. See also ibid., June 12, 1970.

quently, or accepting a pass-fail grade based on their work to date. The Law School allowed its students to put off final examinations but not avoid them. The School of Business offered both regular final and pass-fail exams. In Agriculture and Engineering, where there was considerably less protest activity, most students took the regular final examinations.[155]

The University faculty held two emergency special meetings during what came to be called the Cambodia-Kent State riots. The first, on May 8, was a mass committee-of-the-whole discussion called by the University Committee at the Stock Pavilion and attended by an estimated 1,200 faculty and 1,000 students. Conceived mostly as an opportunity to let off steam, during more than three hours of emotional debate the meeting adopted six non-binding resolutions. Upon reflection, most of the participants—faculty and students alike—agreed it was not the faculty's finest hour. Afterward Chancellor Young told reporters he would consider but not be bound by the faculty's advice.[156] Three weeks later on May 26, at the end of the turbulent semester, the faculty held another special meeting in the Union Theater. This time 630 faculty members gathered to review the recent troubles. After voting down a motion to adjourn and a number of resolutions and amendments, the group adopted the following carefully balanced statement:

---

[155]Ibid., June 12, 1970. Chancellor Young told the Board of Regents he was docking the pay of some twenty faculty members who had canceled their classes during the strike—certainly a low estimate of the number of faculty supporters of the strike. It was nearly impossible, however, to determine whether a class was canceled for lack of students, inability to meet under the riotous conditions, or in support of the protest. It should not be assumed that because there was less protest activity on the western part of the campus that students in engineering and agriculture supported the war; opposition to the war was general across the student body.

[156]The resolutions were adopted by ever-dwindling numbers and the vote tallies indicated many abstentions. The first, adopted by the widest margin (600-72) but obviously with many abstentions, declared that "the U.S. should immediately cease all military operations in S.E. Asia." Another resolution (adopted 329-232) called for the campus to be closed until May 16 "because of our outrage over the widening war in Asia and the recent events at Kent State University," with another faculty meeting set for the afternoon of May 15 to assess the situation. Another (adopted 430-207) called for a two-week free period just prior to the coming November elections to enable students to take part in political activity and attend University workshops on political issues. Still another (voted 197-170) called on the University administration "to make an effective public demonstration of concern and moral leadership, by joining in *representative fashion*" a mass march from Bascom Hall to the state capitol on May 11. UW Faculty Minutes, May 8, 1970.

We deplore and condemn all acts of personal injury, destruction and obstruction that have taken place on or near the campus, in recent days and in recent months and years.

There have also been use of invective and personal attack, and some coercion and intimidation. We deplore and condemn these practices. They are hostile to the central idea of a free university, which finds civility and mutual respect to be useful aids toward advancing truth and improving policy.

To attain greater understanding and support for these principles, a committee shall be established on Civil Peace in the University community. The committee shall consist of faculty and student members to be appointed by the Chancellor. The committee shall study conditions on the campus which promote or encourage disruption of civil peace and make recommendations to appropriate agencies of the student body, the faculty or the administration.[157]

The statement and proposed committee were harmless, but whether they could restore peace to a shattered campus community was an open question.

A somber commencement ceremony went off as scheduled at the stadium on Monday, June 8, with extra police on hand to guard against further violence. Anti-war placards were much in evidence, and many members of the senior class declined to wear the traditional cap and gown as a mark of their protest against the war and the University's continuation of business as usual. Class President David S. Zucker told the assemblage the seniors were donating the rental fees for their spurned academic attire and making other contributions to a fund to help elect peace candidates in the fall elections:

We as seniors should not be wearing academic costumes while the Vietnamese people and their land is [sic] being destroyed in a senseless war of genocide. We should not be wearing costumes while our government is systematically slaying Black Panthers and repressing all black people. We cannot wear costumes while our fellow students are murdered by National Guardsmen. And we cannot wear their costumes while the war and the military devour huge sums that could be put toward giving every American citizen the decent standard of living to which we are all entitled as human beings.[158]

---

[157]Ibid., May 26, 1970.

[158]David S. Zucker remarks, UW press release, June 8, 1970, Series 4/21/1, Box 41, UA; "Again Graduation Numbers Set Records," *WAM*, 71 (June, 1970), 19.

Anti-war demonstration, *Capital Times* photo, 1967, UA, X25-2624.

Keeping order during Kent State-Cambodia protests, May, 1970. UA, X25-2122.

Tear gas on Bascom Hill. UA, X25-3413.

Sterling Hall after the bombing, August, 1970, photo
by Gary Schulz. UA, 4332-J-1.

Former Secretary of the Interior Stewart Udall, a prominent environmentalist and the chief commencement speaker, hailed the graduates as the "conscience of the country."[159] Remembering their smashed windows and firebombed homes, not all of faculty members present shared Udall's enthusiasm.

The Bomb

As an uneasy peace returned to the troubled campus, student militants reviewed the recent rioting and planned their next action to "bring the war home." They were convinced that rallies and peace marches were useful only in mobilizing mass support. Only by escalating the violence at home could they get the politicians in Washington to see that their evil war in Vietnam was too costly and divisive to continue. Although only a small minority of the student body, and some of them not even active students, the extremists now openly advocated civil war. The underground newspaper *Kaleidoscope*, which was hawked around the campus and circulated among Madison radicals, printed directions on how to make and use bombs safely.

> Remember, dynamite is easier to get in Wisconsin than firecrackers. We must make the transition from trashing and mass street actions at lengthy intervals to systematic sabotage by innumerable groups if we wish to grow, if we wish to really put muscle behind our slogans and ideas.[160]

In an article headed "Get a Gun and Learn to Use It!" the paper lamented that the campus buildings housing such offensive programs as ROTC, MRC, and computer science, were still standing.

> They may be occupied now, but they won't be for long. . . .
> Now that things have died down around the campus, time bombs that explode hours after the buildings are empty is the best mechanism. Fire bombs are cool, too—but be in groups of two or three. Molotov cocktails anyone?[161]

Karleton Armstrong, the New Year's bomber now back in Madison, shared this militancy. Likewise did Leo Burt, the *Daily*

---

[159]*Daily Cardinal*, June 19, 1970.
[160]*Kaleidoscope*, May 15, 1970.
[161]Ibid., May 19, 1970.

Cardinal's SDS expert, whose radicalism had been further steeled by beatings received from the Madison police while he covered the recent campus riots. He discovered that his *Cardinal* press badge made him even more of a target for police attention. Burt had by this time learned that Armstrong was the New Year's bomber, and readily accepted his invitation to join an attempt to eradicate the hated Army Math Research Center once and for all time. Burt brought another recruit–David Fine, a young *Cardinal* reporter whose role model at the paper was the fiery activist Jim Rowen. Armstrong was skeptical of Fine's youth and apparent immaturity, but recognized that the undertaking he contemplated would require group action. The New Year's Gang now numbered four: Karl Armstrong and his brother Dwight, plus the new recruits, Leo Burt and David Fine.[162]

The Math Research Center was located on the second, third, and fourth floors of Sterling Hall, which also housed the offices and laboratories of the physics and astronomy departments as well as some classrooms. The conspirators eventually concluded it would be impossible to destroy the center from within because access to it was restricted. They would have to attack the building in which it was located. They first considered planting a bomb in the steam tunnel beneath the building, but concluded it would be difficult to plant enough explosive in such a restricted space. Armstrong decided they would again have to use a mixture of ammonium nitrate fertilizer and fuel oil, the only explosive he could afford on the $200 profit he had gained from the bulk sale of some marijuana. His ill-fated air attack on the BOW plant on New Year's Eve had taught him that an ANFO bomb must be ignited by an explosion. Because he and the others wanted to avoid casualties, they set their attack for late August when campus activity was at a low ebb. After reconnoitering the site for several nights, they decided the best time would be on a weekend, specifically between 2:00 and 4:00 a.m. on a Monday morning, when the building appeared to be deserted. Without knowing how much explosive power was needed to accomplish their objective, they made a huge bomb of 1,750 pounds of ammonium nitrate and 20 gallons of fuel oil, which Karl calculated would equal 3,400 sticks of dynamite. They packed the ANFO mixture into a number of barrels placed in a white Econoline van stolen randomly from computer science Professor Larry Travis, who had made the mistake of leaving his keys in his van while dropping some

---

[162]Bates, *Rads*, pp. 254–66.

papers off at his office. Karl armed the ANFO barrels with sticks of dynamite and a ten-foot fuse, which he figured would give them about six-and-a-half minutes lead time.

Shortly after 3:30 a.m. on August 24 they parked the Travis van in the driveway next to Sterling Hall directly under the MRC, signaled the waiting David Fine in a nearby public booth to telephone a warning to the Madison police dispatcher, and sped away in the Armstrong family Corvair, borrowed for the weekend from the brothers' unknowing mother. They were only a few blocks away when the shock wave from the explosion seemed to lift their car off the ground. Looking back at a fireball mushrooming hundreds of feet in the air, an amazed Dwight Armstrong likened it to an atom bomb. His brother Karl later recalled that all he could muster was the shocked one-word comment, "Fuck."[163]

Armstrong's bomb did massive damage to Sterling Hall and nearby buildings, including the cardiac wing of University Hospital across the street where miraculously no one was hurt. Instantly killed in Sterling Hall was Robert Fassnacht, a young physics postdoctoral fellow who was working through the night on his superconductivity experiment; several others in the building were seriously injured. Ironically, the target of the bombers, the Mathematics Research Center, had no laboratories and little equipment and was scarcely affected by the destruction around it. The hated center was quickly back in business in new quarters in the Wisconsin Alumni Research Foundation building on the western edge of the campus. For MRC's Sterling Hall neighbors, physics and astronomy, it was a far different story. Both departments' space and equipment were heavily damaged, with several graduate students losing part or all of their thesis research when their professors' laboratories disintegrated. After pondering the destruction of their labs and the loss of decades of research data, two senior physics faculty, Henry Barschall and Joseph Dillinger–the latter with whom Fassnacht was working–eventually concluded they were too old to rebuild an active research program anew.[164] For them Armstrong's bomb was intensely personal.

The bombing had a chilling and polarizing effect on the campus community. Most student demonstrators had not expected their protest activity to lead to murder and massive destruction. Hard-core radicals no doubt agreed with *Kaleidoscope*'s assessment that the bombing was

---

[163]Ibid., pp. 278-308.
[164]See "Sterling Hall Bomber Kills One, Injures Three," *WAM*, 71 (August, 1970), 14-15.

inevitable, "the logical outcome of Dow '67, of departmental and dorm organizing in '68 and a strike by the TAA in '69. It is the result of confronting the University with its pig capitalist nature for four years."[165] Rena Steinzor and her colleagues at the *Daily Cardinal* had more trouble explaining the event, especially because two of the suspected bombers were soon identified as *Cardinal* staffers. The paper declined to judge them, however: "We are with Leo and David now because they are people we care for very deeply and know very well." Students must decide for themselves how to make the most of this traumatic act:

> The AMRC was a physical and symbolic installation whose sole purpose was to serve the strong arm of American economic interests across the globe. This military arm of our government has been the most violent instrument in the history of the world and has stolen from murdered and destroyed the lives of people in the countries from Cuba to Vietnam, as well as those at the bottom of the social ladder within its own turf. . . . In order for its physical and symbolic destruction to have any meaning beyond this specific point in time, the movement from which the bombing sprang must be expanded.[166]

Most UW faculty members were considerably less ambivalent about the meaning of this assault against their campus. Although the bombing had occurred during the late summer vacation period when many UW staff members were away from Madison, within a few days more than a thousand faculty members signed a hastily drafted statement denouncing violence and intimidation and pledging to defend their University.[167] Chancellor Young cautioned the Board of Regents against panic or any vindictive reaction:

> We believe it is possible to deal with advocates of violence, to punish those who put their theories to practice and break the law, to stand firm against attempts to disrupt and destroy—and at the same time, proceed with enlightened and responsible programs for change. . . .
> In its crisis, the University needs to be able to rely on courageous support from its alumni, its friends and, above

---

[165]*Kaleidoscope*, August 30, 1970.

[166]"Where Do We Go from Here?" *Daily Cardinal*, registration issue, September, 1970.

[167]Copy in UHP; *Daily Cardinal*, September 22, 1970; *Badger Herald*, September 24, 1970.

all from the members of its own community. Only with such support can it stand solidly against terrorism and move with imagination to new standards of greatness. If it gets such support–and I am confident it will–there is no way the forces of intimidation can prevail.[168]

The End of Violent Revolution

In the days and months ahead it became increasingly evident that the New Year's Gang had killed not only Bob Fassnacht but the strategy of revolutionary violence as well, in Madison and to a considerable extent in the nation as a whole. The gaping hole in Sterling Hall was a continuing reminder of the enormous explosion that shocked the campus community as had few events in the University's long history. Student radicals could and did point out that the bombing had merely brought the war home, that it was but an example of what the United States was daily inflicting on the Vietnamese people, and that, as a *Cardinal* columnist noted, "if Fassnacht had been drafted and killed in Vietnam none of us would stir."[169] True enough, but to the anti-war but peace-loving idealists who comprised the great bulk of the UW student body, Armstrong's bomb also brought home the horrors of violence, whether in Vietnam or Madison.

Following the MRC bombing it proved more difficult to attract the sizable protest crowds necessary to provide cover for those bent on trashing, harder to recruit the small affinity groups willing to undertake such violence. There were, in fact, fewer calls now for violent revolution and fewer listeners taking them seriously. Washington's gradual reduction in draft calls, moreover, and even more the decision in the fall of 1969 to reduce the selective service jeopardy period to a one-year lottery had also lessened the importance of this issue in fueling anti-war protests. Though the American role in the Vietnamese civil war continued on an ever-diminishing basis for nearly three more years, in January, 1973, the Nixon administration finally concluded its peace negotiations in Paris with the North Vietnamese government, accepting terms that probably could have been agreed upon years earlier. The resulting American withdrawal was quickly followed by the collapse of the South Vietnamese government and the occupation of the entire

---

[168]Young, Statement on "The State of the Campus," UW BOR Minutes, Exhibit B, September 11, 1970.

[169]*Daily Cardinal*, registration issue, September, 1970.

country by Hanoi's forces. With peace came the end of the longest and most unpopular war in the nation's history, a military defeat that had traumatized a generation, cost more than 58,000 American lives and $150 billion, and seriously damaged the morale and effectiveness of the United States military forces. Because of it, neither the nation nor the University of Wisconsin would ever be the same again.

9.

The UW System Merger

In addition to the University in Madison, beginning with Platteville in 1866 during the latter part of the nineteenth century the Wisconsin Legislature began developing another, more specialized form of state-funded higher education–a system of normal schools located in various parts of the state to train teachers for the public schools. Eventually there were nine of these institutions after a legislative reorganization in 1955. Like the University, the Normal Schools were authorized under a separate but parallel chapter of the statutes and governed by their own board of regents. Over time this board authorized a name change for its institutions to suggest a broadening mission: from Normal Schools to Teachers Colleges in 1927, to State Colleges (WSC) in 1951, to Wisconsin State Universities (WSU) in 1964.

Prior to World War II it was relatively easy for the public and the legislature to distinguish between the University of Wisconsin and the state's teacher training institutions. The latter were smaller and had more specialized missions and quite different budgetary needs than the University, the state's only comprehensive doctoral institution. As the University grew into a diverse multi-campus system during the 1950s and 1960s, however, and even more as the former teachers colleges simultaneously evolved into universities offering more than teacher training and even some graduate programs, it became harder for legislators and the governor to make a sharp distinction between what were increasingly two competing and seemingly similar systems of public higher education. By the early 1960s the combined undergraduate enrollment of the WSC campuses exceeded that of UW-Madison and UW-Milwaukee together and was growing at a faster rate as the WSU system moved well beyond its original mission. To Wisconsin political leaders, this was a development needing attention and control.

Integration to Coordination

With the return of peace in 1945, it was clear that Wisconsin badly needed to modernize its infrastructure and improve basic public services after a decade and one-half of severe economic depression and war. At a time when most economists were predicting a resumption of the Great Depression, it also was obvious that tax revenues would be insufficient to meet every challenge. Accordingly, the watchword among Wisconsin politicians was fiscal prudence combined with efficiency and effectiveness in all public expenditures. Because of the substantial portion of the state budget devoted to higher education, a succession of governors and legislatures after the war turned a critical eye on the funding requests of the University and the Teachers College system, both experiencing unprecedented enrollment growth. The elderly Republican Governor Walter Goodland, a former Racine editor and legislator, pointed to the problem in an address to the legislature in January, 1947. "A duplicity of higher educational boards creates an overlapping and duplication of efforts," he declared, and then added with some puzzlement, "It seems to be a haphazard system."[1] Goodland's commonsense remedy was to substitute a single State Board of Higher Education for the two regent boards governing the University and the Teachers Colleges, and additionally include the Stout Institute in Menomonie and the Wisconsin Institute of Technology in Platteville in the new system. The legislature had higher priorities in other areas, however, and failed to give the governor's proposal serious attention.

Goodland was not around to witness the rebuff. Only two months after making this recommendation he died of a heart attack and was succeeded by the Republican Lieutenant Governor, Oscar Rennebohm, who had built up a prosperous chain of drug stores in Madison. Governor Rennebohm shared his predecessor's concern about the anomalous state educational structure and persuaded the legislature to authorize a study of the situation. In the fall of 1947 he appointed a Commission on Education, consisting of four legislators and five private citizens, to look

---

[1]Governor Walter Goodland, Message to the Legislature, *Senate Journal*, 68th session, 1947, p. 31; Vernon W. Thomson, "Education Reform," *WAM*, 48 (March, 1947), 21.

into Wisconsin education "at all levels." To meet its reporting deadline in late 1948, the commission enlisted all of the targeted agencies to provide information and advice.[2]

UW President E.B. Fred responded by naming a high-level Committee on University Functions and Policies under the leadership of the widely respected Letters and Science Dean Mark H. Ingraham. As an indication of the importance attached to the undertaking, Ingraham took a leave of absence from his administrative duties to concentrate on it. The committee issued its "First Report" in October, 1948. Most of the narrative–covering 59 of its 74 pages–consisted of a "status report" that comprehensively described the complex higher education structure in Wisconsin. Had this been the committee's only contribution, the effort would have been fully justified as providing a solid factual grounding for subsequent political debates. The "First Report" depended heavily for its data and analysis on a wide-ranging series of commissioned studies by other UW staff members and groups, several of them operating directly under the guidance and close scrutiny of President Fred. The overall effort was an excellent example of the faculty's continued allegiance to the Wisconsin Idea of University public service.[3]

The functions and policies exercise also illustrated the faculty's significant involvement in University governance by this time. As a member of the University Committee in 1932-33, Ingraham had played an instrumental role in devising a way to absorb a drastic state budget cut without violating any faculty employment contracts or tenure. Now he and UW Vice President Ira L. Baldwin and their committee colleagues again faced a major policy challenge. Aware of Governor Goodland's view of the problem and his suggested solution, the Functions and Policies Committee addressed straight-on the highly charged question of a single state higher education governing board. With considerable daring, they concluded that a merger of the University of Wisconsin and the Wisconsin State Teachers Colleges, if done properly, promised the best results for the state "as a whole."[4]

---

[2]"Administration: For UW, An Analysis," *WAM*, 49 (January, 1948), 6-7.

[3]Committee on University Functions and Policies, "First Report," October, 1948, UHP. For examples of support studies, see John Guy Fowlkes and Henry C. Ahrnsbrak, *Junior College Needs in Wisconsin, Bulletin of the University of Wisconsin*, Serial No. 2907, General Series No. 2681, April, 1947, and *State-Supported Institutions of Higher Education and Their Governing Boards: A Digest of Facts, Trends, and Developments, With Implications for Wisconsin*, mimeographed, March, 1948. See above, p. 80.

[4]Committee on University Functions and Policies, "First Report," p. 3.

The committee chose this recommendation from three alternatives outlined in the report. The first, which envisioned a "superboard, or commission, above the present governing boards," seemed entirely unworkable by virtue of its too limited ability to coordinate such important functions as budgeting and planning for capital improvements. The committee predicted that "educational jockeying would take the place of educational planning, and bickering the place of cooperation." The second alternative called for ad hoc cooperation between the two current regent boards. Something like this had apparently succeeded in Ohio since 1939 and seemed at the moment to be developing nicely in Wisconsin. Finally, the committee's favored option called for a single regent board empowered to open and close campuses, a central administration for the merged system, and a combined faculty. The governor would appoint the regents subject to confirmation by the Wisconsin Senate and would serve long and staggered terms to assure they represented the interests of Wisconsin as a whole. "Constant vigilance" would be required of the board to safeguard the Madison campus traditions of high-quality research, scholarship, and public service in addition to the generally accepted importance of teaching excellence. These qualities were essential to the committee's merger recommendation. If all of them could not be assured, the idea of a state-wide system should be abandoned in favor of the relatively limited but perhaps more realistic second alternative.[5]

Probably because this visionary proposal went well beyond the Ingraham Committee's charge, its "First Report" had little immediate influence, even though much of its thinking would eventually prove to be prescient. The UW Board of Regents received the report in November of 1948, took a few minutes to criticize its admittedly extreme proposal, and filed it specifically "without endorsement or approval."[6] After years of seemingly unending emergency challenges and only now beginning to sense a return to something like "normal" times, the board was in no mood to consider any fundamental tinkering with its job of watching over the state's prestigious University. Governor Rennebohm and his Commission on Education were more sympathetic to the merger idea, however. In January of 1949, having recently been elected governor in his own right, Rennebohm told the legislature, "In the realm of higher education . . . there is great need for a closer integration of the state's services." He agreed with his commission's conclusion "that the interests of Wisconsin citizens can be served best by an integrated system," and

[5]Ibid., pp. 65-73.
[6]UW BOR Minutes, November 20, 1948, UA.

proposed that the legislature follow the commission's recommendations to this end.[7]

Governor Rennebohm's initiative was translated into identical bills 263S (in the senate) and 356A (in the assembly). They called for the establishment of a University of Wisconsin System, to include the existing UW, the State Teachers Colleges, and the Stout and Platteville institutes. The non-Madison units would function under a provost, who would report to the UW president in Madison. Not surprisingly, both existing boards of regents opposed these bills, which, although not as extensive as the proposal from the Functions and Policies Committee, nevertheless threatened major changes. The legislature cooperated by declining to approve the bills. In a further rebuff to the governor, the legislature authorized the Teachers College Regents to offer liberal arts baccalaureate degrees at all of their campuses. Rennebohm reluctantly concurred, with the understanding that no changes would be made at the Milwaukee State Teachers College until the larger issue of public higher education in the city was resolved.[8]

Rennebohm's concern with the Milwaukee situation reflected his sensitivity to an issue that had first emerged early in the twentieth century and whose intensity had recently been growing. University of Wisconsin officials had long resisted pressures to establish a branch campus in the state's largest city. They were skeptical of obtaining adequate state funding for two campuses when there never seemed enough for Madison alone. They also worried lest the original campus in Madison might eventually be overshadowed by the new branch. Following World War I, the University responded to pressures to provide classes for returning veterans in the Milwaukee area, establishing the downtown Extension Center that soon developed a resident faculty offering day and evening freshman-sophomore courses in the liberal arts, commerce, and engineering, in addition to a variety of non-credit instruction.[9] At the same time, the Milwaukee State Teachers College, located in a residential area near Lake

---

[7]Governor's Message, *Senate Journal*, 69th session, 1949, p. 47. See also "University System?" *WAM*, 50 (December, 1948), 8; "Consolidation Coming?" ibid. (February, 1949), 14; and J. Martin Klotsche, *The University of Wisconsin-Milwaukee: An Urban University* (Milwaukee: University of Wisconsin-Milwaukee, 1972), p. 3.

[8]Ibid., p. 6. Because of its isolated location in the far northwestern corner of the state, the campus at Superior had received special legislative approval in 1945 to offer bachelor degrees in the liberal arts.

[9]See E. David Cronon and John W. Jenkins, *The University of Wisconsin: A History*, vol. 3, *Politics, Depression, and War, 1925-1945* (Madison: University of Wisconsin Press, 1994), pp. 251-54, 792-98, 804-15, 842.

Michigan, was evolving beyond its original teacher training mission. While these two state institutions served separate clienteles and together were providing substantial post-secondary educational services to the area, there continued to be many Milwaukee boosters who believed the state's only metropolis deserved a full-fledged University of Wisconsin campus. Governor Rennebohm evidently found their arguments persuasive.

Following the legislative session of 1949, the frustrated governor, who had decided not to run for reelection in 1950 because of health concerns, appointed a special Commission on Public Higher Education in the Lake Shore Area. Its members included Rennebohm himself as well as state legislative and educational leaders. Early in 1950 the commission set up an advisory committee of Milwaukee citizens and hired Arthur Klein, the emeritus dean of the School of Education at Ohio State University, to prepare an analysis and recommendations. At the same time Milwaukee advocates of a four-year branch of the University formed the Committee for a Lake Shore College. It consisted of numerous civic, business, labor, and government leaders. This group managed to persuade the Republican and Democratic state parties to include a plank in their platforms that summer supporting this goal. Dean Klein's report, submitted on the first of August, recommended that a new semi-autonomous undergraduate institution be established on the outskirts of Milwaukee. In contrast, the commission's advisory committee recommended a short time later that the downtown UW Extension Center be transformed into a four-year college with a significantly expanded campus. Governor Rennebohm pondered these and other ideas, and as part of his farewell address in late November urged the establishment of a state-funded Lake Shore College in western metropolitan Milwaukee. It would replace Milwaukee's UW Center and State Teachers College and initially be financed by the sale of the two abandoned campuses.[10]

Rennebohm was succeeded by a prominent Republican industrialist, Walter J. Kohler, Jr., who in his first address to the legislature on January 11, 1951, followed his predecessor's lead. Acknowledging a general consensus in favor of expanded higher educational opportunities in Milwaukee and noting the bewildering array of plans to attain that goal, Kohler proposed the "sensible" idea merging the two current Milwaukee institutions into a single, four-year UW branch campus. This suggestion was consistent with the preference of UW Regent Leonard J. Kleczka, a Milwaukee resident. His colleagues on the board disagreed, however.

[10]Klotsche, *University of Wisconsin-Milwaukee*, pp. 7-12; "Wisconsin, A Two-Campus University?" *WAM*, 52 (October, 1950), 11.

Instead they, in conjunction with the Teachers College regents, responded to Kohler with a counter-proposal that the Milwaukee State Teachers College add a full four-year liberal arts curriculum while the UW Extension Center be left unchanged. Nevertheless, by the end of January identical bills 148S and 133A, embodying Governor Kohler's proposal, were introduced for legislative consideration. After several hearings and considerable parliamentary maneuvering, on May 21 the senate passed 148S by a 2-to-1 margin and sent it to the assembly, where on June 1 it was rejected. The assembly refused to reconsider its vote and the legislature adjourned without resolving anything about higher education in Milwaukee.[11]

Following his reelection in November, 1952, Governor Kohler turned his attention to the state-wide "integration" questions as a step toward settling the Milwaukee issue. An early indication of the governor's change in focus had come in November, 1951, when, as chairman of the State Building Commission, he temporarily refused to release $2.6 million of appropriated funds for construction, remodeling, and real estate acquisition at the Milwaukee Extension Center and the newly renamed Milwaukee State College.[12] A year later, during a building commission hearing on the capital budget requests from the University and the State Colleges, the governor declared:

> I feel we should do nothing until the legislature can consider integration. . . . These institutions are competing here for money, just as they are competing for students, and this tugging and hauling must be stopped. I don't see that we can have a sensible plan for developing these institutions until we get integration.[13]

In his state-of-the-state address to the legislature in January, Kohler reiterated his call for integration and proposed the merger of all twenty-one "of our institutions of higher learning into a state University system." Each unit would be headed by a president who would report to a University chancellor. As for the campus in Madison, it would "devote greater attention to specialized instruction, such as engineering, law and medicine, as well

---

[11]Governor's Message, *Senate Journal*, 70th session, 1951, pp. 32-33; Klotsche, *University of Wisconsin-Milwaukee*, pp. 12-16; UW BOR Minutes, February 17, 1951.

[12]Kohler released the funds in January of 1952 after receiving assurances that they would not be used to provide duplicative facilities. Klotsche, *University of Wisconsin-Milwaukee*, p. 16; "Milwaukee Building Fund Release Gets Approved," *WAM*, 53 (February, 1952), 22.

[13]Quoted in Klotsche, *University of Wisconsin-Milwaukee*, pp. 16-17, with reference to "Kohler Urges Ultimatum on College Plan," *Milwaukee Journal*, November 22, 1952.

as the bulk of graduate instruction and research." The "outlying institutions," on the other hand, would emphasize undergraduate instruction, their degrees gaining "prestige" through association with the University in Madison.[14]

During the ensuing legislative session, key officials and regents of the University and the State Colleges organized a tenuous but cooperative relationship that combined, as in previous years, to fend off merger. Within the University, a faculty Committee on Integration of Higher Education in Wisconsin carried on the work of the earlier Ingraham Committee on University Functions and Policies. Unlike the latter, its approach was largely defensive. One of its members was history Professor Fred Harvey Harrington, who was beginning to envision the University as operating prominently in a national and even international context, a view that subsequently would infuse his actions as UW president. Harrington thus tended to view any efforts by the state to restrict the University's growth and mission, as did Kohler's merger proposal, as deserving of strong opposition. Although the governor failed to achieve his higher education merger in 1953, he did succeed in pushing through a major budget reduction for the University. Kohler claimed the cut was a necessary response to a shortfall in state revenue, but UW authorities understandably viewed it at least partially as punishment for their opposition to merger.[15]

The 1953 legislative debate over merger did stimulate some movement toward resolution of the integration question. In mid-June, for example, in response to a joint legislative resolution the UW regents agreed to participate in the deliberations of a new Inter Higher Education Boards Committee. Additionally, both the legislature and the Wisconsin Alumni Association formed special study committees to look into integration/merger. In October, after prompting from the University Committee, the UW faculty voted to continue the work of its Committee

---

[14]Governor's Message, January 15, 1953, *Senate Journal*, 71st session, 1953, pp. 59-60. See also, "Governor Proposed Legislature Integrate Higher Education," *WAM*, 54 (February, 1953), 14-15; Klotsche, *University of Wisconsin-Milwaukee*, p. 17. The institutional breakdown involved the UW campus in Madison, nine UW centers, nine State Teachers Colleges, and the Platteville and Stout Institutes.

[15]Ira L. Baldwin, *My Half Century at the University of Wisconsin* (Madison: Ira L. Baldwin, 1995), p. 480; Gale Loudon Kelly, "The Politics of Higher Educational Coordination in Wisconsin, 1956-1969" (Ph.D. dissertation, University of Wisconsin-Madison, 1972), p. 57. Our discussion in this chapter on the Coordinating Committee for Higher Education is based heavily on Kelly's dissertation, along with the excellent research and analytical work of UHP graduate research assistant, Greg Summers. See also above, pp. 82-88.

on Integration of Higher Education in Wisconsin, which soon was sharing data with its legislative counterpart. Unfortunately such cooperation could not by itself overcome the genuinely thorny problem Kohler had sought to solve. This became evident in July of 1954, when the Inter Higher Education Boards Committee failed to agree on any substantial recommendations about integration, proposing instead, with the UW regent members opposed, a merger of the two Milwaukee institutions under the State College regents. Governor Kohler rejected this idea as an inadequate "piecemeal solution," while most of the Milwaukee constituencies came out in opposition because they favored UW control of any new institution. At the same time, the UW faculty Integration Committee recommended the development of "a more nearly complete branch of the University of Wisconsin in Milwaukee, either by expansion of the Milwaukee Extension Division, or, better, by expansion in conjunction with a merger of the Extension Division with the State College at Milwaukee."[16]

Throughout the rest of 1954 discussions continued about the future of higher education in. Most notable was the UW regents meeting on August 7, at which the board considered and rejected the recommendation of the Inter Higher Education Boards Committee, while generally affirming the faculty committee's suggestion though without any mention of merger with the State College campus in the city. As the regents put it, "a more appropriate solution would be for the Legislature to authorize the University to develop a more nearly complete branch of the University of Wisconsin in Milwaukee." For the first time in history, the UW Board of Regents was on record as at least being grudgingly amenable to the establishment of a second, full-fledged branch of the University.[17] The State College regents, who had supported the Inter Boards Committee recommendation, naturally opposed any such UW development.

The two boards outlined their positions at a legislative hearing on October 6. The WSC regents argued they had a proven record of attentiveness to Milwaukee needs and were well-qualified to provide further educational services. The UW regents responded that for several decades

---

[16]UW Faculty Minutes, October 5, 1953, UA; Administrative Committee Minutes, October 27, 1953, Series 5/13, UA; "Four Groups Plan Surveys of UW," *WAM*, 55 (October, 1953), 15; "Faculty Will Study Integration, Too," ibid. (November, 1953), 12; "Statement Agreed Upon by the University of Wisconsin Faculty Committee on Integration, in Consultation with the University Committee," July 22, 1954, included with Administrative Committee Minutes, July 23, 1954; *Milwaukee Journal*, July 5, 1954; Klotsche, *University of Wisconsin-Milwaukee*, pp. 19-20.

[17]UW BOR Minutes, August 7, 1954; "Regents Don't Like Merger Plan," *WAM*, 56 (October, 1954), 20; Klotsche, *University of Wisconsin-Milwaukee*, p. 20.

they, too, had been offering a good variety of instruction in Milwaukee and were now on record as favoring a substantial expansion of the downtown Extension Center. For its part, the legislative Inter Boards Committee managed only to agree that a Milwaukee merger made good sense, but under whose auspices and what form it should take remained problematic. Apart from recommending that the Platteville and Stout institutes be placed under the State Colleges board, the committee had nothing to suggest regarding integration.[18]

Reelected to a third term late in 1954, Governor Kohler doggedly pushed the higher education integration issue again in his state-of-the-state address to the legislature on February 2, 1955. The demographic trend was plain for all to see, he observed: in the next few years there would be a massive surge of baby boom young people inundating Wisconsin's colleges and universities and possibly disrupting the state's economy. This challenge would require solid planning, coordination, and restraint. Kohler feared the State Colleges and the University would concentrate on their own development rather than coordinate their efforts for the public good. He therefore repeated his recommendation that the two systems be merged.[19] On February 17 a delegation of UW regents and staff met with Governor Kohler to discuss his proposal. No minds were changed, and the next day the regent delegation unanimously approved a statement prepared by the faculty Integration Committee, the University Committee, and top UW administrators. It read in part:

> The State cannot afford to take any action which might lower the effectiveness, the quality, or the reputation of the University of Wisconsin.... Any changes in the organizational patterns of higher education in this State should be taken slowly, one step at a time, and not abruptly in a single all-inclusive step. Any sudden and pronounced changes in this organization might be disastrous to the University and the State.[20]

While maintaining a strong stand against merger, the statement went on to affirm the regents' earlier compromise position on the Milwaukee situation: "If the Legislature desires to combine the State College in Milwaukee and the University Extension Division in Milwaukee, the

---

[18]Ibid., pp. 20-21; "Agreement on Milwaukee Merger Is Hard to Find," *WAM,* 56 (January, 1955), 6.

[19]Governor's Message, *Senate Journal,* 72nd session, 1955, pp. 227-240.

[20]"Position of the University on Coordination of public Higher Education in Wisconsin," February 18, 1955, attached to UW BOR Minutes, March 12, 1955.

University believes that the Legislature should direct such a combination as a part of the University of Wisconsin." The regents agreed to issue this statement upon the introduction of the governor's merger proposal into the legislature.

This came to pass on February 22, when Senator W.W. Clark, Republican from Vesper, offered bill 279S. It provided for the creation of a "Board of Regents of the University and State Colleges" to replace the current two boards, and would consist of fourteen citizen members appointed by the governor, plus the superintendent of public instruction. On March 9 UW Regents Charles D. Gelatt, Wilbur N. Renk, and Oscar Rennebohm (Kohler had appointed the former governor to the board), President Fred, and faculty Integration Committee Chairman Fred Harvey Harrington appeared at a joint hearing of the senate and assembly education committees to present the UW case for maintaining the status quo. Kohler supporters countered with two assertions: first, merger would enable the state to "meet future needs at the lowest possible cost," and second, coordination required a single board "because it is a practical impossibility to achieve co-operation otherwise."[21] On April 13, by a vote of 28-4 the senate adopted a compromise substitute amendment to 279S that would accomplish consolidation but also direct the new board to establish two seven-member subcommittees that separately would superintend the day-to-day operations of the University and the State Colleges. The amendment also provided for the merger of the Milwaukee Extension Center and State College, with the new institution placed under UW control.[22]

Continuing University opposition to a merger led assembly Speaker Mark Catlin, Republican from Appleton, to introduce a substitute amendment, 1A, on June 8. It embodied a considerably less extreme alternative to Kohler's integration plan, something more in line with the UW regents' stated step-by-step preference. Rather than consolidating the two regent boards, Catlin's proposal left them intact while establishing an overarching "co-ordinating agency for institutions of higher education" to set policy for educational programming, facilities, and budgetary

---

[21]Quoted in Kelly, "Politics of Higher Educational Coordination," p. 70.

[22]Proceedings of the Board of Regents of State Colleges (hereafter WSC/WSU BOR Minutes), February 9, 1955, Government Publications, SHSW; "State College Board Supports Integration," *Capital Times*, February 9, 1955; [Special regents' committee consisting of Charles Gelatt, John Jones, Carl Steiger, and A. Matt. Werner], "Position of the University on Coordination of Public Higher Education in Wisconsin," dated February 17, 1955, and adopted by the full board the next month, UW BOR Minutes, March 12, 1955; "Governor Again Seeks Coordination," *WAM*, 56 (February, 15, 1955), 11; "Regents Open Fight on Integration Plan," *Wisconsin State Journal*, February 19, 1955.

planning. This eleven-member coordinating body would consist of five delegates each from the UW and State College boards, plus the state superintendent of public instruction. Unlike the governor's plan, there were no citizen appointees representing the public. The University and the State Colleges would pay the expenses and provide staff support for the new agency, whose chairmanship would alternate annually between the two regent presidents. In essence, Catlin's substitute mandated the voluntary cooperation that University officials had occasionally advocated in response to calls for integration, even as they failed to implement it on a continuing basis. The behind-the-scenes politicking, which involved Speaker Catlin, several UW regents and administrative officers, and other state officials, is poorly documented, but the result was the passage, 60-34, on June 14 of bill 1A, the assembly's amended version of Kohler's 279S.[23]

Although assembly passage of bill 1A seemed to indicate the distance between the University and the Kohler administration on integration was narrowing, a full compromise remained elusive. The governor instructed Senate Majority Leader Paul Rogan, a Republican from Ladysmith, to offer yet another substitute amendment, 1S, to counter the assembly bill. The changes were significant: Kohler added four citizen members to the assembly plan's coordinating committee, retained the four-year Milwaukee college provision, and mandated in forceful language that all policies decided by the coordinating body "shall be carried out" by the respective regent boards. Furthermore, the coordinating committee's authority would "supersede" that of the regent boards in the case of any conflict between them. In short, the senate bill transferred the real power from the regents to the new oversight committee, in effect accomplishing integration without a formal action. Interpreting 1S from this perspective, UW Regent President Gelatt and Vice President Renk issued a statement on June 20 in support of Catlin's 1A. The next day, Senator Rogan withdrew 1S and the senate rejected 1A by a vote of 21-12, creating a legislative deadlock.[24]

---

[23]Kelly, "Politics," p. 71; Klotsche, *University of Wisconsin-Milwaukee*, pp. 21-23; Joseph C. Rost, "The Merger of the University of Wisconsin and the Wisconsin State University Systems: A Case Study in the Politics of Education," (Ph.D. dissertation, University of Wisconsin-Madison, 1973), pp. 163-64. Rost recounts that prior to offering 1A, Catlin, UW Regent Renk, and LeRoy Luberg, E.B. Fred's representative, had met to discuss an alternative to 279S. Apparently the two sides could not agree on a plan, and so Catlin proceeded with his own. Subsequently, again according to Rost, UW supported Catlin's 1A in the hopes of producing a legislative deadlock rather than accomplishing an actual solution to the problem of coordination.

[24]The quotes are from Kelly, "Politics," p. 73. In endorsing 1A, the UW regent

Even though Governor Kohler had again failed to accomplish integration, it was apparent to UW and State College officials that legislative support was building toward some form of statutory coordination. The time had come for a genuine compromise. Apparently UW Regent President Gelatt took the initiative in arranging a meeting with William D. McIntyre, his counterpart on the State Colleges board, to try to work something out. Discussions quickly expanded to include individual regents and top administrators from both sides. Major responsibility for drafting a bill fell to UW Vice President Ira Baldwin, who enlisted the expert help of economics Professor Edwin E. Witte, an experienced legislative adviser and member of the faculty Committee on Integration, along with University legislative lobbyist LeRoy Luberg. The two regent boards met jointly in Milwaukee on August 30 and approved the Baldwin-Witte draft presented by Gelatt and McIntyre. A series of legislative formalities ensued, resulting in senate passage, 29-1, on October 11, and assembly approval, 96-0, the next day. "Every Wisconsin parent and every prospective student . . . can look forward to greater educational opportunity which will be provided at a minimum expense to the citizens of the state," a pleased Governor Kohler observed as he signed the compromise into law on October 13.[25]

"Review and Coordination"

The compromise integration bill became Chapter 619 of the *Laws of Wisconsin*, 1955. It established a permanent fifteen-member Coordinating Committee for Higher Education (CCHE), consisting of five UW regents, five State College regents, four citizens appointed by the governor, and

statement by board leaders Charles Gelatt and Wilbur Renk complained that 1S "places the authority in the hands of a committee which will have power to supersede actions of the present boards."

[25] Luberg to Percy and Taylor, February 26, 1971, Series 40/1/2/3-2, Box 2, UA. Witte had been instrumental in formulating the U.S. Social Security Act during the 1930s and previously had managed the Wisconsin Legislative Reference Bureau. For a good treatment of Witte's career at the University, see David B. Johnson, "Edwin E. Witte's Years on the Faculty, 1933-1957," in Robert J. Lampman, ed., *Economics at Wisconsin, 1892-1992* (Madison: Board of Regents of the University of Wisconsin System, 1993), pp. 106-117. Governor Kohler subsequently credited Regent Gelatt with "bringing about this meeting of minds with respect to the future of higher education in Wisconsin." Kohler to Gelatt, September 22, 1955, Kohler Papers, SHSW Archives. The regent vote breakdown was: UW, 6 yes, 2 no; State Colleges, 6 yes, 5 no; state superintendent of public instruction, yes. UW Faculty Minutes, September 10, 1955; UW Faculty Documents 1183 and 1183A, UA; UW BOR Minutes, September 1, 1955; Baldwin, *My Half Century*, pp. 480-481; Kelly, "Politics," 77-79.

the superintendent of public instruction, who served as an ex officio member of both regent boards. Its provisions for membership and responsibilities, as well as for the creation of a four-year public college in Milwaukee under UW direction, followed closely Senator Rogan's 1S substitute amendment. Only the final, open-ended assertion of Coordinating Committee authority over the two boards was omitted, replaced instead by a provision that limited the committee's powers to areas explicitly delineated in the statute. This was the governor's major concession, which he probably interpreted as minor in light of CCHE's stated control over educational program, budget, facilities planning, and responsibility for presenting the two systems' biennial budget requests to the legislature.

From the regents' perspective, too, the outcome could have been much worse. As UW Regent Gelatt put it while the final legislative compromise was taking shape, CCHE would be "a committee of review and coordination rather than a committee of initiation and direction."[26] Even if the four citizen members remained faithful to the governor's wishes on any particular issue, the ten regent members would always have it in their power collectively to prevail. Additionally, according to the final bill, the regent members would be designated annually and would include the two board presidents, who would alternately serve as chairman and vice chairman, along with eight others chosen by majority votes of their respective colleagues. Thus the membership structure favored dependable and timely regent influence in CCHE deliberations. Similarly, as initially proposed in Catlin's 1A, all committee funding and staff would be provided by the University and State Colleges. These provisions seemed to buttress Gelatt's friendly view of the new oversight agency.

The Coordinating Committee's early actions affirmed this expectation. Even prior to the committee's first formal meeting in January of 1956, University officials–chief among them Vice President Baldwin–had already made considerable progress in merging the University Extension Center and State Teachers College in Milwaukee.[27] Although CCHE was ultimately responsible for developing the state's new four-year institution (soon know variously as the University of Wisconsin-Milwaukee and UWM), the committee was left with little to do but approve decisions made on Bascom Hill. In the crucial matter of committee staffing, the regent boards designated top-level leaders Eugene Kleinpell, president of WSC-River Falls, and UW's Ira Baldwin as co-directors. Formerly

---

[26]Quoted in Kelly, "Politics," p. 77, with references to *Milwaukee Sentinel* and *Milwaukee Journal*, August 31, 1955.

[27]See above, pp. 98-103. Also see Baldwin, *My Half Century*, pp. 486-87.

opponents, Kleinpell and Baldwin were now committed to achieving genuine cooperation. To this end they organized staff support in such a way as to involve numerous faculty members and administrators in all phases of CCHE's background studies. This was a traditional UW practice, though less well-developed among the WSC institutions, which operated along more authoritarian lines. As CCHE established its procedures and began to address important issues, its members easily fell into the habit of relying on the staff for data, analysis, and recommendations, certainly a comfortable arrangement for the University and the State Colleges.[28]

Over the next few years the committee staff produced numerous studies providing solid quantitative data and analysis upon which CCHE deliberations could proceed. They addressed a whole range of relevant issues, including "Economic and Educational Relationships," "Wisconsin Population Trends," "Geographic Origins of Wisconsin College Students," "The Junior College," "Retention of Students in the State Colleges and the University," and a "Physical Facilities Study." Beginning in 1957 the Coordinating Committee began issuing a series of easily readable semi-annual reports for general public and legislative consumption that framed the major issues of the day and suggested that CCHE had them well in hand. With no natural constituency of its own, CCHE tried to use its publications to establish an image as a legitimate and effective oversight agency promoting the public interest even as it largely functioned as an arm of the two collegiate systems.[29]

CCHE's coordinative function also was put to use. It early became apparent, for example, that the state would benefit from a comprehensive

---

[28]Baldwin's appointment did not derive from a formal action and did not appear in the UW BOR Minutes. Baldwin speculated that he and Kleinpell had been "drafted" into this work as "just retribution" for their former argumentative behavior before the legislature. Ibid., pp. 482-83.

[29]For a list of 28 studies prepared for CCHE by its staff, see CCHE, *Education Beyond High School: The Changing Picture of Higher Education in Wisconsin*, Semi-Annual Report (December, 1958), pp. 22-23. The semi-annual reports were entitled *Higher Education* and carried various subtitles: *An Investment In People– Wisconsin's Most Precious Resource* (June, 1957), *Wisconsin's Opportunities–Their Availability and Use* (December, 1957), *The Changing Picture of Higher Education in Wisconsin* (December, 1958), and *Financial Aid to Students Attending Wisconsin's Colleges* (June, 1959). "You had to study the character and the adequacy of the programs you had in all these institutions [including private colleges and public technical and county teacher training institutions] that were serving post-high school students. You had to study the space needs and the financial needs of the institutions under your control, meaning the state colleges and the University. And these were the first studies that were ever really made of this kind of thing." Baldwin, *My Half Century*, p.483.

approach to post-secondary educational issues. This led to CCHE proclamations asserting the virtue of "diversity" across a wide range of educational institutions, particularly the private colleges and the emerging statewide system of technical and adult education programs, which were funded primarily at the county level. And even as CCHE welcomed the participation of the twenty-two county-based two-year normal schools, it also encouraged these institutions to accommodate the national trend toward four-year teacher licensing requirements. While this portended the eventual closing of these local teacher-training schools, it also led to much discussion and some organization of cooperative instructional arrangements across the several systems, all with the objective of providing the best and most affordable educational opportunities possible.

CCHE was notably successful in its early efforts to coordinate important functions of the University and the State Colleges, its central responsibility. With regard to academic programming, the challenge was to establish basic policy guidelines. Thus in early 1956 the committee agreed to maintain the "historical functions" of the State Colleges and the University. In succeeding years this helped justify decisions limiting most Ph.D. degree programs to the Madison campus, allowing for joint-master's degree programming between the State Colleges and UW, and providing for the expansion of "liberal arts and teacher training programs" throughout the State Colleges, with future master's level programs envisioned but not yet operational. Among other things, the Coordinating Committee also tried to strengthen nurses training across the state, authorized an undergraduate degree program in commerce at UWM, set up a Joint Committee in Engineering Education to plan cooperative UW-State College bachelor's degree programming, and approved a new Master of Fine Arts degree program at Madison. The period also witnessed the beginnings of a debate over the future of UW's freshman-sophomore extension centers and their potential for combining with local technical and adult education schools under county auspices to form what in other states were known as community or junior colleges.[30]

Finally, CCHE asserted, or seemed to assert, a welcome degree of order in the perennially troublesome biennial budgeting process. Thus in 1957 and 1959 the Coordinating Committee earned praise from the

---

[30]For a summary of early CCHE actions regarding the centers and current policy as of early 1960 see Joint Staff Working Paper #19, "Actions of the Coordinating Committee for Higher Education Upon Which the Master Plan Will be Based," July 22, 1960, CCHE Studies, SHSW Archives, and *Design for the Future Development of Public Higher Education in Wisconsin: Semi-Annual Report*, (CCHE, December, 1960), pp. 14-16.

governor and legislature simply for presenting combined UW-WSC requests for operations and for capital improvements. The specific features and priorities of the original University and the State College proposals, however, remained essentially unchanged by the committee. Very little in the way of true compromise or cutting was involved in the CCHE review. Thus, as with the decisions regarding programming, cooperation was easy at this time because few tough decisions were yet needed. Several years still remained before the baby boomers would begin graduating from high school and heading for college. The goodwill and intentions of the University and the State Colleges remained essentially untested, and CCHE's decisions were easy for everyone to live with. In January, 1960, CCHE proclaimed two guiding principles: first, to "improve the effectiveness and efficiency" of the two collegiate systems, and second, to "prepare for the greatly increased demands and needs . . . which will occur within the next decade."[31] Only as the enrollment deluge arrived and state resources truly became scarce relative to demand, and as new regent and CCHE leadership replaced the old, would the legislative compromise of 1955 be tested.

Competition Renewed

For the University, in the early 1960s inter-system cooperation under CCHE began to give way to an institutional dynamic emphasizing UW expansion and diversification. This was partly the result of greatly expanded funding for research and instruction provided by the big national foundations and the federal government. As we have seen in prior chapters, this massive infusion of resources from outside Wisconsin was helping to support a growing student body and faculty and a major expansion of the scholarly disciplines themselves. UW faculty members at all levels were encouraged to concentrate on publishable research and scholarship and increasingly viewed themselves as operating primarily within national, and frequently international, professional networks. Local UW and state citizenship suffered by comparison. UW departments and administrators found themselves searching a frenzied national academic market for the best new faculty, obliged to adjust teaching loads and provide competitive salaries and support, while trying to retain what positive features they could of the older, smaller, more personal University of Wisconsin.

---

[31] Joint Staff Working Paper #8, "Review of the First Four Years of the Activities of the Coordinating Committee," January, 1960, p. 3, CCHE Studies, SHSW Archives.

Changing UW leadership also was involved. President Conrad Elvehjem (1958-1962), was largely content to follow the lead of his predecessor, E.B. Fred (1945-1958), and continued to rely on Ira Baldwin as the University's primary liaison with the Coordinating Committee. Following President Elvehjem's fatal heart attack in mid-1962, the much more dynamic Fred Harvey Harrington ascended to the UW presidency (1962-1970) and promptly began to reshape the University in a variety of expansive ways. Meanwhile, in January of 1959 Gaylord Nelson became the first Democratic governor of Wisconsin since 1935. A UW alumnus and acknowledged "friend" of the institution, Nelson immediately began appointing regents from his own party. The new board members tended be liberal Democrats who shared Harrington's vision of the University and identified with the Kennedy-Johnson administrations in Washington. To Harrington and the new regents, the 1955 CCHE compromise, which had been largely engineered and thereafter managed by Republicans, seemed of questionable value. For them the challenge was largely how to clear the way for unhindered UW expansion in the dawning age of massive governmental and educational activism. This was far more important than developing a collegial relationship with what seemed in their view to be a Wisconsin cast of academic and political lightweights. More than anyone else, Park Falls attorney Arthur DeBardeleben, Nelson's first appointment to the UW board, enthusiastically embodied this perspective.[32]

Support for the Coordinating Committee as a University priority began to decline almost as soon as E.B. Fred left the president's office in 1958. While Ira Baldwin retained his CCHE co-directorship, his position within the University administration was downgraded from vice president to special assistant to the president. He no longer participated in any important University administrative activity, but instead split his time between CCHE and the bacteriology department. Simultaneously, Fred Harvey Harrington, who had narrowly lost out to Elvehjem for the presidency, moved to the vice presidency. As a faculty leader in the fight against Governor Kohler's integration initiatives in 1953 and 1955, Harrington did not share Fred's and Baldwin's commitment to making CCHE work, and in contrast soon was promoting an expansionist view. Although Baldwin and Elvehjem had initially agreed that the former would remain at CCHE only long enough for the latter to designate a suitable replacement, the passive UW president never got around to this.[33] It fell

---

[32]For Ira Baldwin's view of the significance of regent turnover, see Baldwin, *My Half Century*, pp. 484-85.

[33]Baldwin claimed he did not wish to continue as vice president after Fred retired.

to President Harrington to make the change in 1963 by designating law Professor Carlisle P. Runge as UW's new CCHE co-director.[34] As Ira Baldwin later reflected on the Coordinating Committee of these years, "the original cooperative spirit had disappeared, and it was just another arena in which each group was trying to gain the advantage."[35]

A significant issue for CCHE at this time was the University's determination to expand and upgrade its system of two-year extension centers. From the UW point of view, its actions seemed both a matter of tradition and inevitability. The centers (excluding the Milwaukee unit, which was established about 1908) dated from the 1920s and especially the 1930s, when they enabled many freshmen and sophomores to live at home while attending the University. Although the centers were essentially dormant during World War II, they flourished again after the war as University authorities set up dozens of temporary outposts across Wisconsin to relieve the severe enrollment pressures swamping the campus in Madison. As the number of war veterans seeking collegiate instruction declined by the early 1950s, the University Extension Division (UED) reduced the number of centers to eight, all of them regularly attracting adequate enrollments (usually in the range of 200 students) and occupying temporary space in local educational facilities (primarily high schools, technical institutes, and county normal schools). Thereafter the University began encouraging the host communities to provide dedicated permanent buildings and grounds for their centers, with the University responsible for the curriculum and instructional staff. In 1963 Harrington, now president, obtained regent approval to split the centers from their parent University Extension Division and designate them collectively as the free-standing UW Center System. CCHE was largely a bystander to these changes, which UW officials viewed as an internal matter.[36]

The regents therefore appointed Elvehjem president and Harrington vice president. Elvehjem wanted Baldwin to remain as vice president and split the work with Harrington, but Baldwin would only agree to remain at CCHE while working half-time at Bacteriology. Ibid., pp. 265, 271-2.

[34]Runge had served on the UW Law School faculty since 1951. In 1961 and 1962, during the Kennedy administration, he served as assistant secretary of defense for manpower. For a good overview of Runge's career, see UW Faculty Document 543, "Memorial Resolution of the Faculty of the University of Wisconsin on the Death of Emeritus Professor Carlisle P. Runge," December 5, 1981.

[35]Baldwin, *My Half Century*, p. 485.

[36]UW BOR Minutes, September 6, 1963; "Recommendation Concerning Organization of University Center System," September 3, 1963, Series 4/18/1, Box 40, UA.

Far from an isolated housekeeping move, the decision to create the Center System was part of Harrington's larger restructuring of the University, which fragmented the institution into a number of separate units, each headed by a chancellor: the two campuses at Madison and Milwaukee, the two-year centers, and a new University of Wisconsin Extension, which combining UED, the Cooperative (agricultural) Extension Service, and WHA radio and television. Control over these separate UW units was retained in the president's Central Administration offices in Madison. Though not yet officially designated as such, Harrington had thus by 1965 effectively transformed the University into a University of Wisconsin system. From an organizational point of view, the parent campus in Madison was now only one of several equal units. These administrative changes seemed to make eminently good sense for Harrington's aspiring world-class University of Wisconsin, but they were undertaken without significant CCHE or other state review. Few observers at the time noted or cared that they also were distancing the Madison campus administration and faculty from the state-wide political and educational context.

The two-year centers were important to the University in several respects. They had met a clear state need in times of unusual social or economic stress, such as the Great Depression and the post-war reconversion period. University publicists found them a convenient illustration of the venerable Wisconsin Idea of University service across the state. As UW leaders planned for the anticipated enrollment growth generated by the baby boomers, they naturally thought of expanding and upgrading the system. This also was attractive to a sizable part of the Madison faculty, particularly in those departments of the College of Letters and Science that maintained close control over their fields of study at the centers and used them as employment opportunities for advanced graduate students. As the University and the State Colleges competed for limited state resources, the centers appealed as a low-cost way to maximize enrollment and therefore state funding. Indeed, critics sometimes charged this was the University's primary motivation in expanding the centers. Others believed the Harrington administration used the Center System as a means of enhancing grass-roots political support for the University.[37]

As we have seen, CCHE began considering the freshman-sophomore centers during the 1950s and thereafter sought to establish policies governing the orderly and reasonable expansion of such educational services. After a long and complex debate the Coordinating Committee

---

[37]Kelly, "Politics," pp. 160, 162.

ultimately decided against the creation of a state-wide system of public junior colleges. UW officials favored, and helped force, this decision because such an enterprise would have meant its loss of the centers, an unacceptable option. The proposal received only mild support from the WSC regents, who were more concerned with developing their four-year campuses. Even in the face of serious concern expressed by both the legislature and Governor Nelson in 1961 and 1962, the Coordinating Committee managed only to develop a policy supporting the creation of additional two-year centers by the University and the State Colleges but failing to assert crucial guidance as to where and under which system. At one point in 1960, for example, the CCHE position was that local communities were responsible for petitioning either the University or the State Colleges for a campus. Not surprisingly given its greater experience and prestige, UW usually turned out to be the preferred agency.[38]

Without serious regard for either the State Colleges or CCHE, the University proceeded substantially to develop its two-year centers. State College officials responded that expansion was intruding upon the service regions of their nine four-year campuses. They therefore began advocating WSC control over any new two-year campuses that might be located in their regions. Their argument was weakened somewhat by the fact that they had not previously initiated such programs on their own. In mid-1962 the Wood County cities of Marshfield and Wisconsin Rapids each petitioned for a permanent UW center, which the UW regents approved. This forced the ultimate decision on the Coordinating Committee, which easily approved the Marshfield center, bringing the number of UW centers to nine. The State College regent members succeeded in blocking the Wisconsin Rapids proposal, however, arguing that it fell within the service area of WSC-Stevens Point. More than the particular decision, this episode was notable for the acrimonious exchange between the two sets of regent members of CCHE and the several party-line roll call votes, both rarities in earlier Coordinating Committee deliberations. The 1955 compromise that produced CCHE was breaking down. Increasingly, the committee found itself in the thankless role of trying to moderate the competitive drives of the two collegiate systems while also serving the complex interests of each and the state as a whole.[39]

[38]CCHE Minutes, July 23, 1960, Government Publications, SHSW; Kelly, "Politics," pp. 132-37.

[39]UW BOR Minutes, June 5, 1962; CCHE Minutes, July 20, 1962; "Hocus-Pocus Won't Dissuade Extension Center Boosters," Wisconsin Rapids *Daily Tribune*; John C. Thompson to Richard A. Davis, December 10, 1962, John K. Kyle Papers, SHSW Archives;

In April, 1964, WSC Regent John C. Thomson, a strong junior college advocate, convinced his board to request that the Coordinating Committee "take a new look at plans for developing two-year post high school public higher education opportunities." The State College regents went on to suggest "the possibility of some form of unified effort in program implementation." The CCHE plans and policies subcommittee took up this request on April 23. But due to strong opposition from UW representatives, the subcommittee voted to table the WSC request, along with an accompanying document written by Thomson, entitled "A Proposal for A System of Two-Year Colleges." Instead, the subcommittee merely recommended that CCHE carry on with its "long-range plans as presently adopted." The State College regents responded on May 22 with a request that the Coordinating Committee declare a moratorium on two-year campus expansion and study the possibility of organizing all such institutions into a single system under the State Board of Vocational and Adult Education (SBVAE). This obviously was unacceptable to the University (as well as to SBVAE), and in June the CCHE plans and policies subcommittee rejected the follow-up WSC request by a 4-3 vote, instead "reaffirming further development" as previously defined.[40] Unrelenting UW pressure had produced these WSC defeats and allowed the UW Center System to proceed with its development largely unchecked, while the stature of CCHE as an effective coordinating agency correspondingly declined.[41]

Kelly, "Politics," pp. 146-47, 159. The problem got so serious that when CCHE issued its December, 1963, semi-annual report, it listed six additional sites throughout the state potentially appropriate for the establishment of two-year campuses between 1965 and 1969, but failed to make a definite decision as to which system might operate each new center. As of fall, 1963, the official CCHE list of potential host communities and operating systems were: Waukesha (UW), Rock County (UW), Rice Lake (WSC), West Bend (UW), Baraboo (UW), and Clintonville-Shawano (WSC). CCHE Working Paper #44, "Proposal for the Distribution and Establishment of Two-Year University Centers and State College Branch Campuses," October, 1963, SHSW Archives.

[40]John C. Thomson, "A Proposal for a System of Two-Year Colleges," appendix II, CCHE Minutes, April 24, 1964; "To Get a Junior College Just Change a Name!" *Wisconsin State Journal*, June 8, 1964; Angus B. Rothwell, Resolution, CCHE Minutes, June 12, 1964; Kelly, "Politics," pp. 161-162, 164, 165.

[41]The Coordinating Committee did apparently manage to assert itself in 1965 by engineering a compromise between the State Colleges and the University in authorizing three "experimental" community college campuses (Rice Lake, Wisconsin Rapids, and Rhinelander) in northern Wisconsin. The fact was, however, that the University's main concern was to carry on with its expansion throughout the more populous areas of southern and eastern Wisconsin, an objective left unaffected by the so-called compromise. Meyer M. Cohen to Duane Smith, December 15, 1964, CCHE Correspondence and Subject File, SHSW Archives; David F. Behrendt, "First of Three State Community Colleges Proposed

As the debate over two-year campuses continued, more general program-related conflicts arose at CCHE between the University and the State Colleges. In 1961, for example, a bitter dispute unfolded over a UW-Milwaukee plan to add two new physical education majors. WSC regents argued that WSC-La Crosse had long specialized in physical education and filled its impressive sports teams with student-athletes who frequently majored in physical education and often came from the Milwaukee metropolitan area. Although the Coordinating Committee staff, still led to a great extent by UW co-director Ira Baldwin, recommended delay, UW Regent DeBardeleben, closely aligned with Vice President Harrington, forced a divided vote approving the UWM request. The growing use of hard-nosed lobbying and bloc voting, often initiated by UW representatives, was a rejection of the earlier Baldwin cooperative style of CCHE decision-making. Less partisan members of the Coordinating Committee tried to respond to this episode by requiring the State Colleges and the University to obtain CCHE approval before establishing new degree programs or majors. In 1963, however, with President Harrington now fully engaged in turning the Milwaukee campus into a major urban university, the Coordinating Committee without comment granted permission to establish the first UWM Ph.D. program, in mathematics. In the process CCHE tacitly declined to notice, let alone to question or challenge, the substantial expansion of the original Milwaukee mission implied by the decision. As one staff member confided to an out-of-state colleague, "we have not assumed our responsibility in this area in the past."[42]

Two decisions by the WSC regents in 1964 indicated the by-now untenable position of CCHE as the supposed coordinator of public higher

for Central, North Areas," *Milwaukee Journal*, February 7, 1965; CCHE Minutes, February 12, 1965; David F. Behrendt, "Politics Played Role in College Agreement," *Milwaukee Journal*, February 14, 1965; Kelly, "Politics," pp. 165-80.

Added to the UW Center System were Marinette in 1965, Rock County and Waukesha County in 1966, and Baraboo-Sauk County and Washington County in 1968. Added to WSU were Barron County Branch of Stout in 1966, Richland Center Branch of Platteville in 1967, Fond du Lac Branch of Oshkosh in 1968, and Medford Branch of Stevens Point in 1969. Rost, "Merger," pp. 49, 54; Adolfson gives different dates for the opening of some of the UW Centers: Marshfield in 1964; Janesville (Rock County) and Waukesha in 1966; and West Bend (Washington County) and Baraboo (Sauk County) in 1968. With the opening of four-year campuses at Parkside and Green Bay, five center campuses were closed: Racine and Kenosha going to Parkside; Marinette, Fox Valley, Green Bay, and Manitowoc going to Green Bay. L. H. Adolfson, "University of Wisconsin Centers, 1946-1972," *Wisconsin Academy Review*, vol. 19, no. 3 (1973), 28.

[42]CCHE Minutes, January 20, May 19-20, 1961; Kelly, "Politics," pp. 180-86; the quotation is from p. 186.

education in Wisconsin. First came the committee's decision not to concern itself with the action of the WSC regents on May 22 upgrading the titles of their institutions from Wisconsin State Colleges to Wisconsin State Universities (WSU). (The legislature did not get around to updating the WSC board's official name until 1968.) Although UW President Harrington considered this move innocuous and gave it his blessing, the name change in fact reflected the transformation of the former teachers colleges into genuine university-level institutions. Total WSU enrollments now rivaled those of the University, their physical plants were burgeoning, their libraries were developing more substantial if not yet comprehensive collections, new departments were expanding the available fields of study, and their faculties were being upgraded with Ph.D. appointees from prestigious institutions, including the University of Wisconsin itself.[43] The State College regents further asserted an independent CCHE agenda by replacing their experienced co-director, Robert DeZonia, with Jim Dan Hill, a former major general and president of WSC-Superior. DeZonia, like UW's Baldwin, had earned a reputation as competent, cooperative, and even-handed; Hill, on the other hand, was partisan, tough, and an accomplished lobbyist. Announced as a surprise fait accompli, the Hill appointment produced a minor furor as observers lamented the Coordinating Committee's transformation into a highly combative political arena.[44]

The 1965 Restructuring

UW Regent Gelatt's 1955 depiction of the Coordinating Committee as an agency of "review and coordination" was clearly no longer valid a decade later. Unrestrained inter-institutional conflict was accompanying the rapidly growing boomer enrollments. Governor Warren Knowles and the legislature responded in 1965 by restructuring CCHE in several important ways, all intended to produce a more independent and powerful

---

[43]WSC BOR Minutes, May 22, 1964; "Colleges Grab 'U' Title," *Capital Times*, May 22, 1964. Stated President Harrington several days later: "My own individual view is that it was bound to come sooner or later, since the equivalent institutions in Michigan and Illinois have moved to the university label. I cannot believe that the change in title will hurt us in any way." Harrington to Each Regent, May 27, 1964, Series 4/18/1, Box 58, UA.

[44]CCHE Minutes, January 24, 1964; David F. Behrendt, "Official Shifts Protested by College Unit," *Milwaukee Journal*, January 25, 1964; David F. Behrendt, "Controversy Follows Hill to Madison Post," *Milwaukee Journal*, January 26, 1964; "Statement by Board of Regents of State Colleges," February 28, 1964, included in CCHE Minutes, April 3, 1964.

oversight agency. The 1965 changes increased the number of citizen members and gave them a voting majority; required that a citizen member, rather than one of the regent board presidents, serve as CCHE chairman; created a new top staff position of executive director paid by and reporting exclusively to CCHE; for the first time funded CCHE through its own appropriation in the state budget; and expanded the committee's mission to include some degree of unspecified "direction" over educational operations. These changes amounted to a repudiation of the original Baldwin-crafted compromise creating CCHE as essentially a voluntary coordinating mechanism of the University and State Colleges.[45]

All three Wisconsin governors between 1960 and 1965–two Democrats and one Republican–were alert to and unhappy with the evolving situation. In early 1962, for example, Democratic Governor Gaylord Nelson (1959-1963) took the unusual step of convening a joint meeting of the UW and WSC regent boards and CCHE. Through his department of administration head Joe Nusbaum, Nelson had earlier encouraged CCHE to engage in detailed long-term planning for the additional college and university facilities that soon would be necessary. The committee had demurred, however, instead referring Nelson's concerns to the two regent boards. Frustrated over CCHE's inaction, Governor Nelson called this joint meeting to proclaim an approaching "crisis" in higher education and to offer twenty-three suggestions for meeting the challenge.[46] Little if any change resulted, however. Nelson's successor, Democrat John W. Reynolds (1963-1965), was more content to support UW President Harrington's aggressive lead. He viewed CCHE as an appropriately passive agency and did not pursue Nelson's more activist vision for it. But the WSC move in the Jim Dan Hill affair got Reynolds' attention, and he eventually welcomed a legislative initiative establishing the so-called Committee of 25 to conduct a comprehensive investigation into the

---

[45]"Final Report of the Subcommittee on Education to the Committee of 25," January 18, 1965, CCHE Correspondence and Subject File, SHSW Archives.

[46]CCHE Minutes, April 27, 1962. The Department of Administration had been established during Nelson's administration to centralize budgeting and personnel policies for state agencies under the governor's office. Early in his administration, Nelson had worked behind the scenes to deal with the CCHE problem. In July of 1960, for example, Nelson had assigned Joe Nusbaum, his commissioner of administration, to serve as liaison between the governor's office and CCHE. Nelson to Carl E. Steiger, CCHE Chairman, July 19, 1960, Governor Gaylord A. Nelson Papers, Box 106, Folder 9, SHSW Archives. A few months later, Nelson had concluded that the long-range planning process was inadequate. Robert C. Bassett, UW Regent Member of the CCHE to Nelson, September 21, 1960, ibid., Box 131, Folder 6.

expenditure of state funds. Recommendations coming out of an educational sub-committee of this group in 1964 eventually formed the basis of the 1965 CCHE reorganization.[47] Meanwhile, Republican Warren P. Knowles became governor in January, 1965 (and would served through the remainder of the decade). Like Nelson, Knowles favored rigorous control of state spending and centralized long-term planning for all state agencies. An experienced legislator before his election as governor, he was familiar with CCHE and the state's two higher education systems. Indeed, as we have seen in Chapter 2 of this study, he was a strong UW supporter and had defended the University during the 1950s McCarthy era. As governor, he grew increasingly critical of CCHE and recommended its reorganization to the legislature in March of 1965.[48]

UW Regent and CCHE member Arthur DeBardeleben led the Coordinating Committee's resistance to reorganization. Ironically, he had in the past consistently objected when the committee tried to take any action he interpreted as meddling with the University. In fact, he had been the primary agent for changing the modus operandi at CCHE from cooperative to competitive to sometimes outright confrontational.[49] In light of the Committee of 25's recommendations for a major CCHE reorganization, the CCHE citizen members themselves began to push for a more independent Coordinating Committee. DeBardeleben now switched positions and defended the status quo. In September of 1964 he proposed that CCHE appoint a panel to evaluate the Committee of 25 recommendations. He chaired this group, whose report accused the Committee of 25 of trying fundamentally to pervert CCHE, whose responsibility was primarily to represent the needs and interests of the "operating systems" before the state government and public. While friction between system representatives had occasionally developed, CCHE had in fact remained loyal to its mission, deliberating and acting constructively. The result, according to the DeBardeleben Committee, had been effective and efficient educational programming. If the Committee of 25 had its way, DeBardeleben's group warned, the proposed independent board and staff would "gravitate to the power centers of higher levels of government." This would be disastrous. In the view of DeBardeleben and his fellow panel members,

[47]Committee of 25 Minutes, July 25-26, 1963, February 13, April 2 and 30, June 18, 1964, CCHE Correspondence and Subject File, SHSW; Kelly, "Politics," p. 196.

[48]Governor Warren P. Knowles, "Special Message: Crisis In Education," March 24, 1965, State of Wisconsin, Government Publications, SHSW.

[49]CCHE Minutes, May 19, 1961, July 20, 1962, and February 12, 1965; Robert DeZonia to John W. Jenkins, November 17, 1998.

nothing was wrong; no changes were needed. The full Coordinating Committee, including three reluctant citizen members, voted unanimously to affirm the DeBardeleben Committee report. In so doing, CCHE tacitly declared itself irrelevant in the political debate over how to manage higher education growth in Wisconsin.[50]

CCHE and the DeBardeleben Committee notwithstanding, by mid-1965 the legislature had voted for reorganization. The changes reduced Coordinating Committee membership from 19 to 17, now with only two representatives each from UW and WSU. Governor Knowles appointed six new citizen members (bringing the total to 9), including former Governor Walter J. Kohler, whom he designated as CCHE chairman. Knowles sought leaders who he thought could assert the restructured Coordinating Committee's new powers. Walter Kohler seemed ideally suited for this leadership role, since more than anyone he had been responsible for the creation of CCHE in 1955. Although he had originally overestimated the Coordinating Committee's effectiveness, he appreciated the current challenges and enthusiastically accepted his new assignment.[51]

True to form, Regent DeBardeleben denied that the legislature had intended any significant expansion of CCHE's authority, and he was largely successful in limiting the powers of the newly created executive director's position. Furthermore, in 1966 following a direct confrontation between DeBardeleben and Chairman Kohler, CCHE settled on the compromise appointment of Angus Rothwell, who had previously served ex officio on the Coordinating Committee and on the two boards of regents by virtue of his position as state superintendent of public instruction. A competent and respected schoolman, Rothwell shunned the public spotlight, preferring instead to work things out quietly behind the scenes. He was, in short, a conciliator in the mode of Ira Baldwin. The problem was, of course, that the University and the State Universities were no longer committed to cooperation. Instead, they were aggressively moving ahead with competing and frequently conflicting expansionist agendas. Thus

---

[50]CCHE Minutes, September 14, 1964; CCHE Working Paper #83, "Report of the Ad Hoc Committee on the Report of the Committee of Twenty-Five on Organization for Higher Education," October, 1964, Government Publications, SHSW. Apparently Carlisle Runge, the UW co-director of CCHE, drafted the report. Kelly, "Politics," pp. 202-203.

[51]Knowles' six citizen appointments included: Kohler, G. Kenneth Crowell, Harold A. Konnak, William Kraus, Frank H. Ranney, and C. O. Wanvig, Jr. Ibid., 240. See also "Ex-Gov. Kohler Named to New Education Unit," *Wisconsin State Journal*, September 14, 1965; "Good Choices to Higher Education Body by Knowles," ed., *Milwaukee Journal*, September 14, 1965.

UW Regent and CCHE member
Arthur DeBardeleben. UA,
X25-3386.

Van Hise Hall above the clouds,
1975, photo by Norman Lenburg.
UA, X25-3385.

although the 1965 reorganization envisioned a more powerful and directive CCHE functioning through a strong executive director, Rothwell was not well suited for such a role. He was, however, perfect from the point of view of Regent DeBardeleben, President Harrington, and WSU Director Eugene McPhee. The law might have changed, but CCHE was as marginal and ineffective as ever.

CCHE's Last Stand

Without consulting CCHE, which was in the process of reorganizing, the legislature approved the establishment of two new University centers, one at Green Bay and the other between Racine and Kenosha, eventually designated UW-Green Bay and UW-Parkside. The UW regents at first authorized them to offer only junior-senior work in conjunction with nearby freshman-sophomore centers, but their status was quickly changed to be four-year, degree-granting branch universities. While the primary initiative for this expansion had been local, the Harrington administration had early recognized its potential political benefits and offered encouragement. The new branch campuses, located as they were at the north and south ends of Wisconsin's Lake Michigan urban corridor, promised to enhance the University's base vis-à-vis the State Universities. Managed wisely, this might indeed have been the outcome. Instead, President Harrington's "single university-branch campuses" philosophy led him and his lieutenants to apply UW-Madison workloads, salaries, and practices in the development of UW-Green Bay and UW-Parkside. When questioned about the justification for this approach for what were clearly undergraduate institutions, UW officials replied glibly that the University's statutory mission was broader than that of the WSU system, involving not only instruction, but also research and public service. Yet to WSU authorities and faculty, as well as many observers outside the University, it seemed clear that the new UW campuses were much more comparable to the WSU institutions than to Madison or Milwaukee. Such critics saw no reason why professors at Green Bay and Parkside should be paid more and teach less than their WSU counterparts. The newly strengthened CCHE was largely ineffective in resolving any of the bitter discussion over this issue.[52]

---

[52]"Area University Plan Fund Bill Passed by Legislature," *Green Bay Press-Gazette*, July 29, 1965; CCHE #53, "First Report on the Planning for the New Third and Fourth Year Campuses," November 9, 1965, CCHE Correspondence and Subject file, SHSW Archives; UW BOR Minutes, November 4, 1966; CCHE Minutes, March 9, 1967; "Urge

The Harrington administration's ongoing effort to build the Milwaukee campus to major university status also created problems for Coordinating Committee. UW authorities seemed to expect automatic CCHE authorization for anything they proposed. In reviewing a UW request to approve a UWM master's degree in pediatric nursing in June, 1966, for example, CCHE discovered the program had been operating for two years and already had granted four degrees. Explained UW Vice President Clodius lamely, "It's not been clear what programs have to be taken to the co-ordinating committee."[53] Another difficult issue centered on competition between Milwaukee and the State University campuses at Platteville and Stevens Point for approval of an architectural degree program. CCHE ultimately avoided a difficult choice by allowing undergraduate pre-professional programs at the two WSU campuses and a comprehensive master's level program at UWM.[54] When the Coordinating Committee received applications to approve Ph.D. programs in chemistry and anthropology at Milwaukee, it became apparent that the UWM

Equal Quality Level for States' Universities," *Racine Journal Times,* July 16, 1967; Matt Pommer, "Many Questions Must Be Answered on New Campuses," *Capital Times,* December 13, 1967; Tim Wyngaard, "Harrington Says UWGB Plans Dormitories, Graduate Program," *Green Bay Press-Gazette,* January 13, 1968; "Public Dormitories Sought for Kenosha, GB Campuses," *Appleton Post-Crescent,* January 17, 1968; CCHE Minutes, March 16, 1968; "Debate on Academic Programs Deplored," *Wisconsin State Journal,* March 15, 1968; Matt Pommer, "State U Protests High Parkside Wage," *Kenosha News,* August 29, 1968; "An Unfortunate Decision," Kenosha Evening News, October 1, 1968; Matt Pommer, "Gelatt Suggests Parkside Be in State 'U' System," *Kenosha News,* October 5, 1968; "Senator Backs Putting UW-GB in State System," *Green Bay Press-Gazette,* October 9, 1968; "No Time to Change the Rules," *Appleton Post-Crescent,* October 15, 1968; "Panel Blamed for Faculty Loss," *Milwaukee Journal,* October 17, 1968; "Kohler Defends CCHE Guides for University," *Green Bay Press-Gazette,* November 8, 1968; 12/16/68 "Budget Information Paper B-4: New Campus Development (Green Bay and Parkside)," December 16, 1968, CCHE Correspondence and Subject File, SHSW Archives; David F. Behrendt, "Green Bay Academic Plans Defy Council, Kohler Says," *Milwaukee Journal,* June 6, 1969; William White to Edward Weidner, June 11, 1969, CCHE Correspondence and Subject File, SHSW Archives; "Green Bay, Parkside U Campuses Open," *Daily Cardinal,* September 16, 1969.

[53]Quoted in Kelly, "Politics," p. 267, with reference to *Milwaukee Sentinel,* July 30, 1966.

[54]CCHE Minutes, December 14, 1966, March 9, 1967; Walter J. Kohler to Carl E. Steiger, December 19, 1966, CCHE Correspondence and Subject File, SHSW Archives; "The Need for a School of Architecture in the State of Wisconsin–A Second Look.," December 28, 1966, ibid.; UW BOR Minutes, March 11, 1967; see also Rost, "Merger," 69, with reference to James Gilbert Paltridge, *Conflict and Coordination in Higher Education: The Wisconsin Experience* (Berkeley, CA: Center for Research and Development in Higher Education, University of California, 1968), pp. 84-89.

anthropology department had for several years been making faculty appointments as if its full graduate program were already in effect. To some extent this was the academic version of the old chicken-egg question, but it demonstrated CCHE's essential inability to control UWM development beyond what its leaders, faculty, and resources determined.[55]

The Coordinating Committee found it particularly difficult to deal with academic developments at UW-Madison, the oldest and most comprehensive university in the state. One example involved simultaneous proposals to establish baccalaureate degree programs in forestry at WSU-Stevens Point and in Madison's College of Agriculture. During an early phase of this discussion citizen member William Kraus raised an important and troubling general point:

> When UW and any other institution go head-to-head on a curriculum item, how can UW lose? The Forestry case, for example, is built on and around UW's historical and continuing advantages. They can do it better because they are bigger, broader, deeper, and more respected. And they are. So, taking this reasoning to its logical conclusion, UW should do everything, preferably on one campus. What's the answer? Or is there one?[56]

The debate on this issue was long and contentious, including testimony from a number of professional experts that not even one, let alone two, such programs were warranted. Yet CCHE ultimately approved both proposals, on the dubious ground they would fill highly specialized niches in the state's economy.[57] Another thorny question involved proposals from

[55]CCHE Minutes, March 5, 1968; Matt Pommer, "UW-M Grad School Buildup Faces Close CCHE Study," *Capital Times*, May 1, 1968; Matt Pommer, "Rothwell's Plea Defeats UW-M Proposal for Ph.D.," *Capital Times*, September 20, 1968; "'Bridge-Building' Education Parley Endorsed," *Wisconsin State Journal*, September 20, 1968; "UWM Loses Appeal for New Ph.D. Course," *Milwaukee Journal*, September 20, 1968; "UW-M Unit Hits CCHE Staff Action," *Capital Times*, September 23, 1968; "A Disservice," *Milwaukee Sentinel*, September 26, 1968; "New UWM Doctoral May Be Reconsidered," *Milwaukee Journal*, September 27, 1968; "How Much Graduate Duplication?" *Appleton Post-Crescent*, September 28, 1968; David F. Behrendt, "State Council Bests UW in Ph.D. Battle," *Milwaukee Journal*, September 29, 1968; Angus Rothwell, "An Educator Speaks Out," *Milwaukee Journal*, February 1, 1970.

[56]Kraus to Runge, November 15, 1965, CCHE Correspondence and Subject File, SHSW Archives.

[57]See CCHE #9, "Staff Recommendations on Forestry Education," March, 1968, CCHE Correspondence and Subject File, SHSW Archives; J. W. Macon, Advisory Committee for Forestry Education, to Walter J. Kohler, March 5, 1968, ibid.; John Gruber, "Unit Approves Forestry Majors," *Wisconsin State Journal*, March 6, 1968; Howard S. Lovestead

WSU-River Falls and UW-Madison to establish a school of veterinary medicine. While fairly substantial arguments were made for such a program in the state (Wisconsin veterinary students had to obtain their training outside the state), CCHE in this case opted to approve neither. The decision may in fact have represented wise stewardship, but the way it was determined in reality only revealed the Coordinating Committee's continuing division and weakness.[58]

All of the foregoing reflected badly on CCHE, but it was the committee's failure to exercise effective control of the UW and WSU biennial budget requests that raised the most concern at the state capitol. To a great extent CCHE had no choice. Because of its inadequate legislative appropriation, it lacked both the staff and the time to prepare a thorough analysis of the funding requests submitted by the two systems. This of course was fine with Harrington and McPhee and their respective regents, who did little to make the CCHE review easier. The Coordinating Committee therefore essentially passed along the UW and WSU funding requests with only slight cuts in spending or changes in priorities. Later, at the budget hearings, legislators and reporters tended to daydream through CCHE testimony while they waited to hear firsthand from the system representatives themselves. This left any serious review up to the governor and the legislature, and with it the unwelcome challenge of establishing state educational priorities and adjudicating between two collegiate systems. Increasingly, state political leaders concluded the CCHE experiment had failed to live up to their expectations.[59]

---

to Walter J. Kohler, March 12, 1968, CCHE Correspondence and Subject File, SHSW Archives; CCHE Minutes, March 14, 1968; "On, Wisconsin: We Go from None to Two Schools of Forestry," Milwaukee Journal, March 20, 1968; John Wyngaard, "CCHE Is Accused of 'Horse-Trading,'" *Waukesha Daily Freeman*, April 30, 1968 ;Angus Rothwell to All Members of the Coordinating Council for Higher Education., May 17, 1968, CCHE Correspondence and Subject File, SHSW Archives.

[58] CCHE Minutes, April 3, 1969; "UW Pushed As Site of Veterinary School," *Milwaukee Journal*, May 10, 1969; "Veterinary School at UW Recommended," LaCrosse *Leader Tribune*, May 18, 1969; Neil H. Shively, "Bypassing CCHE on Vet School Hit," Milwaukee Sentinel, May 29, 1969; "Veterinary School Site Creates Rift," *Milwaukee Journal*, May 29, 1969; "Political Gamesmanship," ed., Portage *Daily Register,* June 9, 1969; CCHE Minutes, June 5, 1969, January 29, 1970.

[59]See, for example, "CCHE Plans Strong Role in Budget-Cutting," Appleton *Post-Crescent*, May 1, 1968; Matt Pommer, "New Round in UW-CCHE Struggle," *Capital Times*, May 13, 1968; Roger A. Gribble, "CCHE Nears 'Muscle Test,'" *Wisconsin State Journal*, August 11, 1968; "Knowles Asks Restraints in Budgeting," *Milwaukee Sentinel*, September 7, 1968; "Sharp Cuts Urged in New UW Budget," *Milwaukee Journal*, September 17, 1968; 01/24/69 "Statement by University of Wisconsin President Fred Harvey Harrington," to Joint Legislative Committee on Finance, January 24, 1969, CCHE

A final blowup came in 1969 when CCHE members voted to replace retiring Executive Director Rothwell with UW Associate Vice President Donald Percy. In many ways the decision made excellent sense. Percy was probably the only person capable of wrestling control over the budgeting process from the two educational systems CCHE was supposed to coordinate. Smart, disciplined, and creative, he had spent much of his working life dealing with academic budgets. Few people had his detailed knowledge of the UW central and Madison campus budgets and budgeting processes. Percy was tainted, however, by his involvement with the University and his close association with the increasingly unpopular Harrington administration. As the University's primary budget spokesman, he had sometimes offended with his detailed knowledge and his facile and hardball responses at Coordinating Committee and legislative hearings. Legislative reaction to his appointment, especially among conservative Republicans, was swift and negative: Percy, "the fox in the henhouse," was persona non grata. He quickly removed his name from consideration. Chastened, CCHE turned instead to Arthur D. Browne of the Illinois Board of Higher Education. Browne might have been quite competent under more congenial circumstances, but he simply was incapable of providing the leadership needed at this extraordinary juncture. Chairman Kohler also left at this time.[60] Renamed the Coordinating *Commission* for Higher Education in 1968 as part of a general restructuring of state agencies, CCHE was effectively dead and only waited to be buried.

Correspondence and Subject File, SHSW Archives; "Education Leaders Repeat Budget Warnings," Appleton *Post-Crescent*, May 6, 1969; "Undaunted CCHE Looks Ahead," ibid., June 26, 1969; CCHE Minutes, May 28, 1970.

[60]John Keefe, "UW Man to Get Ex-Rothwell Post," *Wisconsin State Journal*, June 11, 1969; Tim Wyngaard, "UW Administrator Accepts Job As New Chief of CCHE," Green Bay *Press-Gazette*, June 11, 1969; Matt Pommer, "Percy Appointment As CCHE Head Seen Despite Opposition," *Capital Times*, June 11, 1969; Tim Wyngaard, "Legislative Heat Could Weld or Melt CCHE," Green Bay *Press-Gazette*, June 12, 1969; John Keefe, "Percy's CCHE Post Touches Off Storm," *Wisconsin State Journal*, June 12, 1969; Matt Pommer, "Solons Nix CCHE Choice for Director," *Capital Times*, June 13, 1969; Matt Pommer, "Will Percy Affair Set Back CCHE Recruiting Efforts?" ibid., June 16, 1969; John Wyngaard, "CCHE Directorship," Stevens Point *Daily Journal*, June 23, 1969. In October of 1971, after CCHE had been abolished in favor of a merged UW and WSU system, one newspaper observed: "He [Percy] was the first choice of the Coordinating Council for Higher Education as staff director two years ago when the ill-fated CCHE missed its last chance for success and survival. Percy was knocked out of the race after he had it won by a political reaction from legislative conservatives, who charged that allowing a former UW man to run the CCHE was like 'letting the fox watch the chickens.'" "UW Regents Have Puzzle Pieces Ready for Merger with State Universities," *Green Bay Press Gazette*, October 10, 1971.

Changing Leadership

By 1970, the Vietnam War and its turbulent effects on campuses across the state but especially in Madison were engaging the attention of lawmakers and the public far more than the problems of an ineffective CCHE. In May, UW President Fred Harvey Harrington, the state's most prominent educator and war casualty, announced his resignation, effective October 1. The following month a rumor circulated that the WSU regents intended soon to name a successor to Eugene McPhee, their system's top administrator, who planned to retire within a year or so. It was in this context that Patrick J. Lucey called a capitol square news conference on June 11. A long-time liberal Wisconsin Democratic activist and state party chairman who had worked on the presidential campaigns of Robert Kennedy and Eugene McCarthy, Lucey was a front-runner candidate to receive his party's nomination for governor.[61] He declared:

> I strongly urge the delay of these appointments until there is an opportunity for the new governor and Legislature to reconsider the structure of higher education in Wisconsin.
> . . . While the dual University system has served Wisconsin well during the period of dramatic increases in student enrollments, the time may very well have arrived for a consolidation and simplification of the higher education structure in Wisconsin.
> This is a critical time to consider this problem because the leaders of both University systems will soon retire. The study of reorganization can proceed without becoming entangled with the personalities of men in high educational posts.[62]

Lucey did not point out that because of Governor Knowles' six years in office both regent boards were now dominated by Republican appointees who were likely to install top administrators congenial with their political orientation. Nor did he refer to a widely circulated "Preliminary Report of the Governor's Commission on Education," issued the previous March. Also known as the Kellett Commission Report for its prominent Republican industrialist chairman, William R. Kellett, this document called for the abolition of CCHE in favor of a comprehensive and powerful State Education Board and the eventual merger of the two university systems. Thus, for any number of reasons change was in the air, and Patrick Lucey

---

[61]For a biographical sketch of Lucey, see Rost, "Merger," pp. 168-170.

[62]Dave Zweifel, "Lucey Asks Delay in Choice of U. System Chiefs: Says Next Governor and Legislature May Want to Combine Regents," *Capital Times*, June 12, 1970.

apparently believed the time was right for a Democrat to capture the initiative.

Lucey also outlined a merger plan, which had been worked out by David Adamany, a young campaign adviser. Harvard-educated, Adamany had worked for several years in Wisconsin as a Democratic Party activist while teaching at WSU-Whitewater and studying for his Ph.D. in political science at UW-Madison. In addition to merging UW and WSU while eliminating CCHE, Adamany's plan favored the current WSU governance structure, which featured campus presidents reporting directly to their regent board. By implication this arrangement rejected President Harrington's chancellor system, by which the campus chancellors reported to the system president, who then was responsible for working with the regents. In the months ahead participants in the merger debate would tend to frame the issues in terms of the institutions they represented, while Lucey would remain flexible about the structural details as long as merger in some form remained part of the equation.[63]

Lucey's June 11 press conference received almost no notice, either in the press or among Wisconsin politicians. And as the weeks and months of the campaign passed, Lucey failed to do or say anything else to make merger an issue. Nor did his opponent, Republican Lieutenant Governor and Wisconsin Dells businessman Jack Olson, pick up on the theme.[64] Both candidates' concern was more with the violence and seeming chaos at UW-Madison, particularly following the murderous bombing of Sterling Hall on August 23. In a September 3 "Statement on Campus Unrest," for example, Lucey commented on what he saw as the University's major problem:

> Only the determination of some faculty and students as well as the University administration preserved the continuity of the University by fulfilling as best they could their respective responsibilities. Despite their efforts, the University of Wisconsin as a renowned institution of higher learning is near death. Another semester of violence and disruption will surely kill it as a great public university.

---

[63]Rost, "Merger," pp. 41-42, 172-75.

[64]Lucey was not the only politician to consider merger; the idea surfaced regularly at the capitol. Bills proposing some sort of major restructuring of Wisconsin public higher education had previously been introduced at the legislature in 1897, 1911, 1913, 1915, 1917, 1921, 1923, 1927, 1931, 1933, 1937, 1939, 1943, 1947, 1949, 1953, 1955, 1961, 1963, 1965, 1967, and 1969. See ibid., p. 105.

Although "left-wing" radicals deserved much of the blame, the regents also were liable for a share:

> Attempts by the Board of Regents to take political reprisals against a member of the University faculty with whom they disagree is a counter-threat to freedom from the right which poses an equal danger to the University.[65]

Lucey intended as governor to address "the problem of campus unrest." Whatever his thoughts on merger, it was an issue that could wait.

Meanwhile, CCHE Chairman Harold A. Konnack and William Kraus, chairman of the commission's Finance Committee, made a last-ditch effort to capture control of the budget review process for the moribund agency. On October 1, the day after President Harrington left office, Acting UW President Robert Clodius appeared before Kraus's committee, stating he was prepared to defend UW's proposed 1971-73 biennial budget line by line. UW Vice President Donald Percy also was present and privately told Kraus that he could and would demonstrate the perfunctory job done by the CCHE staff in analyzing the UW proposal. If these were threats, they evidently worked, because the next day CCHE approved the UW and WSU requests essentially as presented. Through his campaign lieutenant Joe Nusbaum, candidate Lucey was made aware of this episode and the ensuing storm of charges and recriminations about the superficial CCHE review, including a growing consensus among Wisconsin legislators and others that the Coordinating Commission had outlived its usefulness.[66]

On October 26, eight days before the gubernatorial election, the UW Board of Regents named John C. Weaver to succeed Harrington as president of the University of Wisconsin. While this action obviously contradicted Lucey's June 11 request, it is unknown whether anyone on the regent board took cognizance of it. In announcing the appointment, Regent President Bernard C. Ziegler, described a wide-ranging search-and-screen process that had considered 195 names. A 16-member Advisory Committee, chaired by UW-Madison biochemistry Professor Robert H. Burris, had submitted a list of 17 finalists, all of whom a regent sub-

---

[65]Quotes from Patrick J. Lucey, "Statement on Campus Unrest," September 3, 1970, typed manuscript, on file with UW Clip Sheet, Series 40/00/3, Box 15, UA. Also see "Speech on Higher Education by Patrick J. Lucey, Democratic Candidate for Governor," n.d., ibid.

[66]For a summary of this controversy, see Rost, "Merger," pp. 72-79, 182. According to Rost, when Joe Nusbaum, subsequently Lucey's secretary of the Department of Administration and manager of the merger campaign, spoke with legislators about CCHE he found near unanimity that the coordinating agency's usefulness was over. Ibid., p. 200.

committee had interviewed and ranked. Subsequently the entire board had agreed unanimously on Weaver, whose family background and academic training were solidly Wisconsin. He subsequently had taught geography at the Universities of Minnesota and Oregon, Harvard, and the University of London, and had held high administrative posts at Kansas, Iowa, and Ohio State universities, as graduate dean at the University of Nebraska, and most recently as system president at the University of Missouri. Regent Ziegler read a statement from Weaver expressing his "humility" and "enthusiasm" for his new assignment, and proclaiming, "I have known Wisconsin by heart! My heart tells me to return." Although the University possessed great traditions, he believed it now faced severe challenges. "The heartbeat of this vital institution deserves protection," declared the president-elect, "both from those destructive forces that can bring disruption from within and from those potentially crippling forces of repression that may bear down upon it from without." Weaver indicated he would make frequent trips to Madison but would not be available to tackle his new assignment on a full-time basis until the end of the 1970-71 academic year.[67]

On November 3 the Democrats, in the words of the Republican speaker of the assembly, Appleton conservative Harold Froehlich, won "nearly a landslide in view of the state's voting history." Not only did Patrick Lucey handily defeat the lackluster Jack Olson, but his party wrested control of the assembly from the GOP.[68] The new Lucey administration faced severe problems, however, particularly in dealing with a serious economic recession that promised to force tough state budget limits and require tax increases. Concerning the "higher education stew," as *Milwaukee Sentinel* reporter Roger A. Stafford put it, Lucey's June 11 merger suggestion might be timely. Rather than the Kellett Commission's "major structural changes in the administration of education in Wisconsin," the governor-elect's ideas were "much more limited in scope," indeed essentially intended to accomplish the goals already sought through CCHE.[69]

---

[67]UW BOR Minutes, October 26, 1970. In reality, Weaver was in the Van Hise president's office full-time by January. When he informed the Missouri Board of Curators, or governing board, that he had accepted the Wisconsin presidency but offered to stay at his post for the remainder of the year in order to minimize any transition problems, the curators listened in stony silence, then asked him to leave the room. In his absence they voted to relieve him of his duties immediately, appointed an acting president, and gave Weaver a day to clear out his office!

[68]"Froehlich Puzzled by Assembly Upset," *Green Bay Press-Gazette*, November 4, 1970.

[69]Roger A. Stafford, "Lucey Election Adds Spice to Higher Education Stew,"

While Lucey remained publicly silent on the issue, his friend and WSU-Stevens Point President Lee S. Dreyfus called for merger at a budget hearing on December 8. His argument, which he would repeat and expand throughout the coming months, focused on the need for "equity" and the end of "discrimination" against the State Universities vis-à-vis the University.[70]

The New Governor and Merger

Patrick J. Lucey assumed the Wisconsin governorship on January 4, 1971, and on January 21 he delivered his state-of-the-state address before a joint session of the legislature. His introductory comments were somber: "We are all painfully aware of the disastrous deterioration of the national economy. Inflation has increased the cost of governmental services. Unemployment and declining business profits have reduced our tax yield. Hard times have increased the demand for public services from many who in better times would be self-reliant. In the face of this economic reality, I have pledged an austerity budget."Lucey promised to discuss "education, mental health, and welfare" in his upcoming budget message, where he planned "to recommend not only the level of services in these areas for the next biennium, but also certain changes in program and departmental organization."[71] Two days later, on February 23, the governor issued Part I of his three-part budget message. This printed document analyzed "The Fiscal Problem" by weaving its argument around the central fact that the total of state agency budget requests exceeded projected state revenue by more than a half billion dollars!

Early in February, Governor Lucey appeared on a television program and revealed he might include a higher education merger plan in his executive budget proposal to be presented to the legislature in March.[72] He essentially confirmed this intention in a private meeting with William Kellett by asserting he intended to ignore the Kellett Commission's education recommendations.[73] Simultaneously, for reasons that are unclear,

Milwaukee Sentinel, November 5, 1970.

[70]Dreyfus framed his argument in terms of institutional "discrimination" and "equity." Rost, "Merger," pp. 42-43, 178-180. For a short sketch of WSU system enrollment, breadth of academic programs, and faculty qualifications at this time, see Ibid., p. 52.

[71]Governor's State of the State Message to the Legislature, *Senate Journal*, 80th session, January 21, 1971, pp. 102, 113.

[72]Rost, "Merger," p. 45.

[73]*A Forward Look: Final Report of the Governor's Commission on Education* (Madison: Wisconsin Department of Administration, November, 1970).

UW Vice President Donald Percy prepared an in-house "confidential" document entitled "A Proposed 'Third Alternative' for Wisconsin Higher Education."[74] Percy proposed the establishment of a single University of Wisconsin System that would provide the regulation CCHE had been unable to achieve. Percy's "Third Alternative" called for merging the present UW and WSU regent boards, eliminating CCHE, distinguishing among and assuring the several types of collegiate institutions, and providing for a central administration similar to the UW's. Except for the central administration recommendation, Percy's scheme was quite similar to the one suggested by candidate Lucey the previous June. Several days after completing his confidential proposal, which he probably shared with President Weaver, Percy testified before the senate Education Committee. In response to a direct question but emphasizing he was speaking as a private citizen, he surprised his listeners by stating that perhaps merger was warranted. "Anything that eliminates one bureaucracy and tears down two others can't be all bad," he observed.[75]

Governor Lucey presented Part II of his budget message, "Policy Changes and Cost Reductions," to the legislature on February 25. Under the heading "Reorganization and Program Changes in Higher Education," he declared: "We can no longer afford to support an archaic organization of higher education which is a product of historic accident and ignores the converging social missions of the two systems that have been developing over recent decades." Accordingly, he had "eliminated" from his executive budget funding for the UW and WSU central administrations and CCHE. In their place he proposed "a single Board of Regents" to formulate "broad public policy for higher education." The reorganized board would consist of six current UW regents, four current WSU regents, and four new members appointed by the governor, plus the state superintendent of public instruction and the chairman of the State Board of Vocational, Technical and Adult Education. Lucey also designated new UW President Weaver to head the consolidated system. At the operating level, each campus would have an "assigned mission," grant degrees from "the University of

---

[74] [Donald Percy] "A Proposed 'Third Alternative' for Wisconsin Higher Education," n.d. but stamped Feb. 9, 1971, and marked "CONFIDENTIAL," Series 5/96/3, Box 8, UA.

[75] Matt Pommer, "Frank Talk on Merger of U. Systems by Donald Percy Jars Lawmakers," *Capital Times*, February 15, 1971, quoted in Rost, "Merger," pp. 96-97. What implications, if any, Percy's testimony held for official UW policy cannot be determined. In light of his recent "Third Alternative" plan, perhaps he was launching a trial balloon. Or perhaps he really was just speaking as a private citizen. In any event, thereafter the UW Vice President kept his opinions about merger to himself.

Wisconsin," be "headed" by a chancellor, and maintain an eleven-member "campus council." The latter would "consist of citizen, student and faculty members and would have advisory and consultative functions."

Lucey asserted the merger would produce several benefits. Most specifically, he thought President Weaver could save at least $4 million over the biennium through cutting out the three former administrative staffs. To accomplish this, the governor promised that Weaver would have a "free hand" in organizing his new central administration. Lucey also claimed the merger would help end "costly and unseemly rivalries between the two systems," and added that "in these days of austerity, Wisconsin taxpayers cannot be asked to finance projects dictated by bureaucratic competition." Equally important, merger would assure more rational planning and efficient use of resources: "the integrity of the mission of every university would be better protected by a single board which will not permit competition, duplication and overlapping among individual institutions. This is the kind of intelligent, rational and efficient educational planning that Wisconsin needs." Finally, the status quo was no longer an alternative:

> Let me add that if a rational restructuring of higher education fails to pass, then we as elected officials will be required to take into our hands the review of planning and budgeting throughout higher education that should ordinarily be the responsibility of an effective, consolidated leadership of the universities themselves.

Having dealt with "reorganization," the governor turned to "program changes." "As with all major agencies," he announced, "I have built into my budget a reduction in the continuing cost of higher education." While not at this time providing dollar figures, Lucey listed three "policy recommendations" that would determine them:

> * Senior faculty should devote a larger proportion of their time to classroom teaching, especially at the undergraduate level;
> * State support for comparable types and levels of instruction in the present two systems should move toward equality;
> * We cannot at this time burden Wisconsin taxpayers with excessive costs for graduate programs when a recent study suggests that by 1980 we will graduate 50,000 academic Ph.D.'s in this country, with an anticipated national need for only 9,000.

Regarding the third point, Lucey planned to recommend "a cutback in graduate programs in both present systems." Sugar coating this unpalatable news for the Madison campus was the governor's intention to provide substantial salary increases for UW faculty of 8 percent in the first year of the biennium and 8.5 percent in the second; WSU faculty would receive 9 percent and 11.5 percent respectively.[76]

President Weaver was appropriately circumspect as he promptly reacted to the governor's merger plan. "I favor anything that furthers educational opportunities for the young people of the state," he declared. "I favor anything that can accomplish this goal at the lowest cost consistent with quality education" Yet the UW president clearly was skeptical of the potential value or success of a merger, which he said would "require careful study and evaluation by all concerned." Even if Lucey's plan were enacted, moreover, implementing it would involve a "significant transitional period" and "should not risk the homogenization of higher education nor the leveling of the peaks of excellence." Weaver also found Lucey's recommended reduction in UW graduate instruction disturbing, but he promised immediately to "designate a senior member of my staff" to work with CCHE and the Department of Administration "in exploring in depth the many facets of the proposals advanced by Governor Lucey." Subsequently he gave Donald Percy, his top lieutenant, this assignment.[77]

UWM Chancellor J. Martin Klotsche also spoke out on Lucey's budget message. He focused his remarks on the possible implications of merger for his institution. Anticipating questions "relating to the clarification of existing missions and to the elimination of duplicating programs," Klotsche argued that the Milwaukee campus had already gone "through this process," obtaining both UW regent and CCHE approval "as *the* urban university of Wisconsin." During its fifteen-year history, UWM had become "an integral part" of the metropolitan area, serving a locality comprising over one-third of the state's population. "It is essential that the merger not change this," declared Klotsche. On March 27 and 28 the UWM chancellor presented the "Guest Comment" on Milwaukee's WTMJ television and radio stations, reiterating these remarks and, further, expressing a desire to use merger as a means to free his campus from UW-Madison domination: "UWM . . . is the urban campus of the state and must continue as such. Its mission has now been clearly established and nothing must be done to destroy it. . . . it must be permitted to seek its own level of quality as a teaching, research, and service center for this

[76]Governor's Budget Message, Part II. Policy Changes and Cost Reductions," *Senate Journal*, 80th session, February 25, 1971, pp. 395-396.

[77]"Statement by University of Wisconsin President John C. Weaver," February 25, 1971, and Weaver to Lucey, February 26, 1971, Series 40/1/2/3-2, Box 6, UA..

area of the state. These are the ingredients that must be protected in the event of a merger."[78]

Assembly Bill 414

On March 3 Lucey's executive budget was introduced to the legislature as Assembly Bill 414 (or 414A). The provisions for merger were few and general. Following the governor's stated plan, the bill created a "board of regents of the University of Wisconsin." Its sixteen members included the state superintendent of public instruction, the president of the Board of Vocational, Technical and Adult Education, and fourteen citizen appointees serving staggered seven-year terms. Initial appointments on the new board would include six current members of the UW regent board, four from the WSU board, and four appointed by the governor. The reorganization would not affect tenure in either system until new rules were promulgated. The new University of Wisconsin would encompass all of the former University of Wisconsin and Wisconsin State University units. Finally, an eleven-member campus council would be established at each institution "to bring student, faculty and community viewpoints to bear on university campus operations, academic programming and mission and student affairs." Each campus chancellor "shall make wide use of the councils as advising and deliberating mechanisms." This, in essence, was the Lucey administration's entire merger initiative. As expected, Assembly Bill 414 also severely reduced spending for graduate and undergraduate instruction from the University's request.

President Weaver limited his initial comments about 414A to the proposed funding cuts, which he thought would threaten the quality of UW undergraduate teaching "to meld more agreeably with the State University system."[79] This observation quickly elicited an angry response from Marshall Wick, a mathematics professor at WSU-Eau Claire and president of the Association of Wisconsin State University Faculties (TAWSUF), the WSU faculty union, who claimed undergraduate instruction at the WSU campuses already surpassed that of the University.[80] Madison

---

[78]"Statement by University of Wisconsin-Milwaukee Chancellor, J. Martin Klotsche," February 25, 1971, ibid. Klotsche sent a copy of this statement to UW President Weaver on February 26, 1971, with the cover note stating, "For your information." WTMJ Editorial, March 27 and 28, 1971, ibid., Box 2.

[79]Quoted in Rost, "Merger," p. 220.

[80]Rost quotes Wick's response, citing Matt Pommer, "U. Merger Project Begins to Show Traces of Stress," *Capital Times*, March 4, 1971. For background on the Association of Wisconsin State University Faculties and Wick, see Ibid., pp. 274-278.

Vice Chancellor Irving Shain reacted to Wick a few days later: "The Madison undergraduates get a damn good education. Look at the jobs they get. What we don't provide is a babysitting service which some of the state universities seem to provide."[81] Clearly, the debate over merger would occur not only in the legislature, but also between and within the two collegiate systems.

The UW Board of Regents first officially reacted to Governor Lucey's merger proposal on March 12. Regent President Ziegler opened the discussion by stating that inasmuch as the WSU board had not yet taken a position, he would not at this time push his board to do so. Regent Nellen asked about similar consolidations in other states. President Weaver responded that only the State University of New York came to mind, and it really was not comparable. Wisconsin, suggested Weaver, would probably have to focus "on the merits of its own circumstances and needs." Regent Sandin thought campus missions should be included in the legislation as safeguards to institutional "diversity." Regent Gelatt concurred, arguing that although UW and WSU campuses had during the past five or six years become more "comparable," any single board responsible for governing a merged system would tend toward imposing "standardization" throughout. Regent Ody Fish, recently appointed to the board by outgoing Governor Knowles, stated he would support any measure that would improve the quality of higher education at reasonable expense, and urged careful study of the alternatives.[82] Regent Walker predicted increased influence by the Central Administration because a merged citizen board would be unable to manage in detail the many issues confronting it. Whatever happened, said Walker in betraying more wishful thinking than prophesy, the decision regarding merger "is going to take some thought, and some time, and some time, and some time."[83]

Regent Pelisek said he preferred a single, properly structured system that might better allocate state resources and control internal competition. Furthermore, "what is good for a UW or the WSU system is not really

---

[81]Quoted in ibid., p. 228. Rost's reference is Matt Pommer, "Shain Calls Lucey's UW Budget Cuts 'Short-Sighted,'" *Capital Times*, March 10, 1971.

[82]Fish, a successful businessman and influential Republican national committeeman, was initially reluctant to accept the regent appointment because he was not a college graduate. Knowles was insistent, however, and Fish eventually agreed after Democratic gubernatorial candidate Lucey privately and strongly urged him to accept.

[83]Excerpts from a rough draft transcript of a portion of the UW BOR meeting, March 12, 1971, regarding a "Report on Governor's Proposal for Merger of the University of Wisconsin and the Wisconsin State University Systems," March 16, 1971, Series 40/1/2/3-2, Box 2, UA.

the critical question. The true issue is what is best for the State as a whole."
For Pelisek, a merged system should involve a single board of regents
committed to maintaining institutional diversity, a strong chief executive
answerable to the board, some level of "operational autonomy" for each
campus, faculty and student participation "in institutional affairs," and
official campus mission statements that might or might not appear in the
statutes. Whether or not coincidental, Pelisek's requirements for a merged
system were fully consistent with Vice President Percy's "Third
Alternative" plan. In the event of merger, they both made considerable
sense from the UW point of view.

After each regent had spoken, Regent President Ziegler, who
definitely was not assuming that a merger bill would pass the divided
legislature, noted what he believed was the single point of consensus among
his fellow board members: "anything that will improve the quality of our
educational programs here in the State we are for." He mentioned concern
expressed by UW alumni and the recent intensive involvement by the
regents in the operation of the University as potential stumbling blocks
for the effective management of an even larger system. "I don't like to
see us give up that quick on the Coordinating Council," Ziegler said. Regent
Sandin then offered a resolution asserting the board's support of any
measure that furthered educational opportunity in Wisconsin "at the lowest
cost consistent with quality education," encouraging full and open debate,
and recommending that as an early step in the process the UW and WSU
regent boards should hold a joint meeting to discuss the matter. Following
a somewhat acrimonious exchange between Regents Pelisek and Fish,
the board adopted the Sandin resolution.

At the March 12 meeting, the regents also approved a significant
reorganization of the UW Central Administration. The new arrangement
put forward by President Weaver established Donald Percy, who had
succeeded Vice President Clodius, as clearly second in command. Percy,
unlike his predecessor, did not have a doctorate and had never held a
professorial appointment. He was therefore named Executive Vice President
to imply less responsibility for academic affairs. More significantly,
however, the reorganization downgraded several other vice presidential
slots, the key ones occupied by men with longstanding allegiance to the
Madison campus. The changes, along with the regents' increasing
inclination to manage the University, consolidated administrative authority
at the very top of the system. They also tended further to fragment the
original University into its Harrington-devised components, each
administered by a chancellor and organized to operate quite independently

of its sister institutions. While probably neither intended nor even recognized by anyone involved, this administrative restructuring continued to weaken the informal shared governance structure that had traditionally involved the Madison faculty in helping to solve basic University-wide problems. Furthermore, the UW president and his top lieutenants no longer consulted regularly with the Madison University Committee to get a faculty perspective and advice on important policy issues. This erosion of Madison campus influence, on the other hand, was welcomed in Milwaukee, where UWM Chancellor Klotsche and his colleagues, as we have seen, sought to weaken rather than maintain the traditional University-wide ties.[84] All of this potentially detracted from the University's traditional ability to marshal its forces effectively against perceived outside threats like the Lucey merger initiative.

During the next few days President Weaver expressed increasing skepticism about the budget bill and its merger plan. On March 23 he delivered an address in Milwaukee, noting vaguely that the Lucey merger proposal "raises a lot of very complicated questions."[85] But in this early part of the debate, Weaver's major concern seemed to be the governor's proposed instructional policy changes and their attendant funding implications. A statement issued by the Lucey administration had declared that one of the governor's key objectives was to equalize the instructional funding support of the two collegiate systems:

> Teaching, particularly the teaching of undergraduates, is the most important activity conducted on university campuses. Other activities, while often more dramatic, must be viewed as subordinate functions which are permitted only because they enrich the ability of the faculty to teach. When this perspective is lost, teaching suffers as the glamour of other activities steals the time of the most qualified staff.[86]

President Weaver was himself a long-time advocate of improving instructional quality. But he also knew the Lucey policy statement seemed to contradict a long-held University ideal, stretching back to the Van Hise administration, that research and public service, along with but not exclusive of teaching, were fundamental and interrelated elements of UW's mission.

---

[84]UW BOR Minutes, March 12, 1971; Klotsche, *University of Wisconsin-Milwaukee*, p. 124; Rost, "Merger," p. 227.

[85]Quoted in ibid., p. 244, with reference to "Weaver Ponders Merger's Merit," *Milwaukee Journal*, March 24, 1971.

[86]"Governor's Policy Positions, 1971-1973," February, 1971, p. 156, Series, 5/2/14-2, Box 11, UA.

Lucey's apparent narrow emphasis on undergraduate teaching helped to confirm serious doubts among Madison campus leaders as to the academic depth and soundness of his plans. These suspicions would negatively shape the Madison faculty's view of merger throughout the legislative debate and well beyond.

Governor Lucey assigned his Department of Administration secretary, Joe E. Nusbaum, the job of shepherding the merger bill through the legislature. Nusbaum, it will be recalled, had earlier served as Governor Nelson's emissary to CCHE in the early 1960s, and he was familiar with the complicated issues and players involved. At the suggestion of WSU Executive Director Eugene McPhee, himself a brilliant political strategist, he convened groups of public higher education leaders to elicit suggestions on how to make the merger, should it come to pass, as palatable as possible. The first such gathering, on March 8, involved a "wrinkle committee" consisting of UW Vice President Donald Percy and Madison Chancellor Edwin Young and WSU campus Presidents Leonard Haas (Eau Claire) and George Field (River Falls).[87] Nusbaum also invited a separate group of UW and WSU faculty representatives to meet on March 18 to "discuss the implications of merger for the two systems." WSU participants at this faculty session included Marshall Wick (WSU-Eau Claire and TAWSUF president), George R. Gilkey (WSU-La Crosse and TAWSUF secretary), and Robert Berg (WSU-River Falls and TAWSUF chairman of Committee on Academic Freedom). UW participants included J. Ray Bowen (member of Madison University Committee and chairman of the UW-wide Faculty Council), James B. Bower (chairman of the Madison University Committee), and Wilder W. Crane (chairman of the UWM University Committee).[88] Out of these and other conferences, on March 25 Nusbaum drafted and circulated a memorandum outlining "suggested changes to the current merger language."[89]

---

[87]The meeting covered five topics: (1) WSU tenure; (2) "existing policies and practices" of the two systems; (3) preferred titles for campus and system administrative heads; (4) strong or weak central administration; and (5) campus councils. For Nusbaum's effort to smooth over the disagreements, see Nusbaum to George Field, Leonard Haas, Don Percy, and Ed Young, March 10, 1971, Series 40/1/2/3-2, Box 1, UA.

[88]Elaine M. Staley to Members of the University Faculty Council, March 19, 1971, Series 5/2/14-2, Box 11, UA; Rost, "Merger," p. 236. The quote is from Staley.

[89]For an approving response from UWM, see Wilder Crane to Nusbaum, April 1, 1971, Series 4/21/1, Box 61. See also Percy to Regents, Central Staff and Chancellors regarding Suggested Amendments to A.B. 414 (Gov'r's Budget Bill) Relative to Merger of UW and WSU Systems," March 29, 1971, Series 40/1/2/3-2, box 2, UA.

Nusbaum's March 25 memorandum proposed a number of modifications of the Lucey plan as presently defined. First, he recommended including a statement of legislative intent setting forth the basic goals of fostering equality of educational opportunity while promoting diverse and high quality undergraduate programming and preserving Wisconsin's graduate training and research centers. All of this would occur in the context of maximum autonomy for the individual campuses. Second, UWM would continue to be designated as the state's preeminent urban university. Third, the Madison campus would retain its status as Wisconsin's single top-flight comprehensive institution of higher education. Fourth, each campus would assure access to qualified applicants. Fifth, the merged regent board would report to the governor and legislature by January 1, 1973, with a list of recommended campus missions. Sixth, current general operating policies for each of the campuses would be retained throughout the 1971-73 biennium. Seventh, existing tenure guarantees would remain in effect and any changes in the rules would involve consultation with the affected faculties. Eighth, as a concession to the WSU presidents who felt strongly about their titles, whoever led the merged system would be designated "chancellor" of the University of Wisconsin System and each of the campus administrative heads would be called "President of the University of Wisconsin: _____ Campus." Nusbaum concluded this document by acknowledging it needed "considerable polishing." He stated that none of its content had been "cleared" by Governor Lucey, "but I am sure he would be in general agreement with most of the points."[90] Clearly Nusbaum's strategy was to accommodate the various constituencies while maintaining the political momentum for merger.

On March 26, the Madison University Committee weighed in with a statement entitled "The Impact of the Proposed Executive Budget on the Instructional Programs of the Madison Campus." It strongly criticized Lucey's funding recommendations, which in the committee's view failed to account for the substantial educational differences between the WSU and UW campuses, especially Madison. The committee declared: "If programs are truly comparable, they deserve equity in support. But it has yet to be established that the undergraduate programs in any area, to say nothing of those in engineering, physical sciences, agriculture, and life sciences, are in fact comparable."[91] This was a tricky line of argument

---

[90]Nusbaum to Bower, Bowen, Berg, Crane, Field, Gilkey, Haas, Percy, Wick, and Young, March 25, 1971, Series 5/2/14-2, Box 11, UA.

[91] UW Faculty Senate Document 46, "The Impact of the Proposed Executive Budget on the Instructional Programs of the Madison Campus: A Statement by the University

for the University Committee, because a strong defense of Madison's academic programs required, or at least implied, criticism of the other campuses. Still, the governor's objective seemed to be to force the reorganized University to institute "comparable" instructional programming and to do so partially by adjusting, and perhaps downgrading or even eliminating, other elements of UW scholarly activity, especially at Madison. The University Committee consequently interpreted the Lucey budget recommendations as threatening to the fundamental nature of their institution and responded accordingly.

The University Committee also offered some thoughts on the proposed merger: "We believe that high quality education at low cost can be obtained under either a merged or a separate system. In either case, an optimum system requires that a specific mission be established for each institution and that each be funded at a level appropriate to its mission." The committee therefore suggested categories reflecting "the system which has presently evolved under the coordination of CCHE." Without naming the units, the breakdowns were: "full-program" Madison; "urban" UWM; "four-year," meaning UW's Green Bay and Parkside campuses as well as the WSU degree-granting schools; "two-year undergraduate centers"; and "an extension division." While the Madison campus clearly retained its preeminent position in this mix, the implicit compromise was that the controversial UW-Green Bay and UW-Parkside campuses might eventually be downgraded to WSU budgetary levels:

> If we are to merge, it would be wiser to do just that, keeping all programs at their present level for the moment. When the dust has settled, and when faculty, administration and regents have had a period in which to reorient their outlook and their loyalties toward the merged system, they can set about the task of developing an optimum educational system for Wisconsin.

Thus what the University Committee seemed willing to accept was the assurance of state budgetary support appropriate for the comprehensive nature and mission of the Madison campus, abolition of CCHE, and a statewide institutional status quo under a single administration and board of regents.

Convened by UW Regent President Ziegler and WSU Regent President Roy Kopp, the joint meeting of the two regent boards was held on March 27. As planned, discussion covered three areas of concern

Committee," March 29, 1971. It should be noted that one of the authors, E. David Cronon, was a member of the University Committee and the UW Faculty Council during 1969-72.

regarding merger: education, organization and administration, and finances. The statements and exchanges were frank and wide-ranging, covering such topics as the relative quality of undergraduate instruction at WSU and UW institutions, campus missions and program diversity, differences in admission and program requirements, research versus instruction, the proposed campus councils (and possible "acute councilitis"), campus autonomy and the relative strength of the two central administrations, and the likelihood of financial savings through a merged system. Only one regent, UW's Nellen, explicitly mentioned the failure of CCHE as having created and conditioned the difficult problem they now were confronting. Two regents advocated the old idea of greater voluntary cooperation between their boards as an alternative to merger, but no one, with the possible exception of UW Regent Gelatt, seemed aware of the past failure of this strategy or its intimate connection with the origin and history of CCHE. The only formal action of the meeting was the adoption of a resolution offered by UW Regent Fish setting up a Joint Committee of the regent boards "to immediately develop informative input to the two Boards detailing the advantages and disadvantages not of merger as such but of the varying factors involved."[92] The next day the *Wisconsin State Journal* ran an interview with Governor Lucey in which he took a hard stand for merger. Rather than fighting it, which Lucey thought the regents were doing, they "ought to get their heads together and help us."[93]

On March 29 the Madison Faculty Senate considered a resolution from its University Committee. After accepting two minor amendments, the senate voted unanimously to express "grave concern over the crippling effect of the interrelated funding and merger proposals contained in the Governor's 1971-73 executive budget recommendations." The resolution explained that while the faculty did not "in principle" oppose merger, "we strongly oppose proposals for uniformity in funding and in teaching which fail to take into account the different roles of the various campuses of the University of Wisconsin and the Wisconsin State University systems." And although the senate was aware of the "serious fiscal problems" facing Wisconsin, it nevertheless feared the adoption of the governor's proposals

---

[92]"Joint Meeting of the UW and WSU Boards of Regents, March 27, 1971, UWM, Chapman Hall," minutes, March 29, 1971, Series 40/1/2/3-2, Box 2, UA. Only one administrator from each system was invited to attend the meeting, and then only to provide requested information; presidents and chancellors were specifically excluded. See Ziegler to [UW] Board of Regents, March 17, 1971, ibid.

[93]"Lucey: No Budget Without UW Merger," *Wisconsin State Journal*, March 28, 1971, quoted in Rost, "Merger," p. 247.

would have "a destructive impact upon the quality of the educational programs offered on the Madison campus."[94]

A few days later, on April 1, UW President Weaver testified at a hearing before the legislature's Joint Committee on Finance about the budget and stressed the importance of "Strengthening Undergraduate Education at the University of Wisconsin." He expressed concern over the proposed cuts in the governor's budget for graduate programs at Madison and for UW undergraduate instruction generally. The latter recommendation, he said, was:

> calculated on the basis of equity with the WSU per credit costs, [which] does not take into account significant differences in programs. It reflects the apparent determination that undergraduate teaching in the public university, wherever it occurs and whatever the content and scope of the program, ought to be supported by the State at a single level.

The UW president strongly defended the quality of undergraduate instruction at Madison and throughout the University, arguing that Lucey's approach was seriously flawed because it did not recognize that Madison offered numerous high-cost academic majors not available elsewhere in the state. Added Vice President Percy: "We're not trying to be sanctimonious about being better than some other institutions. We're just trying to say we are different. . . . If we are given WSU support, we can teach WSU level courses."[95]

Merger Amendments

On April 6 DOA Secretary Nusbaum appeared before the legislature's Joint Committee on Finance to recommend several changes in the administration's merger proposal. This brought home to many at the University in Madison the genuine threat of merger and ultimately led to the passage of a UW regent resolution in mid-June opposing the Lucey initiative. As would be expected, Nusbaum's amendments reflected the suggestions he had received from various elements of Wisconsin's higher education establishment, including students and alumni. They indicated Governor Lucey was both serious about accomplishing merger

---

[94]UW Faculty Minutes, March 29, 1971.

[95]"Statement by President John C. Weaver on Strengthening Undergraduate Education at the University of Wisconsin, Joint Finance Committee Hearing," April 1, 1971, Series 5/1/14-2, Box 11, UA. Percy was quoted in Rost, "Merger," p. 251.

and willing to accept a considerable number of modifications to his initial proposal as long as its basic objective was achieved. For example, the administration now proposed to include in the statute the most recent CCHE mission statements for each UW and WSU unit. Another important recommendation reflected strong lobbying by Wisconsin State University interests. While 414A originally placed six UW and four WSU regents on the new board, the numbers now were five from each. It appeared University of Wisconsin supporters had not taken the likelihood of a merger as seriously as their rivals.[96]

If Secretary Nusbaum's April 6 recommendations were not enough to sensitize the University's leadership to the real possibility of merger, there were other straws in the wind. On April 7 CCHE Executive Director Arthur D. Browne wrote President Weaver about his testimony before the legislature's Joint Committee on Finance and his fears for UW-Madison under a merged system. Most telling was Browne's final observation: "I do not expect to gain much concurrence except possibly among a few in Joint Finance. Indeed, I am well aware that the critical outcomes stem from negotiations between the Governor and the Boards of Regents."[97] Later that month, on April 16, Lucey publicly justified his initiative in blunt language and without reference to his controversial educational policy recommendations:

> All we're doing is recognizing the obvious–you don't need three citizen boards wrangling over higher education and a matching staff for each of them. But the big saving in merger is not the administrative costs, but the elimination of the rivalry between the two systems and the educational tradeoffs. We just can't afford, anymore, that kind of foolishness.[98]

---

[96]Joe E. Nusbaum to Joint Committee on Finance, "A Single Governing Board for Wisconsin's Public Universities," April 6, 1971, Series 5/2/14-2, Box 11, UA; Nusbaum memorandum to Joint Committee on Finance, "A Single Governing Board for Wisconsin's Public Degree-Granting Higher Education Institutions," April 6, 1971, marked "Sunday Draft," Series 5/96/3, Box 8, UA. See also Rost, "Merger," pp. 253-256, with references to Joe E. Nusbaum, "A Single Governing Board for Wisconsin Public Universities," A memo to the Joint Committee on Finance, April 6, 1971; and Joe E. Nusbaum, "Governor Lucey's Proposed Single Governing Board for Public Universities," April 6, 1971.

[97] Browne to Weaver, April 7, 1971. Weaver replied to Browne on April 14, concluding: "It is a complex and difficult array of problems, that's for sure." Both in Series 40/1/2/3-2, Box 6, UA. See also [Browne,] "Reorganization of Higher Education: A Suggested Approach," a Presentation to the Joint Finance Committee, April 6, 1971, ibid., Box 2.

[98]Quoted in Rost, "Merger," p. 267 with reference to Eugene C. Harrington, "Lucey Riding Herd on Budget, Merger," *Milwaukee Journal*, April 19, 1971.

Striking, too, was an internal UW memo from John F. Newman, director of the University News and Publications Service, reporting his informal sampling of "merger sentiments" during recent visits with "a few key newspaper and radio executives in the La Crosse-Wausau-Fond du Lac areas." Newman found:

> —Virtually unanimous support for the merger concept;
> —No strong expectation of dollar savings;
> —But general feeling that a single system is "logical," with one observing, "After all, we don't have *two* departments of agriculture;
> —Awareness of quality difference between UW and WSU, with one commenting, "Just about any high school graduate or undergraduate can make it at the State Universities";
> —Desire that UW-Madison be protected from damage to its graduate or undergraduate educational programs;
> —But apparent lack of information on proposed budget cuts and how they equate funding for junior-senior instruction in the two systems.

Concluded Newman: "These men feel a strong personal identification with the Madison campus. All are alumni; all have children who are graduates or current students here."[99] The merger initiative was evidently striking a responsive chord even among well-informed, indeed partisan, friends of the University.

It now also became increasingly evident the University was seriously divided over merger. At UWM, for example, Chancellor Klotsche and his faculty senate offered strong support for the Lucey initiative, as long as the legislation supported UWM's central goal of attaining President Harrington's goal of "major urban university status." The UWM stand therefore called for clearly differentiated campus mission statements, differential funding according to mission, and a strong central administration to keep the various campuses in line.[100] On the other hand, considering

---

[99]Jack Newman to Young, April 16, 1971, Series 4/21/1, Box 61, UA. Young sent copies to Robert Taylor, Harvey Breuscher, and Arthur Hove.

[100]During an April 8 hearing of the Senate Education Committee at UWM, for example, Chancellor Klotsche indicated his price for supporting merger was the guarantee that the urban mission of his campus would be retained. "If the answer is yes, then merger would be acceptable. If it is no, then it would be intolerable." J. Martin Klotsche, "Statement on Merger Before Senate Committee on Education," April 8, 1971; Klotsche to Regents, Weaver, Percy, Clarke Smith, April 8, 1971, both in Series 40/1/2/3-2, Box 6, UA.

On April 22, the UWM Faculty Senate considered a recommendation from its University Committee backing merger if five conditions were met. These included: (1)

the heated controversy over the favored status of UW-Green Bay and UW-Parkside vis-à-vis the WSU campuses, probably no one was surprised when Green Bay Chancellor Edward W. Weidner came out strongly against merger. His comments reflected negatively on his WSU counterparts, who recently had released a list of "requirements" for obtaining their support for merger, including the need for a weak central administration.[101]

differentiation of campus missions, (2) differential funding according to mission, (3) strong central administration of programming with unit autonomy for operations, (4) faculty involvement in university governance, and (5) continued tenure system based on demonstrated competence. The senate approved this document 27-2. On May 4, the full UWM faculty votes 300-85 to endorse merger. After praising the governor for "seeking a solution to the problems of wasteful proliferating and duplicating academic programs by proposing a merger," the UWM faculty declared:

> We agree that the Coordinating Council of Higher Education has failed to provide for effective program planning because its goals were often different from the two boards of regents. . . .
>
> Only a strong Board of Regents and a strong Central Administration can develop the goals, objectives, and functions of higher education and make the painful decisions to eliminate wasteful programs and to determine areas of excellence for each of the units of higher education.

From the UWM perspective, merger was an opportunity. UWM Faculty Document 660, "Statement on Merger of the University Systems Proposal for the Faculty Senate, University of Wisconsin-Milwaukee," April 22, 1971, ibid., Box 2, UA; Rost, "Merger," pp. 269-271.

[101]"Requirements for a Sound Merger of the UW and WSU Systems," typed, n.d. but marked "received" by the Madison Chancellor's Office, April 16, 1971, Series 4/21/1, Box 61, UA. For an early WSU-based argument for a weak UW System administration, see David Witmer memorandum to Robert Polk [scratched out and handwritten Don Percy], "First thoughts on the administration of a state university of Wisconsin (should it gain legislative approval)," February 26, 1971, Series 40/1/2/3-2, Box 1, UA. Also see WSU-Stevens Point Faculty, "Recommendations and Resolutions on Merger of Wisconsin State Universities and University of Wisconsin," May 18, 1971, ibid., Box 6.

On April 19 Weidner wrote UW Regent Frank Pelisek declaring he saw "no advantages" and "many disadvantages" to merger. Not only did he view the WSU Council of Presidents' requirements as "bad enough in and of themselves," he thought they demonstrated that the group was "rather impossible":

> I am afraid that if merger came about in any close period of time, there would be the greatest political shenanigans, lobby groups, and irresponsible going around that any state ever saw. I fear it will bring higher education down into the gutter. Instead of removing competition, it will create the biggest cutthroat competition that one could conceive. It is apparent that the nine presidents are not a disciplined group, and it is apparent that they would be impossible to control by any Board or any President under merger conditions.

After several further observations, Chancellor Weidner concluded "that we should indefinitely

The UW-Madison University Committee also issued a strongly worded statement on the proposed merger. It supported a strong central administration, a point favored throughout the University, and official mission statements, which everyone on all sides thought were appropriate. The statement also argued for a relatively small board of regents whose members would have statewide allegiances and general policy responsibilities. This implied a rejection of the WSU model, in which each regent represented and helped govern a particular campus. As would be expected, the University Committee's vision also included parochial elements designed to protect Madison campus interests. The statement thus called for continued faculty control over educational policy, faculty tenure based only on "demonstrated competence and performance," and "unit autonomy." To the committee, this latter requirement was crucial, as it included guaranteed local control over important Madison financial resources–such as the Wisconsin Alumni Research Foundation, the University of Wisconsin Foundation, and various campus endowment funds. If such assurances were not received, "the University Committee must *actively oppose* the merger."[102] The 1948 Madison faculty vision of a truly unitary state-wide

---

postpone the matter of merger, although a study committee to point out the advantages and disadvantages would be acceptable." Referring to this "strong statement," President Weaver later told Weidner, "I find myself in considerable agreement with its substance." Weidner to Pelisek, April 19, 1971; Weaver to Weidner, May 4, 1971, both in ibid.

[102]UW-Madison Faculty Senate Document 47A, "Proposed Merger–Additional Comments: A Statement by the University Committee," April 26. This document included a copy of University Committee to Regent Frank J. Pelisek, April 18, 1971. On April 26, 1971, on the motion of University Committee Chairman Bower, the Madison Faculty Senate voted to file Faculty Senate Documents 47A and 47, "Proposed Merger: A Statement by the University Committee," April 26, 1971. UW-Madison Faculty Senate Minutes, April 26, 1971. See also UW News release regarding the University Committee statement to Regent Pelisek, April 20, 1971, Series 4/21/1, Box 61, UA.

The system-wide University Faculty Council issued a "Position on Merger" on April 24 that expressed sentiments similar to those of the Madison University Committee, although the statement omitted any reference to the disposition of campus-specific resources such as WARF. "Position on Merger by the University Faculty Council," April 24, 1971, Series 40/1/2/3-2, Box 6, UA.

The UW Board of Visitors held its monthly meeting on April 27 and discussed the various merger proposals. The group complained that "we find many major questions about merger as yet unanswered." Four seemed especially troublesome: First, there was "no evidence" that a "decentralized system" of thirteen institutions would be cheaper to run than the present "two complete systems"; second, there was "no evidence" to support the conclusion that the quality and opportunity of education would improve under merger; third, direct access to one board of regents by thirteen separate institutions, not to mention the establishment of thirteen campus councils, might result in increased competition; and fourth, accomplishing merger in 120 days seemed hasty in view of UW's 120 years of

University of Wisconsin, as expressed in the report of the Ingraham Committee on University Functions and Policies, had vanished.

On May 5 the Joint Regent Committee issued an "Interim Report." The committee, it will be recalled, had been directed to consult widely and then detail the advantages and disadvantages of merger. It turned out this charge had been difficult to meet because of the "skeletal" quality of the Lucey administration's proposal, even with the recommended Nusbaum amendments of April 6. Consequently only "the abstract concept of merger itself" could be evaluated. The Joint Regent Committee said it appreciated the governor's intention to leave "a great deal of flexibility in the structure of the new system" to the "newly formed" Board of Regents. But there remained a "great deal of uncertainty" and "concern" among the "members of both systems." The report listed three basic reasons for merger as offered by the governor: "operating economies," "elimination of CCHE," and "elimination of competition." The Joint Committee discussed each and tentatively concluded the first was unlikely, the second was unnecessary, and the third might actually be harmful. After listing numerous other potential "problem areas" that had come to light during the Joint Committee's work, the report concluded:

> Despite the many obstacles, there is no question that a merger can be accomplished. The question remains, however, whether or not a merger can be administratively structured to the satisfaction of a majority of those concerned and still meet the goals of reduced cost, elimination of duplication and competition within the system, while still protecting the quality of education which this state has enjoyed.

Although the committee did not offer an explicit answer, taken as a whole its report implied a negative conclusion.[103] While satisfactory to the members of the Joint Regent Committee, their analysis must have appeared biased and self-serving to the state officials who were familiar with CCHE's inability to prevent wasteful duplication or provide effective coordination of the two systems.

Meanwhile, the merger initiative gained strength in the legislature. In the senate, Bill 213S, previously submitted by Senator Raymond F. Heinzen, one of the rare Republican advocates of merger, was amended

---

development. The visitors transmitted these concerns to the parent UW Board of Regents. Robert Howell to Ziegler, April 27, 1971, ibid., box 2; "Visitors Board Raises Questions About Lucey's U Merger Proposal," *Wisconsin State Journal*, April 30, 1971.

[103]"Interim Report of Joint Regent Committee on Merger," [May 5, 1971] Series 40/1/2/3-2, Box 2, UA.

on May 19 by its author and Dane County Democratic Senator Carl W. Thompson, to make it essentially identical with the modified Lucey version imbedded in the larger executive budget.[104] This seemed of little consequence at the time, because the governor had insisted that merger must occur as part of the biennial budget. On May 20 Governor Lucey delivered an invited address before the Republican-controlled senate to defend his merger initiative. He offered the beguiling argument that merger "will give the legislature only one University to deal with. Will save money on lobbying. Will be one lobby group instead of three. Higher education should be working together." In the question-and-answer period, he tried to dispel fears over the future of the Madison campus by noting that he expected the merged regent board to regard and protect Madison as the "one jewel in the crown." Concerning his proposed local campus councils, which had raised concerns among both UW and WSU leaders, the governor said he was "flexible" on that point.[105] His performance was masterful.

Soon both houses of the legislature were debating merger. On May 21 the Joint Finance Committee, on a straight party-line vote of 8-6, released amended bill 414A for debate and action in the assembly. Two weeks later, on June 3, Senators Heinzen and Thompson offered substitute amendment 2 to their bill 213S that incorporated recommendations from UW-Madison Chancellor Edwin Young, who characteristically was working quietly behind the scenes to defend the interests of his campus.[106] On June 10, seemingly of greater significance at the time, Republican Senator James C. Devitt proposed substitute amendment 3 to 213S. This so-called semi-merger plan was primarily the work of UW Vice President Percy and Regent Ody Fish, who because of his Republican connections had informally been designated by his board colleagues to defeat merger in the senate, where the G.O.P. held a comfortable 20-12 margin.[107] The Devitt

---

[104]Rost, "Merger," pp. 283-284.

[105]"Governor's Statement (not verbatim!)," n.d., typed, Series 40/1/2/3-2, Box 6, UA. Rost, "Merger," pp. 285-287, refers to a document prepared by the Senate Republican Caucus Staff, "Senate Committee of the Whole Meeting with Governor Patrick J. Lucey Regarding Merger of University Systems," May 20, 1971, a verbatim transcript that has not come to light for this study.

[106]State of Wisconsin Senate Substitute Amendment 2 [As Revised in Joint Finance (Compromise Proposal)] to 1971 Senate Bill 213, June 3, 1971–Offered by Senators Heinzen and C. Thompson, Series 40/1/2/3-2, Box 1, UA; Thompson to Young, May 19, 1971; Young to Thompson, May 26, 1971; Thompson to Young, June 4, 1971, all in Series 4/21/1, Box 61, UA.

[107]On April 23 Executive Vice President Percy sent President Weaver and Regent Fish an incomplete draft proposal for an alternative to merger. This plan was quite different from the generally pro-merger plan Percy had constructed in February and may have been

amendment rejected merger and instead mandated regular consultation among the two existing regent boards and top state government leaders. The "semi-merger" amendment never had any real chance of passage, but it did provide Regent Fish with an alternative as he lobbied senate Republicans against the Lucey initiative.[108] Finally, and as expected, on the evening of June 11 the assembly, with its 67-33 Democratic majority, easily passed the executive budget, including its merger provisions.[109]

developed according to guidelines laid down by Regent Fish. In his introductory "Rationale" section, Percy acknowledged the state's concern, in light of growing "disenchantment" over CCHE, "to assure that adequate planning, coordination and control characterize" UW and WSU operations. On the other hand, he noted a "growing feeling that separate systems under separate board direction may be the most effective means of assuring citizen control and guarding against monolithic political influence and bureaucratic control." Furthermore, continued Percy, "most everyone agrees" that "there is a need for coordination of planning and prevention of unnecessary program duplication and proliferation. There is also a need for improved legislative and executive understanding of the universities" and exchanges between the two regent boards. Percy thus offered an alternative to merger that was reminiscent of UW arguments against "integration" during the early 1950s.

The plan had four parts. First, CCHE would be eliminated as of June 30, 1971. Second, the UW and WSU boards must meet jointly at least three times annually, including once following individual board actions on the biennial budget requests. Among other things, this would "assure that program and planning efforts of the two Systems are coordinated and that unnecessary program duplication is avoided." Third, the key regent committees for each system (business, budget, education, and facilities) also would meet jointly from time to time. And in the case of the joint education committee deliberations, they would be required to "certify" that each program or degree proposal was in conformance with campus mission and did not cause "unnecessary proliferation." If this were not accomplished, the sponsoring regent board would be required to reconsider and reaffirm the proposal before it could go into effect. Fourth, the legislature would establish a University Education Commission, consisting of such officials as the senate and assembly education committee chairmen, the co-chairmen of joint finance, and the state budget officer. The commission would "conduct preliminary review" of the UW and WSU biennial budget proposals and receive semi-annual reports from the two regent boards on anticipated major actions and future developments. This arrangement would "keep the legislative and executive branches *informed* and . . . provide a forum for *explanation*." Percy latest plan, in other words, would divide up CCHE's responsibilities between the universities, on the one hand, and the state government, on the other. Typed statement without heading, handwritten at top: "JOHN & ODY—HERE ARE MY FIRST THOUGHTS ON AN *ALTERNATIVE* TO MERGER D 4/23/71," Series 40/1/2/3-2, Box 6, UA.

[108]Rost, "Merger," pp. 299-301. Rost, pp. 302-7, 310, praises Fish's efforts and speculates about his reasons for leading the Republican fight against merger.

[109]The Assembly vote followed an argument in the Assembly lobby on June 9 between Dick Weening, a young Lucey aide, and Harvey Breuscher of the UW central administration. Weening claimed Breuscher was lobbying against merger, which the UW president had supposedly agreed not to do. The Lucey forces were also concerned that Weaver had entertained the senate Republicans at the president's home on the 8th and was hosting the senate Democrats on the 9th. Weaver responded with a press statement

As the legislative focus shifted to the state senate, the higher education establishment began shaping an official stand on merger. A joint meeting of the two regent boards took up a "Second Interim Report" from the Pelisek Committee on June 11. It consisted primarily of analyses of the various merger proposals before the legislature.[110] During the discussion, Regent Fish, supported by both regent presidents, argued that the boards should formally back the Devitt amendment. This a majority of the regents refused to do. Instead, the boards directed the Joint Committee to canvass the usual groups for their views on all the legislative options and to evaluate these according to criteria set down in the first interim report. On June 16 the committee distributed its "Third Interim Report," which concluded "mandatory merger has not yet been proved."[111] The same day Senator Thompson, a Madison area Democrat and friend of the University, wrote President Weaver stating: "it now seems . . . that a single University system is inevitable. Therefore, I urge everyone interested in the proposal to actively become a partner in the legislative process so that the best possible measures can finally be enacted."[112] Nevertheless, two days later the two regent boards met separately, each passing a resolution stating their "fundamental opposition to the merger of the University of Wisconsin and Wisconsin State University systems at this time." The boards also identified the Devitt's "semi-merger" plan as the best option currently available. Arlie Mucks, secretary of the Wisconsin Alumni Association, quickly followed up on this vote by sending out nine hundred letters urging University alumni to let their senators know they supported the boards' decision.[113] Governor Lucey commented the

on June 10 proclaiming, "The irresponsible claim that an agreement exists which would muzzle the University in discussions of the proposed merger . . . is absolutely false. The Governor has never sought such an agreement, nor would I have agreed to such an arrangement." Typed, untitled statement with handwritten note: "Telecopied to Governor's Office, June 10, 1971, 1:30 p.m.," Series 40/1/2/3-2, Boxes 2 and 6, UA; "U. Merger Tensions Spill Out; Lucey Ranks Torn," *Capital Times*, June 10, 1971; "Fight Over Merger Breaks Into Open," *Wisconsin State Journal*, June 10, 1971; James D. Selk, "Heinzen Rips Attack on Weaver; UW Chief Denies Neutral Stand," ibid., June 11, 1971; "Lucey Aide Asked to Apologize," *Milwaukee Journal*, June 11, 1971.

[110]Joint Regent Committee on Merger, "Second Interim Report," June 11, 1971, Series 40/1/2/3-3, Box 2, UA.

[111]Joint Regent Committee on Merger, "Third Interim Report," June 16, 1971, Series 5/2/14-2, Box 11, UA.

[112]Thompson to Weaver, June 16, 1971, Series 40/1/2/3-2, Box 6, UA.

[113]Rost, "Merger," p. 331. Mucks was accused of taking this action because of his Republican connections. He replied that the WAA Executive Committee had instructed him on May 15 to support whatever action the regents took on the question. See Mike Miller, "Mucks in Alumni Anti-Merger Push," *Capital Times*, July 9, 1971. See also L.E.

regent action "came as no surprise and I doubt that it will have much effect."[114]

The Governor Comes to Campus

Just as it appeared the regents had provided a rallying point against merger, the senate approved its own budget bill, formally a substitute amendment for Assembly Bill 414A. Reflecting the tax policy being promoted by conservative Republicans, it called for major cuts in the governor's already tight budget, including a reduction of UW's operating budget by $11 million and its capital budget by $33 million! On the other hand, it eliminated Governor Lucey's merger proposal.[115] While the latter action was welcome, the further budget cuts were not. On June 30 President Weaver called a special meeting of the UW regent Budget Committee. He noted that Lucey's budget "already calls for university belt tightening beyond the last notch. The senate substitute would be no less than devastating and would serve to establish one pole of a compromise position so removed from reality insofar as the University is concerned as to make any midpoint compromise untenable." The alarmed Madison University Committee also reacted: "It makes no sense to construct buildings and then to eliminate funds to equip and operate them."[116] As the senate debated the Republican budget, it killed numerous Democratic amendments, then easily passed the bill 18-15 and adjourned for the Fourth of July weekend.[117] As things now stood, UW supporters faced a Hobson's choice between a considerably better-funded assembly budget that included merger, or a senate budget with drastic funding cuts but no reorganization. A further

---

Luberg to President Weaver, Don Percy, Wally Lemon, Bob Taylor, and Harvey Breuscher, July 22, 1971, Series 40/1/2/3-2, Box 6, UA, in which Luberg reported that Milwaukee attorney and alumni leader David Beckwith had asserted that Mucks was not authorized by the alumni directors to speak for WAA on the issue.

[114]Quoted by Rost, "Merger," p. 315, citing James D. Selk, "Lucey Sticks to His U Merger Plan," *Wisconsin State Journal*, June 22, 1971.

[115]Rost, "Merger," pp. 321-322.

[116]"Statement by President John C. Weaver to U.W. Regent Budget Committee on Impact of Proposed Senate Substitute Amendment to Assembly Budget Bill 414," June 30, 1971, Series 40/1/2/3-2, Box 6, UA. Also see "Editor's Memo: To U.W. Regents," ed., *Capital Times*, June 30, 1971; Mike Miller, "Regents Find GOP Budget Even Worse than Dems'," ibid.; "UW Regents Panel Raps GOP Budget," *Milwaukee Journal*, July 1, 1971.

[117]Rost, "Merger," pp. 323-324, referring to Knutson to Weaver, July 1, 1971; *Senate Journal*, July 1, 1971, p. 1370; John Keefe, "As Usual, Legislature Personified by Inaction," *Wisconsin State Journal*, July 4, 1971.

complication was Governor Lucey's pledge not to sign any budget bill that did not also provide for merger.

With the legislature effectively deadlocked over the budget and with both regent boards officially opposing merger, Governor Lucey asked Madison University Committee Chairman J. Ray Bowen to arrange a "frank and open exchange of ideas between interested faculty members and myself." The University Committee responded by calling an unprecedented special Madison faculty meeting with the governor for the afternoon of July 8.[118] Anticipating the event, on July 7 the *Capital Times* published an editorial strongly supporting merger; the next morning the rival *Wisconsin State Journal,* which generally opposed merger, offered a list of questions the faculty should "start with."[119] At the least, an interesting confrontation with considerable media coverage seemed assured.

The meeting convened at 3:30 p.m. in room B-10 Commerce, one of the largest campus lecture halls. Fully six hundred faculty members and other UW staff were present, along with numerous print and electronic media reporters. Broadcast across the state via WHA radio, the meeting opened with remarks by the governor. Lucey alluded to the generally hostile public environment in which the University currently found itself, resulting from difficult economic times, the perceived under-emphasis on undergraduate instruction at Madison, and the recent campus "disorders" combined with the prevalent "youth culture":

> In a democracy . . . the only measure of a public institution is its credit with the voters. The fact is that the credit of higher education has sagged badly and it is now at a lower point than in any other time in my public career, which goes back to the historical days of Joe McCarthy in the early 1950s. It is against this background that I present my present budget and the merger proposals that I have submitted to the Legislature.

The governor then reviewed figures contrasting the relatively generous character of his higher education budget with those of most other Big Ten states as well as with the outrageously tight-fisted budget recently adopted by the senate.

Turning to his merger proposal, Lucey noted the growing similarities between UW and the WSU systems. These featured expanded

---

[118]Quoted in Rost, "Merger," p. 317, referring to "Lucey Seeks Meeting With Critics on Faculty," *Capital Times,* June 24, 1971.

[119]Quoted by Rost, "Merger," p. 326, referring to "Merger: Bests Hope for Higher Education in State," ed., *Capital Times,* July 7, 1971; "Time for UW Merger Answers," ed., *Wisconsin State Journal,* July 8, 1971.

graduate offerings along with multiple two-year and four-year undergraduate campuses that had resulted from both healthy competition and unwise political logrolling. He argued that Wisconsin had reached the point where:

> the expensive competition, the duplication, the wastefulness, can only be curbed if we have a single Board of Regents which can be held accountable for setting priorities for higher education in the State. The alternative, I might say, is to allow the Governor and the Legislature to become more active in the management and oversight of higher education and this is a prospect that I do not believe would serve the interests of higher education or the interest of the State of Wisconsin.

The governor pointed out that Wisconsin voters could not get "very enthused about the construction of Phy[sical] Ed[ucation] buildings or swimming pools. Yet, this is the kind of competition that develops every time we call a meeting of the Building Commission."

According to Lucey, most of the wasteful competition and duplication came as a result of inter-system rivalry. Within their separate structures the two systems planned sensibly and allocated resources "to preserve the individual strengths and missions of each campus, and this is as it ought to be." It therefore seemed reasonable to assume that a merged board of regents under UW President Weaver would impose a similar process across the state. "Upon the advice of faculty leaders in both University systems," the governor continued, "we have included in the merger legislation the explicit mission statement for each campus. These statutory provisions will protect the special strengths of each campus in the allocation of funds and of responsibilities." Thus the Lucey merger proposal was workable and a positive reform that would particularly benefit the Madison and Milwaukee campuses, whose graduate programs currently were facing severe curtailment due to the economic downturn, not to mention the aspirations of the WSU campuses to move beyond their traditional professional education offerings.

Governor Lucey's further arguments for merger were less appealing to the Madison faculty audience, which by its nature reflected elitist sentiments. Lucey deplored what he called "a vicious discrimination among our young people" that resulted from the differing prestige (and job prospects) that attached to degrees from the University and WSU systems. This was an indication of the negative fallout from President Harrington's determined acquisition of the new undergraduate campuses at Green Bay and Parkside:

>A merger proposal would give every graduate a degree from the University of Wisconsin. If employers and if graduate schools wish to make evaluations reflecting the work of each individual campus, we certainly have no objection to that. But I think it objectionable and unfair for the State to encourage irrational discrimination by giving out a more prestigious degree in some institutions than others without regard to the merits of the respective institutions but with respect only to the administrative system that they happen to be a part of.

Furthermore, "this discrimination tends to work against certain groups in our State, certain geographic groups, certain economical and racial groups who are more heavily enrolled in one system than in the other."

Regarding University governance, Lucey continued to defend his proposed "Campus Councils" as a means of eliciting advice from the "broad public." Nevertheless, he promised the merged system would have "the broadest possible discretion . . . to work out the details. The proposed merger respects your competence to devise internal governing arrangements and internal standards for higher education." To this end he had included a provision requiring the new system to report back to the governor and legislature with recommended statutory changes that "might be needed to make the merger effective." A more detailed initiative would have obviated the need for such an exercise, but it also would have faced widespread and substantial objections. "The lack of detail is deliberate because we have confidence that most of these issues are better spelled out by the university community than by the Governor and the Legislature." Lucey concluded by asserting: "You and I are partners and not adversaries in the battle to bring quality higher education to the people of Wisconsin. . . . We must create a 'New Wisconsin Idea' that can cope with the new challenges of the 1970s."

There followed forty minutes of questions and answers.[120] The dialogue initially focused on faculty salaries and must have struck at least some observers as evidence of the Madison faculty's self-centered arrogance. Mathematics Professor Anatole Beck, a frequent and usually caustic faculty spokesman, told the governor, "To us it is extremely important . . . that our salaries be raised." Beck bolstered his argument by pointing out that UW-Madison was the tenth most distinguished American university but ranked one hundred and fifty-forth in faculty

---

[120]"Question and Answer Period following Governor Patrick J. Lucey's Address to the UW-Madison Faculty," July 8, 1971, typed transcript, Series 40/1/2/3-2, Box 6, UA.

pay. Lucey replied that in view of the state's current weak economic condition, his willingness to provide raises of at least eight percent during each of the next two years was unmatched among Wisconsin politicians. In fact, "I regret that there was not greater faculty support for those increases." Professors Robert Kingdon (history), Louis Rossi (French and Italian), and Robert Ozanne (economics and School for Workers) pressed the governor further on his stated objective of equalizing the cost of instruction for students across all UW and WSU institutions for any given course, particularly at the freshman-sophomore level. How, the three asked, could Madison recruit and retain top-flight scholars at these significantly reduced wage rates? Lucey's rather obscure reply was that "comparability" factors, involving such things as experience and scholarly distinction, should of course be taken into account in setting salaries, which thus would be higher at Madison. As for the cost-per-student, "economy of size" at Madison would translate into larger classes per instructor, so the relatively higher faculty salaries would cover more students than at other campuses. Ultimately, stated the governor: "I think comparability is the byword of salary structure and I think that comparability will enter into negotiations between the two Systems without merger. I think that it can be dealt with more orderly with a single Board of Regents and a single Central Administration." Lucey's comments may not have reassured the Madison faculty, but they probably played well elsewhere in Wisconsin, especially among those who had given up on CCHE.

Other clarifications were forthcoming. Regarding "duplication" of programs, for example, Lucey contended it made sense to eliminate those graduating few students when larger ones were also available. "It would be up to the new Board of Regents and the new Central Administration to do it," he said. Responding to comments from Professor Edmund Zawacki (Slavic languages), the governor acknowledged the challenge of nurturing excellence in the context of modern mass education, shrewdly relating the problem to preserving UW-Madison's quality:

> I think that we have reached the point now where the only way to preserve the "jewel in the crown"– . . . that is the Madison campus–is by going to one system, one board of regents, and one central administration; the elimination of that whole tier of bureaucracy called the CCHE; and the elimination of all duplication of the wasteful courses that we have now, and introduce economy of scale in some of the other campuses. I think that the excellence of this campus depends on the

administrative efficiency that would come through a well planned and well executed merger plan.

Later, following a query from Professor Joseph Heffernan (social work), Lucey summarized his case for merger:

> I think that a single board of regents will give autonomy to the 13 campuses, which they need, and I think that a single Board of Regents is adequate to provide broad public policy and to set long range objectives for higher education in this State. I also think that a single Board of Regents can maintain differences, can permit peaks of excellence among the 13 campuses that now exist and can enhance these peaks of excellence.

Whether the governor succeeded in overcoming the widespread Madison faculty opposition to his merger proposal was doubtful, but most observers gave him high marks for making this face-to-face effort.[121]

Toward a Resolution

Events occurring throughout the remainder of July finally convinced key UW Central Administration authorities that merger probably could

---

[121]See "Gov. Lucey's Address to University Faculty," *Capital Times*, July 12, 1971; Roger A. Gribble, "Faculty Hears Salesman Lucey," *Wisconsin State Journal*, July 9, 1971. Rost's summary appears at pp. 328-331, including the number in attendance, which is not recorded in the official minutes of the meeting, referenced as Special Faculty Meeting, Minutes, July 8, 1971. A few days after his meeting with the Madison faculty, Lucey stated in part: "It is evident that there will be a direct and not insubstantial economy which will be accomplished by consolidating the present, duplicative administrative structures; and this savings is one which will be repeated during each biennium. Of still greater impact, however is the savings which I believe will accompany the elimination of the rivalry between the two systems." Lucey to David Fellman, July 16, 1971, Series 40/1/2/3-2, Box 2, UA.

On July 12, Governor Lucey spent the evening at the Milwaukee University Club with a group of prominent UW alumni, including attorney and merger advocate, David Beckwith and Allen and Donald Slichter, whose father had been a longtime Madison faculty member and Graduate School dean. Not surprisingly, Lucey made the same arguments he had earlier with the Madison Faculty Senate. More significantly, he confided off the record to Allen Slichter that he would be willing to have one regent board for the Madison campus, or possibly for Madison and UWM, and another for all the other campuses. He did not, however, think this was politically feasible. Luberg to Weaver re: "Meeting of Governor Lucey with a Milwaukee Group Last Evening at the University Club," July 13, 1971, ibid., Box 6.

not be avoided and therefore they needed a more constructive strategy. As late as July 13, however, President Weaver had not determined what course to follow. During an appearance before the Joint Finance Committee, he was asked whether he preferred the assembly or the senate budget bill. "As to which arm I should cut off," he replied, "my overriding concern is to not damage the distinction of a great university either through inadequate financial support or by a yet undefined system of reorganization."[122] After the assembly rejected the senate budget on the 15th, a legislative conference committee was set up to reconcile the two bills.[123] On July 21, after rejecting the senate's budget, the committee voted unanimously to delete the merger provision from the assembly alternative. Suddenly, Devitt's bill 213S was the only piece of legislation carrying the merger banner.

Two days later Republican Assemblyman Walter G. Hollander and Democratic Assemblyman George Molinaro, co-chairmen of the Joint Finance Committee and both longtime supporters of the University, met with President Weaver and Vice President Percy. They came directly to the point: merger was destined to pass and therefore it was time to minimize the damage. Percy, who during the previous months had thought about many options, brought out a draft amendment for 213S that seemed appropriate. Hollander thereafter modified and submitted it to his committee for consideration. Simultaneously, WSU supporters came forward with their own amendment. By July 28 it was clear to Hollander that his proposal would fail, so he offered softening amendments to the WSU plan. The resulting compromise would allow the new regent board to open (but not close) two-year campuses, retain the original two central administrations through the 1971-1973 biennium, and somewhat alter the composition of a so-called merger implementation committee charged with developing detailed plans for completing the merger. After some additional maneuvering, on July 28 the Joint Finance Committee endorsed the amended WSU proposal by a 9-4 vote. The next day Governor Lucey announced his support of this separate merger bill. Assemblyman Hollander predicted senate passage.[124]

---

[122]Rost, "Merger," pp. 332-333, referring to Eugene C. Harrington, "UW Takes a Swing at GOP Budget," *Milwaukee Journal*, July 14, 1971.

[123]Rost, "Merger," p. 333.

[124]Ibid., pp. 353-354, referring to Charlotte Robinson, "Lucey Hails U. Merger Compromise," *Ccapital Times*, July 29, 1971; John Keefe, "Hollander's Sure of Merger Nod," *Wisconsin State Journal*, July 30, 1971.

Early the next day, July 29, Vice President Percy wrote a frank, confidential, "morning-after" memo to President Weaver before leaving "these 'wilds' for the wilds of northern Wisconsin."[125] Percy now was almost completely persuaded that merger would pass and he urged Weaver to grasp the initiative in shaping the new administrative structure. Otherwise, he said, Joe Nusbaum and his Lucey administration colleagues or perhaps the WSU leadership would do so. "McPhee is probably at work on this project this morning," warned Percy. He also speculated that Weaver's own UW chancellors might join a coalition in favor of making campus autonomy "a complete reality," one that would render "the central administration a pale copy of the CCHE." Never one to leave a vacuum unfilled, Percy offered "my thoughts on a possible administrative structure . . . we might pursue" in the context of "vague" statutory language regarding the interim "dual central administration." Percy's latest plan envisioned two system vice presidents, one each for the UW and WSU institutions, reporting to the president, who alone would speak to the regents for the administration. Another option had vice presidents for graduate-professional campuses, undergraduate campuses, extension, and centers all reporting to the president. In each case the strong Central Administration would continue to look after business affairs, facilities, budget, planning, and university relations. "I have a folder somewhere outlining clusters of institutions in case of merger," added the president's chief assistant.

Vice President Percy's July 29 memo also provided some tantalizing hints about prior University strategy: "Since [Regent] Ody [Fish] 'guided' us through the early months on this issue," noted Percy, "maybe he can figure a way to head off complete merger when the matter comes to the senate. I doubt whether we can head it off, but it's worth a try provided we're really willing to settle for" the failed Hollander/Percy plan. Percy further intimated his disenchantment with Fish's judgment: "If Ody advises that there's 'no way' to beat it with the same vigor he used four months ago in advising in 'no way' can it pass the senate, then our thinking *must* move toward making the most of it." Something more realistic was needed:

> John, you were not convinced that merger was in the best interests of the University of Wisconsin–but now merger *is* the University of Wisconsin . . . assuming we can't turn it around. In light of this, can we protect what we sought to protect from the beginning by dragging our feet and delaying a move to assert leadership (as you have been invited to do)?

---

[125]Percy to Weaver, July 29, 1971, Series 40/1/2/3-2, Box 2, UA.

Percy clearly believed the time had come to take the initiative on merger.

On August 3 President Weaver called a Van Hise Hall press conference and read a statement attacking senate substitute amendment 5, which that had prevailed at joint finance on July 28. Weaver argued four main points: first, it did not make sense to pass merger and then later work out the details; second, the weak central administration described in this bill would produce chaos, for "in the name of autonomy this proposal recommends something akin to anarchy"; third, the required "campus council" for each degree-granting institution and the retention of both present regent boards contradicted Governor Lucey's goal of reducing the number and complexity of governing bodies; and finally, it made no sense to introduce doctoral work at the WSU campuses while "crippling" the graduate programs at Madison and Milwaukee. Weaver said he realized that by offering these criticisms he might have "disqualified" himself from the merged system presidency, but in accordance with "faculty consensus," he believed it important to warn that the adoption of amendment 5 could place the University "in genuine peril."[126]

Later that day Governor Lucey defended substitute 5 as a "bipartisan product of months of research, public debate, and legislative review":

> It would have been helpful for President Weaver, as my designee to head the merged system, to have clearly set forth his position on the details of merger at an earlier date so that the Senate authors and my office might have considered it carefully. Instead he has chosen to reveal his objections on the eve of legislative action.

Weaver had, of course, frequently expressed his administration's negative view of merger privately through Vice President Percy. In any case, the governor went on to urge that "in spite of this inconvenience," he was sure the senate would consider those "positive suggestions implicit in President Weaver's comments."[127]

[126]"Press Conference Statement by President John C. Weaver," August 3, 1971, ibid., Box 1. See also Rost, "Merger," references Howard Cosgrove, "Weaver Tries to Scuttle 'Agreed' U. Merger Move," *Capital Times*, August 3, 1971; "The GOP-Weaver Game," ed., ibid., August 4, 1971; Roger A. Gribble, "UW Head Attacks State Merger Plan," *Wisconsin State Journal*, August 4, 1971; "Lucey's Merger Plan Threatens Future of Education in State," ed., ibid., August 4, 1971; "Merger Bill Denounced by Weaver," *Milwaukee Journal*, August 3, 1971. For an interesting analysis of the conference press coverage see "Steve" to President Weaver, "News Conference Report," August 4, 1971, Series 40/1/2/3-2, Box 6, UA.

[127]"Gov. Lucey Defends Merger Plan, Says Weaver Timing Inconvenient,"

Lucey's aides soon contacted the UW president's office and arranged for the two antagonists to hold negotiations at the governor's mansion on the morning of August 4. During a long meeting the two men agreed to nineteen amendments, including a proviso that TAWSUF, the WSU faculty union, must approve everything. The next day Governor Lucey and President Weaver appeared at a joint news conference to announce this list of amendments, which Weaver characterized as making amendment 5 "workable." Lucey agreed. "The consensus can best be expressed in this way: if there is to be merger, this proposal is the most workable and effective way to consolidate the governing boards and the systems." Even so, Weaver still emphasized, "I agree with my Board's position that merger is not in the best interests of the University of Wisconsin, the Wisconsin State University system, or the people of this State."[128]

The Lucey-Weaver amendments added up to four substantial changes in the legislation. First, the new mission statements contained in the present bill would be replaced by the missions adopted by CCHE on July 1, 1971. Second, the merged central administration would be similar to the strong pre-merger UW arrangement. Third, the campus councils were retained, but strictly as advisory bodies with no influence over academic programming. Fourth, unlike Lucey's original plan, the two boards were to be merged immediately, even as the two systems would continue to function separately until the regents and a merger implementation committee determined the specific details of the new University of Wisconsin System. As Lucey told the senate floor leaders, "While I am reluctant to postpone the administrative reorganization, this proposal does have the merit of allowing the Legislature to act on the basic policy question while leaving the details for further consideration by both higher education personnel and representatives of appropriate legislative committees."[129]

The *Capital Times* report of the August 5 press conference gave the impression that Lucey and Weaver had not only agreed to "workable" amendments to the bill but also that they believed it *ought* to pass. Observed reporter Howard Cosgrove, "Merger of the state's two University systems

Wisconsin State Journal, August 4, 1971. Also see Rost, "Merger," pp. 359-360, referring to "Lucey Grave, GOP Joyous on Weaver Merger Blast," *Capital Times*, August 4, 1971.

[128]Rost, "Merger," pp. 360-364, referring to John Keefe, "Merger Accord Still Hanging," *Wisconsin State Journal*, August 6, 1971; Ralph D. Olive, "Lucey Courts Weaver's Support," *Milwaukee Journal*, August 6, 1971. Weaver spelled out his continuing opposition to merger in a "Statement by President John C. Weaver, University of Wisconsin to the Board of Regents," August 6, 1971, Series 40/1/2/3-2, Box 6, UA.

[129]Rost, "Merger," pp. 365-366.

took a giant step forward today with the announcement that Gov. Patrick J. Lucey and the University of Wisconsin President John Weaver have agreed on a merger bill." An accompanying photo caption observed erroneously that Lucey and Weaver had "announced today that Weaver will withdraw his opposition to merger."[130] Meanwhile, the senate Republicans met in caucus decide their next step in light of President Weaver's apparent capitulation. UW Regent Ody Fish participated, urging delay on the two key issues at hand: taxation policy and merger. The Republicans decided to adjourn until August 24, unless the conference committee should overcame its impasse on these two questions.[131] After learning of Fish's participation in the caucus, Lucey publicly charged him with injecting partisan politics into the matter, surely a contrived reaction in light of all of the complicated maneuvering to date.[132]

The UW Board of Regents convened on Friday, August 6, to review the situation. That morning, prior to the full board meeting, Weaver and Regents Fish and Ziegler met to discuss the recent developments. Fish criticized Weaver for undermining the regents' anti-merger stand, and he handed the president a statement to read at the board meeting affirming Weaver's continued opposition to merger. Weaver agreed to this but also reminded the two regents he had checked with both of them prior to the Lucey-Weaver conference.[133] At the board meeting President Weaver raised the question of merger and Regent President Ziegler requested a chronological summary of recent developments. Weaver recounted the legislative actions and his subsequent reactions, including his consultations with the regent Executive Committee. He then read Fish's statement reaffirming his and the board's continued opposition to amended 213S and the entire concept of merger. According to the board minutes, Regent Ziegler explained he had asked Weaver:

> to reaffirm, for the benefit of the Regents, what had happened during the past week, because of the conflicting reports; and he stated that he wanted to emphasize that President Weaver had not, either on his own, or representing the Board, taken a different position that the Board had agreed upon a month ago. He expressed sympathy with the awkward position that

---

[130]Quoted in ibid., p. 372.

[131]Ibid., pp. 374-375.

[132]Patrick J. Lucey Press Release, August 6, 1971, Series 40/1/2/3-2, Box 6, UA; Charlotte Robinson, "Lucey Says Fish Puts Politics Into U. Merger Issue," *Capital Times*, August 6, 1971; "Regent Ody Fish in Disgraceful Tactics," ed., ibid.

[133]This follows the undocumented account of Rost, "Merger," pp. 378-379.

President Weaver was put in, but complimented him on the way he handled it.[134]

Unfortunately for Weaver, he would remain in that "awkward position" for some time.

Observers interpreted the Weaver statement variously. The pro-merger *Capital Times* commented, "Weaver, it seems, was one of the few persons who did not interpret his joint press conference with Gov. Lucey as the first step toward a compromise."[135] In contrast, a *Wisconsin State Journal* editorial concluded that no substantial progress had been made toward settling merger. As for Lucey's complaint that Fish had introduced partisan politics into the matter, "The charge is ludicrous because it is so obvious to everyone that the governor, in trying to save face, has been playing frantic politics for weeks with this issue."[136] Eugene Harrington of the *Milwaukee Journal* perhaps most accurately described Weaver as caught in a difficult position between his Republican board of regents, which opposed merger, and Lucey, who had adapted his proposal to Weaver's criticisms and wanted the UW president to head the new system.[137] Amid the press discussion, Republican Assemblyman Helgeson from Manitowoc wrote the UW president saying he had "questioned whether you were wavering in your opposition against the merger," but was now reassured: "your statement to the Board of Regents certainly clears this question and clearly explains your position."[138]

Next President Weaver assigned LeRoy Luberg the job of organizing a last-ditch fight against merger. Luberg in turn recruited WAA President Robert Wilson, a Madison banker and popular former Badger athlete, to help.[139] Wilson issued a statement on August 20 asserting that merger was "far too important a matter of educational policy to be decided

---

[134]UW BOR Minutes, August 6, 1971; "Statement by President John C. Weaver, University of Wisconsin, to the Board of Regents," August 6, 1971, ibid., Exhibit D.

[135]Rost, "Merger," p. 381, referring to Dave Maraniss, "Merger Power Struggle Dents Weaver Credibility," *Capital Times*, August 7, 1971.

[136]Rost, "Merger," p. 382, referring to John Keefe, "Governor's Tactic Puts Weaver in Political Box," *Wisconsin State Journal*, August 8, 1971; "Lucey's Merger Still Bad Idea," ed., ibid., August 9, 1971.

[137]Rost, "Merger," pp. 383-384, referring Harrington, "Tug of War Over Merger," *Milwaukee Journal*, August 8, 1971.

[138]Helgeson to Weaver, August 11, 1971, Series 40/1/2/3-2, Box 6, UA.

[139]Rost, "Merger," pp. 397-398. Rost did not document Luberg's campaign or his influence with Wilson. Rost also failed to explain why Weaver would organize such an effort after supposedly deciding that a compromise would be better for UW-Madison than a complete defeat leaving the WSU system to define and implement the merger.

on political terms."[140] About this same time Weaver told a UW Center System faculty member, "My growing concern is that the ultimate decision regarding the University's future will be based upon political rather than educational considerations."[141] Assembly Speaker Robert Huber responded to the UW anti-merger campaign on August 24, complaining that "every effort to develop an acceptable merger proposition has been met by the cynical strategy of the University, a strategy that shows no regard for the taxpayer who funds the University's bloated budget." Huber also expressed dismay that "the University seems shocked that in return for taxpayers' money, a better organized system of administration be established."[142] Madison Assemblywoman Midge Miller, a fellow Democrat but staunch University defender, countered that she disagreed with the speaker because a good case for merger had not yet been made; she thought caution and further study were warranted.[143]

The next day, August 25, Governor Lucey spoke about "The Political Requirements of Higher Educational Coordination" at a UW-Madison seminar for visiting academic administrators. He pointed out that the University's good public image had vanished over the preceding five years of campus unrest and violence. Furthermore, the unwillingness of UW to focus on undergraduate education and to agree to merger misjudged current political realities and ultimately could jeopardize a healthy future.[144] According to a friendly *Capital Times* report, Lucey later commented to a seminar participant that the UW and WSU systems were "the worst managed public services in state government, and that they were an administrative monstrosity that cannot be justified."[145] Former UW Regent and CCHE critic Arthur DeBardeleben, a longtime Democrat, responded that Lucey was making "irrelevant" and inaccurate statements about what might be accomplished through merger. "The overriding and unanswerable objection to merger," DeBardeleben declared, "is that it

---

[140]Quoted in Rost, "Merger," pp. 397-398, referring to "Merger Plan Opposed by UW Alumni Assn.," *Wisconsin State Journal*, August 21, 1971.

[141]Weaver to Robert Biederwolf, August 10, 1971; for the same view see Weaver to Reverend J. Ellsworth Kalas, August 10, 1971, both in Series 40/1/2/3-2, Box 6, UA.

[142]"Huber Puts Pressure on GOP for Merger," *Wisconsin State Journal*, August 25, 1971.

[143]Rost, "Merger," p. 401, referring to John Keefe, "Linking Budget and Merger Is Criticized by Rep. Miller," *Wisconsin State Journal*, August 26, 1971.

[144]Rost, "Merger," pp. 402-403, referring to Lucey, "The Political Requirements of Higher Education Coordination," a Speech Given to a University of Wisconsin Seminar in University Administration and Operations, August 25, 1971.

[145]Rost, "Merger," p. 403, referring to "Lucey Tells Foreign Group 2 U. Systems 'Monstrosity'," *Capital Times*, August 26, 1971.

will pull down the pre-eminent quality of the world-renowned Madison campus of the University to the level of the state universities."[146]

Also on August 25 UW Board of Visitors Chairman Lawrence J. Fitzpatrick issued a report from his group: "Our Board has met with students, faculty, and administration on the 16 campuses of the University, plus members of the general public. We have carefully assessed the product and the nature of the University and conclude that the present system should be maintained."[147] A short while later, the *Wisconsin Alumnus* carried an editorial by Arlie Mucks reporting that President Weaver had declared merger "conceptually unacceptable" and warning that the legislature was moving toward passage. The time had come, Mucks urged the UW alumni, "to speak out."[148] President Weaver maintained his opposition, telling a UW graduate student that he agreed with the UW and WSU regent boards "that the two existing systems are doing an excellent job of fulfilling their educational missions, and that merger would not improve higher education nor reduce educational costs."[149]

Merger

On August 30, William Kellett, the chairman of the Commission on Educational Reform, issued a statement advocating merger as a way of surmounting the deadlock blocking legislative approval of the great bulk of the commission's recommendations. This statement, whether or not orchestrated by Governor Lucey and his Democratic colleagues, set the stage for the final act of the merger drama. Early in September the two houses of the legislature reconvened and began sparring over several issues, particularly the long-delayed budget and tax reform. On September 16 the senate approved amendments embodying the Weaver-Lucey merger agreements, eliminated the local campus councils, and dealt with other minor amendments. Thereafter the primary problem for the pro-merger coalition was to keep merger supporters from adding amendments that

---

[146]DeBardeleben to Lucey, with copies to *Milwaukee Journal*, *Milwaukee Sentinel*, *Wisconsin State Journal*, and *Captial Times*, August 26, 1971, Series 40/1/2/3-2, Box 2, UA; "DeBardeleben Blasts U Merger Plan," *Wisconsin State Journal*, August 28, 1971; "A Democrat on Merger," *Capital Times*, September 1, 1971.

[147]Quoted in Rost, "Merger," p. 403, referring to "UW's Board of Visitors Strongly Opposes Merger," *Wisconsin State Journal*, August 26, 1971.

[148]Rost, "Merger," pp. 432-533, referring to Arlie M. Mucks, Jr., "On Wisconsin: August 11," *WAM*, 72 (August-September, 1971), 2.

[149]Weaver to Margaret Johnson, September 15, 1971, Series 40/1/2/3-2, Box 6, UA.

would cost votes for the bill. One amendment, for example, would have shortened regent terms from seven to five years. By the end of debate on the 17th, the bill had survived its third reading by a one-vote margin, which meant the senate could no longer amend it and now must vote it up or down. Adjourning for the weekend, merger opponents sought to convince Republican Senator Clifford W. "Tiny" Krueger, to withdraw his unexpected support of merger and join his GOP colleagues in opposition. Krueger, meanwhile, consulted with UW-Stevens Point President and staunch merger advocate Lee Sherman Dreyfus and concluded he would stay the course, even against his fellow party members. Debate resumed on Tuesday the 21st, and the next day, at 11:45 a.m., the final vote was taken. The Republican-controlled senate approved amended bill 213 by a vote of 18-15.[150] Although merger still formally required the approval of the Democratic-controlled assembly, this was assured, and all sides agreed Governor Lucey had won a great victory. Many of the staunchest opponents, meanwhile, particularly at UW-Madison, quietly lamented Krueger's defection and began speculating endlessly about what might have been.

Public reactions of high UW and WSU officials varied. President Weaver said the close vote did not "dissolve" the concern of UW faculty, administrators, and regents, and that it would be "entirely premature and inappropriate" for him at this early moment to issue a more substantive statement.[151] The disappointed Madison University Committee promised:

> We accept the obligation to implement the provisions of the bill in such a way as to insure the continuation of a strong system of higher education in Wisconsin. We are confident that the faculty of both systems will contribute substantially and positively to the work of the merger implementation study committee during the next two years.[152]

Eugene McPhee, WSU executive director, thought the adopted bill was

---

[150]Percy to Chancellors, September 17, 1971, Series 40/1/2/3-2, Box 2; Rost, "Merger," pp. 405-410, 435-459. James D. Selk, "Preliminary Approval Given to Merger," *Wisconsin State Journal*, September 18, 1971; Charles E. Friederich, "Merger Clears Major Hurdle," *Milwaukee Journal*, September 18, 1971; Friederich, "UW, WSU Marriage Near, Honeymoon May Be a Battle," ibid., September 19, 1971.

[151]"Statement by President John C. Weaver, September 22, 1971, Series 40/1/2/3-2, Box 6, UA.

[152]"Statement by the Madison Campus University Committee 9/22/71," release, ibid.

UW President John Weaver, press conference to oppose UW System merger compromise bill, August 3, 1971, photo by Norman Lenburg. UA, X25-3409.

UW System merger bill signing; l-r: Martin J. Schreiber, Patrick J. Lucey, John Weaver, Lee Sherman Dreyfus, October, 1971. UA, 6252-J-1.

better than Governor Lucey's original version. UW-Madison Chancellor Young observed cryptically that "out of this could come a better system." Regent Fish, on the other hand, predicted no improvements from merger.[153]

The assembly voted its approval on October 5 by a comfortable margin of 56-43. The *Milwaukee Journal* commented:

> An entirely new self-concept will be needed among regents, many of whom had come to seeing their role largely as advocates for a particular system in dealing with the Co-ordinating Council for Higher Education. There will be no CCHE now. The regents themselves take on all the power–and thus the grave responsibility for public accountability–that formerly was vested in the CCHE.[154]

Governor Lucey signed the merger bill into law on Friday, October 8, 1971, hailing it as "the beginning of a new era in the education of Wisconsin's young people. Merger is now a reality and we will all benefit because of it, through the new University of Wisconsin system." Merger went officially into effect four days later, and with it the original University of Wisconsin disappeared.[155]

Green Bay Press-Gazette reporter Tim Wyngaard pointed out the irony that the University of Wisconsin System might "become one of the lasting legacies of the man who dominated higher education in the state for the past decade and more: Fred Harvey Harrington." For it was Harrington who had transformed the University structure into something closer to and comparable with the multi-campus Wisconsin State University, creating "a sprawling, state-wide system of basic, undergraduate education." Thus, in a sense Governor Lucey had merely capitalized on what President Harrington had put in place.[156]

---

[153]Rost, "Merger," pp. 460-61, referring to "U. Officials' Reactions to Merger Is Like That After Game's Lost," *Wisconsin State Journal*, September 23, 1971.

[154]Quoted in Rost, "Merger," p. 467, referring to "New Era of Higher Education," ed., *Milwaukee Journal*, October 6, 1971. Donald Percy expressed much the same sentiment when he urged the State Department of Administration "to exercise . . . restraint with regard to CCHE functions and responsibilities set to transfer to the new board. I make particular reference to program planning, enrollment projections and the myriad other important functions of CCHE that fall to the jurisdiction of the new board and the staff which supports it." Percy to Nusbaum, September 29, 1971, Series 40/1/2/3-2, Box 2, UA.

[155]Quoted in Rost, "Merger," p. 469.

[156]Quoted in ibid., p. 462, referring to Tim Wyngaard, "Merger Passage Viewed As Harrington Legacy," *Green Bay Press-Gazette*, September 26, 1971. Another irony involved Lucey's later statement that he would not have attempted his merger initiative if Harrington had still been the UW president, because he thought Harrington was the

The 1948 "First Report" of the Ingraham Committee on University Functions and Policies had accurately predicted the problems CCHE ultimately was unable to resolve. The Ingraham Committee had also discussed voluntary cooperation, which turned out not to work in practice. Its recommended option–merger–ultimately came about. The 1971 legislation did not, however, follow the committee's model of a carefully integrated merged system under University leadership and control. This idea, in fact, had not been seriously considered for a number of years. For one thing, the creation of UW-Milwaukee in 1955 and its subsequent development as a semi-autonomous graduate-level institution worked against any unitary concept. President Harrington's chancellor system also tended to fragment, rather than unite, the growing multi-campus University. Finally, Governor Lucey's emphasis in 1971 on undergraduate instruction as the primary *raison d'être* for a public university aroused grave suspicions among UW-Madison faculty members, who responded by trying to wall off their prestigious comprehensive institution as much as possible from the rest of the new University of Wisconsin System. The result was surely not what Mark Ingraham and his colleagues had in mind a quarter of a century earlier.

---

one UW leader who could have mobilized enough political support to defeat it. Patrick J. Lucey, oral history interview, 1985, UA.

10.

End of an Era

The University of Wisconsin changed more in the quarter century after the Second World War than at any time in its history, culminating in its disappearance as a distinct legal entity in 1971. At the beginning of the period, everyone in the state and the country understood the University of Wisconsin to mean the campus in Madison, including any subordinate outlying UW activities around the state. By the 1960s, the University had become a multi-campus system, a "multiversity," with its name sometimes applied just to the parent campus in Madison and sometimes confusingly used to embrace the whole. Within this emerging system the Madison campus became administratively and symbolically only one of a half dozen separate units, its greater academic stature sometimes proudly hailed and sometimes grudgingly conceded, but its parental role and long history increasingly ignored or forgotten. The decision in 1971 by state political leaders to combine all of the state's higher education institutions into a new University of Wisconsin System thus merely enlarged a structure the original University of Wisconsin had developed earlier. The difference was significant, however. UW officials had led in the creation and development and had determined the structure of their initial smaller system. The 1971 merger was imposed by state political leaders over the deep misgivings of most UW regents, administrators, and Madison faculty members, alumni, and students . Of all the many changes of the post-war years, this one was the most profound and unsettling. It was to force UW-Madison administrators and faculty members to reexamine their role in Wisconsin higher education and their relationship to the other units of the new UW System.

597

The Golden Age in Retrospect

A pivotal development of the post-war years was the shift in the sources of University funding and the relative decline in the importance of traditional state support. The impact of federal and other external funds on the University in the quarter century following World War II was enormous. They helped transform the campus physical plant, shaped the curriculum, and revolutionized the funding and nature of faculty research and of student support. This change was not unique to Wisconsin, of course; all major U.S. universities experienced the same thing in greater or lesser degrees. Some figures will illustrate the magnitude of this shift in the funding of American higher education after the war. Between 1949 and 1971 federal research and development (R&D) spending totaled more than $183 billion for the country as a whole. These expenditures doubled–from $3.2 billion to $6.4 billion–the year after the Soviet Union launched its first Sputnik satellite in 1958 and continued to grow thereafter at an accelerated rate. By 1970 federal agencies were budgeting $15.8 billion annually for research and development, and channeling nearly $1.5 billion of it to American colleges and universities.[1] At first defense-related R&D grants predominated by a wide margin, but by the end of this period the extent of defense over non-defense R&D spending had declined to a ratio of only about 8 to 7.[2]

As a leading research and graduate university, the University of Wisconsin at Madison was a major beneficiary of this federal spending, a fact noted in 1962 by a special UW Committee on Federal and Industrial Grants and Contracts in a report to President Elvehjem and the Board of Regents. During the decade of the 1950s, the committee pointed out, the University's operating budget increased two-and-a-half times. In the same period budgeted research quadrupled, and federal support of research (not even counting Land Grant funds) jumped thirteen-fold.[3] In 1965-66, mid-way through the Harrington era, UW-

---

[1]U.S. Government, *Special Analyses: Budget of the United States, Fiscal Year 1972* (Washington: Government Printing Office, 1971), pp. 273-74.

[2]Ibid., *Budget of the United States Government: Historical Tables - Fiscal Year 1995* (Washington: Government Printing Office, 1994), Table 10.1, p. 140.

[3]"Report to the Administrative Committee by Its Ad Hoc Committee on Federal and Industrial Grants and Contracts," UW BOR Minutes, February 9, 1962, UA. The committee was chaired by Graduate Dean John Willard and included Vice President A.W. Peterson, Deans Mark Ingraham and Kurt Wendt, and George R. Field. The report offered a number of insightful policy suggestions about how to deal with the increasing

Madison ranked 11th in the country in receipt of federal R&D funding and 12th nationally in total federal support, amounting that year to $38,756,000.[4] By the time President Harrington left office in late 1970, the yearly total of federal R&D funding received by the University had climbed to $62,512,000 and the campus ranked seventh nationally in such support.[5] It was an improved standing Harrington had worked hard to achieve.

Although substantially less in dollar totals, the support provided by the major foundations for research, instruction, and academic programming was also highly significant. It helped to move the University into a number of new curricular areas and brought a wider, more international perspective to its activities. Foundation and National Defense Education Act funds were largely responsible for transforming this seemingly unlikely Midwestern university—one located far from either coast and in a state with a strong isolationist tradition—into an institution whose global outlook and reach stood out nationally. One should not minimize the importance of UW leaders—President Harrington, Vice President Clodius, and Chancellor Young in particular, along with interested UW faculty members—in promoting an international agenda, but without the external funding they surely would have accomplished far less.

University officials deserve high marks for their aggressive pursuit of funds and other means to accommodate the explosive growth they confronted in the quarter century after World War II. On the whole, they did a good job of planning campus construction, recruiting the necessary additional faculty, and maintaining and even improving academic quality. Indeed, the construction and hiring booms of the fifties and sixties brought a spectacular transformation of the physical face and intellectual breadth of the campus unrivaled in any previous period.

At the same time, these changes were not entirely beneficial. The splendid new buildings usually included meeting rooms and lounges where faculty members could enjoy informal brownbag

---

flow of external research and program funds.

[4]National Science Foundation, *Federal Support to Universities and Colleges: Fiscal Years 1963-66* (Washington: Government Printing Office, 1967), Chapter III, Table 19, p. 38, and Appendix B, Table B-4, pp. 59-61.

[5]Ibid., *Federal Support to Universities, Colleges, and Selected Nonprofit Institutions, Fiscal Year 1972* (Washington: Government Printing Office, 1974), Table B-9, p. 53.

lunches, thus reducing their use of the University Club or the Memorial Union and with it the opportunity to mix with faculty colleagues from other parts of the campus. As departments expanded in size, it became harder for the faculty to know one another well or to keep up with, and sometimes even understand, their colleagues' scholarly research. Nor was it any longer easy and in some cases simply impossible for them to become acquainted with very many of the growing number of graduate and undergraduate student majors in the larger departments. The history department provided probably the most extreme example of the downside of overwhelming student growth. Even though the department's faculty grew more than fivefold in the quarter century after World War II, it was simply impossible for 61 history professors, even if none was ever on research or other leave, to provide close mentoring and effective academic advising to the approximately 650 graduate and 900 undergraduate student majors enrolled in the department in 1970. It was no wonder the department thereafter took steps to reduce and control its enrollment, especially at the graduate level.

Another extreme but quite different illustration of the negative effects of growth was provided by the Department of Zoology, whose 9 faculty members in 1945 were housed together in the Biology Building (renamed Birge Hall in 1950) atop Bascom Hill. By 1970 the department had grown to 27 faculty, housed in three widely scattered buildings. Its whole organism or traditional field researchers had remained in Birge Hall along with the Zoology Museum; the molecular-cell specialists had moved their offices and laboratories to the new Zoology Research Building on Johnson Street; and the limnologists were located in the recently constructed Limnology Laboratory on Lake Mendota. The completion of the Noland Zoology Building in 1972, moreover, provided space for the department's administrative offices and some of its classrooms, along with the striking example of a medium-sized but widely dispersed department now unfortunately housed in four separate buildings.

Zoology's experience reflected the revolutionary but also divisive developments in the biological sciences after World War II. Probably no area of knowledge progressed more rapidly and changed more profoundly than biology in the post-war years. The descriptive study of whole organisms was increasingly augmented by the examination of their cell-molecular-genetic-DNA structures, whether involving plants, animals, or humans. Faculty concerned with the traditional study of the general and external characteristics of whole organisms tended to become "outsiders" in more than one sense, for biomedical research funds increasingly flowed more readily and generously to their "insider" colleagues concerned with the internal makeup of organisms. It was no accident that the Zoology "insiders" were located in the new Zoology Research Building after 1964, for their research had helped to secure the federal and WARF funds that made the building's construction possible.[6] As the revolution in biology developed across the University, the "insider" specialists as a group tended to have more in common with similar researchers in other departments than with their immediate whole organism colleagues.

Another divisive influence stemmed from the University's policy of channeling some of the overhead money derived from external grants back to the departments generating the grants. This could create problems of how to spend the funds: for what and by whom? Within departments receiving sizable overhead returns, tension sometimes arose over how to allocate these funds, because the overhead from individual researchers' grants was not generated evenly across the department. Thus, not only the increasing size but also the expanding expertise and research activity within departments tended to fragment their faculties, introduce new sources of conflict, undermine institutional loyalty, foster identification with national funding agencies, and encourage association with professional colleagues and organizations outside the University. None of these developments was bad as such; they merely combined to undermine Van Hise's ideal of a close collegial enterprise.

Changing Student Life

A large-scale survey in 1965 comparing the views of UW-Madison students with those of Wisconsin adults as a whole revealed some major differences. More than twice as many students as adults (42 percent to 19 percent) believed the attainment of a basic general education rather than vocational training should be the students'

---

[6]In 1959 the Department of Zoology applied for a grant of $750,000 from the National Institute of Health (NIH), to be matched by a similar WARF grant, to construct a new $1,500,000 research facility. NIH eventually awarded $381,500, matched by $750,000 from WARF and $368,500 from the National Science Foundation. The Board of Regents approved the final plans on October 5, 1962, and the building was completed in mid-1964. See Jim Feldman, *The Buildings of the University of Wisconsin* (Madison: Jim Feldman, 1996), p. 368.

primary academic goal. Over half the students but only about a third of the adults (51 percent to 35 percent) believed that important social reforms, usually identified as civil rights, were needed in American society.[7] Although college students have traditionally tested their parents' values, some significant attitudinal differences in the state's population seemed to be emerging as the baby boom generation matured. These differences became ever more pronounced in the years ahead.

Student extracurricular concerns and activism took many forms after World War II, with most of the traditional student organizations and activities remaining throughout the period. Regrettably, those disappearing as the student body grew larger and more diffuse included the impressive women's Senior Swingout spring ceremony, the symbolic men's Pipe of Peace transfer of authority and responsibility between the senior and junior classes, the colorful lakefront Venetian Nights celebration, and the annual spring student work days. By the late sixties much student energy was going into protest marches and demonstrations aimed mostly at correcting problems in the larger society beyond the University.

UW leaders were not notably successful in addressing student concerns in the latter part of this period, especially the unrest and confrontations arising out of the Vietnam War. Their strategies and record in handling violent student demonstrations were probably not much better or worse than those of other campuses experiencing similar uprisings–Berkeley, Cornell, Columbia, Oberlin come to mind. To its everlasting credit, however, throughout several years of campus turmoil that included two periods of unprecedented military occupation, the University of Wisconsin managed to preserve due process in handling student and faculty discipline cases, while at the same time maintaining and even extending the structures of student and faculty self-government. While the student policy reforms may have lagged behind the aspirations of some faculty and students, they were none the less significant.

UW athletes continued to take part in a wide range of intercollegiate competition, with Badger teams experiencing their usual varying success. A major change was the revived popularity and success of men's ice hockey under Coach Bob Johnson, which became the third

---

[7]Marvin Jacobson and Harry Sharp, "The College Student and the Public," University Extension, Wisconsin Survey Research Laboratory, July, 1966, Series 4/21/1, Box 17, UA.

UW varsity sport after football and basketball to generate significant spectator income after the team moved its games to the new Dane County Coliseum. Badger football teams struggled for often elusive success throughout the period, but were sustained by two Rose Bowl appearances, the second an unforgettable come-from-way-behind near victory in 1963 through the superb passing of Badger quarterback Ron VanderKelen. The memory of this might-have-been had to suffice for years thereafter. The growth of the student body led the University in the mid-1960s to expand the stadium's capacity to 79,000 seats by means of an upper deck over the west stands. Recruitment of the legendary pre-war UW football star Elroy Hirsch as athletic director at the end of the decade promised a revival of varsity sports and spirit. Hirsch's efforts were aided by the growing popularity of the marching band under its charismatic new director, music Professor Michael Leckrone, who succeeded the considerably more traditional Raymond Dvorak after the latter's retirement in 1968. Following a controversial three-year experiment in the early 1950s, women rejoined the cheerleading squad permanently in 1956. Both men and women students enjoyed active programs of recreational and intramural sports, and by the end of this period the Athletic Board began to consider supporting women's varsity teams.

The editors of the *Badger* continued to produce expensive glossy yearbooks, although in the latter sixties these took on a more political character reflecting the pervasive anti-war and activist sentiments of the student body. Conservative students tried several times to start a rival campus newspaper to counter what they considered to be the increasingly leftist outlook of the *Daily Cardinal*. With some outside financial help in 1969, they finally succeeded in launching a weekly *Badger Herald*, promising to keep their editorial views separate from news coverage. Impressed and gratified, as well as upset by the *Cardinal*'s unrestrained radical militancy at this time, the Board of Regents voted the next year to permit the new paper to be printed on the *Cardinal*'s press, which had earlier been acquired by the School of Journalism's typographical laboratory in exchange for University office space for the paper.[8]

UW students in the sixties were significantly influenced by an emerging counter culture among the baby boom generation in the United States and Europe. The movement included many things: new

---

[8]UW BOR Minutes, June 12, 1970.

forms of popular and folk music expressing disdain for authority and societal norms, unrestrained personal freedom, sexual liberation, and unconventional dress and behavior, including experimentation with a variety of mind-altering drugs. In Madison and elsewhere the boomers' counter culture movement gave rise to a drive for student power dedicated to abolishing the traditional University *in loco parentis* policies governing extracurricular student conduct and activities. The student power movement enjoyed considerable success in changing the University's policies governing student life, but much less in academic matters. Under student pressures a few UW faculty members experimented with relaxed grading standards and participatory democracy in the classroom, but the faculty as a body firmly rejected any mandatory sharing of its responsibility for the curriculum and instruction, and showed little interest in most of the trendy curricular experiments undertaken elsewhere. There was a widespread faculty determination, shared by many students, to maintain the quality and integrity of UW academic programs and degrees.

On the other hand, campus unrest and the student power movement produced a viable if untraditional student trade union, the Teaching Assistants Association, which conducted the first strike of instructional staff in the University's history in the spring of 1970. It resulted in a negotiated contract with the first group of unionized graduate students in the country. Student power advocates also succeeded in ending the faculty's parent-like Committee on Student Life and Interests (SLIC), which had closely supervised most student extracurricular activities since 1914. A major thrust of the campaign against SLIC was to relax or even abolish University restrictions on the hours and living arrangements of undergraduate women. In this area University housing policies lagged well behind the growing popularity of the new birth control pill in the late 1950s and the resulting sexual revolution in the next decade. By the end of the period, SLIC was a thing of the past and student preference for unsupervised apartment living had obliged the University to convert two of the new Elm Drive dormitories to other uses. The same forces, augmented by the earlier University campaign against discriminatory membership requirements, put a considerable strain on the Langdon Street sororities and fraternities. By the end of the sixties several of the Greek chapters had lost their houses and gone out of existence.

Organizational Changes

In some respects the most profound University changes of the period 1945-71 were structural, with effects that are yet to be determined fully. This was the expansion from a single comprehensive campus in Madison with outlying activities, into a system of two- and four-year branch UW campuses spread strategically around the state. The change was launched in 1955 when state political leaders, with the reluctant approval of UW leaders, decided to improve public higher education in Milwaukee by merging the University's Milwaukee Extension Center and staff with the Wisconsin State College-Milwaukee, a primarily teacher training school, and placing the new institution under the direction of the UW Board of Regents. The resulting University of Wisconsin-Milwaukee (UWM) was soon encouraged to develop urban-related graduate programs and authorized to achieve major university status. Closely linked to the Madison campus initially, within a decade UWM was operating in a parallel and semi-autonomous fashion under the leadership of its own chancellor. This was a truly revolutionary change, because prior to this UW leaders had always opposed efforts to establish another state university in Milwaukee, fearing it might come to rival Madison's status as the Wisconsin's only comprehensive graduate and research institution.

Equally important was the University's decision in the 1950s to develop permanent freshman-sophomore branch campuses in a number of cities around the state. These two-year UW centers grew out of a temporary jerry-built system created initially by the University Extension Division to meet local needs during the Great Depression and subsequently expanded to handle the enrollment pressures of the early post-war years. By the early 1960s the growth and permanent character of the two-year centers seemed to justify combining them in a separate administrative structure. It also prepared the way for the creation of two "senior" UW centers near Green Bay and Kenosha, conceived initially as offering junior-senior undergraduate work in combination with the freshman-sophomore centers in their immediate areas. Even before UW-Green Bay and UW-Parkside opened in 1969, however, their missions had been enlarged to full baccalaureate degree-granting status and each enjoyed the same degree of institutional autonomy granted UW-Milwaukee. Thus, through a combination of institutional growth and restructuring aided by a good deal of local and legislative logrolling, in the quarter century after the Second World War the University of Wisconsin expanded from a single University in Madison to a sprawling multi-campus system spread across the state.

This University expansion seemed at the time to be a natural, even predictable, and highly commendable response to the enrollment pressures and funding opportunities of the post-war years. Actually, the decisions taken by UW leaders in the circumstances, especially those of President Fred Harvey Harrington in the 1960s, were neither entirely natural nor necessarily predictable as to substance and details. In fact, they represented a considerable departure from past UW experience and policy.

When Harrington took over the presidency in 1962, he offered a bold academic vision requiring aggressive action and a certain amount of imperial implementation. He was convinced the next few years offered unparalleled opportunities for UW development. Steadily increasing enrollments and sharply rising outside funding opportunities would enable the parent campus in Madison to become one of the handful of top U.S. research universities, even potentially world-class, he believed. In Milwaukee, as UWM developed graduate programs and research capabilities, it could become a demonstration model of how a specialized urban university might serve all parts of its metropolitan community. Harrington thought the larger UW enterprise would prosper in the long run only if it continued to be the innovative leader of Wisconsin higher education. To this end it must see that its outreach activities served the expanding urban population of the state as effectively as agricultural extension had traditionally helped farmers and rural families. The times called for major University expansion to meet the new challenges and take advantage of the new opportunities. And while the UW president was not one to look over his shoulder at what he considered negligible academic competition, his goals also had the effect of keeping pace with the concurrent growth of the rival Wisconsin State College system.

Harrington accomplished a truly impressive amount of his activist agenda during his eight year-presidency, in the process certainly rivaling and perhaps exceeding Van Hise's achievements in the early years of the century. Harrington's support for expanded academic programming and research in Madison paid off hugely. The Madison campus improved steadily after the war but its quality by 1970 was unquestionably higher because of his stimulus and support as vice president and president. If progress at UW-Milwaukee was slower than

Harrington would have liked, he nevertheless deserves major credit for pushing UWM toward genuine university status. He enlarged the earlier tradition of bringing the opportunity for UW credit instruction and degrees to other Wisconsin communities through the network of permanent UW centers and the two new baccalaureate campuses near Green Bay and Kenosha. His merger of the two UW extension services and WHA radio and television into a new agency to bring more breadth and efficiency to University outreach activities turned out to be more problematic. This was partly because of local digestive problems, but even more because of inadequate federal support for urban extension which the UW president had lobbied hard to set in place.

President Harrington's plans did not seem unrealistic in the early 1960s, given the favorable funding and political support he and others believed the University could count on to achieve his ambitious goals. Still, they went well beyond previous University aspirations. It seems quite unlikely that President Fred or President Elvehjem would have undertaken such a challenging program, at least in the same way or to the same degree. The expansion and structural changes put in place in the 1960s were very much the vision and legacy of Fred Harrington, the most creative and imperial of all UW presidents.

In positioning the University to take advantage of the growth possibilities of the 1960s, Harrington seems not to have given much if any consideration to a possible merger of all state-funded higher education institutions under the leadership of the UW president and Board of Regents. He was certainly aware that this idea had been recommended by the Ingraham Committee on University Functions and Policies in 1949. There were only two UW leaders with sufficient statewide stature to generate the political and public support needed for such a bold move in this period. One–the soft-spoken and courtly President E.B. Fred–instinctively thought small and tried to avoid controversy. The other–Fred Harrington–welcomed controversy and instinctively thought big, but evidently was not so ambitious as to want to try to put together a fully merged system. He preferred Clark Kerr's California model of two separate collegiate systems, one consisting of genuine universities and the other of primarily undergraduate colleges of lesser academic standards and stature. The problem with the California model was that it required California-style budgets, and it was highly questionable whether Wisconsin possessed the resources to develop and support two competing collegiate systems. If not, then some sort of coordination and control was essential. State leaders had reached this conclusion by 1955 when they created the Coordinating Committee for Higher Education (CCHE). Toward the end of his administration Harrington apparently decided that some sort of merger of Wisconsin higher education was inevitable. By that time, however, he and his associates had fatally weakened CCHE's coordination efforts and in the process had lost any capacity to put something in its place.

The great expansion of the University and its activities during the 1960s, while involving some decentralization, inevitably required a restructuring of the UW administration. To this end, Harrington created a new layer of administration to provide chief executives–six chancellors–for the major components of his new organization: one each for the two doctoral universities in Madison and Milwaukee, the two new four-year baccalaureate campuses at Green Bay and Kenosha, the University centers, and University Extension. On the UW president's organization chart the six units were structurally co-equal. This meant that although Madison staff and students might think of their campus as first among unequals, UW-Madison was no longer the parent and headquarters of University activities throughout the state. And in spite of its original status as Wisconsin's land grant university, it had lost its administrative ties and control over University Extension and the University centers. Madison might be described as the flagship campus, but there was no denying that under Harrington it had become part of a fleet, all of whose six ships-of-the-line were now symbolically co-equal and expected to take orders from a superior admiral. These administrative changes had the effect of upgrading the status and autonomy of five of the six major units, but they clearly downgraded the position, role, and influence of the Madison campus in Wisconsin higher education.

A perennial theme of Wisconsin governors and legislators after World War II was concern about the structural anomalies, the rising costs, and the duplication inherent in operating two increasingly parallel systems of public higher education. State politicians clearly would have welcomed University assistance and leadership in addressing these very real problems. With hindsight, one can argue that Fred Harrington's imperial strategy was in the end short-sighted and misguided. Instead of trying to checkmate the growing WSC/WSU system by employing the University's greater stature to build a rival multi-campus system, he might have strengthened rather than undermined CCHE's coordinating efforts. This might well have resulted in bolder CCHE decisions to emphasize the primarily undergraduate mission of the nine state colleges/universities, to restrict graduate programs to Madison and Milwaukee, and to limit the development of new campuses on the ground that Wisconsin already had in place a broadly based, multi-campus system of public higher education. This in fact is what Wisconsin political leaders had hoped and expected CCHE to deliver.

Or consider a more extreme option: At a time in the early 1960s when President Harrington's stature as a Wisconsin educational leader was unsurpassed, he might have pushed for some sort of UW-WSC merger under UW leadership. This probably would have required more willingness to accept and work with the WSC administrators and faculty as co-equal colleagues than either Harrington or most Madison faculty members were ready to undertake at the time. Still, Harrington might have pulled it off, for almost alone among UW administrators he had from the beginning worked to build up UWM from a state college to genuine university status.

Instead, balanced against his considerable achievements, we must assign to Harrington a considerable share of the blame for the failure of CCHE to bring about any meaningful coordination and direction of the state's two rival higher education systems. The turning point was the president's push for the creation of UW-Green Bay and UW-Parkside. Although these new universities were to have a primarily undergraduate baccalaureate mission, Harrington insisted they should be funded and staffed on the same basis as the doctoral campuses in Madison and Milwaukee, that is, more generously than the nearby competing WSU campuses. This differential understandably infuriated WSU staff members and supporters and was a constant reminder to them that UW people evidently thought the WSU competition was second rate. More than any other development of the 1960s, the two new universities highlighted the failure of CCHE coordination and paved the way for Governor Lucey's state-mandated merger in 1971.

Harrington had resigned the UW presidency by this time, and his chancellor system had so diffused the University's voice and weakened its political influence that the several UW units were divided and ill-prepared for the merger debate in the legislature. The result was a different sort of merger than might have been possible had UW leaders been more understanding of the concerns of a succession of Wisconsin governors and more supportive of their goals to control state spending on higher education. In short, what was needed throughout was a less parochial and more balanced UW view of state needs, along with wiser leadership to address them.

Without a doubt, Fred Harvey Harrington ranks as one of the great leaders of the University of Wisconsin, a giant who stands with Charles Van Hise for his accomplishments in reshaping the physical face and strengthening the academic and research programs of the Madison campus, while at the same time extending University services more widely to the people of Wisconsin. It is thus supremely ironic that Harrington's greatest but unintended presidential legacy was the legal demise of the University of Wisconsin he had presided over so confidently, and its replacement by an over-arching University of Wisconsin System that even such an unabashed academic imperialist as this UW president had always hesitated to propose.

Appendix

Campus Map
of the
University of Wisconsin
1971

1. Agriculture Bulletin
2. Agriculture Engineering
3. Agriculture Engineering Lab
4. Agricultural Hall
5. Agronomy Seed
6. Alumni House
7. Armory-Gym
8. Athletic Practice
9. Athletic Ticket Office
10. Audio-Visual Instruction, Bureau of
11. Babcock Hall
12. Bacteriology
13. Bank Building Offices
14. Bardeen Medical Lab
15. Barley and Malt Lab
16. Bascom Hall
17. Baseball Field
18. Beef Barn
19. Biochemistry
20. Biotron
21. Birge Hall
22. Bradley Hospital
23. Carillon Tower
24. Chemistry
25. Children's Hospital
26. Commerce
27. Communication Arts
28. Computer Sciences-Statistics
29. Crew House
30. Dairy Barn
31. Dairy Cattle Instruction and Research Center
32. Dairy Science
33. Downstairs Cafeteria
34. Education
35. Elvehjem Art Center
36. Engineering: Chemical, Civil, Electrical, and Engineering Mechanics
37. Engineering Research
38. Enzyme Institutes
39. Extension
40. Extension Services: Duplicating and Photography Lab
41. Field House
42. Fleet Car Office
43. Food Research Institute
44. Forest Products Lab
45. Fur Research Lab
46. Genetics
47. Genetics Research Lab
48. Greenhouses: Walnut Street
49. Greenhouses: Old
50. Gymnasium: New
51. Heating Plant: New
52. Heating Station: Old
53. Highway Lab, State

54. High Energy Lab
55. Hiram Smith
56. Historical Society, State
57. Home Economics
58. Home Management House
59. Horse Barn
60. Horticulture
61. Hospital Records Office
62. Housing Services
63. Humanities
64. Hygiene Lab, State
65. Hydraulic Lab
66. Information Booth, Union
67. King Hall
68. Lathrop Hall
69. Law
70. Limnology Lab
71. Meats/Animal Research Lab
72. Mechanical Engineering
73. Medical Library
74. Medical Sciences
75. Memorial Library
76. Memorial Union
77. Meteorology and Space Science
78. McArdle Lab for Cancer Research
79. Minerals and Metals Engineering
80. Molecular Biology-Biophysics
81. Moore Hall
82. Music Hall
83. Naval ROTC Armory
84. Nielson Tennis Stadium
85. North Hall
86. Nursing
87. Observatory
88. Observatory Hill Office
89. Parking: Hospital, Paid
90. Parking for Visitors: Lot 60
91. Parking for Visitors: City Ramp
92. Parking for Visitors, Paid
93. Peterson Office Building
94. Pharmacy-Physics
95. Poultry Research Lab
96. Preschool Lab
97. Primate Center
98. Primate Lab
99. Protection and Security
100. Psychology
101. Radio
102. Russell Labs
103. Science Hall
104. Service
105. Service Memorial Institutes
106. Short Course Dorms
107. Social Science
108. Soils
109. Solar Energy Research Lab
110. South Hall
111. Stadium
112. Steenbock Memorial Library
113. Sterling Hall
114. Stock Pavilion: Meat and Animal Science
115. Stores
116. Studio: Artist in Residence
117. Swine Barn
118. T-16: Army ROTC
119. T-22: Food Services
120. T-23: Nuclear Engineering
121. T-24: Engineering Graphics
122. T-27: Motor Vehicles Lab
123. Toilet Facilities
124. Towers Office
125. Undergraduate Library
126. University Club
127. University Health Service
128. University Hospitals
129. University Press
130. University Press Warehouse
131. Van Hise
132. Van Vleck

133. Veterinary Science
134. Wisconsin Alumni Research
     Foundation (WARF)
135. Wisconsin Center
136. Wisconsin Union South
137. YMCA: University Branch
138. Zoology Research
139. 215 North Brooks
140. 228 North Charter St.
141. 307 North Charter St.
142. 420 North Charter St.
143. 425 Henry Mall
144. 936 West Johnson St.
145. 938-940 West Johnson St.
146. 1120 West Johnson St.
147. 427 Lorch St.
148. 720 State St.
149. 811 State St.
150. 917 University Ave.
151. 929 University Ave.
152. 935 University Ave.
153. 1815 University Ave.

RESIDENCE HALLS
154. Adams
155. Barnard
156. Chadbourne
157. Cole
158. David Schreiner
159. Carson Gulley Commons
160. Elizabeth Waters
161. Elm Drive A, B, C and
     Commons
162. Gordon Commons
163. Holt Commons
164. Kronshage
165. Ogg
166. Rust
167. Sellery
168. Slichter
169. Sullivan
170. Susan Davis
171. Tripp

172. Witte
173. Zoe Bayliss

Bibliographical Note

Source materials for the period covered by this volume are abundant and easily available in Madison. The great bulk of the documentation is to be found in the University Archives and Records Management Services, referred to throughout this volume simply as *UA,* headquartered in the UW-Madison Memorial Library with a major outpost at the Steenbock Library. The UA collections include: official institutional papers and publications; correspondence of leading campus officials; related periodicals such as the *Daily Cardinal, Wisconsin Alumni Magazine/Wisconsin Alumnus,* and the *Badger Herald*; and substantial oral history and iconographic collections. The State Historical Society of Wisconsin, located across the Library Mall from the Memorial Library, contains records of official state legislation and budgets, papers of numerous Wisconsin citizens and political leaders, microfilm copies of most newspapers of the state, American and local civil rights movement materials, the papers of the Coordinating Committee for Higher Education, and Board of Regents' materials from the Wisconsin State Colleges/Wisconsin State University system, all of which entered significantly into the story told in this volume. Secondary source materials pertaining to the University of Wisconsin during our period are only beginning to appear. Among the most notable are: Tom Bates, *Rads: The 1970 Bombing of the Army Math Research Center at the University of Wisconsin and Its Aftermath* (New York: Harper Collins, 1992); Paul Buhle, ed., *History and the New Left: Madison, Wisconsin, 1950-1970* (Philadelphia: Temple University Press, 1990); Jim Feldman, *The Buildings of the University of Wisconsin* (Madison: Jim Feldman, 1997); and Arthur Hove, *The University of Wisconsin: A Pictorial History* (Madison: University of Wisconsin Press, 1991). These and other published materials consulted or cited in this volume are available from the UW-Madison General Library System or the Library of the State Historical Society of Wisconsin. The University History Project has also developed a specialized collection of published and unpublished materials used for this volume and cited herein as UHP.

Index

The 50-Year Story of the Wisconsin Idea in Education, 306

Academic freedom, 385; not to extend to administrative matters, 158; and Cold War, 90-98, 133-35, 304, 400-411, 431; and "sifting and winnowing" plaque on Bascom Hall, 93, 111, 159, 404n, 407, 407-8; and student protests, 214-15; support for, 4, 91-94, 111, 304; threat to, 133. *See also* Loyalty oaths

Adamany, David, 555

Adams, Charles Kendall, 2, 411

Adams Hall, 3, 16, 17, 414

Administration: reorganization under E. B. Fred, 57-66; style of Elvehjem, 117-18, 120, 123-27; style of E. B. Fred, 66-69. *See also* Central administration

Administration Building, Old, 374

Admissions: limits placed on non-residents, 18-19, 450, 455n, 465, 465n, 485, 494, 494n-95n; limits placed on non-resident, non-veterans, 18, 18-19, 25, 450, 455n, 465, 465n, 485, 494, 494n-95n; increasing high-school graduates applying for, 18; and Jewish students, 4, 18; openness of, 4; raising standards for, 129n; restrictions on non-resident women, 25; and WW II veterans, 13, 15, 17-18. *See also* Enrollment

Adolfson, Lorentz H., on University Extension committee for Adult Education and Public Service, 97n; as dean of University Extension, 138, 301, 303-6, 312; as candidate for dean of merged UED and CES, 322; on importance of education TV, 307; illustrations of, 212, 351; and Medical School Bowers Affair, 158n; nominated to succeed E. B. Fred as president, 303; suspicious of merger of UED and CES, 317, 317n, 318, 318n

Adult education, 96, 313-14, 318, 320, 325, 536; and UW extension, 209-10; expanded need for, 316; federal support for, 327; offered in Milwaukee, 3; via radio and television, 314n. *See also* Correspondence courses

Advisory Committee on Future Campus Development, 60

Affirmative action programs, 323

African-Americans, 325; and civil rights issues on Madison campus, 215, 384, 432, 434, 448, 450-51, 602; opposition to discrimination of, 52, 385-86, 387, 388-89, 432, 433, 450; education programs for, 323n, 346n; demands for increased enrollment of, 467-67, 474n, 478; UWM to address civil rights issues, 198-99; given preference in University Houses, 78n. *See also* Black student movement

African Languages and Literature, Department of, 229, 233, 281

African Studies Program, 281

Afro-American Studies, Department of, 229, 289; creation of, 483-84, 483n; demand for, 288-89, 383, 479, 482-83. *See also* Black student movement

Agard, Walter R., 282, 282n, 389, 393, 393n, 394

Agency for International Development. *See* U.S. Agency for International

Development (AID)
Agricultural and Life Sciences, College of (CALS), 230, 286. *See also* Agriculture, College of
Agricultural Hall, 234
Agricultural Records Cooperative, 301
Agriculture, College of, 65, 68, 68n, 274; and agricultural extension agencies, 96, 606; construction needs of, 135; creation of, 2; forestry program, 551; growth of, 228; influence on E. B. Fred administration, 59, 65, 106, 120; Hill Farms, 61, 135; and Land Tenure Center, 271, 280, 487, 488; opposes merger of CES and UED, 333-35, 336-37; organizational changes in, 230; renamed, 230. *See also* Cooperative Extension Service (CES); University Extension Division (UED); University Extension (merged CES and UED)
Agriculture Library, 238
Agronomy, 296
Ahearn, A. F., 97n
Ahlgren, Henry L.: on Adult Education and Public Service Committee of University Extension, 97n; as candidate for dean of College of Agriculture, 68; on Administrative Committee of University Extension, 330n, 334n, 335; biography of, 296n; as associate director of CES, 296-301, 303, 308, 312, 317, 318; on guest speakers' policy, 409n; and leave of absence, 371-72; memoirs of, 372n; passed over as director of University Extension, 317, 317n, 322, 325, 328n; undermined by McNeil, 325; as assistant chancellor of University Extension, 337, 338n, 339-40, 343, 350, 352; as vice chancellor of University Extension, 359, 362n; as chancellor of University Extension, 366-72; on University Committee, 80n
Airplanes: University-owned, 211
Alberty, Robert A., 182, 182n, 266, 266n, 267, 268

Alexander, Edward P., 70
Allhiser, Norman C., 343n
Alperovitz, Gar, 129
Alt, Agnes L., 406, 406n
Alumni: and search for successor for E. B. Fred, 110; importance of politically, 195; reaction against controversial guest speakers, 403; and merger, 564, 570, 572, 578, 584n, 592; oppose student protests, 214, 364-65; support from needed, 518; and UW Foundation, 249; and WARF, 239, 242. *See also* Wisconsin Alumni Association
Alumni House, 211
Alumni Records Office, 70
Ambrose, Stephen, 93n-94n
Ameche, Alan (the Horse), 376, 424
American Cancer Society, 240
American Council on Education (ACE), 14, 176
American Jewish Committee, 260
American Legion (David Schreiner Post), 52, 384, 411
American Veterans Committee (AVC), 52, 384
American Youth for Democracy (AYD), 400
Ammerman, Robert, 287n
Anderson, C. J., 66n
Andre, Floyd, 68, 68n
Anesthesiology, Department of, 231
Angevine, D. Murray, 97n, 141n
Anonymous Trust Fund, 191, 191n, 255n
Anthropology, Department of, 229, 233, 274, 281; at UWM, 550
Anti-Dow Coordinating Committee, 452
Anti-Semitism, 215; and admissions policy, 4, 18; in housing, 385, 387; in employment with University, 387
Architectural program, 550
Arlington-Leeds farm, 62, 135, 135n, 137, 253
Armstrong, Dwight, 490, 516, 517. *See also* Mathematics Research Center, bombing of
Armstrong, Karleton, 489-91, 493, 494n, 515, 516, 517, 519. *See also* Mathematics Research Center,

bombing of
Army Air Corps, 9, 33
Army Cooks and Bakers School, 8-9
Army Mathematics Research Center (AMRC). *See* Mathematics Research Center (MRC)
Army Specialized Training Program, 8
Art, Department of, 233
Art History, Department of, 233
Articulated Instructional Media (AIM), 280
Arts Foundation Act, 327
Arveson, Raymond G., 141, 373, 396n
Association of American Universities (AAU), 81, 176
Athletics, 602-3; and female cheerleaders, 424, 603; football, 447, 603; ice hockey, 602-3; Board considers women's varsity sports, 603. *See also* Ameche, Alan; Rose Ball; VanderKelen, Ron
Atmospheric and Oceanic Sciences, 274-79
Atomic Energy Commission (AEC), 272-73
Atom smasher vacuum tank, 262
Atwell, Robert H., 185, 187, 189, 189n, 466
Audio-visual enhancement, 279

Baby boom generation students: counter-culture of, 603-4; disillusionment of, 227, 432; expected enrollment of, 103, 110, 111, 136, 172, 187-88, 205, 432, 435, 530, 537, 540, 544
Backus, Myron P., 8
Bacteriology, Department of, 230, 233
Badger, 603
The Badger Bulletin, 46
Badger Herald, 492, 502, 603
Badger Ordnance Works (BOW), 38-39; bombing of, 490, 490n, 493, 516; building from moved to UW, 21; dances at, 46; description of Badger Village, 41-46, 85; housing secured at for married veterans, 38; illustrations of housing at, 42; North Badger housing, 39, 41-42, 46; nursery school at, 45; as satellite campus, 40, 40n; South Badger Village, 39, 43; trailers from moved to UW for student housing, 28-33; transportation to, 39-40, 41, 43-45
Badger Wives' Club, 46
Badura-Skoda, Paul, 251
Baier, Joseph G., 100n, 110, 158n, 197
Baldwin, Ira L., 80n, 97n, 100n, 141, 238, 242, 373; and academic freedom, 406; biography of, 60n; and Coordinating Committee for Higher Education, 139, 139-40, 196, 534-35, 535n, 538, 539, 539n, 543; directs executive committee of CPC, 60-61; and legislative investigation of UW, 95, 96, 97-98; and construction of Library, 234, 237n; and creation of UWM, 99, 100-102, 102, 534; as vice president of academic affairs, 63-64, 64, 68, 120, 523, 533; and WW II, 8
Baran, Gary L., 463
Barbash, Jack, 324
Bardell, Ross H., 100n
Barnard Hall, 21
Barr, A. S., 409n
Barracks: used as classrooms, 21; as men's housing, 36
Barschall, Henry, 517
Barstow, Bonnie, 418
Bascom, John, 2, 237
Bascom Hall, 21, 104, 187, 211, 213, 501; "sifting and winnowing" plaque on, 93, 111, 159, 404n, 407, 407-8. *See also* Lincoln, Abraham, statue of
Bascom Hill, 1, 212, 220, 221, 381, 455, 480, 514
Bascom Memorial Cemetery, 221
Bataglia, Francis, 476n
Baumann, Robert F., 27
Beach, Kathryn, 427n
Bear, Ralph, 434
Beck, Anatole, 218, 582
Beckwith, David, 579n, 584n
Bedrosian, Armina, 419
Beeman, William W., 442n
Bequests and gifts, 75. *See also* Anonymous Trust Fund; Brittingham Trust Funds; Knapp grants; University of Wisconsin Foundation; Vilas Trust

Funds
Berg, Robert, 566
Berge, John, 70, 75, 77
Berkowitz, Leonard, 287n
Berry, Abner, 91, 92, 405
Beuscher, Jacob H., 394
Billings, Ned, 100n
Biochemistry, Department of, 230, 233
Biochemistry Building, 247
Bio-Core, 283-84
Biology Building: renamed Birge Hall, 600
Biology Curriculum Committee, 283-84, 284n
Biotron, 136, 211, 247-48, 256, 264-66
Birch, Frank V., 107
Bird, R. Byron, 287n
Birge, Edward A., 74, 277
Birge Hall, 247, 600
Bivens, Gordon, 356n
Bjorklund, Robert, 329, 364
Black Peoples Alliance, 478
Black student movement, 478-86; strike, 485-86
Blaesser, Willard W., 13
Blockstein, William L., 352n, 367n
Blum, Lawrence, 352n
Boardman, Eugene, 232
Board of Regents (BOR): and academic freedom, 4, 304, 408; and *Badger Herald*, 603; and beginning of UW, 1; favors balanced research and scholarly effort, 124n; approves BOW as satellite campus, 40; and Bowers affair, 155-59, 160; interprets GI Bill broadly, 47-48; and state budget cycle, 83; and building construction after WW II, 16, 24; creates Campus Planning Committee, 59-60; and Centennial celebration of UW, 69-71; criticism of, 556; opposes discrimination, 390-91, 393, 396; disposes of University farm land, 62; fires Glenn Frank, 5; elects Harrington president, 164-65; and opposition to Harrington, 222, 366, 509; supports Harrington and Fleming on student protests, 458; hosting meetings of,

176; and Hill Farms housing development, 253-54; restricts admissions because of housing shortage, 25-26; joint committee with WSU on merger, 568, 569, 575, 578; approves L&S honors program, 130; supports internationalization of UW, 133; investigates Klotsche leave of absence from UWM, 202-3; and management of University, 564; supports merger of CES and UED, 316n, 337; opposes merger of UW and WSU, 570, 578-79, 588, 589, 597; opposes student protests, 218, 218n, 462, 463; and limits on non-resident students, 485, 494n-95n; Republicans control, 554; responds to Sputnik, 128; searches for successor to E. B. Fred, 109-13; orders suspension of three student protesters, 481; approves contract ending TAA strike, 505; and trailer housing for married veterans, 28-33; and creation of UWM, 100, 529; fears competition of a Milwaukee campus, 3, 98-99, 99n, 525, 605; and WARF support for social sciences and humanities, 244, 245-46, 246n; and WARF support for UWM, 245n; elects Weaver president, 556-57
Board of Visitors, 574n-75n, 592
Bock, Robert M., 182n
Bögholt, Carl M., 40
BOR. *See* Board of Regents
Borchers, Gladys, 100n
Botany, Department of, 233, 274
Bousel, Barbara, 375
BOW. *See* Badger Ordnance Works
Bowen, J. Ray, 462n, 566, 580
Bower, James B., 566, 574n
Bowers, John Z., 66, 68-69, 231
Bowers Affair, 140-61, 231
Boyle, Patrick, 330, 338, 338n, 340, 341, 342, 343-44, 344, 352, 352n, 356, 369, 370
Bozak, Irene M., 100n
Bradley, Harold C., 70n
Bradley, General Omar, 47
Brandt, Willard, 356n

Breuscher, Harvey, 577n
Brewere, Dick, 427n
Bridge over Park Street, 378, 461
Bridgman, Charles S., 328n, 343n
Brink, R. A., 70n, 80n, 97n
Brittingham, Thomas E., Jr., 373; and
    Brittingham Trust, 243, 251, 257;
    and UW Foundation, 76n; and
    WARF, 241, 242, 251
Brittingham, Thomas E., Sr., 251
Brittingham Family Trust, 190n, 192,
    243-44, 251, 257-58, 310
Brotslaw, Irving, 343n
Browne, Arthur D., 553, 571
Bruck, Richard H., 389
Bruns Garage and Volkswagen, 451
Bryan, George Smith, 418
Bryson, Reid A., 266n, 274, 275-78,
    275n, 278, 286, 290n
Bubolz, Gordon A., 91-95, 406
Buck, R. Creighton, 287
Buck Committee, 287-88, 477n
Bucklew, Neil, 496, 496n, 500
Buddhist studies, 132
Buildings: use of barracks, 21, 36; none
    at beginning of UW, 1; and budget
    cycle, 83; churches used as
    classrooms, 20, 20n, 22; post-war
    construction of, 16, 58, 59-60; con-
    structed during E. B. Fred
    administration, 106; destruction of
    obsolete buildings, 137; funding for,
    135-39, 598; constructed during
    Harrington administration, 210; on
    Milwaukee campus, 138; Quonset
    huts, 21, 23, 33, 52, 61; use of
    temporary buildings, 21-24, 135;
    WARF grants for construction of,
    136, 247. *See also* Housing, student;
    Residence halls; individually listed
    buildings
Bullis, Harry A., 75n, 76n
Bunn, Charles, 80n
Burcalow, Vic, 297
Bureau of Community Development,
    306
Bureau of Government, 306
Bureau of Information and Program
    Services, 306

Bureau of Lectures and Concerts, 306
Burgess, James E., 129n
Burke, L. C., 235
Burns, Lee, 41
Burris, Robert H., 265, 556
Burt, Leo F., 488, 507n, 515-16, 518. *See
    also* Mathematics Research Center,
    bombing of
Buses: from Badger Village, 39-40, 41,
    43-45; from Truax Field housing, 37;
    and wrong-way lane on University
    Avenue, 461, 461n
Business, School of, 230-31; no separate
    departments in, 231; and truncated
    semester caused by protests, 511. *See
    also* Commerce, School of

Cafeteria, 21, 24
Cafferty, Neil G., 63n, 88, 97n, 169,
    169n, 187, 189
Cambodia: students protest bombing of,
    508, 508-9, 511, 513
Cameron, Eugene N., 439n
Campbell, William J., 87, 92, 373, 391
Camp Randall Memorial Park, 28, 28n
Camp Randall Stadium, 377
Camp Randall Trailer Park: for married
    veterans, 28-33; co-op grocery store
    at, 30
Campus Digest, 500, 500-501
Campus Planning Commission (CPC),
    59-61, 106
Campus Report, 500
Campus Student Housing Committee, 443
Capital Times, 93, 111, 114, 134, 148,
    155, 157, 218n, 261; on merger, 580,
    588, 590, 591
Carnegie Corporation, 119, 255, 259-60,
    281, 313, 318
Carstensen, Vernon, 70, 71n
Catlin, Mark, 531-32, 532n
CCHE. *See* Coordinating Committee for
    Higher Education
Cech, Sue, 418
Centennial celebration of UW, 69-77, 106
Centennial Committee, 69-70, 70n, 73
Centennial Fund, 70-71, 249
Center, Charles C., 409n
Center for Action on Poverty, 330, 340,

346, 347, 363
Center for Climatic Research, 277
Center for Luso-Brazilian Studies, 132
Central Administration: under Elvehjem, 119-23; under E. B. Fred, 58-61, 63-68, 88-90; under Harrington, 179-81, 608; UED under McNeil, 329-30, 337-38; under Weaver, 560, 564-65. *See also* Administration
Central Intelligence Agency (CIA): and campus job interviews, 461
CES Cooperative Extension Service
Chadbourne, Paul A., 1
Chadbourne Residence Hall, 136, 137
Chamberlin, Thomas C., 2
Chamber of Commerce, Wisconsin: opposes construction of library, 236
Charmany-Rieder Farm, 177, 178
Cheerleaders, female, 424
Chemical Engineering, Department of, 233
Chemical Engineering Building, 247
Chemistry, Department of, 233, 274; at UWM, 550
Chemistry Research Building, 211, 247
Churches: used as classrooms by UW, 20, 20n, 22; and sanctuary for Ken Vogel, 452n
"C.I.A., Why?-Speak Out Teach-In," 452
Civil Engineering, Department of, 233
Clarenbach, Kathryn F., 319n
Clark, Robert C., 297n, 319n, 325
Clark, William W., 95n, 96n, 531
Classes: increased in number of and size of, 20. *See also* Curriculum
Cleary, James W., 185, 187
Cleary, Michael J., 76n
Clifton, Chester V. (Ted), 71-72
Clifton, Kelly H., 284
Clinical Sciences Center, 231
Clodius, Robert L., 122, 337, 564; and Bio-Core, 284; illustration of, 173; and merger of CES and UED, 317n, 319, 320n, 322, 325, 326; and NASA, 266, 266n, 267; and policy on federal overhead funds, 362; as acting president, 556; as acting provost, 183; as vice president,

163-64, 168-69, 170, 179, 179n, 179-80, 182, 186, 189, 190, 191, 200, 201-2, 219n, 368n, 550, 599; supports UWM use of Vilas funds, 252
Code, Arthur, 266n, 267, 268
Cohen, Philip P., 141n, 151n, 156n, 157, 160-61
Cohen, Robert, 463, 465, 465n
Cole, John W., 147, 148-49, 153
College Qualification Test, 454
Collins, Jim, 308n
Colston, Marshall H., 346, 346n
"Combination University," 2, 3-5, 58; transformation of, 5
Commerce/Business, School of, 21, 65, 66, 106; creates honors program, 131, 284-85; growth of, 228, 230-31; renamed Business School, 230-31
Commerce Building, 217
Commission on Education, 522-23, 524
Committee on Federal and Industrial Grants Contracts, 598, 598n-99n
Commission on Public Higher Education in the Lake Shore Area, 526
Committee Against Army Recruitment, 452
Committee Against Discrimination (CAD), 386, 387
Committee for a Lake Shore College, 526
Committee for Direct Action, 452
Committee for Student Rights, 452
Committee of Thirty, 100-101, 496n, 506n
Committee of Twenty-Five, 545-46, 546
Committee on Enrollment Policy, 24n
Committee on Environmental Studies, 278
Committee on General Education for Adults (UED), 318
Committee on Human Rights, 392, 393-94, 395, 397, 398, 412, 433, 445
Committee on Human Relations, 389
Committee on Integration of Higher Education in Wisconsin, 528, 528-29, 529, 530
Committee on Loans and Undergraduate Scholarships, 397-98
Committee on Non-Curricular Life of Students, 435, 436

Committee on Quality of Instruction and Scholarship, 80

Committee on Space Sciences, 266, 266n, 267

Committee on Student Conduct, 401

Committee on Student Life and Interests (SLIC), 4, 93, 386, 387-88, 389, 400, 404-5, 407-8, 408n, 410, 412, 419, 424-31, 433, 437, 439, 440, 443, 444, 444n, 604

Committee on Student Organizations, 444

Committee on Studies and Instruction in Race Relations. *See* Thiede Committee

Committee on the Educational Program at the Badger Ordnance Works, 40n

Committee on the Reorganization of Adult Education and Extension Activities, 318

Committee on the Roles of Students in the Government of the University, 442-46

Committee on Undergraduate Education, 288

Committee on the University and the Draft, 452, 455

Committee on University Functions and Policies, 79-82, 102, 175, 523-24, 528, 574-75, 596, 607

Committee system, 63, 63n. *See also* Faculty governance

Committee to Defend Individual Rights, 452

Committee to End the War in Vietnam (CEWV), 452, 458

Committee to Liberate the Southeast Area Dorms, 452

Commons, John R., 285

Communication Arts, Department of, 229

Communicative Disorders, Department of, 229, 233

Communist threat: opposition to anti-Communist restrictions, 90-98, 133-35, 304, 400-411. *See also* McCarthy, Joseph R.; McCarthyism

Community: UW as, 225-26

Community Center Project (UWM), 357

Comparative Literature, Department of, 233

Comparative Tropical History, 259-60, 260n

Computer Science Building, 211

Computer Sciences, 229, 233, 269, 515

Conant, James B., 12, 264

Conference of midwestern colleges and universities (1944), 15-16

Connections, 481n

Connors, Edward J., 153, 155

Continuing education. *See* Adult education

Cook, Thomas, 354

Cooperative Extension Service (CES), 209-10, 295, 296-301; and county-based extension agents, 297, 298, 302; and department-based specialists, 297; and job titles in, 298, 298n; and merger with University Extension Division, 209-20, 257, 258-59, 295, 311n, 314-28, 328-40, 341-44, 540

Cooperative grocery store, 30, 32

Coordinating Committee for Higher Education (CCHE), 99, 100, 103, 139, 170, 193n, 195-97, 205, 208, 465n, 485, 533-37, 595, 595n, 608-9; competition within, 537-44; cannot control UW-Madison on curriculum matters, 551-52; cannot control development of UWM, 551; continuation of wanted, 564; creation of, 533, 533n, 607-8; death of, 553, 577n, 609; funding for, 545; ineffectiveness of, 575, 583, 596, 608; decides against statewide junior college system, 540-41; Kellett Commission calls for abolition of, 554; renamed, 553; restructuring of, 544-49

Correspondence courses, 295, 303, 303-4, 304n, 353. *See also* Adult education

Cosgrove, Howard, 588-89

Council of Graduate Schools, 176

Council of Ten, 496n, 504, 506n

Counseling and Guidance, Department of, 229

Counseling services: for veterans, 13

CPC. *See* Campus Planning Commission

Crane, Wilder W., 566

Cronon, E. David, 191n-92n, 290, 290n, 292n, 462n; as chair of History Department, 473, 473n, 475

Crow, James F., 149n, 156n, 160n, 442-46

Crow Committee, 442-46, 466, 467

Crowell, G. Kenneth, 547n

Curreri, 'Anthony R., 80n; and Bowers affair, 141n, 145, 147, 148, 149, 152, 153, 155, 156, 160, 231n

Curriculum: broadened by outside funding, 238-39, 250-51, 281, 598, 599; CCHE cannot control UW-Madison on matters of, 551-52; enrichment of, 229; reform of, 281-86, 471; students want to set requirements, 289, 471, 479, 604

Curriculum and Instruction, Department of, 229

Curriculum Review Committee, 289-94, 290n

Curti, Merle, 70, 71n, 80n, 249, 256; pessimism of at end of Fred administration, 107-8

Curtin, Philip D., 232, 259-60, 260n

Cutlip, Scott, 67-68, 72

Daily Cardinal, 38, 95, 112, 120n, 128, 129n, 130, 184, 203, 422, 427, 429, 441, 603; and academic freedom, 400, 402, 404, 404n; support black students' demands, 479; and budget cuts for University, 485; and campus police, 416, 417; and discrimination in housing, 385, 392, 394, 395, 396, 399, 412, 432, 441; and anti-draft sit-in, 455; and female cheerleaders, 424; on Harrington's resignation, 509-10; praises Harrington's vision, 172; leadership of, 505; and loyalty oaths, 134, 134-35; and panty raid and water fights, 412, 414, 415; increasingly radical, 486, 487, 488, 491-92, 492n, 507, 508, 519; and search for successor for E. B. Fred, 111; opposes University social restrictions, 430; and Chancellor

Sewell, 461, 468-69; and William Sewell's resignation, 218, 218n; critical of SLIC, 426; and student power, 413; and student protests, 216, 451, 460, 481; and student suspensions, 481n-82n; supports TAA strike, 499-500, 499n-500n, 505; endorses terrorism, 491-92; criticizes Thiede Committee report, 483; and undergraduate women's housing, 425; veterans dominate, 53-54; and Vietnam, 452n, 453

Dairy Building, 16

Dairy Science, Department of, 230

Dane County: Coliseum, 603. *See also* Police, sheriff's deputies

Daniel, Mary Lou, 129n

Daniels, W. W., 275

Daniels Chemistry Building, 211, 247

David, Martin H., 286

Davidson, Carl, 288

Davis, Lloyd H., 350n

Davis, Rennie, 487

Davis, Susan Burdick, 35, 38

Davis House, Susan Burdick, 137

Dawe, Helen, 80n

Day, Richard H., 286

Day of Concern, 509

DeBardeleben, Arthur, 327; opposes reorganization of CCHE, 546-49; weakens CCHE, 196, 538, 543; and Dow protests, 218n; helps obtain additional state funds, 124n; supports Harrington, 179; illustration of, 548; opposes merger, 591-92; and WARF support for social sciences and humanities, 244, 245-46, 246n

Declaration of Student Rights, 439

Deloret, Richard, 296

Democratic National Convention (Chicago, 1968), 486

Departments: election of chairmen of, 150-51; creation of, 229-33; and inter-departmental studies programs, 281, 601; and control over fields at UW centers, 540; student associations in, 472-77. *See also* Faculty

Devitt, James C., 576, 578, 585

DeZonia, Robert, 544

Dick, Robert N.: and UED, 317n, 319-20, 343; on UED Administrative Committee, 330; heads UED Community Programs, 338, 349, 349n, 352, 353n; and UWM Extension, 356n

Dillinger, Joseph, 517

Discrimination on campus. *See* African-Americans; Anti-Semitism; Fraternities and sororities; Jews

Divisional Student-Faculty Conference Committees, 444

Division of Community Programs, 349-54, 353n

Division of Educational Communications, 344-45. *See also* WHA Radio; WHA-TV

Doane, Gilbert H., 237n

Dohse, Genevieve, 418, 420

Dolbeare, Kenneth M., 442n

Dow Chemical Company: anti-war protests, 216-17, 364, 442, 459, 462-65, 465n, 470, 518; recruiters return to campus from, 468

Downer Seminary, 138

Doyle, James E., 157n, 481n-82n

Doyle, Ruth, 479n

Draft. *See* Selective Service Administration

Dresang, Dennis L., 290n

Dreyfus, Joyce, 47

Dreyfus, Lee Sherman, 46, 308, 344, 435n, 558, 593, 594

Dreyfus, Susan, 46-47

DuBois Club, 452

Duffie, John A., 266n

Dunwiddie, Jean E., 290n

Durrand, Loyal, 308n, 309

Dvorak, Raymond, 603

Dyke, William, 509

Dykstra, Clarence A., 301; and Centennial celebration of UW, 69-71; as president of UW, 5, 8-9, 59, 69; and planning for post-WW II, 9-10, 15, 25; resignation of, 55

Dylan, Bob, 432, 435, 446

Eagle Heights apartments, 136, 137, 177, 251, 373

Early, James S., 253n, 282n

Earth Day, 287

East Asian Languages and Literature, Department of, 229

East Asian Theater Program, 251

East Hill Farm, 61-62

East Hill trailer park, 33, 44, 61-62

Eaton, Donald, 502

Eckhardt, August G., 328n, 439n

Economic Opportunity Act, 330

Economic Redevelopment Act, 330

Economics, Department of, 280, 281, 285

Education, School of, 65, 66, 274, 280; growth of, 228; runs nursery school, 32, 45; reorganization of, 229; SDS associations in, 470-71; student association in, 472; and TAA strike, 501

Educational Administration, Department of, 229

Educational communications, 344-46. *See also* WHA Radio; WHA-TV

Educational Teleconference Network (ETN), 307, 344

Educational Policy Studies, Department of, 229

Educational Psychology, Department of, 229

Educational Science Building, 211

Eichman, Peter L., 166, 188-89

Eisenhower, Dwight D., 81, 448, 449

Eisler, Gerhard, 92-93, 400, 404, 406n

Ekern, Herman L., 75n, 76n

Electrical Engineering, Department of, 233

Eley, Lynn, 357n

Elizabeth Waters Hall, 3, 16

Elliott, Ben G., 409n

Elliott, Elizabeth A., 352n

Elm Drive dormitory complex, 136, 137, 604

Elvehjem, Conrad A., 80n, 97n, 100n, 110, 264; administration practices of, 117-18, 120, 123-27; biography of, 115-17; and Bowers affair, 140, 141, 143, 145, 148-61; central administration of, 119-23; death of, 161-62, 246; compared with E. B. Fred, 117-18, 538; as Graduate

School dean, 65, 84-85, 107, 113, 117; vows to support humanities, 124, 124n, 127, 244; illustrations of, 116, 125; favors support for natural sciences, 242; praise of, 164, 165; chosen as president, 112, 113, 114, 303n, 539n; as president of UW, 5, 113n, 117-18, 120, 123-30, 130n, 132, 310; and problems with retired E. B. Fred, 121, 121n

Elvehjem, Constance Waltz (Connie), 117-18, 142n, 162

Elvehjem, Robert, 162

Elvehjem Art Center (Elvehjem Museum of Art), 114, 191, 211, 212, 247, 249, 251, 380

Elwell, Fayette H., 66, 105

Ely, Richard T., 285

Endicott, Kenneth M., 263

Engineering, College of, 65, 106, 280; growth of, 228, 230

Engineering Experiment Station, 230

Engineering Graphics, Department of, 230

Engineering Library, 238

Engineering Mechanics, Department of, 230

Engineering Research Building, 211, 216, 234, 236, 247, 459

English, Department of: drops freshman courses, 290-92, 293, 475-76; growth of, 233; new program areas in, 233; student association in, 472, 476

Engman, Charles A., 180, 204n, 366

Enrollment, 606; and Army and Navy programs, 8-9; baby boom generation anticipated, 103, 110, 111, 136, 172, 187-88, 205, 432, 435, 530, 537, 540, 544; balanced range of students sought, 24, 24n; President Harrington opposes limits on, 178; huge increases by end of century, 171; increase in requires new library, 236; limits might be needed, 210; growing at Madison campus, 210, 227-28; maximized through center system, 540; demand for increase in minority and poor

students, 466-67, 474n, 475n, 478; increase in summer sessions, 17; post-war estimates of, 9-10, 12, 16, 16-17, 90; WSU surpasses UW-Madison, 195, 521-22, 544; growth of at UWM, 204; of veterans, 17-25, 51; remains high after veterans graduate, 58; World War II impact on, 7, 14, 17-25, 69

Entomology, Department of, 230, 233

Entomology-Plant-Science Building (the Harry L. Russell Laboratories), 211

Environmental Studies, Institute for, 286, 287

Enzyme Institute, 137, 247, 260, 274

Epstein, Leon D., 266n, 277, 484

Everest, Clark, 75n

Experimental College, 281

Extension Administrative Committee, 360

Extension Committee on Organization and Policy (ECOP), 298-300, 352n

Extension services: creation of, 3

Extension Services Building, 137

Eye, Glen G., 80n

Faculty: accused of betrayal by radical students, 456, 463, 481; attempts to bring regular and extension faculty together, 304; and AEC, 272; and correspondence courses for U.S. Armed Forces Institute, 94, 303-4; and selection of department chairmen, 150-51; lack of collegiality among, 225, 599-600, 601; disciplinary procedures against, 602; four divisions of, 225; response to handling of Dow protest, 462; elimination of junior positions, 86; in English Dept. denounce dropping freshman courses, 291; support choice of Elvehjem as president, 114; support Harrington and Fleming handling of student unrest, 457; expansion of international activities of, 132, 280; and external research funds, 227, 246, 250-51, 537, 598, 599; freeze on hiring in merged UED, 353; glut of, 256n; and grading experiments, 287, 476-77, 604;

growth in numbers of, 10, 24-25, 58, 211, 228-29, 537; need for housing in recruiting of, 78, 78n; improvement of, 78; lead radical students, 214; legislature alludes to non-Wisconsinites as, 465; delay in Library construction angers, 236; oppose loyalty oaths, 92, 133-35; loyalty to university diminishes, 226; Mathematics Research Center recruits, 270; meeting against draft, 455-56; meeting of over student protests, 216; demand for increase in number of minorities as, 478-79; on NSF panels, 264; meet with Gov. Lucey, 580-84; oppose research by UED staff, 361, 361n; recruitment of high quality, 599; suspicious of merger of UW and WSU, 566, 569-70, 597; oppose limits of non-resident students, 484; outside income of, 91; and personnel matters in merger of UED and CES, 321; recruitment of at UWM, 204; resolutions of on students protests, 511-12, 511n; retention of, 123; role of with private industry, 178; role of during WW II, 7-8; oppose Rose Ball participation, 86; salaries of, 52, 561, 582-83; senate created on Madison campus, 294, 294n; shared appointments across departments and colleges, 225; specialization of, 226, 229, 231-33, 250-51, 600; and student involvement in faculty appointments, promotions and salaries, 288-89, 444, 474n, 479; oppose student radicals, 224, 469-70, 481-82, 482n, 486, 515, 518; suspend classes during protests, 510, 511n; and TAA strike, 503-4, 505n; teaching as primary responsibility, 560, 565; teaching loads of, 537; tenure guaranteed after merger, 567; support for tenure, 574; and University control over student social relationships, 430-31; upgraded at WSU, 544; votes not to admit suspended students from Osh-

kosh, 482, 482n; at UW centers, 138-39; at UWM fear control by Central Administration, 203; oppose Vietnam war, 270-71; WHA Radio division of radio education supervised by committee of, 307; disparage WSU faculty, 609. *See also* Faculty governance

Faculty governance, 602; beginnings of, 3; and budget advisory committee, 85-86; committee system, 63, 63n; Elvehjem less willing to work with than Fred, 118; UED operates outside of, 322n; growth of, 4, 5, 62-63, 225; importance of, 82, 523; Mark Ingraham advocates, 65; maintained under merged system, 582; and policies with space program, 266n; and search and screen committee for top appointments, 184n, 328, 328n; structure of on Madison campus, 185n-86n, 187; structure of at UWM, 99, 186n; faculty oppose students sharing in, 288-89, 444, 472, 474n, 479, 482n, 483-84, 500, 503; support for, 574; faculty at UWM demand more, 203; Chancellor Young eschews in settling TAA strike, 506, 506n; weakened under Weaver, 565. *See also* Committee on University Functions and Policies; Faculty

Faia, Michael A., 477
Fain, Haskell, 462n
Falk, Philip H., 76n
Family Resources and Consumer Sciences, School of, 230
Farm Bureau Federation, 316, 336, 367
Farm Museum Committee (SHSW), 301
Fassnacht, Robert, 517, 519
Federal Public Housing Authority, 28, 31n-32, 34, 35, 37, 39, 40, 41, 44
Feinsinger, Nathan P., 501, 501n, 505
Feierman, Steven, 232
Fellman, David, 186
Female College, 1
Ferry, John D., 439n
Festge, Otto, 479
Fewster, Jean, 308n
Field, George R., 180, 182-83, 566, 598n

Field House, 173
Finch, Verner, 275
Fine, David, 516, 517, 518. *See also* Mathematics Research Center, bombing of
Fine Arts, Master of, program at UW, 536
Finley, Robert W., 343n
Fiorita, Alfred F., 100n
Firebombings, 507, 509; of faculty and E. B. Fred's homes, 509; of Krogers' Food Store, 493, 509, 510; of Old Red Gym, 490-91, 491; of ROTC's T-16 building, 489; of South Hall, 467, 467n. *See also* Badger Ordnance Works, bombing of; Mathematics Research Center, bombing of
First Congregational Church, 22, 452n
Fish, Ody: appointed to Board of Regents, 563; considers merger on Board of Regents, 563, 564, 569, 576, 576n-77n, 577, 578, 586, 589, 595
Fisher, Burton R., 427, 427n
Fitzpatrick, Lawrence J., 592
Fleming, Robben W., 179n, 182n; and Bio-Core, 284; as chancellor, 183-84, 185, 186, 187, 189, 189n, 223, 278n, 283, 438; and Industrial Relations Center, 285; leaves Madison, 216, 461; and student protests, 215, 215-16, 215n, 455, 455n, 457, 458, 458-59, 459-60, 460
Flinn, John H., 155n, 159
Fontanne, Lynn, 74
Folk Arts Club, 424-25
Food Research Institute, 230
Food Science, Department of, 230
Football, 447, 603. *See also* Amache, Alan; Camp Randall Stadium; Rose Ball; VanderKelen, Ron
Football stadium: used for student housing, 27
Ford Foundation, 119, 127-28, 133, 199, 255-59, 265, 280, 310-12, 325, 348n. *See also* Funding, from foundations
Foreign language: requirement, 293,

293n; studies, 132-33, 281
Forestry, Department of, 230
Forster, Francis M., 155n
Foss, Robert, 72-73
Foundations, private. *See* Carnegie Corporation; Ford Foundation; Funding, fund raising from foundations; Johnson Foundation; Kellogg Foundation; Kennedy Foundation; Rockefeller Foundation
Fowler, Murray, 110
Fowlkes, John Guy, 66, 66n, 70n, 80n, 97n
Fox, Phillip G., 15n
Francis, Roy, 355
Frank, Glenn, 4-5, 55, 57, 69
Fraternities and sororities: and discrimination, 385-86, 388, 394-95, 395-96, 398, 399, 412, 433, 441, 604; houses of converted for wartime use, 17, 25; slow to reopen houses after WW II, 17; effect of veterans on, 53; and visiting hours for women, 423, 427
Fred, Edwin B. (E. B.), 80n, 100n, 523, 531, 538; and academic freedom, 304, 400, 404, 406, 408-9, 410, 411; administrative reorganization under, 57-66; administrative style of, 66-69, 607; on administrative support committee, 5; and housing at Badger Ordnance Works (BOW), 38; visits BOW, 47; and BOW as satellite campus, 40; biography of, 55n-56n; and Bowers affair, 141-42, 142n, 143n; central administration of, 58-61, 63-68, 88-90; compared with Elvehjem, 117-18; and state budgets for the UW, 82-90; given authority to obtain surplus federal buildings, 21; and Campus Planning Commission, 59-61; and Centennial celebration of UW, 71-77, 78, 81; opposes discrimination, 385-86, 387, 393; end of term, 13-8; and enrollment increases after WW II, 18-19, 19, 19-20; attempts to bring regular and extension faculty together, 304; praises GI Bill, 48-49; home of

firebombed, 509; housing (non-trailer) for married veterans, 33-34, 34n; illustrations of, 81, 87, 104, 105, 235, 382; and construction of Memorial Library, 234-38; and National Science Foundation, 264; and nursery school, 32; and panty raids, 414; supports natural sciences over social studies, 107-8, 112, 174, 242, 244; and post-war planning, 13, 28; and creation of UW Foundation, 75-77; and University Houses, 78-79; and creation of UWM, 98-103; as UW president, 5, 58-108, 122n, 132; elected UW president, 55-57; post-presidency problems, 121, 121n; and restrictions on admissions of non-residents and non-veterans, 18, 18-19; retirement of, 109, 113-14, 114n, 114-15; and trailer housing for married veterans, 28n, 33; and support for urban studies, 258; and WW II, 8

Freedman, Francesca, 473n

Freeman, Maxwell, 100n

Friedrick, Jacob F., 164-65, 165

Friends of the University, 95

Froehlich, Harold K., 485, 557

Froker, Rudolph K., as dean of College of Agriculture, 65, 68, 110, 158n, 277n, 296, 297, 297n, 298, 317, 319n, 325; on search committee for successor for E. B. Fred, 110; on lack of academic freedom for administrators, 158n

Frykenberg, Robert E., 232

Fulbright grants, 281

Fullwood, Michael, 438, 439, 468

Funding: and autonomy of campus chancellors, 176; budget cuts, 5, 522, 523, 528, 562, 565, 570, 579-80, 585, 598; budget delays, 527; budget increases, 210; for buildings, 135-39; CCHE coordination of budget process, 140, 536-37, 552; Centennial celebration of UW, 70-71, 249; for CES, 303; and competition between UW and State College/University System, 194; and federal support for research, 127, 133-35, 144, 169, 172, 176, 183, 188, 198, 209, 210, 215, 227, 228, 238, 243, 246, 248, 250-51, 261-73, 280, 320-21, 326-27, 329, 537, 598-99, 606; and decrease in federal support for urban problems, 204-5, 210, 347-48, 347n, 353, 362-63; and federal support for land grant universities, 175-76; and federal support for buildings, 136, 210; under E. B. Fred, 82-90; from foundations, 119, 144, 172, 209-10, 210, 228, 238, 246, 248, 255-61, 280, 323, 537, 598, 599, 606; President Harrington aggressively seeks state and federal funds, 169-70, 172; legislature refusing separate support for honors program, 131; Madison and Milwaukee campuses considered separate for obtaining federal and foundation grants, 177; for merged system, 560, 566; and overhead on federal grants, 88, 188-89, 188n, 201, 250, 362, 601; salary savings, 190; trust funds, 190-93; tuition balances, 190; UED fails to get increase, 303, 607; for WHA Radio and WHA-TV, 345-46, 345n. *See also* Brittingham Trust Funds; Carnegie Corporation; Ford Foundation; Kellogg Foundation; State Emergency Board; University of Wisconsin Foundation; Wisconsin Alumni Research Foundation; Rockefeller Foundation; Vilas Trust Funds

Gabelman, Warren H., 283n, 334n

Gadjah Mada University (Indonesia), 256, 280

Gale, Joseph W., 152

Gallistel, Albert F., 60n, 63n, 97n

Gardner, John, 313

Garrison, Lloyd K., 8, 66

Gaumnitz, Erwin A., 66, 80n, 158n, 319n, 415

Gaus, John M., 301

GE Day, 492-93, 493n, 507

Gelatt, Charles D.: and Bowers affair,

156; and CCHE, 534, 544; and search for new UW president, 109-13; and appointment of Harrington as president, 165; criticizes Chancellor Sewell, 218n; on BOR search committee for chancellor of University Extension, 367n; on housing rules, 396n; on merger, 208, 531, 533, 533n, 563, 569; and creation of UWM, 531n, 532

General Electric Company. *See* GE Day

Genetics, Department of, 230

Genetics Building, 137

Genetics Laboratory, 247

Geography, Department of, 281

Gerlach, Arch C., 282n

Gerloff, Gerald, 287n

GI Bill of Rights, 10-13; Board of Regents advocates broad interpretation of, 47-48; criticism of, 12-13, 49; educational provisions of, 47-51; opens opportunities for education, 384; helps prepare college teachers, 24; lowers need for state public funds, 49

Giese, William C., 95n

Gifted students, 128, 129, 255. *See also* Honors program

Gifts and Bequests Council, 75

Gilkey, George R., 566

Gilligan, James, 360n

Goldberg, Harvey, 457, 473n

Goldberger, Arthur S., 286

Goldstein, Marty, 434

Good, Andrew H., 463n

Goodland, Walter S., 522, 523

Gordon Commons, 381, 502

Graber, Laurence F., 296

Grading system: changes in, 287-88, 471, 474n, 474n-75n, 476-77, 477n, 604

Graduate School: administers both Madison and Milwaukee, 101; cutbacks proposed for, 560; duties of dean of, 121-22; encourages faculty to seek outside funds, 246; and history requirement for graduation, 232, 232n; funding cutback for in

merger bill, 562, 570; grade requirements of, 287n; importance of to stature of UW, 123; at different UW campuses, 536; opposition to reduction in program of, 561; programs of after merger, 567, 572. *See also* Research Committee; Wisconsin Alumni Research Foundation

Graduate students: view faculty favorably, 471; and Ford Foundation grants to speed up completion of work of, 256, 256n; grade requirements for, 287n; growth in numbers of assistants, 24, 24n, 228; and Knapp scholarships, 253; no need for so many, 560; placed in teaching positions at UW centers, 540; survey of in 1968, 471-72, 472n; do not support TAA, 494; and Vilas fellowships for graduate students, 252; want more control over curriculum, 471

Grady, Daniel H., 87, 391-92

Gray, Carl, 51

Great Depression, 7, 83, 540, 605; and decline of UW's reputation, 69; fear of return of, 11-12, 522; and WARF, 3, 75

Green Bay Press-Gazette, 595

Greene, Howard T., 75n, 76n, 105

Greenquist, Kenneth L., 218n

Gregg, Allan, 142n

Gregg, Russell T., 422n

Gregg Committee, 422-23

Grogan, Paul J., 97n

Gronouski, John A., 52

Groves, Harold M., 31-32, 392, 393n

Guest speakers policy, 93, 93n, 403, 404, 406, 407-11

"A Guide to Extension Programs for the Future," 300

Gurda, George, 427n

Gym Unit 1 (the Natatorium), 137, 211

Gym Unit 2, 137

Gynecology and Obstetrics, Department of, 231

Haas, Leonard, 566

Haberman, Fred, 308

Haerberli, Willy, 262
Haferbecker, Gordon, 100n
Hagenah, William J., 76, 76n, 77, 105, 249
Hagenah Fountain, 77
Hagenah Plan, 76, 77
Hagensick, A. Clarke, 356n
Hager, Douglas F., 290n
Hagglund, George, 352n
Haight, George I., 75, 75n, 76, 76n, 242
Halbert, C. A., 97n
Haldeman, H. R., 372
Haley, Bill, 432
Halle, Lawrence E., 40-41, 46
Halleck, Seymour, 435n
Halvorson, Donald L., 25, 41, 63n
Hamalainen, Pekka K., 232
Hamann, Albert D., 417
Hamerow, Theodore S., 504
Hammer, Preston, 124
Hammersley, Joe, 415-16, 417, 420
Hammes, Robert E., 63n, 97n
Hanley, Wilbur M., 301, 305n
Hansen, Lee C., 350n
Hanson, Ralph, 478
Hardiman, Percy S., 367
Hargraves, Priscilla, 367n
Harley, William, 307
Harlow, Harry, 136, 263, 272n, 273
Harlow, Margaret, 263
Harootunian, Harry, 232
Harriman, John E., 129n
Harrington, Eugene, 590
Harrington, Fred Harvey, 97n, 121n, 528, 531, 595; administration of as president, 178-93, 608; as assistant to E. B. Fred, 65, 119-20, 198, 243, 250; and Bowers affair, 154, 160; as candidate to succeed E. B. Fred, 112, 113, 114, 119, 303n, 538, 539n; favors campuses at Green Bay and Parkside, 549; and diminished role of CCHE, 549, 552; and Center system, 540; recommends firing Robert Cohen, 463, 465; criticism of, 203, 481, 506, 509, 553; and federal funding, 243, 250-51, 261-73, 598-99; and foundation funding, 243, 255-61, 310-14;
descriptions of, 166-68, 607; and disciplinary authority of University, 481n-82n; and draft inequities, 456; faculty support for, 482n; favors development of UWM, 138, 165, 190-93, 197-205, 543, 550, 606-7, 609; returns to History Department, 232; illustrations of, 167, 173, 221, 324, 382; and internationalization of UW, 131-33, 280, 599; opposes Gov. Kohler's merger attempts, 538; and merger of CES and UED, 295-372 *passim*, 540; only one who could have prevented merger of UW and WSU, 595n-96n; and NASA, 266; calls for national guard on campus, 479; opposes limits on non-resident students, 485; accepts position as president of University of Hawaii, 163; named acting president of UW, 164; as president of UW, 5, 164, 246, 538, 607-10; opposes research park for Charmany-Rieder area, 178; opposes separate campus for merged University Extension, 361-632; opposition to, 222, 366, 553; refuses to crack down on student protests, 214-24, 455, 457-58, 460, 463, 466; resignation of, 222-24, 223n-24n, 257, 371, 509, 554, 609; and social sciences and humanities funding, 65, 119-20, 198, 243, 244, 246-47; supports new four-year campus, 205-9; supports urban studies, 257-59; as vice president for academic affairs, 120, 127, 127n, 190; publicly stays neutral on Vietnam War, 223, 460; vision of, 168-78, 606-10; disparages faculty of WSU, 609; and name change for Wisconsin State Colleges, 544, 544n
Harris, Bernard, 271n
Harris, Chester W., 97n
Hart, E. B., 115
Hart, Edmund J., 157n
Hartshorne, Richard, 282n, 407, 409-10, 409n, 412, 412n, 428
Haslach, Henry, 505
Hasler, Arthur D., 272n

Hassan, Ihab, 252
Haugen, Einar, 259
Havey, O. T., 87
Hay, William H., 442n
Health services: for returning veterans, 13
Heber, Richard, 274
Hebrew and Semitic Studies, Department of, 229, 260-61
Heffernan, Joseph, 584
Heidelberger, Charles, 240
Heil, Julius P., 5, 69
Heinzen, Raymond F., 575-76, 576
Helgeson, Assemblyman, 590
Hensen, Nelson, 50n
Herrick, Virgil, 97n
Higham, John, 52
High Energy Physics Laboratory, 137
Higher Education Act of 1965: Title 1 of, 315, 323, 327, 330, 331, 331n, 342, 348, 349, 353, 354
Hill, Donald, 100n
Hill, Herbert B., 133
Hill, Jim Dan, 544, 545
Hilldale, Inc., 254-55
Hilldale Shopping Center, 135n, 137, 253, 254-55, 255n
Hill Farms, 61; real estate development, 135, 135n, 136, 137, 177, 253, 253-54
Hirsch, Elroy (Crazylegs), 603
Hirschfelder, Joseph O., 266n
History, Department of: broadening of course offerings internationally, 131-32, 280, 281; enrollment in courses of increases, 20, 232n; faculty petition supports administration, 481; and grading changes, 287, 476-77; growth of and specialization in, 231-33, 600; and History Students Association (HSA), 472-75, 474n; and History Students for Reform (HSF), 474, 474n-75n; radical students activism in, 455n-56n, 472-75; requirement of courses in for graduation, 232, 232n, 403; rules for meetings, 474
History of Medicine, Department of, 231
History of Science, Department of, 229, 233
Ho Chi Minh, 448, 449
Hodge, Edwin R., 100n
Hodgkins, Walter J., 56n, 69-70, 75, 76n
Hollander, Walter G., 585, 586
Holloway, Claude, 85
Holst, Edward D., 100n
Holt, Charles C., 266n, 286
Holt, Frank O., 70n, 75, 76n
Holzhueter, John O. (Jack), 426-27, 429
Home Economic building, 16
Honors program: in Commerce/Business, 131, 284-85; in L&S, 127, 129, 130-31, 130n-31n, 284; in L&S at UWM, 131. *See also* Gifted students
Hooper, Nancy, 427n
Hoover, J. Edgar, 408n
Hopkins, Andrew, 71
Horlick, A. J., 75n, 76n
Horn, Lyle, 277
Horowitz, Vladimir, 74
Horswill, C. B., 63
Housing, student: barns used for, 27; barracks used for men, 36; discrimination in, 385-87, 388-89, 391-92, 433, 450; large dorm rooms divided into two, 26; need for married housing, 27-34, 52; post-war needs, 16, 18, 25-47; private homes opened to students, 26; veterans in housing office, 29; restrictions on undergraduate women, 386, 423-24. *See also* Residence halls; Trailer parks
Housing Bureau: and discrimination, 386, 395, 397
Howells, W. W., 282n
Huber, Robert, 591
Huitt, Ralph K., 176, 183, 317-22, 317n
Human Ecology, School of, 230
Humanities, Institute for Research in, 120, 261
Humanities Building, 211, 212, 380, 501
Humanities-Elvehjem Art Center Fence, 211, 214
Human Oncology, Department of, 231
Hurwitz (Hur), Kenneth, 46
Huskins, C. Leonard, 80n, 282n
Hutchins, H. Clifton, 427, 427n
Hutchins, Robert M., 12

Hutchins Committee, 427, 430
Hyde, Grant M., 67
Hydrobiology Laboratory (limnology), 137, 600

Iacocca, Lee, 173
Ihde, Aaron J., 282n
Independent Student Association, 419
Independent study, 292
Indian Home Management and Community Development Project, 346
Indian Studies Program, 132, 229, 233, 260, 281
Industrial Engineering, Department of, 230
Industrial Management Institute, 306
Industrial Relations Center, 285
Industrial Relations Research Institute, 285
Ingraham, Mark H., 80, 80n, 97n, 100n, 102, 121n, 175, 409n, 598n; on academic freedom, 409-10; and Bowers affair, 158, 158n; chairs Committee on University Functions and Policies, 523-24, 528, 574-75, 596, 607; on CPC, 60n; as dean of L&S, 56, 59, 59n, 64-65, 122; describes Elvehjem, 118; and construction of Library, 236, 237n; illustration of, 235; and meteorology studies, 275, 277; and search for successor to E. B. Fred, 110; and University Houses, 78n
Insheivitz, Louise, 375
Institute for Research in the Humanities, 120, 261
Institute of Environmental Studies (IES), 278
Institute of Human Relations, 357
Integrated Liberal Studies (ILS), 282
Inter-departmental studies programs, 281
Inter-Fraternity Council, 396, 399, 441, 455, 455n
Inter Higher Education Boards Committee, 528, 529
Internal Security Act of 1950, 407
Internationalization of UW, 131-33, 280, 599

Jackson, Joseph W., 28
James, Bernard J., 319n, 330, 367n, 368, 369
Jensen, Ellis, 105, 164
Jews: activism of, 450; admissions policy toward, 4, 18; discriminated against, 215, 385, 387; and Jewish ``houses,'' 398
Job Corps, 330n, 341, 347, 364
Johansen, Milo V., 343n
Johnson, Bob, 602-3
Johnson, Jay A., 364
Johnson, Lyndon B., 324, 449, 453, 456, 538; Great Society programs of, 315, 323, 330, 341, 346, 347
Johnson, William, 122
Johnson Foundation, 261
Joint Committee in Engineering Education, 536
Joint Council on Human Rights, 394, 396, 397
Joint Finance Committee (Wis. legislature), 194n, 570, 576, 585, 587
Joint Interim Committee, 95-98
Jones, John D., 114, 373, 396n, 531n
Journalism, School of, 67, 603
Journal of Extension, 299
Junior colleges, 536, 540-41, 542

Kaplan, Louis, 94n, 238
Kaplan, William (Billy), 473n, 475n, 488-89
Karpat, Kemal, 232
KasaKaitas, William, 367
Kasten, Lloyd, 132
Kauffman, Joseph F., 185, 216, 453, 455n-56n, 458, 469
Kauffman, Robert, 287n
Kearl, Bryant E., 286n, 322
Kelab, Inc., 254
Keliher, J. Jay, 85, 88
Kellett, William R., 554, 558, 592
Kellett Commission, 370, 554, 557, 558
Kellogg, John, 431
Kellogg Foundation, 299, 342n
Kelly, John B., 232
Kennedy, Edward, 458
Kennedy, John F., 266, 449, 538
Kennedy Foundation, Joseph P., 274

Kenosha, Wis. *See* University of Wisconsin-Parkside
Kent State University shootings, 223, 292n, 508, 511, 512, 513
Kerouac, Jack, 432
Kessler, Warren, 494
Kiekhofer, William H. (Wild Bill), 418n, 421; and Centennial celebration of UW, 70, 71, 73
Kiekhofer Wall, 21, 214
Kies, William S., 75, 75n, 76n, 78
Kimball, Spencer L., 368n
Kimbrough, Robert, 476n
King, Martin Luther, Jr., 433, 466-67, 479
Kingdon, Robert, 583
Kintz, Milford C., 95n
Kirchoff, Roger, 234n
Kirkpatrick, Donald L., 352n, 356n
Kissinger, C. Clark, 451
Kisslow, Mark, 427n
Kivlin, Vincent E., 15n, 26-27, 68
Klagos, Harland R. (Harley), 330, 330n, 338, 340, 340n, 361, 362
Kleczka, Leonard J., 63-64, 373, 396n, 526
Kleene, Stephen C., 289, 290n, 292n, 462n, 499
Klein, Arthur, 526
Kleinpell, Eugene, 139, 534-35, 535n
Klotsche, J. Martin, 183; illustration of, 212; and creation of UWM, 100, 100n; as provost (chancellor) of UWM, 103, 183n, 186, 190, 190n, 197-204, 338-39, 355, 356-57, 356n; and merger of UW and WSU, 561-62, 565, 572, 572n
Knaplund, Paul, 70, 70n, 232; and construction of Library, 236, 237n
Knapp, Kemper K., 190, 253
Knapp grants, 190, 253, 253n
Knight, W. D., 97n
Knops, Mark, 490n
Knowles, Robert P., 485
Knowles, Warren P., 554; chairs UW Policies Committee (Interim Committee), 95n, 97-98; elected governor, 180; sends national guard to campus, 222, 289, 509; opposes

anti-University legislation, 485; and restructuring CCHE, 544, 546, 547; and TAA as bargaining agent, 495; and University Extension, 330, 369, 370, 479, 481; on Wisconsin Legislative Council, 96n
Koehler, Glenn, 307
Koenig, Helga, 393
Kohler, Herbert V., 106, 107
Kohler, Walter J., Jr., 83, 84-90, 418, 533; and budget reduction for UW, 528; on CCHE, 547, 547n, 553; illustration of, 87, 376; favors merger, 99, 102, 139, 526, 527, 528, 529, 530, 532, 533, 534, 538
Konnak, Harold A., 159, 547n, 556
Koop, Roy, 568
Korach, Robert S., 37
Korean War, 227, 401, 453
Kotch, Alex, 503
Kraus, William, 547n, 551, 556
Kreisler, Fritz, 74
Kreuger, Clifford W. (Tiny), 593
Krill, Karl E., 180-81, 183, 355
Kroeber, Clifton, 232
Krogers' Food Store: firebombing of, 493, 509, 510
Kronshage Hall, 3, 16, 17
Kunz, Jeffrey R. M., 290n
Kutchera, Father Alvin, 105

Laboratory of Molecular Biology and Biophysics, 247
Labor Youth League (LYL), 91-92, 95, 402, 405, 411
La Follette, Philip F., 5, 157n
La Follette, Robert M., 2
La Follette, Robert M., Jr., 28, 33, 34
Laird, Helen, 418
Laird, Melvin, 263, 396n
Lake Mendota, 277
Lamb, Luke F., 345, 369
Lampman, Robert J., 290n, 442n
Landscape Architecture, Department of, 230
Land Tenure Center, 271, 280, 487, 488
Langer, Rudolph E., 86, 97n, 269
Language and Area Center for Latin American Studies, 132

Larson, Adlowe, 367n
Lash, John S., 324
Lathrop, John H., 1
Lathrop Hall, 3
Latin-American Area Studies, 281
Lattimore, Owen, 403
Law School, 65, 231; construction of
library wing for, 16; grade re-
quirements in, 287n; no separate
departments in, 231; growth of, 228;
and truncated semester caused by
protests, 511
Leckrone, Michael, 603
Legislation: Arts Foundation Act, 327;
Economic Opportunity Act, 330;
Economic Redevelopment Act, 330;
Higher Education Act of 1965 (Title
1), 315, 323, 327, 330, 331, 331n,
342, 348, 349, 353, 354; Internal
Security Act of 1950, 407; Public
Law 16, 10; Public Law 346 (GI Bill
of Rights), 10-11; Smith-Lever Act,
300; Technical Services Act, 327,
330. *See also* GI Bill of Rights;
National Defense Education Act
Legislative investigation of UW, 91-98,
481, 485
LeGrand, Roger W., 165n
LeMasters, E. E., 435n
Lemon, Wallace L., 181
Lenroot, Arthur A., Jr., 89
Lerner, Max, 402
Lettau, Heinz, 277
Letters and Science, College of:
dissatisfaction over research funds
allocated to, 65, 114-15, 119, 119n,
123-24, 127, 242-43, 244, 245;
curriculum committee, 293; and
curriculum and staff of UW centers,
138-39; departments created in, 229;
growth of, 228; honors program in,
127, 129, 130-31, 130n-31n; loses
oversight over Pharmacy and
Nursing, 230; soft money used for
faculty in, 250; and formation of
SDS associations, 470-71; and TAA
strike, 501; and truncated semester
caused by protests, 510-11
Levenick, Leo B., 49

Levine, Margo, 488n
Library: addition to, 238; auxiliary
libraries created, 234, 238; need for
construction of, 16, 135; construction
of, 87, 233-38; development of
research collections of, 119-20;
McCarthy criticizes, 93n-94n; mall,
88; opening of Memorial Library, 77,
106, 235; Quonset hut used for, 21;
site for, 61; at Truax Field, 35;
undergraduate, 211
Liddle, Clifford S., 393
Liebert, Roland, 463n
Lin, Yu-Sheng, 232
Lincoln, Abraham: statue of, 251, 375
Linguistics, Department of, 229
Link, Karl Paul, 115, 240, 241
Little, J. Kenneth, 15n, 26, 64, 80n, 97n,
100n, 409n
Liveright, Sandy, 313
Lord, John S., 112
Lorenz, Reuben H., 363n
Loyalty oaths, 92, 94-95, 133-35, 134n
Luberg, LeRoy, 183; as administrative
assistant to E. B. Fred, 59, 59n, 64; as
dean of students, 426-27, 430; and
legislative investigation of UW, 96;
and merger, 532n, 533, 579n, 590,
590n
Lucey, Patrick J., 372, 594; elected
governor, 557; illustration of, 594;
meets with UW faculty, 580-84; calls
for merger, 554-96, 609; signs merger
bill, 594, 595
Ludvigsen, Alfred R., 89
Luhman, George, 75n, 76n
Lunt, Alfred, 74

McCaffrey, Maurice E., 75
McCamy, J. L., 80n
McCardle Laboratory for Cancer Re-
search, 211, 240, 263, 274
McCarthy, Joseph R.: speaks on UW
campus, 93-94, 402, 404; visits UW's
library, 93n-94n; censured by U.S.
Senate, 98
McCarthyism, 92, 133, 232, 401, 403,
404, 431, 450, 580
McCarty, Donald J., 229

McCarty, Harold B., 97n, 307, 308, 317, 330n, 338, 345
McDougal, Charles, 319n
McElvain, S. M., 80n
McGilvery, Robert W., 144
McIntyre, William D., 533
MacKendrick, Paul L., 80n, 282n
McMurray, Howard, 400n
McNeil, Donald R., 181, 181n, 182, 204n, 322; and adult education, 313, 318, 325; as chancellor of merged CES and UED, 323-72 *passim*; illustrations of, 212, 324, 351; replacement for as chancellor of University Extension, 366-69; salary of, 327n
McNelly, John, 53
McPhee, Eugene R.: biography of, 194; as director of WSU System, 180, 194n, 195; and CCHE, 196, 549, 552; on merger, 566, 586, 593, 595; and name change of WSC, 193n; retirement of, 554; wants new four-year campus as part of WSU system, 206
Madison, City of: expansion of airport of, 211; and outlying university lands, 177, 253, 254; zoo, 273, 273n-74n. *See also* Hill Farms; Police, City of Madison
Madison Academic Computing Center (MACC), 279
Madison Club, 215
Madison Female Academy, 1
Madison Kaleidoscope, 490, 492, 515, 517-18
Madison Transportation Company, 37
Magnuson, John J., 290n
Major, Charlotte, 100n
Malcolm X, 433
Manhattan Project, 7-8, 272
Mansoor, Meneham, 260, 261
Mao Zedong, 449
"March against State Interference," 452
Marching band, 603
Marine Studies Center, 277
Marketti, James, 497n
Marquette University, 99
Married housing, 27-34, 52. *See also*

Eagle Heights apartments; Trailer parks
Marshall, Douglas G., 435n, 439n
Marshall, E. Robert, 361
Marshall, William P., 97n
Marsh Farm, 275
Marshfield Center, 541
Marty, James E., 463n
Marzani, Carl, 93, 400, 404, 406n
Masterson, Norton E., 96n
Mathematics, Department of, 233, 269
Mathematics Research Center (MRC), 224, 269-72; bombing of, 6, 24, 271, 514, 515-20, 555; seminar of disrupted, 488; student opposition to, 487, 487n, 488, 493, 502, 515
Matheson, Jean, 418, 418n, 422
Mathews, Lee, 100n
Mathews Chemistry Building, 137
Meat and Animal Science, Department of, 230
Mechanical Engineering Building, 16, 137
Medical School, 65, 66, 68-69, 106, 274; and the Bowers affair, 140-61; growth of, 228, 231
Medical Genetics, Department of, 231
Medical Microbiology, Department of, 231
Meggers, John F., 330n
Meiklejohn, Alexander, 281, 282
Meisner, Maurice J., 232
Meloche, Villiers W., 15n, 80n, 393, 394, 395
Memorial Library. *See* Library
Memorial Union, 600; cafeteria, 24; creation of, 3, 225; declining use of, 452n; and faculty meeting in, 456; food line outside of, 22; fund raising for, 249; and student night life, 412; overnight accommodations in, 106; non-discrimination in hiring, 387; Rathskeller, 418, 418n, 421, 452, 489; shows movie twice a week, 38; and TAA strike, 501; terrace, 378; Theater, 16, 20, 74, 93, 511; Tripp Commons, 17
Merger of Extension with Cooperative Extension Service, 209-20, 257,

258-59, 295, 311, 314-28, 328-40, 540

Merger of UW and Wisconsin State University System, 6, 80n, 99, 139, 175, 175n, 208, 597, 607-10; Board of Regents opposes, 570, 578-79, 588, 589, 597; and Committee on University Functions and Policies, 523-24, 574-75, 596; modifications and amendments of, 562-93

Mermin, Samuel, 462, 462n, 466-68

Mermin Committee, 462-63, 467-68

Merriman, Curtis, 16

Meserow, Joseph T., 509

Metallurgical and Mineral Engineering, Department of, 229

Meteorology, Department of, 229, 233, 267, 268, 274-79

Meteorology and Space Science Building, 211, 274, 279

Meyer, Karl E., 53-54

Meyer, Ovid O., 160n

Meyerson, Martin, 202

Middleton, William S., 66, 143, 147; retirement of, 140-41; and WW II, 8

Middleton Medical Library, 211

Mifflin-Bassett Streets, 485, 507

Miller, Edward, 287n

Miller, Eric R., 275

Miller, Lyle, 388, 393, 393n

Miller, Midge, 591

Milwaukee: adult education courses offered in, 3; beautification agent for, 350n; boosters want university campus in, 3; State Teachers College, 99, 197, 306, 525, 525-26, 526, 527, 532; and merger of State Teachers College (Milwaukee) and University Extension (Milwaukee), 530, 531. *See also* University Extension Center (Milwaukee); University of Wisconsin-Milwaukee

Milwaukee Downer Seminary, 138

Milwaukee Journal, 203, 329, 457, 590, 595

Minahan, Anne, 356n

Molecular Biology and Biophysics, Laboratory of, 247

Molinaro, George, 166, 206, 585

Monkmeyer, Peter L., 442n

Monroe Park trailer park, 31-33

Montross, Harold W., 330, 330n, 338, 340, 356n, 368, 369

Morrill Land Grant Act (1862): UW as land grant university, 11, 170-71, 171, 172, 175-76, 257, 311, 598, 608

Mortensen, Otto A., 155, 157

Mosse, George L. 442n, 457

Mother Jones Revolutionary League, 451, 487, 502, 507

MRC. *See* Mathematics Research Center

Muckenhirn, Robert J., 97n, 297n

Mucks, Arlie, 214, 214-15, 215n, 297n, 364; opposes merger, 578, 578n, 579n, 592

Muehlenkamp, Robert, 502, 504

Mueller, Gerald C., 283n

"Multiversity," 175, 187, 597

Mulvihill, E. Robert, 504

Murray Street Mall, 106

Music, School of, 179, 421

Music Hall, 216, 456n

Nafziger, Ralph O., 67, 110

Najem, Robert, 352n

Natatorium, 137, 211

National Aeronautics and Space Administration (NASA), 265, 266-68, 277, 279

National Agricultural Extension Center for Advanced Study, 298-99

National Association for the Advancement of Colored People (NAACP), 395

National Association of State Universities and Land Grant Colleges (NASULGC), 176, 298, 315, 348

National Defense Education Act (NDEA), 127, 132-33, 133-34, 177, 201-2, 281, 431, 599

National Farmers Union, 316

National Guard: on campus, 222, 227, 289, 292n, 479, 480, 481, 482n, 491, 509, 510, 602; non-segregated, 387

National Institutes of Health (NIH), 136, 265, 274, 601n

National Mobilization Committee to End the War in Vietnam, 487

National Regional Primate Center, 136, 211, 247, 273, 274. *See also* Primate Laboratory
National Science Foundation (NSF), 136, 244, 261-66, 270, 271, 277, 278-79, 279, 601n
National University Extension Training Center, 342
Natural Resources, School of, 230, 278n, 286
Navy Radio School, 8, 17
Navy programs, 8, 9n
Nellen, James W., 218n, 484, 563
Nelson, Gaylord, 95n; as governor, 124, 155n, 178, 244, 316, 538, 541, 545, 545n
Nelson, Vesper, 95n
Nestigen, Ivan, 52
Neurology, Department of, 231
Neurophysiology, Department of, 231
Newburger, Joy, 393, 393n
Newcomb, Eldon H., 283n, 290n
Newman, John F., 572
Newspapers, 510. *See Badger Herald; Capital Times; Daily Cardinal; Green Bay Press-Gazette; Milwaukee Journal; New York Times;* Public relations; *Wisconsin State Journal*
New Year's Gang, 492, 493, 494, 502, 507n, 516, 519
New York Metropolitan Museum of Art, 74
New York Philharmonic Orchestra, 74
New York Times, 198
Niedermeier, R. P., 334n
Nielson Tennis Stadium, 211
Nigeria, 256, 280
Nitty Gritty bar, 452
Nixon, Richard M., 506, 508, 519
Noland Zoology Building, 211, 600. *See also* Zoology, Department of; Zoology Research Building
Nollendorfs, Valters, 287n
Normal Department: creation of, 1
Normal schools, 521, 536
Norris, Robert, 100n
North Hall, 275, 277
Novotny, Donald, 435n

Nuclear Engineering, Department of, 230, 273
Numerical Analysis Laboratory, 124
Nursery school, 31, 32, 32n, 33, 45, 52, 65, 66
Nursing, School of, 230, 231, 388
Nusbaum, Joe E., 545, 545n, 556, 556n, 566, 567, 570, 571, 586
Nutritional Sciences, Department of, 230

Obey, David, 134n
O'Brien, James, 486
O'Brien, Judy, 427n
Octopus, 425
Office of Conferences, Institutes, and Short Courses (OCISC), 354
Office of Naval Research, 267, 277
Ogg Hall, 381
Ohlson, Sue, 287n
Ohst, Ken, 308n
Old Red Gym. *See* Red Gym
Olsen, Ann, 418
Olson, Frederick I.: on search committee for successor for E. B. Fred, 110; as candidate for chancellor of University Extension, 322; on Administrative Committee of University Extension, 330n, 332n, 333n; as chief administrator of University Extension in Milwaukee, 338-39, 356n
Olson, Jack B., 466, 555, 557
Oncology, Department of, 231
Ophthalmology, Department of, 231
Orcutt, Guy H., 285-86, 285n
Orth, O. Sidney, 160n
Our Group (dining club), 296
Overhead on federal grants, 88, 188-89, 188n, 201, 250, 362, 601
Owens, Lloyd, 336n-37n
Ozanne, Robert, 583

Palmer, Orville H., 339n
Panty raids, 374, 396, 412, 414-15, 417, 428, 447
Pappas, Peter, 96n
Parent, R. J., 267
Parentis, in loco, 4, 384, 415, 419, 422-31, 433, 435; ends, 437, 443, 604
Parkin, Robert C., 97n

Parkinson, George A., 100n
Patterson, Cecil, 324
Payne, Stanley, 489
Peace Corps, 132
Peckham, Ben M., 155n, 157n, 160, 160n
Pediatrics, Department of, 231
Pelisek, Frank, 563-64, 564, 573n, 578
Penniman, Clara, 442n
Percy, Donald E., 556; and budget hearings before Joint Finance Committee, 194n; and CCHE, 553, 553n, 595n; describes Harrington, 166; becomes assistant to Harrington, 181; illustration of, 382; opposes merger, 570, 576, 576n-77n, 587; concedes merger will pass, 585, 586; drafts "A Proposed 'Third Alternative' for Wisconsin Higher Education," 559, 559n, 564; and investigation of University Extension, 370; as Weaver's top assistant, 561, 564
Perrow, Charles, 287n
Peterson, A. W., 80n, 97n, 100n, 417, 598n; on administrative support committee, 5, 59; as director/vice president of business and finance, 62-64, 64, 122n, 127, 169, 169n; on Gifts and Bequests Council, 75; given authority to obtain surplus federal buildings, 21; secures housing at Badger Ordnance Works (BOW), 38; on CPC, 60n; and GI Bill, 49n, 50; and transportation to BOW, 39-40
Peterson, E. L., 299n
Peterson, Martha E., 183, 424, 425, 427n
Peterson, William H., 8
Peterson Administration Building, 169n, 187, 211; identification cards seized in, 489; and student sit-in, 215-16, 220, 453, 454-55, 455
Petrovich, Michael B., 232, 279
Pfankuchen, Llewellyn, 282n
Pharmacology, Department of, 231
Pharmacy, School of, 65-66, 230, 231, 274

Phelan, John L., 232
Philosophy, Department of, 233
Physical Sciences Laboratory, 189n
Physics, Department of, 233, 273
Pierce, Lowell, 352n
Pine Bluff Observatory, 247
Pipe of Peace Ceremony, 602
Placement Service (the Big Red Machine), 168n, 467-68, 467n-68n
Plant Pathology, Department of, 230
Platz, Frederick V., Jr., 87
Pochmann, Henry A., 15
Police: City of Madison, 414, 437, 447-48, 462, 479, 486, 507, 509, 516, 517; sheriff's deputies, 447-48, 479, 491; UW-Madison, 415-17, 437, 447-48, 457n, 462, 479, 486, 509, 510
Political Science, Department of, 233, 281, 472
Pooley, Robert C., 282, 282n
Post, Gaines, 282n
Potter, Howard I., 75n, 76n, 107
Potter, Van R., 160n, 266n
Poultry building, 27
Poultry Science, 230
Pound, Glenn S.: as dean of College of Agriculture, 230n, 283n, 286, 360; opposes merger of CES and UED, 317n, 333-34, 357; as candidate for chancellor of University Extension, 322; disagrees with Chancellor McNeil's policies, 360, 361n, 367-68
Poverty program, 330n-31n, 363. *See also* Center for Action on Poverty
Preparatory Department, 1
Preventive Medicine, Department of, 231
Price, James M., 152, 152n
Price controls, 52
Primate Laboratory, 247, 263, 272n, 273; bombing of, 491. *See also* National Regional Primate Center
Pro Arte Quartet, 251
Protection and Security, Department of, 415-17, 437, 441, 447-48, 457n, 462, 478, 479, 509, 510
Psychiatry, Department of, 231
Psychology, Department of, 273, 274, 472
Psychology Building, 137

Public Relations Committee (student-run), 226
Public relations, 69-76; over academic freedom, 403, 405; approve Harrington administration, 457; oppose Harrington's inaction, 457; and construction of Library, 238; McNeil tries to obtain support for autonomous Extension, 358-62; displeasure with quality of undergraduate education at UW, 580, 591; suffer over social activity of initiatives of UED, 363-64; and student protests, 214, 364-65, 370, 458, 485, 580, 591
Public Works Administration, 16
Pulver, Glen C., 338, 340, 346, 347, 356n, 368

Quonset huts, 21, 23, 33, 52, 61

Racine, Wis. *See* University of Wisconsin-Parkside
Radar: atop North Hall, 277
Radio. *See* WHA Radio
Ragotskie, Robert, 277, 278
Ramsberger, Albert G., 15n
Randall-Monroe Nursery School, 31, 32n, 33
Rankin, Glenn, 324
Ranney, Frank H., 547n
Ratchford, C. Bryce, 318
Ratcliff, Richard U., 100n, 254
Rathskeller, 418, 418n, 421, 452, 489
Raushenbush, Elizabeth Brandeis, 342n
Raushenbush, Walter B., 442n
Red Gym: firebombing of, 490-91, 491
Reeder, William G., 283n
Regan, Elizabeth, 367n
Rehabilitation Medicine, Department of, 231
Reinecke, Harold, 367n
Remington, Frank, 435n
Remington Committee, 435-37, 445
Renk, Walter, 369
Renk, Wilbur N., 107, 121n, 218n, 367n, 530, 532, 532n, 533n
Rennebohm, Oscar, 62, 76n, 88, 106, 396n, 522; and Hill Farms housing

development, 253, 254; illustrations of, 81, 105, 235; and construction of Memorial Library, 236, 237; recommends Lake Shore College, 526; recommends merger, 524-25, 531
Rennebohm, Robert B., 77, 249
Research Committee, 121, 124, 124n, 174, 192, 242, 246, 248
Research park: President Harrington opposes, 178
Residence halls: Chadbourne Residence Hall, 136, 137; construction of, 136; opposition to discrimination in, 387, 388, 433; Eagle Heights apartments, 136, 137, 177, 291, 373; Elizabeth Waters, 3, 16; Elm Drive dormitory complex, 136, 137, 604; Gordon Commons, 381; lack of public financial support for, 3; doubling up, 26; Ogg Hall, 381; post-war need for student housing, 16, 18, 25; Sellery Hall, 126, 211; Southeast Dormitory Area, 126, 136, 137, 211, 381, 502; Tripp-Adams-Kronshage dormitories, 3, 16, 17; Truax Base hospital converted into dorm, 34-38; Van Hise Commons, 3; visiting hours for opposite sex, 423, 426, 427, 430, 440, 441. *See also* Housing, students; Trailer parks
Retraining program, 342
Reynolds, John W., 154n, 158, 178n, 545
Reynolds, Robert L., 282n
Rhinelander Community College, 542n
Rice, Barbara, 356n
Rice, Ora R., 96n
Rice, William G., 389
Rice Lake Community College, 542
Richards, Hugh T., 262, 266n, 462n
Richards, John F., 232
Rieck, Robert, 343, 343n, 360, 360n
Rieder Farm, 177, 178
Riegel, Sieghardt M., 399
Rifkin, Wendy K., 463n
Ritchie, John, 66, 97n
Roark, Glen V., 75n, 76n, 80n
Roberson, William N., 358, 358n
Roberts, Cliff, 308n

Robertson, Ellis James, 308, 345, 367n
Rockefeller Foundation, 255, 259, 260, 261, 281. *See also* Funding, from foundations
Rodman, George B., 80n
Roessler, Robert L., 155n, 159
Rogan, Paul, 532, 534
Rohde, Gilbert, 316
Rohlich, Gerard, 110, 319n
Roosevelt, Eleanor, 12
Rose Bowl, 86, 376, 377, 411, 603
Rosenberg, Mark, 473n
Rosenbloom, Judy, 422-23
Rosser, J. Barkley, 269, 270
Rossi, Louis, 583
Rost, Joseph C., 532n, 556n, 590n
ROTC, 14, 52, 64, 384, 472; firebombing of T-16 building, 489; loyalty oaths for cadets, 94-95; protest against, 401, 415-16, 420, 450, 487, 488, 490, 493, 515
Rothwell, Angus, 547, 549, 553
Rowen, James: as *Cardinal* columnist, 271, 271n, 486, 487, 487n, 493, 507, 516; arrested for GE Day activities, 493n
Rowlands, Walter A., 97n
Ruedisili, Chester, 324
Rundell, Oliver s., 66
Runge, Carlisle, 196, 319n, 539, 539n
Rural Community Action Program, 341, 346
Rusch, Harold P., 263
Russell Laboratories, 211
Rust House, Henry, 137
Ryder, Norman B., 462n, 467n
Ryearson, Stanley, 356n

Sachjten, William, 502-3, 503n
Samoff, Joel, 463n
Sandin, Mrs. Howard V., 563, 564
Sarles, William B., 58-59, 59n
Scandinavian studies, 259
Schenk, Quentin, 317n, 356n
Schmelzer, H. M., 63n
Schmidt, Erwin R., 147, 148
Schmidt, John R., 334n
Schmidt, Karl F., 308n, 330, 343n
Schmitt, John, 498, 498n

Schoenemann, John A., 317n
Schoenfeld, Clarence (Clay), 73, 75, 98, 302, 329, 332n
Scholarships: demand for financial support for all students, 474n; and discrimination, 397-98; for minorities, 466. *See also* Graduate students
School for Workers, 306, 474n
Schreiber, Martin J., 594
Schreiner, David N., 27
Schueler, Donna, 461n
Schultz, Greg, 287n
Schultz, Lynn, 490, 493
Science, Literature and the Arts, Department of, 1
Scott, Charles, 476n
Sea Grant College, 278
Seeger, Pete, 432
Selective Service Administration, 216, 287, 506, 519; attempted bombing of Madison headquarters of, 491; and draft, 384, 452n, 453-54, 455n, 456, 458, 486, 506, 519
Sellery, George C., 5, 59, 64-65
Sellery Hall, 126, 211
Senn, Alfred E., 232
Senn, Harold A., 265
Sensenbrenner, Frank J., 75n, 76n, 94, 237n
Seraphim, Christ J., 411
Service Memorial Institutes, 247
Servicemen's Readjustment Act of 1944. *See* GI Bill of Rights
Settlage, P. H., 272n
Sewell, William H., 97n, 174, 439n; as chancellor, 217-18, 218n, 223, 461-62, 462, 463, 466; resignation of, 462, 468, 468n
Shabaz, John C., 494-95
Shain, Irving, 563
Shannon, Theodore J.: on Administrative Committee of University Extension, 330n; as candidate for chancellor of University Extension, 322, 368-69; and general extension programming in UED, 301; illustration of, 302; on Huitt Committee, 317n-18n; accepts two-year appointment with Ford Foundation, 337n

Shaw, J. Thomas, 290n
Shea, Donald, 198, 356n
Sheirbeck, Helen M., 346
Shorewood Hills, Wis., 78, 79
Siff, David, 476n
Simonis, Eileen, 424
Singer, 266n
Sipple, G. E., 411
Skidmore, Thomas E., 232
Skoog, Folke C., 264, 265, 283n
Skornicka, Joel C., 129n
Sledge, George W., 322
SLIC. *See* Committee on Student Life and Interests
Slichter, Allen, 584n
Slichter, Charles Sumner, professorship, 249, 285n
Slichter, Donald, 203, 584n
Slichter Hall, 25, 137
Smail, John R. W., 232
Smith, Henry Ladd, 67, 388, 393n
Smith, John, 266n
Smith, Leon, 60n
Smith, Nathan J., 155n
Smith, Newell J., 34, 34n, 38, 41
Smith, Peter H., 232
Smith, William Bradford, 452n
Smith-Lever Act, 300
Social action programs, 329
Social Science Building, 126, 137, 262, 502
Social Science Research Committee, 243
Social sciences and humanities: not supported as well as natural sciences under E. B. Fred, 107-8, 112, 114-15, 119, 119n, 123-24, 127, 242-43, 244, 245
Social Work, Department of, 229, 233, 274
Sociology, Department of, 233, 274, 281; opposes grading changes, 287; student association in, 472, 476, 477
Soglin, Paul, 461, 461n-62n
Soil Science, Department of, 230
Solie, Bruce L., 44
Sororities. *See* Fraternities and sororities
South Asian Area Studies, 281
Southeast Dormitory Area, 126, 136, 137, 211, 381, 502

South Hall: and Female College, 1; firebombing of, 467, 467n
Space Management Office, 501
Space Science and Engineering Building, 211
Space Science and Engineering Center, 267, 268, 277
Special Committee on Educational Problems for War Veterans, 15
Sprague, Monroe, 287n
Sputnik, 112, 127, 129n, 284, 431, 598
Stafford, Roger A., 557
State Board of Vocational and Adult Education (SBVAE), 542
State Emergency Board, 88; composition of, 83; funding from, 28, 31n, 34, 37, 43, 83
State Historical Society of Wisconsin (SHSW), 77, 234, 235, 301, 313, 379
"A Statement of Scope and Responsibility: The Cooperative Extension Service Today," 299-300, 350
State Street, 412, 429, 461, 488n, 493, 507, 510
State Teachers College System, 80, 525
Statewide Extension Education Network (SEEN), 307
Stathas, Charles J., 181, 181n
Statistics, Department of, 229, 233, 269
Steenbock, Harry, 115, 239, 240n, 241, 242, 244
Steenbock Memorial Library, 211, 247
Steiger, Carl E., 110n, 155, 156, 157, 179, 246n, 531n
Steiner, Peter O., 285
Steinzor, Rena, 507, 518
Stepner, Mark H., 290n
Sterling, John W., 275
Sterling Hall, 247, 269; bombing of, 6, 24, 271, 514, 516, 519, 555
Stern, Linda, 488n
Stevenson, Adlai, 111, 111n
Stieghorst, Karl, 393n
Stiehl, Jack, 307
Stiles, Lindley J., 66, 100n, 158n, 229
Stilwell, Hamilton, 357n
Stock Pavilion, 27, 75, 458, 511
Stokes, William S., 405n-6n

Stokowski, Leopold, 74
Stone, J. Riley, 96n
Stone, William H., 283n
Stout Institute (Menomonie), 522, 525, 530, 550
Strong, Dorothy, 318n
Strong, Frank M., 283n
Strother, George B., 318n, 320, 330, 337, 339-40, 355, 356n, 359, 369, 371
Stroud, Ray M., 75n, 76n
Strowig, R. Wray, 435n
Structure Agreement, 503, 504
Student Activity Reserve Fund, 441-42
Student Board, 422; and academic freedom, 400; and discrimination, 385, 396, 397
Student Court, 440, 441, 444, 460
Student-Faculty Committee on Academic Standards, 129
Student League for Industrial Democracy, 451
Student Life and Interests Appeal Board, 440
Student organizations, 451; review of campus policy on, 94, 400, 406; women lead during WW II, 7, 53, 418. *See also* American Youth for Democracy; Guest speakers; Labor Youth League; Students for a Democratic Society; Young Republicans
Student Power Bills, 437
Student publications: restrictions on, 91. *See also Badger; Badger Herald; Daily Cardinal; Madison Kaleidoscope*
Students: activism of in changing curriculum, 286-94, 471; activism of politically, 450-52, 465; admission of Jewish students, 4; average age of, 427; clothing of, 51, 425, 604; want to set course requirements, 289, 471; criticize funding of UW from federal government and industry, 239; oppose discrimination, 385-400, 432; disciplinary procedure for, 445, 445n, 602; disillusionment and distrust of, 431-32, 447, 486, 507;

diversity of, 4; not to be involved in faculty appointments, promotions and salaries, 444; and federal loans and loyalty oaths, 134-35; financial support for, 598; first class of at UW, 1; leftist orientation of, 450; legislature proposes punishment for radical leaders of, 485; not allowed legal counsel at disciplinary hearings, 435; attitude of toward merger, 570; oppose UW policies toward private activities of, 412-13; and limit on non-resident students, 450, 455n, 465, 465n, 484, 485, 494, 494n-95n; and Peterson Building sit-in, 215-16, 220, 453, 454-55; petition from seeking more educational challenges, 128-29, 130n, 437-43; power of, 5, 288-89, 383-446, 478, 604; protests against Vietnam War, 6, 185, 186n, 214-24, 227, 270-71, 287, 364-65, 370, 383, 445, 447-79, 486, 513, 580, 591, 602, 603; sent to UW psychiatrists for evaluation, 436; radical leaders among, 5, 486; restrictions on, 4; spring work days end, 602; strike, 288-89, 470; study abroad, 133; survey of comparing with general adult population, 601-2; and truth squads, 226; and underage drinking, 413. *See also* Admissions; Black student movement; Enrollments; Graduate students; Internationalization of UW; Scholarships; Undergraduate education
Student Senate, 433, 435, 437, 438, 439, 440, 455, 458, 465-66; support black students' demands, 479; decertifies SDS, 460; maintained, 602
Students for a Democratic Society (SDS), 215-16, 216, 270-71, 451, 452, 454-55, 459, 460, 486, 488-89, 490n, 492; on grading system, 288; takes more activist role, 469-79
Studies of Behavioral Disabilities, Department of, 229
Study Committee on Student Newspapers (BOR), 510
Stuhldreher, Harry, 27

Sullivan, Benjamin A., 100n
Sullivan cabin court, 33
Summer sessions, 17
Suomi, Verner E., 266n, 268, 274, 275-78
Superconductivity research, 251
Suppan, Adolph, 100n
Survey Research Laboratory, 127, 244, 291, 453
Syamananda, Rong, 302
Sylvers, Malcolm, 473

Tandler, Martin, 453
TAWSUF, 588
Taylor, Fan, 359n
Taylor, Robert, 73, 183, 329n, 364
Teacher education, 127-28, 256, 521, 536`
Teaching: audio-visual enhancement of, 279; and distance instruction, 280; group and individualized credit instruction, 280; multi-media, 279, 344; and radio and telephone linkages, 280. *See also* Adult education
Teaching assistants: and grading experiments, 287; in English Dept. denounce dropping freshman courses, 291
Teaching Assistants Association, 463n, 479, 604; not supported by graduate students, 494; and strike of 1969, 494-506, 604
Technical Services Act, 327, 330
Teter, John W., 100n
Theoretical Chemistry Institute, 267
Thiede, Wilson B., 322, 329, 330, 331, 338n, 466
Thiede Committee, 466-67, 479, 482, 483
Thiesenhusen, William C., 129n
Thompson, Carl W., 576, 578
Thomson, John C., 542
Thomson, Vernon W., 107, 128
Torgerson, Rita, 419
Torkelson, M. W., 60n
Town-gown relations, 117, 118, 225, 273
Trailer parks, 28-35; illustrations of,

29-30; location of, 61. *See also* Badger Ordnance Works; East Hill; Monroe Park; Randall Trailer Park
Trane, Reuben N., 75n, 76n
Travis, Larry, 516-17
Trewartha, Glenn, 275, 277n
Trimester system, 8, 20
Trinko, Curtis V., 290n
Tripp Commons, 17
Tripp Hall, 3, 16, 17
Troxell, Louise, 419, 424
Truax Field: building from used as UW cafeteria, 21, 24; cafeteria at as married housing facility, 35; and housing for married veterans, 33-38; illustrations of housing at, 36; student association at, 38; transportation to, 39, 44; women's club at, 38
Trubek, David, 415
TRUE program (Teaching, Research, Urban Extension), 258
True Axe, 38
Truman, Harry, 75, 448
Trump, Paul L., 53, 386
Trust funds: Anonymous Trust Fund, 191, 191n, 255n; Brittingham Family Trust, 190n, 192, 243-44, 251, 257-58, 310; Knapp grants, 190, 253, 253n; Vilas Trust Fund, 190n, 192-93, 252-53. *See also* Wisconsin Alumni Research Foundation
Truth squads, 226
Tuition and fees: and GI Bill, 48-49, 50; setting of undergraduate levels, 88-89; support for low level of, 174. *See also* Admissions; Scholarships
Turner, Frederick Jackson, professorship, 249

Udall, Stewart, 515
Uhl, Arthur H., 66, 158n, 319n
Uihlein, Robert, 75n, 76n
Undergraduate education: and creation of Committee on Undergraduate Education, 288; and curriculum reform, 281-86, 604; funding for cutback in merger bill, 562; and history requirement for graduation, 232, 232n; improvement of under

Elvehjem, 127-35; and independent study, 292; and Knapp scholarships, 253; loss of sense of community among, 227; under merged system, 567, 572; as main mission of university, 560, 565; quality of at UW and WSU, 569, 570, 580, 591, 604; study abroad, 133; and Vilas scholarships, 252. *See also* Curriculum; Grading system; Honors program

Undergraduate Library, 211, 238, 380

Union, Memorial. *See* Memorial Union

Union Forum Committee, 403, 404

Union South, 211, 274, 452n-53n

United Campus Action, 452

University Club, 3, 225, 600

University Committee (Madison), 523, 530, 565; and administrative appointments, 328n; and cooperation with black universities, 346n; to assist in naming members of Committee on University Functions and Policies, 80; recommends end to discriminatory practices, 389, 390, 391, 392; and appointment of Fleming as Madison provost, 184n; and grading practices, 287, 477; and selection of Harrington as president, 164; critical of Lucey's proposed funding, 567-68, 574, 579; and Medical School, 150, 161; accepts merger, 593; wants to reject all NDEA funds, 134; to identify likely post-war problems, 9; and anti-war protests, 459, 462, 467, 468, 511; asked to evaluate standing committees, 63; on student governance, 438, 442, 443, 461; students petition for improvement in undergraduate education, 129; UWM faculty serve on, 103; and search for successor to E. B. Fred, 109, 110; for UED, 343; and organizational changes in UED, 359; UWM University Faculty Council modeled on, 186

University Extension Building, 137, 351

University Extension Center (Milwaukee), 99, 305-6, 526, 527, 530; campus, 138; creation of, 3, 175n, 305, 525; merger with State College in Milwaukee, 530, 605

University Extension Division (UED), 605, 608; and group and individualized credit instruction, 280; urban mission of, 306, 306n; and U.S. Armed Forces Institute (USAFI), 303-4, 304n. *See also* University of Wisconsin Centers; WHA Radio; WHA-TV

University Extension (merged CES and UED), 85, 175n, 176, 179, 195, 238, 301-6; accomplishing merger, 209-20, 257, 258-59, 295, 311n, 314-28, 328-40, 341-44, 540; AID funds international programs of, 362; separate campus for, 361-62, 368, 369; and Department of Youth Development, 364; directory of programs, 352; Division of Staff Training and Development, 352; extension league, 358; faculty government plan of, 343; first faculty meeting of, 343; faculty senate of, 358; freeze on hiring faculty in, 353; Madison faculty oppose research by staff of, 361, 361n; funding problems at, 362-63, 365; Chancellor McNeil strives for autonomous status, 358-62; under merger, 568; and overhead funds, 362; bad publicity on social action initiatives of, 363-64; Research Committee of, 361; Space Committee of, 361; proposal for "University School," 370-71; UWM objects to Madison control of, 354-58; and WARF funds for, 361

University Hospital, 231, 517

University Health Service Building, 211

University Hill. *See* Bascom Hill

University Houses, Inc., 78-79, 81, 177, 247

University of Michigan-Berkeley Solidarity rally, 452

University of the Air, 280. *See also* WHA Radio

University of Wisconsin Center for

Development, 280
University of Wisconsin Center System, 80, 86, 96, 99, 140, 175n, 295, 305, 315, 539, 540, 607, 608; debate over future of, 536; post-war growth of, 20, 24n, 138, 171, 179, 195, 539, 541, 605; graduate students placed in teaching positions at, 540; existence of in southeastern Wisconsin works against new four-year campus, 205; under merger, 568
University of Wisconsin Extension Center, 99
University of Wisconsin Foundation (UWF), 83, 98, 106, 107, 121; capital campaign of, 76-77; creation of, 75-76, 249; first directors of, 76, 76n; and Hilldale Shopping Center, 254-55; Madison campus fears having to share with WSU after merger, 574
University of Wisconsin-Green Bay, 205-9, 210n, 331, 549, 568, 573, 581, 605, 607, 609
University of Wisconsin-Milwaukee (UWM), 165, 171; and architectural program at, 550; buildings of, 138; creation of, 98-103, 120, 175n, 526, 529, 534, 596, 605; and development of, 138, 175n, 197-205, 543, 550, 605, 606-7; extension program at, 331; faculty of support merger, 572n-73n; graduate program of, 208, 550, 606; creates honors program in L&S, 131; separated from Madison campus, 185-86; and merger of UW and WSU, 561-62, 567, 568, 572; opposes merger of CES and UED, 338-39, 354-58; physical education major at, 543; to address urban issues, 197-201, 605, 606; UW and WSU vie to control, 196; vice provost created for, 200-201; use of Vilas funds at, 252, 252n; WARF funds for faculty at, 3, 75, 123, 127, 242, 238-48
University of Wisconsin News, 72-73
University of Wisconsin-Parkside, 205-9, 210n, 331, 549, 573, 581, 605, 607, 609
University of Wisconsin Policies Committee, 95n
University of Wisconsin Upham Woods Committee, 301
University of Wisconsin Veterans of World War II, 51-52
University Park Corporation, 254
University Placement Service. *See* Placement Service
"University School," 370-71
Upham Woods, 239n, 301
Urban Affairs, Department of (at UWM), 258, 310n
Urban and Regional Planning, Department of, 229, 233
Urban mission; of UED, 306, 306n, 315; foundation support for, 323. *See also* University of Wisconsin-Milwaukee
Urban Research Committee, 310n
Urban Research Program; supported by Brittingham Trust Funds, 257-58, 310; Ford Foundation grant for, 257-59, 310-12; and TRUE program, 258
U.S. Agency for International Development (AID), 271, 280, 362, 487
U.S. Armed Forces Institute (USAFI), 303-4, 304
U.S. Army. *See* Mathematics Research Center
U.S. Department of Agriculture (USDA): and merger of CES and UED, 336, 341, 350
U.S. Department of Health, Education, and Welfare, 241
U.S. House Committee on Un-American Activities, 91, 93. *See also* McCarthyism
U.S. National Student Association (NSA), 384-85
U.S. Office of Economic Opportunity (OEO), 326-27, 330, 346
U.S. Public Health Service, 240, 241, 273, 274
U.S. Veterans Administration, 12, 13; interprets GI Bill, 47-48, 50, 51

U.S. War Department, 12, 21, 34, 39, 41
U.S. Weather Bureau, 277

VandeBerg, Gale L.: on Administrative Committee of University Extension, 330n, 333n; as candidate for chancellor of University Extension, 322, 369; on search committee for chancellor for University Extension, 367n; as dean in University Extension, 338, 340, 340n, 354, 356n, 360n-61n; on Huitt Committee, 318n; on Thiede Committee, 330
VanderKelen, Ron, 377, 603
VanderMeulen, Judy, 427n
Vanguard of the Revolution, 490, 491, 494
Van Hagen, Leslie F., 15n
Van Hise, Charles R.; as president of UW, 2, 2-4, 57, 58, 172, 209, 214, 225, 227, 254, 342, 601, 606, 610
Van Hise Commons, 3
Van Hise Hall, 187, 211, 213, 501, 548, 565
Van Pelt, C. F., 75n, 76n
Vansina, Jan, 232
Van Vleck Hall, 136, 137, 247
Van Vleet, James G., 100n
Vaughn, C. W., 63n
Venetian Nights celebration, 602
Veterans; academic credit given to for wartime service, 14, 14n; and admissions, 13, 15, 17, 18, 19, 26, 539; and American Veterans Committee (AVC), 52, 384; applying for housing, 29; bonus, 384; Business Office for, 13; help construct prefabricated buildings, 21; counseling services for, 13; bring new culture to campus, 383-84; disabled come to campus, 10; grades of, 52-53; health services for, 13; non-trailer housing for those married, 33-38; refresher courses for, 17; attempt to integrate into student body, 15; as percentage of student body, 51; registration of at UW, 19; and Special Committee on

Educational Problems for War Veterans, 15; and status of a students, 15; as student leaders, 53; and summer sessions, 17; trailer park for married veterans, 28-33; and University of Wisconsin Veterans of World War II, 51-52. *See also* GI Bill of Rights
Veterans of Foreign Wars, 384
Veterinary Science, School of, 552
Veterinary Science Research Building, 136, 137, 247
Vevier, Charles: as assistant to Harrington, 181; description of, 181n, 357n; as Harrington liaison at UWM, 197-99; on Committee on Space Sciences, 266n; objects to merged UED, 354, 355; as vice chancellor of UWM, 332-33, 338, 356n; as vice provost of UWM, 191, 200-204, 204n
Vietnam War, 204-5, 353, 362, 432, 554; Vietnam Moratorium, 487, 488; protests against, 6, 185, 186n, 214-24, 227, 270, 287, 364-65, 370, 383, 445, 447-79, 486, 513, 580, 591, 602; support for, 453-54
Vilas, William F., 252
Vilas Hall for the Communication Arts, 211
Vilas Trust Fund, 190n, 192-93, 252-53; graduate fellowships, 252; research professorships, 252-53; undergraduate scholarships, 252; use of funds at UWM, 252, 252n
Vilas Zoo, 273, 273n-74n
Villemonte, James R., 217n, 439n
Vilstrup, Richard, 360, 360n
VISTA, 330n, 341, 346, 347, 363
Vlasin, Raymond, 367n
Voegli, Donald J., 46, 352n
Vogel, Ken, 452n
Vogelman, Roy, 308n
Voices of Protest, 364

Waisman, Harry, 274
Waisman Center, 274
Walker, Gordon R., 563
Walsh, Leo M., 352n
Walter, Toni L., 463n

Wanvig, C. O., Jr., 547n
WARF. *See* Wisconsin Alumni Research Foundation
WARF Building, 211, 248, 517
Warren, Lindsay, 51
Warren, Robert W., 505-6, 506n
Washburn Observatory, 275
Wasow, Wolfgang, 272
Water fights, 412, 414-15, 417
Watson, George, 396n
Watts, Harold W., 286
Weathermen, 451, 487
Weaver, Andrew T., 70n
Weaver, John C., 559; and budget cuts, 579; central administration of, 560; illustrations of, 382, 594; and merger, 561-95 *passim;* to head merged system, 581; opposes reduction in graduate program, 561; elected president, 556-57, 557n; and quality of undergraduate education, 570
Webb, James, 266
Weber, Ed, 355
Webster, Anita, 95n
Weck, Alice, 338, 358
Wedemeyer, Charles A., 338, 344
Wee, Morris, 105
Weening, Dick, 577n
Weidner, Edward W., 207-8, 212, 573
Welfare sit-in in Wisconsin capitol, 222
Wendt, Kurt F., 65, 80n, 97n, 100n, 105, 158n, 267, 598n
nominated to succeed E.B. Fred, 303n
Werner, A. Matt., 165, 177, 373, 396n, 531n
We Want No Berkeley Here Committee, 460
WHA Radio, 47, 64, 195, 209, 280, 297, 307-9, 370, 607; and adult education, 314n; division of radio education supervised by faculty committee, 307; and "Freshman Forum," 373; broadcasts faculty meeting with Gov. Lucey, 580-84; funding for, 345-46, 345n, 363; and merger with CES and UED, 295, 315-16, 321, 332, 344-46, 540; popular radio programs in the sixties, 308n; professionalization of, 344; and WHA-FM (WERN) and other statewide stations, 307
WHA-TV, 195, 209, 280, 307-9, 370, 607; and adult education, 314n; wins Emmy, 345; funding for, 345-46, 345n, 363; and merger with CES and UED, 295, 315-16, 321, 332, 344-46, 540; professionalization of, 344
Wheeler, Floyd, 95n
White, Alden, 97n
White, Barry, 287n
White, Helen C., 80n, 129
White, Helen C., Hall, 211, 379
White, Maurice, 354
Whitley, Alvin, 130-31
Wick, Marshall, 562-63, 566
Wildlife Ecology, Department of, 230
Willard, John E., 122, 124, 127n, 158n, 182, 182n, 246, 246-47, 598n
Williams, William Appleman, 456
Wilson, Joe B., 283, 283n, 286
Wilson, Robert, 590-91
Winter Carnival, 375
Wirka, Herman, 152n
Wisconsin Agricultural Savings Bond Committee, 301
Wisconsin Alumni Association (WAA), 121, 129n, 195, 214, 248-49, 364, 528; on merger, 578, 578n, 579n, 590
Wisconsin Alumni Research Foundation (WARF), 65, 77, 83, 121-22; and Brittingham visiting professorships, 251, 285, 285n; opened to competitive application from all segments of UW, 174; and construction of buildings, 136, 247, 269, 601, 601n; creation of, 3, 192; provides UW financial support during Depression, 3, 75; funds for University Extension, 361; Madison campus fears having to share after merger, 574, 574n; funds meteorology studies, 275; real estate holdings of, 239n; social sciences and humanities dissatisfied with support from, 65, 112, 114-15, 119, 119n, 121-22, 123-24, 174, 217, 223n-24n, 242-43, 245; sub-contracts to run MRC, 269;

supports social sciences and humanities, 127, 244, 461; and creation of University Houses, 78; supports research at UWM, 3, 75, 123, 127, 192, 238-48; limited to Madison campus, 192; and WARF Building, 211, 248, 517

Wisconsin Alumnus, 90, 97, 149, 592

Wisconsin Association of Agricultural and Extension Committees of County Boards, 301

Wisconsin Building Commission, 265, 527

Wisconsin Center building, 77, 98, 103, 105, 106, 107, 121, 249, 303, 488, 488n

Wisconsin Department of Economic Development, 341

Wisconsin Department of Public Instruction (DPI), 341

Wisconsin Draft Resisters Union (WDRU), 452

Wisconsin Educational Bonus Act of 1919, 10

Wisconsin Employment Relations Commission, 495

Wisconsin Exposition Council, 301

Wisconsin Farm Progress Days, 301

Wisconsin Idea, 77, 107, 171-72, 174, 195, 316, 326, 540; *The 50-Year Story of the Wisconsin Idea in Education*, 306; broadening of internationally, 132; faculty's commitment to, 523; forerunner of, 3; reshaping of, 295-372 *passim*, 582; slogan of, 73

Wisconsin Idea Theater, 307

Wisconsin Institute of Technology (Platteville), 522, 525, 530, 550

Wisconsin Legislative Council, 89, 90, 95, 406

Wisconsin legislature: Assembly passes merger, 577; and merger bill, 562-85; Senate deletes merger from budget bill, 579-80; radical students critical of, 481; upset over campus disruptions, 481, 485, 494, 506, 554. *See also* Funding; Joint Finance Committee

Wisconsin Players, 74

Wisconsin Power and Light Company, 493

Wisconsin Radio Council, 308

Wisconsin Rapids Center, 541

Wisconsin Rapids Community College, 542n

Wisconsin Rural Development Committee, 301

Wisconsin Social System Research Institute, 285, 285n

Wisconsin State College System/Wisconsin State Universities (WSU), 84, 139, 178, 193-97, 341, 573n; enrollment of surpasses UW-Madison, 195, 521-22, 544; expansion considered, 206; faculty salaries at, 583; and faculty union (TAWSUF) on merger, 588; faculty of disparaged by UW faculty and Harrington, 609; faculty upgrading, 544; graduate program limited by CCHE, 208; and joint board of regents on merger, 569, 575, 578; Milwaukee added to, 306; under merger, 568; and name change, 544, 544n; political influence of, 195, 206; poor management of, 591; and undergraduate education at, 562; and veterinary science program at WSU-River Falls, 552

Wisconsin State College-Superior, 525n

Wisconsin State College-Whitewater, 205

Wisconsin State Journal, 148, 149, 155, 155n-56n, 156, 329, 364, 369, 457n; on merger, 569, 580, 590

Wisconsin State Soil and Water Conservation Committee, 300-301

Wisconsin State University-Oshkosh, 482

Wisconsin State University-Stevens Point, 551

Wisconsin Student Association (WSA), 418, 435, 437, 455n, 467, 492; Summer Board, 440, 443; "Student Power Report, 1967," 443

Wisconsin University Building Corporation, 137

Withey, Morton O., 60n, 65, 70n

WITI-TV, 165n

Witmer, David, 573n
Witte, Edwin E., 342n, 409, 409n, 533, 533n
Witte Hall, 211
Wolfe, Pat, 427n
Wolff, Robert L., 232
Wollaeger, Charlotte, 100n
"Women Say **Yes** to Men Who Say **No**" march, 452
Women's Field House: first floor of turned into men's cooperative house, 27
Women's club at Truax project, 38
Women students: admission of, 1, 7; admission restrictions on after WW II, 18, 25; as cheerleaders, 424, 603; and Female College, 1; housing for, 25, 419, 425; restricted hours for, 422, 423-24, 427, 440, 441, 443, 604; Senior Swingout ends, 602; separated from men in classrooms, 418, 418n, 421; as student leaders, 7, 53, 418; and visiting hours for, 423, 426, 427, 430, 440, 604; and varsity athletics, 603
Women's liberation movement, 418
Women's Self-Government Association (WSGA), 419, 422
Woodburn, James G., 60n
Woodbury, Coleman, 258, 310, 310n, 311, 311n, 312
Woolsey, Clinton N., 142n, 249
World Food and Agricultural Foundation, 301
World Student Congress, 384-85
World War II: impact on enrollment, 7-9, 14, 17-25, 69; and post-war construction of buildings, 16; and post-war planning, 9-17. *See also* GI Bill of Rights; U.S. Veterans Administration; Veterans
Writing Laboratory, 290, 290n
WTMJ (Milwaukee), 561
Wyllie, Irvin G., 206-7, 207-8, 212
Wyngaard, Tim, 595

Xerographic copy machines, 280

Yaillen, Earl, 412n

Yank magazine, 19
Ylvisaker, Paul, 310n, 311, 312n, 325. *See also* Ford Foundation
YMCA Building (campus), 452, 493
Youmans, William B., 156
Young, H. Edwin, 110, 110n, 114, 122-23, 283n, 285; as candidate for Madison chancellor, 217n, 286, 473; as chancellor, 219, 219n, 222, 223, 277, 292n, 469, 487, 518-19, 599; illustrations of, 212, 382, 480; and merger, 566, 576, 595; calls for national guard on campus, 479, 482n; returns to Madison campus, 219n, 366n; and TAA strike, 494-506; vows to keep University open, 481, 510
Young, George H., 66, 158n, 409n
Young, Louise A., 343n
Young, William H., 88-90, 97n, 122, 182-83, 183n; and Bowers affair, 154, 156, 160; and construction of Library, 236; as counter-balance to A. W. Peterson, 122
Young Republicans, 400, 405
Young Socialist Alliance, 452, 492

Zawacki, Edmund, 583
Ziegler, Bernard C., 218n, 367n, 510, 556, 557, 563, 564, 568, 589
Zillman, Theodore, 414, 415, 424, 426, 427n
Zoology, Department of, 274, 284n, 600
Zoology Museum, 600
Zoology Research Building, 136, 137, 247, 600, 601, 601n. *See also* Noland Zoology Building
Zucker, David S., 512

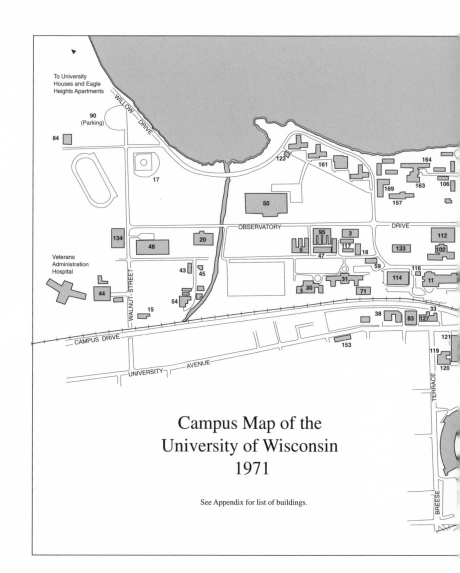

To University
Houses and Eagle
Heights Apartments

WILLOW DRIVE

90
(Parking)

84

17

123

161

164

163

106

169

157

50

OBSERVATORY DRIVE

134

48

20

95

3

117

18

133

112

102

5

47

59

116

Veterans
Administration
Hospital

43

45

WALNUT STREET

44

54

30

31

71

114

11

15

38

83

127

33

CAMPUS DRIVE

153

121

119

120

UNIVERSITY AVENUE

TERRACE

BREESE

Campus Map of the
University of Wisconsin
1971

See Appendix for list of buildings.